ASHGATE
**RESEARCH**
COMPANION

# THE ASHGATE RESEARCH COMPANION TO INTERNATIONAL CRIMINAL LAW

ASHGATE
**RESEARCH**
COMPANION

The *Ashgate Research Companions* are designed to offer scholars and graduate students a comprehensive and authoritative state-of-the-art review of current research in a particular area. The companions' editors bring together a team of respected and experienced experts to write chapters on the key issues in their speciality, providing a comprehensive reference to the field.

# The Ashgate Research Companion to International Criminal Law
## Critical Perspectives

*Edited by*

WILLIAM A. SCHABAS
*Middlesex University, UK*

YVONNE MCDERMOTT
*Bangor University, UK*

NIAMH HAYES
*Institute for International Criminal Investigations, The Netherlands*

LONDON AND NEW YORK

First published 2013 by Ashgate Publishing

2 Park Square, Milton Park, Abingdon, Oxfordshire OX14 4RN
52 Vanderbilt Avenue, New York, NY 10017

*Routledge is an imprint of the Taylor & Francis Group, an informa business*

First issued in paperback 2018

Copyright © William A. Schabas, Yvonne McDermott and Niamh Hayes and the contributors 2013

All rights reserved. No part of this book may be reprinted or reproduced or utilised in any form or by any electronic, mechanical, or other means, now known or hereafter invented, including photocopying and recording, or in any information storage or retrieval system, without permission in writing from the publishers.

Notice:
Product or corporate names may be trademarks or registered trademarks, and are used only for identification and explanation without intent to infringe.

**British Library Cataloguing in Publication Data**
The Ashgate Research Companion to International Criminal Law: Critical Perspectives.
   1. International criminal law.
   I. International criminal law II. Schabas, William, 1950– III. McDermott, Yvonne.
   IV. Hayes, Niamh.
   345-dc23

**Library of Congress Cataloging-in-Publication Data**
Schabas, William, 1950-
   The Ashgate Research Companion to International Criminal Law: Critical Perspectives/
by William A. Schabas, Yvonne McDermott, and Niamh Hayes.
      p.    cm.
   Includes bibliographical references and index.
   1. International criminal law. I. McDermott, Yvonne. II. Hayes, Niamh. III. Title.
   KZ7050.S33 2012
   345–dc23                                                                    2012038188

ISBN-13: 978-1-4094-1918-1 (hbk)
ISBN-13: 978-0-367-19191-7 (pbk)

 Printed in the United Kingdom
by Henry Ling Limited

# Contents

| | |
|---|---|
| *List of Abbreviations* | *vii* |
| *List of Cases* | *ix* |
| *Notes on Contributors* | *xxxi* |
| *Preface* | *xl* |

Introduction     1
*Niamh Hayes, Yvonne McDermott and William A. Schabas*

## PART I: INTERNATIONAL CRIMES AND MODES OF LIABILITY

1    Sisyphus Wept: Prosecuting Sexual Violence at the International Criminal Court     7
*Niamh Hayes*

2    Creating a Framework for the Prosecution of Environmental Crimes in International Criminal Law     45
*Tara Smith*

3    Alleged Aggression in Utopia: An International Criminal Law Examination Question for 2020     63
*Roger S. Clark*

4    The Special Tribunal for Lebanon and Terrorism as an International Crime: Reflections on the Judicial Function     79
*Ben Saul*

5    Damned If You Don't: Liability for Omissions in International Criminal Law     101
*Christopher Gosnell*

6    Joint Criminal Enterprise Liability: Result Orientated Justice     133
*Wayne Jordash*

## PART II: THE INTERNATIONAL CRIMINAL PROCESS

7  Rights in Reverse: A Critical Analysis of Fair Trial Rights under
   International Criminal Law   165
   *Yvonne McDermott*

8  Victims' Participation at the International Criminal Court:
   Benefit or Burden?   181
   *Lorraine Smith-van Lin*

9  A Shifting Scale of Power: Who is in Charge of the Charges at the
   International Criminal Court   205
   *Dov Jacobs*

10 Distinguishing Creativity from Activism: International Criminal
   Law and the 'Legitimacy' of Judicial Development of the Law   223
   *Joseph Powderly*

11 Equality of Arms in International Criminal Law:
   Continuing Challenges   251
   *Charles Chernor Jalloh and Amy DiBella*

12 Protecting the Rights of the Accused in International Criminal
   Proceedings: Lip Service or Affirmative Action?   289
   *Colleen Rohan*

13 Reconciliation and Sentencing in the Practice of the ad hoc Tribunals   307
   *Silvia D'Ascoli*

## PART III: COMPLEMENTARITY AND SENTENCING: A DISCUSSION

14 A Sentence-Based Theory of Complementarity   335
   *Kevin Jon Heller*

15 'Sentencing Horror' or 'Sentencing Heuristic'? A Reply to
   Heller's 'Sentence-Based' Theory of Complementarity   357
   *Carsten Stahn*

16 Three Theories of Complementarity: Charge, Sentence or
   Process? A Comment on Kevin Heller's Sentence-Based
   Theory of Complementarity   369
   *Darryl Robinson*

## PART IV: INTERNATIONAL CRIMINAL JUSTICE IN CONTEXT

17  The Short Arm of International Criminal Law  387
    *William A. Schabas*

18  Palestine and the Politics of International Criminal Justice  407
    *Michael Kearney and John Reynolds*

19  Lions and Tigers and Deterrence, Oh My: Evaluating Expectations
    of International Criminal Justice  435
    *Kate Cronin-Furman and Amanda Taub*

20  Hybrid Courts in Retrospect: Of Lost Legacies and Modest Futures  453
    *Pádraig McAuliffe*

21  'Political Trials'? The UN Security Council and the Development of
    International Criminal Law  475
    *David P. Forsythe*

22  Expanding the Focus of the 'African Criminal Court'  499
    *Kai Ambos*

23  The Future of International Criminal Law and Transitional Justice  531
    *Mark A. Drumbl*

Index  547

# List of Abbreviations

| | |
|---|---|
| ACHPR | African Commission for Human and People's Rights |
| *AJIL* | *American Journal of International Law* |
| ASP | Assembly of State Parties of the International Criminal Court |
| AU | African Union |
| AUPD | African Union High-Level Panel on Darfur |
| CAR | Central African Republic |
| *CLF* | *Criminal Law Forum* |
| CUP | Cambridge University Press |
| DRC | Democratic Republic of the Congo |
| *EJIL* | *European Journal of International Law* |
| *HRQ* | *Human Rights Quarterly* |
| ICC | International Criminal Court |
| *ICLR* | *International Criminal Law Review* |
| ICRC | International Committee of the Red Cross |
| ICTR | International Criminal Tribunal for Rwanda |
| ICTY | International Criminal Tribunal for the former Yugoslavia |
| *JICJ* | *Journal of International Criminal Justice* |
| *LJIL* | *Leiden Journal of International Law* |
| NGO | non-governmental organisation |
| OAU | Organisation of African Unity |
| OTP | Office of the Prosecutor of the International Criminal Court |
| OUP | Oxford University Press |
| PTC | Pre-Trial Chamber |
| SC | United Nations Security Council |
| SCSL | Special Court for Sierra Leone |
| UN | United Nations |

# List of Cases

## International

### International Criminal Court

a. Situation in the Central African Republic
*Situation in the Central African Republic: Prosecutor v Bemba* (Decision on the Prosecutor's Application for a Warrant of Arrest Against Jean-Pierre Bemba Gombo) ICC-01/05-01/08 (10 June 2008)
*Situation in the Central African Republic: Prosecutor v Bemba* (Fourth Decision on Victims' Participation) ICC-01/05-01/08 (12 December 2008)
*Situation in the Central African Republic: Prosecutor v Bemba* (Désignation d'un représentant légal commun pour les victimes autorisées à participer à la procédure dans l'affaire Le Procureur c. Jean-Pierre Bemba) ICC-01/05-01/08 (5 January 2009)
*Situation in the Central African Republic: Prosecutor v Bemba* (Decision Pursuant to Article 61(7)(a) and (b) of the Rome Statute on the Charges of the Prosecutor Against Jean-Pierre Bemba Gombo) ICC-01/05-01/08 (12 January 2009)
*Situation in the Central African Republic: Prosecutor v Bemba* (Decision Pursuant to Article 61(7)(a) and (b) of the Rome Statute on the Charges of the Prosecutor Against Jean-Pierre Bemba Gombo) ICC-01/05-01/08 (15 June 2009)
*Situation in the Central African Republic: Prosecutor v Bemba* (Decision defining the status of 54 victims who participated at the pre-trial stage, and inviting the parties' observations on applications for participation by 86 applicants) ICC-01/05-01/08 (22 February 2010)
*Situation in the Central African Republic: Prosecutor v Bemba* (Corrigendum to Decision on the participation of victims in the trial and on 86 applications by victims to participate in the proceedings) ICC-01/05-01/08 (12 July 2010)
*Situation in the Central African Republic: Prosecutor v Bemba* (Judgment on the appeal of Mr Jean-Pierre Bemba Gombo against the decision of Trial Chamber II of 24 June 2010 entitled 'Decision on the Admissibility and Abuse of Process Challenges') ICC-01/05-01/08 (19 October 2010)

*Situation in the Central African Republic: Prosecutor v Bemba* (Decision on common legal representation of victims for the purpose of trial) ICC-01/05-01/08 (10 November 2010)

*Situation in the Central African Republic: Prosecutor v Bemba* (Decision on the legal representation of victim applicants at trial) ICC-01/05-01/08 (19 November 2010)

*Situation in the Central African Republic: Prosecutor v Bemba* (Notification of designation of common legal representatives) ICC-01/05-01/08 (22 November 2010)

*Situation in the Central African Republic: Prosecutor v Bemba* (Decision setting a timeline for the filing of observations on pending victims' applications) ICC-01/05-01/08 (9 September 2011)

## b. Situation in Darfur, Sudan

*Situation in Darfur, Sudan* (Summary of the Prosecutor's Application under Article 58) ICC-02/05 (20 November 2008)

*Situation in Darfur, Sudan* (Judgment on victim participation in the investigation stage of the proceedings in the appeal of the OPCD against the decision of Pre-Trial Chamber I of 3 December 2007 and in the appeals of the OPCD and the Prosecutor against the decision of Pre-Trial Chamber I) ICC-02/05 (2 February 2009)

*Situation in Darfur, Sudan: Prosecutor v Abu Garda* (Decision on the 34 Applications for Participation at the Pre-Trial Stage of the Case) ICC-02/05-02/09 (29 September 2009)

*Situation in Darfur, Sudan: Prosecutor v Abu Garda* (Decision on the Confirmation of Charges) ICC-02/05-02/09 (8 February 2010)

*Situation in Darfur, Sudan: Prosecutor v Harun and Kushayb* (Warrant of Arrest for Ahmad Harun) ICC-02/05-01/07-2-Corr (27 April 2007)

*Situation in Darfur, Sudan: Prosecutor v Harun and Kushayb* (Warrant of Arrest for Ahmad Harun and Ali Kushayb) ICC-02/05-01/07-3-Corr (27 April 2007)

*Situation in Darfur, Sudan: Prosecutor v Harun and Kushayb* (Decision on the Prosecution Application under Article 58(7) of the Statute) ICC-02/05-01/07 (27 April 2007)

*Situation in Darfur, Sudan: Prosecutor v al Bashir* (Warrant of Arrest for Omar Hassan Ahmad al Bashir) ICC-02/05-01/09 (4 March 2009)

*Situation in Darfur, Sudan: Prosecutor v al Bashir* (Decision on the Prosecution's Application for a Warrant of Arrest against Omar Hassan Ahmad Al Bashir) ICC-02/05-01/09 (4 March 2009)

*Situation in Darfur, Sudan: Prosecutor v al Bashir* (Decision on the Second Application by Victims a/0443/09 to a/0450/09 to Participate in the Appeal against the 'Decision on the Prosecution's Application for a Warrant of Arrest against Omar Hassan Ahmad Al Bashir') ICC-02/05-01/09 (28 January 2010)

*Situation in Darfur, Sudan: Prosecutor v al Bashir* (Judgment on the appeal of the Prosecutor against the 'Decision on the Prosecution's Application for a Warrant

of Arrest against Omar Hassan Ahmad al Bashir') ICC-02/05-01/09 (3 February 2010)
*Situation in Darfur, Sudan: Prosecutor v al Bashir* (Second Warrant of Arrest for Omar Hassan Ahmad Al Bashir) ICC-02/05-01/09 (12 July 2010)
*Situation in Darfur, Sudan: Prosecutor v al Bashir* (Decision Pursuant to Article 87(7) of the Rome Statute on the Failure by the Republic of Malawi to Comply with the Cooperation Requests Issued by the Court with Respect to the Arrest and Surrender of Omar Hassan Ahmad al Bashir) ICC-02/05-01/09 (12 December 2011)
*Situation in Darfur, Sudan: Prosecutor v al Bashir* (Decision Pursuant to Article 87(7) of the Rome Statute on the Failure by the Republic of Chad to Comply with the Cooperation Requests Issued by the Court with Respect to the Arrest and Surrender of Omar Hassan Ahmad al Bashir) ICC-02/05-01/09 (13 December 2011)
*Situation in Darfur, Sudan: Prosecutor v Banda and Jerbo* (Report recommending a decision concerning the common legal representation of victims participating in the case) ICC-02/05-03/09 (15 April 2011)
*Situation in Darfur, Sudan: Prosecutor v Banda and Jerbo* (Report on the implementation of the Chamber's Order instructing the Registry to start consultations on the organization of common legal representation) ICC-02/05-03/09 (21 June 2011)
*Situation in Darfur, Sudan: Prosecutor v Banda and Jerbo* (Order instructing the Registry to start consultations on the organisation of common legal representation) ICC-02/05-03/09 (21 June 2011)
*Situation in Darfur, Sudan: Prosecutor v Banda and Jerbo* (Proposal for the common legal representation of victims) ICC-02/05-03/09 (25 August 2011)

c. Situation in the DRC

*Situation in the DRC* (Decision on the applications for Participation in the Proceedings of VPRS 1, VPRS 2, VPRS 3, VPRS 4, VPRS 5 and VPRS 6 (Public redacted Version)) ICC-01/04 (17 January 2006)
*Situation in the DRC* (Decision on the Applications for Participation in the Proceedings of a/0001/06, a/0002/06 and a/0003/06 in the case of the Prosecutor v Thomas Lubanga Dyilo and of the investigation in the Democratic Republic of the Congo) ICC-01/04 (31 July 2006)
*Situation in the DRC* (Decision on the Requests of the Legal Representative of Applicants on application process for victims' participation and legal representation) ICC-01/04 (17 August 2007)
*Situation in the DRC* (Décision sur les demandes de participation à la procédure déposées dans le cadre de l'enquête en République démocratique du Congo par a/0004/06 à a/0009/06, a/0016/06 à a/0063/06, a/0071/06 à a/0080/06 et a/0105/06 à a/0110/06, a/0188/06, a/0128/06 à a/0162/06, a/0199/06, a/0203/06, a/0209/06, a/0214/06, a/0220/06 à a/0222/06, a/0224/06, a/0227/06 à a/0230/06, a/0234/06 à a/0236/06, a/0240/06, a/0225/06, a/0226/06, a/0231/06 à a/0233/06, a/0237/06 à a/0239/06 et a/0241/06 à a/0250/06) ICC-01/04 (24 December 2007)

*Situation in the DRC* (Décision sur les demandes de participation à la procédure déposées dans le cadre de l'enquête en République démocratique du Congo par a/0004/06 à a/0009/06, a/0016/06 à a/0063/06, a/0071/06 à a/0080/06 et a/0105/06 à a/0110/06, a/0188/06, a/0128/06 à a/0162/06, a/0199/06, a/0203/06, a/0209/06, a/0214/06, a/0220/06 à a/0222/06, a/0224/06, a/0227/06 à a/0230/06, a/0234/06 à a/0236/06, a/0240/06, a/0225/06, a/0226/06, a/0231/06 à a/0233/06, a/0237/06 à a/0239/06 et a/0241/06 à a/0250/06) ICC-01/04 (31 January 2008)

*Situation in the DRC* (Judgment on victim participation in the investigation stage of the proceedings in the appeal of the OPCD against the decision of Pre-Trial Chamber I of 7 December 2007 and in the appeals of the OPCD and the Prosecutor against the decision of Pre-Trial Chamber I) ICC-01/04 (19 December 2008)

*Situation in the DRC: Prosecutor v Katanga and Chui* (Decision on the Applications for Participation in the Proceedings of Applicants a/0327/07 to a/0337/07 and a/0001/08) ICC-01/04-01/07 (2 April 2008)

*Situation in the DRC: Prosecutor v Katanga and Chui* (Decision on the Set of Procedural Rights Attached to Procedural Status of Victim at the Pre-Trial Stage of the Case) ICC-01/04-01/07 (13 May 2008)

*Situation in the DRC: Prosecutor v Katanga and Chui* (Decision Requesting Observations Concerning Article 54(3)(e) Documents Identified as Potentially Exculpatory or Otherwise Material for the Defence's Preparation for the Confirmation Hearing) ICC-01/04-01/07 (2 June 2008)

*Situation in the DRC: Prosecutor v Katanga and Chui* (Decision on the Confirmation of Charges) ICC-01/04-01/07 (1 October 2008)

*Situation in the DRC: Prosecutor v Katanga and Chui* (Decision on the treatment of applications for participation) ICC-01/04-01/07 (26 February 2009)

*Situation in the DRC: Prosecutor v Katanga and Chui* (Reasons for the Oral Decision on the Motion Challenging the Admissibility of the Case (Article 19 of the Statute)) ICC-01/04-01/07 (16 June 2009)

*Situation in the DRC: Prosecutor v Katanga and Chui* (Report of the Registry on the organisation of the common legal representation of victims) ICC-01/04-01/07 (14 August 2009)

*Situation in the DRC: Prosecutor v Katanga and Chui* (Judgment on the Appeal of Mr Germain Katanga against the Oral Decision of Trial Chamber II of 12 June 2009 on the Admissibility of the Case) ICC-01/04-01/07-1497 (25 September 2009)

*Situation in the DRC: Prosecutor v Katanga and Chui* (Directions for the conduct of the proceedings and testimony in accordance with rule 140) ICC-01/04-01/07 (20 November 2009)

*Situation in the DRC: Prosecutor v Katanga and Chui* (Directions for the conduct of the proceedings and testimony in accordance with rule 140) ICC-01/04-01/07 (1 December 2009)

*Situation in the DRC: Prosecutor v Katanga and Chui* (Defence Request with Regard to Private Session Hearings) 01/04-01/07 (1 June 2010)

# LIST OF CASES

*Situation in the DRC: Prosecutor v Katanga and Chui* (Decision on the 'Prosecution's Application Concerning Disclosure Pursuant to Rules 78 and 79(4)') ICC-01/04-01/07 (14 September 2010)
*Situation in the DRC: Prosecutor v Katanga and Chui* (Decision on the Prosecutor's Bar Table Motions) ICC-01/04-01/07 (17 December 2010)
*Situation in the DRC: Prosecutor v Lubanga* (Warrant of Arrest) ICC-01/04-01/06 (10 February 2006)
*Situation in the DRC: Prosecutor v Lubanga* (Decision on the Prosecutor's Application for a Warrant of Arrest, Article 58) ICC-01/04-01/06 (10 February 2006)
*Situation in the DRC: Prosecutor v Lubanga* (Decision on the Prosecutor's Application for a Warrant of Arrest) ICC-01/04-01/06 (24 February 2006)
*Situation in the DRC: Prosecutor v Lubanga* (Decision on the Applications for Participation in the Proceedings of a/0001/06, a/0002/06 and a/0003/06 in the case of the Prosecutor v Thomas Lubanga Dyilo and of the investigation in the Democratic Republic of the Congo) ICC-01/04-01/06 (28 July 2006)
*Situation in the DRC: Prosecutor v Lubanga* (Decision on the Prosecutor's 'Application for Leave to Reply to "Conclusions de la défense en réponse au mémoire d'appel du Procureur"') ICC-01/04-01/06 (12 September 2006)
*Situation in the DRC: Prosecutor v Lubanga* (Judgment on the Prosecutor's Appeal Against the Decision of Pre-Trial Chamber I entitled 'Decision Establishing General Principles Governing Applications to Restrict Disclosure Pursuant to Rule 81(2) and (4) of the Rules of Procedure and Evidence') ICC-01/04-01/06 (13 October 2006)
*Situation in the DRC: Prosecutor v Lubanga* (Decision on applications for participation in proceedings a/0004/06 to a/0009/06, a/0016/06, a/0063/06, a/0071/06 to a/0080/06 and a/0105/06 in the case of The Prosecutor v Thomas Lubanga Dyilo) ICC-01/04-01/06 (20 October 2006)
*Situation in the DRC: Prosecutor v Lubanga* (Décision sur la demande d'autorisation d'appel de la Défense relative a la transmission des Demandes de Participation des Victimes) ICC-01/04-01/06 (6 November 2006)
*Situation in the DRC: Prosecutor v Lubanga* (Decision on the Confirmation of Charges) ICC 01/04-01/06 (29 January 2007)
*Situation in the DRC: Prosecutor v Lubanga* (Decision of the Presidency upon the document entitled 'Clarification' filed by Thomas Lubanga Dyilo on 3 April 2007, the requests of the Registrar of 5 April 2007 and the requests of Thomas Lubanga Dyilo of 17 April 2007) ICC-01/04-01/06 (2 May 2007)
*Situation in the DRC: Prosecutor v Lubanga* (Decision on 'Demande de déposition du représentant légales demandeurs des victimes') ICC-01/04-01/06 (25 October 2007)
*Situation in the DRC: Prosecutor v Lubanga* (Decision on Victims' Participation) ICC-01/04-01/06 (18 January 2008)
*Situation in the DRC: Prosecutor v Lubanga* (Corrigendum to the 'Decision on the Applications for Participation Filed in Connection with the Investigation in the Democratic Republic of the Congo by a/0004/06 to a/0009/06, a/0016/06 to a/0063/06, a/0071/06 to a/0080/06 and a/0105/06 to a/0110/06, a/0188/06, a/0128/06

to a/0162/06, a/0199/06, a/0203/06, a/0209/06, a/0214/06, a/0220/06 to a/0222/06, a/0224/06, a/0227/06 to a/0230/06, a/0234/06 to a/0236/06, a/0240/06, a/0225/06, a/0226/06, a/0231/06 to a/0233/06, a/0237/06 to a/0239/06 and a/0241/06 to a/0250/06') ICC-01/04-01/06 (31 January 2008)

*Situation in the DRC: Prosecutor v Lubanga* (Decision on the Defence and Prosecution Requests for Leave to Appeal the Decision on Victims' Participation of 18 January 2008) ICC-01/04-01/06 (26 February 2008)

*Situation in the DRC: Prosecutor v Lubanga* (Decision, *in limine,* on Victim Participation in the appeals of the Prosecutor and the Defence against Trial Chamber I's Decision entitled 'Decision on Victims' Participation') ICC-01/04-01/06 (16 May 2008)

*Situation in the DRC: Prosecutor v Lubanga* (Decision on certain practicalities regarding individuals who have the dual status of witness and victim) ICC-01/04-01/06 (5 June 2008)

*Situation in the DRC: Prosecutor v Lubanga* (Public Redacted Version of the 'Decision on the 97 Applications for Participation at the Pre-Trial Stage of the Case') ICC-01/04-01/07 (10 June 2008)

*Situation in the DRC: Prosecutor v Lubanga* (Decision on the Consequences of Non-Disclosure of Exculpatory Materials Covered by Article 54(3)(e) Agreements and the Application to Stay the Prosecution of the Accused, Together with Certain Other Issues Raised at the Status Conference on 10 June 2008) ICC-01/04/01/06 (13 June 2008)

*Situation in the DRC: Prosecutor v Lubanga* (Judgment on the appeals of The Prosecutor and The Defence against Trial Chamber I's Decision on Victims' Participation of 18 January 2008) ICC-01/04-01/06 (11 July 2008)

*Situation in the DRC: Prosecutor v Lubanga* (Judgment on the appeals of The Prosecutor and The Defence against Trial Chamber I's Decision on Victims' Participation of 18 January 2008: Dissenting Opinion of Judge Pikis) ICC-01/04-01/06 (11 July 2008)

*Situation in the DRC: Prosecutor v Lubanga* (Judgment on the appeals of The Prosecutor and The Defence against Trial Chamber I's Decision on Victims' Participation of 18 January 2008: Partly Dissenting Opinion of Judge Kirsch) ICC-01/04-01/06 (11 July 2008)

*Situation in the DRC: Prosecutor v Lubanga* (Order issuing public redacted version of the 'Decision on the request by victims a/ 0225/06, a/0229/06 and a/0270/07 to express their views and concerns in person and to present evidence during the trial') ICC-01/04-01/06 (26 June 2009)

*Situation in the DRC: Prosecutor v Lubanga* (Decision Giving Notice to the Parties and Participants that the Legal Characterisation of the Facts May be Subject to Change in Accordance with Regulation 55(2) of the Regulations of the Court) ICC-01/04-01/06 (14 July 2009)

*Situation in the DRC: Prosecutor v Lubanga* (Decision Giving Notice to the Parties and Participants that the Legal Characterisation of the Facts May be Subject to Change in Accordance with Regulation 55(2) of the Regulations of the Court: Dissenting Opinion of Judge Adrian Fulford) ICC-01/04-01/06 (17 July 2009)

LIST OF CASES

*Situation in the DRC: Prosecutor v Lubanga* (Judgment on the Appeals of Mr Lubanga Dyilo and the Prosecutor against the Decision of Trial Chamber I of 14 July 2009 Entitled 'Decision Giving Notice to the Parties and Participants that the Legal Characterisation of the Facts May be Subject to Change in Accordance with Regulation 55(2) of the Regulations of the Court') ICC-01/04-01/06 (8 December 2009)

*Situation in the DRC: Prosecutor v Lubanga* (Prosecution Proposed Procedure for Dealing with Intermediaries) ICC-01/04-01/06 (19 March 2010)

*Situation in the DRC: Prosecutor v Lubanga* (Redacted Decision on Intermediaries) ICC-01/04-01/06 (31 May 2010)

*Situation in the DRC: Prosecutor v Lubanga* (Decision on the Prosecution's Urgent Request for Variation of the Time-Limit to Disclose the Identity of Intermediary 143 or Alternatively to Stay Proceedings Pending Further Consultations with the VWU) ICC-01/04-01/06 (8 July 2010)

*Situation in the DRC: Prosecutor v Lubanga* (Judgment on the Appeal of the Prosecutor Against the Decision of Trial Chamber I of 8 July 2010 Entitled 'Decision on the Prosecution's Urgent Request for Variation of the Time-Limit to Disclose the Identity of Intermediary 143 or Alternatively to Stay Proceedings Pending Further Consultation with the VWU') ICC-01/04-01/06 (8 October 2010)

*Situation in the DRC: Prosecutor v Lubanga* (Redacted Decision on the 'Defence Application Seeking a Permanent Stay of Proceedings') ICC-01/04-01/06 (7 March 2011)

*Situation in the DRC: Prosecutor v Mbarushimana* (Warrant of Arrest for Callixte Mbarushimana) ICC-01/04-01/10 (11 October 2010)

*Situation in the DRC: Prosecutor v Mbarushimana* (Proposal on victim participation in the confirmation hearing) ICC-01/04-01/10 (6 June 2011)

*Situation in the DRC: Prosecutor v Mbarushimana* (Request to access documents in the case record in relation to the Defence Challenge to the Jurisdiction of the Court) ICC-01/04-01/10 (19 June 2011)

*Situation in the DRC: Prosecutor v Mbarushimana* (Decision on the Confirmation of Charges) ICC-01/04-01/10 (16 December 2011)

*Situation in the DRC: Prosecutor v Mbarushimana* (Decision on the Confirmation of Charges: Dissenting Opinion by Judge Hans-Peter Kaul) ICC-01/04-01/10 (16 December 2011)

*Situation in the DRC: Prosecutor v Ntaganda* (Warrant of Arrest) ICC-01/04-02/06 (22 August 2006)

d. Situation in the Republic of Kenya

*Situation in the Republic of Kenya* (Decision Pursuant to Article 15 of the Rome Statute on the Authorization of an Investigation into the Situation in the Republic of Kenya) ICC-01/09 (31 March 2010)

*Situation in the Republic of Kenya* (Decision Pursuant to Article 15 of the Rome Statute on the Authorization of an Investigation into the Situation in the Republic of

Kenya: Dissenting Opinion of Judge Hans-Peter Kaul) ICC-01/09 (31 March 2010)

*Situation in Kenya: Prosecutor v Muthaura et al* (Decision on the Prosecutor's Application for Summonses to Appear for Francis Kirimi Muthaura, Uhuru Muigai Kenyatta and Mohammed Hussein Ali) ICC-01/09-02/11 (8 March 2011)

*Situation in the Republic of Kenya: Prosecutor v Muthaura et al* (Decision on the Application of the Government of Kenya challenging the Admissibility of the Case Pursuant to Article 19(2)(b) of the Statute) ICC-01/09-02/11-96 (30 May 2011)

*Situation in the Republic of Kenya: Prosecutor v Muthaura et al* (Proposal for the common legal representation of victims) ICC-01/09-02/11 (5 August 2011)

*Situation in Kenya: Prosecutor v Muthaura et al* (Prosecution's Amended Document Containing the Charges and List of Evidence Submitted Pursuant to Article 61(3) and Rule 121(3) (4) and (5)) ICC-01/09-01/11 (19 August 2011)

*Situation in the Republic of Kenya: Prosecutor v Muthaura et al* (Judgment on Defence Appeal Challenging Admissibility of Case) ICC-01/09-02/11 (30 August 2011)

*Situation in the Republic of Kenya: Prosecutor v Muthaura et al* (Judgment on the appeal of the Republic of Kenya against the decision of Pre-Trial Chamber II of 30 May 2011 entitled 'Decision on the Application by the Government of Kenya Challenging the Admissibility of the Case Pursuant to Article 19(2)(b) of the Statute') ICC-01/09-02/11 (30 August 2011)

*Situation in Kenya: Prosecutor v Muthaura et al* (Decision on the Confirmation of Charges Pursuant to Article 61(7)(a) and (b) of the Rome Statute) ICC-01/09-02/11 (23 January 2012)

*Situation in the Republic of Kenya: Prosecutor v Ruto et al* (Decision on the Application of the Government of Kenya challenging the Admissibility of the Case Pursuant to Article 19(2)(b) of the Statute) ICC-01/09-01/11 (30 May 2011)

*Situation in the Republic of Kenya: Prosecutor v Ruto et al* (Proposal for the common legal representation of victims (including annexes)) ICC-01/09-01/11 (1 August 2011)

*Situation in the Republic of Kenya: Prosecutor v Ruto et al* (Urgent Defence Application for Postponement of the Confirmation Hearing and Extension of Time to Disclose and List Evidence) ICC-01/09-01/11 (11 August 2011)

*Situation in the Republic of Kenya: Prosecutor v Ruto et al* (Decision on Urgent Defence Application for Postponement of the Confirmation Hearing and Extension of Time to Disclose and List Evidence) ICC-01/09-01/11 (12 August 2011)

*Situation in the Republic of Kenya: Prosecutor v Ruto et al* (Henry Kosgey's Contingent Request for Extension of Time Limit for Disclosure in Compliance with the E-Court Protocol with Confidential Annexes 1-3) ICC-01/09-01/11 (15 August 2011)

*Situation in the Republic of Kenya: Prosecutor v Ruto et al* (Decision on the Defence Requests for Extension of Time Limit for Disclosure in Compliance with the E-Court Protocol) ICC-01/09-01/11 (16 August 2011)

LIST OF CASES

*Situation in the Republic of Kenya: Prosecutor v Ruto et al* (Decision on the Issuance of the Decision Pursuant to Article 61(7) of the Rome Statute) ICC-01/09-01/11 (26 October 2011)

*Situation in Kenya: Prosecutor v Ruto et al* (Decision on the Confirmation of Charges Pursuant to Article 61(7)(a) and (b) of the Rome Statute) ICC-01/09-01/11 (23 January 2012)

e. *Situation in the Republic of Côte d'Ivoire*

*Situation in the Republic of Côte d'Ivoire* (Decision Pursuant to Article 15 of the Rome Statute on the Authorisation of an Investigation into the Situation in the Republic of Côte d'Ivoire) ICC-02/11 (3 October 2011)

*Situation in the Republic of Côte d'Ivoire* (Decision Pursuant to Article 15 of the Rome Statute on the Authorisation of an Investigation into the Situation in the Republic of Côte d'Ivoire: Separate and Partially Dissenting Opinion of Judge Fernandez de Gurmendi) ICC-02/11 (3 October 2011)

*Situation in the Republic of Côte d'Ivoire: Prosecutor v Gbagbo* (Decision on the Prosecutor's Application Pursuant to Article 58 for a Warrant of Arrest Against Laurent Koudou Gbagbo) ICC-02/11-01/11 (30 November 2011)

f. *Situation in Uganda*

*Situation in Uganda* (Decision on Victims' Applications for Participation a/0010/06, a/0064/06 to a/0070/06, a/0081/06 to a/0104/06 and a/0111/06 to a/0127/06) ICC-02/04 (10 August 2007)

*Situation in Uganda* (Decision on the Prosecution's Application for Leave to Appeal the Decision on Victims' Applications for Participation a/0010/06, a/0064/06 to a/0070/06, a/0081/06 to a/0104/06 and a/0111/06 to a/0127/06) ICC-02/04-01/05 (19 December 2007)

*Situation in Uganda: Prosecutor v Kony et al* (Warrant of Arrest) ICC-02/04-01/05 (8 July 2005)

*Situation in Uganda: Prosecutor v Kony et al* (Decision on Prosecutor's Application for Leave to Appeal in part Pre-Trial Chamber II's Decision on the Prosecutor's Applications for Warrants of Arrest under Article 58) ICC-02/04-01/05 (19 August 2005)

*Situation in Uganda: Prosecutor v Kony et al* (Decision on the Prosecutor's Application for Leave to Appeal Dated the 15th day of May 2006) ICC-02/04-01/05 (10 July 2006)

*Situation in Uganda: Prosecutor v Kony et al* (Decision on victims' applications for participation a/0010/06, a/0064/06 to a/0070/06, a/0081/06 to a/0104/06 and a/0111/06 to a/0127/06) ICC-02/04-01/05 (10 August 2007)

*Situation in Uganda: Prosecutor v Kony et al* (Decision on victims' applications for participation a/0010/06, a/0064/06 to a/0070/06, a/0081/06, a/0082/06, a/0084/06 to a/0089/06, a/0091/06 to a/0097/06, a/0099/06, a/0100/06, a/0102/06 to a/0104/06, a/0111/06, a/0113/06 to a/0117/06, a/0120/06, a/0121/06 and a/0123/06 to a/0127/06) ICC-02/04-01/05 (14 March 2008)

*Situation in Uganda: Prosecutor v Kony et al* (Decision on the admissibility of the case under article 19(1) of the Statute) ICC-02/04-01/05 (10 March 2009)

*Situation in Uganda: Prosecutor v Kony et al* (Judgment on the appeal of the Defence against the 'Decision on the admissibility of the case under article 19(1) of the Statute' of March 2009) ICC-02/04-01/05 (16 September 2009)

## International Criminal Tribunal for the Former Yugoslavia

*Prosecutor v Ademi and Norac* (Decision for Referral to the Authorities of the Republic of Croatia pursuant to Rule 11bis) IT-04-78-PT (14 September 2005)

*Prosecutor v Aleksovski* (Appeal Judgment) IT-95-14/1-A (24 March 2000)

*Prosecutor v Alekovski* (Decision on Prosecutor's Appeal on Admissibility of Evidence) IT-95-14/1-AR73 (16 February 1999)

*Prosecutor v Aleksovski* (Trial Judgment) IT-95-14/1-T (25 June 1999)

*Prosecutor v Babić* (Sentencing Judgment) IT-03-72-S (29 June 2004)

*Prosecutor v Blagojević and Jokić* (Trial Judgment) IT-02-60-T (17 January 2005)

*Prosecutor v Blagojević and Jokić* (Judgment) IT-02-60-A (9 May 2007)

*Prosecutor v Blaškić* (Decision on the Production of Discovery Materials) IT-95-14-T (27 January 1997)

*Prosecutor v Blaskić* (Trial Judgment) IT-95-14-T (3 March 2000)

*Prosecutor v Blaškić* (Appeals Judgment) IT-95-14-A (29 July 2004)

*Prosecutor v Bralo* (Sentencing Judgment) IT-95-17-S (7 December 2005)

*Prosecutor v Brđanin* (Decision on Objections by Talić) IT-99-36-T (20 February 2001)

*Prosecutor v Brđanin and Talić* (Decision on the Prosecutor's Oral Request for the Separation of Trials) IT-99-36-T (20 September 2002)

*Prosecutor v Brđanin* (Trial Judgment) IT-99-36-T (1 September 2004)

*Prosecutor v Brđanin* (Judgment) IT-99-36-A (3 April 2007)

*Prosecutor v Brđanin* (Judgment: Partially Dissenting Opinion of Judge Shahabuddeen) IT-99-36-A (3 April 2007)

*Prosecutor v Delalić et al* (Trial Judgment) IT-96-21-T (16 November 1998)

*Prosecutor v Delalić et al* (Appeal Judgment) IT-96-21-A (20 February 2001)

*Prosecutor v Delalić et al* (Sentencing Judgment) IT-96-21-T*bis* (9 October 2001)

*Prosecutor v Deronjić* (Sentencing Judgment) IT-02-61-S (30 March 2004)

*Prosecutor v Deronjić* (Sentencing Judgment: Dissenting Opinion of Judge Schomburg) IT-02-61-S (30 March 2004)

*Prosecutor v Dordević* (Appeals Judgment) IT-05-87/1 (23 February 2011)

*Prosecutor v Erdemović* (Sentencing Judgment) IT-96-22-T (29 November 1996)

*Prosecutor v Erdemović* (Judgment) IT-96-22-T*bis* (7 October 1997)

*Prosecutor v Erdemović* (Judgment: Joint Separate Opinion of Judges McDonald and Vohrah) IT-96-22-T*bis* (7 October 1997)

*Prosecutor v Erdemović* (Judgment: Separate and Dissenting Opinion of Judge Li) IT-96-22-T*bis* (7 October 1997)

## List of Cases

*Prosecutor v Erdemović* (Sentencing Judgment) IT-96-22-T*bis* (5 March 1998)
*Prosecutor v Furundžija* (Judgment) IT-95-17/1-T (10 December 1998)
*Prosecutor v Galić* (Trial Judgment) IT-98-29-T (5 December 2003)
*Prosecutor v Galić* (Appeal Judgment) IT-98-29-A (30 November 2006)
*Prosecutor v Hadžihasanović and Kabura* (Decision on urgent motion for ex parte oral hearing on allocation of resources to the defence and consequences thereof for the rights of the accused to a fair trial) IT-07-47-PT (17 June 2003)
*Prosecutor v Hadžihasanović and Kabura* (Decision on Joint Challenge to Jurisdiction) IT-01-47-PT (16 July 2003)
*Prosecutor v Hadžihasanović and Kabura* (Decision on defence access to EUMM archives) IT-07-47-PT (12 September 2003)
*Prosecutor v Hadžihasanović and Kabura* (Decision on joint defence application for certification of decision on access to EUMM archives of 12 September 2003) IT-01-47-PT (25 September 2003)
*Prosecutor v Halilović* (Judgment) IT-01-48-T (16 November 2005)
*Prosecutor v Haradinaj et al* (Decision on Prosecution's Urgent Application for Authorisation to Exceed Page Limit for Responses) IT-04-84-PT (5 May 2005)
*Prosecutor v Haradinaj et al* (Decision on Ramush Haradinaj's Motion for Provisional Release) IT-04-84-T (6 June 2005)
*Prosecutor v Haradinaj et al* (Decision on Defence Motion on Behalf of Ramush Haradinaj to Request Re-assessment of Conditions of Provisional Release Granted 6 June 2005) IT-04-84-T (12 October 2005)
*Prosecutor v Haradinaj et al* (Order recalling Ramush Haradinaj from provisional release) IT-04-84-T (1 February 2007)
*Prosecutor v Haradinaj et al* (Decision on Whether to Resume Hearing Testimony of Witness 8 and Call Chamber Witness) IT-04-84-T (20 June 2007)
*Prosecutor v Haradinaj et al* (Decision on Motion on Behalf of Ramush Haradinaj for Provisional Release) IT-04-84-T (20 July 2007)
*Prosecutor v Haradinaj et al* (Decision on Defence Motion on Behalf of Ramush Haradinaj for Urgent Provisional Release) IT-04-84-T (3 October 2007)
*Prosecutor v Haradinaj et al* (Decision on the Admission of a Prosecution Witness Statement under Rule 92*bis* and Prosecution's 17th Motion for Protective Measures) IT-04-84-T (29 October 2007)
*Prosecutor v Haradinaj et al* (Decision on Fourth Batch of 92*bis* Witnesses and Protective Measures for One of These Witnesses) IT-04-84-T (6 November 2007)
*Prosecutor v Haradinaj et al* (Decision on Prosecution's 30th and 31st Motions for Trial-Related Protective Measures) IT-04-84-T (6 November 2007)
*Prosecutor v Haradinaj et al* (Scheduling Order for Final Trial Briefs and Closing Arguments) IT-04-84-T (30 November 2007)
*Prosecutor v Haradinaj et al* (Judgment) IT-04-84-T (3 April 2008)
*Prosecutor v Haradinaj et al* (Judgment) IT-04-84-A (19 July 2010)
*Prosecutor v Haradinaj et al* (Corrigendum to Judgement of 19 July 2010) IT-04-84-A (23 July 2010)
*Prosecutor v Haradinaj et al* (Decision on Haradinaj's Appeal on Scope of Partial Retrial) IT -04-84bis-AR 73.1 (31 May 2011)

*Prosecutor v Jelisić* (Trial Judgment) IT-95-10-T (14 December 1999)
*Prosecutor v Kabashi* (Sentencing Judgment) IT-04-84-R77.1 (16 September 2011)
*Prosecutor v Kordić and Čerkez* (Decision on Appeal regarding the Admission into Evidence of seven Affidavits and one formal Statement) IT-95-14/2-A (18 September 2000)
*Prosecutor v Kordić and Čerkez* (Appeal Judgment) IT-95-14/2-A (17 December 2004)
*Prosecutor v Kordić and Čerkez* (Decision on application by Mario Čerkez for extension of time to file his respondent's brief) IT-95-14/2-A (11 September 2011)
*Prosecutor v Krajisnik* (Trial Judgment) IT-00-39&40-T (27 September 2006)
*Prosecutor v Krajišnik* (Decision on Krajišnik Request and on Prosecution Motion) IT-00-39-A (11 September 2007)
*Prosecutor v Krajisnik* (Appeals Judgment) IT-00-39 (17 March 2009)
*Prosecutor v Krnojelac* (Judgment) IT-97-25-T (15 March 2002)
*Prosecutor v Krnojelac* (Judgment) IT-97-25-A (17 September 2003)
*Prosecutor v Krstić* (Trial Judgment) IT-98-33-T (2 August 2001)
*Prosecutor v Krstić* (Appeals Judgment) IT-98-33-A (19 April 2004)
*Prosecutor v Kunarac* (Trial Judgment) IT-96-23-T (22 February 2001)
*Prosecutor v Kupreskić* (Trial Judgment) IT-95-16-T (14 January 2000)
*Prosecutor v Kupreškić et al* (Appeals Judgment) IT-95-16-A (23 October 2001)
*Prosecutor v Kvočka* (Appeal Judgment) IT-98-30/1 (28 February 2005)
*Prosecutor v Kvočka et al* (Trial Judgment) IT-98-30/1-T (2 November 2001)
*Prosecutor v Limaj* (Judgment) IT-03-66-T (30 November 2005)
*Prosecutor v Lukić & Lukić* (Trial Judgment) IT-98-32/1-T (20 July 2009)
*Prosecutor v Martić* (Judgment) IT-95-11-T (12 June 2007)
*Prosecutor v Martić* (Judgment) IT-95-11-A (8 October 2008)
*Prosecutor v Milošević* (Reasons for Decision on Assignment of Defence Counsel) IT-02-54-T (22 September 2004)
*Prosecutor v Milošević* (Decision on Preliminary Motions) IT-02-54-PT (8 November 2001)
*Prosecutor v Milošević* (Decision in relation to severance, extension of time and rest) IT-02-54-T (12 December 2005)
*Prosecutor v Milutinović et al* (Decision on interlocutory appeal on motion for additional funds) IT-99-37-AR73.2 (13 November 2003)
*Prosecutor v Milutinović et al* (Decision on second application of Dragoljub Ojdanić for binding orders pursuant to Rule 54bis) IT-05-87-PT (17 November 2005)
*Prosecutor v Milutinović et al* (Decision on Prosecution's Request for Certification of Rule 73bis Issue for Appeal) IT-05-87-T (30 August 2006)
*Prosecutor v Milutinović et al* (Judgment) IT-05-87-T (26 February 2009)
*Prosecutor v Mrkšić et al* (Judgment) IT-95-13/1-T (27 September 2007)
*Prosecutor v Mrkšić* (Appeal Judgment) ICTR-95-13/1-A (5 May 2009)
*Prosecutor v Mrkšić* (Review Judgment) ICTR-95-13/1-R.1 (8 December 2010)
*Prosecutor v D Nikolić* (Sentencing Judgment) IT-94-2-S (18 December 2003)
*Prosecutor v D Nikolić* (Judgment on Sentencing Appeal) IT-94-2-A (4 February 2005)
*Prosecutor v M Nikolić* (Sentencing Judgment) IT-02-60/1-S (2 December 2003)
*Prosecutor v Obrenović* (Sentencing Judgment) IT-02-60/2-S (10 December 2003)

*Prosecutor v Orić* (Interlocutory decision on length of defence case) IT-03-68-AR73.2 (20 July 2005)
*Prosecutor v Orić* (Judgment) IT-03-68-A (3 July 2008)
*Prosecutor v Perišić* (Trial Chamber Judgment) IT-04-81-T (6 September 2011)
*Prosecutor v Plavšić* (Sentencing Judgment) IT-00-39&40/1-S (27 February 2003)
*Prosecutor v Popović et al* (Trial Judgment) IT-05-88-T (10 June 2010)
*Prosecutor v Rajić* (Sentencing Judgment) IT-95-12-S (8 May 2006)
*Prosecutor v Šainović* (Decision on Ojdanić's Motion Challenging Jurisdiction – Joint Criminal Enterprise) IT-99-37-AR72 (21 May 2003)
*Prosecutor v Semanza* (Trial Judgment) ICTR-97-20-T (15 May 2003)
*Prosecutor v Simić* (Sentencing Judgment) IT-95-9/2-S (17 October 2003)
*Prosecutor v Simić et al* (Judgment) IT-95-9-A (28 November 2006)
*Prosecutor v Stakić* (Trial Judgment) IT-97-24-T (31 July 2003)
*Prosecutor v Stakić* (Appeal Judgment) IT-97-24-A (22 March 2006)
*Prosecutor v Strugar* (Trial Judgment) IT-01-42-T (31 January 2005)
*Prosecutor v Tadić* (Appeals Chamber Decision on the Defence Motion for Interlocutory Appeal on Jurisdiction) IT-94-1-AR72 (2 October 1995)
*Prosecutor v Tadić* (Opinion and Judgment) IT-94-1-T (7 May 1997)
*Prosecutor v Tadić* (Appeals Judgment) IT-04-1-A (15 July 1999)
*Prosecutor v Tadić* (Sentencing Judgment) IT-94-1-T*bis*-R117 (11 November 1999)
*Prosecutor v Tadić* (Sentencing Judgment) IT-94-1A*bis* (26 January 2000)
*Prosecutor v Todorović* (Sentencing Judgment) IT-95-9/1-S (31 July 2001)
*Prosecutor v Vasiljević* (Judgment) IT-98-32-A (25 February 2004)
*Prosecutor v Zelenović* (Sentencing Judgment) IT-96-23/2-S (4 April 2007)

## International Criminal Tribunal for Rwanda

*Prosecutor v Akayesu* (Trial Judgment) ICTR-96-4-T (2 September 1998)
*Prosecutor v Aleksovski* (Appeal Judgment) IT-95-14/1-A (24 March 2000)
*Prosecutor v Bagaragaza* (Decision on Rule 11*bis* Appeal) ICTR-05-86-Ar11bis (30 August 2006)
*Prosecutor v Bagaragaza* (Sentencing Judgment) ICTR-05-86-S (17 November 2009)
*Prosecutor v Barayagwiza* (Decision on Prosecutor's Request for Review or Reconsideration) ICTR-97-19-AR72 (31 March 2000)
*Prosecutor v Bisengimana* (Judgment and Sentence) ICTR-00-60 (13 April 2006)
*Prosecutor v Bizimungu et al* (Decision on Prosper Mugiraneza's Application for a Hearing or Other Relief on his Motion for Dismissal for Violation of his Right to a Trial without Undue Delay) ICTR-99-50-T (3 November 2004)
*Prosecutor v Bizimungu et al* (Decision on Prosper Mugiraneza's Second Motion to Dismiss for Deprivation of his Right to Trial without Undue Delay) ICTR-99-50-AR73 (29 May 2007)
*Prosecutor v Bizimungu et al* (Decision on Prosper Mugiraneza's Third Motion to Dismiss Indictment for Violation of Right to Trial without Undue Delay) ICTR-99-50-AR73 (10 February 2009)

*Prosecutor v Bizimungu et al* (Decision on Jérôme-Clément Bicamumpaka's Motion Seeking Permanent Stay of Proceedings) ICTR-99-50-AR73 (27 February 2009)
*Prosecutor v Bizimungu et al* (Decision on Prosper Mugiraneza's Fourth Motion to Dismiss Indictment for Violation of Right to Trial without Undue Delay) ICTR-99-50-AR73 (23 June 2010)
*Prosecutor v Bizimungu et al* (Judgment and Sentence) ICTR-99-50-T (30 September 2011)
*Prosecutor v Bizimungu et al* (Judgment and Sentence: Partially Dissenting Opinion of Judge Emile Francis Short) ICTR-99-50-T (30 September 2011)
*Prosecutor v Gacumbitsi* (Judgment) ICTR-2001-64-T (17 June 2004)
*Prosecutor v Gacumbitsi* (Appeals Judgment) ICTR-2001-64-A (7 July 2006)
*Prosecutor v Kajelijeli* (Judgment and Sentence) ICTR-98-44A-T (1 December 2003)
*Prosecutor v Kajelijeli* (Appeal Judgment) ICTR-98-44A-A (23 May 2005)
*Prosecutor v Kalimanzira* (Judgment) ICTR-05-88-A (20 October 2010)
*Prosecutor v Kambanda* (Judgment and Sentence) ICTR-97-23-S (4 September 1998)
*Prosecutor v Kamuhanda* (Trial Judgment) ICTR-95-54A-T (22 January 2004)
*Prosecutor v Kamuhanda* (Appeals Judgment) ICTR-99-54A-A (19 September 2005)
*Prosecutor v Karemera et al* (Decision on Severance of André Rwamakuba and Amendments to the Indictment) ICTR-98-44-PT (7 December 2004)
*Prosecutor v Kayishema and Ruzindana* (Judgment and Sentence) ICTR-95-1-T (21 May 1999)
*Prosecutor v Kayishema and Ruzindana* (Appeals Chamber Judgment) ICTR-95-1-A (1 June 2001)
*Prosecutor v Mugiraneza* (Decision on Prosper Mugiraneza's Motion to Dismiss the Indictment for Violation of Article 20(4)(C) of the Statute, Demand for Speedy Trial and for Appropriate Relief) ICTR-99-50-T (2 October 2003)
*Prosecutor v Mugiraneza* (Decision on Prosper Mugarineza's Interlocutory Appeal from Trial Chamber II Decision of 2 October 2003 Denying the Motion to Dismiss the Indictment, Demand Speedy Trial and for Appropriate Relief) ICTR-99-50-AR73 (27 February 2004)
*Prosecutor v Muhimana* (Judgment and Sentence) ICTR-95-1B-T (28 April 2005)
*Prosecutor v Musema* (Judgment and Sentence) ICTR-96-13-T (27 January 2000)
*Prosecutor v Muvunyi* (Trial Judgment) ICTR-2000-55A-T (12 September 2006)
*Prosecutor v Muvunyi* (Judgment) ICTR-2000-55A-A (29 August 2008)
*Prosecutor v Nahimana et al* (Judgment and Sentence) ICTR-99-52-T (3 December 2003)
*Prosecutor v Nahimana et al* (Appeal Judgment) ICTR-99-52-A (28 November 2007)
*Prosecutor v Ndayambaje et al* (Decision on Joseph Kanyabashi's Appeal against the Decision of Trial Chamber II of 21 March 2007 concerning the Dismissal of Motions to Vary his Witness List) ICTR-98-42-AR73 (21 August 2007)
*Prosecutor v Ndindabahizi* (Trial Judgment) ICTR-2001-71-I (15 July 2004)
*Prosecutor v Niyitegeka* (Judgment and Sentence) ICTR-96-14-T (16 May 2003)
*Prosecutor v Niyitegeka* (Appeals Judgment) ICTR-96-14-A (9 July 2004)
*Prosecutor v Ntagerura* (Judgment and Sentence) ICTR-99-46-T (25 February 2004)
*Prosecutor v Ntagerura et al* (Judgment) ICTR-99-46-A (7 July 2006)

*Prosecutor v Ntakirutimana* (Trial Judgment) ICTR-96-10 & ICTR-96-17-T (21 February 2003)

*Prosecutor v Ntakirutimana* (Appeals Judgment) ICTR-96-17-A (13 December 2004)

*Prosecutor v Nyiramasuhuko et al* (Decision in the matter of proceedings under Rule 15bis(D)) ICTR 98-42-T (15 July 2003)

*Prosecutor v Nyiramasuhuko et al* (Decision in the Matter of Proceedings under Rule 15bis(D)) ICTR-98-42-A15bis (24 September 2003)

*Prosecutor v Nyiramasuhuko et al* (Judgment and Sentence) ICTR-98-42-T (24 June 2011)

*Prosecutor v Nzabirinda* (Trial Judgment) ICTR-2001-77-T (23 February 2007)

*Prosecutor v Rugambarara* (Sentencing Judgment) ICTR-00-59-T (16 November 2007)

*Prosecutor v Ruggiu* (Trial Judgment) ICTR-97-32-I (1 June 2000)

*Prosecutor v Rutaganda* (Judgment and Sentence) ICTR-96-3-T (6 December 1999)

*Prosecutor v Rutaganda* (Appeals Judgment) ICTR-96-3-A (26 May 2003)

*Prosecutor v Semanza* (Judgment and Sentence) ICTR-97-20-T (15 May 2003)

*Prosecutor v Seromba* (Judgment) ICTR-2001-66-A (12 March 2008)

*Prosecutor v Serugendo* (Judgment and Sentence) ICTR-2005-84-I (12 June 2006)

*Prosecutor v Serushago* (Sentencing Judgment) ICTR-98-39-T (5 February 1999)

*Prosecutor v Uwinkindi* (Decision on Prosecutor's Request for Referral to the Republic of Rwanda) ICTR-2001-75-R11bis (28 June 2011)

*Prosecutor v Uwindindi* (Decision on Defence Appeal Against the Decision Denying Motion Alleging Defects in the Indictment) ICTR-01-75-AR72(C) (16 November 2011)

## Special Court for Sierra Leone

*Prosecutor v Brima et al* (Decision on Brima-Kamara Defence Appeal Motion against Trial Chamber II Majority Decision on Extremely Urgent Confidential Joint Motion for the Re-Appointment of Kevin Metzger and Wilbert Harris as Lead Counsel for Alex Tamba Brima and Brima Bazzy Kamara) SCSL-2004-16-AR73 (8 December 2005)

*Prosecutor v Brima et al* (Trial Judgment: Partly Dissenting Opinion of Justice Doherty on Count 7 (Sexual Slavery) and Count 8 (Forced Marriages)) SCSL-04-16-T (20 June 2007)

*Prosecutor v Brima et al* (Appeals Judgment) SCSL-2004-16-A (22 February 2008)

*Prosecutor v Fofana* (Decision on the Preliminary Defence Motion on the Lack of Personal Jurisdiction Filed on Behalf of the Accused Fofana) SCSL-2004-14-PT (3 March 2004)

*Prosecutor v Fofana et al* (Reasoned Majority Decision on Prosecution Motion for a Ruling on the Admissibility of Evidence) SCSL-04-14-PT (24 May 2005)

*Prosecutor v Fofana et al* (Dissenting Opinion of Justice Pierre Boutet on Decision on Prosecution Motion for a Ruling on the Admissibility of Evidence) SCSL-04-14-PT (24 May 2005)

*Prosecutor v Fofana and Kondewa* (Judgment) SCSL-04-14-A (28 May 2008)

*Prosecutor v Gbao* (Decision on the Prosecution Motion for Immediate Protective Measures for Witnesses and Victims and for Non-Public Disclosure) SCSL-2003-09-PT (10 October 2003)

*Prosecutor v Norman et al* (Decision on the Application for a Stay of Proceedings and Denial of Right to Appeal) SCSL-2003-09-PT (4 November 2003)

*Prosecutor v Norman et al* (Decision on Presentation of Witness Testimony on Moyamba Crime Base) SCSL-04-14-T (1 March 2005)

*Prosecutor v Sesay* (Decision on Defence Motion Seeking the Disqualification of Justice Robertson from the Appears Chamber) SCSL-2004-14-AR 15 (13 March 2004)

*Prosecutor v Sesay et al* (Decision on Sesay Defence Application I—Logistical Resources) SCSL-04-15-T (24 January 2007)

*Prosecutor v Sesay et al* (Decision on the Sesay Defence Team's Application for Judicial Review of the Registrar's Refusal to Provide Additional Funds for an Additional Counsel as Part of the Implementation of the Arbitration Agreement of the 26th of April 2007) SCSL-04-15-T (12 February 2008)

*Prosecutor v Sesay et al* (Written Decision on Sesay Defence Application for a Week's Adjournment—Insufficient Resources in Violation of Article 17(4)(b) of the Statute of the Special Court) SCSL-04-15-T (5 March 2008)

*Prosecutor v Taylor* (Decision on 'Defence Notice of Appeal and Submissions Regarding the Majority Decision Concerning the Pleading of JCE in the Second Amended Indictment') SCSL-03-1-T (1 May 2009)

## Special Tribunal for Lebanon

*Case No STL-11-01/I* (Interlocutory Decision on the Applicable Law: Terrorism, Conspiracy, Homicide, Perpetration, Cumulative Charging) STL-11-01/I/AC/R176bis (16 February 2011)

*Case No STL-11-01/I* (Order on Preliminary Questions Addressed to the Judges of the Appeals Chamber pursuant to Rule 68, paragraph (G) of the Rules of Procedure and Evidence) STL-11-01/I/AC-R176*bis* (21 January 2011)

*In the Matter of El Sayed* (Decision on Mr El Sayed's Motion for the Disqualification of Judge Riachy from the Appeals Chamber Pursuant to Rule 25) CH/PRES/2010/08 (5 November 2010)

## European Court of Human Rights

*Al-Skeini* et al *v United Kingdom* (Judgment) App No 55721/07 (7 July 2011)

*Bulut v Austria* (Judgment) App No 17358/90 (22 February 1996)

*Case of 97 Members of the Gldani Congregation of Jehovah's Witnesses and 4 Others v Georgia* (Judgment) App No 71156/01 (3 May 2007)

*Doorson v The Netherlands* (Judgment) App No 20524/92 (26 March 1996)

## Inter-American Commission of Human Rights

*Garza v United States*, Report No 52/01, Case 12.243 (4 April 2001)

## United Nations Human Rights Committee

*B. d. B. et al v Netherlands* (1989) UN Doc Supp No 40 (A/44/40) (30 March 1989)
*Larranaga v The Phillipines* UN Doc CCPR/C/87/D/1421/2005 (14 September 2006)

## Post-World War II Proceedings

*Hostages Trial (Wilhelm List and Others)* (1948) 8 *Law Reports of Trials of War Criminals* 66
*Trials of the Major War Criminals before the International Military Tribunal, Nuremberg, 14 November 1945 – 1 October 1946* Vol 1, Judgment (International Military Tribunal, Nuremberg, 1947–1949)
*United Nations War Crimes Commission*, Case No 7150, 496 (1948)
*United States of America v Alstötter et al* ('the *Justice* case') Judgment (4 December 1947), in *Trials of War Criminals before the Nuremberg Military Tribunals under Control Council Law No. 10*, Vol III
*Zyklon B Case (Trial of Bruno Tesch and Two Others)* Case No. 9 (British Military Court, Hamburg, 1946) 102

## International Court of Justice

*Application of the Convention on the Prevention and Punishment of the Crime of Genocide (Bosnia and Herzegovina v Serbia and Montenegro)* (Judgment) 2007 ICJ Reports 43 (26 February 2007)
*Legality of the Use by a State of Nuclear Weapons in Armed Conflict* (Advisory Opinion), 1996 ICJ Reports 66 (8 July 1996)
*Military and Paramilitary Activities in and against Nicaragua* (1986) *ICJ Reports* 14
*North Sea Continental Shelf Cases*, 1969 ICJ Reports 3 (20 February 1969)
*Questions of Interpretation and Application of the 1971 Montreal Convention arising from the Aerial Incident at Lockerbie (Libyan Arab Jamahiriya v United Kingdom)* (Judgment on Preliminary Objections) 1998 ICJ Reports 9 (27 February 1998)

## Domestic

### Argentina

*Enrique Lautaro Aranclbta Clavel Case* Supreme Court Case No 259 (2004) (24 August 2004)

### Belgium

*EHL case*, Cass: 15 février 2006, RG P.05.1594.F, Pas. 2006, No. 96

### Canada

*Cassady v Reg Morris Transport Ltd* [1975] RTR 470A
*Dunlop & Sylvester v The Queen* [1979] SCR 881
*R. v Hibbert* [1995] 2 SCR 973
*R v Nixon* 57 CCC (3d) 97(British Columbia CA 1990)
*R v Roach* (2004) 192 CCC (3d) 557 (Ont CA)
*Suresh v Canada* [2002] 1 SCR 3
*Zrig v Canada* (Minister of Citizenship and Immigration) (CA) [2003] 3 FC 761

### France

*Ghaddafi* case, Bulletin des arret de la Cour de Cassation, Chambre criminelle, mar 2001, No 64, 218–219

### India

*Madan Singh v State of Bihar* [2004] INSC 225 (2 April 2004)

### Italy

*Bouyahia Maher Ben Abdelaziz et al*, Corte di Cassazione (11 October 2006)

### Mexico

*Cavallo case*, Supreme Court Case No 140/2002 (10 June 2003)

## Uganda

Constitutional Petition No 036/11, *Thomas Kwoyelo alias Latoni v Uganda* (22 September 2011)

## United Kingdom

*Al-Sirri v Secretary of State for the Home Department* [2009] EWCA Civ 364
*R v Coney* (1881-82) 8 QBD 534, 537
*R v Dytham* [1979] QB 722
*R v Miller* [1983] 2 AC 161
*R v Pitwood* (1902) 19 TLR 37
*R v Stone and Dobinson* [1977] QB 354
*R v Sussex Justices, Ex parte McCarthy* [1923] All ER Rep 233

## United States of America

*Attorney General v Tally*, 102 Ala 25
*Burnett et al v Al Baraka Investment and Development Corporation et al*, Civil Action No 02-1616 (JR), US District Court, District of Columbia, 25 July 2003, 274 F Supp 2d 86
*Commonwealth v Kern*, 1 Brewst 350
*Jerue v Alaska*, 1994 WL 16196278 (Alaska App) 2
*People v Green*, 130 Cal App 3d 1
*State v Moreno*, 104 P3d 628, 631 (Or Ct App 2005)
*Tel-Oren v Libyan Arab Republic* 726 F.2d 774 (DC Cir 1984)
*US v Irwin*, 149 F.3d 565, 572 (7th Cir 1998)
*US v Peoni*, 100 F.2d 401, 402 (2nd Cir 1938)
*US v Yunis*, 924 F.2d 1086 (DC Cir 1991), 1092; (1991) 30 ILM 403

# Notes on Contributors

**Kai Ambos** is Professor of Criminal Law, Comparative Law and International Criminal Law and Head of the Department for Foreign and International Criminal Law at the Georg August University, Göttingen. He is also Member of the Office of Examination (*Justizprüfungsamt*) of the Ministry of Justice of Lower Saxony. Professor Ambos participated in the negotiations on the creation of the International Criminal Court on behalf of Germany, and is a member of the German Federal Ministry of Justice's expert working group on the implementation of the Rome Statute. He is a member of the editorial board of several noted international criminal journals, both in Europe and Latin America.

**Roger S. Clark** is the Board of Governors Professor at Rutgers University. He served as a member of the United Nations Committee on Crime Prevention and Control between 1987 and 1990. Before joining the Rutgers faculty in 1972, he had worked at the New Zealand Justice Department and Ministry of Foreign Affairs, Victoria University of Wellington in New Zealand and the University of Iowa. He has been a visiting or adjunct professor at numerous institutions, including the University of Pennsylvania, the University of Miami, the University of Graz in Austria and the University of the South Pacific (Fiji). Professor Clark serves on the editorial boards of various publications, including the *Criminal Law Forum*, the *Human Rights Review* and the *International Lawyer*. He has been the general editor of the *Procedural Aspects of International Law* monographs since 2004. In 1995 and 1996, he represented the Government of Samoa in arguing the illegality of nuclear weapons before the International Court of Justice in The Hague. Since 1995, he has represented Samoa in negotiations to create the International Criminal Court. He was very active in Court's Special Working Group on the Crime of Aggression which had the task of drafting an amendment to the Court's Statute to activate its nascent jurisdiction over the crime of aggression. A New Zealander by birth, he is a graduate in history and law from Victoria University of Wellington and has graduate degrees form Columbia University School of Law in New York.

**Kate Cronin-Furman** received her JD in 2006 from Columbia Law School and has practiced law in New York and Cambodia. In 2008-2009, she served as a law clerk on the International Court of Justice for Judges Keith and Sepúlveda-Amor. Kate is currently completing a PhD in Political Science from Columbia University. Her research focuses on justice and accountability in the aftermath of mass atrocity. Her work has appeared in the *Columbia Law Review* and the *American University International Law Review*. Along with Amanda Taub, she blogs about international law and human rights at *Wronging Rights*.

**Silvia D'Ascoli** is currently a Legal Officer in the Trial Division of the Office of the Prosecutor at the International Criminal Tribunal for the Former Yugoslavia (ICTY). She has previously worked as an Associate Legal Officer in the Appeals Division of the Office of the Prosecutor at the ICTY. Silvia received her doctorate from the European University Institute in Florence in 2008 for her thesis, which focussed on sentencing practice before international criminal tribunals. She is the author of *Sentencing in International Criminal Law: The UN ad hoc Tribunals and Future Perspectives for the ICC* (Hart Publishing, 2011). She has also published in the *Journal of International Criminal Justice*.

**Amy DiBella** currently practises criminal defence in Pittsburgh, Pennsylvania. She is a former intern of the Office of Public Counsel for Defence at the ICC. Amy received her JD from the University of Pittsburgh where she was awarded the Faculty Award for Excellence in Legal Scholarship for her paper 'The Right to Confrontation; Reconciling the Constitution with International Criminal Proceedings'. She received her LLM in the International Law of Human Rights and Criminal Justice from Utrecht University, where she wrote her Masters' thesis on the topic 'Statements of Guilt and the Presumption of Innocence: A Comparative Approach for the International Criminal Court'.

**Mark A. Drumbl** is the Class of 1975 Alumni Professor at Washington & Lee University School of Law, where he also serves as Director of the Transnational Law Institute. His scholarly interests include public international law, international criminal law and transitional justice. He recently published *Reminagining Child Soldiers in International Law and Policy* (Oxford University Press, 2012). His 2007 book, *Atrocity, Punishment and International Law* (Cambridge University Press), has been widely reviewed and has earned critical acclaim. Drumbl's research has received scholarly excellence commendations from the International Association of Criminal Law, the American Association of Law Schools, and the American Society of International Law. He has represented genocide suspects in Rwandan jails; has served as an expert for U.S. courts; and has taught in a number of jurisdictions, including Pakistan, Finland, Uganda, Australia, France, Argentina, The Netherlands, Italy, and Brazil. His work has been cited by courts in the United States, United Kingdom, and Canada. He holds degrees in law and politics from McGill University, University of Toronto, and Columbia University, and served as law clerk to Justice Frank Iacobucci of the Supreme Court of Canada.

**Chile Eboe-Osuji** is currently serving as a judge in the Trial Division of the International Criminal Court, having been appointed to the bench in March 2012. He previously served as Legal Advisor to the United Nations High Commissioner

# Notes on Contributors

for Human Rights, Navanathem Pillay, and was involved in filing *amicus curiae* briefs on behalf of the Office of the High Commissioner before the European Court of Human Rights and the United States Supreme Court. He has worked at the International Criminal Tribunal for Rwanda and the Special Court for Sierra Leone, both as prosecuting counsel and in senior positions within Chambers. Judge Eboe-Osuji has taught international criminal law as an adjunct professor at the University of Ottawa and is a member of both the Nigerian and Canadian Bar. He provided legal advice to the Nigerian delegation to the ICC ASP Special Working Group on the Definition of the Crime of Aggression. Judge Eboe-Osuji holds a PhD in international criminal law from the University of Amsterdam.

**David P. Forsythe** is Professor Emeritus in Political Science at the University of Nebraska-Lincoln, USA. He is the author of *Human Rights in International Relations*, now in its third edition with Cambridge University Press. In 2011, he published a monograph entitled *The Politics of Prisoner Abuse: US Policy Toward Enemy Prisoners After 9/11*, also with Cambridge University Press. He is the general editor of the five-volume *Human Rights Encyclopedia* for Oxford University Press. His research interests include international human rights, international law and organisations, American foreign policy and international relations.

**Christopher Gosnell** is a counsel in private practice who has appeared on behalf of accused before the ICTY, SCSL and ICTR. He has acted on behalf of victims at the STL, and as part of the Office of Public Counsel for Victims at the International Criminal Court. He has also worked in the Office of the Prosecutor at the ICTY, and as Legal Officer in Chambers at the ICTR. Chris is admitted in New York, where he was previously in private practice and was a Lecturer in Law at Columbia Law School.

**Niamh Hayes** is Head of Office for the Institute for International Criminal Investigations, an NGO based in The Hague which provides specialised professional training in the investigation of international crimes and widespread human rights violations. She is completing a PhD at the Irish Centre for Human Rights, National University of Ireland on the investigation and prosecution of sexual violence by international criminal tribunals, for which she received a Government of Ireland Postgraduate Scholarship. She has an LLM in International Human Rights Law from the Irish Centre for Human Rights and an LLB from Trinity College Dublin. For two years, she was a Legal Consultant to Women's Initiatives for Gender Justice, a women's rights NGO based in The Hague. Niamh has lectured International Criminal Law and International Law in Trinity College Dublin, worked as a defence intern on the Karadžić trial at the ICTY, and was involved in the development by the United Nations of a standardised curriculum for investigating sexual violence to be used in pre-deployment training of all UN Police personnel. She is co-editor with Dr Éadaoin O'Brien of *Forensic Science and International Law: Cases, Problems and Perspectives* (TMC Asser Press, forthcoming 2013) and has contributed over 45 case reports to the *Oxford Reports on International Criminal Law*.

# The Ashgate Research Companion to International Criminal Law

**Kevin Jon Heller** is currently an Associate Professor and Reader at Melbourne Law School. He holds a PhD in law from Leiden University and a JD with distinction from Stanford Law School. His book *The Nuremberg Military Tribunals and the Origins of International Criminal Law* was published by Oxford University Press in June 2011. From December 2008 until February 2011, he served as one of Radovan Karadžić's formally-appointed legal associates.

**Dov Jacobs** is an Assistant Professor in International Law at the Grotius Centre for International Legal Studies at Leiden University. Previously, he was a postdoctoral researcher at the University of Amsterdam, a PhD Researcher at the European University Institute in Florence and a lecturer in Public International Law at the University Roma Tre. He is currently a senior editor on the editorial board of the *Leiden Journal of International Law* and an Expert Associate on the SHARES Project of the University of Amsterdam. He has published extensively in the field of international law and international criminal law. His current research interests cover international criminal law, public international law (particularly state responsibility) and legal theory.

**Charles Chernor Jalloh** is an Assistant Professor at the University of Pittsburgh School of Law, Pennsylvania, USA. A member of the Ontario Bar, he has been a Legal Counsel in the Crimes Against Humanity and War Crimes Section, Canadian Department of Justice. He was formerly the Legal Advisor to the Office of the Principal Defender (OPD) in the Special Court for Sierra Leone, where he acted as court-appointed Duty Counsel in the trial of former Liberian President Charles Taylor; an Associate Legal Officer at the International Criminal Tribunal for Rwanda and a Visiting Professional at the International Criminal Court. He is an active member of the international criminal bar serving, inter alia, on the Advisory Panel to the President of the International Criminal Tribunal for the Former Yugoslavia. He earned his LL.B. and B.C.L. degrees from McGill University and his M.St. in International Human Rights Law, with distinction, at Oxford University, where he was also a Chevening Scholar. Charles has published widely on issues of international criminal justice in prestigious scholarly journals. The Founding Editor-in-Chief of the *African Journal of Legal Studies*, he is the lead editor of the first multi-volume *Law Reports of the Special Court for Sierra Leone* (Brill), editor of *Consolidated Legal Texts of the Special Court for Sierra Leone* (Brill) and *The Sierra Leone Special Court and Its Legacy: The Impact for Africa and International Criminal Law* (Cambridge University Press, 2013).

**Wayne Jordash** is a barrister at Doughty Street Chambers, London, specialising in criminal defence and human rights law. Currently Wayne is lead counsel at the ICTY defending Jovica Stanišić, the first intelligence chief to be tried by an international criminal tribunal. Stanišić is alleged to have been the second in command in the Milošević regime during the civil war in the former Yugoslavia, charged with crimes against humanity and war crimes in Bosnia and Herzegovina and Croatia. Wayne is also acting as a consultant to the Appellant team in the case of *Sagahutu* convicted in 2011 at the ICTR for the crime of genocide. His practice also includes a wide range of consultancies, e.g., advising on domestic prosecutions of international crimes and related humanitarian law issues. This advisory work has included the Extraordinary Chambers in the Courts of Cambodia (ECCC) (advising on a range of international law issues relevant to the defence of former Khmer Rouge members of the Pol Pot regime, including the deputy to Pol Pot (*Nuon Chea*) and the former Minister of Foreign Affairs (*Khieu Samphan*), the Libyan Ministry of Justice (on issues relevant to domestic prosecutions), the International Commission of Jurists (prosecution of international crimes), and to the Cambodian Centre for Human Rights (CCHR) (advising on a range of international, criminal and human rights law issues for the NGO that works to promote democracy and human rights throughout Cambodia).

**Michael Kearney** is a Lecturer in Law at the University of Sussex. Michael studied law at University College Cork, and obtained an LLM from the Irish Centre for Human Rights, National University of Ireland Galway. His PhD dissertation, also awarded by NUI Galway, was published by Oxford University Press in 2007 as *The Prohibition of Propaganda for War in International Law*. The book was awarded the 2008 Lieber Certificate of Merit (for a work in the area of the law of armed conflict) by the American Society of International Law. Michael lectured in the Department of Politics and the Centre for Applied Human Rights at the University of York, where he was RCUK Fellow in Law and Human Rights, and was Fellow in Law at the London School of Economics. He has also worked in advocacy and research roles for Al-Haq, a Palestinian human rights NGO based in Ramallah.

**Pádraig McAuliffe** is a graduate of University College Cork. In 2009, he was awarded his doctorate for his research on the Special Panels for Serious Crimes in East Timor. He held a visiting research fellowship at the University of California, Los Angeles in 2007. From 2008 to 2009, Pádraig worked as a researcher in the Legal Division of the Irish Department of Foreign Affairs. In 2009, he was appointed to a lectureship in law at the University of Dundee where he teaches international human rights law. His research interests are primarily in the fields of transitional justice and international criminal law and has published a book entitled *Transitional Justice and Rule of Law Reconstruction: A Contentious Relationship* (Routledge, 2013)

**Yvonne McDermott** is a Lecturer in Law at Bangor Law School, Wales, where she is Deputy Director of the Bangor Centre for International Law and the School's Director of Teaching and Learning. She is completing a PhD at the Irish Centre for Human Rights, National University of Ireland, on the potential of international criminal law to develop the highest standards of fairness for the conduct of criminal proceedings, and its failure to embrace that potential standard-setting function. She is the managing editor of the Oxford University Press *Oxford Reports on International Criminal Law* database, expert researcher on the *International Criminal Procedure Expert Framework: Towards the Codification of General Rules and Principles* project, and Assistant Editor of the *Criminal Law Forum* journal. Yvonne was awarded the inaugural Böhler Franken Koppe Wijngaarden Advocaten/Hague Academic Coalition Award for Young Professionals in June 2009. She has worked professionally with the Irish Department of Foreign Affairs and as a consultant to the United Nations High Commissioner for Refugees. Her research interests include international criminal law, international criminal procedure, human rights and refugee law.

**Joseph Powderly** is Assistant Professor of Public International Law at the Grotius Centre for International Legal Studies, Leiden University. He is a PhD candidate and Government of Ireland Postgraduate Scholar at the Irish Centre for Human Rights, researching theories of judicial interpretation and the development of international criminal and humanitarian law. Joseph holds an LLM in International Human Rights Law from the Irish Centre for Human Rights, as well as a BA and an LLB from the National University of Ireland Galway. Along with Dr Shane Darcy, he was co-editor of and a contributor to *Judicial Creativity in International Criminal Tribunals*, an edited collection published by Oxford University Press in 2010. In 2009, he investigated the commission of crimes and widespread human rights violations against the Rohingya, a stateless Muslim ethnic minority living in north-western Burma, and was co-author of the resulting report *Crimes Against Humanity in Western Burma: The Situation of the Rohingyas* (Irish Centre for Human Rights, 2010). He has written over 80 case reports for the *Oxford Reports on International Criminal Law*, as well as numerous book chapters on topics ranging from the principle of complementarity to Irish involvement in the drafting of the Geneva Conventions. He is Managing Editor of the peer-reviewed journal *Criminal Law Forum*.

**John Reynolds** is the National University of Ireland EJ Phelan Fellow in International Law. He is a Ph.D candidate at the National University of Ireland, Galway and Teaching Fellow on the E.MA Programme at the European Inter-University Centre for Human Rights and Democratisation in Venice. John received a Bachelor's degree in Business & Law from University College Dublin and an LL.M in International Human Rights Law from the Irish Centre for Human Rights, National University of Ireland, Galway. For several years, he worked as a Legal Researcher for Al-Haq, a Palestinian human rights organisation based in the West Bank. His doctoral research is on colonialism, states of emergency and international law, and between 2009 and 2012 he was awarded a National University of Ireland Travelling Scholarship and a Government of Ireland Postgraduate Scholarship. John is a co-author of *Beyond Occupation: Apartheid, Colonialism and International Law in the Occupied Palestinian Territories* (Pluto Press, 2012), and was editor of *Human Rights Through the Lens,* a book of photography celebrating the tenth anniversary of the Irish Centre for Human Rights.

**Colleen Rohan** is an attorney who currently practises as an international criminal defence lawyer. She is a member of the International Criminal Law Bureau, providing advice, consultancy and training services to governments, international organisations and private clients. Colleen has represented members of the military and private clients charged with genocide, murder, terrorism and crimes against humanity, in domestic and international courts including the International Criminal Tribunal for the former Yugoslavia. She has also represented clients in extradition and death penalty cases in the United States. She is a Vice President of the Executive Committee of the Association of Defence Counsel Practising Before the International Criminal Tribunal for the former Yugoslavia (ADC-ICTY). She was a focal point for a joint initiative between the ADC-ICTY and the UN Interregional Crime and Justice Research Institute (UNICRI) to develop a manual on defence practice before international tribunals, and was a co-author of the resulting *Manual on International Criminal Defence: ADC-ICTY Developed Practices* (2011). She has lectured extensively on international criminal law at universities in the United States and Europe and has provided training to lawyers in the United States, Europe and at the International Criminal Court.

**Darryl Robinson** is Assistant Professor at Queen's University, Ontario, teaching international law, international criminal law and international human rights law. He received his LLM in International Legal Studies from NYU School of Law, where he was also a Hauser Global Scholar. He clerked at the Supreme Court of Canada under Justice John Major. From 1997 to 2003 he served as Legal Officer for the Canadian Department of Foreign Affairs, for which he received a Minister's Citation and a Minister's Award for Foreign Policy Excellence. He was an advisor to the Chief Prosecutor of the International Criminal Court from 2004 to 2006, and then a Fellow, Adjunct Professor and Director of the International Human Rights Clinic at the University of Toronto Faculty of Law from 2006 to 2008. He is co-editor with Håkan Friman, Rob Cryer and Elizabeth Wilmhurst of the *Introduction to International Criminal Law and Procedure* (Cambridge University Press, 2nd edn, 2010).

**Ben Saul** is Professor of International Law and an Australian Research Council Future Fellow at the University of Sydney. as a leading expert on global counter-terrorism law, human rights, the law of war, and international crimes. He has published six books, 65 scholarly articles, and hundreds of other publications and presentations, and his research has been used in various national and international courts. Ben has taught law at Oxford, the Hague Academy of International Law and in China, India, Nepal and Cambodia, and has been a visiting professor at Harvard Law School. Ben practices as a barrister in international and national courts, has advised various United Nations bodies and foreign governments, has delivered foreign aid projects, and often appears in the media. He has a doctorate in law from Oxford and honours in Arts and Law from Sydney.

**William A. Schabas** is Professor of International Law at Middlesex University in London. He is also Professor of International Criminal Law and Human Rights at Leiden University, Emeritus Professor of Human Rights Law at the Irish Centre for Human Rights of the National University of Ireland Galway, and an honorary professor at the Chinese Academy of Social Sciences in Beijing and Wuhan University. He is the author of more than 20 books and 300 journal articles, on such subjects as the abolition of capital punishment, genocide and the international criminal tribunals. Professor Schabas was a member of the Sierra Leone Truth and Reconciliation Commission. He was a member of the Board of Trustees of the United Nations Voluntary Fund for Technical Cooperation in Human Rights and president of the International Association of Genocide Scholars. He serves as President of the Irish Branch of the International Law Association and Chair of the Institute for International Criminal Investigations. He is an Officer of the Order of Canada and a member of the Royal Irish Academy.

**Lorraine Smith van Lin** has been the Programme Manager for the International Bar Association (IBA) ICC Programme in The Hague since July 2007. She previously served as Judge of the Resident Magistrate's Court in Kingston, Jamaica, conducting preliminary enquiries and presiding over criminal cases. Lorraine worked in the Jamaican Office of the Director of Public Prosecutions for several years, prosecuting serious criminal cases and serving as Assistant Director of Public Prosecutions and Crown Counsel. She received her LLM in International Human Rights Law from the University of Essex and her LLB from the University of the West Indies.

**Tara Smith** is a PhD candidate at the Irish Centre for Human Rights, National University of Ireland Galway. Her doctoral dissertation is on the protection of the environment in non-international armed conflict. Previously Tara has been a Lecturer in Law at Bangor University, Wales. She has also worked as a Teaching Fellow at the Irish Centre for Human Rights and a Research Fellow at the International Institute for Higher Studies in Criminal Sciences, Italy. Tara is also a licensed Attorney-at-Law in the state of New York.

**Carsten Stahn** is Professor of International Criminal Law and Global Justice at Leiden University and Programme Director of the Grotius Centre for International Legal Studies. He previously worked as a Legal Officer in Chambers at the International Criminal Court from 2003 to 2008. He obtained his PhD degree (*summa cum laude*) from Humboldt University Berlin, and holds LLM degrees from New York University and Cologne – Paris I (Panthéon-Sorbonne). He is author of *The Law and Practice of International Territorial Administration: Versailles to Iraq and Beyond* (Cambridge University Press, 2008 and 2010). He has edited several volumes in the area of international criminal justice and published numerous articles in the areas of peace and security, international courts and tribunals, transitional justice and the law of international organisations. He is ICC editor of the *Leiden Journal of International Law*, Executive Editor of the *Criminal Law Forum* and Correspondent of the *Netherlands International Law Review*. His work has been cited in the jurisprudence of the ICC, the ICJ and the European Court of Human Rights.

**Amanda Taub** holds a JD from Georgetown University Law Center, where she was the Senior Articles Editor of the *Georgetown Journal of International Law*. She served as a law clerk to Judge Theodore H. Katz of the United States District Court for the Southern District of New York. Currently, she is an Adjunct Professor of

International Law at Fordham University, teaching courses on international law and human rights. She is also a member of a Columbia University research group investigating the mental health needs of unaccompanied minors in deportation proceedings. In her private practice at the law firm of Buhler Duggal & Henry, Amanda specializes in the representation of startups and emerging companies from around the world. Along with Kate Cronin-Furman, she blogs about international law and human rights at *Wronging Rights*.

# Preface

As everyone knows, there is a certain pampered halo that accompanies most things new that are generally warmly received into the fold. Such is the case with a new addition to the family: usually a child. So, too, a new spouse in a marriage not forged over the vigorous objection of the mother-in-law. But the halo never lasts forever. Sooner or later, critical questions are engaged. They mostly concern whether the addition has lived up to what had been hoped; whether life in the fold has been really improved or actually diminished by it; and so on. Similar observations largely apply to the birth of *modern* international criminal law, which was conceived in Nuremberg and Tokyo in the 1940s and finally delivered in The Hague and Arusha in the early 1990s, after that long a period of gestation. I am constrained to say 'modern' international criminal law here, not least because Jenny Martinez, in her fascinating new book on slavery and the origins of international human rights law, challenges the current assumption that international criminal law and international human rights law were largely post-Second World War phenomena. '[I]n fact', she contends 'the nineteenth-century slavery abolition movement was the first successful international human rights campaign, and international treaties and courts were its central features. Indeed, even the phrase "crimes against humanity"—which came to modern fame based on its use at the Nuremberg trials of Nazi war criminals—was used in the nineteenth century to describe the slave trade'.[1] As she had earlier observed, '[m]ore than a century before Nuremberg, international courts in Sierra Leone, Cuba, Brazil, and other places around the Atlantic heard cases related to the slave trade, the original "crime against humanity"'.[2] The work of these courts and the subject matter of their jurisdiction '[provide] insight into issues faced by modern international tribunals like the International Criminal Court'.[3] Martinez never contends that these prize courts really did exercise a criminal jurisdiction as such, as opposed to admiralty jurisdiction (of a civil nature) to determine whether a captured slave ship was lawfully impounded and therefore liable to forfeiture

---

[1] JS Martinez, *The Slave Trade and the Origins of International Human Rights Law* (Oxford University Press, Oxford 2012) 13–14.
[2] Ibid 6.
[3] Ibid.

as lawful bounty to the captain and crew of the arresting ship.[4] But, in view of the spectre of their subject matter as a crime against humanity coupled with the related old international crime of piracy, 'modern' seems an appropriate modifier to the epoch of international criminal law that commenced with the creation of the ICTY and ICTR.

Indeed, after about a decade and half of operation, it will be strange to maintain a mindset that continues to see modern international criminal law as 'a newcomer in the field of international law'. After all, a decade of practice is generally accepted in the common law world as endowing a lawyer with sufficient seniority for promotion to the rank of a superior court judge. The development of modern international criminal law which began with the establishment of the ICTY and the ICTR respectively in 1993 and 1994, and had taken in the creation of the Special Court for Sierra Leone in 2002, as well as national judicial mechanisms established to try international crimes in Timor Leste, Bosnia-Herzegovina and Cambodia, has now tapered to 'an increasingly unipolar international criminal legal order' in which the International Criminal Court has become the last stop. Even the ICC, as the last major pillar in the edifice of international criminal law, is widely recognised to have come of age. Among the indicia of its maturity was the change of guard that was witnessed in New York in December 2011, when a new chief prosecutor and six new judges were elected, in that order. It is therefore right to engage the critical questions about international criminal law. This volume seeks to do precisely that. The questions explored come in varied forms, in the general order of issues of procedural and substantive law, the place and role of international criminal law in the wider world, and issues to contemplate for the future.

In contemplating critical questions about the substance of international criminal law, its role in the wider world and in the future, we may derive some inspiration from a question posed in the Call for Presentations for the 11th Biennial Conference of the International Association of Women Judges, held in London in May 2012. In the segment entitled 'Violence and the Problem-Solving Court', the question was asked: 'Is judging about resolving private disputes or punishing wrongdoers? Or is it also about finding creative and positive solutions which may *help people lead better lives in future*?'[5] The import of that critical question about judging as a general legal occupation also applies to international criminal law in general. In particular, is international criminal law also about finding creative solutions that may help people lead better lives in future? Serviceable answers may be found in general theories concerning the purpose of criminal law.

---

[4] Quite the contrary, she had disagreed in an earlier writing that these prize courts did not exercise criminal jurisdiction: see JS Martinez, 'International Courts and the US Constitution: Re-examining the History' (2011) 159 *U Penn L Rev* 1069, 1073. Eugene Kontorovich had made the opposite contention: see E Kontorovich, 'The Constitutionality of International Courts: The Forgotten Precedent of Slave-Trade Tribunals' (2009) 158 *U Penn L Rev* 39, 83–86.

[5] Emphasis added.

In an effort to explain the purposes of criminal law, the American Law Institute's Model Penal Code (MPC) suggests the following:

1. to forbid and prevent conduct that unjustifiably and inexcusably inflicts or threatens substantial harm to individual or public interests;
2. to subject to public control persons whose conduct indicates that they are disposed to commit crimes;
3. to safeguard conduct that is without fault from condemnation as criminal;
4. to give fair warning of the nature of the conduct declared to be an offence;
5. to differentiate on reasonable grounds between serious and minor offences.[6]

For their part, Simester et al. tell us that the criminal law, like other types of law, is a means by which the state participates in the ordering of its citizens' lives.[7] Surely, the purposes stated in the MPC are, by any other description, efforts aimed at 'ordering citizens' lives'. Smith and Hogan appear less confident about bold statements on the contemporary purposes of the English criminal law, in view of the passage of many centuries over which it has been developed in that country. Yet, they do agree that the MPC contains what 'might be taken as a statement of the objectives of the substantive law of crime in *a modern legal system*'.[8]

The international criminal law of our times is a modern system of legal norms that undoubtedly seeks to accomplish universally for humanity what criminal law seeks to accomplish for citizens within national borders. If, as a social objective, the creation of conditions that will help people lead better lives seems too ambitious a purpose to ascribe to (international) criminal law, we should be able to settle for the minima of removal of certain human conducts that tend to interfere with that objective. At the appropriate level of abstraction, the proscription of genocide, crimes against humanity, war crimes and the crime of aggression surely aim to achieve that minimum objective. Yet, the proscription of these violent anti-social conducts that inflict direct harm upon its victims ought not be seen as the limit of international criminal law's attainable scope, in its purpose of removing human conducts that tend to interfere with a better life for members of society. Indeed, there are other anti-social conducts of a non-violent nature that inflict just as direct a harm and are just as egregious in ramifications as the proscribed conducts of the violent type. In this connection, it is helpful to keep in mind that the principled basis for international criminal law's proscriptions is not exclusive to violent anti-social conducts. One sees this in the motivations for the creation of the International Criminal Court. The first of these is the consciousness 'that all peoples are united by common bonds, their cultures pieced together in a shared heritage, and ... that

---

[6] American Law Institute, Model Penal Code, §1.02(1).
[7] See AP Simester, JR Spencer, GR Sullivan and GJ Virgo, *Simester and Sullivan's Criminal Law: Theory and Doctrine*, 4th edn (Hart Publishing, Oxford and Portland, Oregon 2010) 1.
[8] See D Ormerod, *Smith and Hogan, Criminal Law*, 12th edn (OUP, Oxford 2008) 3 [emphasis added].

this delicate mosaic may be shattered at any time'.[9] Much can be said about these 'common bonds' and 'shared heritage' that unite 'all peoples'. But, perhaps, the most succinct expression of them is found in the preamble to the Charter of the UN, which recognises the need not only 'to save succeeding generations from the scourge of war' which brings untold sorrow to humanity; but also the need, among other things, 'to reaffirm faith in fundamental human rights, in the dignity and worth of the human person' and 'to promote social progress and better standards of life in larger freedom': all of which have tasked the determination of 'we the peoples of the United Nations'. These ideals engage the determination to suppress not only the misanthropic impulses of men to inflict harmful violence directly on their fellow human beings, but also the impulse to engage in other conducts of a non-violent type that cause just as much harm in their misanthropic effect. There is indeed no convincing reason not to target these types of conduct for international criminal law's proscription, considering that a powerful impetus that worked the mind of the plenipotentiaries that gave the Rome Statute to the world was 'that during this century millions of children, women and men have been victims of unimaginable atrocities that deeply shock the conscience of humanity'.[10] The most memorable and dramatic of these 'unimaginable atrocities' have surely been violent: the Holocaust; the Rwandan genocide; the apartheid regime in South Africa; ethnic cleansing in the former Yugoslavia; torture and enforced disappearances in Latin America; and sundry war crimes committed in the Vietnam war and in every war fought in the recent memory of those who drafted the words of that preamble. Yet, there are other forms of 'unimaginable atrocities that deeply shock the conscience of humanity' – to which millions of children, women and men have been victims in a manner that has diminished their dignity and worth of the human person – that have taken a non-violent shape.

One such atrocity is kleptocracy. Wikipedia describes it as 'rule by thieves' and goes on to provide the following useful definition: 'a form of political and government corruption where the government exists to increase the personal wealth and political power of its officials and the ruling class at the expense of the wider population, often without pretence of honest service. This type of government corruption is often achieved by the embezzlement of state funds.' It 'deprives millions of health care, education and the prospects of a sustainable future'.[11] It is significant to recognise in the definition and description of kleptocracy the cruel fact that the theft in question is of staggering amounts that go beyond what the thief and his family could possibly use in a lifetime; this to be contrasted with the fact that his poor compatriots from whom the wealth is stolen are left to die from lack of basic needs. It surely must shock the conscience to learn that a leader was suspected to have stolen as much as $5 billion of the national wealth of a

---

[9] Rome Statute of the International Criminal Court, 2187 UNTS 90, 17 July 1998, entered into force 1 July 2002 ('ICC Statute'), Preamble.
[10] Ibid.
[11] Transparency International, Press Release, 25 March 2004.

country where citizens, on average, earn $99 per annum in per capita income.[12] But beyond the invariable costs of kleptocracy to the citizen, in terms of deprivation of opportunity for a better life, one must not ignore the kleptocracy's potential for violent social upheaval that likely results in violent political suppression in the manner of crimes against humanity and other violent human rights violations.

Kleptocracy could afford both motive and opportunity to violate human rights violently, and to continue to do so. The motive might come from kleptocracy giving a reason to suppress public exposure and criticism as may come from current or former colleagues, independent media, opposition politicians, social interest groups, and citizens. Suppression of criticisms could potentially take the form of extermination of political opponents and critics, extra-judicial executions, torture, persecution, arbitrary arrests and detentions, enforced disappearances, and so on. Similarly, the kleptocrat, fearing post-incumbency prosecution or loss of the venal privileges of office, might resolve to remain in office until death, regardless of any rule of law militating against him in that regard. Popular movement for regime change – even by constitutional means – may result in his further violent violations of human rights. Tactics employed to maintain may include any measure to divert attention from the need for political change. To this end, resort may be had to such diversionary tactics as the foment of international wars of aggression, civil wars, sectarian conflicts, inter-racial or inter-ethnic strife, and so forth, even resulting in genocide. Coupled with this motive to violate human rights, an incumbent kleptocrat has the opportunity to commit the violation, simply by having the power to do so, as he is in office and has the ability to marshal the coercive forces of the state.

It is commendable that both the African Union and the UN have adopted conventions dedicated to combating and preventing corruption. But these efforts need teeth in the form of international criminal law to make a difference. That is one atrocity to contemplate for the substance of international criminal law, its role in the wider world and in the future.

CHILE EBOE-OSUJI
*The Hague, 2012*

---

[12] Ibid. See also Transparency International, Global Corruption Report 2004, 13.

# Introduction

## Niamh Hayes, Yvonne McDermott and William A. Schabas

International criminal law is frequently presented or discussed as a relative newcomer within the international legal order. It is true that one can follow some of its tendrils back through to the international military prosecutions following the Second World War, and some back to the aftermath of the First World War or even further back to the development of the first standards of international humanitarian law. However, it is equally true, but a fact which is frequently not entirely absorbed, that what we most often mean when we refer to 'international criminal law' – namely, the body of procedural rules and substantive law identified and applied by modern international criminal tribunals – is not yet 20 years old. It is remarkable in many ways that international criminal law has carved out such a prominent position within the international legal framework in such a short space of time. A number of factors have contributed to this remarkable progress: the parallel development and enforcement of international human rights law and international humanitarian law; the creation of numerous ad hoc international criminal institutions capable of identifying, interpreting and applying international criminal law; the existence of sufficient political impetus in a post-Cold War context for the inclusion of judicial mechanisms in the international community's responses to conflict; the establishment of a permanent treaty-based international criminal court; and, of course, the consistent efforts of countless activists, diplomats and scholars to support and advance the project of international criminal justice.

As international criminal law has developed at an exponential rate over the last two decades, international criminal scholarship has had to evolve to keep pace. As the number of international and internationalised criminal tribunals has multiplied, an ever-expanding body of procedural and substantive law has been created. It has been challenging for academics and practitioners merely to maintain a comprehensive overview of the existing law, to say nothing of identifying overarching patterns or trends within its development. However, as international criminal law becomes more established as a distinct discipline, it becomes more imperative for international criminal scholarship to provide a degree of critical analysis, both of individual legal issues and of the international criminal project as a whole. This book represents a modest collective effort to introduce an element of legal realism or critical legal studies into the academic discourse. Not only is this vital for the maturation and continued evolution of international criminal theory, but it also provides an important safeguard for the maintenance of appropriate standards in what is, lest we forget, a penal system.

While international criminal law provides a goldmine of abstract theoretical and legal issues for academics to parse, its essential function is to adjudicate the criminal responsibility of individuals, and as such, it must live up to its due process obligations. The contributions of Yvonne McDermott and Colleen Rohan to this edited collection provide a closer examination of whether the procedural guarantees and fair trial rights provided to defendants and accused persons under international criminal law are actually realised in substance. Charles Jalloh and Amy DiBella analyse the consistent gulf between the endorsement of the principle of equality of arms in judicial decisions and its fulfilment in practice. Chris Gosnell and Wayne Jordash provide a practitioner's perspective on whether the standard of factual pleading and judicial scrutiny of joint criminal enterprise and omissions liability give rise to either good law or fair convictions. It is clear from all the contributions to this volume that there is certainly no basis for complacency or self-congratulation in relation to the maintenance of consistent due process and fair trial rights across all modern international criminal tribunals.

It can be equally instructive to narrow the focus of scrutiny somewhat to provide a more detailed critical analysis of individual legal or practical issues. Some are unique to specific institutions, while some are of relevance to all criminal processes. In relation to the International Criminal Court, Dov Jacobs examines the vexed question of the recharacterisation of facts and charges, Lorraine Smith takes a critical overview of the development of the system of victim participation, and Roger Clark presents a hypothetical application of the newly-added crime of aggression as defined in Kampala. Some of the criticisms most frequently levelled at that Court, particularly the allegation that its investigations and prosecutions to date have been inordinately focussed on Africa, are addressed in the contribution of Kai Ambos. Kevin Jon Heller, Carsten Stahn and Darryl Robinson provide multiple perspectives on a single issue, namely the question of whether sentencing should be a relevant factor for the purposes of complementarity. Some matters have been grappled with by multiple international criminal institutions, often to mutually contradictory effect. The logic and consistency of the sentencing practice of the ad hoc international criminal tribunals is examined by Silvia D'Ascoli, while Joseph Powderly analyses the legitimacy of the judicial interpretation and development of international criminal law. Some chapters scrutinise the ability or efficacy of international criminal law to address specific crimes or situations. Niamh Hayes provides a narrative analysis of the efforts of the first Prosecutor of the ICC to investigate and prosecute sexual violence, and Tara Smith assesses the capability of international criminal law to provide legal redress or accountability for environmental damage. The definition of the international crime of terrorism identified by the Special Tribunal for Lebanon is deconstructed by Ben Saul. Michael

Kearney and John Reynolds position the efforts of the Palestinian Authority to access the jurisdiction of the International Criminal Court within the broader context of its engagement with and acceptance by the international legal community.

International criminal law does not operate in a vacuum; it is itself a political instrument and it remains susceptible to outside influences and the vagaries of international relations and *realpolitik*. The contribution of David Forsythe examines the role of the Security Council in the development of modern international criminal institutions and policy, while William Schabas provides a critical analysis of the priorities and limitations of prosecutorial discretion. The successes, failures, idiosyncrasies and limitations of hybrid international criminal tribunals as transitional justice institutions are assessed in Pádraig McAuliffe's chapter. Kate Cronin-Furman and Amanda Taub discuss the expectations of international criminal justice and the ability of international criminal trials to address the traditional rationales for prosecution and punishment. Finally, Mark Drumbl attempts to predict some of the future challenges and prospects for international criminal justice.

While the focus of this book is to provide a degree of critical engagement which has sometimes been absent or not particularly prominent within academic literature on international criminal law, its intention is not to supply fodder for pessimism or reflexive fault-finding. The very existence of modern international criminal institutions would have been dismissed as a utopian ideal only a few decades ago, and the advances and precedents which have been achieved since that time are fully deserving of praise. However, international criminal law is a system like any other, and a degree of vigilance and self-reflection, both internally and from the wider epistemic community, remains a necessity to minimise or avoid institutional and theoretical dysfunction. It is to be hoped that this book will mark merely the first of many efforts to provide a timely critical overview of both the health and trajectory of international criminal law's continuing evolution.

# PART I
International Crimes and Modes of Liability

# Sisyphus Wept: Prosecuting Sexual Violence at the International Criminal Court

## Niamh Hayes[1]

It would be churlish, even in a book devoted to critical analyses of the subject, not to acknowledge that international criminal prosecutions are an incredibly complex and eye-wateringly difficult undertaking. Establishing jurisdiction and admissibility; selecting defendants or specific incidents for prosecution; conducting investigations, often via translators and frequently several years after the relevant events occurred, in situations of ongoing conflict or fraught post-conflict societies; identifying the most appropriate charges and modes of liability; balancing disclosure requirements with the need to protect vulnerable victims and witnesses; obtaining custody of a suspect: none of these are simple tasks, and all have the potential to act as lightning rods for criticism or as pressure points for any errors or weaknesses in the case. In some respects, international prosecutors are faced with a thankless task. No matter what they do, someone somewhere is waiting to tell them they have done it wrong, or not enough.

In many ways, an examination of an international tribunal's efforts to prosecute sexual violence provides a microcosm of the successes, failures and challenges of all its international criminal prosecutions. The failure to charge even a single count of rape at the Nuremberg trial is emblematic of the International Military Tribunal's deeply compromised position in relation to offences for which the victorious Allied powers, specifically the Soviet Union, did not exactly have clean hands.[2]

---

[1] All opinions expressed in this chapter are the author's alone.
[2] The foundational Charter of the Nuremberg Tribunal did not list rape as a war crime or newly-fledged crime against humanity, but did include provisions on other inhumane acts and enslavement which could have provided a jurisdictional basis for including evidence of sexual violence. The failure to acknowledge this crucial element of the German war campaign has been attributed to a lack of political will and a certain degree of squeamishness on the part of the Soviet delegates to the London Conference, perhaps as a result of the widespread perpetration of rape and sexual violence by Soviet forces in their

The Yugoslavia Tribunal grappled with some initial strategic and investigative hurdles,³ but went on to establish by far the most robust and least dysfunctional body of prosecutions for sexual violence of all the modern international tribunals, a description which could equally be applied to that Tribunal's broader reputation. The Rwanda Tribunal's marquee judgment on rape as an international crime, in the *Akayesu* case, was achieved almost despite itself given that the original indictment had not contained any sexual violence charges,⁴ and an analysis of its prosecutorial strategy reveals a series of problems inherited from its original investigations and a disconcerting tendency to drop rape charges wholesale in exchange for a guilty plea.⁵ The Special Court for Sierra Leone established some fascinating legal precedents, such as identifying and defining the crime against humanity of forced marriage,⁶ but was constrained by a limited range of defendants and a catastrophic decision to exclude all evidence of sexual violence from one of the cases for procedural reasons.⁷

---

final push on Berlin at the end of the war. See for example KD Askin, *War Crimes Against Women: Prosecution in International War Crimes Tribunals* (Kluwer Law International, The Hague 1997) 163; R Copelon, 'Gender Crimes as War Crimes: Integrating Crimes Against Women into International Criminal Law' (2000–2001) 46 *McGill L J* 217, 222.

³    K Engle, 'Feminism and Its (Dis)Contents: Criminalising Wartime Rape in Bosnia and Herzegovina' (2005) 99(4) *AJIL* 778.

⁴    See for example N Hayes, 'Creating a Definition of Rape in International Law: The Contribution of the International Criminal Tribunals' in S Darcy and J Powderly (eds) *Judicial Creativity at the International Criminal Tribunals* (OUP, Oxford 2010) 129, 132–133; B van Schaack, 'Engendering Genocide: The *Akayesu* Case Before the International Criminal Tribunal for Rwanda' (Santa Clara University School of Law Legal Studies Research Paper Series, Working Paper No. 08-55 2008) <http://ssrn.com/abstract=1154259> last accessed 19 December 2011.

⁵    See for example *Prosecutor v Bisengimana* (Judgment and Sentence) ICTR-00-60 (13 April 2006); *Prosecutor v Nzabirinda* (Sentencing Judgment) ICTR-2001-77 (23 February 2007); *Prosecutor v Rugambarara* (Sentencing Judgment) ICTR-00-59 (16 November 2007); *Prosecutor v Serushago* (Sentence) ICTR-98-39-S (5 February 1999).

⁶    *Prosecutor v Brima et al* (Trial Judgment, Partly Dissenting Opinion of Justice Doherty on Count 7 (Sexual Slavery) and Count 8 (Forced Marriages)) SCSL-04-16-T (20 June 2007); see further V Oosterveld, 'The Special Court for Sierra Leone, Child Soldiers and Forced Marriage: Providing Clarity or Confusion?' (2007) 45 *Canadian Yearbook of Int'l Law* 131. In its judgment in the Charles Taylor trial, the Chamber appeared to row back from the position that forced marriage was a distinct crime against humanity under the rubric of other inhumane acts, interpreting it instead as a distinctive sub-category of sexual slavery. See *Prosecutor v Taylor* (Trial Judgement) SCSL-03-01-T (18 May 2012) paras 428–430.

⁷    *Prosecutor v Fofana et al* (Reasoned Majority Decision on Prosecution Motion for a Ruling on the Admissibility of Evidence) SCSL-04-14-PT (24 May 2005); Judge Boutet of Canada dissenting: *Prosecutor v Fofana et al* (Dissenting Opinion of Justice Pierre Boutet on Decision on Prosecution Motion for a Ruling on the Admissibility of Evidence) SCSL-04-14-PT (24 May 2005). See further M Staggs Kelsall and S Stepakoff, '"When We Wanted to Talk About Rape": Silencing Sexual Violence at the Special Court for Sierra Leone' (2007) 1(3) *Int'l J of Transitional Justice* 355; CE Rose, 'Troubled Indictments at the Special Court

Despite their individual foibles, the accumulated efforts of modern international criminal tribunals to prosecute sexual violence had tremendous normative and substantive impact. For the first time, rape and sexual violence were acknowledged as war crimes, crimes against humanity and even constituent elements of the crime of genocide; perhaps more importantly, in practical terms, the *ad hoc* tribunals showed through literal trial and error that successful prosecutions of sexual violence as an international crime could be achieved, even in the context of the inherent systemic difficulties attendant on any international criminal investigation or prosecution.[8] These achievements were hard won, and when the Rome Statute came into force in July 2002, hopes were high that the first permanent international criminal tribunal would capitalise and advance on them.[9] Unfortunately, in the decade since, the rock which had been so painstakingly hauled up the hill by prosecutors and practitioners in the other international criminal tribunals was permitted to tumble back to square one, as the International Criminal Court under Luis Moreno-Ocampo regressed in both strategy and practice and competent, focussed prosecutions of sexual violence became depressingly scarce once again. This regression was not confined to this category of crimes alone, as one of the International Criminal Court's defining features in its initial years was an obstinate failure to learn from the accumulated practice of previously established international criminal tribunals. Several key institutional dysfunctions are revealed by an examination of the ICC's record in relation to sexual violence, and one can only hope that they may be acknowledged and addressed by Fatou Bensouda, the newly elected Chief Prosecutor, as she begins the slow process of rolling the stone, once more, up the hill.

## I. Prosecutorial Strategy at the ICC

From one perspective, prosecutors at the International Criminal Court began their work at a distinct advantage. Although the Court's open-ended jurisdiction did not

---

for Sierra Leone: The Pleading of Joint Criminal Enterprise and Sex-Based Crimes' <http://works.bepress.com/cecily_rose/1/> last accessed 19 December 2011.

[8] KD Askin, 'Prosecuting Wartime Rape and Other Gender-Related Crimes Under International Law: Extraordinary Advances, Enduring Obstacles' (2003) 21 *Berkeley J Int'l L* 288; N Hayes, 'The Impact of Prosecutorial Strategy on the Investigation and Prosecution of Sexual Violence at International Criminal Tribunals' in M Bergsmo (ed) *Thematic Prosecution of International Sex Crimes* (Torkel Opsahl Academic ePublisher, Oslo 2012) 409.

[9] For example, speaking in 2002, the first Prosecutor of the ICTY and ICTR, Richard Goldstone, stated that 'the Rome Statute for the ICC represents the normative benchmark of international criminal law, and gender crimes are now given the recognition they were denied for so many years … It is my hope that the history of impunity for gender crimes under international criminal law will resolutely be replaced in the future by accountability and deterrence and prevention'. R Goldstone, 'Prosecuting Rape as a War Crime' (2002) 34 *Case Western Reserve J Int'l L* 277, 285.

allow for the same degree of immersion in and familiarity with the ethnic and factual aspects of a specific conflict that prosecutors at the ICTY and ICTR were gradually able to develop, the Rome Statute did contain the broadest range of provisions on gender-based crimes of any international criminal tribunal to date. This not only included the most expansive enumeration of sexual and gender-based crimes of any tribunal,[10] but also codified institutional and staffing requirements to ensure that sexual and gender-based violence were prioritised within the work of the Court.[11] In addition, the Rules of Procedure and Evidence contained a number of evidentiary concessions to mitigate some of the problematic issues which have traditionally dogged domestic prosecutions for sexual and gender-based violence, such as the exclusion of evidence relating to the prior sexual conduct of the victim and a waiver of the requirement for corroboration of testimony relating to sexual violence.[12]

## A. The Lubanga Trial, Or How Not to Conduct an International Criminal Prosecution

With such a substantial head-start in terms of substantive law and procedure, and the emergence of the Democratic Republic of the Congo (famously referred to by Margot Wallstrom as 'the rape capital of the world')[13] as the ICC's first Situation country following a self-referral by its Government,[14] one would have been forgiven for expecting sexual violence to feature heavily in the Court's initial investigations

---

[10] The Rome Statute recognises rape, sexual slavery, enforced prostitution, forced pregnancy, enforced sterilisation and other forms of sexual violence as crimes against humanity and war crimes, as well as the crime against humanity of persecution on the grounds of gender. See Rome Statute of the International Criminal Court, 2187 UNTS 90, 17 July 1998, entered into force 1 July 2002, arts 7(1)(g) 7(1)(h) 8(b)(xxii) and 8(c)(vi) ('ICC Statute').

[11] For example, Article 42(9) of the ICC Statute requires the Prosecutor to 'appoint advisers with legal expertise on specific issues, including, but not limited to, sexual and gender violence and violence against children', while Article 54(1)(b) imposes a duty on the Prosecutor to 'take appropriate measures to ensure the effective investigation and prosecution of crimes within the jurisdiction of the Court ... in particular where it involves sexual violence, gender violence or violence against children'. The Prosecutor did not appoint a Gender Advisor until 2008, and the position has not been utilised to its fullest possible extent. See Hayes (n 8), 418-419.

[12] International Criminal Court, Rules of Procedure and Evidence, ICC-ASP/1/3 (Part. II-A) 9 September 2002, Rules 63(4) 70 and 71.

[13] Margot Wallstrom, Special Representative of the Secretary General on Sexual Violence in Conflict, Address to the Security Council on Women, Peace and Security, UNSC Verbatim Record (27 April 2010) UN Doc S/PV/6302, 4.

[14] International Criminal Court, 'The Office of the Prosecutor of the International Criminal Court Opens its First Investigation' ICC-OTP-20040623-59 (23 June 2004) <http://www.icc-cpi.int/menus/icc/press%20and%20media/press%20releases/2004/the%20office%20of%20the%20prosecutor%20of%20the%20international%20criminal%20court%20opens%20its%20first%20investigation?lan=en-GB> last accessed 19 December 2011.

and indictments. However, despite the fact that ICC investigators uncovered preliminary evidence of rape, torture and enslavement in the first 18 months of their initial investigations in the DRC, the Office of the Prosecutor instructed them to pursue evidence relating only to the conscription and use of child soldiers.[15] The decision of the Prosecutor to so drastically limit the charges sought against the ICC's first accused, Thomas Lubanga Dyilo, and to confine the prosecution exclusively to the war crime of the recruitment, conscription and use of child soldiers,[16] was the subject of intense criticism from academics, practitioners and NGOs.[17] Perhaps the Prosecutor merely wanted a small, simple first case to get the Court off the starting blocks; it is worth remembering that the Yugoslavia Tribunal was similarly berated for prosecuting Duško Tadić, a low-level (albeit astonishingly sadistic) detention camp guard, as its first trial. However, the seniority of the ICC's first defendant was not the contentious issue. Thomas Lubanga was alleged to have been the President of the Union of Congolese Patriots (UPC) and the commander in chief of its notorious armed military wing, the Forces Patriotiques pour la Libération du Congo (FPLC). Even a cursory familiarity with the operation of such militia groups in the eastern DRC would give rise to incredulity that the Prosecutor should choose to voluntarily confine his scrutiny to its activities in relation to child soldiers alone.[18]

---

[15] K Glassborow, 'ICC Investigative Strategy Under Fire' (Institute for War and Peace Reporting, 27 October 2008) <http://iwpr.net/report-news/icc-investigative-strategy-under-fire> last accessed 19 December 2011. One former ICC investigator who worked on the case described it in the following terms: '"We interviewed a number of 'wives' (girls forced to live with senior LRA men) but questions were focused on their relationship to commanders, not on rape and sexual enslavement," he said. "We should not have limited ourselves to this kind of witness – we should have widened it out to speak to other victims of sexual violence."'

[16] *Situation in the DRC: Prosecutor v Lubanga* (Warrant of Arrest) ICC-01/04-01/06 (10 February 2006).

[17] See for example Women's Initiatives for Gender Justice, 'Women's Initiatives' Letter to the Prosecutor Stating Concern About the Failure to Investigate and Charge Gender-Based Crimes in the Lubanga Case' <http://www.iccwomen.org/publications/articles/docs/LegalFilings-web-2-10.pdf> last accessed 19 December 2011; Human Rights Watch, *ICC Charges Raise Concern* (1 August 2006) <http://www.hrw.org/news/2006/07/31/dr-congo-icc-charges-raise-concern> last accessed 19 December 2011; D Shermak, 'Justice and Moral Responsibility in the Congo' (2007) 4 *Eyes on the ICC* 65; J Coleman, 'Showing Its Teeth: The International Criminal Court Takes on Child Conscription in the Congo, But Is Its Bark Worse Than Its Bite?' (2007–2008) 26 *Penn St Int'l L Rev* 765; SM Pritchett, 'Entrenched Hegemony, Efficient Procedure or Selective Justice: An Inquiry Into Charges for Gender-Based Violence at the International Criminal Court' (2008) 17 *Transnat'l L & Contemp Probs* 265.

[18] For example, Women's Initiatives for Gender Justice, the first NGO to file an *amicus curiae* brief before the ICC, conducted a field documentation exercise in Ituri in 2006 in which 55 victim survivors of sexual and gender-based crimes were interviewed and 31 reported that they had been the victim of rape or sexual slavery committed by the UPC. A report of these interviews was submitted to the Prosecutor in August 2006 but never acted upon. See *Situation in the DRC: Prosecutor v Lubanga* (Request Submitted Pursuant to Rule 103(1) of the Rules of Procedure and Evidence for Leave to Participate as Amicus Curiae with

As it transpired, the absence of sexual violence charges was only the first in a cavalcade of questionable strategic choices made by the Prosecutor in relation to the *Lubanga* case, which exposed serious systemic issues in prosecutorial strategy and practice at the ICC. The case almost ended before the trial even began, following the imposition of a stay of proceedings by the Pre-Trial Chamber in June 2008, as a result of the Prosecution's inability to disclose potentially exculpatory material to the Defence which had been obtained pursuant to confidentiality agreements under Article 54(3)(e).[19] While the impasse in question was ultimately resolved[20] – at the cost of severely damaged relations with the relevant information providers, including the UN – the Prosecutor should never have found himself in such a potentially fatal predicament to begin with. The text of Article 54(3)(e) itself stipulates that evidence obtained on condition of confidentiality may be used 'solely for the purpose of generating new evidence', but the Office of the Prosecutor under Mr Ocampo took a far more expansive approach to the rule, apparently misinterpreting it as providing *carte blanche* to obtain extensive second-hand information first and unilaterally decide on its potentially exculpatory nature later.

Far from using Article 54(3)(e) cautiously and sparingly to obtain so-called 'lead evidence' only, as was envisaged in the Statute, the Office of the Prosecutor admitted in the *Lubanga* case that it had acquired more than half its evidence by means of confidentiality agreements,[21] and was excoriated by Judge Steiner in the *Katanga* case for similar profligacy:

---

Confidential Annex 2) ICC-01/04-01/06 (10 November 2006) paras 35, 41; see further B Inder, 'The ICC, Child Soldiers and Gender Justice' (The Parliament, 21 November 2011) <http://viewer.zmags.com/publication/5ebbab6d?page=55#/5ebbab6d/55> last accessed 6 January 2012. Indeed, the Prosecutor acknowledged in the press release to announce the opening of the Court's first investigation into the DRC that: 'States, international organizations and non-governmental organizations have reported thousands of deaths by mass murder and summary execution in the DRC since 2002. *The reports allege a pattern of rape, torture, forced displacement and the illegal use of child soldiers.*' See International Criminal Court (n 14) [emphasis added].

[19] *Situation in the DRC: Prosecutor v Lubanga* (Decision on the Consequences of Non-Disclosure of Exculpatory Materials Covered by Article 54(3)(e) Agreements and the Application to Stay the Prosecution of the Accused, Together with Certain Other Issues Raised at the Status Conference on 10 June 2008) ICC-01/04/01/06 (13 June 2008). See further HV Stuart, 'The ICC in Trouble' (2008) 6(3) *JICJ* 409.

[20] International Criminal Court, 'Stay of Proceedings in the Lubanga Case is Lifted – Trial Provisionally Scheduled for 26 January 2009' ICC-CPI-20081118-PR372 (18 November 2008) <http://www.icc-cpi.int/menus/icc/press%20and%20media/press%20releases/press%20releases%20(2008)/stay%20of%20proceedings%20in%20the%20lubanga%20case%20is%20lifted%20_%20trial%20provisionally%20scheduled%20for%2026%20january%20200> last accessed 19 December 2011.

[21] *Situation in the DRC: Prosecutor v Lubanga* (Transcript) ICC-01/04-01/06 (27 January 2009) 8 (stating that the Prosecution had obtained 55 per cent of its evidence via confidentiality agreements); K Ambos, 'Confidential Investigations (Article 54(3)(e) ICC Statute) vs. Disclosure Obligations: The Lubanga Case and National Law' (2009) 12 *New*

At the outset, the Single Judge notes the considerable number of documents (1632 according to the last indication given by the Prosecution on 25 April 2008) that the Prosecution has collected pursuant to article 54(3)(e) of the Statute, and that, according to the Prosecution, 'were considered to be relevant' for the present case. In the view of the Single Judge, this is particularly notable because the present case is confined to the crimes allegedly committed during one attack against one village on a single day.

The Single Judge finds this considerable number of documents to indicate that the Prosecution is not resorting to article 54(3)(e) of the Statute only in exceptional or limited circumstances, but rather is extensively gathering documents under such provision.

This practice, in the view of the Single Judge, is at the root of the problems that have arisen in the present case, as well as in the case of the Prosecutor v. Thomas Lubanga Dyilo, with regard to the disclosure to the Defence.[22]

Former practitioners were equally mystified by the Prosecutor's overt enthusiasm for a provision which, if misapplied and used to obtain substantive evidence rather than merely lead evidence, carried a constant risk of rupturing the proceedings if exculpatory evidence was inadvertently obtained which could not then be disclosed.[23]

Prior to the commencement of the trial, whether as a response to continued criticism of the limited scope of the charges or as a pre-emptive measure to ensure some degree of consistency with the evidence of their own witnesses, the Prosecution's public statements on the *Lubanga* case evolved. Having previously claimed to be considering introducing additional charges of sexual violence or

---

*Crim L Rev* 543, 551. See further *Prosecutor v Lubanga* (Decision on the Consequences of Non-Disclosure) (n 19), para 73.

[22] *Situation in the DRC: Prosecutor v Katanga and Chui* (Decision Requesting Observations Concerning Article 54(3)(e) Documents Identified as Potentially Exculpatory or Otherwise Material for the Defence's Preparation for the Confirmation Hearing) ICC-01/04-01/07 (2 June 2008) paras 9–11.

[23] Richard Goldstone, who introduced the original equivalent to Article 54(3)(e) Rule 70(B) into the Rules of Procedure and Evidence of the ICTY in 1994, spoke of his constant anxiety during his tenure as Chief Prosecutor of the ICTY and ICTR that substantive exculpatory evidence would accidentally be obtained under Rule 70(B), as that would create an irresolvable dilemma between disclosure obligations and undertakings to information providers which could lead to the collapse of a case. R Goldstone, speaking at the International Criminal Court Summer School, Irish Centre for Human Rights, National University of Ireland, Galway, 21–26 June 2008, contemporaneous notes on file with author.

even pursuing a second prosecution on those charges after the close of the trial,[24] Chief Prosecutor Ocampo now maintained that he was pursuing an expansive interpretation of the conscription and use of child soldiers to reflect the gendered nature of the crime and the sexual abuse experienced by its victims. An *amicus curiae* brief was submitted to the Trial Chamber by Radhika Coomaraswamy, the Special Representative of the Secretary General for Children and Armed Conflict, arguing that since 'during war, the use of girl children in particular includes sexual violence', the Trial Chamber should interpret the element of the crime of using children under the age of 15 to 'actively participate in hostilities' as including the abuse of female child soldiers as sexual slaves or so-called 'bush wives'.[25] While there is a lot of merit in Ms Coomaraswamy's submissions, particularly in light of her expertise and knowledge of the reality of female child soldiers' experience of conflict, their co-option by the Office of the Prosecutor to retrospectively justify a clearly inept and insufficient range of charges was unbecoming and reeked slightly of panic. It allowed the Prosecutor to claim that he was pursuing a conscious policy, ostensibly to provide long-overdue recognition of the sexual exploitation of girl child soldiers,[26] rather than attempting to camouflage the gaping omissions in his own indictment.

At the opening of the trial against Lubanga in January 2009, Mr Ocampo spoke at some length about the rape of female child soldiers, their sexual enslavement and abuse as 'wives' and 'sexual prey',[27] claiming that '[i]n this International Criminal Court, the girl soldiers will not be invisible'.[28] I would argue that it would have been a far more fitting and effective tribute to the experience of those children to have investigated and *charged* rape, sexual slavery and forced marriage than merely to have name-checked such crimes for rhetorical and emotive effect.[29] The extent of the disconnect between the Prosecution's evidence and its charges became

---

[24] K Glassborow, 'Lubanga Defence Hits out at ICC' (Institute for War and Peace Reporting, 13 November 2006) <http://iwpr.net/report-news/lubanga-defence-hits-out-icc> last accessed 19 December 2011.

[25] *Situation in the DRC: Prosecutor v Lubanga* (Submission of the Observations of the Special Representative of the Secretary General of the United Nations for Children and Armed Conflict Pursuant to Rule 103 of the Rules of Procedure and Evidence) ICC-01/04-01/06 (18 March 2008). See further K Glassborow, 'Call for Lubanga Charges to Cover Rape' (Institute for War and Peace Reporting, 12 May 2008) <http://iwpr.net/report-news/call-lubanga-charges-cover-rape> last accessed 28 December 2011.

[26] See for example L Moreno-Ocampo, 'Keynote Address – *Interdisciplinary Colloquium on Sexual Violence as International Crime*: Interdiscplinary Approaches to Evidence' 35(4) *Law & Social Inquiry* 839, 845–846.

[27] *Situation in the DRC: Prosecutor v Lubanga* (Transcript) ICC-01/04-01/06 (26 January 2009) 11–13.

[28] Ibid 13.

[29] The sentencing judgment in the Lubanga trial likewise criticised the Prosecutor for advancing 'extensive submissions' on sexual violence in his opening and closing statements but refusing to include it within the charges. See *Situation in the DRC: Prosecutor v Lubanga* (Decision on Sentence Pursuant to Article 76 of the Statute) ICC-01/04-01/06 (10 July 2012) para 60.

inescapably apparent during the initial weeks of the trial. At least 15 of the first 25 prosecution witnesses (including two expert witnesses) provided testimony of gender-based crimes, particularly rape and sexual slavery.[30] Given that the received wisdom in international criminal investigations is that victims and witnesses are frequently reluctant to volunteer evidence of sexual violence, it seems remarkable – and is indicative of the underlying factual context to the case – that the Prosecution succeeded in obtaining such extensive testimony despite its own best efforts.

Unsurprisingly, the Defence in the *Lubanga* case were unimpressed with the leading of evidence relating to crimes which had not been charged against the accused.[31] However, the Legal Representatives of Victims were the ones to ultimately attempt to resolve this discrepancy, by requesting the Trial Chamber to consider revising the legal characterisation of facts in the case pursuant to Regulation 55 to include charges of cruel and inhuman treatment and sexual slavery in light of witness testimony, despite the Prosecution's opposition to this step.[32] By majority,[33] Judge Fulford dissenting,[34] the Trial Chamber issued a decision giving notice to the parties and the participants in the case that the legal characterisation of facts could be subject to change under Regulation 55. This decision was later overturned by the Appeals Chamber on procedural grounds, holding that legal re-characterisation of facts under Regulation 55 could not exceed the facts and circumstances described in the charges.[35] This was the correct decision in terms of fairness to the accused,

---

[30] Women's Initiatives for Gender Justice, *Gender Report Card on the International Criminal Court 2009* <http://www.iccwomen.org/news/docs/GRC09_web-2-10.pdf> last accessed 19 December 2011, 71–85.

[31] For example, counsel for the Defence remarked during her opening statement in the trial: 'I listened to much more than just reference to the crime of enlisting and conscripting. I heard the word "rape" and "sexual slavery" mentioned. However, those aren't charges brought against our client. The Legal Representative of Victims cannot accused our client of crimes which he isn't prosecuted for here.' *Situation in the DRC: Prosecutor v Lubanga* (Transcript) ICC-01/04-01/06 (27 January 2009) 18. For the defence reaction to the attempted recharacterization of facts, see R Irwin, 'Lubanga Defence Warn New Charges Threaten Trial' (Institute for War and Peace Reporting, 3 July 2009) <http://iwpr.net/report-news/lubanga-defence-warn-new-charges-threaten-trial> last accessed 19 December 2011.

[32] *Situation in the DRC: Prosecutor v Lubanga* (Joint Application of the Legal Representatives of Victims for the Implementation of the Procedure under Regulation 55 of the Regulations of the Court) ICC-01/04-01/06 (22 May 2009).

[33] *Situation in the DRC: Prosecutor v Lubanga* (Decision Giving Notice to the Parties and Participants that the Legal Characterisation of the Facts May be Subject to Change in Accordance with Regulation 55(2) of the Regulations of the Court) ICC-01/04-01/06 (14 July 2009); Women's Initiatives for Gender Justice (n 30) 86–90.

[34] *Situation in the DRC: Prosecutor v Lubanga* (Decision Giving Notice to the Parties and Participants that the Legal Characterisation of the Facts May be Subject to Change in Accordance with Regulation 55(2) of the Regulations of the Court: Dissenting Opinion of Judge Adrian Fulford) ICC-01/04-01/06 (17 July 2009).

[35] *Situation in the DRC: Prosecutor v Lubanga* (Judgment on the Appeals of Mr Lubanga Dyilo and the Prosecutor against the Decision of Trial Chamber I of 14 July 2009 Entitled 'Decision Giving Notice to the Parties and Participants that the Legal Characterisation of

but it is illustrative of the shambolic nature of the trial that halfway through the Prosecution's case, the Legal Representatives of Victims and the Trial Chamber were the primary actors attempting to provide some degree of clarity as to what charges the evidence against Lubanga actually supported. It also provided an ideal but disconcerting example for those who had expressed concerns that the system of victim participation at the International Criminal Court had the potential to amount to a 'second Prosecutor' in a trial.[36]

Unfortunately, the comedy of errors was not yet over, as another potentially case-ending issue which had dogged the trial from its inception brought proceedings to a halt for the second time in two years. At the beginning of the trial, the first prosecution witness to take the stand, Witness 298, had recanted his testimony in spectacular fashion, claiming that he had been coached to provide a false statement and to lie about having been abducted and conscripted as a child soldier.[37] When he retook the stand two weeks later, Witness 298 retracted his retraction, testified that he had in fact been a child soldier, and stated that he had not been telling the truth when he claimed in his initial appearance to have been persuaded to tell lies.[38] However, Prosecution Witness 15 also made similar allegations of having been instructed by a specific intermediary working for the Office of the Prosecutor to provide false evidence:

---

the Facts May be Subject to Change in Accordance with Regulation 55(2) of the Regulations of the Court') ICC-01/04-01/06 (8 December 2009); Women's Initiatives for Gender Justice, *Gender Report Card on the International Criminal Court 2010* <http://www.iccwomen.org/news/docs/GRC10-WEB-11-10-v4_Final-version-Dec.pdf> last accessed 19 December 2011, 129–132. These decisions are discussed in greater detail by Dov Jacobs in Chapter 9 of this volume.

[36] See for example M Jouet, 'Reconciling the Conflicting Rights of Victims and Defendants at the International Criminal Court' (2007) 26 *St Louis U Pub L Rev* 249; M Cohen, 'Victim's Participation Rights within the International Criminal Court: A Critical Overview' (2009) 37 *Denv J Int'l L & Policy* 351.

[37] *Situation in the DRC: Prosecutor v Lubanga* (Transcript) ICC-01/04-01/06 (28 January 2009) 40. When asked about his earlier testimony of having been abducted by UPC soldiers on his way home from school and taken to a training camp for child soldiers, Witness 298 replied 'they taught me that over three and a half years. I don't like it. I would like to speak my mind as I swore before God and before everyone … I told myself I would do what I wanted, but in coming here I told myself that I would say what I know to be the truth'. See further D Charter, 'Chaos Reigns at the International Criminal Court Trial of Thomas Lubanga' *The Times* (London 29 January 2009); R Irwin, 'Lubanga Trial, Week 1: Prosecutors Stumble Out of the Gate' (Lubangatrial.org, 30 January 2009) <http://www.lubangatrial.org/2009/01/30/lubanga-trial-week-1-prosecutors-stumble-out-of-the-gate/> last accessed 19 December 2011.

[38] *Situation in the DRC: Prosecutor v Lubanga* (Transcript) ICC-01/04-01/06 (10 February 2009) 58. See also T Gurd, 'When Witnesses Change Their Stories …' (Lubangatrial.org, 10 February 2009) <http://www.lubangatrial.org/2009/02/10/when-witnesses-change-their-stories%E2%80%A6/> last accessed 19 December 2011.

I met the OTP's intermediary [Intermediary 316] who told me the following. He said, You have to change your name, you have to change your identity. Don't give the true story that took place; in other words, there was a story that they were telling to the witnesses. And I say that they're crooks. Why is it that I say that they're crooks and swindlers? Well, instead of letting me tell the true story of what took place and instead of letting me describe all of the events that I lived through, they are inventing statements in order to manipulate the investigation.[39]

This extraordinary allegation from the Prosecution's own witness was supported by the testimony of several defence witnesses, who claimed to have been promised money and other inducements by intermediaries working for the Office of the Prosecutor in exchange for false testimony, to have been given false identities and dates of birth, and to have been coached by the intermediary prior to meeting with investigators from the Office of the Prosecutor.[40]

Following the emergence of this very serious issue, the Trial Chamber acknowledged that the Defence was entitled to know the identity of three specific intermediaries (Intermediary 321, 316 and 143) in order to undertake proper investigations into potential manipulation of witnesses and inducement of false testimony in the interests of a fair trial.[41] Although the Chamber had ordered that the identity of Intermediary 143 was not to be disclosed until appropriate security

---

[39] *Situation in the DRC: Prosecutor v Lubanga* (Transcript) ICC-01/04-01/06 (16 June 2009) 6, 11. In response to a question from Judge Fulford immediately after his testimony, 'So your statement, therefore, the one you provided to the Office of the Prosecutor, is substantially inaccurate; is that correct?', Witness 15 replied 'That's the case. It's a false statement'. See further R Irwin, 'Witness Admits to False Statements' (Lubangatrial.org, 19 June 2009) <http://www.lubangatrial.org/2009/06/19/witness-admits-to-false-statements/> last accessed 19 December 2011.

[40] One defence witness testified that she was the mother of an individual who had earlier taken the stand for the prosecution as a former child soldier and claimed in evidence that his mother was dead; 'Lubanga Witness Testifies from Congo via Video Link' (Lubangatrial.org, 30 March 2010) <http://www.lubangatrial.org/2010/03/30/lubanga-witness-testifies-from-congo-via-video-link/> last accessed 19 December 2011. See further 'ICC Intermediaries Allegedly Concocted Evidence' (Institute for War and Peace Reporting, 12 February 2010) <http://iwpr.net/report-news/icc-intermediaries-allegedly-concocted-evidence> last accessed 19 December 2011.

[41] *Situation in the DRC: Prosecutor v Lubanga* (Redacted Decision on Intermediaries) ICC-01/04-01/06 (31 May 2010) para 138, stating that there was 'a real basis for concern as to the system employed by the prosecution for identifying potential witnesses. On the evidence, there was extensive opportunity for the intermediaries, if they wished, to influence the witnesses as regards the statements they provided to the prosecution, and ... there is evidence this may have occurred. In the circumstances it would be unfair to deny the defence the opportunity to research this possibility with all of the intermediaries used by the prosecution for the relevant witnesses in this trial, where the evidence justifies that course'.

measures had been put in place,[42] the intermediary's name or a diminutive of it was inadvertently revealed in open court during closed session testimony by a Prosecution staff member.[43] Despite some unresolved security issues, the Trial Chamber later ordered the Prosecution to disclose the identity of Intermediary 143 on a strictly confidential basis to the Defence team.[44] In response, over 24 increasingly frantic hours, the Office of the Prosecutor announced its intention to file for leave to appeal, requested the Trial Chamber to use its 'inherent powers' to reconsider the order for disclosure, and pronounced that the Prosecutor had an 'independent statutory obligation to protect persons put at risk on account of the Prosecution's actions'.[45] Crucially, however, the Prosecutor continued to refuse to comply with two direct orders for disclosure from the Chamber.

In response to the continued intransigence of the Prosecutor, the Trial Chamber issued a coldly furious decision on 8 July 2010, once again imposing an indefinite stay of proceedings and suspending the trial.[46] The Chamber held that a fair trial was impossible under circumstances where the Prosecutor refused to accept the authority of the Trial Chamber and disregarded a direct order from the Court, noting that 'it is not for the prosecution to seek to determine … what constitutes fairness for an accused'.[47] The position of the judges was that, by claiming an autonomous statutory obligation to protect those put at risk on account of the Court's activities, the Prosecutor had embarked on a 'profound, unacceptable and unjustified intrusion into the role of the judiciary',[48] and concluded that:

> [the Prosecutor] cannot be allowed to continue with this prosecution if he seeks to reserve to himself the right to avoid the Court's orders

---

[42] Ibid para 143, 150; '[T]he Chamber is sure that in order to enable the defence to conduct necessary and meaningful investigations and to secure a fair trial for the accused, it is strictly necessary for his identity to be disclosed. Without his identity, this will not be possible.'

[43] *Situation in the DRC: Prosecutor v Lubanga* (Redacted Decision on the Prosecution's Urgent Request for Variation of the Time-Limit to Disclose the Identity of Intermediary 143 or Alternatively to Stay Proceedings Pending Further Consultation with the VWU) ICC-01/04-01/06 (8 July 2010) para 4.

[44] *Situation in the DRC: Prosecutor v Lubanga* (Transcript) ICC-01/04-01/06 (6 July 2010) 61.

[45] *Situation in the DRC: Prosecutor v Lubanga* (Prosecution's Urgent Provision of Further Information Following Consultation with the VWU, to Supplement the Request for Variation of the Time-Limit or Stay) ICC-01/04-01/06 (7 July 2010) para 6. See also *Situation in the DRC: Prosecutor v Lubanga* (Transcript) ICC-01/04-01/06 (7 July 2010) 15–22; *Situation in the DRC: Prosecutor v Lubanga* (Prosecution's Urgent Request for Variation of the Time-Limit to Disclose the Identity of Intermediary 143 or Alternatively to Stay Proceedings Pending Further Consultation with the VWU) ICC-01/04-01/06 (7 July 2010).

[46] *Situation in the DRC: Prosecutor v Lubanga* (Redacted Decision on the Prosecution's Urgent Request for Variation of the Time-Limit to Disclose the Identity of Intermediary 143 or Alternatively to Stay Proceedings Pending Further Consultation with the VWU) (n 43).

[47] Ibid para 24.

[48] Ibid para 27.

whenever he decides that they are inconsistent with his interpretation of his other obligations.[49]

Once again, the stay was ultimately lifted by the Appeals Chamber, who noted that the Trial Chamber had been a little too eager to deploy the nuclear option, so to speak, by imposing a stay of proceedings, and should have instead exhausted less severe measures first, such as imposing sanctions for misconduct against the Prosecutor under Article 71.[50] As with the previous stay of proceedings, the Prosecutor had belatedly agreed to disclosure of the contentious information prior to the Appeals Chamber's decision. However, it says a lot about the extent of the breakdown of relations between the bench and the Prosecutor that the Appeals Chamber essentially had to suggest that everyone should take a deep breath and count to 10 before acting in future, and it seems mystifying from a tactical standpoint that Mr Ocampo would allow his first trial to come to the very brink of disaster rather than obey a direct order from the Trial Chamber and officially disclose a name which had already effectively been revealed in open court a month previously.

The *Lubanga* trial was therefore permitted to limp to a close, but not without some additional discomfiture for the Prosecution. After a formal claim of abuse of process was made by the Defence in relation to the intermediaries issue, the Trial Chamber declined to impose a third stay of proceedings but somewhat ominously deferred consideration of the merits of the Defence allegations until its final assessment of the evidence in the case.[51] The Chamber's ultimate assessment in the *Lubanga* trial judgment of the failure of the Office of the Prosecutor to responsibly or sufficiently supervise the activities of its intermediaries was hugely damaging to its case. The Chamber found the evidence of all but one of the alleged former child soldier witnesses called by the Prosecution – including Witness 298,

---

[49] Ibid para 28.

[50] *Situation in the DRC: Prosecutor v Lubanga* (Judgment on the Appeal of the Prosecutor Against the Decision of Trial Chamber I of 8 July 2010 Entitled 'Decision on the Prosecution's Urgent Request for Variation of the Time-Limit to Disclose the Identity of Intermediary 143 or Alternatively to Stay Proceedings Pending Further Consultation with the VWU') ICC-01/04-01/06 (8 October 2010) paras 55–61, stating at para 60: '[T]o the extent possible, a Trial Chamber faced with a deliberate refusal of a party to comply with its orders which threatens the fairness of the trial should seek to bring about that party's compliance through the imposition of sanctions under article 71 before resorting to imposition of a stay of proceedings.' Trial Chamber I did in fact issue a formal warning for misconduct against the Prosecutor and Deputy Prosecutor as a necessary precondition for the imposition of sanctions under Rule 171. See *Situation in the DRC: Prosecutor v Lubanga* (Transcript) ICC-01/04-01/06 (8 July 2010) 2–4.

[51] *Situation in the DRC: Prosecutor v Lubanga* (Redacted Decision on the 'Defence Application Seeking a Permanent Stay of Proceedings') ICC-01/04-01/06 (7 March 2011); the abuse of process application and the Chamber's deliberations on it are discussed further in Women's Initiatives for Gender Justice, *Gender Report Card on the International Criminal Court 2011* <http://www.iccwomen.org/documents/Gender-Report-Card-on-the-International-Criminal-Court-2011.pdf> last accessed 19 December 2011, 217–221.

the first witness to take the stand – to be unreliable due to the risk that they had been manipulated, coached or suborned by intermediaries into providing false testimony, and concluded that the Prosecution had failed to establish that those witnesses had been enlisted or conscripted into the UPC or used to participate actively in hostilities.[52] After reviewing the Prosecution's strategic approach to its investigation in the DRC, the Chamber came to the following damning assessment of the consequences for the evidence in the case and the witnesses themselves:

> The Chamber is of the view that the prosecution should not have delegated its investigative responsibilities to the intermediaries in the way set out above, notwithstanding the extensive security difficulties it faced. A series of witnesses have been called during this trial whose evidence, as a result of the essentially unsupervised actions of three of the principal intermediaries, cannot safely be relied on. The Chamber spent a considerable period of time investigating the circumstances of a substantial number of individuals whose evidence was, at least in part, inaccurate or dishonest. The prosecution's negligence in failing to verify and scrutinise this material sufficiently before it was introduced led to significant expenditure on the part of the Court. An additional consequence of the lack of proper oversight of the intermediaries is that they were potentially able to take advantage of the witnesses they contacted. Irrespective of the Chamber's conclusions regarding the credibility and reliability of these alleged former child soldiers, given their youth and likely exposure to conflict, they were vulnerable to manipulation.[53]

As a consequence of its finding that there was a risk that Intermediaries 143 and 321 had encouraged or assisted witnesses to give false evidence and that there were 'strong reasons to believe that [Intermediary 316] persuaded witnesses to lie as to their involvement as child soldiers within the UPC', the Chamber concluded that the three individuals employed by the Office of the Prosecutor may have committed criminal offences against the administration of justice under Article 70 of the Statute and instructed the Prosecution to initiate an investigation.[54]

When the trial at last reached its closing arguments, the Prosecution was given one final opportunity to coherently present its case, specifically in relation to the still-unresolved issue of the relevance of evidence of sexual violence to the recruitment, enlistment or conscription of children under the age of 15 and their use to participate actively in hostilities. Although no fewer than six individuals

---

[52] *Situation in the DRC: Prosecutor v Lubanga* (Judgment Pursuant to Article 74 of the Statute) ICC-01/04-01/06 (14 March 2012) paras 478–484.
[53] Ibid para 482.
[54] Ibid para 483.

presented the closing arguments on behalf of the Office of the Prosecutor,[55] this issue was not substantively addressed by any of them, nor was it discussed in the Prosecution's closing brief.[56] Two of the three judges in the case explicitly raised the issue with Prosecution counsel, which was of potentially immense significance for both the gendered interpretation of the elements of the crime and the accurate reflection in the final judgment of the facts underpinning the case and the totality of the evidence.[57] Unfortunately, this opportunity was squandered and the judges' questioning resulted only in a series of uncomfortably charged and occasionally outright hostile exchanges between the Prosecutor and the bench.[58]

Judge Fulford first asked a clarifying question in relation to the submissions by one member of the Prosecution team that, if a child soldier is sent out to procure young women for a commander to sleep with, such actions would constitute active participation in hostilities.[59] The Prosecutor, who had not presented any of the closing arguments for the Prosecution but was observing proceedings from the back of the courtroom, attempted to intervene:

> Moreno-Ocampo: Your Honour, if I may.
>
> Judge Fulford: In a moment, Mr. Ocampo. I'm just asking some questions of Ms. Samson at the moment.
>
> Moreno-Ocampo: Yes, she represents my office.
>
> Judge Fulford: Really, I don't think counsel should be receiving e-mails during the course of closing submissions, Mr. Ocampo.[60]

---

[55] Including Professor Tim McCormack on the correct legal characterisation of the conflict in the DRC as non-international at the time relative to the indictment, and Benjamin Ferencz on the symbolic significance of the ICC's first trial.

[56] For a full summary of the closing arguments of the Prosecution, see further Women's Initiatives for Gender Justice (n 51) 205–211.

[57] See for example B Inder, 'Reflection: Gender Issues and Child Soldiers – The Case of Prosecutor v Thomas Lubanga Dyilo' (Lubangatrial.org, 31 August 2011) <http://www.lubangatrial.org/2011/08/31/reflection-gender-issues-and-child-soldiers-the-case-of-prosecutor-v-thomas-lubanga-dyilo-2/> last accessed 19 December 2011.

[58] Press reports of the closing arguments in the trial noted the 'friction' and 'simmering tensions between prosecutors and judges'. See 'Lawyers Wrap Up International Court's First Trial' (Associated Press, 25 August 2011) <http://hosted2.ap.org/APDEFAULT/cae69a7523db45408eeb2b3a98c0c9c5/Article_2011-08-25-EU-International-Court-Congo/id-9c011aad1c61422a97cd7c0d95564c95> last visited 19 December 2011.

[59] *Situation in the DRC: Prosecutor v Lubanga* (Transcript) ICC-01/04-01/06 (25 August 2011) 22; contemporaneous notes on file with author.

[60] Ibid 23. One report of the closing arguments noted that 'the tension between the bench and the prosecution that has characterized this entire trial was manifest in the courtroom today ... Judge Fulford scolded Mr Ocampo for using email in the courtroom', and also highlighted the 'detectable impatience' and 'notably disturbed' demeanour of Judge Fulford in response to Mr Ocampo's repeated attempts to intervene to answer

A second attempted intervention by the Prosecutor gave rise to further ill-tempered exchanges with the presiding judge.

> Judge Fulford: Mr. Ocampo, really, can we please have some order to how the submissions are advanced. You have selected six advocates to address the Court. Can we remain with them. I'm sure that messages can be passed forward if there's something else that needs to be said at some stage.
>
> Moreno-Ocampo: I'm sorry, your Honour, if I may, the Office of the Prosecutor is represented by me here also and I'd like to answer your question if I may.
>
> Judge Fulford: Mr. Ocampo, no, not at the moment. In due course, if there are supplementary matters that need to be dealt with, we will ask for your assistance, but I'm not going to have different people jumping up and intervening during what needs to be a very tightly controlled hearing.[61]

Judge Odio-Benito then raised the issue for a second time, noting that although evidence of sexual violence had been advanced during the trial, no charges of sexual crimes had been included in the indictment or confirmed by the Pre-Trial Chamber. She therefore put the following question to then-Deputy Prosecutor Fatou Bensouda: 'How is sexual violence relevant to this case, and how does the Prosecution expect the Trial Chamber to refer to the sexual violence allegedly suffered by girls if this was not in the facts and circumstances described in the charges against Mr Lubanga Dyilo?'[62] The Prosecutor once again insisted on responding:

> So what we believe in this case is a different way to present the gender crimes. It presents the gender crimes not specific as rapes. Gender crimes were committed as part of the conscription of girls in – in the militias. And it is important to have the charge as confined to the inscription, because if not – and that's the point that Ms Coomaraswamy did here – if not, the girls are considered wife and ignored as people to be protected and demobilised and cared. That is why the Prosecutor decided to confine the charges – to present the

---

questions which were directed at other members of the Prosecution team. See A Sesay, 'Prosecutors and Victims' Representatives Make Closing Statements in Lubanga Trial' (Lubangatrial.org, 25 August 2011) <http://www.lubangatrial.org/2011/08/25/prosecutors-and-victims-representatives-make-closing-statements-in-lubanga-trial/> last accessed 19 December 2011.
  [61] Ibid 23–24.
  [62] Ibid 53–54.

suffering and the sexual abuse and the gender crime suffered by the girls in the camps just as conscription.[63]

However, shortly after sitting down following this answer, the Prosecutor once again attempted to respond to the question, but now argued contradictorily that sexual violence was an element of using child soldiers to participate actively in hostilities.[64] The closing arguments therefore ended without clarification of a central issue in the Prosecution's case.

Unsurprisingly, when the trial judgment was finally delivered in March 2012, there was scant cause for celebration for the Prosecution beyond the achievement of a conviction on the three counts of enlistment, conscription and use of child soldiers to participate actively in hostilities.[65] Although the judgment contains a summary of testimony relating to sexual violence provided in the course of the trial,[66] the majority concluded that 'given the prosecution's failure to include allegations of sexual violence in the charges ... this evidence is irrelevant for the purposes of the [judgment] save as regards providing context'.[67] The Chamber reasoned that:

> [r]egardless of whether sexual violence may properly be included within the scope of 'using [children under the age of 15] to participate actively in hostilities' as a matter of law, because facts relating to sexual violence were not included in the Decision on the Confirmation of Charges, it would be impermissible for the Chamber to base its [judgment] on the evidence introduced during the trial that is relevant to this issue.[68]

The judges therefore refused to make any findings of fact on the issue of sexual violence, particularly in relation to the individual criminal responsibility of Thomas Lubanga for its commission.[69] Judge Odio-Benito issued a separate and dissenting opinion to the judgment, arguing that sexual violence was an intrinsic part of the criminal conduct of using children to participate actively in hostilities and that it was 'necessary and a duty of the Chamber to include sexual violence within [that] legal

---

[63] Ibid 54 [sic].
[64] Ibid 55.
[65] *Situation in the DRC: Prosecutor v Lubanga* (Judgment Pursuant to Article 74 of the Statute) (n 52).
[66] Ibid paras 890–895.
[67] Ibid para 896.
[68] Ibid para 630.
[69] Ibid para 896.

concept'.⁷⁰ The majority explicitly reserved judgment on whether evidence of sexual violence could be taken into account for the purposes of sentencing and reparations.⁷¹

Notwithstanding the unequivocal and strongly critical nature of the Chamber's findings on this issue, the Prosecutor appeared quite self-congratulatory about the significance of sexual violence evidence in the case at a press conference the day after the judgment was issued, even inaccurately asserting that a majority of the Chamber had agreed that the gendered nature of the crimes could be taken into consideration at the sentencing phase.⁷² However, the sentencing judgment was, if anything, even less subtle in its criticisms of the (now former) Prosecutor's strategy and conduct throughout the trial, stating:

> The Chamber strongly deprecates the attitude of the former Prosecutor in relation to the issue of sexual violence. He advanced extensive submissions as regards sexual violence in his opening and closing submissions at trial, and in his arguments on sentence he contended that sexual violence is an aggravating factor that should be reflected by the Chamber. However, not only did the former Prosecutor fail to apply or include sexual violence or sexual slavery at any stage during these proceedings, including in the original charges, but he actively opposed taking this step during the trial when he submitted that it would cause unfairness to the accused if he was convicted on this basis. Notwithstanding this stance on his part throughout these proceedings, he suggested that sexual violence ought to be considered for the purposes of sentencing.⁷³

While the Chamber held that, as a matter of law, the lack of inclusion of relevant charges in the confirmation decision would not preclude consideration of evidence of sexual violence under Rule 145,⁷⁴ the majority (Judge Odio-Benito dissenting) found that the Prosecution had not advanced sufficient evidence in the course of the trial to permit the Chamber to establish the widespread nature of the sexual violence or to attribute it to the actions or omissions of Lubanga himself.⁷⁵ The Chamber also pointedly emphasised Lubanga's 'respectful and cooperative' conduct throughout the trial, even in the 'particularly onerous circumstances' caused by

---

⁷⁰ *Situation in the DRC: Prosecutor v Lubanga* (Judgment Pursuant to Article 74 of the Statute – Separate and Dissenting Opinion of Judge Odio-Benito) ICC-01/04-01/06 (14 March 2012), paras 17–20.

⁷¹ *Situation in the DRC: Prosecutor v Lubanga* (Judgment Pursuant to Article 74 of the Statute) (n 52) paras 631, 896.

⁷² International Criminal Court, OTP Press Conference, 15 March 2012, <http://www.youtube.com/watch?v=eoj_qCwHePk&list=UU183T5VoMh5wISSdKPaMgRw&index=3&feature=plpp_video> last accessed 10 April 2012.

⁷³ *Situation in the DRC: Prosecutor v Lubanga* (Decision on Sentence Pursuant to Article 76 of the Statute) (n 29) para 60.

⁷⁴ Ibid paras 67–68.

⁷⁵ Ibid paras 74–75.

the Prosecution's actions in relation to gathering evidence under confidentiality agreements, the failure to comply with the Chamber's disclosure orders, and the issuance of 'misleading and inaccurate statements to the press about the evidence in the case and Mr Lubanga's conduct during the proceedings'.[76]

While it is a significant milestone for the Court to have handed down its first conviction, some signal lessons can be drawn from the Prosecution's conduct of its first trial. This case was beset by entirely avoidable problems from the outset, most if not all of which are directly attributable to strategic errors within the Office of the Prosecutor. The truncation of field investigations, misinterpretation of and over-reliance on confidentiality agreements, disastrous charge selection, use of intermediaries without appropriate safeguards and entirely needless refusal to obey disclosure orders of the Trial Chamber have undermined the legitimacy of the trial and engendered far-reaching doubts about the competence of the former Prosecutor. The combined effect of these issues – particularly the unprecedented imposition of two stays of proceedings – has also bloated what may once have been intended as an expeditious, streamlined prosecution, leaving the Court without a verdict in its first case six years after the accused was first brought into custody. Far from being a flagship trial to burnish the embryonic institution's reputation, both within the international legal community and in regions affected by conflict, the *Lubanga* case has set a particularly ignominious precedent for the coherence, efficiency and professionalism of international criminal prosecutions. More importantly, for the purposes of this chapter at least, the trial exposed fundamental errors of prosecutorial strategy in relation to the investigation and prosecution of sexual and gender-based crimes at the international criminal level. As will be discussed in the following section, many of these issues are systemic, and basic mistakes which were learned the hard way at the *ad hoc* tribunals have been needlessly repeated throughout the first 10 years' work at the ICC.

## B. Investigations, Evidence and Charging

Ironically, given the experience of the *Lubanga* trial, the one area in which the ICC has shown significant improvement on the experience of the *ad hoc* tribunals in their initial years is that of charging sexual violence. Out of the seven Situations currently before the Court at the time of writing, charges for sexual and gender-based violence have been sought in six of them, the only exception for now being the investigation in Libya.[77] Sexual and gender-based crimes have been included in

---

[76] Ibid para 91.

[77] Although the Prosecutor has announced his intention to investigate acts of sexual violence committed during that conflict, no charges have been added at the time of writing. See for example E Pilkington et al, 'Gaddafi Faces New ICC Charges for Using Rape as Weapon in Conflict', *Guardian* (London 9 June 2011) <http://www.guardian.co.uk/world/2011/jun/08/gaddafi-forces-libya-britain-nato> last accessed 10 December 2011; Women's Initiatives

13 of the 18 cases pursued by the Court to date.[78] Of the 30 individuals to have been the subject of an arrest warrant or summons to appear to date,[79] gender-based crimes have been charged against 17, including one female accused.[80] Sexual violence has been charged under the rubric of war crimes, crimes against humanity and genocide, and as a constituent element of a range of crimes including rape, sexual slavery, other forms of sexual violence, torture, persecution, other inhumane acts, cruel or inhuman treatment and outrages on personal dignity.[81] These statistics are heartening and deserve to be praised, although it is somewhat less encouraging to consider that, of the 30 individuals indicted by the ICC over the last decade, at least three are now dead,[82] four have had all charges against them dismissed and been

---

for Gender Justice, *Legal Eye on the ICC*, July 2011 <http://www.iccwomen.org/news/docs/LegalEye7-11/LegalEye7-11.html> last accessed 10 December 2011.

[78] Charges have been included in the cases against: Ntaganda, Katanga, Ngudjolo, Mbarushimana and Mudacumura (Situation in the Democratic Republic of the Congo); Bemba (Situation in the Central African Republic); Kony *et al* (Situation in Uganda); Harun & Kushayb, al Bashir and Hussein (Situation in Darfur, Sudan); Muthaura *et al* (Situation in Kenya); and in the cases against both Laurent and Simone Gbagbo (Situation in Côte d'Ivoire). The prosecutions of Lubanga, Abu Garda, Banda & Jerbo, Ruto *et al* and Gaddafi *et al* do not contain charges for sexual or gender-based violence. Although the original indictment against Bosco Ntaganda did not contain any charges of sexual violence, the indictment was amended following the verdict in the *Lubanga* case to include charges of rape and sexual slavery. See further *Situation in the DRC: Prosecutor v Ntaganda* (Decision on the Prosecutor's Application under Article 58) ICC-01/04-02/06 (13 July 2012). Simone Gbagbo is the first woman to be charged with crimes of sexual violence by the ICC. The arrest warrant against her includes one charge of rape and other forms of sexual violence as a crime against humanity. See *Situation in Côte d'Ivoire: Prosecutor v Simone Gbagbo* (Decision on the Prosecutor's Application Pursuant to Article 58 for a Warrant of Arrest Against Simone Gbagbo) ICC-02/11-01/12 (2 March 2012, reclassified as public on 22 November 2012).

[79] The 30 individuals in question are: Thomas Lubanga Dyilo, Bosco Ntaganda, Germain Katanga, Mathieu Ngudjolo Chui, Callixte Mbarushimana, Sylvestre Mudacumura (Situation in the DRC); Jean-Pierre Bemba Gombo (Situation in the CAR); Joseph Kony, Vincent Otti, Raska Lukwiya, Dominic Ongwen, Okot Odhiambo (Situation in Uganda); Ahmed Mohammed Harun, Ali Kushayb, Omar al Bashir, Abdallah Banda Abakaer Nourain, Saleh Mohammed Jerbo Jamus, Bahar Idriss Abu Garda, Abdel-Rahim Mohamed Hussein (Situation in Darfur, Sudan); Francis Kirimi Muthaura, Uhuru Muigai Kenyatta, Mohammed Hussein Ali, William Samoei Ruto, Henry Kiprono Kosgey, Joshua Arap Sang (Situation in Kenya); Muammar Gaddafi, Saif al-Islam Gaddafi, Abdullah al-Senussi (Situation in Libya); Laurent Gbagbo and Simone Gbagbo (Situation in Côte d'Ivoire).

[80] Namely Ntaganda, Katanga, Ngudjolo, Mbarushimana, Mudacumura, Bemba, Kony, Otti, Harun, Kushayb, al Bashir, Hussein, Muthaura, Kenyatta, Ali, Laurent Gbagbo and Simone Gbagbo.

[81] Women's Initiatives for Gender Justice (n 51) 121; full range of charges set out at 123–124.

[82] Vincent Otti, Raska Lukwiya and Muammar Gaddafi.

released without trial,[83] and 15 have never been brought into ICC custody.[84] These are institutional challenges relating to enforcement and arrest and are not exclusive to the issue of sexual and gender-based violence. However, the most intractable problem facing the ICC, and one which appears to affect prosecutions for sexual violence to an inordinate extent, is that of sufficiency of prosecution evidence and attrition of charges before trial.

It has been noted that the Prosecutor's batting average when it comes to the confirmation of charges currently makes for grim reading.[85] Fourteen individuals to date have appeared before the ICC for a confirmation of charges hearing; of those, four have had no charges confirmed for trial.[86] Put another way, this means that almost a third of those who ever come into the ICC's custody are released without charge before even standing trial. The evidentiary reasons behind this phenomenon will be discussed later in the chapter; for now, it will suffice to note that it does not bode well for the future prospects of contemporaneous prosecutions at the ICC if such portentous failures have been encountered at a stage of proceedings which requires a much lower standard of proof than would be necessary to secure a conviction at trial.[87] However, looking beyond the individual outcome, a discernible pattern emerges when one examines the success rate for confirmation of specific charges of sexual and gender-based violence. Women's Initiatives for Gender Justice have noted that, based on current figures, exactly half of all individual charges for

---

[83] Bahar Idriss Abu Garda, Callixte Mbarushimana, Mohammed Hussein Ali and Henry Kosgey.

[84] Namely Ntaganda, Mudacumura, Kony, Otti, Lukwiya, Ongwen, Odhiambo, Harun, Kushayb, al Bashir, Hussein, Muammar Gaddafi, Saif Gaddafi, al-Senussi and Simone Gbagbo.

[85] See for example W Schabas, 'Thoughts on the Kenya Confirmation Decisions' (PhD Studies in Human Rights, 30 January 2012) <http://humanrightsdoctorate.blogspot.com/2012/01/thoughts-on-kenya-confirmation.html> last accessed 30 January 2012, comparing the 'failure rate' at the confirmation stage at the ICC (29 per cent) to the acquittal rate at the ICTY (14 per cent).

[86] While the cases against Lubanga, Katanga, Ngudjolo, Bemba, Banda, Jerbo, Muthaura, Kenyatta, Ruto and Sang proceeded to trial, no charges were confirmed against Abu Garda, Mbarushimana, Ali and Kosgey and they were released. See *Situation in Darfur, Sudan: Prosecutor v Abu Garda* (Decision on the Confirmation of Charges) ICC-02/05-02/09 (8 February 2010); *Situation in the DRC: Prosecutor v Mbarushimana* (Decision on the Confirmation of Charges) ICC-01/04-01/10 (16 December 2011); *Situation in Kenya: Prosecutor v Ruto et al* (Decision on the Confirmation of Charges Pursuant to Article 61(7)(a) and (b) of the Rome Statute) ICC-01/09-01/11 (23 January 2012); *Situation in Kenya: Prosecutor v Muthaura et al* (Decision on the Confirmation of Charges Pursuant to Article 61(7)(a) and (b) of the Rome Statute) ICC-01/09-02/11 (23 January 2012).

[87] The standard of proof at the trial phase at the ICC is 'beyond reasonable doubt'; ICC Statute, art 66(3): 'In order to convict the accused, the Court must be convinced of the guilt of the accused beyond reasonable doubt.' At the confirmation of charges phase, the standard is 'substantial grounds to believe'; ICC Statute, art 61(7): 'The Pre-Trial Chamber shall, on the basis of the hearing, determine whether there is sufficient evidence to establish substantial grounds to believe that the person committed each of the crimes charged.'

gender-based crimes have not survived the confirmation of charges hearings.[88] By contrast, charges for crimes such as murder, pillage or intentionally directing attacks against the civilian population have encountered no such obstacles. Why then are charges relating to sexual or gender-based crimes so vulnerable?

One primary contributing factor relates to investigations. As discussed earlier in relation to the *Lubanga* trial, the Prosecutor relied heavily in his initial investigations on material obtained pursuant to confidentiality agreements under Article 54(3)(e) of the Statute, as well as witness evidence which was sourced via the use of intermediaries. Intermediaries can be an invaluable asset to investigators, and in some cases, such as the investigations in the Central African Republic, have provided vital information which allowed investigators to identify potential victims of sexual violence – both male and female – who would be willing to testify before the ICC.[89] Without sufficient supervision of their activities, however, intermediaries have the potential to taint crucial evidence and inadvertently undermine the work of the Court. The third feature to emerge from Prosecution investigations which has depreciated the standard of evidence produced is an over-reliance on the use of open-source information, such as reports from human rights organisations, media outlets and Government or UN agencies. While such information can be (and has been) used as an important part of pre-deployment preparations and strategic planning for investigators[90] and for the purposes of corroboration, it should never be considered as a viable substitute for first-hand witness testimony or documentary evidence. However, this basic fact is clearly not understood within the Office of the Prosecutor. In the *Mbarushimana* confirmation hearing, for example, the Prosecution did not advance a single insider or crime-base witness, relying solely on indirect evidence sourced from NGOs and other international organisations, in relation to eight of the 15 locations identified in its document containing the charges.[91]

---

[88] Women's Initiatives for Gender Justice, *Gender Report Card on the International Criminal Court 2012* <http://www.iccwomen.org/documents/Gender-Report-Card-on-the-International-Criminal-Court-2012.pdf> last accessed 21 November 2012, 106-107. Following the confirmation of charges hearings in the *Mbarushimana* and Kenyan cases, 15 of a total of 30 charges of sexual and gender-based violence across four cases (Bemba, Katanga & Ngudjolo, Mbarushimana and Muthaura *et al*) have not been confirmed for trial. Prior to those decisions, the failure rate of charges for gender-based crimes at the confirmation of charges phase was 33 per cent; see Women's Initiatives for Gender Justice (n 51) 125.

[89] See for example M Glasius, 'Global Justice Meets Local Civil Society: The International Criminal Court's Investigation in the Central African Republic' (2008) 33(4) *Alternatives* 413.

[90] See for example Glassborow (n 15) on the preparations for investigations in Uganda: 'Before beginning investigations, ICC prosecution analysts received documents from local NGOs and rehabilitation centres where children abducted and held captive as child soldiers, porters and sex slaves gathered when they came out of the bush. They also collected evidence from the Ugandan authorities, which had documented the actions of the LRA over the last 20 years, and rooted through newspaper articles written about attacks.'

[91] *Situation in the DRC: Prosecutor v Mbarushimana* (Transcript) ICC-01/04-01/10 (21 September 2011) 2–4. Somewhat unsurprisingly, no charges were confirmed against Callixte

In both the *Mbarushimana* and Kenyan confirmation decisions, the Pre-Trial Chamber felt the need to explain the ramifications of this simple evidentiary premise to the Prosecution. In *Mbarushimana*, the Chamber stated:

> As a general principle, the Chamber finds that information based on anonymous hearsay must be given a low probative value in view of the inherent difficulties in ascertaining the truthfulness and authenticity of such information. Accordingly, such information will be used only for the purpose of corroborating other evidence.[92]

The Chamber's instruction in the *Ruto* and *Muthaura* confirmation decisions was even more explicit:

> With respect to indirect evidence, the Chamber is of the view that, as a general rule, such evidence must be accorded a lower probative value than direct evidence. The Chamber highlights that, although indirect evidence is commonly accepted in the jurisprudence of the Court, the decision on the confirmation of charges cannot be based solely on one such piece of evidence.[93]

One can only hope that the extent of the Prosecution's reliance on indirect evidence as a substitute for first-hand field investigations will decrease under the current Prosecutor, if these deliberate rebukes from the Pre-Trial Chambers are correctly interpreted. However, the use of third-hand and open-source information is indicative of a more insidious problem within the Office of the Prosecutor; namely a tendency to develop a case hypothesis in the abstract and seek evidence which complements and supports that theory, rather than pursuing evidence-led investigations from the outset. Not only does this approach involve a risk that the Prosecution will overlook significant elements of the fact pattern in an investigation which could have supported charges not initially envisaged in the case hypothesis, as indeed occurred in the *Lubanga* case, it also tends to give rise to weaker evidence and a greater risk that charges will be lost at the various procedural hurdles preceding the trial.

---

Mbarushimana and he was released from ICC custody in December 2011.

[92] *Situation in the DRC: Prosecutor v Mbarushimana* (Decision on the Confirmation of Charges) (n 86) para 78, in relation to Human Rights Watch reports which had been challenged by the Defence.

[93] *Prosecutor v Ruto et al* (Decision on the Confirmation of Charges) (n 86) para 74; *Prosecutor v Muthaura et al* (Decision on the Confirmation of Charges) (n 86) para 86 (quote identical in both decisions). The Pre-Trial Chamber defined 'indirect evidence' as encompassing 'hearsay evidence, reports of international and non-governmental organisations (NGOs) as well as reports from national agencies, domestic intelligence services and the media'; *Prosecutor v Ruto et al* (Decision on the Confirmation of Charges) (n 86) para 69.

The Prosecution's investigative methodology was condemned in astonishingly frank terms by the Pre-Trial Chamber in the *Mbarushimana* case, which are worth repeating in full:

> Finally, the Chamber wishes to highlight its concern at the technique followed in several instances by some Prosecution investigators, which seems utterly inappropriate when viewed in light of the objective, set out in article 54(1)(a) of the Statute, to establish the truth by 'investigating incriminating and exonerating circumstances equally'. The reader of the transcript of interviews is repeatedly left with the impression that the investigator is so attached to his or her theory or assumption that he or she does not refrain from putting questions in leading terms and from showing resentment, impatience or disappointment whenever the witness replies in terms which are not entirely in line with his or her expectations. Suggesting that the witness may not be 'really remembering exactly what was said', complaining about having 'to milk out' from the witness details which are of relevance to the investigation, lamenting that the witness does not 'really understand what is important' to the investigators in the case, or hinting at the fact that the witness may be 'trying to cover' for the Suspect, seem hardly reconcilable with a professional and impartial technique of witness questioning. Accordingly, the Chamber cannot refrain from deprecating such techniques and from highlighting that, as a consequence, the probative value of evidence obtained by these means may be significantly weakened.[94]

The Chamber raises an interesting point, not only by explicitly putting the Prosecutor on notice that evidence collected pursuant to leading questions or questionable investigative practices will be given less weight by the Chamber. Prosecutor Ocampo never appeared to understand the requirement placed on him and his investigative staff by Article 54(1)(a) to deliberately investigate both incriminating and exonerating evidence equally.[95] It is clear, however, from the behaviour described by the Pre-Trial Chamber that, at a minimum, investigators

---

[94] *Prosecutor v Mbarushimana* (Decision on the Confirmation of Charges) (n 86) para 51.
[95] See for example W Schabas, 'Does the Prosecutor Only Investigate Incriminating Evidence?' (PhD Studies in Human Rights, 1 February 2012) <http://humanrightsdoctorate.blogspot.com/2012/02/in-preparation-for-talk-i-am-delivering.html> last accessed 1 February 2012, in relation to public statements by the Prosecutor regarding the investigation in Libya; 'The ICC Under Scrutiny: Assessing Recent Developments at the International Criminal Court' (International Bar Association, November 2008) <http://www.ibanet.org/Document/Default.aspx?DocumentUid=6BB0015D-5E75-4F79-B1D0-C37F91303222> last accessed 10 December 2011, 26, noting that 'Article 54(1)(a) essentially places the Office of the Prosecutor (OTP) under an obligation to investigate all aspects of the case in order to establish the truth, and the wording of Article 54(1) suggests a prosecutor with a "high level of neutrality and impartiality", who should act as an "officer of justice rather than a partisan

have on occasion actively failed to pursue evidence which appears to be relative to exoneration. It is to be hoped that the new Prosecutor will ensure greater compliance with a rule which not only allows for fairness to the defence, but permits prosecution investigators to have a greater understanding of the full parameters and potential weaknesses of their own case well in advance of trial.

The Prosecutor has frequently defended his remote investigative strategy on the grounds of security risks to victims and witnesses and the practical difficulties of gaining access to Situation countries without the cooperation of the governments in question.[96] However, this justification was brought into question by Antonio Cassese as early as 2006, in an *amicus curiae* brief submitted in the Darfur Situation in his capacity as Chairman of the UN Commission on Enquiry on Darfur.[97] Judge Cassese appeared to attempt to provide some basic instruction on the kind of investigative activities which could be conducted without field investigations (such as attempting to identify the military chain of command or obtaining documentary evidence relating to military orders),[98] but also noted that, from his recent first-hand experience, while long-term and complex field investigations such as mass grave excavations could be stymied by the prevailing security conditions on the ground, 'undertaking *targeted and brief interviews* of victims and witnesses in the capital cities of the three States of Darfur (El Fashir, El Geneina and Nyala) could prove to be safe'.[99] UN High Commissioner for Human Rights and former ICTY Prosecutor Louise Arbour likewise criticised the Prosecutor's approach from a position of significant first-hand authority, stating that, in her view, 'it is possible to conduct serious investigations of human

---

advocate" ... Successful prosecution should not be the ultimate aim of the Prosecutor when investigating – this should be "establishment of truth".'

[96] See for example 'BBC Briefed on ICC Gaddafi Probe' (Institute for War and Peace Reporting, 4 March 2011) <http://iwpr.net/report-news/bbc-briefed-icc-gaddafi-probe> last accessed 10 December 2011, quoting the Prosecutor as stating that investigators 'are obviously not going to be allowed in Libya at least for the foreseeable future'; International Criminal Court, Office of the Prosecutor, 'Third Report of the Prosecutor of the International Criminal Court to the UN Security Council Pursuant to UNSCR 1593 (2005)' (14 June 2006) <http://www.amicc.org/docs/OTP_ReportUNSC_3-Darfur_English.pdf> last accessed 10 December 2011, 2: 'The continuing insecurity in Darfur is prohibitive of effective investigations inside Darfur, particularly in light of the absence of a functioning and sustainable system for the protection of victims and witnesses. The investigative activities of the Office are therefore continuing outside Darfur.'

[97] *Situation in Darfur, Sudan* (Observations on Issues Concerning the Protection of Victims and the Preservation of Evidence in the Proceedings on Darfur Pending Before the ICC) ICC-02/05 (25 August 2006).

[98] Ibid 4, 10–11.

[99] Ibid 5 [emphasis in original]. Significantly, Cassese also argued that, given the 'copious and reliable evidence' of rape being committed by Sudanese armed forces and the lack of political will to address the issue on the part of the Sudanese authorities, 'the only way of stopping rape in Darfur, a heinous crime of vast magnitude, that is, to *protect victims of rape*, is to hold accountable under the notion of command responsibility those who would be in a position to prevent or punish its authors'. Ibid 7 [emphasis in original].

rights violations during an armed conflict in general, and in Darfur in particular, without putting victims at unreasonable risk'.[100] Cassese later repeated his frustrations with the Prosecutor's strategy in relation to the Darfur investigations, stating that 'there are some aspects of the Prosecutor's handling of the Darfur situation that cannot help but mystify all those who have laid great stock in the ICC's ability to make rapid and significant headway ... one fails to see why the Prosecutor has not yet requested Sudan to allow his investigators to enter its territory and discharge their duties'.[101] The former Senior Trial Attorney in the Darfur Situation, Andrew Cayley, also expressed frustration and disappointment in the Prosecutor's 'extremely risk averse' strategy in Darfur, arguing that 'it was a mistake that the court did not establish a presence on the ground in Darfur'.[102] Unsurprisingly, absent or insufficient field investigations will have a drastic effect on the quality and amount of victim and witness testimony collected, which can have a disproportionate impact on charges of sexual and gender-based crimes in the absence of documentary or pattern evidence of sufficient probative value.

Unsurprisingly, given the range of recurring problems and strategic errors attaching to the Office of the Prosecutor's investigations, the resulting evidence has been shown on numerous occasions throughout the Court's records to be insufficient, poorly pleaded and therefore incapable of supporting the charges sought. When this is compounded by a frequently deficient charge selection and inappropriate mode of liability, it can result in the attrition of charges and factual circumstances at the various pre-trial procedural stages and, in some cases, the complete failure of a case to proceed to trial. These issues have frequently been at their most immediately apparent in relation to the ICC's investigations of sexual and gender-based violence, but are far from unique to that category of crime. As more of the ICC's cases proceed towards a final verdict, evidence from the initial investigations by the Office of the Prosecutor which may have been deemed satisfactory for the purposes of confirmation of charges (but which have not been subsequently buttressed by additional investigations or by the introduction of supplementary evidence, where procedurally permissible) may well prove to be

---

[100] *Situation in Darfur, Sudan* (Observations of the United Nations High Commissioner for Human Rights Invited in Application of Rule 103 of the Rules of Procedure and Evidence) ICC-02/05 (10 October 2006) para 64. She went on: '[T]he particular case of the ICC investigation in Darfur ... may require amongst other things a determination of whether the possible risks created by victims' contact with ICC investigators are greater than the danger they face daily by the continuation or escalation of the conflict and commission of related crimes'; ibid para 68.

[101] A Cassese, 'Is the ICC Still Having Teething Problems?' (2006) 4 *JICJ* 434, 438–439.

[102] 'Discussion' (2008) 6 *JICJ* 763, 779–780: 'We did not collect evidence in Darfur as the Cassese Commission did extremely successfully in a three months period; more importantly we did not establish a presence on the ground in Darfur ... Professor Cassese, the head of the UN Commission personally went to Khoba prison in Khartoum and interviewed very sensitive witnesses. He demanded access with nothing more than a Security Council resolution in his hand. The OTP ICC got no further than the Hilton Hotel in Khartoum ... The ICC has relied heavily on the information that they [the Cassese Commission] gathered.'

insufficient to establish the guilt of an individual defendant beyond a reasonable doubt or to support the entering of a conviction on a particular charge. It is an illuminating and worthwhile endeavour to examine the fate of charges of sexual and gender-based violence at earlier procedural stages – entailing a far lower standard of proof – as a harbinger of the potential consequences of Prosecutor Ocampo's chosen investigative and prosecutorial strategy on future trial judgments, as the impact of investigative errors made during the Court's first decade of operations will continue to manifest and reverberate at later stages of proceedings. In the confirmation of charges decision in the *Katanga* case, for instance, the Pre-Trial Chamber held that the Prosecutor had provided sufficient evidence to establish substantial grounds to believe that the war crime of outrages upon personal dignity had been committed during the attack on the village of Bogoro, but had 'brought no evidence showing that the commission of such crimes was intended' by the two accused or even that they were foreseeable in the ordinary course of events.[103] This finding foreshadows the issue of individual criminal responsibility which would prove to be so contentious for the eventual verdicts in that case. Crime-base evidence is obviously important to prove the factual allegations underpinning a prosecution; however, it is not exclusively determinative, and in the absence of sufficient evidence to establish the individual criminal responsibility of an accused or the contextual elements of the individual crimes charged, the Prosecutor is unlikely to rack up many convictions.

One of the most high-profile failures of Prosecutor Ocampo's tenure came in the *al Bashir* case, when the Pre-Trial Chamber initially refused to include charges for genocide (committed *inter alia* by means of widespread rape and sexual violence) in the arrest warrant against Sudanese President Omar al Bashir.[104] Although the Appeals Chamber ultimately overturned this decision on the grounds that the Pre-Trial Chamber had applied a higher standard of proof than was strictly necessary under the Statute,[105] it is worth noting that counsel for the Prosecution had acknowledged before the Pre-Trial Chamber that '(i) it does not have any direct evidence in relation to Omar Al Bashir's alleged responsibility for the crime of genocide; and that therefore ii) its allegations concerning genocide are solely based on certain inferences that, according to the Prosecution, can be drawn from the facts of the case'.[106] One does not need to be the Prosecutor to understand that proving specific intent for genocide is a challenging and fraught enterprise,[107] and

---

[103] *Situation in the DRC: Prosecutor v Katanga and Chui* (Decision on the Confirmation of Charges) ICC-01/04-01/07 (1 October 2008) para 570–572.

[104] *Situation in Darfur: Prosecutor v al Bashir* (Decision on the Prosecution's Application for a Warrant of Arrest against Omar Hassan Ahmad Al Bashir) ICC-02/05-01/09 (4 March 2009).

[105] *Situation in Darfur: Prosecutor v al Bashir* (Judgment on the Appeal of the Prosecutor Against the 'Decision on the Prosecution's Application for a Warrant of Arrest against Omar Hassan Ahmad Al Bashir') ICC-02/05-01/09 (3 February 2010) paras 39–42.

[106] *Prosecutor v al Bashir* (Decision on the Prosecution's Application for a Warrant of Arrest against Omar Hassan Ahmad Al Bashir) (n 104) para 111.

[107] See for example C Aptel, 'The Intent to Commit Genocide in the Case Law of the International Criminal Tribunal for Rwanda' (2002) 13(3) *CLF* 273; R Park, 'Proving Genocidal

direct evidence may not always be available or even necessary.[108] It is less than heartening, however, to reflect on the UN Commission of Inquiry's conclusion that genocide could not be proven on the evidence available to it,[109] evidence which was significantly broader than that available to the Prosecutor due to the lack of concerted field investigations. It is even less heartening to consider that the Prosecution took two attempts to drag the genocide charge over the lowest hurdle of proof, merely 'reasonable grounds to believe'. Therefore, without addressing the merits of whether charges of genocide should ever have been advanced in the first place,[110] it should be obvious to the staff of the Office of the Prosecutor that more substantive evidence of specific genocidal intent than has currently been assembled will be required to prove this charge beyond a reasonable doubt should the case ever miraculously get to trial; indeed, as it stands, one would hardly put money on its being confirmed. The foregoing assumes, of course, that additional post-confirmation investigations would be considered permissible within the statutory framework of the Court.[111]

In the *Muthaura* case, the Prosecutor was aiming for significantly less controversial charges of crimes against humanity relating to the post-election violence in Kenya in early 2008. However, the Pre-Trial Chamber was devastating in its assessment of the standard of evidence presented by the Prosecution to support charges of sexual violence in its decision on the issuance of summonses to appear. Regarding allegations of rape and sexual violence committed in the town of Naivasha, the Pre-Trial Chamber found that the Prosecutor had 'failed to provide evidence substantiating his allegation that rape was committed as part of the attack';[112] note

---

Intent: International Precedent and ECCC Case 002' (2010) 63(1) *Rutgers L Rev* 129.

[108] See for example *Prosecutor v Jelisić* (Appeal Judgment) IT-95-10-A (5 July 2001); *Prosecutor v Krstić* (Appeal Judgment) IT-98-33-A (19 April 2004); W Schabas, 'The *Jelisić* Case and the *Mens Rea* of the Crime of Genocide' (2001) 14 *LJIL* 125.

[109] Report of the International Commission of Inquiry on Darfur to the United Nations Secretary-General Pursuant to Security Council Resolution 1564 of 18 September 2004 (25 January 2005) <http://www.un.org/news/dh/sudan/com_inq_darfur.pdf> last accessed 10 December 2011, 4, 124–133, stating at para 518: 'one crucial element appears to be missing, at least as far as the central Government authorities are concerned: genocidal intent. Generally speaking the policy of attacking, killing and forcibly displacing members of some tribes does not evince a specific intent to annihilate, in whole or in part, a group distinguished on racial, ethnic, national or religious grounds.' See further W Schabas, 'Darfur and the "Odious Scourge": The Commission of Inquiry's Findings on Genocide' (2005) 18 *LJIL* 871.

[110] See for example W Schabas, 'New Warrant for Darfur, But Where is the Genocide Charge?' (PhD Studies in Human Rights, 7 December 2011) <http://humanrightsdoctorate.blogspot.com/2011/12/new-warrant-for-darfur-but-where-is.html> last accessed 10 December 2011.

[111] *Situation in the DRC: Prosecutor v Lubanga* (Judgment on the Prosecutor's Appeal Against the Decision of Pre-Trial Chamber I entitled 'Decision Establishing General Principles Governing Applications to Restrict Disclosure Pursuant to Rule 81(2) and (4) of the Rules of Procedure and Evidence') ICC-01/04-01/06 (13 October 2006) paras 49–57.

[112] *Situation in Kenya: Prosecutor v Muthaura et al* (Decision on the Prosecutor's Application for Summonses to Appear for Francis Kirimi Muthaura, Uhuru Muigai Kenyatta

that the Chamber did not find that Prosecutor Ocampo had provided *insufficient* evidence, rather that he had advanced none at all in support of the rape charge in that location. The charge of rape relating to events in Naivasha was reinstated at the confirmation of charges hearing following the submission of additional evidence by the Prosecutor, albeit three second-hand NGO reports rather than direct testimonial evidence.[113] The Prosecution attempted to justify their lack of crime-base witness testimony or documentary evidence of rape in Naivasha by arguing that 'many other cases of rape and other forms of sexual violence went unreported due to the trauma caused by such crimes and societal stigma'.[114] While this is often true with regard to crimes of sexual violence, it hardly seems feasible that the Prosecution could fail to find a single victim or witness willing to testify when three separate Kenyan NGOs were capable of adducing evidence of rape in that location.[115] In relation to the allegations of rape committed in Kisumu and Kibera, although the Pre-Trial Chamber found that the Prosecutor had provided sufficient evidence to establish reasonable grounds to believe that rape had in fact occurred, it found that 'the Prosecutor ... failed to provide an accurate factual and legal submission which would require the Chamber to examine whether the acts of violence were part of an attack pursuant to or in furtherance of a State policy'.[116] Furthermore, the Chamber held that 'it is even more compelling that the material presented by the Prosecutor does not provide reasonable grounds to believe that the events which took place in Kisumu and/or in Kibera can be attributed to Muthaura, Kenyatta and/or Ali under any mode of liability embodied in article 25(3) of the Statute'.[117]

In one of its most high-profile trials, at the earliest stage of proceedings and needing to fulfil only the lowest possible standard of proof, Prosecutor Ocampo was found wanting on such basic prosecution elements as proving the existence

---

and Mohammed Hussein Ali) ICC-01/09-02/11 (8 March 2011) para 26.

[113] Ibid para 259. The Chamber did note, however, that the evidence advanced by the Prosecutor was sufficient to 'reach the threshold required at this stage of the proceedings', implicitly suggesting that it may not be strong enough (without further corroboration) to uphold a conviction.

[114] Ibid para 255.

[115] Admittedly there are many reasons why an individual would feel comfortable giving an unattributed or anonymous account of sexual violence to an NGO or human rights group rather than providing specific testimony to international criminal investigators, particularly in the context of the intensely political opposition to the ICC's activities in Kenya. Bizarrely, however, the Prosecution document containing the charges appears to cite a witness statement (KEN-OTP-0042-0228) in support of their assertion that rape had gone unreported in Naivasha due to trauma and stigma. It is not immediately obvious why the Prosecution witness could state with authority that rape had gone unreported due to specific factors, but could not testify that it had in fact occurred. *Situation in Kenya: Prosecutor v Muthaura et al* (Prosecution's Amended Document Containing the Charges and List of Evidence Submitted Pursuant to Article 61(3) and Rule 121(3) (4) and (5)) ICC-01/09-01/11 (19 August 2011) para 74.

[116] *Prosecutor v Muthaura et al* (Decision on the Prosecutor's Application for Summonses to Appear) (n 112) para 31.

[117] Ibid para 32.

of a crime base in a particular location, establishing linkage evidence to prove the individual criminal liability of the suspects and satisfying the *chapeau* requirements for crimes against humanity. More damningly, however, Judge Kaul issued a separate dissenting opinion to the decision on the confirmation of charges dissecting the strategic failure behind many of the most basic and commonly repeated errors in the Prosecutions' pleadings: phased investigations. Judge Kaul set out the qualities which he held to be crucial in any Prosecution investigation, including promptness, impartiality and comprehensive thoroughness,[118] and concluded that he '[did] not find it difficult to assume that any investigation meeting these standards only partially and unsatisfactorily will probably lead to problems and difficulties not only for an effective and successful prosecution but also for the work of the Chamber concerned and for the Court in general'.[119] Judge Kaul explicitly identified 'scarcity of evidence' as one potential consequence of insufficiently comprehensive investigations, before highlighting another deeply unsatisfactory aspect of the Prosecutor's approach:

> [A]n approach which *de facto* is aiming, in a first phase, (only) at gathering enough evidence to reach the 'sufficiency standard' within the meaning of article 61(7) of the Statute, maybe in the expectation or hope that in a further phase after the confirmation proceedings, additional and more convincing evidence may be assembled to attain the 'beyond reasonable doubt' threshold, as required by article 66(3) of the Statute. I believe that such an approach, as tempting as it might be for the Prosecutor, would be risky, if not irresponsible: if after the confirmation of the charges it turns out as impossible to gather further evidence to attain the decisive threshold of 'beyond reasonable doubt', the case in question may become very difficult or may eventually collapse at trial.[120]

It is deeply embarrassing but hardly coincidental, given the extensive procedural headaches which can be caused by insufficient or tainted prosecution evidence and which were exemplified in the *Lubanga* proceedings, that judges at the ICC have felt the need to make such advice explicit to the Prosecutor. Unfortunately, however, experience has shown that, no matter how explicit, this advice is clearly not being heeded.

Perhaps the most comprehensive evisceration of the Prosecutor's evidence to date was provided in the *Mbarushimana* case. The arrest warrant against

---

[118] *Situation in Kenya: Prosecutor v Muthaura et al* (Decision on the Confirmation of Charges: Dissenting Opinion by Judge Hans-Peter Kaul) ICC-01/09-02/11 (26 January 2012) paras 50, 53.

[119] Ibid para 52.

[120] Ibid, discussed further in B Inder, Speech at 'Justice for All? The International Criminal Court – Ten Year Review' Conference, University of New South Wales and Australian Human Rights Centre, 14 February 2012.

Mbarushimana had contained the broadest range of sexual and gender-based crimes charged in any case before the ICC to date, including rape, torture, mutilation, other inhumane acts, inhuman treatment and persecution on the basis of gender.[121] *Mbarushimana* was also the only case to date to proceed to a confirmation of charges hearing with a majority of gender-based crimes, making it in many ways the ICC's flagship prosecution of sexual and gender-based violence. Unfortunately – albeit entirely predictably to those closely monitoring pre-trial proceedings – not a single charge was confirmed against Callixte Mbarushimana and he was released on 23 December 2011. The confirmation of charges decision makes for instructive (and profoundly depressing) reading. The Pre-Trial Chamber began by critiquing the entirety of the Prosecution's presentation of the case, highlighting that 'the charges and the statements of facts in the DCC [Document Containing the Charges] have been articulated in such vague terms that the Chamber had serious difficulties in determining, or could not determine at all, the factual ambit of a number of the charges'.[122] The Chamber immediately excluded from consideration seven of the locations identified by the Prosecution in its pleadings, on the grounds that 'the evidence is so scant that the Chamber cannot properly assess, let alone satisfy itself to the required threshold, whether any of the war crimes charged by the Prosecution were committed by the FDLR in [those] villages'.[123] The Chamber noted that for some of the locations in question, the Prosecution had advanced only a single UN or Human Rights Watch report (based on anonymous sources) to support their allegations.[124] On numerous occasions throughout the confirmation decision, the Chamber held that the Prosecutor had not provided sufficient evidence (or in some cases any evidence) to establish substantial grounds to believe that the event in question had occurred or that an ancillary element of the offence had been satisfied.[125] The Chamber found substantial grounds to believe that war crimes had been committed in the course of only five of the 25 events alleged by the Prosecutor, but, even more devastatingly, refused to support charges for crimes against humanity on the basis that the Prosecutor had failed to provide substantial grounds to believe that an 'attack against a civilian population' within the meaning

---

[121] *Situation in the DRC: Prosecutor v Mbarushimana* (Warrant of Arrest for Callixte Mbarushimana) ICC-01/04-01/10 (11 October 2010).

[122] *Prosecutor v Mbarushimana* (Decision on the Confirmation of Charges) (n 86) para 110. In relation to the charge of cruel treatment as a war crime, the Chamber noted that a combined reading of the Prosecution's Document Containing the Charges and List of Evidence revealed that the Prosecution had included 'under the heading of cruel treatment several other acts which would not seem to be adequately captured within the term "assault", including: abducting and raping women ... rape and other forms of sexual violence, forcing family members to witness the perpetration of rape, sexual violence and atrocities on their loved ones, and an incident in which a number of women were allegedly captured, raped, tortured and killed by the FDLR'.

[123] Ibid para 113.

[124] Ibid para 117, 194, 232.

[125] Ibid paras 131, 134, 169, 206, 211.

of Article 7 of the Statute had taken place.[126] Finally, the Chamber resoundingly rejected the Prosecutor's characterisation of the mode of liability in the case, holding that Mbarushimana could not be held individually criminally responsible under Article 25(3)(d).[127]

Given the inescapable failure of Prosecutor Ocampo to correctly interpret the damning analysis of his pleadings and standards of evidence emerging from several different Pre-Trial Chambers, it is little wonder that judges at the pre-trial stage have begun to feel the need to provide explicit instructions regarding the weaknesses in the Prosecution's presentation of a case. In the decision on the issuance of an arrest warrant in the *Gbagbo* case,[128] for example, the Pre-Trial Chamber highlighted a number of problematic areas in the Prosecutor's application for an arrest warrant which were likely to exacerbate as the proceedings progressed. The Chamber, doing everything but tapping their nose and suggesting that someone should probably write this down, noted that the Prosecutor had not cited any witness statements, summaries or affidavits in support of the charge of rape, but held that the indirect evidence advanced was sufficient at that stage of proceedings to satisfy 'the low evidential threshold established by Article 58'.[129] The Chamber criticised the pleading of the mode of liability in less subtle terms:

> For the purposes of his Application, therefore, the Prosecutor has focused exclusively on individual criminal responsibility under Article 25(3)(a) of the Statute, as opposed to the other provisions of that Article or, alternatively, command responsibility under Article 28 of the Statute … It is undesirable, particularly at this early stage of the case, for the Chamber to limit the options that may exist for establishing criminal responsibility under the Rome Statute … Until the Chamber has heard full arguments from the parties, it is premature to decide, certainly with any finality, whether Article 25(3)(a) of the Statute is the correct basis for proceeding against Mr Gbagbo (either standing alone or along with other provisions) … [I]t is likely that this issue (i.e. Mr Gbagbo's suggested liability as an 'indirect co-perpetrator' under Article 25(3)(a) of the Statute) may well need to be revisited in due course with the parties and participants.[130]

Following the devastating assessment of the Pre-Trial Chamber in the *Mbarushimana* case, one can only hope that those in a position to affect strategy in the Office of the Prosecutor were paying attention to the Chamber's warnings in the *Gbagbo* case.

---

[126] Ibid para 264.
[127] Ibid paras 291–340.
[128] *Situation in the Republic of Côte d'Ivoire: Prosecutor v Gbagbo* (Decision on the Prosecutor's Application Pursuant to Article 58 for a Warrant of Arrest Against Laurent Koudou Gbagbo) ICC-02/11-01/11 (30 November 2011).
[129] Ibid para 59.
[130] Ibid paras 73–77.

The stunning predictability of many of the strategic blunders made by the ICC's first Prosecutor has not lessened the disappointment that so many unforced errors have been needlessly repeated.

However, in the interests of fairness, it is worth noting that there are many individuals within the Office of the Prosecutor who have likewise tried to emphasise internally that, unless particular strategies were abandoned, the result would be compromised evidence and diminished chances of success at the confirmation of charges and trial stage. While many of these individuals are no longer employed by the Court, it is to be hoped that some may be persuaded to return under the tenure of Fatou Bensouda.[131] It would also be unfair to the efforts of many dedicated and committed individuals within the Office of the Prosecutor not to point out that, even on the (admittedly rare) occasions when the Prosecution have selected the best possible charges to represent the gendered nature of the crime, presented their evidence in a competent and comprehensive manner and put their work product at the mercy of the Pre-Trial Chamber, they have often encountered a remarkable lack of judicial receptiveness. Charges of torture and outrages upon personal dignity, for example, in so far as they have been pleaded in relation to sexual and gender-based violence, have never been successfully confirmed for trial.[132] This extreme reticence to progressively interpret the law on sexual and gender-based crimes – and in some cases, refusal even to acknowledge the law as it currently stands – is at its most virulent, it must be said, in the combined deliberations of Judge Trendafilova, Judge Tarfusser and Judge Kaul.

Events in two cases stand out as worthy of particular criticism. In the *Bemba* case, the Pre-Trial Chamber[133] refused to include factual allegations relating to women who had been forced to undress in public in order to humiliate them within the charge of 'other forms of sexual violence', on the basis that 'the facts submitted by the Prosecutor do not constitute forms of sexual violence of comparable gravity to the other crimes set forth in article 7(1)(g) of the Statute'.[134] The Pre-Trial Chamber did not appear to be aware of, or in any event did not make any reference to, the fact that in the first international criminal judgment to identify and define the crime of 'other forms of sexual violence', the *Akayesu* case at the Rwanda Tribunal in 1998, forced nudity of women for the purposes of humiliation was enumerated as the archetypal example of behaviour which would not meet the definition of rape

---

[131] See generally J Flint and A de Waal, 'Case Closed: A Prosecutor Without Borders' (2009) *World Affairs*, <http://www.worldaffairsjournal.org/article/case-closed-prosecutor-without-borders> last accessed 10 December 2011.

[132] Women's Initiatives for Gender Justice (n 51) 126.

[133] For the decision on the issuance of an arrest warrant, Pre-Trial Chamber III was composed of Judge Dembele Diarra, Judge Kaul and Judge Trendafilova; the decision on the confirmation of charges was issued by Pre-Trial Chamber II, composed of Judge Kaul, Judge Tarfusser and Judge Trendafilova.

[134] *Situation in the Central African Republic: Prosecutor v Bemba* (Decision on the Prosecutor's Application for a Warrant of Arrest Against Jean-Pierre Bemba Gombo) ICC-01/05-01/08 (10 June 2008) para 40.

but would nevertheless constitute an international crime of sexual violence.[135] In its decision on the confirmation of charges in the *Bemba* case, the Pre-Trial Chamber showed an even more inexplicable disregard for the existing body of international criminal jurisprudence when it held that the practice of cumulative charging was inherently detrimental to the rights of the defence.[136] As a result, the Chamber refused to confirm two separate but related charges, one of rape and one of torture, which had as their factual basis the pain and suffering experienced both by those who were raped in front of family members and those forced to endure watching the rape of family members. The Chamber found that, as cumulative charging was apparently offensive to the ICC's legal framework, and as (in its view) rape was the 'most appropriate legal characterisation' of the facts since it encompassed the material elements of the crime of torture in addition to the specific element of penetration, the act of torture identified by the Prosecution was 'fully subsumed by the count of rape'.[137] While one could at least attempt to argue the logic, if not the necessity or wisdom, of this course of action regarding the factual allegations underpinning the charge of torture arising from the public nature of the rape, it is entirely unclear how the Chamber concluded that the specific material elements of severe pain and suffering inflicted on those who were forced to watch their family members being raped in front of them could be accurately or appropriately subsumed within a single charge of rape. Those witnesses were not raped, but they were tortured, and as a result of the Chamber's needless and illogical constriction of the charges and facts presented by the Prosecutor, their suffering and that element

---

[135] *Prosecutor v Akayesu* (Trial Judgment) ICTR-96-4-T (2 September 1998) para 688: 'The Tribunal considers sexual violence, which includes rape, as any act of a sexual nature which is committed on a person under circumstances which are coercive. Sexual violence is not limited to physical invasion of the human body and may include acts which do not involve penetration or even physical contact. The incident described by Witness KK in which the Accused ordered the Interahamwe to undress a student and force her to do gymnastics naked in the public courtyard of the bureau communal, in front of a crowd, constitutes sexual violence.' Although jurisprudence from the *ad hoc* tribunals does not necessarily carry any precedential weight at the ICC, in light of its direct relevance to the interpretational issue in question, the lack of any discussion or even acknowledgement of the ICTR Trial Chamber's finding within the reasoning of the Pre-Trial Chamber on this point appears to be more attributable to judicial oversight, rather than an attempt to distinguish the *Akayesu* case or to deliberately omit to cite it on a point of principle regarding the applicability of jurisprudence from other international criminal tribunals to the interpretation of crimes under the Rome Statute, an issue which, when it does arise at the ICC, is usually addressed directly.

[136] *Situation in the Central African Republic: Prosecutor v Bemba* (Decision Pursuant to Article 61(7)(a) and (b) of the Rome Statute on the Charges of the Prosecutor Against Jean-Pierre Bemba Gombo) ICC-01/05-01/08 (15 June 2009) para 202, apparently basing the entirety of its legal authority for this proposition within the ICC legal framework on an *obiter* remark by the same Pre-Trial Chamber in its decision on the issuance of an arrest warrant, while simultaneously acknowledging that cumulative charging was accepted within national jurisdictions and other international criminal jurisdictions such as the ICTY and ICTR.

[137] Ibid paras 204–205.

of the gendered nature of the crimes will not now be fully captured by the Court's eventual judgment in the case.

In the *Muthaura* case, at both the decision on the issuance of an arrest warrant and the decision on the confirmation of charges phase of proceedings, Pre-Trial Chamber II[138] refused to characterise the forcible circumcision of Luo men as 'other forms of sexual violence', insisting that it should instead be considered as part of the charge of 'other inhumane acts'. In its decision on the issuance of an arrest warrant, the Chamber asserted, without authority or legal reasoning,[139] that 'acts of forcible circumcision cannot be considered acts of a "sexual nature" as required by the Elements of Crimes but are to be more properly qualified as "other inhumane acts" … in light of the serious injury to body that the forcible circumcision causes and in view of its character, similar to other underlying acts constituting crimes against humanity'.[140] The Chamber returned to this theme in its decision on the confirmation of charges,[141] advancing the frankly incomprehensible argument that 'not every act of violence which targets parts of the body commonly associated with sexuality should be considered an act of sexual violence' and that 'the determination of whether an act is of a sexual nature is inherently a question of fact'.[142] The Chamber's assessment of the determinancy of the severity of the violence inflicted as opposed to the deliberate targeting of sexual organs does seem worthy of questioning, given that it could apparently find nothing of relevance to sexual violence about the amateur circumcision and in some cases amputation of the penises of men of a particular ethnicity, frequently committed in public and with makeshift implements such as broken bottles. The Chamber found, quite incredibly, that 'the evidence placed before it does not establish the sexual nature of the acts of forcible circumcision and penile amputation visited upon Luo men',[143] a sentence devoid of even internal logic. Since, in its view, 'the acts were motivated by ethnic prejudice and intended to demonstrate cultural superiority of one tribe over the other',[144] they did not qualify as other forms of sexual violence within the meaning of Article 7(1)(g) of the Statute.

The Chamber's reasoning on this issue is beyond comprehension, unsupported by sufficiently detailed legal reasoning, and demonstrative of an entirely unnecessary hostility and reactionary conservatism towards the concept of

---

[138] Composed of Judge Trendafilova, Judge Tarfusser and Judge Kaul.

[139] Beyond one footnote referring to the Elements of Crimes, cited without discussion.

[140] *Prosecutor v Muthaura et al* (Decision on the Prosecutor's Application for Summonses to Appear) (n 112) para 27.

[141] Despite arguments submitted by the Prosecution in support of the inclusion of forcible circumcision within the legal characterisation of 'other forms of sexual violence', on the grounds that 'these weren't just attacks on men's sexual organs as such but were intended as attacks on men's identities as men within their society and were designed to destroy their masculinity'. *Prosecutor v Muthaura et al* (Decision on the Confirmation of Charges) (n 86) para 264.

[142] Ibid para 265.

[143] Ibid para 266.

[144] Ibid.

progressively interpreting existing criminal provisions to permit the fullest examination and representation of the sexualised nature of violence committed during armed conflict.[145] By the Chamber's logic, if women of a particular ethnicity were consistently targeted for and subjected to crude attempts at female genital mutilation, ostensibly to establish the cultural superiority of another ethnic group which followed the practice, there would be *nothing inherently sexual* about the violent excision of their clitoris or other external sexual organs. I would argue that it is equally ridiculous to assert with a straight face that, as a matter either of fact or of law, there is nothing sexual about the full or partial amputation of a man's penis as it is to argue that the severity of physical injury inflicted by means of sexual violence is a more relevant legal factor than the sexualised nature of the violence itself. In this respect, it is worth emphasising that the definition of 'other forms of sexual violence' in the Elements of Crimes does refer to the commission of 'an act of a sexual nature'. The Chamber's reasoning appears to interpret that provision to include both sexual acts and acts committed with a sexualised purpose or intent, but to exclude acts which have a devastating and permanent impact on an individual's sexual integrity. One can only hope that this restrictive interpretation is revisited in future and does not give rise to a chilling effect on future Prosecution charging strategies.

In addition to the impact the Pre-Trial Chamber's decisions have had on the legal acknowledgement of sexual violence within the relevant cases, they are also a source of immense and profound disappointment to those, like this author, who have previously commended the progressive interpretation of international crimes to reflect the gendered or sexual aspects of the violence by which they were committed.[146] The *ad hoc* tribunals were presented with foundational Statutes which were laconic at best when it came to crimes of sexual violence, but have since held that sexual violence is capable of forming a constituent part of the offences of genocide, extermination, torture, enslavement, persecution, other inhumane acts, grave breaches, outrages on personal dignity and cruel or inhuman treatment. The ICC, on the other hand, began life with the broadest ever range of explicitly sexual crimes included in its Statute, but has since seen at least some of its judges display inordinate amounts of unwillingness even to interpret acts such as forced public nudity or forcible circumcision as falling within the ambit of its existing sexual crimes, not to mention creatively interpreting other crimes without an immediately obvious sexual component to include relevant evidence of sexual violence. This,

---

[145] Both decisions discussed in this context would be very unlikely to pass the test for legitimacy of judicial interpretation proposed by Joseph Powderly in Chapter 10 of this volume.

[146] See for example Hayes (n 4); Copelon (n 1); PV Sellers, 'Gender Strategy is Not a Luxury for International Courts' (2009) 17 *American UJ of Gender, Soc Policy and L* 301; KD Askin, 'Prosecuting Wartime Rape and Other Gender-Related Crimes Under International Law: Extraordinary Advances, Enduring Obstacles' (2003) 21 *Berkeley J Int'l L* 288; Women's Initiatives for Gender Justice, *Gender Report Card 2009* (n 30) *Gender Report Card 2010* (n 35) and *Gender Report Card 2011* (n 51).

perhaps, is one of the most retrograde developments at the ICC to date, and one which gives rise to frustration, regret and a weary suspicion that, despite all the effort expended, the accumulated effects of the Court's activities have contributed more to pushing the rock back down the hill than to edging it further up.

## Conclusion

It is clear from the account above that many of the errors encountered by the *ad hoc* tribunals in their initial efforts to prosecute sexual and gender-based violence have been unnecessarily repeated in the first decade of the ICC's operations. More worryingly, the first Prosecutor appeared incapable of learning even from his own mistakes, as basic systemic flaws at both the investigation and prosecution stage went unaddressed, prosecution evidence was habitually found wanting, and charges of sexual violence were excluded from arrest warrants and summonses to appear or went unconfirmed. The salutary lesson to be drawn from the strategy of the ICC's first Prosecutor is that simply talking a good game about the occurrence of sexual and gender-based violence will not be enough, and that the only meaningful or appropriate way of addressing it through the operation of an international criminal tribunal is to comprehensively, competently and carefully investigate such crimes and to make every effort to ensure that they are pleaded and charged effectively. One can only hope that Prosecutor Bensouda will take determined steps to improve and redirect prosecutorial strategy, and that the ICC will use its unparalleled opportunity as a permanent international criminal court to produce charges of and jurisprudence on sexual violence which are worthy of adding to the growing body of international criminal precedent on this issue. Sisyphus was condemned to repeat his interminable task for eternity; let us hope that the International Criminal Court can escape the same fate.

# Creating a Framework for the Prosecution of Environmental Crimes in International Criminal Law

Tara Smith[1]

The issue of climate change has pushed accountability for environmental damage to the top of the international agenda. However, international criminal law does not attempt to attach criminal liability to environmental damage at present. Although the number of areas of international law concerned with environmental issues has grown significantly over the past three to four decades[2], space has yet to be made within the framework of international criminal law for 'environmental crimes'. While there is some scope at the International Criminal Court for accountability to attach to situations of environmental harm, there is indeed still considerable debate as to whether criminal sanctions are an appropriate form of responsibility for environmental damage at all.[3]

The objective of international criminal law is to provide a means of individual criminal accountability for the most serious atrocities that occur on Planet Earth.

---

[1] Tara Smith is a policy officer in the Environment and Climate Office within Irish Aid, the development cooperation division within Ireland's Department of Foreign Affairs. Tara is also an Attorney-at-Law qualified in the State of New York. Her doctoral thesis on the protection of the environment in non-international armed conflict will be completed in 2013. All views expressed in this chapter are her own.

[2] In particular, the field of human rights is expanding to recognise the impact of environmental conditions on human well-being security and dignity. On this issue see Conor Gearty, 'Do Human Rights Help or Hinder Environmental Protection?' (2010) 1 Journal of Human Rights and the Environment 7 and Dinah Shelton, 'Human Rights and the Environment: Jurisprudence of Human Rights Bodies' (2002) 32 Environmental Policy and Law 158

[3] Cho Byung-Sun, 'Emergence of an International Environmental Criminal Law?' (2000-2002) 19 UCLA Journal of Environmental Law and Policy 11

There is no doubt that rapidly changing environmental conditions can cause catastrophic consequences for both human life and other elements of the natural environment. The effects of tsunamis, hurricanes, typhoons, droughts, floods and other extreme weather events are a constant feature of global news reports. Man-made environmental disasters can have equally devastating effects some of which, it is argued here, should give rise to individual criminal liability. However, given the nature of some environmental damage and the current incarnation of international criminal law, the International Criminal Court or other ad hoc international criminal tribunals may not always provide an appropriate or adequate means of responding to the damage that is caused to the natural environment.

In this chapter, the first step in assessing the value of individual criminal responsibility for environmental damage is a detailed examination of the environmental dimension of the current framework of international criminal law. Noting that there is a distinct absence of environment-specific provisions in international criminal law at present, the discussion below will begin by critically examining the potential for existing international criminal law to give rise to individual criminal liability for environmental damage. Secondly, though ambitious, there is considerable scope for the amendment of existing 'core' crimes - or indeed international criminal law as a whole - to include explicit prohibitions on environmental damage. The second part of this chapter will therefore examine possible ameliorations to existing crimes within the current framework of international criminal law; the specific example of amendments to war crimes provisions will be used to illustrate this point. Finally, there is the possibility that States could agree to a fundamental expansion of international criminal law to respond directly to situations of deliberate environmental damage. This chapter will therefore conclude with an appraisal of the proposals that call for the establishment of a separate and distinct category of environmental crimes – often called 'ecocide' or 'geocide' – within the structure of international criminal law.

## I. Current Responsibility for Environmental Damage in International Criminal Law

In existing international criminal law, environmental damage is only a criminal offence when it can be described in terms of a crime that already exists. The key point in relation to existing international criminal law is that the environmental damage merely amounts to the tool by which atrocity is perpetrated and 'the [environmental] destruction becomes a crime because of its humanitarian consequences'.[4] In other words, the environmental damage *per se* does not yet amount to an offence under

---

[4] T Weinstein, 'Prosecuting Attacks That Destroy the Environment: Environmental Crimes or Humanitarian Atrocities?' (2004–2005) 17(4) *Georgetown Int'l Environmental L Rev* 697, 720.

international criminal law. Essentially, criminal liability arises as a result of the effects of the environmental damage on the human population, as human beings and their security are at the centre of contemporary international criminal law. Though this approach may be somewhat clunky and awkward, there is certainly scope for existing crimes to be interpreted in a 'green' manner, and it is to these interpretations that this discussion now turns.

## A. Genocide and the Environment

In 1948, the Genocide Convention defined the crime of genocide[5] and this definition has since been transcribed *verbatim* into article 6(c) of the Rome Statute of the International Criminal Court.[6] Although a number of actions are enumerated as amounting to acts of genocide, the most pertinent in terms of environmental damage is the proscription on the deliberate infliction of 'conditions of life calculated to bring about [a group's] physical destruction in whole or in part'.[7] The Rome Statute's 'Elements of Crimes'[8] describes the conditions of life amounting to genocide as being the 'deliberate deprivation of resources indispensable for survival'[9]. No stretch of the imagination is required to foresee how environmental conditions, or the calculated and intentional destruction thereof, could be used as a means of effecting the destruction of a specific population, thereby amounting to an act of genocide.

In 1985, the Whitaker Report[10] highlighted the suggestion, made by some members of the Sub-Commission on Prevention of Discrimination and Protection of Minorities, that the scope of the Genocide Convention ought to be expanded to explicitly include environmental destruction. The proposal sought to include 'ecocide' in the Genocide Convention as an act of genocide. This should not be confused with another permutation of ecocide as being perhaps a crime in its own right which will be discussed later in this chapter. Ecocide within the context of the crime of genocide was envisaged to amount to 'adverse alterations, often irreparable, to the environment – for example through nuclear explosions, chemical weapons, serious pollution and acid rain, or destruction of the rain forest – which

---

[5] Convention on the Prevention and Punishment of the Crime of Genocide (1951) 78 UNTS 277, art 2.
[6] Rome Statute of the International Criminal Court, 2187 UNTS 90, 17 July 1998, entered into force 1 July 2002, art 6 ('ICC Statute').
[7] ICC Statute, art 6(c).
[8] International Criminal Court, Elements of Crimes, U.N. Doc. PCNICC/2000/1/Add.2 (2000)
[9] International Criminal Court, Elements of Crimes, U.N. Doc. PCNICC/2000/1/Add.2 (2000), footnote 4
[10] B Whitaker (Special Rapporteur) *Revised and Updated Report on the Question of the Prevention and Punishment of the Crime of Genocide*, UN ESCOR, Human Rights Sub-Commission on the Prevention of Discrimination and Protection of Minorities, 38th Sess., UN Doc. E/CN.4/Sub.2/1985/6 (1985) ('Whitaker Report').

threaten the existence of entire populations, whether deliberately or with criminal negligence'.[11]

The rationale behind this proposition was the feeling amongst some members of the Sub-Commission that 'indigenous groups are too often the silent victims of such actions'[12] and that the 'physical destruction of indigenous communities'[13] amounted to genocide and required 'special and urgent action'.[14] An illustrative example is the situation of the Aché Indians in Paraguay during the 1970s. As a result of State policies to encourage mining and cattle-raising in forests occupied by this indigenous group, the Aché Indians were brutally targeted and their forested area of habitation was destroyed with the aim of removing them from the land.[15] This was done to such an extent that some commentators believe this group no longer exists.[16] In short, it seems as though conditions of life calculated to bring about the physical destruction of a group were used. However, one crucial element in the proof of genocide which is missing in this scenario is that of genocidal intent.

For acts to be recognised as genocide, they must be carried out with genocidal intent: that is, the 'intent to destroy, in whole or in part, a national, ethnical, racial or religious group'.[17] Genocidal intent is indeed a challenge in attempting to prosecute environmental damage as genocide, though it has remained a difficult *mens rea* standard to prove in most circumstances. The proposal for 'ecocide' in the Whitaker Report appears to suggest that a lower 'criminal negligence' standard of intent would be more appropriate where responsibility for environmental damage was in question. Paraguayan officials maintained that the Aché Indians were being targeted and killed 'because their land was desired, and not because they were Indians'[18] and as a result, what occurred 'was not genocide'.[19] In other words, the intent of the alleged perpetrator was to clear the land, not to destroy in whole or in part a national, ethnical, racial or religious group. In the absence of genocidal intent, an act cannot be considered genocide.

This thinly veiled justification appears to easily defeat genocidal intent when it is linked to acts of environmental damage that result in the destruction of a group. Put simply, acts amounting to the *actus reus* of genocide could conceivably occur through environmental damage taking place in the context of development. The *actus reus* of genocide, according to the ICC's Elements of Crimes,[20] requires (i) the

---

[11] Ibid para 33.
[12] Ibid.
[13] Ibid.
[14] Ibid.
[15] M Munzel, *The Aché Indians: Genocide in Paraguay* (International Work Group for Indigenous Affairs, Copenhagen 1973) IWGIA Internal Document No. 11.
[16] P Sharp, 'Prospects for Environmental Liability in the International Criminal Court' (1999) 18 *Virginia Environmental L J* 217, 234–35.
[17] ICC Statute, art 6.
[18] IW Charny (ed) *Encyclopedia of Genocide* (ABC-CLIO, Santa Barbara, CA 1999) 3.
[19] Ibid.
[20] International Criminal Court, Elements of Crimes, U.N. Doc. PCNICC/2000/1/Add.2 (2000)

perpetrator to inflict certain conditions of life upon one or more persons (ii) that such person or persons belonged to a particular national, ethnical, racial or religious group and (iii) that the conduct took place in the context of a manifest pattern of similar conduct directed against that group or was conduct that could itself effect such destruction. However the *mens rea* elements of genocide – the intention to destroy the group and in furtherance of this, the calculated infliction of conditions of life that would result in the group's destruction - would not be satisfied where the intent of the individual was to engage in development. Therefore, while environmental damage caused in the context of development could conceivably cause genocide by proxy in line with the *actus reus* requirements of genocide,

> A country which causes fatal environmental degradation while exercising its right to development now has the conceptual basis for contending that its actions were justified by the greater good of the country as a whole. In the light of this potential, the prospects for proving a specific 'intent to destroy' become increasingly small.[21]

While the case of the Aché Indians remains relevant to this discussion, the most poignant example of the development justification is illustrated by the situation of the 'Marsh Arabs', those native Shi'a Muslims living in the Mesopotamian Marshes in Southern Iraq. Following their participation in an unsuccessful attempt to topple the Hussein government in 1991, the Marsh Arabs were met with sustained attempts by the State to destroy their group. This was done by direct killings, but also by targeting and destroying the very environment upon which the group had traditionally survived for thousands of years.[22] The Iraqi Government drained the Mesopotamian Marshes to such an extent that only 7 per cent of those wetlands remain today. The destruction of this ecosystem has resulted in the deaths of large numbers of Marsh Arabs and the dispersal of many more.[23] The Iraqi government justified the building of dams and canals on the Tigris and Euphrates rivers – actions which directly led to the draining of the marshes – by arguing that it was all done in the name of development and progress. In other words, the stated intent was to effect development; the intent was not to destroy the group. Therefore genocidal intent does not seem to be immediately present. Regardless of how much the act in question seems to satisfy the *actus reus* elements of genocide, without concurrent genocidal intent, the crime of genocide cannot be proved.

However, even in the absence of such justifications, genocidal intent still remains a problem. In Sudan there has been notable evidence of a scorched earth

---

[21] Sharp (n 16) 234.

[22] For a fuller account see A Schwabach, 'Ecocide and Genocide in Iraq: International Law, the Marsh Arabs, and Environmental Damage in Non-International Conflicts' (2004) 15 *Colorado J of Int'l Environmental L and Pol* 1 and Weinstein (n 4).

[23] Schwabach (n 22) 4.

policy employed by Government forces.²⁴ To this end, the Sudanese president, Omar Al Bashir, allegedly stated that he 'did not want any villages or prisoners, only scorched earth'²⁵ to remain in the Darfur region. The International Criminal Court decided in its first arrest warrant for Al Bashir in 2009 that this did not amount to proof of genocidal intent, but rather constituted war crimes or crimes against humanity instead.²⁶ However, there is some promise that this policy and its environmental effects will be addressed in any subsequent prosecution as genocide in light of the Court's revised arrest warrant issued in July 2010.²⁷

Although these examples are mere snapshots of much more complex situations, they nonetheless illustrate the ways in which environmental destruction may be the primary tool or indeed a 'major accelerator'²⁸ of genocide. Because of the terms of the Genocide Convention and article 6(c) of the Rome Statute, there is scope to prosecute environmentally destructive acts as genocide under the current framework of laws. The chances of this occurring, however, remain quite slight because of the difficult *mens rea* requirement associated with the crime of genocide. Perhaps a much stronger case may be made for individual criminal responsibility for environmental damage within the context of crimes against humanity and so it is to this category of crimes that the discussion now turns.

## B. Environmental Crimes against Humanity

The Whitaker Report, discussed above, recorded alternative opinions of the Sub-Commission on Prevention of Discrimination and Protection of Minorities to the effect that environmental destruction would more comfortably fit the description of crimes against humanity than genocide.²⁹ The first attempt to codify crimes against humanity as a separate category of international crimes was made in Article 7 of the Rome Statute in 1998. The four most relevant aspects of this article from an environmental perspective are contained in Article 7(1) and include the prohibitions on extermination,³⁰ forcible transfer of population,³¹ persecution³² and

---

[24] L Polgreen, 'Scorched-Earth Strategy Returns to Darfur' *New York Times* (New York 2 March 2008). See also, S Bloomfield and K Butler, '"Scorched Earth" Unleashed on Darfur, Despite UN Presence' *Irish Independent* (Dublin 12 March 2008) and K Glassborow, 'International Court Urged to Consider Environmental Crimes' *Institute for War & Peace Reporting* (The Hague 4 September 2007).
[25] *Situation in Darfur, Sudan: Prosecutor v al Bashir* (Decision on the Prosecution's Application for a Warrant of Arrest against Omar Hassan Ahmad Al Bashir) ICC-02/05-01/09 (4 March 2009) para 170.
[26] Ibid para 172.
[27] *Situation in Darfur, Sudan: Prosecutor v al Bashir* (Second Warrant of Arrest for Omar Hassan Ahmad Al Bashir) ICC-02/05-01/09 (12 July 2010) 7.
[28] Weinstein (n 4) 719.
[29] Whitaker Report (n.10), para 33.
[30] ICC Statute, art 7(1)(b).
[31] ICC Statute, art 7(1)(d).
[32] ICC Statute, art 7(1)(h).

other inhumane acts[33] which are 'committed as part of a widespread or systematic attack directed against any civilian population, with knowledge of the attack'.[34]

Through these four crimes against humanity, environmental damage which may fall short of the threshold for genocide could potentially be caught in the crimes against humanity safety net. Crimes against humanity do not need to satisfy the challenging genocidal intent requirement. However, any environmental damage which results in extermination, persecution, forcible transfer or other inhumane acts still remains subject to the *mens rea* requirement that the act be committed with the knowledge that it amounts to a widespread and systematic attack on the civilian population. This *mens rea* requirement element is far less elusive than genocidal intent as far as environmental damage is concerned because 'if the foreseeable result of state, individual, or organisational action is to cause severe environmental degradation that destroys or harms civilians, a policy to continue such conduct may be deemed a policy to carry out that action – or "attack" as defined by the [ICC] Statute'.[35]

Going into a little detail on the relevant crimes against humanity identified above, firstly, according to Article 7(2)(b), 'extermination' includes the mass killing of civilians through 'the intentional infliction of conditions of life … calculated to bring about the destruction of part of a population'.[36] This provision is strikingly similar to the crime of genocide discussed earlier in this chapter, but there is no requirement to provide genocidal intent in this instance. The evidence would suggest that the situation of the Marsh Arabs in Iraq could very easily amount to the crime against humanity of extermination since the *actus reus* of the crime is largely the same as described above in the context of genocide, but the *mens rea* requirement of this crime against humanity is somewhat less onerous. According to the Rome Statute's 'Elements of Crimes'[37] the *mens rea* for the crime of extermination is the knowledge that the act was or was intended to be part of a widespread or systematic attack against the civilian population. The difference between this level of intent and that required for genocide is that as long as the alleged perpetrator knew that the act amounted to a systematic attack against the civilian population, they may be guilty of this crime against humanity. Therefore where development policies are pursued aggressively and result in the widespread killing of civilians as a result of serious environmental damage, for example, it may be easier to pursue an alleged perpetrator for the crime against humanity of extermination rather than genocide.

Secondly, the crime against humanity of deportation or forcible transfer of a population amounts to the 'forced displacement of the persons concerned by expulsion or other coercive acts from the area in which they are lawfully

---

[33] ICC Statute, art 7(1)(k).
[34] ICC Statute, art 7.
[35] LA Malone and S Pasternack, *Defending the Environment: Civil Society Strategies to Enforce International Environmental Law* (Island Press, Washington 2004) 236.
[36] ICC Statute, art 7(2)(b).
[37] International Criminal Court, Elements of Crimes, U.N. Doc. PCNICC/2000/1/Add.2 (2000).

present'.[38] The situation in Southern Sudan, where the water supply[39] and land[40] of rural communities was targeted, forcing their exodus from the area to allow oil companies to take advantage of the natural resources there,[41] is exemplary of how environmental damage may be the means by which this crime against humanity is committed. Clearly, the forced displacement of the Marsh Arabs in Southern Iraq could also amount to a crime under Article 7(1)(d) of the Rome Statute.

Thirdly, persecution involves the 'intentional and severe deprivation of fundamental rights contrary to international law by reason of the identity of the group or collectivity'.[42] Where the natural environment is damaged to such an extent that the fundamental rights of a group are affected, this could amount to a crime against humanity. Fourthly, 'other inhumane acts', enumerated as a crime against humanity in Article 7(1)(k) means acts of 'a similar character [to those listed above] intentionally causing great suffering, or serious injury to body or to mental or physical health'.[43] Detailed examination of the environmental conditions inflicted on the habitat of the Aché Indians in Paraguay reveals circumstances that are possibly beyond the proscribed limits of this crime against humanity.

Under the rubric of crimes against humanity, many actions which cause serious environmental damage in the name of development could result in individual criminal responsibility. There are numerous examples of indigenous populations or other vulnerable groups that have been killed or has their way of life destroyed as a result of damage to the natural environment upon which they depended simply because the land had some alternative value or more profitable use: oil, gas or minerals may have been located there; the land may have been particularly lucrative for the growing of certain crops such as biofuels;[44] or the area may have been attractive as a surreptitious waste disposal area. Like genocide, crimes against humanity respond to acts of environmental damage as a result of its impact on the human population.

## C. Environmental War Crimes

Criminal liability for environmental damage in armed conflict is, on paper, a reality. In fact, the environmental war crimes provision in the Rome Statute – Article 8(2)(b)(iv) - is the only example of a direct and explicit environmental crime in the entire framework of international criminal law. However, on closer inspection,

---

[38] ICC Statute, art 7(2)(d).
[39] Second Warrant of Arrest for Omar Hassan Ahmad Al Bashir (n 27) 7.
[40] Decision on the Prosecution's Application for a Warrant of Arrest against Omar Hassan Ahmad Al Bashir (n 25) para 170.
[41] International Association of Genocide Scholars, 'Resolution on Darfur' (July 2007) para 6; Second Warrant of Arrest for Omar Hassan Ahmad Al Bashir (n 27) 7.
[42] ICC Statute, art 7(2)(g).
[43] ICC Statute, art 7(1)(k).
[44] J Borger, 'UN Chief Calls for Review of Biofuels Policy' *Guardian* (London 5 April 2008).

Article 8(2)(b)(iv) and its companion provisions in Additional Protocol I[45] have been an ineffective and inadequate response to a persistent and growing problem in contemporary warfare. A successful prosecution for environmental war crimes seems impossible under the current incarnation of the law.

During the Nuremberg Trials that followed World War II, three significant prosecutions interpreted the laws that then existed to attempt to indirectly prosecute individuals for environmental damage caused during the war. Firstly, charges were brought against General Lothar Rendulic for the implementation of a scorched earth policy in the German retreat from Finnmark.[46] The scorched earth policy was ordered by General Rendulic to avoid annihilation by a superior Russian side that he felt were pursuing the German Army in their retreat. In reality, this belief was unfounded as the Russian Army were not in pursuit of the retreating German Army. However, General Rendulic's sincere but mistaken beliefs were enough to satisfy the Court that the actions he took were justified by military necessity. Lothar Redulic was therefore acquitted of the environmental damage charges,[47] though he was found guilty on all other charges and sentenced to 20 years imprisonment.[48]

Secondly, Alfred Jodl was found guilty of implementing a scorched earth policy in retreat from Norway in 1941. Some 30,000 houses were destroyed in this way and while no human deaths were reported as a result of this method of warfare, the environment was clearly impacted as a result of this destruction. Unlike Lothar Rendulic, General Jodl was found guilty of this charge and as a cumulative result of being found guilty of numerous other serious charges, he was sentenced to death by hanging.[49] Thirdly, natural resource exploitation during World War II was also pursued in post-War prosecutions. In Polish Forestry Case No. 7150, the United Nations War Crimes Commission 'determined that nine of ten German civil administrators could be considered war criminals for cutting down Polish timber.'[50] Each of these cases set landmark precedents for the interpretation of international law to indirectly protect the environment in armed conflict. However, this precedent has not been capitalised on since 'no tribunal since Nuremberg has prosecuted individuals for war-related environmental damage.'[51]

---

[45] Protocol Additional to the Geneva Conventions of 12 August 1949, and relating to the Protection of Victims of International Armed Conflicts (Protocol I), 8 June 1977, 1125 UNTS 3

[46] *Wilhelm List and Others (The Hostages Trial)* (1949) Law Reports of Trials of War Criminals Selected and Prepared by the United Nations War Crimes Committee Vol VIII 34, 45

[47] ibid 67-69

[48] ibid 76

[49] *Trial of Alfred Jodl* (1948) Trial of the Major War Criminals before The International Military Tribunal "Blue Series" Vol XXII , 570-571

[50] Weinstein (n 4), 704

[51] Tara Weinstein, 'Prosecuting Attacks that Destroy the Environment: Environmental Crimes or Humanitarian Atrocities?' (2004-2005) 17 Georgetown International Environmental Law Review 697, 704

Environmental damage became explicitly prohibited in international armed conflict in 1977, as it was included in Additional Protocol I to the 1949 Geneva Conventions.[52] This was almost entirely in response to the means and methods of warfare employed by the US Army in the Vietnam War. Practices of cloud seeding and the use of Agent Orange and other defoliants were strongly condemned due to their long- and short-term effects on the natural environment and human health. Although the provisions in Protocol I could not be retroactively applied, the prohibition of 'methods and means of warfare which are intended, or may be expected, to cause widespread, long-term and severe damage to the natural environment'[53] was expected to prevent this level of environmental damage taking place in future international conflicts. No such provision was included in Protocol II covering non-international armed conflicts.

Despite this explicit prohibition in international humanitarian law, such limitations on environmental harm were not incorporated into international criminal law until 1998. At this point, it was included as a specific war crime in Article 8(2)(b)(iv) of the Rome Statute of the International Criminal Court.[54] The inclusion of this provision in the Rome Statute was probably more in response to the extreme environmental damage witnessed during the Iraqi retreat from Kuwait in 1991[55] than as a result of any compelling argument made by the efficacy of the provisions contained in Protocol I. However, Protocol I was clearly drawn upon for textual inspiration as the construction of the environmental war crime in the Rome Statute is almost identical to the humanitarian prohibition in the 1977 instrument. No provision was made for individual criminal liability for environmental damage in non-international armed conflict.

While environmental humanitarian law provisions did not make it into the statutes of any of the *ad hoc* criminal tribunals established in the 1990s, provisions of this kind have begun to appear in the statutes of tribunals established since the adoption of the Rome Statute in 1998. The Statutes of the Special Panels for Serious

---

[52] Protocol Additional to the Geneva Conventions of 12 August 1949, and relating to the Protection of Victims of International Armed Conflicts (Protocol I) 1125 UNTS 3, 8 June 1977, entered into force 7 December 1979, arts 35(3) and 55.

[53] Protocol I to the Geneva Conventions art 35(3). The text of the ICC Statute reads 'long-lasting' instead of 'long-term', but there is no significant divergence in meaning between these two terms.

[54] Art 8(2)(b)(iv) prohibits: 'Intentionally launching an attack in the knowledge that such attack will cause incidental loss of life or injury to civilians or damage to civilian objects or widespread, long-term and severe damage to the natural environment which would be clearly excessive in relation to the concrete and direct overall military advantage anticipated.'

[55] Where more than 700 oil rigs were set on fire and copious amounts of oil polluted the entire Persian Gulf region. For more information see MA Ross, 'Environmental Warfare and the Persian Gulf War: Possible Remedies to Combat Intentional Destruction of the Environment' (1992) 10 *Dickinson J of Int'l L* 515.

Crimes (Dili District Court of East Timor)[56] and of the Iraqi Special Tribunal[57] contain transcribed versions of the International Criminal Court's environmental war crimes clause.

At present, the levels of damage contemplated by Additional Protocol I and The Rome Statute are extraordinarily high. No prosecutions have been pursued to date under these provisions and as a result no judicial precedent has been set to clarify the levels of environmental harm that need to occur to trigger criminal liability. The prevailing understanding, arrived at through academic examination and discussion, is that an extremely high level of damage is required to trigger individual criminal liability in the Rome Statute. An attack which results in 'widespread, long-term and severe damage to the natural environment'[58] will only be considered criminal under international law if it is intentionally launched with the knowledge that this degree of environmental damage will be caused as a result. In addition, the damage must be disproportionate and 'clearly excessive in relation to the concrete and direct overall military advantage anticipated'.[59] By all standards, this clause imposes impossible conditions for the prosecution of environmental war crimes and it certainly does 'not reflect preventive theories of environmental law'.[60]

Such is the level of environmental damage needed to result in individual criminal responsibility that it may seem as though there is no actual prohibition in international criminal law on environmental damage in times of armed conflict, since no environmental damage since 1977 has reached the required threshold (even though significant environmental damage has indeed occurred in international conflicts). It would appear that the terms of Additional Protocol I (and by association, Article 8(2)(b)(iv) of the Rome Statute place 'the prohibition of ecological warfare incomprehensively higher than what modern weapons could possibly achieve...thus having no limiting or protective effect'.[61] For example, the Committee that was established by the Office of the Prosecutor at the ICTY to review the NATO bombing campaign of the former Yugoslavia in 1999[62] did identify some

---

[56] 'United Nations Transitional Administration in East Timor, on the Establishment of Panels with Exclusive Jurisdiction over Serious Criminal Offences' UNTAET Reg. 2000/15, 6 June 2000, s. 6(1)(b)(iv).

[57] Statute of the Iraqi Special Tribunal for Crimes Against Humanity (10 December 2003) art 13(b)(5).

[58] ICC Statute, art 8(2)(b)(4).

[59] Ibid.

[60] SN Simonds, 'Conventional Warfare and Environmental Protection: A Proposal for International Legal Reform' (1992) 29 *Stanford J of Int'l L* 165, 175.

[61] K Hulme, 'Armed Conflict, Wanton Ecological Devastation and Scorched Earth Policies: How the 1990-91 Gulf Conflict Revealed the Inadequacies of the Current Laws to Ensure Effective Protection and Preservation of the Natural Environment' (1997) 2 *J of Armed Conflict L* 45, 61.

[62] Final Report to the Prosecutor by the Committee Established to Review the NATO Bombing Campaign Against the Federal Republic of Yugoslavia, ICTY 2000 <http://www.icty.org/x/file/Press/nato061300.pdf> accessed 4 January 2013

serious environmental damage that was caused by NATO forces, particularly as a result of the bombing of chemical plants, inadvertently or otherwise. However, the Committee felt that the damage did not cross the Additional Protocol I threshold and therefore should not be pursued as a violation of the laws of armed conflict.[63]

Further limiting the efficacy of Article 8(2)(b)(iv) is the situation created by international law whereby any post-conflict remediation carried out on environmental damage could jeopardise an environmental war crimes prosecution because it would prevent the harm from reaching the required thresholds in the long term. Post-conflict remediation should not be discouraged in this way, but neither should it absolve an individual of criminal responsibility for causing environmental harm in the first place.

Moreover, the terms of the threshold clause in Article 8(2)(b)(iv) are impractical and ambiguous: there is no indication of exactly what constitutes *widespread*, what length of time constitutes *long-term* and what amounts to *severe* damage within the context of the Rome Statute. Points of clarification which were applied to previous treaties with similar terms[64] are explicitly not applicable to the Rome Statute. Karen Hulme has attempted to shed some light on the vagueness of these terms. According to her analysis, widespread could amount to several tens of thousands of kilometers,[65] long-term could amount to decades – 20 to 30 years at a minimum,[66] and severe might amount to significant interference with human life or human utilities.[67] Clearly the level of damage required to breach Article 8(2)(b)(iv) is far too high and provides no real limitation on the amount of environmental damage that can be caused in armed conflict.

It has been argued that even had there been jurisdiction over the environmental damage caused during the 1991 Iraqi retreat from Kuwait, the thresholds of harm in Protocol I and the Rome Statute may still not have been breached[68] – and this is probably the most extreme and deliberate environmental damage that has occurred since the Second World War. Even if this damage could have triggered liability under the Rome Statute, there is always the possibility that the environmental

---

[63] ibid para 25

[64] Specifically the Convention on the Prohibition of Military or any Other Hostile Use of Environmental Modification Techniques, opened for signature on 18 May 1977, entered into force on, 5 October 1978 1108 UNTS 17119 ('ENMOD Convention') where an Understanding Regarding Article I of ENMOD drafted at the Conference of the Committee on Disarmament advanced guidelines for the interpretation of these three terms. 'Widespread' was thought to mean an area of about several hundred square kilometres, 'long lasting' meant a period of months, approximately a season, while 'severe' referred to serious or significant disruption or harm to human life, natural and economic resources or other assets. See Hulme (n 65), 67.

[65] K Hulme, *War Torn Environment: Interpreting the Legal Threshold* (Martinus Nijhoff Publishers, Leiden 2004) 92. See also MN Schmitt, 'War and the Environment: Fault Lines in the Prescriptive Landscape' in JE Austin and CE Bruch (eds) *The Environmental Consequences of War: Legal, Scientific and Economic Perspectives* (CUP, Cambridge 2000) 87, 109.

[66] Hulme (n 65) 94.

[67] Ibid 96.

[68] Hulme (n 65) 70.

damage could be considered to be proportionate collateral damage or required and therefore justified by the demands of military necessity – or military advantage, as contained in the latter part of the Article 8(2)(b)(iv). Precedent exists for the defence of military necessity to wartime environmental damage since charges against German General Rendulic for his scorched earth policy in Norway, done also in retreat, were dropped on grounds of military necessity.

Of course, like other crimes in international criminal law, environmental damage could be indirectly prohibited through international criminal law by non-environment specific provisions. However, the focus of the discussion in this section has deliberately remained predominantly on the enumerated environmental war crimes provisions as they are the only 'green' crimes to exist under international criminal law to date.

## D. Aggression and the Environment

It is difficult to see how the crime of aggression as it stands could be perpetrated by any means of environmental damage falling short of the use of nuclear weapons, or extreme biological or chemical attacks. Clearly the invasion, attack or bombardment of one state by the armed forces of another, as envisaged by Article 8*bis*[69] will cause a certain amount of environmental damage. Given the weakened state of the global environment at present, the environmental consequences of a transboundary attack may become the main purpose of future acts of aggression. However, such acts could easily be transformed into an armed conflict, at which point the relationship between the armed forces and the environment becomes governed by Article 8(2)(b)(iv) of the Rome Statute or Articles 35(3) and 55(1) of Additional Protocol I if the conflict is international in nature. Given the lack of ambition to incorporate direct and enforceable environmental crimes into international criminal law to date, and given the unfinished status of the crime of aggression,[70] it would be unrealistic to read too much into Article 8*bis* as being a feasible route for the prosecution of environmental crimes at the International Criminal Court.

---

[69] ICC Statute, art 8*bis*.
[70] D Scheffer, 'The Complex Crime of Aggression under the Rome Statute' (2010) 23(4) *LJIL* 897.

## II. Developing Environmental Crimes within International Criminal Law

All four crimes in the Statute of the International Criminal Court discussed above could be amended to include effective environment-specific offences if the desire for such change is acted upon by States when next given the opportunity. The addition of new and distinct environmental crimes in addition to the four enumerated International Criminal Court crimes is also a possibility. In this section, both the modification of existing crimes and the enumeration of a new environmental crime will be considered. In discussing the former, war crimes will be taken as an illustrative case study of the ways in which existing crimes can be moulded to create effective criminal sanctions for environmental damage. Discussion of the latter issue will specifically look at calls for the establishment of 'ecocide' as an environment-specific and independent international crime.

### A. The Amelioration of Environmental War Crimes

There have been many proposals put forth to solve the current environmental deficiencies in the laws of armed conflict.[71] At the radical end of the spectrum are suggestions for the creation of a Fifth Geneva Convention[72] or the establishment of an International Environmental Criminal Court.[73] Lingering at the conservative end of the scale are those who suggest minor textual changes or mere clarifications of existing terms. The discussion below focuses on two suggestions for developing pragmatic and enforceable war crimes with individual criminal responsibility for environmental damage caused in armed conflict.

*i. Lower the thresholds of harm*
The degree of environmental damage that must be caused in armed conflict before an individual becomes criminally responsible under international law is prohibitively high. Regrettably, the thresholds of harm contained in Protocol I and

---

[71] See generally H-P Gasser, 'For Better Protection of the Natural Environment in Armed Conflict: A Proposal for Action' (1995) 89(3) *AJIL* 637–44. See also United Nations Environment Programme, 'Protecting the Environment During Armed Conflict: An Inventory and Analysis of International Law' (UNEP Post-Conflict and Disaster Management Branch, Nairobi November 2009) 51.

[72] G Plant (ed) *Environmental Protection and the Law of War: A 'Fifth Geneva' Convention on the Protection of the Environment in Time of Armed Conflict* (Belhaven Press, London and New York 1992).

[73] See S Hockman, 'An International Court for the Environment' (2009) 11 *Environmental L Rev*, 1–4. See also A Abrami, 'Proposal of Two Historical Reforms: An International Environmental Criminal Court (IECC) A European Environmental Criminal Court (EECC)' (International Academy of Environmental Sciences, Venice 2010).

Article 8(2)(b)(iv) of the Rome Statute may be having a greater deterrent effect on prosecutors to pursue environmental war crimes charges against an individual than to individuals engaged in armed conflict on the battlefield. As already discussed, the magnitude of environmental damage required for the war crime that currently exists is 'widespread, long-term and severe' damage, in addition to the knowledge requirements and an absence of military advantage.[74]

One of the major issues in the current environmental war crime is the conjunctive nature of the thresholds of harm in both Additional Protocol I and the Rome Statute. Amending the cumulative requirement of widespread *and* long-term *and* severe damage is one small change that could make a big difference. Lowering the threshold by simply making these terms disjunctive units of evidence – so that only one of the three elements would trigger criminal liability – would be a positive amendment to the current international criminal law framework. The standard would then be similar to that contained in the 1976 Environmental Modification Convention[75]. Secondly, the precise meaning of the terms 'widespread, long-term, and severe' could be revised to define an environmental crime that is in line with contemporary expectations of environmental protection. This would go some way towards ensuring that the burden of proof is not 'stacked heavily against the environment'.[76]

## ii. Make provision for non-international armed conflict

International criminal law currently has no environmental war crimes that apply to situations of non-international armed conflict. This is one of the most frequently cited faults of the existing framework of laws that apply in this category of armed conflict.[77] All of the environmental provisions that exist within the laws of armed conflict apply exclusively to international armed conflict and so there is no option of prosecuting for environmental crimes in non-international armed conflict. Although the ICRC's study on Customary International Humanitarian Law indicates that state practice to date has arguably created customary rules of environmental protection in non-international armed conflict,[78] this remains a contestable issue. The fact remains that non-international armed conflicts vastly outnumber international conflicts in the present day and the environment is just as vulnerable to methods and means of warfare that could result in unacceptable levels of harm. Non-international armed conflict is frequently connected with

---

[74] This is equated with the concept of military necessity in Additional Protocol I art 35(3).

[75] Convention on the Prohibition of Military or Any Other Hostile Use of Environmental Modification Techniques, 10 December 1976, 1108 UNTS 151

[76] Sharp (n 16) 241.

[77] J Kellenberger, 'Strengthening Legal Protection for Victims of Armed Conflicts' (Address by President of the ICRC: The ICRC Study on the Curent State of Internaitonal Humanitarian Law, 21 September 2010).

[78] J-M Henckaerts and L Doswald-Beck (eds) *Customary International Humanitarian Law Volume I: Rules* (ICRC/CUP, Cambridge 2005) Chapter 14, Rules 43–45.

environmental damage to natural resources and so an international crime in this regard would be very appropriate.

There is the option to interpret existing non-international crimes in the Rome Statute in ways that result in individual criminal liability indirectly for environmental damage. A 'green' interpretation of, Articles 8(2)(c)–(f) of the Statute of the International Criminal Court – not to mention the customary law concepts of proportionality, distinction, humanity and military necessity – may provide a certain level of indirect environmental accountability in the absence of specific provisions. However, the potential for existing laws to provide adequate environmental protection in non-international armed conflict is extremely limited. However, to model any changes on existing provisions within the international criminal laws that apply to international conflicts would be a mistake. As discussed above, the existing environmental war crime in the Rome Statute needs thorough revision in its own right.

## B. A New Crime against the Environment?

The term 'ecocide' was coined in the late 1960s as a result of large-scale wartime environmental damage taking place at the time.[79] However it has since come to carry connotations of extensive or excessive environmental damage occurring in times of peace also – the word itself is an obvious play on the term 'genocide', and literally means 'the killing of ecology'.[80] Under the current framework of international criminal law, apart from the environmental war crime in Article 8(2)(b)(iv) of the Rome Statute, environmental damage would not be pursued as a crime in itself - it is instead considered to be a means of committing the crimes of genocide, crimes against humanity or other war crimes. To remedy this lacuna there have been calls for the creation of ecocide[81] as a separate international crime within the jurisdiction of the International Criminal Court.[82]

The very essence of ecocide would be the criminalisation of serious environmental damage that is intentionally, recklessly or negligently caused, so that those most responsible for this damage can be held criminally accountable in an effort to deter

---

[79] LA Teclaff, 'Beyond Restoration – The Case of Ecocide' (1994) 34 *Natural Resources Journal* 933; AH Westing, 'Arms Control and the Environment: Proscription of Ecocide' (1974) 30(1) *Bulletin of the Atomic Scientists* 24–27.

[80] MA Gray, 'The International Crime of Ecocide' (1995) 26 *California Western Int'l L J* 215, 258.

[81] Ecocide is sometimes also referred to as 'geocide' – a killing of the earth. See L Berat, 'Defending the Right to a Healthy Environment: Toward a Crime of Geocide in International Law' (1993) 11 *Boston University Int'l L J* 328.

[82] J Jowit, 'British Campaigner Urges UN to Accept "Ecocide" as International Crime' *Guardian* (London 9 April 2010). In this campaign, the proposed definition of ecocide is 'the extensive destruction, damage to or loss of ecosystem(s) of a given territory, whether by human agency or by other causes, to such an extent that peaceful enjoyment by the inhabitants of that territory has been severely diminished'.

such behaviour in the future. Criminalising environmental damage is not a new concept.[83] Yet as far as international criminal law is concerned, the extent to which pure environmental damage (without any direct or immediate adverse impacts on the human population) could be appropriately responded to by criminal sanctions is questionable.[84] The International Law Commission has recognised that severe environmental damage ought to carry heavy penalties. However, criminal law is not really equipped with the most appropriate penalties to provide redress for harm caused to the environment: in the case of a damaged environment, it is argued here that repairing the damage should be the absolute priority. This would not be possible through international criminal law, as its sanctions focus almost exclusively on penalising the individual perpetrator through a period of incarceration.

Though the term carries no legal meaning or effect in international law at present, ecocide does exist as a crime in the criminal codes of Armenia[85] and Belarus.[86] As to possible definitions of a crime of ecocide, in its Draft Code on State Responsibility, the International Law Commission equates 'serious acts of environmental degradation with crimes such as aggression ... slavery, genocide and apartheid'.[87] Yet, as a result of competing interests and different standards of environmental integrity across the globe it has been 'a little difficult to decide upon the precise limits of ecocide'.[88] Some definitions rely heavily on the right to a healthy environment;[89] a concept which is still in gestation in international human rights law. Other proposals see ecocide as an extension to the Genocide Convention,[90] though the association of ecocide so closely with genocide could weaken the Genocide Convention and its associated provisions.[91] Perhaps a more useful definition could be modelled on the existing limitations of environmental harm in international criminal law's war crimes provisions. While the 'long-term,

---

[83] See Convention on the Protection of the Environment through Criminal Law, ETS No. 172, Council of Europe (Strasbourg, 4 November 1998).

[84] M Halsey, 'Against "Green" Criminology' (2004) 44 *British J of Criminology* 833.

[85] Art 394 of the Armenian Criminal Code defines ecocide as '[m]ass destruction of flora or fauna, poisoning the environment, the soils or water resources, as well as implementation of other actions causing an ecological catastrophe, is punished with imprisonment for the term of 10 to 15 years'.

[86] Art 131 of the Belarusian Criminal Code prohibits ecocide as such: 'Intentional mass destruction of flora or fauna, or poisoning of the atmosphere or water, or committing other intentional acts that could cause an environmental catastrophe (ecocide) – shall be punishable with imprisonment for a term of ten to fifteen years.'

[87] See Berat (n 81) 344.

[88] Westing (n 79) 26.

[89] Berat (n 81) 342.

[90] Whitaker Report (n 10) para 33. See also RA Falk, 'The Inadequacy of the Existing Legal Approach to Environmental Protection in Wartime' in JE Austin and CE Bruch (eds) *The Environmental Consequences of War: Legal, Economic, and Scientific Perspectives* (CUP, Cambridge 2000) 137, 155. See also Westing (n 79) 26 and Berat (n 81) 343.

[91] WA Schabas, *Genocide in International Law: The Crime of Crimes* (CUP, Cambridge 2000) 201.

widespread and severe' requirements are too high a threshold of harm to be of any real use in preventing environmental damage in the theatre of war, they may be just the right standard by which to judge the magnitude of environmental damage understood to amount to ecocide. Widespread, long-term and severe damage caused recklessly might be something that the international community would accept as being an international crime.

The value of enumerating a single crime against the environment is certainly apparent. International criminal law could offer a satisfactory means of holding individuals criminally liable for extensive environmental damage,[92] thereby potentially removing some of the political or corporate shields that have prevented accountability in the past. However, it is not plainly obvious that the crime of ecocide would be a success. At the most fundamental level, the types of remedy required by environmental damage are not to be found in the mechanisms of accountability offered by international criminal law[93] and this is something to be borne in mind throughout future discussion on this issue.

## Conclusion

There is no greater challenge facing the world than that of climate change and environmental degradation. As our global climate continues to increase in temperature, and as the effects of this change begin to manifest in more extreme weather patterns and more frequent sudden onset and slow onset environmental disasters, it seems inevitable that environmental concerns will be reflected in almost every aspect of international law in the future. In this regard, international criminal law will most certainly eventually evolve to recognise specific environmental crimes. However, the time for that kind of progress has not yet arrived. Environmental international criminal law will continue to develop incrementally as the environmental dimension of existing crimes becomes more frequently raised in international criminal prosecutions of the future. Big gestures, such as the development of a stand-alone crime against the environment, will not exist for some time yet. While international criminal law may not be the right mechanism to respond to all instances of serious environmental damage, the outlook for it to become a strong and integral part of the developing jigsaw of environmental protection is good.

---

[92] Berat (n 91) 345.
[93] MA Drumbl, 'Waging War against the World: The Need to Move from War Crimes to Environmental Crimes' in JE Austin and CE Bruch (eds) *The Environmental Consequences of War: Legal, Economic, and Scientific Perspectives* (CUP, Cambridge 2000) 620, 636–46.

# Alleged Aggression in Utopia: An International Criminal Law Examination Question for 2020

Roger S. Clark

## Introduction

*It is 2020. Because you took this course, you have obtained an internship at the Office of the Prosecutor at the International Criminal Court. The Prosecutor is contemplating the first prosecution for the crime of aggression. She has accumulated specific memos from members of her staff, but wants you to take a fresh look at the big picture. She needs a memorandum setting out what you think are the major issues that she will need to confront, both in the first instance and in response to what will be raised inevitably by the defence.*

*This is an open book exam. You should have with you the Rome Statute of the International Criminal Court and Resolution 6 adopted by the 2010 ICC Review Conference in Kampala [hereinafter the Kampala Amendments]. The Elements of Crimes and Understandings annexed to the Amendments may be especially relevant. Do not make any extensive references to secondary sources. The main idea is to examine the language of the Statute and the Kampala Amendments (of course, in light of relevant general international law). If you learned nothing else in this course, remember this: READ THE STATUTE!*

*Thirty ratifications or acceptances of the Kampala Amendments were received by 1 January 2016. Early in 2017, the Court's Assembly of States Parties adopted, by consensus, a resolution entitled 'Definitive Activation of the Court's Jurisdiction over the Crime of Aggression'.*

*Here is the basic factual situation, although investigators are still studying the nuances. Utopia is a small absolute monarchy adjoining the, slightly larger, Republic of Tapu. Both countries have surprisingly large militaries and have contributed to United Nations Peacekeeping Operations. The potential defendant, General Pickens, was at relevant times Chief of the General Staff of Tapu. Early in 2020, he was ordered by the President to invade Utopia, capture the capital and effect a regime change. The order was approved by Cabinet. General Pickens and the press were told that the Utopian regime was in the early stages of commencing an organised genocide (or at least crimes against humanity) against an ethnic* minority in Utopia related to the majority population of Tapu. General Pickens advised Cabinet that he might not have sufficient forces to intervene quickly and successfully. He was also concerned about the legality of the operation. His own military legal team thought the legal justification weak. The President, however, presented General Pickens with a one-paragraph statement by the Attorney-General (a Cabinet member) that the operation was completely legal as an example of the responsibility to protect, which the statement described as 'a unilateral obligation of all States'. In light of this document, General Pickens concluded that his only options were to resign and lose his pension or comply with the order. The invasion did not go well. Utopia's army responded fiercely. There were many casualties on both sides. General Pickens was captured by Utopian forces deep into Utopian territory. He managed to escape to another neighboring country, Activia. This also proved unfortunate. Activia has legislation containing a definition of the crime of aggression very similar to that in the Kampala Amendments and providing for universal jurisdiction over it. Activia is a major military power and the former colonial master of Utopia and Tapu. Activia has a Special International Prosecutions Unit which is actively preparing the case for prosecution. General Pickens is languishing in prison. Activia refuses to hand him over either to Utopia or to Tapu, with whom it has no extradition treaties. Meanwhile, the President and the entire Cabinet of Tapu committed mass suicide in a bunker, in shame at the failed invasion. The United Nations Security Council was seized of the matter at the commencement of hostilities. Disagreement among the Permanent Members of the Council meant that no resolutions were adopted.

The Prosecutor has received a request from Utopia for the prosecution of General Pickens for the crime of aggression. Given the 'impunity' achieved by the civilian leadership of Tapu (by their suicide), Utopia contends it is especially important that the military leader of the operation be brought to international justice. Utopia has no domestic legislation on aggression and does not wish to prosecute him itself.

Utopia and Tapu became States Parties to the ICC well before Kampala. Neither has taken any action to ratify the Kampala Amendments, nor has either state deposited an 'opt-out' declaration thereto. Activia is not a party to the Rome Statute. It has an aversion to international criminal tribunals. It takes the position, though, that States are entitled, and perhaps even have a customary law obligation, to mount fair prosecutions domestically on behalf of the international community in cases involving crimes like those in the Rome Statute.

# Memorandum from Intern

### I. Can the General's Actions Fit within the Definition of the Crime?

My criminal law professor always said that one cannot go wrong by starting with the elements of the crime.[1] So I turn to the language of the Statute and the Elements.

---

[1] ICC Review Conference, 'The Crime of Aggression', Resolution RC/Res.6 (adopted by consensus at the 12th plenary meeting, 11 June 2010) ('Resolution 6') Annex II: Amendments

Article 8*bis*(1) of the Rome Statute, as adopted in Kampala, defines the crime of aggression as the 'planning, preparation, initiation or execution, by a person in a position effectively to exercise control over or to direct the political or military action of a State, of an act of aggression which, by its character, gravity and scale, constitutes a manifest violation of the Charter of the United Nations'. A 'crime of aggression', using the drafting convention followed in the Amendment, is what an individual does; an 'act of aggression' is what a State does. The latter is defined in detail in paragraph 2 of Article 8*bis*. Seven exemplary subparagraphs follow a general *chapeau* to the effect that an act of aggression 'means the use of armed force by a State against the sovereignty, territorial integrity or political independence of another State, or in any other manner inconsistent with the Charter of the United Nations'.[2]

For now, it is necessary to refer only to subparagraph (a) of that paragraph. It gives as one of the examples of an act of aggression, '[t]he invasion or attack by the armed forces of a State against the territory of another State, or any military occupation, however, temporary, resulting from such invasion or attack'. As I understand the facts, there is little doubt that the military activity undertaken on behalf of Tapu comes within this language. There was both an 'invasion' and an 'attack' by the armed forces. Since the drafters of the Kampala definition eschewed any reference to a requirement that there be a 'war', the definition probably does not require any resistance on the part of Utopia. Be that as it may, there was clearly a substantial clash of arms. As we shall see later, in spite of any specific references to 'defences' in Article 8*bis* or its Elements, there may be arguable bases in the

---

to the Elements of Crimes, lists the Elements:

- 'The perpetrator planned, prepared, initiated or executed an act of aggression.
- The perpetrator was a person [footnote omitted] in a position effectively to exercise control over or to direct the political or military action of the State which committed the act of aggression.
- The act of aggression – the use of armed force by a State against the sovereignty, territorial integrity or political independence of another State, or in any other manner inconsistent with the Charter of the United Nations – was committed.
- The perpetrator was aware of the factual circumstances that established such a use of armed force was inconsistent with the Charter of the United Nations.
- The act of aggression, by its character, gravity and scale, constituted a manifest violation of the Charter of the United Nations.
- The perpetrator was aware of the factual circumstances that established such a manifest violation of the Charter of the United Nations.'

[2]  ICC Review Conference, 'The Crime of Aggression', Resolution RC/Res.6 (adopted by consensus at the 12th plenary meeting, 11 June 2010) ('Resolution 6') Annex I: Amendments to the Rome Statute of the International Criminal Court on the crime of aggression, para 8*bis*(2). The examples are (in summary): invasions and annexations; bombardments of another state; blockades, attack on the land sea or air forces of another state; use of armed forces that are within another's territory by agreement contrary to the terms of the agreement; a state allowing its territory to be used by another state for aggression; sending of armed bands, groups, irregulars or mercenaries to carry out acts of armed force.

Rome Statute and in customary international law for avoiding responsibility for this invasion and temporary occupation. Such bases may apply to the State itself (thus taking matters out of the definition of act of aggression) or may be specific to General Pickens. I doubt that these defences would succeed; the important point is that the general is entitled to make the arguments and the prosecution needs to be able to refute them.

For the moment, let us examine the language of Article 8*bis*(1). Do the General's actions fit one or more of the conduct words in the definition?[3] Did he engage in planning, preparation, initiation or execution? 'Execution' is probably the closest. He carried out somebody else's policy. 'Initiation' seems unpromising, given his reluctance. But, good soldier that he was, he apparently did some planning. There is probably enough here to meet the conduct requirement. There is, next, a circumstance element following the conduct words that I find difficult to apply to him. The actor must be 'a person in a position effectively to exercise control over or to direct the political or military action of a State'. Preparatory work for Kampala is replete with assertions that aggression is a 'leadership crime'. How have the drafters expressed that? No question that the general was a leader; he was the head of the military, as we understand it. Was he in a position to 'exercise control over or to direct' the *political* action of the State? It appears not. He did express some views, but his views did not seem to carry much weight with the political leadership. I doubt the words of the Statute about political action are met by the General. Was he in a similar position in respect of the *military* action of the State? The case is closer and we need to think very carefully about what these words mean and do further research about the structure of the bureaucracy (civilian and military) in Tapu. Who really 'directs' in this scenario: the head of the military or the politicians?[4]

---

[3] Rome Statute of the International Criminal Court, 2187 UNTS 90, 17 July 1998, entered into force 1 July 2002 ('ICC Statute') art 30 contemplates that the structure of a typical offence includes at least a mental element (normally 'intent and knowledge') and 'material' elements, notably conduct, circumstance and consequence elements. The Elements are drafted on this understanding. Elements of a crime are those items which are necessary and sufficient to constitute 'the crime'. Each must be proved beyond reasonable doubt, per art 66(3) of the Rome Statute. Moreover, art 67(1)(i) adds that a defendant is entitled 'Not to have imposed on him or her any reversal of the burden of proof or any onus of rebuttal'.

[4] Probably out of an abundance of caution, the leadership point is repeated in art 25 of the ICC Statute, as amended. Art 25(3) sets out the various ways in which an actor may be associated with a crime, including committing it (as a principal) and other modes such as aiding or abetting. Art 25(3*bis*) contained in the Kampala Amendments, provides: 'In respect of the crime of aggression, the provisions of this article shall apply only to persons in a position effectively to exercise control over or to direct the political or military action of a State.' If the General fits the category of leader, he also appears to fit the category 'commits' in art 25(3)(a) of the ICC Statute, so other modes of participation are irrelevant to him. A footnote to Element 2 of the Elements of Aggression, Annex II to Resolution 6 (n 1) (the leadership requirement) adds (again *ex abundante cautela*) that 'With respect to an act of aggression, more than one person may be in a position that meets these criteria'.

We must then delve a little deeper into the elements of the crime of aggression. Paragraph 2 of the Introduction thereto informs us that '[t]here is no need to prove that the perpetrator has made a legal evaluation as to whether the use of armed force was inconsistent with the Charter of the United Nations'.[5] This is helpful to us. It is something on which we do not need to carry any initial or final onus of proof. On the other hand, the legal analysis is germane in several ways to the General's efforts (in his account, genuine) to obtain legal advice within the Government. One is the 'circumstance' element contained in the last phrase of Article 8*bis*(1), 'which, by its character, gravity and scale, constitutes a manifest violation of the Charter of the United Nations'. These words have two apparent objectives. One, demonstrated primarily by 'gravity and scale', aims at eliminating 'minor' cases of aggression from individual criminal responsibility, although they will probably still give rise to some degree of state responsibility. The second, captured by 'character', attempts to remove from criminal responsibility the honestly arguable cases falling within a 'grey area'. Humanitarian interventions were a typical example of such an area raised in the negotiations.[6] Both these objectives were controversial, but nevertheless became part of the final compromise.

There seems little problem on the facts with establishing gravity and scale. The crucial consideration in our case is that of character. Paragraph 3 of the Introduction to the Elements asserts that '[t]he term "manifest" is an objective consideration'. We need to encourage the Court to develop some sort of 'reasonable statesman or soldier' test for what is manifest. In addition, paragraph 4 of the Introduction helps us by insisting that there is no requirement to prove that the perpetrator has made a legal evaluation as to the 'manifest' nature of the violation of the Charter.[7] There are two provisions in the Elements themselves that help us, but will be subject to

---

[5] Annex II to Resolution 6 (n 1) Introduction, para 2.

[6] The customary law status or otherwise of 'R2P' was a matter of intense debate when the Kampala Amendments were being negotiated. It was too much to expect that this controversial issue, debated also in several forums in the United Nations, could be resolved in the ICC negotiations. Out of necessity, the matter had to be left to the evolution of general law. I doubt that the law is now settled. The point is that the 'manifest' requirement facilitates arguments about a margin of error. The 'pre-emptive' nature of the intervention in the present case, however, creates difficulties for the argument.

[7] In proving the act of aggression and its manifest nature, the prosecution should take into account Understandings 6 and 7 in ICC Review Conference, 'The Crime of Aggression', Resolution RC/Res.6 (adopted by consensus at the 12th plenary meeting, 11 June 2010) ('Resolution 6') Annex III, Understandings Regarding the Amendments to the Rome Statute of the International Criminal Court on the crime of Aggression:

'6. It is understood that aggression is the most serious and dangerous form of the illegal use of force; and that a determination whether an act of aggression has been committed requires consideration of all the circumstances of each particular case, including the gravity of the acts concerned and their consequences, in accordance with the Charter of the United Nations.

7. It is understood that in establishing whether an act of aggression constitutes a manifest violation of the Charter of the United Nations, the three components of character,

further defence legal scrutiny. Element 4 requires us to prove, not that the accused knew that there was a breach of the United Nations Charter, but merely that '[t]he perpetrator was aware of the factual circumstances that established that such a use of armed force was inconsistent with the Charter of the United Nations'. Element 6 reverts to the 'manifest' problem. It requires the prosecution to prove that '[t]he perpetrator was aware of the factual circumstances that established a manifest violation of the Charter of the United Nations'. According to these provisions in the Elements, we need to prove matters of fact, not of law.

These provisions in the Elements have their origins in discussions on the Elements for the other offences within the jurisdiction of the Court in the Preparatory Commission for the Court. Article 32(2) of the Rome Statute permits a defence of mistake of law in certain circumstances.[8] The drafters of the Elements were concerned that disingenuous reliance on dubious legal advice might lead to unjustified acquittals. Accordingly, the finesse of re-structuring a potential legal element as a 'factual element' was used in several of the elements of war crimes. A similar effort was made here.[9] The defence will probably argue that such provisions are *ultra vires* the Statute. The Elements of Crimes are meant to 'assist' the judges, but the Statute itself is what ultimately governs, should the judges conclude that a particular Element is inconsistent with it.[10] Nonetheless, one would expect the judges, as they have done until now, to show significant deference to the work of the Preparatory Commission and the Kampala process in negotiating the Elements.

There is another way to inject the alleged reliance on the responsibility to protect into the argument. A significant feature of the Statute and the Kampala Amendments is use of a 'general part' to deal with questions that cut across the various provisions contained in the definitions of particular crimes (the 'special part'). In particular, the war crimes provisions are sometimes open to defences that have to be gleaned from the general part. Given the complexity of the definitional task, not all the defences could be agreed upon and codified. Thus Article 31(3), which codifies several significant grounds for the exclusion of responsibility, creates a procedure whereby the defence can argue in advance of trial that other grounds are supported by the general law. This provides an opportunity to make such arguments as claiming that the State was entitled to a justification based on the responsibility to protect. If that is the case, then there is no 'act of aggression' and one of the elements of the crime of aggression is missing. The argument that the responsibility to protect provides a justification under customary international law was hotly debated in 2010 and is

---

gravity and scale must be sufficient to justify a "manifest" determination. No one component can be significant enough to satisfy the manifest standard by itself.'

[8] 'if it negates the mental element required by such a crime'.

[9] Informal inter-sessional meeting on the crime of aggression, 8–10 June 2009, 'Non-paper by the Chairman on the Elements of Crimes' ICC-ASP/8/INF.2 (25 June 2009) Annex II, Explanatory note, paras 18–19 (requirement of 'knowledge of law' may 'encourage a potential perpetrator to be willfully blind as to the legality of his or her actions, or to rely on disreputable advice').

[10] ICC Statute, art 9(3) requires that the Elements be 'consistent with the Statute'.

still hotly debated. The defence is much more likely to succeed with a 'grey area' argument than with one based on established customary law.

## II. The Security Council and Article 15bis

Another hotly contested issue was the role of the Security Council in state or *proprio motu* referrals. The ultimate resolution of this is found in paragraphs 5, 6 and 7 of Article 15*bis*. It will be necessary to follow the procedure therein. Where the Prosecutor concludes that there is a reasonable basis to proceed with an investigation of aggression, she must first ascertain whether the Security Council has made a determination of an act of aggression by the State concerned.[11] The Prosecutor must also notify the Secretary-General of the United Nations of the situation before the Court. The Article continues that, where the Security Council has made such a determination, the Prosecutor may proceed with the investigation.[12] Since no such determination has been made here, paragraph 8 applies:

> Where no such determination is made within six months after the date of notification, the Prosecutor may proceed with the investigation in respect of a crime of aggression, provided the Pre-Trial Division has authorised the commencement of the investigation in respect of a crime of aggression in accordance with the procedure contained in article 15, and the Security Council has not decided otherwise in accordance with article 16.[13]

Thus it will be necessary to wait out the six-month period and the unlikely possibility that the Security Council will act one way or the other.[14] Then, if the Council again does nothing, action by the full Pre-Trial Division (a majority of the six judges therein) will be required.

## III. Admissibility: Do Activia's Serious Efforts to Prosecute Domestically on a Universal Jurisdiction Theory Involve the Complementarity Principle, Precluding the Court from Proceeding?

This issue arises under Article 17(1) of the Statute:

---

[11] ICC Statute, art 15*bis*(6).
[12] ICC Statute, art 15*bis*(7).
[13] ICC Statute, art 15*bis*(8). Art 15 requires that the prosecutor show a 'reasonable basis to proceed' and that the case 'appears to fall within the jurisdiction of the Court'.
[14] If it does now make a determination, this is useful procedurally but not definitive on the merits. See art 15*bis* (9): 'A determination of an act of aggression by an organ outside the Court shall be without prejudice to the Court's own findings under this Statute.'

> Having regard to paragraph 10 of the Preamble and article 1, the Court shall determine the case is inadmissible where:
>
> The case is being investigated or prosecuted by a State which has jurisdiction over it, unless the State is unwilling or unable genuinely to carry out the investigation or prosecution;
>
> The case has been investigated by a State which has jurisdiction over it and the State has decided not to prosecute the person concerned, unless the decision resulted from the unwillingness or inability of the State genuinely to prosecute.[15]

A threshold question arises because Activia is not a party to the Statute. Does complementarity still apply? There is little doubt that a non-State Party can invoke complementarity. Article 17 refers to a 'State'. There are many other instances in the Statute where the reference is to a 'State Party'. The drafters knew how to distinguish between states generally and those states which are party to the Statute. Here the reference is to any state, party or otherwise.[16] There are two more difficult sub-issues to this question: is there universal jurisdiction over aggression, and does a State which is exercising universal jurisdiction constitute 'a State which has jurisdiction over it'?[17] There is little enlightenment on these questions in the preparatory work or in the commentaries on the Statute. Clearly 'has jurisdiction over it' contemplates that steps have been taken domestically to assert such jurisdiction. This will normally mean, as in Activia, appropriate legislation. But does the language also measure the legitimacy of that jurisdiction under general international law?

When the Statute was being drafted, there was significant discussion about universal jurisdiction, especially in the context of the prerequisites for ICC jurisdiction. Negotiators regarded the states of territoriality and nationality as having the strongest jurisdictional claims, and the Statute requires as a prerequisite to the Court's jurisdiction that either the state of nationality or the state of territoriality be party to the Statute. This hardly precludes the possibility that universal jurisdiction might be appropriate for other purposes, including complementarity.[18] There is little dispute that genocide, crimes against humanity and war crimes attract

---

[15] There is no case 'being investigated or prosecuted' in either Utopia or Tapu, so no question of complementarity arises there.

[16] ICC Statute, art 17 does not seem to require that the Activia legislation be exactly the same as the Statute's. Substantial similarity is enough.

[17] There is a further practical question as well. If the Court concludes either that there is no universal jurisdiction over aggression or that a State acting on the basis of universal jurisdiction is not one that 'has' jurisdiction within the meaning of art 17, how does it persuade Activia to cede?

[18] Indeed a substantial number of states argued before and at Rome that, since there was universal jurisdiction over all the potential crimes, it was not necessary that any particular state be party – universal jurisdiction possessed by all could be delegated to an

universal jurisdiction, but there may be some special considerations about universal jurisdiction over the crime of aggression. The International Law Commission's Draft Code of Crimes against the Peace and Security of Mankind, controversially, seemed to confine jurisdiction over aggression to the courts of an aggressor state or to an international tribunal.[19] There is some (limited) state practice asserting universal jurisdiction over aggression.[20] On the other hand, Understanding 5 in the Kampala Amendments asserts that 'the amendments shall not be interpreted as creating the right or obligation to exercise domestic jurisdiction in respect of an act of aggression committed by another State'. That the amendments themselves do not create such a right is, I would suggest, neutral on the question of whether the general law permits such exercise of jurisdiction. The propriety of universal jurisdiction over aggression is debated. There is, however, not much debate in the literature about whether the phrase 'has jurisdiction' includes a State exercising universal jurisdiction.

Nonetheless, the Statute does not give the Court any clear trumping power over what a non-State Party chooses to do. Persuasion appears to be the order of the day. I doubt that much can be made of the word 'has' and the arguments become ones of policy. Does the Court really want to force its way into cases where there is a domestic prosecution (or legitimate decision not to prosecute)? Article 17 applies across the board to all crimes within the jurisdiction of the Court. There will surely be cases where the Court is content to let a state deal with the situation through universal jurisdiction. This may not be the case to force the question.

## IV. Does the Court have Jurisdiction where Neither the Alleged Aggressor State nor the Alleged Victim State has Ratified or Accepted the Kampala Amendments?

This question really involves two parts: what do the Kampala Amendments say? Do they apply at all here? If they are interpreted to apply in circumstances like ours where neither relevant State Party has ratified them, are they valid or are they *ultra vires* the amendment procedures of the Statute? This is the thorniest problem left from Kampala. First, some background. Article 5 represented a compromise in Rome between those who wanted aggression within the jurisdiction of the Court and those who either did not want it in or saw no possibility of reaching agreement there on the details. Thus, aggression was listed in Article 5(1) as one of the four crimes within the subject matter jurisdiction of the Court. But Article 5(2) states that '[t]he Court shall exercise jurisdiction over the crime of aggression once a

---

international entity. The non-party issue sharpened after Rome because of the attitude of the United States.

[19] See discussion in *Yearbook of the International Law Commission, Vol. I* (1996) 49–53.

[20] A Reisinger-Coracini, 'Evaluating Domestic Legislation on the Customary Crime of Aggression under the Rome Statute's Complementarity Regime', in C Stahn and G Sluiter (eds.) *The Emerging Practice of the International Criminal Court* (Brill, The Hague 2009) 725.

provision is adopted in accordance with articles 121 and 123 defining the crime and setting out the conditions under which the Court shall exercise jurisdiction with respect to that crime'. Unfortunately this formula, adopted without careful debate in the dying stages of the Rome Conference, left ambiguous just which parts of Article 121 were being referenced.[21] Seizing on the word 'adopt', used both in Article 5(2) and in Article 121(3), one participant-observer argued that all that was needed was approval by the Review Conference.[22] This view was in a minority. 'Adopt' in Article 5(2), it was said by the majority, must mean approval of the text and then subsequent ratification, in accordance with standard multilateral practice. 'Adopt' in Article 121(3) means approving the text. This then shifted the argument to whether paragraph 4 or paragraph 5 of Article 121 applies. Paragraph 4 is the general rule on amendments. It says that, except as provided in paragraph 5, 'an amendment shall enter into force for all States Parties one year after instruments of ratification or acceptance have been deposited with the Secretary-General of the United Nations by seven-eighths of them'. No one is bound until everyone is bound. Paragraph 5, provides that:

> Any amendment to articles 5, 6, 7 and 8 of this Statute shall enter into force for those States Parties which have accepted the amendment one year after the deposit of their instruments of ratification or acceptance. In respect of a State Party which has not accepted the amendment, the Court shall not exercise its jurisdiction regarding the crime covered by the amendment when committed by that State Party's nationals or on its territory.

In this case, the amendment applies only to those states that accept it.[23] The issue of interpretation then shifts to the question of whether the aggression provision is functionally an amendment to Article 5(2), removing an existing state of affairs, i.e. the Court cannot currently 'exercise jurisdiction' over one of the crimes listed within its jurisdiction in Article 5(1). If this is the case, the amendment applies only to those who accept it. Or is Article 5(2) a facilitative clause which provides a mechanism for completing the work of Rome? On this reasoning, the amendment is *to the Statute* in general (or to other particular provisions) rather than *to Article 5*, and the seven-eighths rule applies. Against this historical background, I turn to what happened in Kampala.

Since the Utopia proceedings arise from a State referral, the relevant jurisdictional provisions are in Article 15*bis* of the Statute, added in Kampala. Article 15*bis* states that the Court may exercise jurisdiction only with respect to crimes of aggression committed one year after the ratification or acceptance of the amendments by 30

---

[21] RS Clark, 'Ambiguities in Articles 5(2) 121 and 123 of the Rome Statute' (2009) 41 *Case Western Reserve J Int'l L* 413.
[22] Ibid 416–18.
[23] See also text to n 37 below.

States Parties.[24] This condition is met on the facts we are given. The article adds that the Court shall exercise jurisdiction over the crime of aggression, in accordance with the Article, subject to a decision taken after 1 January 2017 by the same majority of States Parties as is required for the adoption of an amendment to the Statute.[25] This condition is also met. The timing is right and the required majority is two-thirds of the States Parties at the relevant time.[26] We are told that the 2017 decision of the Assembly of States Parties was by consensus. There is no suggestion that there was not a quorum of at least two-thirds of the Parties present when the decision was taken. The conditions contained in the Article are met.[27]

We then reach the crucial jurisdictional provision in the Article, namely paragraph 4:

> The Court may, in accordance with article 12, exercise jurisdiction over a crime of aggression, arising from an act of aggression committed by a State Party, unless that State Party has previously declared that it does not accept such jurisdiction by lodging a declaration with the Registrar. The withdrawal of such a declaration may be effected at any time and shall be considered by the State Party within three years.

This language could hardly be plainer: once the other conditions just discussed are met, there is jurisdiction as long as the (alleged) crime arises from an act of aggression[28] committed by 'a State Party'. It does not say 'a State Party which has ratified or accepted the Amendment'. 'A State Party' must be any state that has ratified or acceded to the Rome Statute. If the drafters had meant something else, they could surely have found words to say so. Tapu's actions are alleged to be 'an act of aggression committed by a State Party'. Since Tapu ('that State Party') has not

---

[24] ICC Statute, art 15*bis*(2).
[25] ICC Statute, art 15*bis*(3).
[26] ICC Statute, art 121(3).
[27] See also Understanding 3, in Annex III to Resolution 6 (n 7) headed 'Jurisdiction *ratione temporis*': 'It is understood that in case of [State or *proprio motu* referrals] the Court may exercise jurisdiction only with respect to crimes of aggression committed after a decision in accordance with article 15 *bis*, paragraph 3 is taken, and one year after the ratification or acceptance of the amendments by thirty States Parties, whichever is later.' This is merely a restatement of the conditions in the Article; they have been met.
[28] An 'act of aggression' is thus both jurisdictional and one of the elements of the crime that must be established beyond reasonable doubt.

exercised its right to opt out,[29] the plain language of paragraph 4 suggests that there is jurisdiction in the present circumstances.[30]

The defence will no doubt respond with paragraph 1 of the Kampala adopting resolution. The Conference:

> Decides to adopt, in accordance with article 5, paragraph 2, of the Rome Statute of the International Criminal Court (hereinafter: 'the Statute') the amendments to the Statute contained in annex I of the present resolution, *which are subject to ratification or acceptance and shall enter into force in accordance with article 121, paragraph 5*; and notes that any State Party may lodge a declaration referred to in article 15 bis prior to ratification or acceptance.[31]

Note my italicised clause. Does it mean,[32] as the Prosecutor must contend, that the references to 'ratification and acceptance' and to 'entry into force' merely relate to the need for 30 ratifications or acceptances of the amendment on aggression, and that the reference to Article 121(5) goes to the first sentence of that provision and not to the second sentence? This argument emphasises the question of entry into force, as set out in the first sentence of Article 121(5). Or does the clause mean that, although nobody is bound by the amendments on aggression until the 30 ratifications are received[33] and the ASP adopts the necessary resolution, an aggressor State that fails to accept the amendments is not ever bound by them for events on its territory or the actions of its citizens? Recall the language of the second sentence of Article 121(5): '[i]n respect of a State Party which has not

---

[29] During the Kampala negotiations, some States contended for 'reciprocity', i.e. that both victim and aggressor states consent specifically. There is no reference to this requirement in the final product. To the extent that the parties created a 'State consent regime', the course for potential aggressor States wishing to protect their nationals from ICC jurisdiction is clear: lodge an opt-out declaration. (Note: ratifications and accessions go to the UN Secretary-General as the depositary of the Rome Statute; opt-out declarations go to the Court's Registrar.)

[30] I discuss in the next paragraph of the text the effect of para 1 of the empowering resolution adopted in Kampala. In the final clause of that paragraph, the Conference 'notes that any State Party may lodge a declaration referred to in article 15*bis* prior to ratification or acceptance'. I understand that this attempt at clarification does not mean that it is *only* before ratification or acceptance that such a declaration may be made. Moreover, a reasonable interpretation of it supports the argument about to be made in the text: that a State Party to the Statute does not need to opt in, in order to opt out. It needs to opt out to avoid the effect of the words 'State Party' in subjecting its citizenry to jurisdiction over aggression.

[31] ICC Review Conference, 'The Crime of Aggression', Resolution RC/Res.6 (adopted by consensus at the 12th plenary meeting, 11 June 2010) operative para 1.

[32] I discuss questions of *vires* later; here the issue is one of meaning.

[33] This modifies the effect of para 5 which, in respect of other amendments to which it relates (such as those made to art 8 of the Statute in Kampala) applies to the first and subsequent ratifying parties *seriatim*, one year after each deposits its instrument. Here, 30 ratifications are required before any are bound.

accepted the amendment, the Court shall not exercise its jurisdiction regarding the crime covered by the amendment when committed by that State Party's nationals or on its territory'. The argument for applying this second sentence to the Kampala Amendments perhaps relies on the words 'in accordance with' before 'paragraph 5'. The phrase 'in accordance' could be interpreted as emphasising the whole of that paragraph, including its second sentence. Of course, if that result is what they wanted, the drafters could have clarified matters by avoiding a vague phrase like 'in accordance with'[34] and saying something like 'subject to all the requirements of article 121, paragraph 5'.[35]

Indeed, there were drafters present in Kampala who faced the Article 121(5) issue head on for amendments to Article 8 of the Statute.[36] Relevant amendments (adding provisions on proscribed weapons in the material dealing with non-international armed conflict) were deemed amendments to Article 8 within the meaning of Article 121, paragraph 5. Accordingly, the second preambular paragraph of the Conference's adopting resolution provides:

> Noting article 121, paragraph 5, of the Statute which states that any amendment to articles 5, 6, 7 and 8 of the Statute shall enter into force for those States Parties which have accepted the amendment one year after the deposit of their instruments of ratification or acceptance and that in respect of a State Party which has not accepted the amendment, the Court shall not exercise its jurisdiction regarding the crime covered by the amendment when committed by that State Party's nationals or on its territory, and confirming its understanding that in respect to this amendment the same principle applies in respect of a State Party which has not accepted the amendment applies also in respect of States that are not parties to the Statute.[37]

---

[34]  Which, after all, helped create some of the problems with art 5(2) itself!

[35]  Note that the first paragraph of the Kampala Amendments asserts: 'Article 6, paragraph 2, of the Statute is deleted.' How can that be squared with a literal application of art 121(5)? How can the paragraph be deleted for some parties, but not all?

[36]  'Amendments to article 8 of the Rome Statute', Resolution RC/Res.5 (adopted by consensus at the 12th plenary meeting, 10 June 2010) <http://www.icc-cpi.int/iccdocs/asp_docs/Resolutions/RC-Res.5-ENG.pdf> last accessed 2 December 2011.

[37]  The next preambular paragraph addresses an issue discussed inconclusively in the aggression negotiations but not mentioned ultimately in the aggression amendments: 'Confirming that, in light of the provision of article 40, paragraph 5, of the Vienna Convention on the Law of Treaties, States that subsequently become States Parties to the Statute will be allowed to decide whether to accept the amendment contained in this resolution at the time of ratification, acceptance or approval of, or accession to the Statute.' The Vienna Convention on the Law of Treaties (1979) 1155 UNTS 331, art 40(5) is a default rule that must be subject to being set aside, expressly and perhaps impliedly. There will no doubt be some debate in the future about whether the aggression amendments apply to future parties who do not expressly accept them. I think they do, subject to opting out.

Can any indications be drawn from the obvious differences between language here and in the aggression provision? Personally, I think that the plain language of Article 15*bis*(4) and its reference to a 'State Party', coupled with the right to opt out, overrides any inferences to be gleaned from the less than clear statement in the adopting resolution. If there is no requirement that a state opt in, why give it a right to opt out?

Again, there is a defence response. Article 15*ter*, which deals with Security Council referrals, also requires 30 ratifications and a later resolution by the Parties. One could contemplate a state (especially a Permanent Member of the Security Council) wishing to support the possibility of Security Council referrals – at least in relation to other countries – but not state or *proprio motu* referrals involving itself. It might then rationally ratify the amendment package to help bring it into force, but also opt out of jurisdiction triggered other than through the Security Council.[38]

It is finally time to turn to the '*vires*' question, discussed inconclusively before and at Kampala.[39] There was a fundamental ambiguity in the Statute on how the aggression amendment should be done. Did Article 121(4) or 121(5) apply? Neither view was entirely persuasive; it was not possible to form a consensus around either in Kampala. I read what was done at Kampala as an attempt to finesse these problems. Is the finesse 'constitutional'?

From the point of view of the defence, the best argument here is that the only way to proceed was through paragraph 5, including at least the ratification of the aggressor state. If this is not what happened, then the effort is simply void. We are talking about criminal responsibility and there can be no responsibility based on an invalid amendment! From its point of view, the defence might (somewhat deviously) argue that paragraph 4 was the correct way to go, and that obviously has not happened. Or it might argue that one or other of those was necessary and neither has been followed. After all, it is both normal and legally required to follow amendment procedures in a treaty, at least until those procedures are themselves duly amended.

Can the Prosecution justify what happened in Kampala (if the 'finesse' interpretation is correct)? One simple argument is that the participants accepted

---

[38] The second sentence of art 121(5) could be read on its face to preclude jurisdiction involving a State not accepting an amendment, even in the case of a Security Council resolution, but the Kampala Amendments contemplate that the Security Council may refer both cases involving non-Parties to the Statute and cases involving Parties to the Statute which have not accepted the Kampala Amendments (assuming that such acceptance is necessary for some purposes). This has to be the effect of Understanding 2, in Annex III to Resolution 6 (n 7): 'It is understood that the Court shall exercise jurisdiction over the crime of aggression on the basis of a Security Council referral in accordance with article 13, paragraph (b) of the Statute, irrespective of whether the State concerned has accepted the Court's jurisdiction in this regard.'

[39] The Court would surely find that it has express or implied power to decide this fundamental question. See ICC Statute, art 119 and *Prosecutor v Tadić* (Appeals Chamber Decision on the Defence Motion for Interlocutory Appeal on Jurisdiction) IT-94-1-AR72 (2 October 1995).

that Paragraph 3 of Article 121 ('adoption') was sufficient, but nonetheless erected some further barriers to opening up the exercise of jurisdiction over aggression. These required 30 ratifications and the later vote. The reference to 'conditions' in Article 5(2) probably provided authority for doing that. But the drafters did not expressly say anything about paragraph 3. Could it be that there was simply a conclusion that Article 121 was so dysfunctional when read with Article 5 that it was necessary to find a unique solution for a unique situation by consensus – a 'fix'?[40] How can an amendment procedure be applied if there is no agreement on what it means? Doing the amendment by consensus overcame any potential arguments based on the consensual nature of state obligation.

## V. Summary and Conclusions

I believe that the General's actions can be fitted into the basic definition of an 'act of aggression', either as an 'invasion', an 'attack', or both. More difficult is the question of whether all the elements of the 'crime of aggression' are present. General Pickens does not appear to be one who directs the 'political' action of the state, although he does seem to meet 'the military' criterion in the definition. He can argue that the 'humanitarian' or 'protective' nature of the military action means that the requirement of a 'manifest' violation of the Charter is not met. He also has a weak argument based on mistake (especially weak if the Court finds the relevant element as adopted in Kampala consistent with the Statute).

Since the Security Council has not spoken on whether an aggression occurred, it would be necessary to inform the UN Secretary-General of your intentions, then wait six months for any action from the Council before seeking the Pre-Trial Division's authorization to proceed.

There is a strong argument that Activia's domestic prosecution, albeit by a non-State Party, engages the complementarity provisions of the Statute. You may want to use this situation as an opportunity to argue that universal jurisdiction by a state over the crime of aggression is incompatible with international customary law, and thus that Activia is not a state which 'has' jurisdiction. I suspect, however, that there will be occasions when you will be content to defer to a state that is mounting a genuine prosecution. (This may, indeed, be such a case.)

Finally, there is the problem that neither the alleged aggressor state nor the alleged victim has ratified the Kampala Amendments, nor have they opted out. I believe that the better interpretation of the Amendments is that this is no bar to the Court's jurisdiction. Both states are parties to the Rome Statute, and Article 15 *bis*(4) speaks of jurisdiction 'over a crime of aggression, arising from an act of aggression committed by a State Party'. 'State Party' must mean a party to the Statute. We are left then with the fundamental problem of whether the Kampala Amendments were validly adopted. Given that there was no consensus on what the amendment

---

[40] See C Kress and L von Holtzendorff, 'The Kampala Compromise on the Crime of Aggression' (2010) 8 *JICJ* 1179, 1215–16.

provisions of the Statute required, I would argue that the Court should defer to the judgment of the Review Conference in adopting its 'fix' by consensus. The first 'aggression defendant' will inevitably raise these issues and now may be the time to try to resolve them.

# The Special Tribunal for Lebanon and Terrorism as an International Crime: Reflections on the Judicial Function

## Ben Saul

The surprise decision by the Special Tribunal for Lebanon that transnational terrorism is a customary international law crime[1] sparked considerable controversy in 2011. Until then there was a widespread belief that there existed neither an agreed definition nor an international crime of terrorism. For many, the decision did not change that long-held belief, because of the unsatisfactory nature of the Tribunal's reasoning about customary law. This chapter first outlines how international law dealt with terrorism in a criminal context up until the decision of the Tribunal in 2011. It then briefly critiques the Tribunal's assessment of the various material sources (national laws and judicial decisions, international and regional treaties, and United Nations resolutions) purportedly evidencing a customary international law crime of transnational terrorism.[2] That critique demonstrates that even on the Tribunal's own criteria for identifying customary law, there is no international crime of terrorism.

The core of the chapter then asks a series of background questions about what the Tribunal's decision reveals about its approach to judging and the judicial function. Here the chapter considers in turn the expansive judicial definition of contested issues; the confused methodological approach to custom formation which led the Tribunal into error; the fatal inattention to utilising the writings of jurists

---

[1] *Case No STL-11-01/I* (Interlocutory Decision on the Applicable Law: Terrorism, Conspiracy, Homicide, Perpetration, Cumulative Charging) STL-11-01/I/AC/R176bis (16 February 2011) para 85 (hereinafter, 'Decision').

[2] A more detailed critique can be found in B Saul, 'Legislating from A Radical Hague: The UN Special Tribunal for Lebanon Invents an International Crime of Transnational Terrorism' (2011) 24 *LJIL* 677.

and *amicus* briefs in an area of chronic indeterminacy; the issue of disqualifying a judge (President Cassese) for perceived lack of impartiality in respect of his prior academic publications on the subject matter at hand; and the vexed line between acceptable and unacceptable judicial 'law-making'. The chapter ends by pointing to some factors which may affect the future persuasive value of the decision in relation to the customary law status of terrorism.

## I. The Conventional Wisdom

While transnational terrorism has long posed problems for international law, prior to the terrorist attacks of 11 September 2001 ('9/11') the conventional view was that 'terrorism' as such was not an international or transnational crime. Terrorism was regarded not as 'a discrete topic of international law with its own substantive legal norms', but as 'a pernicious contemporary phenomenon which ... presents complicated legal problems'.[3] Being both vague and undefined, the term terrorism was long thought to serve 'no operative legal purpose'.[4] It was considered 'merely a convenient way of alluding to activities ... widely disapproved of and in which either the methods used are unlawful, or the targets protected, or both'.[5] Relatively few domestic legal orders specifically criminalised terrorism either.

Rather, existing *general norms* of international law were thought capable of dealing with terrorism, such as principles of non-intervention, the non-use of force, State responsibility, the law of armed conflict, international human rights law, and international criminal law. While those principles might face occasional difficulty in their specific or practical application to the factual phenomenon of terrorism in given contexts, it was nonetheless thought that they largely covered the field. As such, many thought there was little need for a more specific, discrete international crime of terrorism *per se*.

Where general norms were found to be inadequate, they were supplemented by numerous 'sectoral' treaties on transnational criminal cooperation, adopted since the 1960s, which targeted the common methods of violence used by terrorists (such as hijacking, hostage taking, endangering maritime facilities, and so on),[6]

---

[3] R Higgins, 'The General International Law of Terrorism' in R Higgins and M Flory (eds) *Terrorism and International Law* (Routledge, London 1997) 13–14; see also R Baxter, 'A Skeptical Look at the Concept of Terrorism' (1974) 7 *Akron L Rev* 380, 380; G Guillaume, 'Terrorism and International Law' (2004) 53 *ICLQ* 537; MC Bassiouni, 'A Policy-Oriented Inquiry into the Different Forms and Manifestations of "International Terrorism"' in MC Bassiouni (ed) *Legal Responses to International Terrorism* (Dordrecht, Martinus Nijhoff 1988) xv, xvi; B Saul, *Defining Terrorism in International Law* (OUP, Oxford 2006).
[4]    Baxter (n 3) 380.
[5]    Higgins (n 3) 28.
[6]    Convention on Offences and Certain Other Acts Committed on Board Aircraft, 704 UNTS 219, 14 September 1963, entered into force 4 December 1969; Convention for the Suppression of Unlawful Seizure of Aircraft, 860 UNTS 105, 16 December 1970, entered

but did not create a new international crime of terrorism.[7] At a practical level, such frameworks were supplemented by technical assistance and transnational cooperation, facilitated by a range of specialised agencies.[8]

This pragmatic approach enabled the repression of terrorism while sidestepping the irreconcilable problem of defining it, at a time when States were unable to agree on the legitimacy of violence committed by self-determination movements or by State forces. This disagreement was particularly acute during debates in the General Assembly during the 1970s, driven by the politics of decolonisation and the Cold War. The result has been a functional transnational cooperation against terrorism, even if there remain regulatory gaps because of the reactive, ad hoc nature of treaty making (for example, terrorist attacks by small arms, as in Mumbai in 2008, are not prohibited by treaty law).

After 9/11, in Resolution 1373 (2001), adopted under Chapter VII of the UN Charter, the Security Council required all States to domestically criminalise 'terrorist acts'. Resolution 1373 did not define terrorism for the purpose of national criminalisation, resulting in decentralised and haphazard national implementation. Many States utilised the authority of the Resolution to define terrorism to suit their own political purposes and sometimes to legitimise assaults on fundamental rights, or to deviate from procedural protections ordinarily accorded in criminal proceedings. Later, Security Council Resolution 1566 (2004) suggested a narrow guideline definition of terrorism, but this did not cure the inconsistencies in national laws because it was non-binding and of limited influence in practice. The combination of the above legal developments has led quite a few international lawyers to believe that '[m]ost of the normative work [in regulating terrorism] has

---

into force 14 October 1971; Convention on the Prevention and Punishment of Crimes against Internationally Protected Persons, including Diplomatic Agents, 1035 UNTS 167, 14 December 1973, entered into force 20 February 1977; International Convention against the Taking of Hostages, 1316 UNTS 205, 17 December 1979, entered into force 3 June 1983; Convention for the Suppression of Unlawful Acts against the Safety of Maritime Navigation, 1678 UNTS 221, 10 March 1988, entered into force 1 March 1992; Protocol for the Suppression of Unlawful Acts against the Safety of Fixed Platforms Located on the Continental Shelf, 1678 UNTS 304, 10 March 1988, entered into force 1 March 1992; Protocol on the Suppression of Unlawful Acts of Violence at Airports Serving International Civil Aviation, 974 UNTS 177, 24 February 1988, entered into force 6 August 1989; Convention on the Marking of Plastic Explosives for the Purpose of Detection, 30 ILM 721, 1 March 1991, entered into force 21 June 1998; 1997 International Convention for the Suppression of Terrorist Bombings, 2149 UNTS 256, adopted 15 December 1997 by UN GA Resolution 52/164 (1997), entered into force 23 May 2001; International Convention for the Suppression of the Financing of Terrorism, 2178 UNTS 229, adopted 9 December 1999 by UN GA Resolution 54/109, entered into force 10 April 2002; International Convention for the Suppression of Acts of Nuclear Terrorism, adopted 13 April 2005 by UN GA Resolution 59/290 (2005), entered into force 7 July 2007.

[7] Saul (n 3) chapter 3.

[8] Such as the International Maritime Organization, International Civil Aviation Organization, International Criminal Police Organization, and the United Nations Office on Drugs and Crime.

been accomplished'.⁹ Nonetheless, the international community has continued to feel compelled to pursue a more general anti-terrorism framework. Since 2000, efforts have been underway to negotiate a Comprehensive Anti-Terrorism Convention under the auspices of the United Nations. The ongoing efforts to define a general international crime of terrorism suggest that the international community places some importance on the symbolic, expressive function of the criminal law in condemning terrorism as such, beyond its ordinary criminal characteristics, as well as in plugging the substantive gaps in the coverage of the sectoral treaties.

The practical significance of adopting such a treaty has diminished somewhat since 9/11, given that many countries have already criminalised terrorism in accordance with UN Security Council Resolution 1373. Yet, there is still value in finalising a comprehensive framework, since the definition in the new treaty would bring greater precision and certainty in the definition of terrorist offences and thus strengthen the rule of law in responding to terrorism. It would also provide a more secure basis for transnational legal cooperation in relation to extraterritorial jurisdiction, prosecution and extradition (including as regards restricting the political offence exception to an extradition request), mutual legal assistance, intelligence sharing, and potentially in establishing the jurisdiction of international tribunals.

## II. The Emerging Normative Controversy

The conventional view of 'terrorism' as lacking independent normative content in international law has come under strain with distance from 9/11. The boldest scholarly claim came from the leading jurist, the late Professor Antonio Cassese, who argued since about 2003 that there exists a customary international crime of terrorism,[10] with distinct elements deriving from various sources: prohibitions on terrorism in international humanitarian law;[11] the 1999 Terrorist Financing

---

[9] Guillaume (n 3) 547.
[10] A Cassese, *International Criminal Law* (OUP, Oxford 2003) 120–131; A Cassese, 'Terrorism is Also Disrupting Some Crucial Legal Categories of International Law' (2001) 12 *EJIL* 993, 994.
[11] 1949 Fourth Geneva Convention relative to the Protection of Civilian Persons in Time of War, 75 UNTS 287, 12 August 1949, entered into force 21 October 1950, art 33(1); 1977 Protocol (I) Additional to the Geneva Conventions of 12 August 1949, and Relating to the Protection of Victims of International Armed Conflicts, 1125 UNTS 3, 8 June 1977, entered into force 7 December 1978, art 51(2); 1977 Protocol II Additional to the Geneva Conventions of 12 August 1949, and Relating to the Protection of the Victims of Non-International Armed Conflicts, 1125 UNTS 609, 8 June 1977, entered into force 7 December 1978, arts 4(2) and 13(2).

Convention;[12] a much-reiterated 1994 General Assembly Declaration;[13] the 1937 League of Nations Convention;[14] treaties of regional organisations; converging national law definitions; and the statements and practice of States and international organisations since 11 September 2001.[15]

In Cassese's view, the essence of terrorism is the commission of serious, politically motivated, criminal violence, aimed at spreading terror, regardless of the status of the perpetrator.[16] Such conduct must also have a nexus with armed conflict, or be of the magnitude of crimes against humanity, or involve State authorities and exhibit a transnational dimension, such as by jeopardising the security of other States.[17] For Cassese, there is general agreement on a definition, but the scope of exceptions remains contentious.[18]

At first sight, the claim that terrorism is now a customary international law crime may seem compelling, given the apparently impressive mass of practice in support of it. The claim is also pragmatically attractive, because it short-circuits the enduring failure of the international community to define and criminalise terrorism in any international treaty, ever since efforts began in the 1920s. Since 2000, the UN's Draft Comprehensive Terrorism Convention, an initiative of India, has been mired in disagreements about the legal position of 'freedom fighters', self-determination movements and 'State terrorism'. Being able to point to a customary crime of terrorism allows international lawyers to extol the flexibility, adaptability and responsiveness of international law as a regulatory field, and to provide a more structured and rights-respecting alternative to more militant and violent State responses to terrorism.

At the same time, an overly elastic conception of custom formation brings its own risks: 'the quest for softness amounts to an endeavour by scholars to broaden the international law discipline beyond its original ambit with a view to expanding the potential objects that they can seize and study'.[19] Evidence of custom must be cautiously appraised if international law is to retain its normative purchase and

---

[12] International Convention for the Suppression of the Financing of Terrorism, 2178 UNTS 229, adopted 9 December 1999 by UN General Assembly resolution 54/109, entered into force 10 April 2002.

[13] UN GA Resolution 49/60 (9 December 1994): Declaration on Measures to Eliminate International Terrorism, annexed Declaration, para 3.

[14] 1937 League of Nations Convention for the Prevention and Punishment of Terrorism (adopted 16 November 1937, never entered into force; (1938) 19 League of Nations Official Journal 23; LoN Doc. C 546 (I) M 383 (I) 1937 V (1938); 7 Hudson 862; in League of Nations, International Conference Proceedings on the Repression of Terrorism, Geneva, 1–16 November 1937, LoN Doc. C.94.M.47.1938.V, annex I, 5).

[15] Cassese, *International Criminal Law* (n 10) 120–131; Cassese, 'Terrorism is also Disrupting …' (n 10) 994.

[16] Cassese, *International Criminal Law* (n 10) 129.

[17] Ibid 125–126, 129.

[18] Ibid 121.

[19] J d'Aspremont, 'Softness in International Law: A Self-Serving Quest for New Legal Materials' (2008) 19 *EJIL* 1075, 1076.

legitimacy; in the criminal law field particularly, there are also potential human rights implications involved in too readily jumping to conclusions about the existence of vague new crimes. Cassese's claims about the existence of a customary international crime of terrorism, and his method of assessing custom formation, have been strongly contested,[20] and indeed lay on or beyond the margins of mainstream scholarship. The evidence that Cassese points to is neither sufficiently dense nor of the requisite character to establish customary agreement on an international crime of terrorism.[21]

The disagreement nonetheless suggests a lingering degree of indeterminacy about the conceptual and normative status of terrorism in international law. As Higgins observes, '[w]hether one regards terrorism ... as new international law, or as the application of a constantly developing international law to new problems — is at heart a jurisprudential question'.[22] At this juncture the Appeals Chamber of the UN Special Tribunal for Lebanon entered the fray in its interlocutory decision of February 2011 – with Cassese as President.

## III. The UN Tribunal Creates Law

In its Decision, the Appeals Chamber identified a customary international crime of transnational terrorism in peacetime, in interpreting the scope of domestic terrorism offences under Lebanese law.[23] The elements of the crime were found to be as follows:

> (i) the perpetration of a criminal act (such as murder, kidnapping, hostage-taking, arson, and so on), or threatening such an act; (ii) the intent to spread fear among the population (which would generally entail the creation of public danger) or directly or indirectly coerce a national or international authority to take some action, or to refrain from taking it; (iii) when the act involves a transnational element.

Its assessment of customary law is, however, highly controversial and has been generally criticised by scholars.[24] A close analysis of the sources relied upon by

---

[20] Saul (n 3) chapter 4; M di Filippo, 'Terrorist Crimes and International Cooperation: Critical Remarks on the Definition and Inclusion of Terrorism in the Category of International Crimes' (2008) 19 *EJIL* 533.

[21] Saul (n 3) chapter 4.

[22] Higgins (n 3) 13.

[23] Decision (n 1) para 85.

[24] Saul (n 2); K Ambos, 'Judicial Creativity at the Special Tribunal for Lebanon: Is There a Crime of Terrorism under International Law?' (2011) 24 *LJIL* 655 (author of an *amicus* in this case); M Gillett and M Schuster, 'Fast-track Justice: The Special Tribunal for Lebanon Defines Terrorism' (2011) 9 *JICJ* 989 (accepting some aspects of its analysis); S Kirsch and A Oehmichen, 'Judges Gone Astray: The Fabrication of Terrorism as an International Crime by

Appeals Chamber[25] demonstrates that its conclusion was mistaken: there is no customary international crime of transnational terrorism. Each category of source is briefly considered below.

## A. The Absence of a Framework Convention

As regards treaties referred to by the Tribunal, an obvious but decisive starting point is that numerous efforts by the international community since the 1920s have not produced agreement on a general international crime of terrorism.[26] While there are numerous sector-specific treaties which address particular criminal means or methods used by terrorists, none of those treaties – individually or collectively – contains a comprehensive definition of terrorism[27] or establishes a general international crime of transnational 'terrorism'. At most, specific offences in some treaties may have entered into customary law, such as aircraft hijacking or hostage taking.[28]

In the absence of a general crime of terrorism in treaty law, no parallel customary rule can arise out of those treaties. The sectoral approach was adopted precisely because states could not reach agreement on 'terrorism' as such. The decades of deadlock – continuing in the negotiations for a UN Draft Comprehensive Terrorism Convention since 2000 – demonstrate a lack of consensus amongst the international community on defining and criminalising terrorism. Even the 1999 Terrorist Financing Convention – sometimes pointed to as a generic definition of terrorism – only defines and criminalises terrorist *financing*, not terrorism *per se*.

## B. Regional Conventions

The Appeals Chamber also invoked the treaties of certain regional organisations to support its conclusion that there exists an international consensus on a customary

---

the Special Tribunal for Lebanon' (2011) 1 *Durham L Rev* 32; compare M Ventura, 'Terrorism According to the STL's Interlocutory Decision on the Applicable Law' (2011) 9 *JICJ* 1021 (former legal intern to President Cassese at the STL; largely supporting the Tribunal's customary law analysis).

[25] Including regional anti-terrorism treaties, General Assembly Resolutions, UN Security Council Resolution 1566 (2004) the UN Draft Comprehensive Anti-Terrorism Convention, the Terrorist Financing Convention 1999, 37 national laws, and nine national judicial decisions; see Decision (n 1) paras 83–113.

[26] Saul (n 3) chapters 3–4; Guillaume (n 3); Higgins (n 3) 13–14.

[27] Report of the Special Rapporteur (Martin Scheinin) on the promotion and protection of human rights and fundamental freedoms while countering terrorism, UN Doc E/CN.4/2006/98 (28 December 2005) para 28.

[28] *US v Yunis*, 924 F.2d 1086 (DC Cir 1991) 1092; (1991) 30 ILM 403; *Burnett et al v Al Baraka Investment and Development Corporation et al*, Civil Action No 02-1616 (JR) US District Court, District of Columbia, 25 July 2003, 274 F Supp 2d 86.

international crime.²⁹ Yet, an accurate reading of those conventions establishes exactly the opposite: enormous variation in regional conceptions of terrorism and no consensus on a common definition.³⁰

Some regional treaties focus on specific terrorist methods, without defining terrorism;³¹ others contain (often wide or conflicting) generic definitions,³² or define terrorism only to criminalise ancillary conduct;³³ and yet others do not create offences at all, but serve other purposes (such as extradition or law enforcement cooperation).³⁴ Some of the treaties do not enjoy wide participation by members of the regional organisation (as with the Organisation of Islamic Conference ('OIC')), and even where states are parties, the treaty may not have influenced national practice much at all (as with the Organisation of African Unity, now the African Union).

## C. United Nations Resolutions

The Appeals Chamber invoked a series of General Assembly Resolutions to support its position.³⁵ Yet, the core of those Resolutions, the 1994 Declaration on Measures against International Terrorism,³⁶ must be viewed cautiously. The Declaration itself

---

29   Decision (n 1) paras 88–89.
30   Saul (n 3) chapter 4.
31   Organisation of the American States, Convention to Prevent and Punish Acts of Terrorism Taking the Form of Crimes against Persons and Related Extortion that are of International Significance; 2002 Inter-American Convention against Terrorism adopted at the second plenary session (3 June 2002) AG/Res 1840 (XXXII-O/02).
32   League of Arab States, Arab Convention for the Suppression of Terrorism, 22 April 1998 (entered into force on 7 May 1999); Organisation of the Islamic Conference (OIC) Convention of the Organisation of the Islamic Conference on Combating International Terrorism, 1 July 1999, Res 59/26-P, Annex; Organisation of African Unity, Convention on the Prevention and Combating of Terrorism, 14 July 1999, 2219 UNTS 179; Council of the European Union, Council Framework Decision 2002/475/JHA on Combating Terrorism, 2002 OJ (L 164).
33   Council of Europe, Convention on the Prevention of Terrorism (15 May 2005) <http://conventions.coe.int/Treaty/en/treaties/html/196.htm> last accessed 2 January 2012; South Asian Association for Regional Cooperation (SAARC) Additional Protocol to the SAARC Regional Convention on Suppression of Terrorism, 6 January 2004.
34   Inter-American Convention against Terrorism (n 31); South Asian Association for Regional Cooperation (SAARC) Regional Convention on Suppression of Terrorism, 4 November 1987, <http://treaties.un.org/doc/db/Terrorism/Conv 18-english.pdf> last accessed 2 January 2012; Commonwealth of Independent States, Treaty on Cooperation among the States Members of the Commonwealth of Independent States in Combating Terrorism, 4 June 1999. Although not cited by the judgment, the Council of Europe, European Convention on the Suppression of Terrorism (27 January 1977) <http://conventions.coe.int/Treaty/en/Treaties/Html/090.htm> last accessed 2 January 2012 would be another example.
35   Decision (n 1) para 88.
36   The 1994 Declaration states that: 'Criminal acts intended or calculated to provoke a state of terror in the general public, a group of persons or particular persons for political

emphasises the need to progressively develop and codify the law on terrorism,[37] far from reflecting existing rules. Many States argued that there was still a need to define terrorism and/or to adopt a comprehensive treaty criminalising it,[38] and to distinguish self-determination struggles[39] – including the 118 States of the Non-Aligned Movement and 56 OIC states.[40] At most, the Declaration reflects a political agreement on the wrongfulness of terrorism which falls short of evidencing a customary international crime, particularly against a background of continuing inconclusive UN treaty negotiations on point since 2000.

Moreover, the Declaration's definition of terrorism (requiring terror for a political purpose) is, in any case, different to that in the UN Draft Comprehensive Convention (which does not require a political motive, and instead focuses on intimidation or coercion);[41] different again from that in Security Council Resolution 1566 (which is limited to underlying offences, and does not catch all forms of terrorism); different from the definitions in recent treaties such the 1999 Terrorist Financing Convention (requiring intimidation or coercion, but no political motive); and different from those many different definitions in national laws and regional treaties (as shown below). All of this suggests that the legal definition of terrorism, and such criminal liability as may attach to it, remains deeply contested.

---

purposes are in any circumstance unjustifiable, whatever the considerations of a political, philosophical, ideological, racial, ethnic, religious or any other nature that may be invoked to justify them': UN GA Resolution 49/60 (9 December 1994): Declaration on Measures to Eliminate International Terrorism, para 2.

[37] UN GA Resolution 49/60 (n 36) para 12.

[38] UN GA (49th Session) (6th Comm) 14th meeting (20 October 1994) para 5 (Sudan) 13 (India) 27 (Algeria) 71 (Nepal); 15th meeting (21 October 1994) para 4 (Sri Lanka) 9 (Iran) 18–19 (Libya).

[39] Ibid 14th meeting (20 October 1994) para 6 (Sudan) 20 (Syria) 24 (Pakistan); 15th meeting (21 October 1994) para 9 (Iran) 18–19 (Libya).

[40] Non-Aligned Movement ('NAM') XIV Ministerial Conference Final Document, Durban, 17–19 August 2004, paras 98–99, 101–102, 104; NAM, XIII Conference of Heads of State or Government, Final Document, Kuala Lumpur, 25 February 2003, paras 105–106, 108, 115; NAM, XIII Ministerial Conference Final Document, Cartagena, 8–9 April 2000, paras 90–91; OIC Resolutions 6/31-LEG (2004) para 5; 7/31-LEG (2004) preamble, paras 1–2; 6/10-LEG(IS) (2003) para 5; 7/10-LEG (IS) (2003) paras 1–2; OIC, Islamic Summit Conference (10th Session) Final Communiqué, Malaysia, 16–17 October 2003, para 50; OIC (Extraordinary Session Foreign Ministers) Declaration on International Terrorism, Kuala Lumpur, 1–3 April 2002, paras 8, 11, 16 and Plan of Action, paras 2–3.

[41] Draft art 2(1) proposes an offence if a person 'unlawfully and intentionally' causes: '[d]eath or serious bodily injury to any person'; '[s]erious damage to public or private property'; or '[d]amage to property, places, facilities, or systems ... resulting or likely to result in major economic loss'. The purpose of any such conduct, 'by its nature or context', must be 'to intimidate a population, or to compel a Government or an international organization to do or abstain from doing any act'. Possible exceptions to the Draft Convention remain contentious, particularly as regards violence by non-State groups and State military forces.

There have been few extradition requests or prosecutions pursuant to the 1994 definition, which has only marginally influenced national laws.[42] At best, the definition reflects nascent political agreement on a shared concept of terrorism, but not legal agreement evidencing a customary crime. For many States, voting support for such resolutions was conditioned on an understanding that they did not generate criminal liability.[43] It would be surprising if the protracted disputes on definition in the treaty context could be circumvented by a relatively recent series of non-binding resolutions, unsupported by State behaviour in conformity.

## D. National Laws

In relation to national laws, the Appeals Chamber claimed that 'the national legislation of countries around the world consistently defines terrorism in similar if not identical terms to those used in the international instruments'.[44] This is plainly not accurate and national laws do not evidence any customary law agreement on a shared definition and crime of terrorism. In the first place, the Appeals Chamber conflated national laws which address *domestic terrorism* with those concerning *international terrorism*, when only the latter are relevant in evidencing the Appeals Chamber's supposed crime of *transnational* terrorism.

Secondly, the Appeals Chamber relied upon national definitions of terrorism used for *criminal offence* purposes in conjunction with definitions used for *non-criminal* purposes, when only the former may be evidence of a customary international *crime* of terrorism. Thirdly, while the Appeals Chamber argued that the many national laws converge on a common definition of terrorism,[45] that reductive assertion conceals the reality of fundamental conceptual disagreements about terrorism which are clearly evident even on the face of those 37 laws – let alone in the more than 160 other divergent national laws which are not mentioned by the Appeals Chamber.

I have demonstrated the acute differences in detail elsewhere.[46] But to put it starkly by reference to just a few examples, the Appeals Chamber is wrong to suggest that there is a common concept of terrorism in the national laws it cites when terrorism variously means 'the violation of honour' (Saudi Arabia), sectarian strife (Iraq), subverting the constitution (Peru), armed conflict (Uzbekistan), harm to public order (Egypt) and so on.[47] These are fundamentally different conceptions of what constitutes terrorism, with many definitions bleeding entirely different species of violence into the notion of 'terrorism'.

---

[42] Saul (n 3) chapter 4.
[43] Ibid 212.
[44] Decision (n 1) para 91; see paras 91–98 on national laws.
[45] Ibid para 97.
[46] Saul (n 2); Saul (n 3) chapter 4.
[47] Decision (n 1) para 93.

It is disingenuous to pretend that there is genuine commonality among them – and these are the best examples the Tribunal managed to find, to say nothing of the 160 or more national laws *not* mentioned. Such divergence has not been cured by the UN Security Council's edict in Resolution 1373 (2001) requiring states to criminalise terrorism; rather, the Security Council has seemingly tolerated a wide variety of national law approaches to terrorism without creating uniformity. The Tribunal's lack of a critical eye and attention to detail is somewhat disturbing for a judicial body.

Fourthly, the Appeals Chamber invokes some national (and regional) laws which patently violate international human rights law, such as by being too vague to satisfy the principle of legality and freedom from retroactive criminal punishment under Article 15 of the International Covenant on Civil and Political Rights.[48] Such unlawful acts are not accompanied by any *opinio juris* to the effect that rights-violating definitions of terrorism are now permissible forms of international anti-terrorism law: they remain simply unlawful.

## E. National Judicial Decisions

The final category of sources invoked by the Appeals Chamber – nine national judicial decisions – also fails to support its contention that terrorism is a customary law crime.[49] The Appeals Chamber misreads, exaggerates, or misrepresents each decision. One case did not concern terrorism at all,[50] while in various other cases, the customary law status of terrorism was not an issue in their disposal.[51] One decision explicitly refrains from ruling on the point.[52] One matter was a civil case and did not involve criminal liability,[53] while others concerned national law contexts

---

[48] For human rights critiques of national laws, see, e.g., 'Concluding Observations of the UN Human Rights Committee': United States of America (15 September 2006) UN Doc CCPR/C/USA/CO/3, para 11; Algeria (18 August 1998) UN Doc CCPR/C/79/Add.95, para 11; Egypt (9 August 1993) UN Doc CCPR/C/79/Add.23, para 8; Democratic Peoples' Republic of Korea (27 August 2001) UN Doc CCPR/CO/72/PRK, para 14; Portugal (Macao) (4 November 1999) UN Doc CCPR/C/79/Add.115, para 12; Peru (25 July 1996) UN Doc CCPR /C/79/Add.67, para 12; and Report of the Special Rapporteur (Martin Scheinin) on the promotion and protection of human rights and fundamental freedoms while countering terrorism, UN Doc E/CN.4/2006/98, 28 December 2005, paras 27–28, 45–47, 56, 62.

[49] Decision (n 1) para 86.

[50] *Enrique Lautaro Aranclbta Clavel Case*, Argentina Supreme Court, Case No. 259 (2004) (24 August 2004).

[51] *Cavallo Case*, Mexico Supreme Court, Case No. 140/2002 (10 June 2003) quoted in Decision (n 1) para 86; *US v Yunis*, 924 F.2d 1086 (DC Cir 1991); *EHL* case, Cass. 15 février 2006, RG P.05.1594.F, Pas. 2006, No. 96; RDP2006, 795, cited in *Rapport annuele la Cour de cassation de Belgique 2009*.

[52] *Zrig v Canada (Minister of Citizenship and Immigration)* (CA) [2003] 3 FC 761, para 180.

[53] *Almog v Arab Bank*, 471 F. Supp. 2d 257 (EDNY 2007).

such as extradition⁵⁴ or exclusion from refugee status.⁵⁵ One decision identifies 'the essence' of terrorism for the limited purpose of interpreting a domestic immigration law statute, but acknowledges that 'there is no single definition that is accepted internationally' and that '[o]ne searches in vain for an authoritative definition'.⁵⁶

At best, some of the decisions accept that certain forms of terrorism may have attracted international consensus⁵⁷ (for instance, hijacking or hostage taking), but that falls far short of support for the existence of a comprehensive, universal crime of terrorism as such. In those few cases which mention customary law, the methodology of analysing custom formation is minimal to say the least and 'rest[s] upon a very inadequate use of the sources'.⁵⁸

While one decision appears to squarely identify a customary crime of terrorism,⁵⁹ it then proceeds to define such crime quite differently from the notion presented by the Appeals Chamber – specifically by requiring a political, religious or ideological motivation (or further 'special intent').⁶⁰ On that view, terrorism is simply *not* terrorism unless it is defined to include the motive element. This is not a trivial or marginal difference of opinion. The Appeals Chamber's assessment of the customary crime of terrorism is directly at odds with the judgment it invokes in its support. The Appeals Chamber also ignores other national judicial decisions which cast doubt on the customary law status of terrorism.⁶¹

## IV. Some Comments on Judging

From the above analysis, it is fairly clear that the Appeals Chamber's assessment of customary law is unsupportable. A more interesting question is what the Decision reveals about approaches to judging and the judicial function.

---

[54] *EHL* case, Cass. 15 février 2006, RG P.05.1594.F, Pas. 2006, No. 96; RDP2006, 795, cited in *Rapport annuele la Cour de cassation de Belgique 2009*.

[55] *Al-Sirri v Secretary of State for the Home Department* [2009] EWCA Civ 364.

[56] *Suresh v Canada* [2002] 1 SCR 3, 53, para 94.

[57] *Zrig* (n 52); *US v Yunis*, 924 F.2d 1086 (DC Cir 1991).

[58] Ian Brownlie, *Principles of Public International Law* (6th edn OUP, Oxford 2003) 22 (speaking of the value of national decisions generally).

[59] *Bouyahia Maher Ben Abdelaziz et al*, Judgment of 11 October 2006, Corte di Cassazione.

[60] On this 'motive' element in terrorism definitions, see B Saul, 'The Curious Element of Motive in Definitions of Terrorism: Essential Ingredient – Or Criminalizing Thought?' in A Lynch, E MacDonald and G Williams (eds) *Law and Liberty in the War on Terror* (Federation Press, Sydney 2007) 28.

[61] *US v Yousef et al*, 327 F.3d 56 (US Crt App, 2nd Cir) 4 April 2003 at 34, 44, 46, 53–60, affirming *Tel-Oren v Libyan Arab Republic* 726 F.2d 774 (DC Cir 1984) at 795 (Edwards J) and 806–807 (Bork J) (USA); *Ghaddafi* case, Bulletin des arret de la Cour de Cassation, Chambre criminelle, mar 2001, No. 64, 218–219; *Madan Singh v State of Bihar* [2004] INSC 215 (2 April 2004).

## A. Judicial Activism in Defining the Issues

In the first place, neither the prosecution nor the defence argued that terrorism is a customary international crime, yet the Appeals Chamber proceeded to determine the question and to establish the existence of such a crime. In fact, both the prosecution and defence argued 'forcefully' that that there is no settled definition of terrorism under customary international law.[62] There was no apparent ambiguity in the Statute, which simply stated that Lebanese criminal law applies, yet the Tribunal constructed elaborate arguments by which to import elements of customary international criminal law into domestic substantive law. In an adversarial criminal trial in common law systems, the usual expectation is that it is for the parties themselves to define the issues in their submissions, and not for judges, of their own motion, to answer incidental questions or to place non-dispositive issues at the centre of the case. As Higgins notes, judging only 'in respect of the particular issue it is required to decide or upon' is part of 'the discipline of relevance and pertinence' of judging, which in turn 'is part of the authoritativeness which commands international respect'.[63]

That conventional view of the judicial function may, however, be qualified. The parties will not necessarily always accurately identify the issues. If there is a glaring omission in the parties' submissions, it may well be appropriate for a more activist, inquisitorial bench to use its initiative to get to the 'truth' rather than restricting its inquiry to issues conveniently agreed between the parties.

Such circumstances will be relatively rare, but would include, for example, situations where there is a mutual interest amongst the parties not to raise a particularly uncertain or troublesome issue in which neither party is confident. Where the court raises such issues of its own volition, and where the parties themselves may not have made extensive submissions on those issues, a special burden falls on the court itself to diligently ventilate, research and reason the issues. In such circumstances the court is acting less as an adjudicator of contested issues and more as an advocate or pleader of a particular position: special caution is therefore warranted, particularly where there is no further appeal from an appellate court.

## B. Approach to Customary Law

A second issue about judging arising from the decision concerns the quality of the Appeals Chamber's reasoning about customary law formation. At first sight, the Appeals Chamber seems to do everything right. The decision invoked the usual legal tests for custom formation from the key cases of the International Court of Justice. Thus, the Tribunal searches for 'general' *opinio juris* accompanied by

---

[62] Decision (n 1) para 83.
[63] R Higgins, *Problems and Process: International Law and How We Use It* (Clarendon, Oxford 2003) 204.

'consistent' practice;[64] discounts mere discrepancies by invoking the *Nicaragua* case;[65] considers the relevance of treaties in custom formation from the *North Sea Continental Shelf* case;[66] and even emphasises its mainstream credentials by aligning itself with a 'strictly positivist construction of custom'.[67]

The Tribunal then purported to assess the various relevant material sources against those conventional (albeit slippery in practice)[68] tests. A relatively detailed and lengthy analysis of an impressive array of sources then ensued. Indeed, the analysis is considerably more fortified than some judgments of other international courts and tribunals in recent years (including the ICJ and ICTY), where the existence of custom has been occasionally asserted with little serious analysis of sources.[69]

As the earlier critique suggests, however, the conclusions drawn by the Appeals Chamber in applying the legal tests to the material sources simply do not add up. It is, of course, well accepted that identifying customary law is an evaluative process, not a scientific one 'the accuracy of which can be measured'[70] in any dogmatic way. It is obvious too that there are 'political, value choices' involved in determining customary law.[71] Some commentators have argued that the Appeals Chamber's approach to custom formation was appropriate, because a 'line of best fit' approach to identifying a common definition of terrorism is preferable to a paralysing, formalistic approach which insists on identical definitions worldwide.[72]

But, even allowing wide latitude for such considerations, the Appeals Chamber stepped over the most elastic line for custom formation. The problem is not that the national laws invoked are not identical, but that they are often entirely outside the same ballpark: the differences are not merely 'peripheral'[73] but fundamental. The UN Resolutions do not stand for what is claimed; the international and regional treaty practice is all over the place; Security Council measures have not produced convergence, and so on. The superficial similarities between the various sources do not survive rigorous, nuanced scrutiny, or the 'extensive empirical investigation'[74] that is needed to properly ground customary law. As a result, the Appeals Chamber

---

[64] Decision (n 1) para 85.
[65] Ibid para 100.
[66] Ibid para 108.
[67] Ibid para 99.
[68] A Boyle and C Chinkin, *The Making of International Law* (OUP, Oxford 2007) 280 (noting the inconsistencies in judicial application of agreed methodology for custom formation).
[69] Ibid 280.
[70] Ibid 279, 285.
[71] Ibid 278.
[72] Gillett and Schuster (n 24) 1, 19 ('As regards methodology, the Appeals Chamber took a measured and reasonable approach'); see also Ventura (n 24) 11–12.
[73] Decision (n 1) para 97.
[74] D Regan, 'International Adjudication: A Response to Paulus – Courts, Custom, Treaties, Regimes, and the WTO' in S Besson and J Tasioulas (eds) *The Philosophy of International Law* (OUP, Oxford 2010) 225, 228.

elided the undoubted international consensus that terrorism is *wrongful* with a far more dubious consensus it claims exists about what terrorism *is*.

On top of the clear divergence in state practice, the Tribunal did not succeed in demonstrating that state practice is driven by a sense of international legal obligation, as opposed to domestic convenience in throttling one's own terrorists, or procedural compliance with UN Security Council resolutions. In this respect there is a problem with some authority cited by the Tribunal. The Tribunal invokes the academic view of Max Sørensen for the proposition that 'one should assume as a starting point the *presumption* of the existence of *opinio juris* whenever a finding is made of a consistent practice'.[75] The Tribunal claims that such proposition amounts to 'legal criteria' based on 'international case law'.[76]

Yet, in the very next paragraph, the Tribunal states that it is '[r]elying on the notion of international custom as set out by the International Court of Justice in the *Continental Shelf* case'.[77] It is well known that Judge Sørensen's suggestion of presuming *opinio juris* from consistent practice was a dissenting view in that case, in which the majority insisted on a stricter requirement of separately evidencing *opinio juris*.[78] The Tribunal cannot have it both ways. Its invocation of Sørensen's view may be a tacit admission that evidence of *opinio juris* concerning *an international obligation to criminalise terrorism in the particular way identified by the Tribunal* is not sufficiently strong to establish such a customary rule.

## C. The Failure to Utilise Subsidiary Means: Jurists and Amicus Briefs

As Rosalyn Higgins observes, judgments must be 'fully reasoned',[79] even if there is a 'difficult line between the maintenance of the highest quality judgments and the achievement of an efficient throughput of work'.[80] In an area of such acute controversy as the legal status of terrorism, and where the parties have not pleaded the issue, one might expect a court to utilise every reasonably available source. A striking omission in the decision is a failure to seriously consider the writings of jurists. At best, a fleeting mention of a few scholars is made in footnote 127 of the decision, but there is no serious engagement of the prevailing substantive arguments in the literature as to why terrorism is *not* a customary international crime.

It is plain that '[a] judge is not an academic and judicial opinions should not be academic articles'.[81] But the purpose of consulting the writings of jurists is not to

---

[75] Decision (n 1) para 101.
[76] Ibid.
[77] Ibid para 102.
[78] *North Sea Continental Shelf Cases*, 1969 ICJ Reports 3 (20 February 1969) paras 77–78.
[79] R Higgins, 'Reflections from the International Court' in MD Evans (ed) *International Law* (OUP, Oxford 2003) 3, 4.
[80] Ibid 4.
[81] Ibid 4.

titillate academics, but to apprise the court of the fullest range of legal arguments on a given topic – all the more vital in this instance where there are no formal treaty provisions supporting the legal position adopted, no prior relevant decisions of international tribunals, and where national decisions are marginally relevant and State practice is highly variable. Seriously engaging with the scholarly literature would have helped to make the court aware of the fatal shortcomings in the case for the existence of a customary international law crime. The writings of jurists are precisely of most significance in novel areas where the law is chronically unsettled. While there is a profusion of academic writings on terrorism, it is still possible to separate the wheat from the chaff to identify the key sources which elaborate upon the point in question.

The same can be said of the need for genuine use of *amicus* briefs. To its credit, the Special Tribunal called for *amicus* briefs on the issues in question. But the call was not widely publicised, little time was given for them to be filed, and the deadline for briefs closed days before the judgment was due to be issued. The call for briefs was made on Monday 7 February 2011. The date for filing was Friday 11 February 2011. There were thus less than five days for any interested organisation to file a brief on 15 complex questions which the parties and the Tribunal itself had been considering for many months.

Unsurprisingly, only two briefs were received, and one was refused,[82] and these two addressed only some of the relevant questions. The 154-page decision was then issued on Wednesday 16 February – less than three working days after the *amicus* briefs were filed, and with scant reference to the *amicus* briefs. Weirdly, the Appeals Chamber invoked passages from one *amicus* brief, from a German university, to support its contention that terrorism is a customary international crime, despite that brief itself arguing no such thing, and its author subsequently disagreeing with that conclusion.[83] It is clear that the *amicus* procedure was a formalistic afterthought, and not taken especially seriously in the judgment writing process.

## D. The Academic's Shadow: Disqualification of President Cassese

Such review of the academic writing and a fuller *amicus* process may have alerted the Appeals Chamber to another potential problem. In his prior capacity as an academic, President Cassese had repeatedly, recently and in some detail published scholarly writings which concluded that terrorism was indeed a customary international law crime.[84] An issue therefore arises as to whether President Cassese's extra-curial opinions gave rise to an appearance of 'issue' bias which compromised his perceived independence and thus the legitimacy of and public confidence in the Tribunal.

---

[82] Decision (n 1) para 2. On the *amicus* refused, see Saul (n 2).
[83] K Ambos, 'Amicus Curiae Brief Submitted to the Appeals Chamber of the Special Tribunal for Lebanon: Introductory Remarks' (2011) 22 *CLF* 398, 390–391.
[84] See above (n 10).

Having been such a vocal, influential, albeit solitary proponent of the view that terrorism is a customary international crime, there is *prima facie* a credible view that President Casssese may have brought a closed mind to the issue on the bench, perhaps driven by his enthusiasm to confirm the correctness of his own academic view, or to mark out a new territory of international criminal law against terrorism. President Cassese did not voluntarily recuse himself, but nor did any party seek his disqualification.

Certainly the decision bears the distinctive drafting hand of President Cassese, who plainly took the lead in relation to the international law questions at issue. One cannot know the influence of the other four judges behind the scenes, although it is fair to observe that some of the other international and Lebanese judges were not necessarily international law experts. Rule 25 of the Rules of Procedure and Evidence of the UN Special Tribunal for Lebanon deals with the disqualification of judges in the following terms:

> A Judge may not sit on a trial or appeal in any case in which he has a personal interest or concerning which he has or has had any association that might affect or appear to affect his impartiality. The Judge shall, in any such circumstance, withdraw, and the President shall assign another Judge to the case.[85]

This general test for disqualification does not specify any particular grounds for recusal, including the pertinent question of the relevance of previous academic writings. Evidently, if international judges are typically drawn from the most qualified international lawyers, then they will almost certainly have published scholarly opinions on a wide range of topics.

Yet, it does not follow that those same academic writings which qualify a scholar for judicial office cannot also give rise, in a given case, to grounds for

---

[85] Rules of Procedure and Evidence of the Special Tribunal for Lebanon (adopted 20 March 2009, as amended 10 November 2010) STL/BD/2009/01/Rev. 3, Rule 25(A). President Cassese ruled in 2010 on a different proceeding to disqualify another judge of the tribunal: *In the Matter of El Sayed* (Decision on Mr El Sayed's Motion for the Disqualification of Judge Riachy from the Appeals Chamber Pursuant to Rule 25) CH/PRES/2010/08 (5 November 2010). A similar test appears in Rule 15(A) of the Rules of Procedure and Evidence of the International Criminal Tribunal for the former Yugoslávia, UN Doc IT/32/Rev.44 (10 November 2009). The test also reflects the International Law Association's *Burgh House Principles on the Independence of the International Judiciary*, para 9.2, <http://www.ucl.ac.uk/laws/cict/docs/burgh_final_21204.pdf> last accessed 20 December 2011. It differs in terms from the tests used by the International Court of Justice. ICJ Statute, article 24(1) provides that: 'If, for some special reason, a member of the Court considers that he should not take part in the decision of a particular case, he shall so inform the President.' See S Rosenne, 'International Court of Justice', *Max Planck Encyclopaedia of Public Int'l L* (online subscription service) para 27, online (accessed 7 December 2011) (most disqualification challenges have concerned a judge's prior diplomatic activities).

disqualification on the basis of actual or apprehended bias.[86] President Geoffrey Robertson, for instance, was disqualified from the Special Court for Sierra Leone precisely because of emotive views he had earlier expressed about the defendants' organisation in one of his books. Applying an impartiality standard similar to that in the rules of the ICTY (and now the Special Tribunal for Lebanon), the Special Court determined that 'the reasonable man [sic], reading those passages will have a legitimate reason to fear that Justice Robertson lacks impartiality'.[87]

Academic writings will not normally impel disqualification. International Bar Association Guidelines on arbitration, for instance, suggest that the prior publication of general opinions (such as in law journal articles or public lectures) about an issue arising in a case is not ordinarily a basis for disqualification, unless the opinion is specifically focused on the case at hand.[88] In Geoffrey Robertson's case, his book had pointedly applied the law to the facts of the defendants' situation, and went beyond merely giving a general legal view on an aspect of treaty interpretation or customary law. Factors arguably relevant to a contextual analysis include the proximity of prior opinions to the issue at hand, whether such opinion is recent, and how definitive is the conviction expressed.[89]

There is certainly a credible, albeit finely balanced, case to be made that President Cassese ought to have recused himself. He had forcefully and repeatedly expressed the view over almost a decade that terrorism is a customary international law crime, and he was known as a leading international criminal lawyer, including on the subject of terrorism (which he had written about over some decades). While the decision did not concern the facts of the cases of individual defendants (on which he had expressed no prior opinion), the focus of the interlocutory proceedings was precisely the issue on which he had previously expressed a firm view: the status of terrorism as a customary international law crime. His views were proximate, recent, definitive and influential, undermining his perceived impartiality.

My own view, however, is that President Cassese need not have recused himself, particularly since the parties made no objection (though that is not the litmus test, given the judge's own duty to voluntarily step aside in the appropriate case). In fact, while the decision concurs with President Cassese's prior academic writings as to the existence of an international crime of terrorism, the arguments in the judgment about the sources – that is, about how to reason to that result – differ somewhat from Cassese's own prior writings: more elaborate, different emphases, new sources, and so on. That indicates that he was not wedded to judicially stamping his academic articles, but approached the issue openly *as a judge*. It is entirely possible for a person to wear different hats.

---

[86] J Brubaker, 'The Judge Who Knew Too Much: Issue Conflicts in International Adjudication' (2008) *Berkeley J Int'l L* 111, 143.

[87] *Prosecutor v Sesay* (Decision on Defence Motion Seeking the Disqualification of Justice Robertson from the Appears Chamber) SCSL-2004-14-AR 15 (13 March 2004) para 15.

[88] *International Bar Association Guidelines on Conflicts of Interest in International Arbitration* (2004) 4.1.1.

[89] Brubaker (n 86) 134.

But I do think that where President Cassese did not recuse himself, or was not otherwise disqualified by the bench, it was incumbent on him to squarely and formally disclose in the judgment his prior academic views on the subject. Such disclosure is not an admission of bias, but gives fair notice to the public and aids transparency and confidence in the judicial process. Without such disclosure, reasonable people – most of whom would personally know nothing about the integrity or otherwise of a particular judge – might perceive that the judge was concealing an agenda, or that some deal was done between the parties not to mention it. Such speculation, which corrodes confidence in justice, can be avoided through disclosure.

## E. From Identifying Custom to Law-Making

It is clear that judges 'make' law (up to a point) and do not merely 'apply' it,[90] despite the awkward view of the ICJ in the *Nuclear Weapons Advisory Opinion* that the Court merely 'states the existing law and does not legislate ... even if, in stating and applying the law, the Court necessarily has to specify its scope and sometimes note its general trend'.[91] Judging is not the mechanical application of rules and necessarily involves value-determinations[92] and even political compromises between competing values or sub-systems.[93] Gap-filling of various kinds is part of judging.[94] A long judicial leash should be tolerated in a decentralised international legal order where relatively few decisions are still made, yet international social life demands legal answers.

Yet, there are limits to judicial creativity. The Appeals Chamber should have concluded that terrorism is not yet a customary international law crime both because state practice is too divergent (that is, there is no consensus on definition) and *opinio juris* is not evident. It might have properly observed that there are specific customary criminal rules addressing particular manifestations of terrorism (such as hijacking, hostage taking, or terrorist financing), and general obligations on States not to support terrorism and so forth. It could have done precisely what the ICJ did in the *Nuclear Weapons Advisory Opinion*: concede that sometimes there is just a gap in the law, even if there is a penumbra of norms surrounding a given subject (including natural law standards such as 'humanity' and so on), and that more specific norms simply cannot be plucked out of the political chaos in hard cases.

---

[90] Boyle and Chinkin (n 68) 268, 310.
[91] *Legality of the Use by a State of Nuclear Weapons in Armed Conflict* (Advisory Opinion) 1996 ICJ Reports 66 (8 July 1996) para 18.
[92] Higgins (n 79) 5.
[93] A Paulus, 'International Adjudication' in S Besson and J Tasioulas (eds) *The Philosophy of International Law* (OUP, Oxford 2010) 207, 219–220.
[94] Ibid 222.

As Paulus writes, 'international adjudication cannot, and should not, disregard the legal sources from which it derives its authority'.[95] The Appeals Chamber attempted to squeeze new anti-terrorism norms through the aperture of customary law, when even widely-crafted apertures have structural limits. A more open approach to adjudication might acknowledge that customary law does not provide an answer, admit the legal indeterminacy, and instead 'distinguish between the constraints of the law and the reasons for their adoption of a particular solution and their preference for one principle over another'.[96]

A failure to judge by reference to law ultimately results in 'arbitrariness and thereby in a dereliction of duty'.[97] It fuels and vindicates often unfounded state anxiety about judicial law-making[98] and intrusion on sovereign autonomy to make law. It manifests as a lack of transparency and indeterminacy which 'enables the (ab) use of international law for political purposes hidden under the alleged objectivity of legal analysis'.[99] Judges are undoubtedly wedded to the ideological apparatus of values which constitutes the international legal order, but they have to play by the rules, and should not substitute fidelity to law for their own ideological convictions or preferences as to what the ideal law ought to be.

## Conclusion

While the Appeals Chamber's decision is inadequate in its use of sources, ultimately it is unsatisfactory because it imposes retrospective criminal liability, contrary to general principles of law, international criminal law and human rights law. It was hardly foreseeable to a person in Lebanon in 2005 that terrorism as such was an international customary law crime, or that such crime would be used ostensibly in 'interpreting' domestic offences, but in reality to import a wholly new offence. This is so even if the conduct of such persons is morally abhorrent. The decision in some ways is an instance of institutional bias towards its own regime – favouring international criminal liabilities over human rights values. Incorrect and rights-violating decisions are not good for international law or public confidence in its institutions and processes.

The authority of the decision does not end with its publication. As others note, 'the law-making effect of all judicial decisions is contingent on the response of a broader international community and cannot be presumed in advance'.[100] The

---

[95] Ibid 219.
[96] Ibid 221.
[97] Ibid 224.
[98] Boyle and Chinkin (n 68) 267.
[99] Paulus (n 93) 218.
[100] Boyle and Chinkin (n 68) 311.

decision may be subsequently endorsed as a statement of customary law,[101] or states may push along its emergence over time if the decision is thought a little premature. But a number of factors will likely limit its authoritativeness and precedent-like effects. The Tribunal is a hybrid court, not an international one, even if its judicial composition tilts slightly towards international over national, and its establishment derived in part from the Security Council.[102] It was established on an ad hoc basis to deal with a very small number of violent acts in one country in a very short space of time, rather than being of wider global significance.

Further, its statutory mandate explicitly specified Lebanese criminal law as the substantive applicable law, and reference to substantive international criminal law was not envisaged at the time of drafting. Its views (as a hybrid-domestic tribunal empowered to apply domestic law) on international criminal law must necessarily be taken with a grain of salt, even if the President happened to be a very eminent international criminal lawyer – whose passing is mourned by all, and whose towering legacy will survive him and this last wobbly judgment. Moreover, the decision was not made in respect of a particular defendant in a criminal trial on foot, but was a preliminary proceeding to clarify certain legal matters.

As individual cases later proceeded to trial, in July 2012 the Appeals Chamber rejected a defence request to reconsider its earlier decision that terrorism is a customary law crime.[103] It found that the Defence had failed to show any prejudice to the accused because they had not been charged with acts falling within the extended international definition of terrorism, and were instead only charged with more conventional terrorism offences under Lebanese law. It was therefore unnecessary to reconsider whether terrorism was an international crime. The earlier decision that terrorism is a customary crime thus remains of theoretical but as yet no dispositive effect in real cases, further marginalizing its precedential significance. On balance, an international crime of terrorism is far from established, but the story is far from finished.

---

[101] As soon occurred in the English case of *Regina v Mohammed Gul*, Court of Appeal (Criminal Division), 22 February 2012, [2012] EWCA Crim 280

[102] UN SC Resolution 1757 (2007) UN Doc S/RES/1757 (30 May 2007) and Annex ('Agreement between the United Nations and the Lebanese Republic on the establishment of a Special Tribunal for Lebanon').

[103] *Prosecutor v Ayyash et al*, Decision on Defence Requests for Reconsideration of the Appeals Chamber's Decision of 16 February 2011, 18 July 2012, STL-11-01/PT/AC/R176bis.

# Damned If You Don't: Liability for Omissions in International Criminal Law

## Christopher Gosnell

In 2009, the ICTY Appeals Chamber upheld Veselin Šljivančanin's conviction for torture, and added a conviction for murder, on the basis of 'aiding and abetting by omission'. Šljivančanin was not convicted of superior responsibility because his subordinates, a military police unit that had transferred the victims into the custody of a group of militiamen who killed the victims; he was instead found to have been an accessory of the perpetraitors for having failed to prevent the transfer. A three-part test of liability was applied: (i) knowledge of the likely crime of the perpetrator; (ii) a duty of action arising from a rule of international humanitarian law; and (iii) a 'capacity to act'.[1] Along the way, the Appeals Chamber abandoned the requirement that the assistance of an aider and abettor be 'specifically directed' towards the crime.[2] Šljivančanin was therefore not required to have withdrawn the military police for the purpose of facilitating the crime, nor, according to the Appeals Chamber, was there any need to show that the militiamen were aware, much less encouraged, by the alleged inactivity.[3] At least two other accused have been convicted under the same form of liability.[4]

Aiding and abetting, by virtue of this jurisprudential expansion, has now emerged as the widest and most permissive form of liability in international criminal law. The accused need neither intend that the crime be accomplished, nor

---

[1]   *Prosecutor v Mrkšić & Šljivančanin* (Appeal Judgment) ICTR-95-13/1-A (5 May 2009) paras 148–159.

[2]   *Prosecutor v Mrkšić & Šljivančanin* (Appeal Judgment) (n 1) para 159. See *Prosecutor v Lukić & Lukić* (Appeal Judgment) IT-98-32/1-A (4 December 2012) para 424.

[3]   Šljivančanin's sentence was later reduced after a review hearing, but without calling into question the legal standards established: *Prosecutor v Mrkšić & Šljivančanin* (Review Judgment) IT-9-13/1-R.1 (8 December 2010).

[4]   *Prosecutor v Popović et al.* (Trial Judgement) IT-05-88-T (10 June 2010) paras 1543-1563 (convicting Borovčanin, for whom the author acted as counsel, of aiding and abetting murder by omission) and paras 1985-1991 (convicting Pandurević on the same basis).

coordinate in any fashion with the perpetrators, as is required in respect of joint criminal enterprise ('JCE'). Nor need the aider and abettor, unlike a superior, have effective control over the perpetrators. The 'assistance' rendered may be no more than a failure to discharge a legal duty that of which might otherwise have impeded the commission of the crime. Šljivančanin, for example, was found liable despite having no *de jure* authority over he military police because he could 'likely' have prevailed on them not to withdraw, or could 'at the very least' have circumvented the chain of command and reported the improper transfer of custody to a higher authority.[5] The implication is that a mere failure to try gives rise to criminal liability.

This chapter suggests that such a doctrine of aiding and abetting by omission is misconceived. This doctrine, unlike that of JCE, has emerged without any comparative analysis of the domestic law of States, much less the traditional sources of customary international law. It has been elaborated by analogy, without verifying whether these analogies can be found in domestic or international law. In particular, the Appeals Chamber has failed to analyse how domestic legal systems categorize different types of omission; how liability is assessed in relation to those different categories; and whether aiding and abetting has any place in that analysis.

Such an analysis reveals that the form of omission liability defined by the Appeals Chamber is virtually unknown in domestic legal systems. Omission liability in domestic law encompasses two distinct situations: (i) a failure to act directly perceived by the perpetrator, or pre-arranged by agreement, where there is an encouraging effect, or understanding, between the omitter and the perpetrator in respect of the crime; and (ii) a failure to fulfill a legal duty to avert harm, regardless of whether the physical perpetrator was encouraged or even aware of the omission. The first category may give rise to accessorial liability, including aiding and abetting. The second category, in contrast, is usually treated in one of two ways: as (i) 'commission by omission' in respect of the ultimate crime; or as (ii) 'pure omission' or 'statutory breach' in respect of a prescribed duty. The latter does not lead to liability for the acts of third parties – such as, for example, a murder committed by a third party subsequent to a breach of a statutory duty by an accused; liability may instead be imposed for the duty breached. 'Commission by omission' can indeed lead to liability for the outcome, but only where there is: (i) *mens rea* in relation to the result; and (ii) a particularly intense and precise legal duty to act. Not all duties of action give rise to criminal liability for the acts of third parties who take advantage of the situation; on the contrary, very few duties can give rise to such liability. Some legal systems prohibit this form of liability entirely, or require that this consequence be expressly specified by statute.

The doctrine of 'aiding and abetting by omission,' as articulated by the Appeals Chamber, confuses the categories described above. The failure to consider 'commission by omission' is particularly curious given that the Appeals Chamber, in *Blaškić* and *Ntagerura*, had so analyzed the omissions of those accused. The

---

[5] *Prosecutor v Mrkšić & Šljivančanin* (Appeal Judgment) IT-95-13/1-A (5 May 2009) para 96, 98. See *Prosecutor v Lukić & Lukić* (Appeal Judgment) IT-98-32/1-A (4 December 2012) paras 95-100.

abandonment of that approach is not even discussed in the *Mrkšić & Šljivančanin* Judgement. States, given the position of their own legal systems, cannot be taken in the absence of any significant practice, to have agreed to such a sweeping and unprecedented form of liability. Many would probably view it as repugnant. One eminent English commentator, who more than twenty years ago hypothesized about a similar concept of aiding and abetting liability, characterized it as 'monstrously unjust'.[6]

## I. The General Standards of Aiding and Abetting Liability

The ICTY, ICTR, SCSL and ICC Statutes all expressly recognize 'aiding and abetting' as a form of criminal participation.[7] The precise elements of this form of liability, especially in relation to the ICTY, ICTR and SCSL statutes, are left for elaboration by the judges.

Defining the *mens rea* of aiding and abetting can be more complex than other forms of liability because of the uniquely bifurcated nature of the *actus reus*. The *actus reus* of aiding and abetting has been defined as 'provid[ing] practical assistance, encouragement, or moral support to the perpetration of a crime or underlying offence' that has 'a substantial effect upon the commission of a crime or underlying offence.'[8] The unusual aspect of the *actus reus*, is that the *actus reus* involves two separate actions by two different actors: the perpetrator's commission of the crime; and the assistance thereto provided by the aider and abettor. Since a criminal act is traditionally defined as the 'union, or joint operation, of act and intent,'[9] one would expect that the mental state must relate to the assistance as such, not to the crime. On the other hand, the quality of the action as 'assistance' must depend in some way on knowledge of the assisting character of one's actions, which implies some mental state vis à vis the perpetrator's intentions.

The minimum threshold of liability is articulated in the French Criminal Code which defines complicity (*complicité*) as 'knowingly facilitat[ing] the preparation or consummation of the offence'.[10] Liability can therefore arise where the alleged

---

[6] G Williams, 'Letting Offences Happen' (1990) *Crim LR* 780, 788.

[7] 'Complicity' is the general form of accessorial liability in the STL Statute. The word is sometimes taken to imply meanings that go beyond accessorial liability, and is there not used in the present discussion. The terms 'accessorial liability' and 'aiding and abetting' are used as synonyms.

[8] *Prosecutor v Milutinović et al* (Judgment) IT-05-87-T (26 February 2009) para 89. See *Prosecutor v Gacumbitsi* (Judgment) ICTR-2001-64-T (17 June 2004) para 286.

[9] Section 20, California Penal Code (defining a criminal act as the 'union, or joint operation, of act and intent'); B Bouloc, *Droit pénal général* (Dalloz, Paris 2009) 234 ('*Il faut que l'élément moral se joigne a l'élément material (qu'il apparaisse avant ou au même moment) pour que l'infraction soit constitué*').

[10] French Code pénal, art 121-7 ('*Est complice d'un crime ou d'un délit la personne qui sciemment, par aide ou assistance, en a facilité la préparation ou la consommation*'); Bouloc (n 9)

accessory is indifferent – or even opposed – to the subsequent crime, but nevertheless knowingly goes along with providing the assistance. Oskar Schindler's laudable ulterior motives would thus in no way negate his liability as an accessory to the Nazis who enslaved and then killed his workers.[11] The harshness of this outcome can be particularly acute where, as in some national systems, even minimal assistance is viewed as sufficient to satisfy the *actus reus*.[12] Not only would Oskar Schindler be liable of aiding and abetting slavery, murder and other crimes, but so would anyone else with even a relatively minor role in supporting that system. The net of prima facie liability is cast even wider in some legal systems, such as South Africa, Germany and Isreal, where 'knowledge' is defined accord to what a person can foresee is the probable effect of their conduct, and yet consciously proceeds to give the assistance with that foresight (*dolus eventualis*).[13]

Many other legal systems have balked at the imposition of such a broad form of criminal liability and have insisted on more than mere 'knowledge' of the assisting character of one's acts. This debate emerged sharply in the United States in the middle of the 20th Century, where Judge Learned Hand declared in one of his opinions that the accessory must 'associate himself with the venture, that he participate in it as something that he wishes to bring about, that he seek by his action to make it succeed'.[14] American jurists divided sharply over this issue. Professor Herbert Wechsler, as reporter of the Model Penal Code, proposed

---

300. See also AP Simester and GR Sullivan, *Criminal Law: Theory and Doctrine* (3rd edn Hart Publishing, Oxford 2007) 208; *Dunlop & Sylvester v The Queen* [1979] 2 SCR 881, 13–14 ('A person cannot properly be convicted of aiding or abetting in the commission of acts which he does not know may be or are intended … One must be able to infer that the accused had prior knowledge that an offence of the type committed was planned').

[11] Simester and Sullivan (n 10) 208; D Ormerod, *Smith and Hogan Criminal Law* (12th edn OUP, Oxford 2008) 195.

[12] Simester and Sullivan (n 10) 199 ('the assistance need not be substantial'); J Pradel, *Droit pénale comparé* (3rd edn Dalloz, Paris 2008) 129 ('*Une assistance très restreinte de la part d'un participant suffit à en faire un complice*'); M Ferrante, 'Argentina' in Heller and Dubber (eds) *The Handbook of Comparative Criminal Law* (Stanford University Press, Stanford, 2011) 33 ('it takes very little for an action to ground as accomplice liability'); I Kugler, 'Israel' in KJ Heller and M Dubber (eds) *The Handbook of Comparative Criminal Law* (Stanford University Press, Stanford 2011) 370 ('it is sufficient that the act could have potentially facilitated the commission of the crime').

[13] JM Burchell and J Milton, *Principles of Criminal Law* (3rd edn Juta, Landsdowne 2005) 605; M Dubber, 'Criminalizing Complicity' (2007) 5 *JICJ* 977, 992;

[14] *US v Peoni*, 100 F.2d 401, 402 (2nd Cir 1938). See US Model Penal Code, s. 206(4) ('When causing a particular result is an element of an offense, an accomplice in the conduct causing such result is an accomplice in the commission of the offense if he acts with the kind of culpability, if any, with respect to that result that is sufficient for the commission of the offense'); *State v Moreno*, 104 P3d 628, 631 (Or Ct App 2005) (acquitting a person selling large number of over-the-counter drugs to purchasers whom he knew were likely to concentrate the products into illegal drugs, on the basis that 'the mental state required for criminal liability on and aid and abet theory is essentially the same as for the principal's liability in this circumstance').

that accessorial liability should follow the approach later adopted in the French code – simply knowledge of the crime plus voluntariness of the assistance. He also proposed, however, mitigating the harshness of the doctrine by elevating the *actus reus* threshold to 'substantially facilitat[ing] commission of the crime'.[15] The American Model Penal Code as ultimately adopted reflected a compromise that partly adopted Judge Hand's approach, requiring that the accomplice act 'with the purpose of promoting or facilitating the commission of the offence'. Most American jurisdictions have interpreted this language to mean that the assister must have the 'conscious object' of furthering or achieving the crime.[16] Hong Kong and India appear to require that as well.[17] Andrew Ashworth has explained the policy justifications for these different standards:

> the 'knowledge' standard 'would also lead to the conviction of a shopkeeper who knows that his customer plans to use a certain item for a crime and who nevertheless sells the item, and it is dissatisfaction with this outcome which led the framers of the American Model Penal Code to impose the more stringent requirement that the accomplice should have acted with the purpose of promoting or facilitating the offence. The effects of that narrower doctrine is to ensure that citizens

---

[15] As quoted in N Abrams, 'The Material Support Terrorism Offenses: Perspectives Derived from the (Early) Model Penal Code' (2005) 1 *Nat'l Security L & Policy* 5, 17.

[16] *US v Irwin*, 149 F.3d 565, 572 (7th Cir 1998); J Decker, 'The Mental State Requirement for Accomplice Liability in American Criminal Law' (2008) 60 *SCL Rev* 237, 247–248. A minority of States have adopted a lower standard: *People v Green*, 130 Cal App 3d 1, 6 ('Under California case law, the only facts necessary to convict a person of aiding and abetting are (1) that the person aid in the commission of a crime (2) with the knowledge of the perpetrator's unlawful purpose or intent'); C Courteau, 'The Mental Element Required for Accomplice Liability: A Topic Note' (1998) 59 *La L Rev* 325, 334.

[17] Jackson, M., 'Criminal Law', in M. Gaylord et al., *Introduction to Crime, Law and Justice in Hong Kong*, Hong Kong University Press (Hong Kong 2009) 28; *Halsbury's Laws of Hong Kong*, s. 130.055 ('there must be a common purpose between the principal and the aider and abettor and an intention to aid or encourage the persons who commit the offence or, a readiness to aid and encourage them if required.'); *R. v Lam Kit*, [1988] 1 HKC 679, 680 ('it is not only necessary to prove that he was present while the offence is committed, that he knew an offence was being committed and that his presence, in fact, gave encouragement to the perpetrators but it must be proved that he intended to give that encouragement, that he *wilfully* encouraged'); *R. v Leung Tak-yin* [1987] 2 HKC 250 ('But the fact that a person was voluntarily and *purposely* present witnessing the commission of a crime, and offered no opposition to it, though he might reasonably be expected to prevent and had the power so to do, or at least to express his dissent, might, under some circumstances, afford cogent evidence upon which a jury would be justified in finding that he wilfully encouraged and so aided and abetted') (italics added) (citing to *R. v Clarkson* 1971 55 Cr. App. R. 445); Yeo, S., 'India' in Heller and Dubber (n 12) 296, citing *Mohd Jamal v Emperor*, A.I.R. 1953 All 668. ('The offence of abetment, however … cannot be made out. Appellant 2 certainly aided appellant 1 in driving the car but it cannot be said that he intended that it should be driven rashly and negligently.')

are not treated as their fellow citizens' keepers, a sturdy individualist approach.[18]

German doctrine, which applies a *dolus eventualis* standard of knowledge, has been responsive to the same concern in its own way. An exception to liability is recognized where the assistance involves 'neutral acts' or 'vocation-specific' conduct (*berufstypisches Verhalten*), i.e. acts that the potential aider and abettor performs as part of his general professional duties or daily routines (such as, to stay with the example above, a hardware store owner who sells tools for a living which are used by some of his customers to commit crimes). The assistance in such cases must be 'intentionally render[ed]' and 'aimed at a criminal act'. As explained by the German Federal Court of Justice (BGH) in acquitting two former East German deputy border commanders of aiding and abetting the murder of individuals while attempting fleeing from East to West Germany, despite their significant roles in maintaining the border control system:

> [T]he BGH has established the following principles in cases of vocation-specific ('*berufstypisch*') 'neutral' acts: If the acts of the principal offender are solely aimed at a criminal act, and the person assisting him knows this, then the assistance should be regarded as aiding and abetting. Under these circumstances, his acts lose the ordinary, everyday character and should instead be viewed as solidarity with the principal offender. Otherwise, the assistance is not unlawful. The annual orders [by the border commander] did not solely concern criminally relevant conduct in relation to the border crossing, but also legitimate matters of national security of the former GDR, as well as external border protection. The contribution of the two accused to the issuance of order no. 40 was limited to their military tasks which had been delegated to them, and which were not connected to the laying of mines along the border. The contribution was therefore vocation-specific and, in relation to the crimes, 'neutral'... In light of these facts, the conduct of the accused in relation to the giving of the annual orders did not unlawfully contribute to the crimes.[19]

---

[18] A Ashworth, *Principles of Criminal Law* (6th edn OUP, Oxford 2009) 417.

[19] German Federal Court of Justice (BGH), Case No. 4 StR 453/00, Judgement of 8 March 2001, 10. See also I. Strafsenat Urteil vom 14. November 1904 g. B. u. Gen. Rep. 1178/04, 323-324 (acquitting a lawyer who had given incorrect advice to the wife and son of a prison inmate on furlough that they were legally permitted to assist his escape: 'To establish knowledge (*Wissentlichkeit*) equivalent to intention (*Vorsätzlichkeit*) it is not sufficient that the aider is aware that the perpetrator intends to commit the relevant offence. For the subjective element of the offence it is necessary that the perpetrator gives his help and advice in the knowledge that through his acts the commission of the offence intended by the principal offender is furthered, and that thereby also the intention (*Wille*) of the person giving advice is directed towards this commission (*Erfolg*).... If the lawyer ... intends nothing more than to give his professional and advice in accordance with his duty, and he is aware that his

A slightly less robust definition of 'purpose' is found in some other jurisdictions. The Canadian Criminal Code requires that any assistance be 'provided for the purpose of aiding' another to commit a crime,[20] but the courts have generally interpreted this as being satisfied when there is no less than actual knowledge or 'wilful blindness' as to the assisting character of the act.[21] Australian courts, applying similar statutory language, have apparently adopted the same approach.[22] English courts, not bound by any statutory definition, appear to have vacillated between the Canadian approach and the American approach to 'purpose'.[23]

The first significant pronouncement by a large number of States on the definition of aiding and abetting in international criminal law is Article 25(3)(c) of the ICC Statute. The 1945 IMT Charter, after all, says nothing about the standards for assessing aiding and abetting; post-World War II caselaw is, at best, contradictory[24]

---

expert opinion leads to the commission of an offence, but his intention (*Wille*) has nothing to do with the consequence of his legal advice, then knowing/deliberate (*wissentlichen*) aiding is out of the question. But if his conscious and deliberate/intentional acts (*Geistes und Willenstätigkeit*) are not only directed to practicing his profession in giving advice, but also to promote the commission of a crime by means of his professional advice, then, and only then, does aiding exist within the meaning of the criminal code.')

[20] Criminal Code of Canada, s. 21(1): 'Everyone is a party to an offence who ... does or omits to do anything for the purpose of aiding any person to commit it, or (c) abets any person in committing it'; *R. v Hibbert* [1995] 2 SCR 973 (Sup Ct Canada) para 39 ('For these reasons, I conclude that the expression 'for the purpose of aiding' in s. 21(1)(*b*) properly understood, does not require that the accused actively view the commission of the offence he or she is aiding as desirable in and of itself').

[21] *R v Roach* (2004) 192 CCC (3d) 557 (Ont CA) ('[Knowledge] will include actual knowledge or willful blindness, but will not include recklessness'); D Stuart, *Canadian Criminal Law* (5th edn Thompson, Scarborough 2007).

[22] S Bronitt, 'Australia' in Heller and Dubber (n 12) 61; J Dietrich, 'The Liability of Accessories under Statute, in Equity, and in Criminal Law: Some Common Problems and (Perhaps) Some Common Solutions' (2010) 34 *Melb UL Rev* 106, 121–122, 128–129 ('Actual knowledge clearly suffices. The courts have gone a little further, however, and it has been held that willful blindness suffices as 'actual knowledge' but that recklessness or carelessness do not').

[23] A Ashworth (n 18) 416–418 (describing 'cases in which recklessness is relied upon have been rare' although not unprecedented, and that 'English courts have not always felt comfortable with the proposition that knowledge of the principal's intention (without purpose) should suffice for accomplice liability'); Ormerod (n 11) 199; *Gillick v West Norfolk and Wisbech A.H.A.*, [1986] AC 112.

[24] At least two cases applied a robust version of the 'purpose' standard described above. In *The Ministries Case*, a banker, Karl Rasche, was acquitted by a U.S. military court of aiding and abetting enslavement and other crimes notwithstanding that he had provided money to the SS knowing that it would be used in their business activities, which employed criminal means. The court held: 'Bankers do not approve or make loans in the number and amount made by the Dresdner Bank without ascertaining, having, or obtaining information or knowledge as to the purpose for which the loan is sought, and how it is to be used. It is inconceivable to us that the defendant did not possess that knowledge, and we find that he did. The real question is, is it a crime to make a loan, knowing or having good

and, in the case of decisions made by national military courts, of dubious relevance to State practice;[25] and the 1996 ILC Draft Code of Crimes, promulgated by a committee of experts and having never received any State approval, must be taken to have been superseded by the Rome negotiations leading to the ICC Statute. Article 25(3)(c) of the ICC Statute is all the more significant as an indicator of customary international law given that the provision was apparently hotly and closely debated. As one participant has written:

> It was a very contentious provision, with some delegations seeking explicit reference to intention, notwithstanding the important complication that the word 'intention' has different meanings in different legal systems ... Other delegations were wedded to the term 'knowledge,' believing that it better reflected the standard that was employed in their national practice and that had been endorsed in the [international] jurisprudence ... Negotiators struggled to find compromise wording and ultimately settled on using neither 'intent' nor 'knowledge' but 'purpose'.[26]

Article 25(3)(c) prescribes criminal responsibility for anyone who *'for the purpose of facilitating* the commission of such a crime, aids, abets, or otherwise assists in its commission or its attempted commission, including providing the means for its commission'. The language uncannily reflects that of the United States Model Penal Code. At least one participant in the Rome Conference confirms that this is the source for the language adopted.[27] Although not every provision in the ICC Statute can be automatically accepted as declaratory of customary international law, the very least that can be said is that there was no consensus amongst State

---

reason to believe that the borrower will us[e] the funds in financing enterprises which are employed in using labor in violation of either national or international law? .... Loans or sale of commodities to be used in an unlawful enterprise may well be condemned from a moral standpoint and reflect no credit on the part of the lender or seller in either case, but the transaction can hardly be said to be a crime.' *United States v Ernst von Weizsaecker, et al.*, Judgment of 31 July 1948, reprinted in Trials of War Criminals before the Nurnberg Military Tribunals under Control Council Law No. 10, Vol. XIV (1949), 622. See also the *'Hechingen Case'* as translated in: A Cassese, 'Modes of Participation in Crimes Against Humanity,' (2009) 7 *JICJ* 131..

[25] The often-cited 'Zykon B' case was decided by a British military court that neither explained the standards it was applying, nor identified the body of law that it purported to apply. *The Zyklon B Case, Trial of Bruno Tesch and Two Others*, Case No. 9 (British Military Court, Hamburg, 1946) 102.

[26] Brief of David J Scheffer, *Presbyterian Church of Sudan v Talisman Energy* (19 May 2010) 12.

[27] K Ambos 'Article 25' in O Triffterer (ed) *Commentary on the Rome Statute* (3rd edn Beck, Munich 2008) 757; *Prosecutor v Mbarushimana*, (Transcript) ICC-01/04-01/10 (20 September 2011), 5 ('I was a part of the German delegation in Rome and I was participating in the working group of general principals which negotiated, among others, this provision.')

representatives at the Rome Conference in favour of a *mens rea* standard of aiding and abetting based purely on a knowledge standard. 'Purpose' appears to have been the only common denominator mental element for aiding and abetting liability acceptable to States.[28] In contrast, the provision says nothing about the minimum quantum of assistance required to satisfy the *actus reus*.

The first significant definition of aiding and abetting in ICTY jurisprudence, the *Furundžija* Trial Judgement, was pronounced some six months after the adoption of the Rome Treaty, before it had been ratified as the ICC Statute. The Trial Chamber did refer to Article 25(3)(c) of the Rome Treaty, but only in passing and only in the context of its discussion of *actus reus*.[29] After a short discussion of various post-World War II cases and the ILC's Draft Code, the Trial Chamber concluded that the appropriate *mens rea* standard is 'the knowledge that [one's own] actions will assist the perpetrator in the commission of the crime'.[30] The Trial Chamber, curiously, refers to a general provision on *mens rea* in the ICC Statute but without considering the element of 'purpose' enshrined in Article 25(3)(c). Subsequent ICTY and ICTR cases have adopted the reasoning in the *Furundžija* Trial Judgement without significant discussion, other than to bifurcate the required knowledge into two

---

[28] Some may argue that Article 25(3)(d) reflects a lower standard of aiding and abetting liability, as it prescribes liability for a person who 'contributes to the commission or attempted commission of such a crime by a group of persons acting with a common purpose.' But Article 25(3)(d) also requires that the 'contribution shall be intentional', implying that the person providing the assistance might need to share the intent of the group. This is how the provision has been interpreted by ICTY Trial Chambers that have considered the provision, and is implied by the drafting history of the provision, which apparently started as a typical common law conspiracy provision, before it was modified after objections from civil law countries. *Furundžija* (Judgment) IT-95-17/1-T (10 December 1998) para 216; K Ambos 'Article 25' in O Triffterer (ed) *Commentary on the Rome Statute* (3rd edn Beck, Munich 2008) 757-758. The need for a joint criminal enterprise provision in the ICC Statute may derive from the fact that Article 25(3)(a) is a pure perpetration, co-perpetration and indirect perpetration provision that always requires that the accused play an 'essential' role in the crime, whereas a participant in a JCE need only make a 'significant' contribution to the crime. *Prosecutor v Lubanga* (Judgement pursuant to Article 74 of the Statute) ICC-01/04-01/06-2842 (14 March 2012) para 999. Further, interpreting Article 25(3)(d) as merely 'aiding and abetting a group' would lead to the anomalous proposition that whether or not the purpose standard applies depends on whether one is assisting an individual or a group. There is not apparent justification for such a distinction.

[29] *Furundžija* (Trial Judgment) (n 28) paras 193–235; *Prosecutor v Tadić* (Opinion and Judgment) IT-94-1-T (7 May 1997) paras 688–796.

[30] *Furundžija* (Trial Judgment) (n 28) para 245; *Tadić* (Opinion and Judgment) (n 29) para 692 ('knowingly participated'); *Prosecutor v Blagojević et al* (Judgment) IT-02-60-A (9 May 2007) para 127 ('the requisite mental element of aiding and abetting is knowledge that the acts performed assist the commission of the specific crime of the principal perpetrator'); *Prosecutor v Ntagerura et al* (Judgment) ICTR-99-46-A (7 July 2006) para 370. STL Statute, Art 3(1)(b) (setting the minimum mental state for aiding and abetting a criminal group as being the 'the knowledge of the intention of the group to commit a crime'); *Prosecutor v Brima et al* (Judgment) SCSL-2004-16-A (22 February 2008) paras 242–243.

prongs: (i) knowledge that one's own acts provide assistance to a crime; and (ii) knowledge of the essential elements of the crime, and that at least one crime is within the perpetrator's contemplation.[31] Never has there been any discussion as to whether the 'knowledge' standard is established as a matter of customary international law.

The absence of any such discussion in ICTY jurisprudence may be attributed to a subsequent development in the definition of the *actus reus* of aiding and abetting. Shortly after the *Furundžija* Trial Judgement, the Appeals Chamber in *Tadić*, consisting of two of the judges who had rendered the *Furundžija* Trial Judgement, added an element to aiding and abetting: that the acts of the aider and abettor be 'specifically directed to assist, encourage or lend moral support to the perpetration of a specific crime.'[32] This phrase subsequently came to be associated with discussions of *actus reus*, even though it implies a state of mind rather than a characteristic of the action itself. It is hard to conceive of assistance 'specifically directed' to a crime that would not also have been performed by the actor for that purpose. Furthermore, the *Furundžija* Trial Chamber had concluded that the minimum threshold for the *actus reus* is that the assistance 'have a substantial effect on the crime' which would require that the an accused have the capacity 'either to influence' the assisting action 'or to prevent it'.[33] The 'substantial effect' or 'substantially contributed to' standard, combined with 'specific direction,' would in substance, appear to exclude any assistance not rendered with the purpose of assisting the crime. With the *Tadić* 'specific direction' element, there was no need

---

[31]   *Milutinović et al* (Judgment) (n 8) para 93; *Prosecutor v Kunarac* (Judgment) IT-96-23-T (22 February 2001) para 392 ('he must know of the essential elements of the crime (including the perpetrator's *mens rea*) and take the conscious decision to act in the knowledge that he thereby supports the commission of the crime'); *Blagojević et al* (Appeal Judgment) (n 30) paras 127, 221-223; *Popović et al* (Judgement) (n 4) para 1017.

[32]   *Prosecutor v Tadić* (Judgment) IT-94-1-A (15 July 1999) para 229 ('The aider and abettor carries out acts specifically directed to assist, encourage or lend moral support to the perpetration of a certain specific crime (murder, extermination, rape, torture, wanton destruction of civilian property, etc.) and this support has a substantial effect upon the perpetration of the crime'); *Prosecutor v Simić et al* (Judgment) IT-95-9-A (28 November 2006) para 85; *Prosecutor v Vasiljević* (Judgment) IT-98-32-A (25 February 2004) para 102; *Ntagerura et al* (Appeal Judgment) (n 30) para 370; *Prosecutor v Krnojelac* (Judgment) IT-97-25-A (17 September 2003) para 33; *Prosecutor v Nahimana et al* (Appeal Judgment) (n 37) para 482; *Prosecutor v Muvunyi* (Judgment) ICTR-2000-55A-A (29 August 2008) para 72.

[33]   *Furundžija* (Trial Judgment) (n 28) paras 223, 234. See *Prosecutor v Orić* (Judgment) IT-03-68-A (3 July 2008) para 41; *Prosecutor v Fofana and Kondewa* (Judgment) SCSL-04-14-A (28 May 2008) para 71; *Nahimana* (Appeal Judgment) insert ICTR-99-52-A (28 November 2007) para 482 ('substantially contributed to').

for anyone to challenge the non-inclusion of the purpose standard[34] from the definition of aiding and abetting in ICTY or ICTR jurisprudence.[35]

That all changed in 2007. Blagojević argued before the Appeals Chamber that his assistance to a crime had not been 'specifically directed' because his acts all fell within the ambit of his regular duties. Not only was the argument rejected on the facts, it induced the Appeals Chamber to question whether 'specific direction' was a separate element from the requirement that the assistance to the crime must be 'substantial'.[36] The criterion was then unambiguously abandoned for the first time in the *Mrkšić & Šljivančanin* Appeal Judgment, without any justification or explanation, and without any further consideration as to whether the remaining elements of aiding and abetting complied with customary international law.[37] The 'specific direction' requirement has re-emerged in at least four subsequent appeals judgments of the ICTR,[38] but the most recent ICTY Appeals Judgement on the issue – over two sharp dissenting opinions -- has reaffirmed that 'specific direction' is not an element of aiding and abetting.[39]

These general issues of 'purpose' and 'specific direction' are, of course, highly relevant in the specific circumstance of omissions. An omission designed to facilitate a crime is one thing, whereas, as discussed in the next section, imposing liability for failing to prevent an unwanted crime quite another. A further preliminary issue, however, is whether the *actus reus* of 'helping' or 'encouraging' has to be known to the perpetrator. The scenario almost never arises in respect of positive acts, and is even difficult to imagine in theory: people seldom assist others covertly to commit crimes. Words typically used to describe the *actus reus* of accessorial liability – such as 'encourage', 'assist', 'help', 'incite' or 'give moral support' – suggest that assistance typically requires, or involves, some level of mutual awareness. Similarly, assistance given after the crime must be based on advance or contemporaneous

---

[34] The 'substantial' threshold has already been foreshadowed as the standard that will likely be applied at the ICC as well: *Situation in the DRC: Prosecutor v Mbarushimana* (Decision on the Confirmation of Charges) ICC-01/04-01/10-465-Red (16 December 2011) paras 277–285 (*obiter* comment that 'a substantial contribution to the crime may be contemplated' in respect of accessorial liability under 25(3)(c) and finding that 25(3)(d) whatever its essential requirements may be, requires at least a 'significant contribution')'; WA Schabas, *The International Criminal Court: A Commentary on the Rome Statute* (OUP, Oxford 2010) 435.

[35] The early jurisprudence also implied that the 'substantial effect' requirement would be applied robustly. The 'substantial effect' requirement, though it has been consistently applied in ICTY and ICTR jurisprudence has been gradually accorded less and less significance.

[36] *Blagojević et al* (Appeal Judgment) (n 30) para 189.

[37] *Mrkšić & Šljivančanin* (Appeal Judgement) (n 1) para 159 ('specific direction' is not an essential ingredient of the *actus reus* of aiding and abetting').

[38] *Prosecutor v Kalimanzira* (Judgement) ICTR-05-88-A (20 October 2010) para 74; *Prosecutor v Ntawukulilyayo* (Judgement) ICTR-2005-82-A (14 December 2011), paras 214, 216; *Prosecutor v Rukundo* (Judgement) ICTR-01-70-A (20 October 2010) para. 52.

[39] *Lukić & Lukić* (Appeal Judgement) (n 2) (Dissenting opinions of Judges Guney and Agius).

agreement with the perpetrator, also implying that it must somehow impact on the perpetrator's decision to go forward with the crime.[40] On the other hand, the *Tadić* Appeals Chamber, in an effort to distinguish JCE and accessorial liability, remarked in passing that 'the principal may not even know about the accomplice's contribution'.[41] This statement, unimportant in its context and unsupported by even a single source, was then regurgitated by the *Milutinović* Trial Chamber for the much more consequential claim that nothing prevents culpable omissions from constituting the *actus reus* of aiding and abetting in the absence of any knowledge by the perpetrator.[42] No further substantiation is offered for this claim, even though the question was nowhere close to the Appeals Chamber's contemplation in *Tadić*. A parenthetical remark is elevated to a statement of law and, *presto*, without any reference to domestic law the way is opened to a new category of international criminal liability.

Domestic law says little about whether the perpetrator needs to be aware of the assistance. No English case whatsoever supports this view of accessorial liability.[43] French doctrine, as we shall see below, expressly rejects the claim to the extent that it applies to omissions. German law does seem to accept it as a theoretical possibility in respect of positive actions, but without providing specific examples or asserting whether it applies to omissions.[44] The only precedents in respect of positive acts of assistance mentioned in American literature are two nineteenth-century cases, one from Pennsylvania, the other from Alabama.[45] The paucity of support is striking, and comes nowhere close the standard of State practice required for reception into international criminal law.

ICTY jurisprudence, in summary, requires: (i) assistance that has a substantial effect on (i.e. makes a substantial contribution to) the perpetration of the crime (*actus reus*); which was (ii) provided with (a) actual knowledge of, rather than with mere recklessness as to, the assisting character of the act, and (b) with knowledge that the perpetrator will commit one of a number of possible crimes. As the foregoing discussion shows, this standard has never been properly analysed in relation to customary international law. In particular, the ICTY Appeals Chamber has never analysed whether the knowledge standard, denuded of either the 'specific direction' or 'purpose' requirement, complies with customary international law.

---

[40]   *Blagojević et al* (Appeal Judgment) (n 30) paras 179–180; *Prosecutor v Blagojević et al* (Judgment) IT-02-60-T (17 January 2005) para 730; *Prosecutor v Mbarushimana* (Decision on the Confirmation of Charges) (n 34) para 287.

[41]   *Tadić* (Appeal Judgment) (n 32) para 229.

[42]   *Milutinović et al* (Trial Judgment) (n 8) para 92. See *Prosecutor v Simić et al* (Judgment) IT-95-9-T (17 October 2003) para 161.

[43]   Simester and Sullivan (n 10) 200–205 ('there is no English case establishing the point').

[44]   A Schönke and H Schröder, *Strafgesetzbuch*, 28th edn (2010) § 27, marginal nos 14, 15; K Kühl, *Strafgesetzbuch*, 27th edn (2011) 743, 744.

[45]   S Kadish, 'Complicity, Cause and Blame: A Study in the Interpretation of Doctrine' (1985) 73 *Cal L Rev* 323, 345 (citing an Alabama case from 1894 – *Attorney General v Tally*, 102 Ala 25 – and a Pennsylvania case from 1867 – *Commonwealth v Kern*, 1 Brewst 350).

That standard is particularly significant to omissions, which, by their nature, are often ambiguous in relation to the crime perpetrated.

The primary purpose of the foregoing discussion, however, is not to challenge the current definition of aiding and abetting as erroneous, although it probably is. The primary purpose, instead, is to define the parameters of aiding and abetting liability as it has so far been defined in relation to the paradigmatic case of positive actions. The discussion in the following sections is equally valid regardless of which view of the minimum *mens rea* threshold is adopted – whether purpose (specific direction) or knowledge, and whether knowledge is defined as 'conscious' knowledge or could be satisfied according to a *dolus eventualis* standard. Regardless of which of these standards is adopted, the overall question remains is whether omission liability is properly analyzed under the rubric of aiding and abetting, rather than as a species of direct perpetration.

## II. Four Types of Omission and How They Are Treated In Domestic Law

A first type of omission that poses no great difficulty of assessment is when a person commits an initial action that sets in train events leading to a prohibited result without the person intervening to prevent the result. The action of locking a child in a sound-proof dungeon, followed by the inaction of failing to feed or care for the child, is perpetration of murder. The natural and foreseeable consequences of one's initial act remain attributable to the perpetrator regardless of the subsequent inaction.[46] In such cases, the mental and material elements of the crime can be assessed according to the initiating action, and the omissive component of the action poses no great difficulties. The relationship between the ultimate harm and the initial action may often be more complex than in the foregoing example, but the principle remains the

---

[46] The importance of the initiating act, even when not initially recognised by the perpetrator as wrongful, is starkly illustrated in *R v Miller*. A vagrant in a drunken stupor inadvertently set fire to the mattress in the house where he was squatting. Roused by the fire some time later, the vagrant moved to another room without bothering to extinguish it. In convicting the accused, the House of Lords placed great emphasis on the importance of the vagrant's awareness that it was his own act that had started the fire and, thus, created the risk of fire: 'I cannot see any good reason why, so far as liability under criminal law is concerned, it should matter at what point of time before the resultant damage is complete a person becomes aware that he has done a physical act which, whether or not he appreciated it at the time when he did it, does in fact create a risk that property of another will be damaged.' This is not to say that the initial act and the subsequent failure should be viewed as a 'continuing act' – indeed, that approach has been heavily criticised; but the case does illustrate the responsibility for one's own acts 'which sets in train events', as opposed to the acts of others or a natural condition. [1983] 2 AC 161, 176, 179. The special rules in the Model Penal Code for omissions are only applicable when 'unaccompanied by action'; § 2.01(3)(b).

same. This is a first type of omission that could apply to actions that either constitute the direct perpetration of a crime, or assistance thereto.

A second type encompasses omissions that are agreed upon in advance by two people in order to further a crime. A customs officer agrees not to prevent a group of thieves from stealing merchandise from the back entrance of a warehouse. Whether access is facilitated by failing to lock the back door, or actively unlocking it, is immaterial. Either way, the prior agreement is itself an action, of which the failure to lock (or unlocking) is both evidence and execution.[47] Assistance of this kind can also arise spontaneously and can include moral support or encouragement. The mere presence of a person during a rape can tacitly reinforce the perpetrator's behaviour. Physical movement or vehement exhortation is not necessarily required for this effect to arise.[48] By the same token, mere presence is not always sufficient to convey tacit encouragement. The impact of the presence is a factual evaluation to be made in light of all the circumstances.

'Approving bystanders' of this sort are a common feature of international cases. Political or military leaders often seem to show up where crimes are taking place and give implicit support for those crimes by choosing to be present without registering any protest or disagreement. Aiding and abetting liability arises in such circumstances not because of an unfulfilled duty to intervene, but rather because of the encouraging effect of their choice to be present.[49] Liability in such cases is always predicated on the perpetrator's awareness of the bystander's presence, since a person cannot be encouraged by an omission of which he or she is unaware.[50]

---

[47]   Crim 27 Oct 1971 (Bull no 284) (Cour de cassation) (while acknowledging that complicity can arise only from positive and material facts, a customs officer had nevertheless engaged in a 'positive action' by agreeing to the fraudulent removal or merchandise from a warehouse, even though he did not need to engage in any positive action, such as affixing his signature on an authorisation, to permit its removal).

[48]   Bouloc (n 9) 292 ('*la jurisprudence a condamné comme complice l'amant qui avait seulement assisté a l'avortement de sa maitresse, parce que, par sa presence et par son attitude, il avait apporté un appui moral a l'auteur de l'avortement*'); *Jerue v Alaska*, 1994 WL 16196278 (Alaska App) 2 ('a person's failure to act when given the opportunity to obstruct or prevent someone else's criminal conduct may tend to prove that the person was not merely a bystander by, instead was present to facilitate or promote that criminal conduct'); *R v Coney* (1881–1882) 8 QBD 534, 537 (Eng Divisional Court) (overturning the trial judge's charge that mere presence of two passersby at a prize fight 'if unexplained, [is] conclusive proof that he was aiding and abetting the assault' of the fighters on one another, finding instead that it was a matter for the jury to assess whether non-accidental presence in the particular case encouraged the crime).

[49]   *Prosecutor v Seromba* (Judgment) ICTR-2001-66-A (12 March 2008) para 64 ('the crime of aiding and abetting genocide for which he was convicted in not premised on any duty owed to the victims … This fact is only relevant for the assessment of possible aggravating circumstances in the determination of sentence'); *Prosecutor v Ndindabahizi* (Judgment) ICTR-2001-71-I (15 July 2004) para 457 ('It is not the position of authority itself that is important, but rather the encouraging effect that a person holding the office may lend to events').

[50]   *Prosecutor v Akayesu* (Judgment) ICTR-96-4-T (2 September 1998) para 705; *Prosecutor v Furundžija* (Trial Judgment) (n 28) para 207 ('an approving spectator who is held in such respect by the other perpetrators that his presence encourages them in their conduct, may

Some international cases have thus expressly held that 'actual presence' or 'physical presence' is a condition of liability,[51] thus excluding the case of someone who is known to be nearby but does not intervene. The encouraging effect of a failure to intervene may indeed be reinforced by the bystander's position of authority, but liability rests on the encouraging effect of the inaction, not the breach of the legal duty. As the *Brdjanin* Appeals Chamber explained in 2007:

> Aiding and abetting by tacit approval and encouragement ... is not, strictly speaking, criminal responsibility for omission. In the cases where this category was applied, the accused held a position of authority, he was physically present on the scene of the crime, and his non-intervention was seen as tacit approval and encouragement. The Trial Chamber in *Kayishema and Ruzindana* held that 'individual responsibility pursuant to Article 6(1) ... is based, in this instance not on a duty to act, but from the encouragement and support that might be afforded to the principals of the crime from such an omission'. In such cases the combination of a position of authority and physical presence on the crime scene allowed the inference that non-interference by the accused actually amount to tacit approval and encouragement.[52]

The first two categories of omission might incidentally involve the breach of a legal duty. Parents, for example, would surely violate their duty to ensure the well-being of their children by locking them in a dungeon without food. Commanders present during the commission of crimes by their subordinates have a legal duty to stop

---

be guilty of complicity'); *Prosecutor v Limaj* (Judgment) IT-03-66-T (30 November 2005) para 517 ('where the presence bestows legitimacy on, or provides encouragement to, the actual perpetrator, that may be sufficient. In a particular case encouragement may be established by an evident sympathetic and approving attitude to the commission of the relevant act'); *Prosecutor v Blaskić* (Judgment) IT-95-14-T (3 March 2000) para 284; *Prosecutor v Krnojelac* (Judgment) IT-97-25-T (15 March 2002) para 89 ('Presence alone at the scene of the crime is not conclusive of aiding and abetting unless it is demonstrated to have a significant legitimising or encouraging effect on the principal offender').

[51] *Prosecutor v Semanza* (Judgment) ICTR-97-20-T (15 May 2003) para 386 ('This encouragement or support may consist of ... mere presence as an 'approving spectator' ... Criminal responsibility as an 'approving spectator' does require actual presence during the commission of the crime or at least presence in the immediate vicinity of the scene of the crime which is perceived by the actual perpetrator as an approval of his conduct. The authority of an individual is frequently a strong indication that the principal perpetrators will perceive his presence as an act of encouragement'); *Prosecutor v Kayishema & Ruzindana* (Judgment) ICTR-95-1-T (21 May 1999) paras 201–202 (an accused may 'incur individual responsibility provided he is aware of the possible effect of his presence (albeit passive) on the commission of the crime. In the case at bar, the Trial Chamber held that the Accused's failure to oppose the killing constituted a form of tacit encouragement in light of his position of authority').

[52] *Prosecutor v Brdjanin* (Judgment) IT-99-36-A (3 April 2007) para 273.

those actions, as well as potentially incurring aiding and abetting liability by way of tacit encouragement. But these legal duties are not the *basis* of liability; they are merely (co-)incidental. Liability of the first type depends on the initiating action that causes the harm, whereas tacit encouragement is the basis of the second type. The legal duties incumbent upon the accused may assist in understanding whether such tacit encouragement was actually given, but is not its basis.

A third and fourth type of omission *does* arise from the breach of the legal duty itself. The first of these is known in some domestic criminal systems as genuine or pure omission (*echte Unterlassungsdelikte, délits de pure omission*). Criminal laws sometimes require specific actions under specific conditions. Failure to respond to a summons, file a tax return, or deliver radioactive waste, are but a few examples of specific acts that domestic criminal law require to be performed.[53] Most obligations of this sort are specific, whereas others relate generally to the suppression of harm or crime. Some legal systems, for example, impose a duty on all citizens to rescue a person in danger, at least where they are able to do so without danger to themselves. The punishment for failing to do so varies significantly from jurisdiction to jurisdiction. Rhode Island permits a maximum prison sentence of six months; Germany, one year; France, five years; and the Northern Territory of Australia, seven years when done 'callously'.[54] The existence of such statutes are more common in civil law than common law jurisdictions, perhaps reflecting different attitudes as to the scope of criminal law in enforcing morality or the potential dangers of using criminal law to compel action according to relatively undefined conditions. These concerns, however, are largely mitigated by the limited sentences available. One is, after all, not guilty of murder merely for failing to discharge the duty to rescue; the crime of failing to rescue is understood as a separate crime and can usually be imposed even if the harm does not ensue.[55]

---

[53] M Bohlander, *Principles of German Criminal Law* (Hart Publishing, Oxford 2009) 40; L Moreillon, *L'infraction par omission* (Geneva: Droz, 1993) 47–56; Pradel (n 12) 66–67; G Fletcher, *Rethinking Criminal Law* (OUP, Oxford 2000) 422–423, 585–586.

[54] Rhode Island Statutes, §11-56-1; Strafgesetzbuch §323c: 'Failure to Render Assistance: Whoever does not render aid during accidents or common danger or need, although it is required and can be expected of him under the circumstances and, especially, is possible without substantial danger to himself and without violation of other important duties, shall be punished with imprisonment of not more than one year or a fine'; French *Code pénal*, 223-6; Criminal Code of the Northern Territory Australia, s 155: 'Any person who, being able to provide rescue, resuscitation, medical treatment, first aid or succour of any kind to a person urgently in need of it and whose life may be endangered if it is not provided, callously fails to do so is guilty of a crime and is liable to imprisonment for 7 years'; D Schiff, 'Samaritans: Good, Bad and Ugly: A Comparative Law Analysis' (2005) 11 *Roger Williams U L Rev* 77.

[55] Some statutes do, however, make liability for these stand-alone crimes conditional upon the harm ensuing. F Feldbrugge, 'Good and Bad Samaritans' (1965–1966) 14 *Am J Comp L* 630, 646 (citing five European countries that require the victim to have suffered either death or serious injuries before liability arises); cf Fletcher's distinction between direct versus derivative liability: Fletcher (n 53) 586.

Duties to rescue from harm can usually apply not only to natural events, such as drowning, but also man-made threats. The duty may arise much less frequently in such circumstances because it is usually dangerous to stop a crime. Some countries therefore regulate the duty to prevent crime separately. Article 223-6 of the French *Code pénal* provides: 'Whoever voluntarily refrains from preventing a crime or a felony against bodily integrity, despite being able to do so by his own immediate action and without risk to himself or others, is punishable by five years in prison and a 75000 Euro fine.'[56] Israeli and Nigerian law allow sentences of up to two years' imprisonment for a similarly-worded offence.[57] Germany imposes a duty to report, for which a sentence of up to five years can be imposed and the general duty to rescue can give rise to a sentence of up to one year.[58] The common law crime of 'misprision of felony' was abolished in England by statute in the 1960s, although many American jurisdictions impose special duties on teachers and others to report suspected crimes against children in their care.[59] Failure to report a crime does not, in itself, make a person an accessory but nor, on the other hand, does it preclude any other form of liability that may properly be available, including accessorial liability.

The fourth, and for present purposes the most important, category of omission concerns those that are treated as equivalent to inflicting the harm by one's own act, even though the accused's conduct is entirely passive in relation to the harm arising. German doctrine calls this 'inauthentic' or 'non-genuine' omissions (*unechte Unterlassungsdelikte*),[60] and French and Spanish law describe it as *commission par omission* and *comisión por omisión*, respectively.[61] No consistent term of art is used in English, although 'commission by omission' has been suggested as an appropriate term.[62] The essential feature of this form of liability is that the passive behaviour is treated as equivalent to an action causing the harm on the basis of the non-fulfilment of a legal duty to avoid the harm.

---

[56] Article 223-6.
[57] Israeli Penal Code, s 262; Nigerian Criminal Code, s 515.
[58] Strafgesetzbuch §138. 323c
[59] Popular opinion in the United States was recently outraged by the case of an alleged act of sexual abuse of a boy witnessed by a former college football player weighing well over 200 pounds. Rather than immediately intervening, he allegedly merely reported the matter to his supervisor, which apparently complied with the legal obligations applicable in that State. Grand Jury Report, 6–7, <http://www.nytimes.com/interactive/2011/11/06/sports/ncaafootball/20111106-pennstate-document.html> last accessed 12 December 2011.
[60] K Gossel, 'Crimes of Omission' (1984) 55 *Revue Int'l de Droit Pénal* 899, 908 ('The violation of an inhibition making a crime of commission 'authentic', the cases of 'commission by omission' consequently were called non-authentic crimes of commission (*unechte Unterlassungsdelikte*): any crime of commission, including that by omission, was considered to be characterized by a violation of an inhibition'); B Schunemann, 'The Principle Governing Crimes of Omission' (1984) 55 *Revue Int'l de Droit Pénal* 879, 886, 888.
[61] Bouloc (n 9) 209; J-M Silva Sanchez, 'Criminal Omissions: Some Relevant Distinctions' (2008) 11 *New Crim L Rev* 452.
[62] Fletcher (n 53).

The doctrine is well-established in civil and common law countries alike, but there are a variety of approaches. French law is formally hostile to the doctrine on the basis that it violates the principle of legality. A notorious 1902 case from Poitiers involved a person accused of battery and homicide for intentionally or recklessly failing to care for his mentally ill brother, who was a shut-in in their mother's house. The accused was acquitted because, in the absence of active conduct, he had not committed the crime.[63] This approach remains good law in French doctrine, although the outcome would be quite different today because the accused could be convicted of the statutory crime of 'abandonment' of a person rendered vulnerable by age or physical or mental infirmity.[64] This reflects the strong preference in French law for dealing with such matters through the mechanism of statutorily-defined 'pure omission,' rather than 'impure omission.' A similar duty of protection is imposed on parents and 'anyone else exercising parental authority' in respect of children.[65] When death ensues, these 'pure omission' crimes carry heavy penalties: 20 and 30 years respectively. The relationships in which an 'abandonment' may occur are not expressly enumerated, but the word does at least convey that there must be a pre-existing relationship of dependence and control that, in turn, justifies criminal liability for passivity in relation to the harm.

The French insistence on the distinction between acts and omissions, and the need for legislative intervention, reflects no fetish for technicality. Imposing liability for commission by omission raises a range of questions that do not arise in respect of commission by action or pure ommissions, and that require value judgments about morality, culpability and the proper scope of criminal law. Which relationships are close enough to give rise to the requisite duty to avert harm? Does it matter if someone else is in a closer relationship? Why did the omission occur? What level of diligence is required? What *mens rea* (knowledge, recklessness, full intent) needs to be proven in relation to the omission? What relieving conditions might there

---

[63] Bouloc (n 9) 209; Moreillon (n 53) 65.

[64] Art 223-3: *'Le délaissement, en un lieu quelconque, d'une personne qui n'est pas en mesure de se protéger en raison de son âge ou de son état physique ou psychique est puni de cinq ans d'emprisonnement et de 75000 euros d'amende.'*; art 223- 4 : *'Le délaissement qui a entraîné une mutilation ou une infirmité permanente est puni de quinze ans de réclusion criminelle. Le délaissement qui a provoqué la mort est puni de vingt ans de réclusion criminelle.'*

[65] Art 227-15 : *'Le fait, par un ascendant ou toute autre personne exerçant à son égard l'autorité parentale ou ayant autorité sur un mineur de quinze ans, de priver celui-ci d'aliments ou de soins au point de compromettre sa santé est puni de sept ans d'emprisonnement et de 100 000 euros d'amende. Constitue notamment une privation de soins le fait de maintenir un enfant de moins de six ans sur la voie publique ou dans un espace affecté au transport collectif de voyageurs, dans le but de solliciter la générosité des passants'* ; art 227-16: *'L'infraction définie à l'article précédent est punie de trente ans de réclusion criminelle lorsqu'elle a entraîné la mort de la victime.'* As Moreillon demonstrates, French law has also softened the impact of this approach by adopting a broad notion of 'negligent action', within which omissions are transformed into negligent conduct. Moreillon (n 53) 66–67.

be in the diverse circumstances that may arise?[66] The French reticence to resolve these questions judicially reflects a deep attachment to a particular conception of legality that should not be lightly dismissed.[67] As one commentator has observed, judges should not 'roam freely about our moral sentiments' in constructing the situations in which a failure is treated as equivalent to causing the harm.[68] The main problem raised by non-genuine omission crimes is not, as some have argued, undue interference with individual autonomy, but rather lack of certainty as to the situations in which omissions are equivalent to acts, and the conditions under which liability should be imposed in such situations. Passivity cannot be equated with action without making a host of value judgments that ought to be left to the legislator.

The English common law, in characteristic fashion, addressed these issues incrementally starting from those cases where the demands of justice appeared undeniable. Thus, it has long been accepted that a parent's failure to care for a child can satisfy the material element of homicide.[69] The intimate relationship of parent and child, and the duty of care owed by the latter to the former, eliminates many of the variables about causation, intent and voluntariness previously mentioned. The relationship, in effect, is the functional equivalent of locking a child in a room: the level of dependence and control is equivalent to the act of physical incarceration. Thus, if a child dies and there is no apparent cause other than a parent's neglect, a presumptive inference can be drawn that the omission was equivalent to an action. English case law has gradually expanded such situations beyond the parent-child context to include undertakings to provide the necessaries of life to a person,[70] or creating or undertaking to control a dangerous

---

[66] Spain apparently recognises that adult children have some kind of duty to provide necessaries of life to their parents, but does not appear to be recognised in other countries. See C Gomez-Jara Diez and L Chiesa, 'Spain' in Heller and Dubber (n 12) 61.

[67] Pradel (n 12) 68; Moreillon (n 53) 65 ('*le droit pénal français est-il extrêment attaché au principe de la legalité des délits et des peines*'); Bouloc (n 9) 210 ('*Mais en dehors de ces cas [des crimes d'omission expressement definis] il n 'y a pas de délit de commission par omission*'); F Desportes and F Le Gunehec, *Droit pénal général* (16th edn Economica, Paris 2009) 65 ('*Les actes d'omission ne peuvent être réprimés que s'ils sont expressément incriminés par un texte spécifique*').

[68] G Fletcher, 'On The Moral Irrelevance of Bodily Movements' (1994) 142 *U Pa L Rev* 1443, 1449 ('My sense of the literature is that most observers are concerned about condemning the injustice of not punishing immoral omissions. There is little concern about the issue of legality in letting courts roam freely about our moral sentiments').

[69] *R v Gibbins and Proctor* (1918) 13 Cr App R 134; A Ashworth, 'The Scope of Criminal Liability for Omissions' (1989) 105 *LQR* 424, 441; Schunemann (n 60) 879, 890; Feldbrugge (n 55) 630, 649.

[70] *R v Stone and Dobinson* [1977] QB 354 (Eng CA) (finding that the two accused had undertaken to care for the sister of one of them whom they had taken in as a lodger; a conviction for manslaughter was upheld on the basis of the finding that their care for her was reckless).

situation.⁷¹ The *mens rea* required can be either intent to kill or recklessness, depending on which form of homicide is charged.

Other common law countries have relied more heavily on the legislator. The Canadian Criminal Code has codified in a presumptively exhaustive manner the special and limited situations in which commission by omission is recognised. These offences have a dual character: (i) crimes of pure omission if the harm does not ensue; (ii) commission by omission if it does. The special character of the obligations is signaled by the title of the section, as being duties 'tending to the preservation of life'. Amongst these is the obligation of heads of households, spouses, and anyone who has charge of another because of 'detention, age, illness, mental disorder or other cause' to provide the 'necessaries of life' to the dependant party.⁷² The common characteristic of such diverse situations as infancy, a debilitated spouse, and a detainee appear to be complete dependence on the one hand, and near-absolute control on the other. Breach of these prohibitions, when it 'endangers' the life or health of a person permanently, is in itself punishable by up to five years in prison as a crime of omission; homicide through commission by omission may also be charged if death ensues.⁷³

The German Criminal Code expressly permits omissions to satisfy the material element of an offence where the accused is 'responsible under law to ensure that the result does not occur, and if the omission is equivalent to the realisation of the statutory elements of the offence through a positive act'.⁷⁴ Generally speaking, the duties to act recognised by German courts concern two groups of persons: (i) caregivers, custodians or others who are expected to protect those for whom they are responsible (so-called 'Beschützergaranten'); and (ii) persons who are responsible for the control or supervision of a potentially dangerous process, activity or thing

---

⁷¹ A gatekeeper at a railway crossing was convicted of manslaughter for failing to close a crossing gate, which contributed to a person's death: *R v Pitwood* (1902) 19 TLR 37. The omission problem could have been avoided by characterising the gatekeeper's conduct as negligent, but in the end the issue is the same: under what circumstances does a duty of careful action arise, failure of which gives rise to criminal liability? See JC Smith, 'Liability for Omissions in the Criminal Law' (1984) 4 *Legal Stud* 88, 91 ('There is no precise borderline between acts and omissions but this is true of many other distinctions in the criminal law. When we have a case which plainly consists in liability for an omission, it is at least unhelpful and possibly dangerous to try to disguise the fact and to describe the occurrence of any act').

⁷² Criminal Code of Canada, s 215(1). The duty to spouses or household members arises only when they are 'in destitute or necessitous circumstances'. As long as the breach of duty 'endangers the life of the person to whom the duty is owed, or causes or is likely to cause the health of that person to be endangered permanently', the sentence may be as much as five years.

⁷³ K Roach, *Criminal Law* (4th edn Irwin Law, Toronto 2009) 107; Criminal Code of Canada, s 215(2).

⁷⁴ German Criminal Code, section 13 (official translation) <http://www.gesetze-im-internet.de/englisch_stgb/index.html> last accessed 16 December 2011.

(so-called 'Überwachergaranten').⁷⁵ This includes, for example, family members living within the same household; members of a dangerous expedition; persons with a contractual or other voluntarily assumed obligation of care for another person, such as doctors or other caregivers; persons who have created harmful situations by prior illegal conduct (so-called 'Ingerenz'); or persons who supervise enterprises that may in some way create dangers to others.⁷⁶ Some commentators have sharply criticised what they perceive as the unduly flexible and fluid approach to guarantorship in German law,⁷⁷ although there are also signs of retrenchment: a recent case determined, for example, that two co-habiting siblings were not in a guarantorship relationship *inter se*.⁷⁸

Not all legal duties in national law are duties of guaranteeship, and even those that are have carefully drawn limits. The general duty to rescue, for example, does not create a guarantorship relationship: a bystander who fails to save a drowning boy may be convicted of failing to assist as a pure omission and sentenced to a year in prison, but is not liable for murder by impure omission.⁷⁹ Husbands and wives are generally expected to protect their spouse from harm by third parties, but are not responsible for failing to stop them from committing crimes against others.⁸⁰ The relevant Spanish provision requires 'a *special* legal duty' as the prerequisite of commission by omission.⁸¹

---

[75] Moreillon (n 53) 79 (identifying eight categories of legal duty that may for the basis of commission by omission, of which four are duties to supervise particular dangers (duties emanating from one's property or possessions, from engaging in a risky activity, the illegal actions of a third party under one's control, or the duty arising from creating a dangerous situation) or to protect certain interests (duties arising from family relations, from state activities, from close community ties, or from a voluntary undertaking to protect someone from harm)).

[76] Bohlander (n 53) 43–45; Moreillon (n 53) 240–309; Schunemann (n 60) 879, 890; H Schumann, 'Criminal Law' in M Reimann and J Zekoll (eds) *Introduction to German Law* (2nd edn The Hague, Kluwer 2005) 407–408.

[77] Moreillon (n 53) 311 (*'Dans d'autres situations, le droit penal n'hesite plus a depasser les frontiers qui lui ont ete assignees par l'ordre juridique : devoirs du restaurateur, du locataire, du possesseur d'un instrument dangereux. Ces tendances, dictees avant tout par des considerations de pure politique criminelle doivent etre rejetees, car violant les principes elementaires de securite du droit. Les derapages sont flagrants, particulierement en droit criminel allemand, alors que l'interpretation par analogie en droit penal est proscrit par le Grundgesetz. Sur ce point, il est etonnant de constater que le droit anglais, pourtant peu attache au principe de la legalite, repugne a faire œuvre de legislateur en l'absence de normes specifiques etendant les conditions objectives de la punissabilite'*); Schunemann (n 60) 879, 890.

[78] N Foster and S Sule, *German Legal System and Laws* (3rd edn OUP, Oxford 2002) 364.

[79] A Cadoppi, 'Failure to Rescue and the Continental Criminal Law' in M Menlowe and S McCall (eds) *The Duty to Rescue, The Jurisprudence of Aid* (Aldershot, Dartmouth 1993) 95; Bohlander (n 53) 41–42 (asserting that commission by omission can arise only when 'that legislation does not provide for genuine omissions liability already'); Fletcher (n 68) 1450.

[80] See Schönke and Schröder (n 44) § 13, para 21.

[81] Article 147, Spanish Criminal Code: '*Los delitos o faltas que consistan en la producción de un resultado sólo se entenderán cometidos por omisión cuando la no evitación del mismo, al infringir*

One domestic situation is particularly relevant to the conduct of soldiers in relation to their duties under international humanitarian law. The statutory duties of public officials do *not* generally qualify as duties of guarantee in favour of citizens who might be harmed by a third party following a breach. The failure of a police officer to prevent crimes does *not* generally make him liable for commission by omission, no matter how egregious the circumstances. English law criminalises such failures as abuse of public office, but no cases are to be found imposing liability for the resulting crime.[82] Not even in South Africa, where there have apparently been some shocking derelictions of duty by police officers, has such liability been imposed.[83] Schunemann's view of German law, to take an example of particular relevance to the context of international criminal law, is that 'the general duty of a police officer to prevent the commission of crimes does not make it possible to treat a failure to prevent the commission of a crime as equivalent to a positive act'.[84] Moreillon's exhaustive comparative review of commission by omission in Germany, Switzerland and England does not cite a single such case.[85] This is not to say that a statutory duty could not coincide with, or directly create, a close relationship of dependence and control so as to create a guarantor relationship; most statutory duties simply do not do so.

The preceding comparative analysis suggests that four different types of liability can arise from conduct that could be described as an omission. The first two types involve passivity that is, in context, equivalent to an action either because it is preceded by some action or because it tacitly encourages the crime; the latter two types arise from a culpable breach of a legal obligation to act. A failure to discharge a legal duty to act can give rise to criminal liability for the harm caused to a victim where there is a special relationship of care, control and protection. This may be described as 'commission by omission' arising from a 'culpable omission'. Some legal systems, such as France, have insisted that such liability be expressly authorised by legislation, whereas other systems have elaborated, at least to some extent, the conditions of liability through case law. The relationship of parent and child, caregiver and patient, and custodian and prisoner are three widely recognised categories of special relationship. The general principle that may be deduced from these categories of relationship is that failures to avert harm may be

---

*un especial deber jurídico del autor, equivalga, según el sentido del texto de la Ley, a su causación.'*

[82] In *R v Dytham* [1979] QB 722, a police officer whose shift was about to end witnessed an assault which ultimately led to the victim's death. Rather than intervening, the defendant went off duty, for which he was convicted of misconduct of an officer of justice, receiving a fine of 150 pounds for an offence that could have attracted imprisonment of up to two years. No charge of commission or complicity was brought against the accused, although Ashworth has argued that the law should be reformed to impose a special duty on law enforcement officers that could give rise to commission by omission. Ashworth (n 69) 455–457.

[83] Burchell and Milton (n 13) 196–201.

[84] Schunemann (n 60) 891. Bohlander (n 53) 42 ('the general duty of care owed by a government to its citizens does not suffice to establish a duty that entails criminal liability').

[85] Moreillon (n 53) 209–311.

deemed equivalent to an action causing harm where the accused is in a relationship of virtually total control over the victim, and the victim is totally dependent on the accused for well-being and protection.

The next section considers how international criminal law has approached the same issue, and whether any of the situations typically confronted in international cases coincide with the principle that may be derived from domestic law.

## III. The Development of Culpable Omission in International Criminal Law and the Mrkšić Deviation

A form of commission by omission that is undoubtedly recognised in international criminal law is superior responsibility. Those possessing effective control over subordinates have a duty to prevent or at least punish their crimes regardless of whether the omission encourages the crime or not.[86] As the *Halilović* Trial Chamber stated, the 'omission is culpable because international law imposes an affirmative duty on superiors to prevent and punish crimes committed by their subordinates'.[87] Further, liability is incurred for the ultimate crime committed, not a separate crime of 'failing to diligently control one's subordinates'. This form of liability is therefore commission by omission, or 'culpable omission' as described in the previous section, although international law gives it the *sui generis* label of 'superior responsibility'. Analogous failures to control arise in domestic legal systems as, for example, when a parent fails to control a child, or when a business owner fails to diligently control a dangerous process or condition.[88]

The express inclusion of superior responsibility cannot be taken to imply, as some have argued,[89] that other forms of omission liability are implicitly excluded. Superior responsibility is addressed narrowly to the situation of commanders, and defined separately from the general forms of individual criminal responsibility. Indeed, the statutes' reliance on well-known terms of art from national legal systems – including committing, instigating and aiding and abetting – suggests that omissions customarily encompassed by these concepts should also exist in international criminal law. The need to explore state practice is therefore particularly significant in respect of these general terms not only to ensure respect for the principle of *nullem crimen sine lege*, but also to adhere to the scope of liability authorised in the statutes. The legitimacy of international criminal law depends on

---

[86] ICTY Statute, art 7(3); ICTR Statute, art 6(3); ICC Statute, art 28.
[87] *Prosecutor v Halilović* (Judgment) IT-01-48-T (16 November 2005) para 54.
[88] Moreillon (n 53) para 225.
[89] G Boas, 'Omission Liability at the International Criminal Tribunals – A Case for Reform' in S Darcy and J Powderly (eds) *Judicial Creativity at the International Criminal Tribunals* (OUP, Oxford, 2010) 204.

anchoring the general rules of individual liability in the state practice from which these terms emerged.

International courts have, regrettably, never made any effort to articulate the state practice in respect of liability for 'culpable omission'. The first two Appeals Judgments to address the question quite properly did address omissions under the rubric of direct perpetration, not aiding and abetting. The first ever finding of culpable omission was decided *proprio motu* by the Appeals Chamber in *Blaškić*. A group of civilian detainees had been used as human shields directly in front of the accused's glass-fronted headquarters. The Appeals Chamber determined that there was no evidence to support the Trial Chamber's finding that this had been done pursuant to Blaškić's orders, but nevertheless felt that superior responsibility did not adequately capture the accused's culpability. Although find that 'criminal responsibility generally requires the commission of a positive act', the Appeals Chamber asserted that an 'exception' arises from the legal duty 'imposed, *inter alia* as a commander, to care for the persons under the control of one's subordinates'. Two articles of the Geneva Conventions were relied upon as the basis for this duty, requiring in substance that detainees must 'at all times be humanely treated, and shall be protected especially against all acts of violence or threats thereof and against insults and public curiosity'.[90] The Appeals Chamber found that Blaškić was 'aware' of the condition of the detainees and yet engaged in 'an intentional omission' and a 'willful failure' to discharge this duty.[91] The Trial Chamber also found that the accused's elevated 'degree of concrete influence' compelled a conviction under Article 7(1) of the ICTY Statute, rather than merely superior responsibility under Article 7(3).[92] The Appeals Chamber commented that the Trial Chamber had been 'correct in substance' in convicting accused under 7(1), although its proper characterisation was not ordering, but rather 'perpetration of a crime of omission pursuant to Article 7(1)'.[93]

The Appeals Chamber's reasoning in *Blaskić*, as in the case of Šljivančanin, can be criticized for failing to substantiate that the duty was analogous to a duty of guarantee, as that concept is understood in domestic law. One may also question whether it was appropriate to impute custody directly to Blaškić via his subordinates. The reasoning is nevertheless substantially more satisfactory than the 'aiding and abetting by omission' approach. Most importantly, the Appeals Chamber understood in that case that Blaškić's alleged failure to protect the prisoners had to be assessed as an alleged perpetration, with the requisite mental state of direct intent. In other words, the passive conduct must be such that it was possible to infer a guilty mind in respect of the criminal harm. No such analysis was undertaken in respect of Šljivančanin. On the contrary, Šljivančanin was convicted simply on the

---

[90] Geneva Convention IV Relative to the Protection of Civilian Persons in Time of War (1949) 75 UNTS 287, art 27; *Prosecutor v Blaškić* (Judgment) IT-95-14-A (29 July 2004) para 663, fn 1384.
[91] *Blaškić* (Appeal Judgment) (n 90) paras 663, 668.
[92] Ibid para 668.
[93] Ibid paras 663, 670.

basis that he had not discharged, or adequately attempted to discharge, the duties that were allegedly incumbent upon him in the circumstances.

The *Blaškić* approach was also followed by the Appeals Chamber in *Ntagerura*. The Prosecution at trial had contended for a far broader duty than recognised in *Blaškić*, claiming that the accused had failed in his duty under Rwandan law to 'ensure the protection and safety of the civilian population with his prefecture'.[94] This was characterised as 'omission as a principal perpetrator'. The Trial Chamber dismissed the claim on factual grounds, namely that the accused did not have adequate means or the legal authority to discharge his supposed obligation.[95] The Appeals Chamber addressed the accused's liability under the rubric of being an alleged 'principal perpetrator' for his 'culpable omission'.[96] It also addressed the Prosecution's argument that the accused's 'knowledge of such massive crimes and his inaction or silence amount to culpable omission or gross negligence or conduct that is tantamount to acquiescence in, or tacit approval of, or aiding and abetting the crimes'. The Appeals Chamber rejected that this form of passivity is encompassed by aiding and abetting:

> [C]riminal responsibility for an omission, which leads to a conviction as the principal perpetrator of the crime, has to be distinguished from aiding and abetting a crime by encouragement, tacit approval or omission, amounting to a substantial contribution to the crime. In the Notice of Appeal, the Prosecution's arguments are exclusively related to the issue of criminal responsibility for an omission. The issue of Bagambiki's responsibility for aiding and abetting the crimes by his tacit approval is raised only in the Appeal Brief, without the Prosecution having first sought leave to vary its grounds of appeal. Accordingly, the Appeals Chamber declines to address this issue further.[97]

The Appeals Chamber, albeit by way of pleading rules, thus excluded culpable omission from the scope of aiding and abetting. The former had been pleaded in the notice of appeal and could be entertained; the latter had not and was rejected.

The Appeals Chamber had nevertheless, even after *Blaškić*, contemplated the possibility that there might be such a thing as 'aiding and abetting by omission proper'. In *Brdjanin*, it remarked in an almost sceptical tone that 'it has so far declined to analyse whether omission proper may lead to individual criminal responsibility for aiding and abetting'.[98] The implication of this phrase is that the existence of this form of liability should not be taken for granted. In contrast, the *Orić* Appeals Chamber seems to have presumed, but without any analysis,

---

[94] *Prosecutor v Ntagerura* (Judgment and Sentence) ICTR-99-46-T (25 February 2004) para 658.
[95] Ibid para 660.
[96] *Ntagerura* (Appeal Judgment) (n 30) paras 331, 333, 335.
[97] Ibid para 338.
[98] *Brdjanin* (Appeal Judgment) (n 52) para 274.

that a failure to discharge a legal duty could, without more, constitute aiding and abetting.[99] The *Blaskić* and *Simić* Appeals Judgments arguably left open the possibility, although the relevant passages are unclear as to whether the type of omission involved is culpable omission or tacit encouragement.[100] The other appeal cases in which omissions to discharge a legal duty to act were discussed – *Tadić* and *Galić* – refer to 'criminal responsibility under Article 7(1)' without distinguishing between perpetration and aiding and abetting.[101] None of these cases engage in the slightest analysis of how culpable omissions are addressed in domestic legal systems, including whether they can properly be assessed as a form of accessorial liability.

The *Mrkšić and Šljivančanin* Appeals Judgment decided for the first time that the failure to discharge a legal duty, in itself, could constitute aiding and abetting even though the perpetrators had no knowledge of the supposed inaction. The accused Šljivančanin, to briefly supplement the description of the case given at the start of this chapter, was found to be responsible for supervising a military police unit that had custody of a group of some 200 prisoners of war. Militia groups attacked the prisoners, but the military police managed to prevent them from being killed.[102] His superior, Mrkšić, then relieved Šljivančanin of his command, ordered the unit's withdrawal, and ordered that the prisoners be handed over to the very militia that had been abusing them. The Appeals Chamber found that Šljivančanin, despite his *de jure* removal, still had some *de facto* authority to stop the unit's withdrawal, which he had not exercised.[103] The same duty of protection for prisoners of war from *Blaškić* was again affirmed, obliging 'each agent in charge of the protection or custody of the prisoners of war'.[104] The *actus reus* of aiding and abetting was found to be fulfilled wherever 'the failure to discharge a legal duty assisted, encouraged or lent moral support to the perpetration of the crime and had a substantial effect on the realization of that crime'.[105] As long as the accused had 'the ability to act, such that there were means available to the accused to fulfil his duty', the failure

---

[99] *Orić* (Appeal Judgment) (n 33) para 43.

[100] *Blaškić* (Appeal Judgment) (n 90) para 47; *Simić et al* (Appeal Judgment) (n 32) para 65, fn 259 (referring to *Blaskić*). The possibility was also contemplated in the *Strugar* and *Simić* Trial Judgments: *Prosecutor v Strugar* (Judgment) IT-01-42-T (31 January 2005) para 349; *Simić et al* (Trial Judgment) (n 42) para 162.

[101] *Prosecutor v Galić* (Judgment) IT-98-29-A (30 November 2006) para 175; *Tadić* (Appeal Judgment) (n 32) para 188.

[102] *Prosecutor v Mrkšić et al* (Judgment) IT-95-13/1-T (27 September 2007) paras 663, 666, 672.

[103] *Mrkšić & Šljivančanin* (Appeal Judgment) (n 1) para 93 ('had he ordered the military police not to withdraw, these troops may well have, in effect, obeyed'); para 98 ('had his attempts to persuade Mrkšić not been successful, when Šljivančanin telephoned Belgrade in order to speak to General Vasiljević, he could have sought the General's assistance on the matter').

[104] Ibid para 71, 73.

[105] Ibid para 49.

could constitute the *actus reus* of aiding and abetting,[106] including 'aiding and abetting murder by omission'.[107]

The Appeals Chamber did not justify, much less consider, whether 'culpable omission' could properly be extended to aiding and abetting liability. The assumption appears to have been that since *Blaškić* had already established that culpable omission could satisfy the *actus reus* of commission, it should also be capable of being the *actus reus* of aiding and abetting. In other words, since 'letting die' in violation of a legal duty can give rise to perpetration liability, then surely it can also constitute assistance to a crime.

This assumption is far from self-evident. There is little to no support, as discussed in Section II of this chapter, for the view that an accessory's actions in support can be unknown to the perpetrator. Indeed, there is significant state practice specifically rejecting the possibility in respect of omissions. French doctrine maintains that accessorial liability cannot arise from a mere failure to discharge a legal duty,[108] unless it is combined with some element of coordination or at least knowledge by the perpetrator.[109] Common law cases likewise require that the omission, whatever it may consist of, serves as a psychological inducement to the perpetrators even if it also violates a legal duty. A police officer who permitted a prisoner in his custody, and in his presence, to be beaten by a fellow prisoner was convicted of aiding and abetting assault. His duty as a police officer was highly relevant to this finding, but the aiding and abetting still consisted of the encouraging effect of the combination of his authority, presence and inaction: 'the accused has been found to have been present when the assault was committed and had a duty to prevent the offence and did not perform that duty. Where an accused has such a duty and fails to act to

---

[106] Ibid 49.

[107] Ibid 103, 141.

[108] Bouloc (n 9) 323 (*'Les actes de complicites ... sont tous des actes positifs, des actes de commissions ... Le seul fait de tolerance ne justifie pas une inculpation de complicite. On n'est pas complice par abstention'*); P Salvage, *Jurisclasseur Penal Code*, Art 121-6 et 131-7, 'Complicité', para 47 (*'La complicité suppose de manière indiscutable l'accomplissement d'un fait positif et l'on conclut qu'il n'y a pas de complicité par abstention'*); Desportes and Le Gunehec (n 67) (*'Celui qui reste passif devant la commission d'une infraction n'en est pas complice'*); Moreillon (n 53) 125 (*'En droit francais, la complicite ne peut s'induire d'un simple inaction ou abstention'*).

[109] Crim 27 Oct 1971 (Bull no 284) (Cour de cassation) (finding that the custom agent's agreement followed by an omission *'avait, par une action positive, apporté, avec connaissance, aux auteurs des soustractions, une aide dans les faits qui avaient preparé ou facilité leur action'*); Cour Cass (No pourvoi 99-80419, 18 January 2000) (*'alors qu'une complicité passive ne saurait rentrer dans aucun cas prévus par les dispositions du Code pénal relative à la complicité; qu'en l'espèce, il resulte des constatations mêmes de l'arrêt, en premier lieu, que, lors de ses interrogatoires, Patrick X ... a declaré avoir 'assisté à trois ou quatres reprises' à la livraison des bidons d'auxines ... [et] qu'ayant ainsi tenu le rôle d'intermediaire auprès du vendeur, il a sciemment facilité la preparation ou la consommation du délit commis'*). See also Belgian law: F Kuty, *Principes Generaux du Droit Penal Belge* (Brussels: Larcier, 2010) v II, 114–115 (implying that actual encouragement of the perpetrator is required).

discharge it, *his failure to act may be held to have encouraged the offence.*'[110] It is not the breach of duty that constitutes the aiding and abetting, but the perception of it by the perpetrator. In this context, Glanville Williams, reviewing the state of English law, explained that:

> [the] cases do not establish that a parent who fails to protect his child from attack is guilty as an accomplice to the attack. Such a rule would be monstrously unjust, besides being contrary to the principles of complicity ... If he is to be brought in, it should be either on account of this neglect of a duty imposed upon him personally (on a charge of manslaughter), or by means of an offence of 'permitting'.[111]

The ICJ has also affirmed this principle, insisting that complicity under the Genocide Convention 'always requires that some positive action has been taken to furnish aid or assistance'.[112] As long as 'positive action' is read as including the positive choice of a bystander to be present during a crime and convey tacit support to the perpetrator, this approach accurately reflects state practice. Letting a crime happen, even when subject to a special duty of protection, does not make a person an accomplice.

Regardless of whether 'culpable omissions' are confined to a perpetration analysis, a more rigorous analysis of the duties underlying omission liability must be undertaken by the Appeals Chamber. The existence of a duty is not sufficient. The essential question is what types of duties might give rise to omission liability and what methodology is applied to make that determination as a matter of customary international law. An omission can only be deemed the equivalent of an action – even assuming that customary international law can rely to a significant degree on comparative law in the absence of distinct State practice – in the clearest of cases of near total dependence and control: parents and children, caregivers and the infirm, jailers and those in their custody. Equating failure to prevent with substantial contribution means that, in principle, any duty should be sufficient to give rise to a culpable omission. *Mrkšić and Šljivančanin* ignores this issue entirely and approaches liability through the lens of 'substantial contribution'. This results in an open-jawed declaration that all duties imposed by international

---

[110] *R v Nixon*, 57 CCC (3d) 97 (British Columbia CA 1990) para 74; Ormerod (n 11) 190 (observing that the omission acts 'a positive encouragement to the other to perform the illegal act').

[111] Williams (n 6) 788. Other cases involve passengers' failures to prevent a driver from driving recklessly, or an employer's failure to stop an employee from committing a crime, the latter of which was explicitly characterised as 'evidence (and not constitutive) of encouragement'; *Cassady v Reg Morris Transport Ltd* [1975] RTR 470A; Simester and Sullivan (n 10) 205–206. Ormerod (n 11) 191 ('a company and its directors may be convicted of abetting the false making of tachograph records by the company's drivers if they knew that their inactivity was encouraging the practice').

[112] *Application of the Convention on the Prevention and Punishment of the Crime of Genocide (Bosnia and Herzegovina v Serbia and Montenegro)* (Judgment) (26 February 2007) para 432.

humanitarian law are duties of guarantee: 'the breach of a duty to act imposed by the laws and customs of war gives rise to individual criminal responsibility'.[113] This reasoning extends the scope of culpable omission far beyond what is recognised in analogous circumstances in national law, and fails to consider the diversity of duties encompassed by international humanitarian law. The key issue, which is completely ignored under the rubric of accessorial liability, is: under what circumstances is the relationship of dependence and control so strong that it is just to equate an omission with an action?

Commission by omission is a better framework for analyzing this issue by recognizing that the level of control and dependence necessary for the recognition of a duty of guarantorship will also characteristically imply that the requisite *mens rea* is direct intent to accomplish the crime. Requiring an intention that the result arises should go hand in glove with the duty of guarantee. Where the relationship of dependence and control is so strong that an omission can be equated with an action, so too could the natural and probable inference to be drawn from such an inaction that the omitter intended the result. Where this remains doubtful, no duty of guarantee should be imposed. Shifting the *mens rea* down towards knowledge has a tendency to over-include all manner of legal duties without a close examination of their content, or whether it is fair, just and moral to say that the defendant's inactions can be equated with inaction.

'Aiding and abetting by omission' has now started to arise in an increasing number of cases.[114] The open-ended potential of omission liability was illustrated in the *Popović* case, where an alleged culpable omission was again assessed through the lens of accessorial liability. One of the accused, Borovčanin, was deemed to have had custody of a group of prisoners even though they were not directly under his control, nor even directly under the control of his subordinates; he was instead deemed to have had custody over them because he was the commander of one of several units in a 'single geographic area' that were 'blended together and had joint custody of the prisoners', part of a 'joint force, guarding and moving the Muslim prisoners'.[115] The notion of 'custody' is treated as a formal threshold triggering a duty recognised under IHL, which automatically – following *Mrkšić & Šljivančanin* – converts omissions into the functional equivalent of a positive action.

No further analysis was required, following *Mrkšić & Šljivančanin*, to consider whether custody was of such a nature as to impose a duty of guarantee in the circumstances. No analysis was required as to whether a duty of guarantee was consistent with the attenuated level of control over the prisoners. No analysis was required as to the extent to which the accused could have mastered the situation such that an omission could justly have been deemed the equivalent of an action. No analysis was required as to whether duties of guarantee could be discerned in State

---

[113] *Mrkšić & Šljivančanin* (Appeal Judgment) (n 1) para 151.

[114] *Prosecutor v Bizimungu et al* (Judgment and Sentence) ICTR-99-50-T (30 September 2011).

[115] *Prosecutor v Popović et al* (Judgment) IT-05-88-T (10 June 2010) paras 1548, 1556. The author was counsel for the accused in this case.

practice, much less reaches the threshold of consistency to qualify as customary international law. No consideration was given as to whether the accused should have been convicted for breach of the duty as such (pure omission, in domestic law) rather than for the acts of the third parties (commission by omission).

The causal equivalence of passivity and action is erroneous, dangerous and deviates markedly from the example set by domestic legal systems. Actions, unlike passivity, are usually indicative of the mental state of the actor. Actions also generally have quantifiable effects on events. Passivity, on the other hand, seldom has either of these attributes. Cowardice, fear, uncertainty, confusion, hesitation in the face of fast-moving events, lack of confidence, introversion, isolation and simple weakness may all contribute to passivity. Assessing the causal significance of passivity necessarily involves a hazardous counter-factual analysis.

No better illustration is available of the fallacious equivalence than the *Mrkšić & Šljivančanin* case itself. The Appeals Chamber imposed liability on the basis that, had Šljivančanin acted, is was 'likely that the military police would have obeyed [his] order to remain in place,'[116] that the unit 'might have kept the TOs and paramilitaries at bay,'[117] and that they 'would likely have been able to regain control of the hangar … and the prisoners of war held therein.'[118] These counter-factual hypotheticals, on their face, do not meet the standard of proof beyond a reasonable doubt. Just as seriously, they reverse the burden of proof – requiring the accused to show that these eventualities were not 'likely' or that they could not have succeeded. The duty to protect prisoners from third parties should, at the very least, require an unambiguous showing that the accused could have prevented the harm without harm to himself or his men. It should follow that custody should not be imputed to an accused unless it can be shown that the accused had the power to exclude the perpetrators; imposing liability on any other basis would be to impute responsibility in the absence of a corresponding authority. Only this level of control permits the inference concerning the *mens rea* – intent to perpetrate the crime – that should be required in the case of what is described in domestic law as 'commission by omission.'

The undefined nature of aiding and abetting by omission is illustrated by a recent ICTR Trial Chamber judgement that convicted a former prefect of aiding and abetting by omission for not stopping crimes committed in his absence but with his knowledge, against civilians who had sought refuge at the prefectural office. The Chamber relied on a 'duty to rescue' statute applying to all Rwandan citizens, and on provisions of the Geneva Conventions and Additional Protocol II concerning prisoners of war.[119] The reasoning dramatically extends omission liability by relying on a domestic 'duty to rescue' statute to impose liability for the ultimate crime, and in failing to require that any of the victims were prisoners

---

[116] *Mrkšić & Šljivančanin* (Appeal Judgment) (n 1) para 96.
[117] Ibid. para 97.
[118] Ibid. para 100.
[119] *Prosecutor v Nyiramasuhuko et al* (Judgment and Sentence) ICTR-98-42-T (24 June 2011) paras 5893–5906.

in the accused's custody. These blatant and unexplained extensions of existing jurisprudence mask a deeper failure to address the basis of the relationships that could give rise to 'commission by omission' and the mental state that would need to be proven to impute responsibility for the ultimate crime.

These errors are directly attributable to approaching omission liability by way of aiding and abetting, rather than 'commission by omission.' The former approach is based on a specious equivalence between actions and passivity that would not be acceptable in any of the domestic jurisdictions discussed above. The ensuing under-analysis fails to address many of the essential issues raised in domestic law, extends omission liability based on a false equivalence of actions and passivity, and deviates from cardinal principles of notice and burden of proof. The current jurisprudence, with its myopic focus on 'substantial contribution' and knowledge, bypasses all of the important questions that should be considered before imposing omission liability.

## Conclusion

The development of 'aiding and abetting by omission' in ICTY jurisprudence is an unfortunate testament to a failure of comparative analysis, and consequent lack of respect for State practice. Not only is there no consensus in State practice supporting such a concept, State practice points the way towards the proper approach: commission by omission. International criminal courts would do well to repudiate the 'aiding and abetting by omission' and return to the starting point of culpable omission set out in *Blaškić*. The law should develop thereafter focusing carefully on the nature of the duty supposedly incumbent on an accused in any particular case with a view to ascertaining whether it is analogous to the strong duties of custodianship, control and dependence that are the hallmarks of such liability in domestic law. A correction along these lines is the only antidote to a fundamentally misguided jurisprudence that could lead to a radical extension of criminal liability.

# Joint Criminal Enterprise Liability: Result Orientated Justice

Wayne Jordash

At the outset of the *Tadić* Judgment, the Appeal Chamber of the International Criminal Tribunal for the former Yugoslavia (ICTY) confirmed the purpose of its mission:

> [A]ll those who have engaged in serious violations of international humanitarian law, whatever the manner in which they may have perpetrated, or participated in the perpetration of those violations, must be brought to justice.[1]

Having paused to sound the briefest of cautionary notes regarding the principle of individual criminal responsibility within international law,[2] the Chamber declared a theory of common purpose liability – Joint Criminal Enterprise (JCE) – that was fit to meet the challenge of this ambitious mission. The late Cassese, one of the most authoritative proponents of JCE, later defended its controversial birth and overweening utility, stating, *inter alia*:

> This notion [JCE] is crucial more in international criminal law than at the domestic level … When such crimes [expressions of collective criminality] are committed, it is extremely difficult to pinpoint the specific contribution made by each individual participant in the collective criminal enterprise, for (i) not all participants acted in the same manner, but rather each of them may have played a different role in planning, organizing, instigating, coordinating, executing or otherwise contributing to the criminal conduct; (ii) the evidence

---

[1]   *Prosecutor v Tadić* (Appeals Judgment) IT-94-1-A (15 July 1999) (hereafter '*Tadić* AC Judgment') para 190.
[2]   *Tadić* AC Judgment, para 186.

relating to each individual's conduct may prove difficult if not impossible to find.³

International criminal law, it seemed, needed a mode of liability that could confront the inconvenience of attempting to prove guilt without evidence. Of course, as at least one commentator has pointed out, this expansive interpretation of Article 7(1) was:

> clever but regrettable ... [it] suggests that we can work backwards from the proposition that the defendants must be punished. Since the defendants must be punished, the Statute must be read in such a way that it will yield the desired result. Of course, the argument is circular. We cannot help ourselves to the proposition that the defendants are guilty until the argument is concluded and we have determined, on some other basis, the level of culpability imposed by the ICTY Statute ... Although it is clear that the framers of the Statute intended to impose criminal liability for perpetrators, this fact alone tells us little about which theory of liability they wanted them prosecuted for and under what factual circumstances.⁴

Given JCE's originating premise, it is unsurprising that it has become the favourite of international prosecutors⁵ and the defence lawyer's *bête noire*. For some, this represents reason enough for celebration. However, for those who seek judgments that carefully assess individual liability through the establishment of a legally authoritative account of complex facts, there may be less reason to applaud. Robust and endurable liabilities tend to emerge from rigorous statutory and jurisprudential interpretation. They are developed and refined through the careful application of law to facts, with the culpability principle as a light to guide the way. In contrast, liabilities such as JCE, that emerge enveloped in teleological considerations, risk remaining blunt instruments, never quite rising to the challenge of accurately assessing individual liability.

---

³ A Cassese, 'The Proper Limits of Individual Responsibility under the Doctrine of JCE' (2007) 5 *JICJ* 109, 110.

⁴ JD Ohlin, 'Three Conceptual Problems with the Doctrine of Joint Criminal Enterprise' *Cornell Law Faculty Publications* (Paper 30, 2007) <http://scholarshilaw.cornell.edu/facpub/30> last accessed 12 January 2012. Ohlin also arguably falls into the same trap, arguing at the same time that, 'No one doubts that those who are charged and brought before international tribunals have fought in wars and engaged in dreadful conduct. But their level of legal liability for collective criminal conduct is precisely what is at issue. Are they guilty for the actions of their co-conspirators or merely guilty for their own actions'?

⁵ See for example AM Danner and JS Martinez, 'Guilty Associations: Joint Criminal Enterprise, Command Responsibility, and the Development of International Criminal Law' (2005) 93 *California L Rev* 75, 107, suggesting that then 34 of the 43 indictments confirmed between 25 June 2001 and 1 January 2004 (81 per cent of the total) incorporate JCE. A perusal of the indictments issued since then suggests that its use has not diminished in the following years.

Previously, in an article discussing the flawed application of JCE at the Special Court for Sierra Leone (SCSL), the present author contended that there appeared to be the signs of a trend towards a more careful application of JCE at the ICTY.[6] Faced with criticisms concerning the tendency of JCE to overreach, the *Brđanin* Appeals Chamber highlighted issues that promised a new determination to ensure the stringent application of the liability in future cases. The Appeals Chamber observed the importance of establishing that the contours of the common criminal purpose are properly defined in the indictment and are supported by the evidence beyond reasonable doubt.[7] The careful application of facts to the elements of JCE, the Appeals Chamber insisted, were the stringent and sufficient 'safeguards' against the danger of JCE overreaching or lapsing into guilt by association.[8] The Judgment provided a useful reminder of some of the risks and the need to apply the burden and standard of proof. However, the Appeals Chamber neglected to provide any practical guidance concerning the deployment of the safeguards in large, cumbersome and complex criminal trials. In order to illustrate the consequences of the dearth of judicial guidance on these essential issues , this chapter surveys the applicable pleading standards with regard to to JCE at the ICTY. Focusing particularly on the *Martić* case, this chapter takes a critical view of the *de minimis* detail required by the jurisprudence of the ICTY when defining the contours of the common purpose and the elements of JCE (and when applying the burden and standard of proof to these impoverished requirements).. Through these issues the chapter seeks to identify the safeguards that the ICTY Appeals Chamber considered were sufficient to ensure that the JCE mode of liability accurately assesses individual responsibility.

Obviously, as an expression of intent, the Appeals Chamber's insistence upon the strict application of JCE can hardly be faulted. In practice, however, the purported safeguards are inadequate. As an analysis of the approach taken to JCE in the *Martić* case shows, the pleading standards at the ICTY are minimal and those that pertain cannot reasonably be considered to be sufficient, let alone stringent. Rather than being carefully and incrementally developed and designed to deal with the practical problems of prosecuting large crime bases[9] the pleading standards demand little from the prosecution and provide even less in furtherance of sensible trial management and fair trial rights.

The standards promulgated do not require the precise detail of the criminal purpose to be pled. Instead, the prosecution has been to plead criminal purposes

---

[6] W Jordash and P van Tuyl, 'Failure to Carry the Burden of Proof: How Joint Criminal Enterprise Lost its Way at the Special Court for Sierra Leone' (2010) 8(2) *JICJ* 591.

[7] *Prosecutor v Brđanin* (Appeals Judgment) IT-99-36-A (3 April 2007) (hereafter '*Brđanin* AC Judgment') para 424 [internal quotations omitted].

[8] *Brđanin* AC Judgment, para 426.

[9] *Brđanin* AC Judgment, para 426. For examples of criticism see E van Sliedregt, *The Criminal Responsibility of Individuals for Violations of International Humanitarian Law* (CUP, Cambridge 2003) 4–5; H Olásolo, 'Reflections on the Treatment of the Notions of Control of the Crime and Joint Criminal Enterprise in the Stakić Appeal Judgment' (2007) 7 *ICLR* 143, 157.

that are defined by their outer geographical and temporal limits, rather than the essential links between the accused, the JCE members, the direct perpetrators, the crimes and any shared intent or alleged forseeability.

Given the judicial acceptance of the paramount importance of clearly defined criminal purposes, it is difficult to escape the conclusion that the minimal pleading requirements are the result, at least in part, of an expectation (or hope) that JCE must not be prevented from serving the ends-orientated objectives that underpinned its conception. In sum, despite many years of JCE trials, the prosecution are still permitted to advance excessively broad and il-defined JCE cases in the (mistaken) belief that asking for too much specificity will hamper effective prosecutions. Accordingly, instead of the criminal purpose and the requisite links between the Accused and the crimes committed by, or at the behest of others, being defined from the outset, the common purpose is allowed to be pled like an open vessel into which the evidence may be poured, providing the Judges with the discretion at the completion of the evidence to define the JCE according to the links which have emerged in the evidence. In reality, rather than the prosecution proving their case, the judges ascertain retrospectively whether one has emerged in the plethora of testimony and documents adduced.

Had the *Brđanin* Appeals Chamber, in its unqualified defence of the liability, examined the jurisprudence, it would have observed pleading standards that allow the Prosecution to omit or obscure the critical details of the JCE essential to provide the requisite framework to ensure that the accused is fairly informed of the nature and cause of the charge, and thereafter ensure a rigorous assessment of individual liability through the application of the burden and standard of proof.

The application of JCE at the ICTY (and its' inevitable demise) should serve as a cautionary tale for the International Criminal Court (ICC). Liabilities that are overloaded with the expectation that they will serve ends-orientated purposes are likely to evade the type of judicial scrutiny that ensures they develop and are used consistent with the principle of individual culpability. The nagging controversy that has plagued JCE since the beginning should have been met with a considered judicial response, highlighting its utility but also robustly acknowledging the practical problems that arise refining its application and limiting its' use where necessary. Unfortunately, , the Appeals Chamber in *Brđanin* spent its time engaged in another, arguably circular, defence of the customary law status of JCE and its applicability for all times and all places. . This was a fraction of the analysis required to ensure that the difficulties encountered over the years were accurately documented and robustly mastered. A comprehensive, careful analysis may have restricted or refined JCE's, use but removed some of the doubts concerning its legitimacy for the betterment of the jurisprudence of the ICTY and international criminal law. Criminal adjudication of individual responsibility must be based on the precise pleading of allegations and the assessment of those stated links between an accused and the crimes. Anything less, in the context of the demands of international criminal trials, is likely to promote the possibility of lapses into attributing guilt by association and the tainting of the inevitable convictions. As the ICC begins developing and clarifying its modes of liabilities, particularly those that seek to assess individual liability arising from collective criminal enterprises, the judiciary must have the confidence to resist an ends orientated approach to justice. Instead, care must be taken to ensure that the liabilities are developed, revisited and refined for one purpose only: the purpose of accurately assessing individual liability.[10]

## I. *Brđanin*: A Missed Opportunity for Analysis and Refinement

In 2007, the *Brđanin* Trial Chamber made an attempt to restrict the use and scope of JCE liability. The Accused was a leading political figure in the Bosnian Serb government charged with having participated in a JCE, the purpose of which was alleged to be the permanent forcible removal of Bosnian Muslim and Bosnian Croat inhabitants from the territory of the planned Bosnian Serb state over a four-year period.[11] The Trial Chamber took the view that JCE was not an appropriate mechanism for assessing the liability of an individual where the Prosecution sought to include within the JCE an accused structurally remote from the commission of the crimes. The Trial Chamber also ruled that, for the purposes of establishing individual criminal responsibility pursuant to the theory of JCE, it was not sufficient to prove an understanding or an agreement to commit a crime between the accused and a person in charge or in control of a military or paramilitary unit committing a crime. Rather, the Accused could only be held criminally responsible if the Prosecution established beyond reasonable doubt that he had an understanding or entered into an agreement with the relevant *physical* perpetrators to commit the *particular* crime eventually perpetrated or if the crime perpetrated by the relevant physical perpetrators was a natural and foreseeable consequence of

---

[10] *Situation in the DRC: Prosecutor v Lubanga* (Decision on the Confirmation of Charges) ICC 01/04-01/06 (29 January 2007). The approach taken in the Lubanga pre-trial decision abandons JCE in favour of a more narrowly tailored liability theory resembling something known in German criminal law as *Mittäterschaft* ('co-perpetration') or *Organisationsherrschaft*, a manner of imputing responsibility to high-level commanders in a criminal organization that requires more direct proof of control and deliberate commission than does the *Tadić* JCE doctrine. For further discussion, see H Olásolo (n 9).

[11] *Prosecutor v Brđanin* (Trial Judgment) IT-99-36-T (1 September 2004) (hereafter '*Brđanin* TC Judgment') paras 10, 355. See also *Prosecutor v Brđanin* (Sixth Amended Indictment) IT-99-36-T (9 December 2003): wherein the Prosecution alleged that the Accused participated in a JCE, the purpose of which was the permanent forcible removal of Bosnian Muslim and Bosnian Croat inhabitants from the territory of the planned Bosnian Serb state by the commission of the crimes alleged in Counts 1 through 12 of the indictment. The JCE came into existence no later than the establishment of the SerBiH Assembly on 24 October 1991 and continued throughout the period of the conflict in BiH until the signing of the Dayton Accords in 1995.

the crime agreed upon by the Accused and the relevant physical perpetrator.[12] On the prosecution appeal, *Brđanin* and the *amicus curiae* (the Association of Defence Counsel) argued that these strictures were required to prevent JCE as a mode of liability from overreaching and lapsing into attributing guilt by association.[13]

The Appeals Chamber disagreed. It considered that JCE was appropriate in all cases, irrespective of the scope or nature of the crimes alleged. The Appeals Chamber, citing the ICTR Appeals Chamber, stated that '[o]n the contrary, the *Justice* Case shows that liability for participation in a criminal plan is as wide as the plan itself, even if the plan amounts to a 'nation wide government organized system of cruelty and injustice'.[14] The Chamber observed that:

> [c]ontrary to what Brđanin alleges, there is no risk that attaching JCE liability to an individual who is structurally remote from the crime increases the possibility of the individual being made guilty by 'mere association'. This is because responsibility pursuant to JCE does require participation by the accused, which may take the form of assistance in, or contribution to, the execution of the common purpose. The Appeals Chamber is also of the view that, whether or not the Trial Chamber is correct in stating that seeking to include structurally remote individuals within the JCE creates difficulties in identifying the agreed criminal object of that enterprise, this does not as such preclude the application of the JCE theory. The requirement, in such cases, is that the contours of the common criminal purpose have been properly defined in the indictment and are supported by the evidence beyond reasonable doubt ...[15][T]he Appeals Chamber is of the view that this doctrine as it stands provides sufficient safeguards against overreaching or lapsing into guilt by association.[16]

Unfortunately, upon closer examination, it appears that the Appeals Chamber's unqualified defence of JCE failed to address the gravamen of the Trial Chamber's concerns. Undoubtedly, the Appeal Chamber's unambiguous clarification of the need to find that the Accused had contributed *significantly* to the crimes before JCE liability could attach was welcome and well overdue.[17] However, as is plain,

---

[12] *Brđanin* TC Judgment, para 347. The Appeals Chamber interpreted this finding as a finding by the Trial Chamber that such agreements or understandings are equivalent to the common plans at the basis of JCEs and therefore logically any direct perpetrators who entered into such an agreement would be a member of a JCE; *Brđanin* AC Judgment, para 389.

[13] *Brđanin* AC Judgment, para 371.

[14] *Brđanin* AC Judgment, para 423.

[15] *Brđanin* AC Judgment, para 424 [internal quotations omitted].

[16] *Brđanin* AC Judgment, para 426.

[17] *Brđanin* AC Judgment, para 430. The Appeals Chamber's previous standard was startlingly minimal: it was 'in general, not necessary to prove the substantial or significant nature of the contribution of an Accused to the joint criminal enterprise to establish his responsibility as a co-perpetrator: it is sufficient for the Accused to have committed an act

the remainder of the Appeals Chamber's comments (concerning the tendency of JCE to lapse into attributing guilt by association) amounted to little more than an analysis of the customary law status of the applicability of JCE to region-wide criminal plans and a recital of the elements of JCE.[18] The Appeals Chamber stated what *should* happen to ensure a proper application of the JCE liability – the criminal object should be properly defined and should be supported by evidence beyond a reasonable doubt – but failed to provide any insight into the practical difficulties that might stand in the way of this desired outcome, let alone the means of maneuvering around or through them[19]

This lack of analysis is particularly significant in light of the Appeals Chamber's decision not to limit an accused's JCE liability to the crimes committed by JCE members, but to allow crimes by non-members to be attributed to the common purpose. The Appeals Chamber found that to hold a member of a JCE responsible for crimes committed by non-members of the enterprise, it only had to be shown that the crime could be imputed to one member of the JCE, and that this member – when using a principal perpetrator – acted in accordance with the common plan. The existence of this link, the Appeals Chamber opined, was a matter to be assessed on a case-by-case basis.[20] On the one hand, this ruling was an attempt to consolidate what had implicitly been found permissible in cases such as *Krstić* and *Stakić*.[21] On the other, it represented the most authoritative endorsement of a controversial extension of JCE liability. As stated by Judge Shahabuddeen in a partially dissenting opinion in the same case, in his view, this extension was akin to attributing criminal responsibility on the basis that the crime committed by the non-JCE member was 'within a certain category', imposing 'criminal responsibility on the accused irrespective of his will'.[22]

---

or an omission which contributes to the common criminal purpose'; *Prosecutor v Kvočka* (Appeal Judgment) IT-98-30/1 (28 February 2005) (hereafter '*Kvočka* AC Judgment') para 421.

[18] See for example *Brđanin* AC Judgment, paras 393–409 wherein the Appeals Chamber considered whether post-Second World War and its own jurisprudence involving common purposes had required that the principle perpetrator be a member of the JCE.

[19] *Brđanin* AC Judgment, para 424 [internal quotations omitted].

[20] *Brđanin* AC Judgment, para 413.

[21] For example, as acknowledged by the *Brđanin* Appeals Chamber at para 408: the principle perpetrators in *Krstić* were not found to be members of the JCE and 'though not mentioned explicitly, were *probably* privates and other low-ranking members of the Drina Corps of the VRS' [emphasis added]. See also A Zahar and G Sluiter, *International Criminal Law* (OUP, Oxford 2008) (hereafter 'Zahar and Sluiter') 237; 'On the question of who constituted the enterprises and what kinds of link existed among their members, the findings of the *Krstić* TC are unclear'.

[22] *Brđanin* AC Judgment (Partially Dissenting Opinion of Judge Shahabuddeen) para 18. See also Antonio Cassese's criticism of the decision in A Cassese, *International Criminal Law* (2nd edn OUP, Oxford 2008) 195, describing the 'broadening of the notion' as excessive and raising 'doubts about its consistency with the nullum crimen principle and principle of personal responsibility ... all the more objectionable ... where crimes are perpetrated on a large scale by individuals who are remote from the accused'.

Unfortunately, the Appeals Chamber appeared more concerned with defending JCE as appropriate for all occasions (through an analysis of its customary law status) than with reflections on its appropriateness in the practical world of criminal adjudication and trial management. Consistent with the principle of legality and personal culpability, a Trial Chamber must approach its assessment of JCE liability concretely and with exactitude – ensuring that the burden and standard of proof remain firmly where they belong. How this is to be achieved is the essential (and controversial) point. However, despite 10 years of JCE application at the ICTY and almost as many at the ICTR, these issues remain scantily addressed. There is a dearth of jurisprudence providing detailed instruction or guidance with regard to these safeguards. As will be discussed below in Section II, this lack of debate and judicial pronouncement has allowed standards to be developed that do not require that the Prosecution pleads the criminal purpose or other elements of JCE with anything close to useful precision. In sum, the Prosecution has been to plead criminal purposes that are defined only by their outer geographical and temporal limits. The essential links between the accused and the crimes of the many can be omitted from the indictment. It is the judges at the end of the trial who are expected to find the links and define the purpose according to the evidence as it has unfolded. The jurisprudence allows the Prosecution to omit or obscure the critical detail of the JCE that would provide the requisite framework to ensure that the Accused is fairly informed of the nature and cause of the charge and thereafter undertake a rigorous assessment of individual liability.

## II. ICTY Pleading Standards: Defining the Contours of the Common Criminal Purpose

The jurisprudence of the ICTY reveals an entirely permissive approach to the pleading of the common purpose and JCE liability. For much of the ICTY's life span the jurisprudence concerning this issue has travelled down the same legal cul-de-sac. Rather than discussing the finer points of JCE pleading, the judiciary has allowed itself to become preoccupied with largely terminological debates, (e.g. whether, for example, the prosecution ought to be able to rely upon JCE despite using wording such as 'acting in concert' rather than 'joint criminal enterprise').[23] Accordingly, instead of articulating the practical requirements for an unambiguous, equitable approach to pleading the elements of JCE in the indictment, ICTY jurisprudence has focused on settling debates over whether the prosecution in fact intended to plead

---

[23] See for example: *Prosecutor v Simić* (Trial Judgment) IT-95-9-T (17 October 2003) (hereafter '*Simić* TC Judgment') paras 148–155; quoting *Prosecutor v Šainović* (Decision on Ojdanić's Motion Challenging Jurisdiction – Joint Criminal Enterprise) IT-99-37-AR72 (21 May 2003); *Prosecutor v Brđanin* (Decision on Objections by Talić) IT-99-36-T (20 February 2001); *Prosecutor v Gacumbitsi* (Appeals Judgment) ICTR-2001-64-A (7 July 2006) para 171.

JCE and whether it was reasonable for the defence to infer that this was a form of liability being pursued at trial.

Of course, that preoccupation and the development of proper pleading standards are not mutually exclusive. As will be discussed below, there may be several associated explanations that cast light on the stunted development of useful minimal standards. However, whatever the cause, the fact remains that, whilst pleading standards in general provide that the charges and the material facts supporting the charges must be pleaded with sufficient precision in the indictment so that the accused can prepare his defence[24] these minimal thresholds are rarely met in a typical JCE case at the ICTY.

The salient JCE jurisprudence demands that the prosecution plead the purpose of the enterprise, the identity of the participants, the nature of the accused's participation in the enterprise and his *mens rea*.[25] Astonishingly, apart from the requirement that these basic elements are *mentioned* in the indictment, the jurisprudence says little else. There are no other specific requirements concerning the details required to efficaciously describe the contours of the criminal purpose. There is no requirement that the indictment pleads the conduct of the JCE members said to demonstrate the shared intent at the heart of the JCE.[26] As concerns the pleading of the accused's contribution to the JCE, the prosecution is not required to be precise. Despite the fact that JCE liability is classified as a form of Article 7(1) commission, the Prosecution is allowed to circumvent the usual requirements that the Accused's role in a course of conduct has to be described so that the constituent acts are particularised.[27] Instead, indictments are permitted to particularise a *précis* of the alleged conduct in the broadest of generic terms (e.g. training, supplying, supporting, authorising, facilitating, failing, etc) designed to encapsulate any possible conduct, rather than pin point suspected acts and omissions.[28] It is

---

[24] *Prosecutor v Semanza* (Trial Judgment) ICTR-97-20-T (15 May 2003) para 44; citing *Prosecutor v Kupreškić et al* (Appeals Judgment) IT-95-16 (23 October 2001) (hereafter '*Kupreškić* AC Judgment') para 88.

[25] *Kvočka* AC Judgment, para 28.

[26] A recent ICTR Appeals Chamber Decision appears to suggest that the Appeals Chamber might be prepared to find this a requirement if the pleading inconsistently describes the conduct of some but not all of the JCE members. The *Uwindindi* Appeals Chamber took the view in the specific circumstances of that indictment the inclusion of incomplete or part details created ambiguity. Unfortunately, it does not appear to create a general rule that all indictments must from thereinafter particularise the conduct of the JCE members; see *Prosecutor v Uwindindi* (Decision on Defence Appeal Against the Decision Denying Motion Alleging Defects in the Indictment) ICTR-01-75-AR72(C) (16 November 2011) (hereafter '*Uwindini* Decision') para 14.

[27] For example, when the Prosecution pleads a case of 'instigation', it must precisely describe the instigating acts and the instigated persons or groups of persons: *Prosecutor v Blaškić* (Appeal Judgment) IT-95-14-A (29 July 2004) paras 213, 226: *Uwindindi* Decision, para 36.

[28] See for example *Prosecutor v Martić* (Amended Indictment) IT-95-11 (9 September 2003) (hereafter '*Martić* Amended Indictment'); *Prosecutor v Brđanin* (Sixth Amended Indictment) IT-99-36 (9 December 2003); *Prosecutor v Krajišnik* (Consolidated Amended

permissible to particularise a course of conduct that is sufficiently vague to include anything (and exclude nothing) that might emerge from hundreds of witnesses and tens of thousands of pages of evidence over the years of a trial.

The attendant failure to demand specific particularisation of the JCE members' conduct at the heart of the JCE has ruinous consequences for the remainder of the indictment. Whilst an accused may be found responsible for crimes committed by non-members of the enterprise providing 'that the crime can be imputed to one member of the joint criminal enterprise, and that this member – when using a principal perpetrator – acted in accordance with the common plan',[29] these links are not required to be explicit in the indictment. A JCE indictment therefore consists of little more than a generic description of the accused's conduct, a list of JCE members and a list of crimes committed on a particular date by a particular group alleged to be associated in some vaguely specified way with the JCE.

Moreover, it is accepted practice for the prosecution to plead the basic (first category) and extended form (third category) of JCE as alternatives.[30] The *Martić* case is a typical example. It was alleged that all crimes were committed pursuant to the basic form or, in the alternative, that the crimes in Counts 1 to 9 and 12 to 19 were committed pursuant to the extended form.[31] Put another way, the *Martić* indictment alleged that the accused acted in concert with hundreds, if not thousands, of alleged (partially identified) JCE members who used hundreds or thousands of (non-identified) non-JCE members to commit the intended crimes; or alternatively the JCE members, themselves or using the non-JCE members, intended only some of the crimes with one or more of the remainder being foreseeable; or, the JCE members, themselves or using the non-JCE members, intended some of the crimes with the remainder being foreseeable but (at some unspecified time) the JCE evolved so that one or more of these latter foreseeable crimes became intended and therefore part of the criminal purpose.[32]

---

Indictment) IT-00-39 (7 March 2002); *Prosecutor v Karadžić* (Third Amended Indictment) IT-95-5/18-1 (27 February 2009).

[29] *Brđanin* AC Judgment, para 413.

[30] Some of the jurisprudence suggests that a Prosecutor need not even identify the form of the JCE in the indictment, providing that it is only '*preferable* for an indictment alleging the Accused's responsibility as a participant in a JCE to refer also to the particular form (basic or extended) of JCE envisaged'. See for example *Prosecutor v Krnojelac* (Appeals Judgment) IT-97-25-A (17 September 2003) (hereafter '*Krnojelac* AC Judgment') para 138 [emphasis added].

[31] *Prosecutor v Martić* (Amended Indictment) IT-95-11 (9 September 2003) para 5.

[32] As found by the *Krajišnik* Trial Chamber and upheld by the Appeal Chamber, the means of realising the common objective of the JCE can evolve over time to embrace expanded criminal means, as long as the evidence shows that the JCE members agreed on this expansion of means. The Appeals Chamber overturned some of the convictions because it determined that the Chamber had not made findings concerning (1) whether the leading members of the JCE were informed of the crimes, (2) whether they did anything to prevent their recurrence and persisted in the implementation of this expansion of the common objective and (3) when the expanded crimes became incorporated in the common objective. The Appeals Chamber considered it even more important that the Chamber had not made

Accordingly, the proposition that an indictment alleging JCE at the ICTY provides an accused with prompt notice of the nature and cause of the charges, a fair opportunity to prepare an effective defence, or a Trial Chamber with a clear idea of what the prosecution hopes to prove, has to be approached with healthy dose of skepticism. Putting aside the fact, as recognised by *Brđanin*, that the contours of the criminal purpose need to be precisely defined to allow an effective final assessment of individual responsibility, an accused taking possession of a typical JCE indictment is hampered from the outset. As noted above, the usual requirements for other liabilities at the ICTY demand that the indictment particularises with a degree of precision the conduct that underpins the charges, especially the constituent acts of the accused. These demands reflect an acknowledgement that the right of an accused to be informed promptly and in detail of the charges through the indictment (to the degree expected of other liabilities) benefits the accused in innumerable ways. Crucially, the defence investigation can begin from the service of the indictment, rather than being delayed or handicapped until the service of the evidence or the disclosure of the prosecution's pre-trial brief. This degree of particularisation is also required to prevent the manifest unfairness that arises from allowing the prosecution to omit material aspects of its case from the indictment to be able to mould the case during the trial depending on how the evidence unfolds.[33] The fact that the prosecution states its case with the type of precision demanded of other liabilities provides the essence of an (ostensibly) adversarial process; that which is stated must be proven. Instead, JCE pleading standards allows much of the essential detail of the allegations to be buried within tens, even hundreds, of thousands of pages of evidence, leaving the Accused with an almost insurmountable task irrespective of the merits of his defence.

Given the manifest stasis in the development of useful pleading standards, it is reasonable to assume that these critical issues have never been at the forefront of the ICTY Appeals Chamber's approach to the JCE liability. In fact, historically, the Appeals Chamber has been more than a little sanguine about upholding indictments (and convictions for JCE) without the pleading of a common purpose or

---

findings concerning at which specific point in time the expanded crimes became part of the common plan and whether the JCE members had any intent. The Chamber noted that 'neither the Appeals Chamber nor the Parties can be required to engage in speculation on the meanings of the Trial Chamber's findings – or lack thereof – in relation to such a central elements of Krajišnik's individual responsibility as the scope of the common objective of the JCE' (*Prosecutor v Krajišnik* (Appeals Judgment) IT-00-39-A (17 March 2009) (hereafter '*Krajišnik* AC Judgment') paras 163–176). Nonetheless, whilst the Appeals Chamber was correct to be concerned, it failed to see the inherent contradiction in its own approach. Logically, if it was unacceptable for an Accused to speculate about the basis for his conviction, it was equally problematic that the indictment failed to particularise these aspects of the common objective from the outset of the trial.

[33] See for example *Prosecutor v Ntakirutimana* (Appeals Judgment) ICTR-96-10-A and 96-17-A (13 December 2004) paras 124–125; *Prosecutor v Rutaganda* (Appeals Judgment) ICTR-96-3-A (26 May 2003) paras 301–303; and *Prosecutor v Niyitegeka* (Appeals Judgment) ICTR-96-14-A (9 July 2004) para 194.

with vaguely defined common purposes.³⁴ The earliest and most obvious example of this is the *Tadić* case.³⁵ Clearly, since JCE did not yet exist, there was no pleading of a well-defined common purpose. Nonetheless, having read the JCE liability into Article 7(1) of the ICTY Statute, the Appeals Chamber went on to find the Accused responsible pursuant to a JCE.³⁶ Similarly Krstić, who at the time of the Srebrenica crimes was the Commander of the Drina Corps,³⁷ was convicted pursuant to Article 7(1) for participation in two JCEs, despite no JCE being pled.³⁸ The Trial Chamber considered it within its discretion to 'convict the Accused under the appropriate head within the limits of the indictment and fair notice of the charges *and insofar as the evidence permits'*.³⁹ It claimed that the Defence had been put on notice of this mode of liability through the Prosecutor's pre-trial brief which 'discussed this form of liability, specifically in the context of ethnic cleansing'.⁴⁰ However the sole reference to this mode of liability in the Prosecution's brief were the following remarks: 'A theory of co-perpetration can also apply to a participation in ethnic cleansing', followed by the observation that this theory had previously been applied in the *Kupreškić* case at the ICTY and one of the Accused had been found guilty 'because he adhered to a common plan for the execution of the cleansing campaign in the village, which by necessity was a highly coordinated effort and required full prior knowledge of the intended activities and subordination to a common plan of action'.⁴¹ Notwithstanding these wholly tangential comments, the Appeals Chamber upheld Krstić's conviction pursuant to one of the JCE's found by the Trial Chamber.⁴²

The same is true of the *Kvočka* case.⁴³ The Trial Chamber rejected the Defence's contention that the absence of JCE pleading precluded it from consideration. It noted that the charges in the Amended Indictment alleging that the Accused instigated, committed or otherwise aided and abetted' crimes included responsibility for participating in a joint criminal enterprise designed to accomplish such crimes. It stated that '[a]lthough greater specificity in drafting indictments is desirable, failure to identify expressly the exact mode of participation is not necessarily fatal to an

---

³⁴ *Prosecutor v Krnojelac* (Trial Judgment) IT-97-25-T (15 March 2002) paras 84–86; *Krnojelac* AC Judgment, para 138.
³⁵ See for example *Prosecutor v Tadić* (Second Amended Indictment) IT-94-1-1 (14 December 1995) paras 4.2 and 4.5.
³⁶ *Prosecutor v Tadić* (Trial Judgment) IT-94-1-T (7 May 1997) paras 366–376; *Tadić* AC Judgment, para 232.
³⁷ The Drina Corps was a formation of the Bosnian Serb Army.
³⁸ *Prosecutor v Krstić* (Trial Judgment) IT-98-33-T (2 August 2001) (hereafter '*Krstić* TC Judgment').
³⁹ *Krstić* TC Judgment, para 602 (emphasis added)..
⁴⁰ *Krstić* TC Judgment, para 602.
⁴¹ *Prosecutor v Krstić* (Prosecution's Pre-Trial Brief) IT-98-33-PT (25 February 2000).
⁴² *Prosecutor v Krstić* (Appeals Judgment) IT-98-33-A (19 April 2004).
⁴³ *Prosecutor v Kvočka et al* (Trial Judgment) IT-98-30/1-T (2 November 2001) (hereafter '*Kvočka* TC Judgment'). See also *Prosecutor v Kupreškić et al* (Trial Judgment) IT-95-16-T (14 January 2000) (hereafter '*Kupreškić* TC Judgment') and *Kupreškić* AC Judgment.

indictment if it nevertheless makes clear to the accused the 'nature and cause of the charge against him'.⁴⁴ Again, the Trial Chamber considered it within its discretion to characterise the form of participation of the Accused, if any, according to the theory of responsibility it deemed most appropriate, within the limits of the Amended Indictment and insofar as the evidence permitted.⁴⁵ The Appeal Chamber agreed with this approach. Even though the Prosecution had failed to plead the category of JCE, let alone the basic elements of the JCE (such as the purpose of the enterprise, the identity of the participants, and the nature of the Accused's participation in the enterprise)⁴⁶ and the common purpose pled in the pre-trial brief was a common purpose to persecute Muslims and Croats in the Municipality of Prijedor,⁴⁷ it, nonetheless, decided that the Accused had received sufficient notice of a common purpose limited to one detention centre within the Municipality.⁴⁸

Perhaps, having set the bar so low in these cases, the Appeals Chamber was left in a judicial quandary concerning creating directly applicable pleading standards that might cast doubt on the safety of these JCE convictions. Equally plausible, bearing in mind JCE's teleological *raison d'être* and the associated benefits to the prosecution of minimal pleading standards, is that the Appeals Chamber has been concerned not to intervene for fear that JCE's utility or unsurpassed ability to find guilt in the absence of evidence might be curtailed – a classic case of 'if it ain't broke, don't fix it'. Indeed, this strain of thinking is inadvertently evidenced in some of the jurisprudence (as well as court practice) in the repeated claim that Trial Chambers should be permitted to apply any theory found applicable to the evidence or find guilt insofar as the evidence permits.⁴⁹ Whilst this may be considered in some instances to be a perfectly sensible call to justice, used as a justification to uphold JCE convictions -where the prosecution have failed to explicitly plead a common purpose or the basic elements of JCE, it raises serious questions of due process: it sits uneasily with the requirement that the contours of the criminal purpose must be precisely defined and the evidence carefully assessed in relation to that pleading to ensure against a lapse into attributing guilt by mere association.

In sum, whatever the reason for the jurisprudential stasis, it is an indisputable fact that most of the links that the Prosecution intends to prove between the Accused, the JCE members, the non-JCE members and the crimes are not required to be defined in the indictment. In contrast to other liabilities,⁵⁰ the jurisprudence

---

⁴⁴ *Kvočka* TC Judgment, para 247 [internal quotations omitted].
⁴⁵ *Kvočka* TC Judgment, para 248 [internal quotations omitted].
⁴⁶ *Kvočka* AC Judgment, para 42.
⁴⁷ *Prosecutor v Kvočka* (Prosecution Pre-Trial Brief) IT-98-30/1-T (14 February 2000) para 216.
⁴⁸ *Kvočka* AC Judgment, paras 39, 44, 45, 196, 198, 246 and others.
⁴⁹ *Prosecutor v Simić* (Trial Judgment) IT-95-9-T (17 October 2003) footnote 244; *Krstić* TC Judgment, para 602; *Prosecutor v Kunarac* (Trial Judgment) IT-96-23-T and IT-96-23/1-T (22 February 2001) paras 388–389; *Prosecutor v Furundžija* (Trial Judgment) IT-95-17/1-T (10 December 1998) para 189; *Kvočka* TC Judgment, para 248 [internal quotations omitted].
⁵⁰ *Kupreškić* AC Judgment, para 88; *Prosecutor v Semanza* (Trial Judgment) ICTR-97-20-T (15 May 2003) para 44.

allows the majority of the material facts to be omitted and the precise links between the accused and crimes to be pled through the evidence. The majority of the conduct that will be alleged at the close of the case to constitute the links that establish the basic elements of JCE liability and therefore the accused's guilt is not particularised in the indictment but remains scattered in the thousands of pages and hundreds of hours of evidence that is led during the prosecution (and defence) case during the trial.[51] This allows an anxious Prosecutor the opportunity to advance multiple (and contradictory) theories at the same time and mould the case against the Accused in the course of the trial depending upon how the evidence unfolds.[52] Both the Accused and the Trial Judge will have to scour this evidence to ascertain the precise links that the Prosecution may seek to rely upon at the close of the case. In a standard JCE case at the ICTY there are hundreds of these links in the evidence, often many are highly inconsistent or even mutually exclusive, making it impracticable, if not impossible, to prepare an effective defence. Further, as will be demonstrated below in Section III, through an examination of the *Martić* case at the ICTY, rather than the criminal purpose being precisely defined in the indictment followed by an assessment of the evidence against this benchmark, the judges are left to define the purpose themselves, 'insofar as the evidence permits',[53] with predictable and far-reaching consequences for the delicate process of assessing individual responsibility.

---

[51] It is habitual practice at the ICTY for the Prosecution to seek to add new witnesses and new evidence during the trial. The jurisprudence makes it practically impossible to exclude the new evidence. Providing the evidence is minimally relevant and probative, the best an Accused can generally hope is that he is granted time to investigate the new material. Of course, with an indictment alleging multiple counts prosecuted through a regional or country wide JCE with thousands of JCE members or non-JCE members and hundreds of charges (or, a distinct basis for conviction) almost any evidence within the temporal framework of the indictment can be argued to fulfil this qualification and therefore becomes admissible.

[52] A process purportedly prohibited according to the jurisprudence: see for example; *Kupreškić* AC Judgment, para 92; *Krnojelac* TC Judgment, para 23. See also WA Schabas, *The UN International Criminal Tribunals: The Former Yugoslavia, Rwanda and Sierra Leone* (CUP, Cambridge 2006) 361–362.

[53] *Kvočka* TC Judgment, para 248 [internal quotations omitted].

## III. The *Martić* Case: Defining the Contours of the Common Purpose

### A. An Ill Defined Campaign of Mass Criminality

The *Martić* case concerned a high-ranking politician from the so-called Autonomous Region of Krajina who was charged with 19 counts of violations of the laws or customs of war and crimes against humanity under Articles 3 and 5 of the Statute of the ICTY respectively,[54] pursuant to the basic and extended forms of JCE liability. Central to the case was a criminal purpose alleged to involve the forcible removal of a majority of the Croat, Muslim and other non-Serb population from thousands of square kilometres in Croatia and Bosnia. The outer limits of the criminal purpose was described in the indictment as 'the forcible removal of a majority of the Croat, Muslim and other non-Serb population from approximately one-third of the territory of the Republic of Croatia ('Croatia'), and large parts of the Republic of Bosnia and Herzegovina ('Bosnia and Herzegovina') through the commission of crimes in violation of Articles 3 and 5 of the Statute of the Tribunal'.[55] For each count, individual criminal responsibility was charged under both Article 7(1) and (3) of the Statute of the ICTY. As mentioned above, it was alleged that all the crimes were committed pursuant to the basic category of JCE. In the alternative, it was alleged that the crimes in Counts 1 to 9 and 12 to 19 were committed pursuant to the extended form.[56] The allegation was that this JCE came into existence before 1 August 1991 and continued until at least August 1995.[57]

The indictment also alleged that 'Milan Martić worked in concert with or through several individuals in the joint criminal enterprise. Each participant or co-perpetrator within the joint criminal enterprise played his role or roles that

---

[54] Article 3: Counts 4 and 16 (Murder); Count 8 (Torture); Counts 9 and 18 (Cruel treatment); Count 12 (Wanton destruction of villages, or devastation not justified by military necessity); Count 13 (Destruction or wilful damage done to institutions dedicated to education or religion); Count 14 (Plunder of public or private property); Count 19 (Attacks on civilians). Article 5: Count 1 (Persecution); Count 2 (Extermination); Counts 3 and 15 (Murder); Count 5 (Imprisonment); Count 6 (Torture); Counts 7 and 17 (Inhumane Acts); Count 10 (Deportation); Count 11 (Other inhumane acts – forcible transfer).

[55] *Prosecutor v Martić* (Amended Indictment) IT-95-11 (9 September 2003) (hereafter '*Martić* Amended Indictment') para 4.

[56] *Martić* Amended Indictment, para 5: Count 1 (Persecution); Count 2 (Extermination); Counts 3, 4, 15 and 16 (Murder); Count 5 (Imprisonment); Counts 6 and 8 (Torture); Counts 7 and 17 (Inhumane Acts); Counts 9 and 18 (Cruel treatment); Count 10 (Deportation); Count 11 (Inhumane Acts); Count 12 (Wanton destruction of villages or devastation not justified by military necessity); Count 13 (Destruction or wilful damage done to institutions dedicated to education or religion); Count 14 (Plunder of public or private property) and Count 19 (Attacks on civilians).

[57] *Martić* Amended Indictment, para 6.

significantly contributed to the overall objective of the enterprise'.[58] The participants or co-perpetrators identified were 19 Serbian civilian, military and paramilitary leaders from the former Yugoslavia (e.g. Milošević, Karadžić, Arkan, etc) and

> other members of the Yugoslav People's Army (JNA), later the Yugoslav Army (VJ); the army of the RSK (SVK); the army of the *Republika Srpska* (VRS); the Serb Territorial Defence (TO) of Croatia, Bosnia and Herzegovina, Serbia and Montenegro; local and Serbian police forces (MUP forces), including the State Security (DB) of the Republic of Serbia, and Serb police forces of the SAO Krajina and the RSK (commonly referred to as 'Martić's Police,' *'Martićevci,'* 'SAO Krajina Police' or 'SAO Krajina Milicija' and hereinafter 'Martić's Police'); and members of Serbian, Montenegrin and Bosnian Serb paramilitary forces and volunteer units, including the 'Wolves of Vucjak' who were trained by Milan Martić and Martić's Police (collectively, 'Serb forces'), and other political figures from the (Socialist) Federal Republic of Yugoslavia, the Republic of Serbia, the Republic of Montenegro and the Bosnian Serb leadership.[59]

In other words, Martić was alleged to have acted in concert with any one of the 19 named and thousands of unnamed co-perpetrators to further the criminal purpose. The remainder of the salient parts of the indictment consisted of a description of Martić's alleged contribution to the common purpose particularised as a non-exclusive range of criminal and non-criminal conduct[60] and a series of specified attacks or crimes in specific locations. The link between Martić and those attacks or crimes was described in a general way as an allegation that Martić was 'acting individually or in concert with other known and unknown members of a joint criminal enterprise',[61] at a time when 'members of Martić's Police and other Serb forces, in particular the JNA and members of the local Serb TO'[62] (or some other variation of these or other militarised formations, e.g. the Republic of Serbia's Ministry of Internal Affairs), had committed the enumerated crimes.

The indictment failed to particularise any role for any other alleged JCE member in relation to the furtherance of the common purpose. Apart from listing them as members of the JCE, their names were not mentioned again in relation to the JCE. How they acted and how their concerted action gave rise to the crimes was not explained. Apart from a global allegation that Martić was the *de jure* and *de facto* commander of some of the forces (e.g. Martić's police) there was nothing to situate him or any member of the alleged JCE in relation to the crimes in the particular place where they occurred and at the particular time in question. The indictment alleged that there was a plan involving every Serbian leader and combatant and somehow, in some way, Martić and they were responsible for the crimes.

---

[58] *Martić* Amended Indictment, para 6.
[59] *Martić* Amended Indictment, para 6.
[60] *Martić* Amended Indictment, para 7; see below for critique of this lack of specificity.
[61] See for example *Martić* Amended Indictment, para 25.
[62] See for example *Martić* Amended Indictment, para 26.

# JOINT CRIMINAL ENTERPRISE LIABILITY

The Prosecution's pre-trial brief was similarly vague and did not provide the accused with notice of the precise elements of the alleged (double) region-wide JCE. Whilst narrating some basic narrative detail concerning the chronology of the criminal events, the majority of the links between the Accused, the JCE members and crime were not particularised. Rather than provide an account of the acts or interaction of individuals, precisely define the plurality, identify the precise conduct of the alleged JCE members or otherwise clarify the nature of the shared intent *of individuals* at the centre of the JCE, the critical focus was on the conduct of the political, military and police groupings whose members were responsible for the crimes. The pre-trial brief studiously avoided identifying individuals (other than Martić, see below) in most instances and repeatedly referred to the conduct of generic groups of combatants, such as 'other members of the JCE' or 'civilian, military, and police organs, and paramilitary/volunteer formations' or 'Martić's police'. Military and police formations such as the Serbian army ('the JNA') numbering thousands of combatants are repeatedly referenced without any further identification of the respective leaders, command structures or rank and file.[63] The pre-trial brief failed to particularise the conduct of prominent politicians or military leaders said to be at the core of the criminal purpose. The upper echelons of the political and military leadership (e.g. Milošević, the President of Serbia, and Karadzić, President of the Bosnian Serbs) or military leaders (such as Adžić, Chief of the JNA and Kadijević, Yugoslav Federal Secretary for Defence) were sparsely referenced in a handful of the briefest paragraphs.[64] The Prosecution's case concerning how the overwhelming vast majority of JCE members had acted and which non-JCE members (even by reference to specific sub-units within the broad groupings) had been used and by whom and how this action gave rise to the crimes was not defined. Individuals were named, but only occasionally did the brief detail their actual roles Of the 20 individuals identified by name (excluding Martić) in the 200 pages of prosecution theory, the majority were not mentioned more than three times.[65]

---

[63] See for example *Martić* Amended Indictment, paras 4, 31, 48, 56, 79, 95, 116. For example, para 31: 'Milan Martić independent of his formal position within the RSK, was the main RSK- player in the relationship with the SFRY/FRY and Serbian leadership and other members of the JCE in securing political and military support from Serbia and SFRY/FRY for the RSK and the SAO Krajina TO, and subsequently the SVK, until the end of the indictment period'; para 37: 'The establishment and existence of this [training] camp shows clearly a direct JCE link between Martić and Serbian State Security, eventually ending up with Slobodan Milošević'; para 43: 'Within the JCE, civilian, military, and police organs and volunteer formations collaborated to take over municipalities and territories throughout Croatia and BiH'.

[64] *Prosecutor v Martić* (Prosecution's Pre-Trial Brief) IT-95-11-PT (7 May 2004) (hereafter '*Martić* Prosecution's Pre-Trial Brief'): Milošević (paras 10, 13, 37, 38, 41, 80) and Karadžić (paras 41, 80, 82).

[65] See for example *Martić* Prosecution's Pre-Trial Brief: Krajišnik (para 41); 'Šešelj's men' (para 98); Opačić (para 54); Dukić (para 96); Novaković (paras 35, 36); Torbica (para

As discussed briefly above, Martić's alleged contribution to the criminal purpose was summarised in the Amended Indictment and pre-trial brief in all-encompassing catch-all phrases alleging that he had participated *inter alia* 'in the planning, preparation and execution of the take-over of territories in the Croatian SAO's and parts of Bosnia and Herzegovina ... and the subsequent forcible removal of the Croat, Muslim and other non-Serb population',[66] or that he 'personally participated in military actions and subsequent crimes of these police and military forces throughout the targeted territories as described in the indictment'.[67] Typical of JCE pleadings at the ICTY, the Accused received notice that *any* evidence of his conduct that emerged during the trial could be assessed as probative of his intent to pursue the crimes: nothing was excluded, everything he did potentially gave rise to criminal responsibility.

The indictment and the pre-trial brief therefore left the majority of the critical questions unanswered. Whilst the jurisprudence (justifiably) permits the prosecution of criminal enterprises involving thousands of JCE members and non-JCE members, thousands of square kilometres, many years of war and a multitude of crime bases and crimes, there are, unfortunately, no requirements that the critical links that must be proven be particularised. Accordingly, whilst Martić was provided with notice of the crimes themselves, his alleged *de jure* position and a global assertion that he was the overall *de facto* commander role at the time, he was deprived of notice of the links alleged to lead from him and the JCE members to the non-JCE members (e.g. particular commanders, sub-commanders or rank and file) and thereafter to the crimes. These are the links that the Prosecution were setting out to prove and the minimum that allow an opportunity to prepare an effective defence without having to forlornly scan thousands of pages of evidence in an n attempt to gauge which of the (often contradictory) links might emerge and be relied upon by the Chamber. These were the signposts that should have guided the parties and the Trial Chamber through the difficult evidential journey ahead, providing the springboard for the precise assessment of individual responsibility required at the final judgment stage.[68]

---

35); Španović (para 35); Koljević (para 41); Adžić (para 41); Vasiljević (para 41); Karadžić (paras 41, 80, 82) and Adžić (para 41); Kadijević (para 41).

66    *Martić* Amended Indictment, para 7. See also *Martić* Prosecution's Pre-Trial Brief, para 52: the Prosecution also provided notice that the events in the indictment are 'only a sample of the serious incidents that occurred between 1991 and 1995 in the Krajina' and that witnesses would also testify to other crimes in other locations to provide 'an overview of the widespread and systematic nature of the atrocities committed by the Serb forces during the relevant period'.

67    *Martić* Amended Indictment, para 7.

68    During the Martić trial, lasting 143 days, 67 witnesses were called to testify and 1,015 exhibits numbering many thousands of pages were tendered.. See *Prosecutor v Martić*, Case Information Sheet <http://www.icty.org/x/cases/martic/cis/en/cis_martic_en.pdf> last accessed 12 January 2012.

## B. The Martić Trial and Appellate Judgments

The Trial Chamber found that Martić had participated in a criminal purpose involving the establishment of an ethnically Serb territory through the forced displacement of the Croat and other non-Serb population.[69] The Trial Chamber concluded that Martić incurred individual responsibility pursuant to Article 7(1) by participating in the JCE through the provision of substantive financial, logistical and military support to the Croatian Serb territory (SAO Krajina and the RSK), by exercising his authority over the Ministry of Interior (MUP) of the Croatian Serbian government (SAO Krajina and the RSK), by fuelling an atmosphere of insecurity and fear through public statements, and by participating in the forcible removal of the non-Serb population.[70] The Trial Chamber convicted Martić under the basic form of JCE for Counts 10, 11 and 1 (in part) and under the extended form of JCE for Counts 3 to 9, 12 to 14 and 1 (in part).[71] The Trial Chamber sentenced Martić to 35 years' imprisonment for the crimes.

Martić complained on appeal, *inter alia*, that the Trial Chamber erred on various occasions[72] in reaching the conclusion that crimes were committed by forces under his control or another member of the JCE's control because the evidence showed 'that they were instead committed by unidentified individuals and/or by unsubordinated or 'renegade' units'.[73] The Appeals Chamber accepted that the Trial Chamber had failed to make the relevant findings that the JCE members,

---

[69] *Prosecutor v Martić* (Judgment) IT-95-11-T (12 June 2007) (hereafter '*Martić* TC Judgment') para 445.

[70] *Martić* TC Judgment, paras 447–455. Martić was convicted of the following crimes: Count 1, persecution as a crime against humanity; Count 3, murder as a crime against humanity; Count 4, murder as a violation of the laws or customs of war; Count 5, imprisonment as a crime against humanity; Count 6, torture as a crime against humanity; Count 7, inhumane acts as a crime against humanity; Count 8, torture as a violation of the laws or customs of war; Count 9, cruel treatment as a violation of the laws or customs of war; Count 10, deportation as a crime against humanity; Count 11, forcible transfer as a crime against humanity; Count 12, wanton destruction of villages or devastation not justified by military necessity as a violation of the laws or customs of war; Count 13, destruction or wilful damage done to institutions dedicated to education or religion as a violation of the laws or customs of war; and Count 14, plunder of public or private property as a violation of the laws or customs of war. More specifically, the Trial Chamber concluded that the crimes under Counts 10, 11 and 1 (in relation to the deportations and forcible transfers) all fell within the common purpose of the JCE, while the crimes under Counts 3 to 9, 12 to 14, and 1 (insofar as it related to those counts) fell outside the common purpose but were 'foreseeable to Martić'.

[71] *Martić* TC Judgment, paras 452–455, 518. The Trial Chamber acquitted Martić of Count 2, extermination as a crime against humanity (paras 406, 517).

[72] In relation to crimes committed during the spring and summer of 1991; also crimes in Hrvastka Dubica, Cerovljani, Bacin and its surroundings; Saborska, Lipovača, Poljanak and Vukovići, Škabrnja, Nadin, Bruška, and those in detention centres; *Prosecutor v Martić* (Judgment) IT-95-11-A (8 October 2008) (hereafter '*Martić* AC Judgment'), para 165.

[73] *Martić* AC Judgment, para 165.

when using the non-JCE members (the JNA, the police and other Serb forces) to commit crimes, were acting in accordance with the common purpose, i.e. the establishment of a unified Serb territory through the forcible removal of the non-Serb population.[74] The Appeals Chamber also accepted that in relation to the crimes committed by 'some armed structures and paramilitary units, including those referred to as 'Martić's men' or 'Martić's police' the Trial Chamber did not reach any definite finding on their link with Martić'.[75] The Appeals Chamber reviewed the findings to ascertain, nonetheless, whether the correct principles were applied and 'whether the factual findings in the Trial Judgment as a whole' warranted 'the conclusion that the interaction of the members of the JCE in the implementation of the common criminal objective, together with other elements of proof', could 'serve as a basis for establishing a link between the crimes committed and Martić'.[76] The Appeals Chamber's approach to the fundamental requirement that a plurality must be found to be acting in furtherance of a criminal purpose, and the *Brđanin* requirement that crimes committed by non-JCE members must be assessed on a case-by-case basis to ascertain whether they were within the criminal purpose before JCE liability can arise, provides a stark demonstration of the consequences of a lack of defined criminal purpose and the lack of safeguards in the application of JCE at the ICTY.

## IV. The Demise of the 'Common Purpose' Requirement

In order to find an accused responsible pursuant to JCE liability, the trier of fact must first find the existence of a common purpose which amounts to or involves the commission of a crime provided for in the Statute[77] and a plurality of persons acting in concert in pursuit of the purpose.[78] In *Martić*, since almost all the JCE crimes were found to be committed through the JCE members using the (non-JCE members) the JNA, the police and other Serb forces to commit the crimes, the question of whether, on a case-by-case basis, this was done in furtherance of the common criminal purpose, ought to have been at the forefront of the Trial Chamber's deliberations. The Trial Chamber's failure therefore to make an explicit finding that the JCE members, when using these non-JCE members to commit crimes, were acting in accordance with the common purpose could not be easily dismissed as a minor judicial slip or typographical error. However, this was the approach the Appeals Chamber appears to have taken to this critical omission. Purporting to review the Trial Judgment, the Appeals Chamber concluded that, despite the lack of explicit findings, the Trial Chamber had been satisfied beyond

---

[74] *Martić* AC Judgment, para 181.
[75] *Martić* AC Judgment, para 181.
[76] *Martić* AC Judgment, para 168 and 174.
[77] *Tadić* AC Judgment, para 227.
[78] *Tadić* AC Judgment, para 227. See also *Krajišnik* TC Judgment, para 884.

reasonable doubt that members of the JCE were acting in accordance with the common purpose.[79] On the face of the Trial Chamber's findings, it is difficult to see how the Appeals Chamber could have fairly reached this conclusion.

Firstly, the Trial Chamber's factual and legal findings concerning the existence of a JCE and Martić's responsibility pursuant to the JCE were analysed in 13 insubstantial paragraphs of the 520-paragraph Judgment.[80] Martić's participation in the JCE was analysed in eight paragraphs of the Judgment.[81] The Chamber analysed the membership of the plurality in a single paragraph.[82] Whilst brevity of legal reasoning may be considered a virtue, the Trial Chamber's analysis of the plurality consisted of an impoverished handful of sentences leading to the overwhelmingly significant conclusion that the cooperation of the political and military leadership in pursuit of the political goal of uniting Serb territories 'necessitated the forcible removal of the non-Serb population'. This was followed by a wholly unreasoned finding that the plurality consisted of 'at least' 11 individuals, namely, Adžić, Babić, Bogdanović, Kadijević, Karadzic, Milošević, Mladić, Seselj, Simatović, Stanišić and Vasiljković.[83] Whilst this finding was referenced to Section III of the Judgment ('Factual Findings'), the Trial Chamber failed to specify which particular factual findings (or, paragraphs) were relevant and how it had reasoned from the factual findings to the legal finding that a particular JCE member's conduct demonstrated his shared criminal intent at the core of the JCE.

Moreover, these deficiencies were not limited to a mere failure to provide detailed analysis or reasoning. The real problem was that Section III of the Judgment ('Factual Findings') failed to detail sufficiently the conduct of JCE members to allow any meaningful insight into the Trial Chamber's summation identifying the plurality. Rather than providing the requisite findings that would substitute for the one-paragraph analysis of the plurality, Section III only found four of the JCE members (Babić,[84] Adžić[85] Kadijević[86] and Milošević) to be acting in furtherance of the common purpose. Further, the conduct outlined concerning the remainder is scant. The most egregious example of this failure to identify relevant conduct concerned one JCE member (Seselj). Section III of the Judgment outlined only one factual finding in relation to this purported JCE member. His membership of the plurality must have been inferred from this single finding, namely that he had visited a detention centre on one occasion and insulted the non-Serb detainees.[87] In sum, rather than the identification of the precise conduct of named individuals and their nexus to the crimes, Section III consisted principally of overarching,

---

[79] *Martić* AC Judgment, paras 174–181.
[80] See for example *Martić* TC Judgment, paras 442–455.
[81] *Martić* TC Judgment, paras 447–455.
[82] *Martić* TC Judgment, para 446.
[83] *Martić* TC Judgment, paras 445–446.
[84] See for example *Martić* TC Judgment, para 333.
[85] *Martić* TC Judgment, para 331.
[86] *Martić* TC Judgment, para 330.
[87] *Martić* TC Judgment, paras 288, 416.

globalised conclusions concerning overall operational coordination at the macro-political level (e.g. presidential or governmental), wholly remote from the crimes,[88] as well as the description of the behaviour of groups, such as the JNA, the TO, the SAO Krajina MUP, the Milicia Krajina, Martić's men, Martić's army, etc, with little else.[89] In other words, the factual findings consisted of descriptions of named groups committing crimes without the identification of the role played by the 11 JCE members or any indication how on a case-by-case basis they had used named non-JCE members to commit the crimes.[90]

As mentioned, notwithstanding, the Appeals Chamber went on to consider and uphold the Trial Chamber finding of a JCE. Firstly, the Appeals Chamber considered Martić's complaint that the Trial Chamber had failed to 'properly establish that a common criminal purpose existed among the eleven alleged participants'.[91] However, with few explicit findings identifying individuals and their conduct and its relationship to crime and the criminal purpose, the Appeals Chamber's endorsement of the Trial Chamber's approach was necessarily equally generalized. First, the Appeals Chamber summarised the Trial Chamber's findings establishing Martić's responsibility for the crimes committed by the police and the TO. It relied upon the finding that Martić had *de jure* and *de facto* control over the police and the TO in general as dispositive of the question of whether it was reasonable to conclude that their crimes had been committed in furtherance of the common purpose.[92] The problem with this analysis is obvious. Rather than illustrating a meaningful analysis into Martić's engagement with these forces on a case-by-case or crime-by-crime basis to ascertain whether these groups had been used by him in furtherance of the common purpose, it merely inferred from the Trial Chamber's global finding (establishing Martić's *de jure* and *de facto* overall control) that all the crimes committed by these forces must have been at the behest of Martić and must have been in furtherance of the common purpose. It was a sweeping, overblown conclusion that suggested that, once Martić had been found to have *de jure* and *de facto* control over these forces generally and had used them to act in furtherance of the criminal purpose on one occasion, then all crimes committed by their members on all subsequent occasions were his responsibility.

As concerns the remaining crime-committing formation (the JNA) and the remaining JCE members the Appeals Chamber's approach was even more presumptive. Taking the same generalising approach, the Chamber purported to summarise the Trial Chamber's findings that they considered must have been critical to attribute the crimes committed by members of the JNA to the JCE members within the common purpose and thereafter to Martić.[93] The Appeals Chamber asserted:

---

[88] *Martić* AC Judgment, para 178.
[89] For example *Martić* TC Judgment, paras 199, 203, 240, 242, 244, 245, 247, 266.
[90] *Martić* TC Judgment, paras 127–160.
[91] *Martić* AC Judgment, para 23.
[92] *Martić* AC Judgment, paras 174–179.
[93] *Martić* AC Judgment, paras 174–180.

With respect to JNA forces active in the region, the Trial Chamber found that the JNA was under the control of a number of the members of the JCE, in particular Ratko Mladić, the Commander of the 9th Corps of the JNA, and General Blagoje Adžić, JNA Chief of the General Staff. Other JCE members with important roles in setting the policy of the JNA and in implementing its objectives were: Radmilo Bogdanović, the Minister of the Interior of Serbia; Jovica Stanišić, the Chief of the SDB; Franko 'Frenki' Simatović, an official of the SDB; and General Veljiko Kadijević, the SFRY Federal Secretary for Defence. The Trial Chamber further found that the SFRY Federal Secretariat of National Defence of the JNA had made unit and personnel changes within the SAO Krajina armed forces, and that the former cooperated with the latter in joint operations.[94]

, It is worthwhile observing that due to the paucity of factual findings in the Trial Judgment, even with this globalizing approach – eschewing a case by case analysis - the Appeals Chamber was only able to find that seven out of the 11 JCE members (Martić, Mladić, Adžić, Bogdanović, Stanišić, Simatović and Kadijević) had been found by the Trial Chamber to be explicitly connected to the military and police formations acting in furtherance of the criminal purpose. Moreover, the Appeals Chamber fell into error in this analysis when asserting that three JCE members (Bogdanović, Stanišić and Simatović) had 'important roles in the policy of the JNA and in implementing its objectives'.

At no stage had the Trial Chamber found that these three (members of the Serbian Ministry of Interior leadership) were responsible for or connected to the JNA. The footnoted reference to the Trial Chamber's finding dealt with a different issue, namely their supply of financial, logistics and military supplies to the Croatian Serb's new government (SAO Krajina).[95] In sum, even with an approach that amounted to little more than upholding findings of JCE membership on the basis of *de jure* titles, the Appeals Chamber was able to (accurately) identify and uphold the Trial Chamber's findings concerning the plurality acting in furtherance of the common purpose when using non-JCE members in relation to four members of the JCE (Martić, Mladić, Adžić and Kadijević). Nonetheless, the Appeals Chamber summarised its review as follows:

> The Trial Chamber considered that the JNA, the police and other Serb forces active on the territory of the SAO Krajina and the RSK were structured hierarchically and closely coordinated one with the other. In conjunction with such findings, and its conclusions regarding the plurality of people sharing the common criminal purpose and Martić's contribution to it, the Trial Chamber explicitly found that

---

[94] *Martić* AC Judgment, para 180.
[95] *Martić* TC Judgment, para 140 (contained under the heading: Support provided to the SAO Krajina).

the objective of establishing a unified Serb territory was implemented 'through widespread and systematic armed attacks [...] and through the commission of acts of violence and intimidation'. Considering in addition the 'scale and gravity of the crimes [...] committed against the non-Serb population', the attacks could not have been carried out by members of the JCE individually, but only by using the forces under their control. Therefore, the only reasonable interpretation of these findings is that the Trial Chamber was satisfied beyond reasonable doubt that members of the JCE, when using these forces, were acting in accordance with the common purpose, *i.e.*, the establishment of a unified Serb territory through the forcible removal of the non-Serb population.[96]

In other words, having failed to identify with precision the JCE members involved, the Appeals Chamber merely inferred from the Trial Chamber's findings concerning the hierarchy and close coordination of the military formations in general and the scale and type of crimes that all crimes committed by these forces must *ipso facto* have been committed by JCE members using non-JCE members in furtherance of the JCE member's common criminal purpose.

As noted above, it is surprising, if not astonishing, that the Appeals Chamber did not regard the Trial Chamber's failure to make explicit findings on these fundamental cornerstones of JCE liability as particularly problematic. The problem was not limited to the absence of explicit findings that the JCE members, when using the JNA, the police and other Serb forces, to commit crimes, were acting in accordance with the common purpose, but extended to the comprehensive failure to identify the conduct of the JCE members that demonstrated the shared intent at the core of the criminal enterprise and link it directly to the non-JCE members, the criminal purpose and the crimes on a case-by-case basis. Instead of focusing on these essential assessments, the Trial Chamber subordinated these safeguards to the identification of group conduct and the crimes themselves and little else. There was little within the Trial Judgment to rebut the presumption that the absence of findings was a systemic problem of analysis. Nonetheless, with little or no analysis, the Appeals Chamber was content to conclude that the Trial Chamber had been satisfied beyond reasonable doubt that members of the JCE were acting in accordance with the common purpose.[97] As the above discussion demonstrates, absent specific findings relating to JCE members and named individuals, the Appeal Chamber had to fall back on the same collectivising analysis, relying on the identification of previous group behaviour, general coordination of the forces and the scale, similarity and gravity of the crimes. All crime committed at any time during the indictment period could be assessed as committed at the behest of the JCE members in furtherance of the criminal purpose and thereafter to Martić

---

[96] *Martić* TC Judgment, para 181.
[97] *Martić* AC Judgment, para 174–181.

provided the perpetrators could be identified as members of the three groupings (TO, police and the JNA).

## V. Crimes by Non-JCE Members: Another Interpretation of the *Brđanin* 'Tools Requirement'

As noted above, the Appeals Chamber accepted that, in relation to some of the crimes committed by 'some armed structures and paramilitary units, including those referred to as 'Martić's men' or 'Martić's police' (*Martićevci*), the Trial Chamber failed to make any definite finding on their link with Martić'.[98] To reiterate, as the Appeals Chamber in *Brđanin* made clear, 'to hold a member of a JCE responsible for crimes committed by non-members of the enterprise, it has to be shown that the crime can be imputed to one member of the joint criminal enterprise, and that this member – when using a principal perpetrator – acted in accordance with the common plan'.[99] In assessing this connection, the 'factors indicative of a sufficient link include evidence that the JCE members explicitly or implicitly requested the non-JCE member to commit such a crime or instigated, ordered, encouraged, or otherwise availed himself of the non-JCE member to commit the crime'.[100] The Appeals Chamber in *Martić* reviewed the Trial Chamber's findings on the crimes to ascertain whether, in light of the factual findings in relation to the specific crimes and the Judgment as a whole, it was open to a reasonable trier of fact to have attributed these crimes to Martić.[101]

Given the paucity of factual findings linking Martić or other JCE members to the crimes committed by non-JCE members on a case-by-case basis, the Appeals Chamber lapsed once more into generalities. The Appeals Chamber's review was predicated upon a globalised view concerning the coordination of the formations in general, Martić's *de jure* status as Minister of Interior, his 'general roles and responsibilities' and his *mens rea*.[102] The Appeals Chambers review consisted of little other than a reiteration of evidence that demonstrated that the crimes had been committed by members of the relevant military formations and the identification of the Trial Chamber findings implicating three JCE members (Martić, Mladić and Seselj) in a handful of the crimes.[103] The logic was reductionist to say the least. Because the Trial Chamber found that the JCE members, including Martić, occupied leadership positions in the military and police (whose members had been found responsible for the crimes), it was, in the mind of the Appeals Chamber,

---

[98] *Martić* AC Judgment, para 181.
[99] *Brdjanin* AC Judgment, para 413.
[100] *Krajišnik* AC Judgment, para 226.
[101] *Martić* AC Judgment, para 182.
[102] *Martić* AC Judgment, paras 187–188.
[103] *Martić* AC Judgment, paras 188–189.

reasonable to attribute any crime committed in any circumstances by any of their members to within the common purpose. Again, the consequence of this stark line of reasoning was that any crime committed by men identified as being associated with these groups, however loosely, could be attributed to Martić without further consideration of whether they had been requested to commit such a crime or instigated, ordered, encouraged, or otherwise availed to do so (or, whether in fact the crime was foreseeable from crimes so availed).

For example, the Appeals Chamber upheld the Trial Chamber's conviction for the intentional killing of nine people in Cerovljani. The Trial Chamber found that the victims were killed either by (unidentified) men from the 'Milicia Krajina, or units of the JNA or TO or a combination of some of them'[104] and that therefore Martić incurred responsibility for the crimes of persecution and murder pursuant to the extended form of JCE.[105] Despite the fact that none of the perpetrators had been identified as belonging to these groups,[106] the Trial Chamber relied on an attack that had taken place on or around the same day in a neighbouring village (Hrvatska Dubica) to conclude that because the attack on Cerovljani was 'almost identical to the events in Hrvatska Dubica' it could be satisfied that the men came from the same groups.[107] Again, the Trial Chamber failed to make any showing that these groups were actually linked to a JCE member at the time of the crimes. Despite the complete absence of a *Brđanin* showing, the Appeals Chamber upheld the conviction for these crimes by relying upon 'the Trial Chamber's findings on Martić's position as Minister of the Interior and his absolute authority over the MUP, his control over the armed forces, the TO and *Milicija Krajine*, the cooperation between the TO, the JNA, the *Milicija Krajine* and the armed forces of the SAO Krajina, and the control over the JNA and the TO exercised by other members of the JCE as well as its findings regarding Martić's conduct and *mens rea*'.[108] This was assumption laid on presumption. The Appeals Chamber's approach collapsed, if not removed, the *Brđanin* dual requirements; that to hold a member of a JCE responsible for crimes committed by non-members of the enterprise, it has to be shown that the crime can be imputed to one member of the joint criminal enterprise, and that this member – when using a principal perpetrator – acted in accordance with the common plan.[109] Using the Martić Appeal threshold, any crime suspected of being committed by a member of the dominant armed group could be assumed to have been procured by one of the JCE members in furtherance of the common purpose or foreseeable from those crimes found to be so procured.[110] Given that

---

[104] *Martić* AC Judgment, para 359.
[105] *Martić* AC Judgment, para 183.
[106] *Martić* TC Judgment, paras 187–188.
[107] *Martić* TC Judgment, paras 359, 363.
[108] *Martić* AC Judgment, paras 187, 205.
[109] *Brđanin* AC Judgment, para 413.
[110] For further examples see *Martić* AC Judgment, paras 183–184, 194–195, 202–206, 209–212. As a contrast, see for example: paras 191–193, 197–201, where the Appeal Chamber declined to uphold the Trial Chamber's findings on the basis that the link to the relevant forces was too tenuous or the identification too uncertain.

almost all Serbian combatants or criminals fought under the banner of these dominant forces at one time or another, this was hugely significant. Martić could be found guilty through the JCE for any crime committed by anyone at any time during the indictment period with little other than a positive identification of this membership: guilt by association cloaked in the language of JCE.

## Conclusion: Inadequate JCE Safeguards

The *Brđanin* Trial Chamber was correct to display discomfort with extraordinarily large JCEs where the accused is structurally remote from the crimes. On the other hand, the Appeals Chamber was probably correct in concluding that a lapse into attributing guilt by association might be avoided by ensuring that the contours of the common criminal purpose are properly defined in the indictment and supported by the evidence beyond reasonable doubt.[111] how this is achieved in a complex trial. Unfortunately, these practicalities have been insufficiently addressed at the ICTY (or the ICTR) in the years since JCE made its entrance onto the international criminal law stage. Whilst general pleading standards have progressed significantly over the life span of the *ad hoc* tribunals,[112] JCE has been stubbornly impervious to these improvements. As this chapter has discussed, the pleading standards for JCE are rudimentary at best. The requirements are focused on the minimal expectation that JCE will *appear* in the indictment, rather than creating any meaningful threshold concerning particularisation of the elements of JCE and the links that are alleged to demonstrate the scope of the criminal purpose. JCE liability requires, *inter alia*, that the accused's participation 'must form a link in the chain of causation' to the crimes and the significance of this contribution to the crime is relevant for determining whether such a link exists.[113] It is the interaction or cooperation among persons – their joint action – in addition to their common objective that forges a group out of a mere plurality. The persons in a criminal enterprise must be shown to act together, or in concert with each other, in the implementation of a common objective. The Chamber also has to be satisfied of a link between the JCE members and the non-JCE members, and that the latter were being used by the former in relation to the crimes, on a case-by-case basis. Unfortunately, international criminal law has procedural guarantees, such as the requirements for specificity in the Indictment and Pre-Trial Brief, that in theory require the links to be particularised, but in practice these are not enforced, leaving them unspecified during the evidential

---

[111] *Brđanin* AC Judgment, para 424 [internal quotations omitted].

[112] W Jordash and J Coughlan, 'The Right to be Informed of the Nature and Causes of the Charges: A Potentially Formidable Jurisprudential Legacy', in S Darcy and J Powderly (eds) *Judicial Creativity at the International Criminal Tribunals* (OUP, Oxford 2010) 286.

[113] *Prosecutor v Blagojević* (Trial Judgment) IT-02-60-T (17 January 2005) para 702; *Brđanin* TC Judgment, para 263; *Prosecutor v Milutinovic* (Trial Judgment) IT-05-87-T (26 February 2009) para 105.

stage of the trial. These are the critical details that constitute the contours of the criminal purpose and the JCE. These provide the basis for the preparation of an effective defence and allow a Trial Chamber to have the optimum chance of being able to accurately assess individual responsibility.

One must query the contradiction between the ICTY jurisprudence that acknowledges with such apparent conviction the need to carefully define the contours of the criminal purpose, whilst simultaneously and comprehensively failing to craft rules to achieve this objective. Unfortunately, JCE has never cast off its' controversial teleological creation. Consequently, since that time, instead of focusing on the creative development of proper pleading standards based on trial practice, the Appeals Chamber became mired in defending the use of JCE on the basis of its customary law status, or alternatively in terminological debates that were case specific and led to little development or change of practice.

Meanwhile, the presumptions underpinning JCE's birth – that it can pinpoint responsibility in circumstances where evidence is difficult to find – still haunt the corridors of the ICTY. Rather than insisting on a defined criminal purpose and the proper pleading of the elements of JCE and the insistence that the prosecution stick to that case, the ICTY judiciary jealously guards the right to define the JCE and therefore the accused's guilt 'insofar as the evidence permits' at the final judgment stage. The conflict between this 'right' and the *Brdanin* requirement of a clearly defined criminal purpose is regrettable. It is a manifestation of the proposition that the defendants must be punished. Since the defendants must be punished, JCE must be used in such a way that it will yield the desired result.

The presumption of innocence requires, *inter alia*, that when carrying out their duties, the members of the court should not start with the preconceived idea that the accused has committed the offence charged. This means that the Judges must commence the trial with a clearly defined criminal purpose and a clear understanding of what links the Prosecution allege. That which is pled – the links between the Accused and the crimes – must be proven beyond a reasonable doubt. There is no doubt, as the *Martić* case amply demonstrates, that JCE trials without these essentials will yield the desired result. However, the *Martić* Trial Chamber's failure to make findings on many of the salient JCE links was directly referable to the Prosecution's failure to identify them at the beginning of the trial and subsequently make use of them as the road map for the trial. Requiring little more than the creation of a cavernous criminal pleading of the purpose into which evidence may be poured until a link of some kind emerges encourages gut determinations that attribute guilt by association, rather than enhancing the careful application of the burden and standard of proof. This is not procedural justice, but result orientated justice. Ultimately the failure of the ICTY to deal with these questions through the explicit development of rules of practice may well have played a defining role in the inevitable demise of JCE in the international criminal law project.

As the ICC begins to develop and employ liabilities, and particularly those that seek to assess individual liability arising from collective criminal enterprises, it must cast aside teleological objectives. The focus should be to ensure that its modes of liability accurately assess individual liability, rather than being designed to achieve a result to satisfy other transitional justice objectives. If the evidence relating to an individual's guilt proves difficult or impossible to find, despite careful investigations and generous prosecutorial resources, then the solution is not to find and reinterpret the law to achieve a result; but to strictly adhere to the principle of culpability, by remaining true to the standard of proof and the presumption of innocence for the betterment of the international criminal process.

# PART II
# The International Criminal Process

# Rights in Reverse: A Critical Analysis of Fair Trial Rights under International Criminal Law

Yvonne McDermott[1]

This chapter examines two key issues which have arisen as regards the international criminal tribunals' interpretation of the right to a fair trial, namely the parties to whom rights at trial attach, and the right to trial without undue delay. The chapter argues that the tribunals' extension of fair trial rights to other actors at trial, but particularly the prosecutor, is unnecessary and unhelpful. It also reveals that the defendant's right to a speedy trial has been used as a bar to the exercise of other rights in some circumstances, whilst in other situations a breach of the right to trial without undue delay has proven almost impossible to assert. These issues ought not to be viewed in a vacuum, but rather as symptomatic of a wider deficiency in international criminal law. They illustrate the piecemeal fashion in which questions on the fundaments of fairness in international criminal law have been answered, the lack of an overarching theory guiding the procedural fairness of trials, and international criminal law's resultant failure to serve a standard-setting function for the fairness of trials.[2]

Section I of this chapter outlines some instances where the ICTY, ICTR, SCSL and ICC have extended rights of the accused to other actors at trial, with a specific

---

[1] The author would like to thank Patricia Sellers, Ian Scobbie, William A. Schabas, Joe Powderly, Niamh Hayes and participants at the Irish Centre for Human Rights annual doctoral seminar 2011 for their valuable comments on an earlier draft.

[2] The potential of international criminal procedure to set the highest standards for the fairness of trials, and its failure to do so, is addressed in part by the present author in 'Double Speak and Double Standards: Does the Jurisprudence on Retrial following Acquittal under International Criminal Law Spell the End of the Double Jeopardy Rule?' in D Keane and Y McDermott (eds) *The Challenge of Human Rights: Past, Present and Future* (Edward Elgar, Cheltenham 2012) 176. For an interesting analysis of international criminal procedure's potential in advancing the rule of law in post-conflict societies, see J-D Ohlin, 'A Meta-Theory of International Criminal Procedure: Vindicating the Rule of Law' (2009) 14 *UCLA J Int'l L & Foreign Affairs* 77, 103.

focus on the prosecutor as a new rights-holder at trial. The irony of this unfounded extension is that it often has a detrimental effect on the rights of the accused, whom the enumerated rights were intended to protect in the first place. On occasion, and in a sporadic fashion, the international criminal tribunals have also elevated certain interests of other parties to the status of 'rights', which can also come to bear on the position of the only true rights-holder at trial – the accused. Section II illustrates the ease with which judges can assert the right to trial without undue delay as a reason for a decision denying a request of the accused, compared to the immense hurdles which an accused must overcome to show that the right to a speedy trial has been violated.

## I. The Prosecutor's Right to a Fair Trial

It is uncontroversial to suggest that the accused is the principal beneficiary of the right to a fair trial. However, the following analysis aims to illustrate that the accused individual ought to be regarded as the *only* actor that holds enforceable rights related to their status at trial. Other actors such as the prosecutor, witnesses, victims, and the international community may be regarded as interest-holders, and holders of personal rights as human rights but not as rights deriving from their status of actor at trial. In other words, there is a distinction to be made under international law between 'status human rights' and 'pure human rights'; whether a person is a refugee, a prisoner, a combatant or an accused person before an international tribunal, their right to be free from torture may never be derogated from, but they may have additional rights or duties attaching to their status. Ergo, there is no tension between recognising a victim or witness's right to life, freedom from fear and other general human rights derived from internationally binding instruments as factors which may need to be balanced against the accused's right to a fair trial,[3] but there is an inherent tension between attaching the status rights of another actor under international law to a person to whom the same status rights simply do not apply. We can see such an extension in a decision of the *Norman* case before the SCSL Appeals Chamber, where the Chamber examined Article 14 of the ICCPR,[4] which delineates the rights of all accused persons to trial without undue delay:

> It appears in the ICCPR as a right guaranteed to a defendant, but for international human rights law it offers a vital and concomitant guarantee to victims of war crimes and crimes against humanity ... Victims and relatives of victims are entitled to have those accused of hideous offences which have caused them so much grief to be tried expeditiously.[5]

---

[3] *Doorson v The Netherlands* (Judgment) App No 20524/92 (26 March 1996) para 70.
[4] International Covenant on Civil and Political Rights, 999 UNTS 171 (19 December 1966).
[5] *Prosecutor v Norman et al* (Decision on the Application for a Stay of Proceedings and Denial of Right to Appeal) SCSL-2003-09-PT (4 November 2003) para 8.

The Appeals Chamber offered no legal justification or reference to its extension of the accused's right to a speedy trial to victims. It went on to observe that the international community also expected tribunals to work efficiently as well as fairly, with the pithy note that 'justice delayed is justice denied is no less true for being a truism'.[6]

Substantively derived from Article 14 ICCPR are Articles 18, 20 and 21 of the SCSL, ICTR and ICTY Statutes respectively.[7] These are the primary statutory provisions on the right to a fair trial, although of course they are complemented by other provisions in the Statutes and Rules which ensure the fairness of proceedings, such as rules on evidence and appeal. Three of the four sub-sections of these articles explicitly state that the '*accused* shall be' entitled to the guarantees therein, rendering their application to the accused alone relatively uncontroversial.[8] The other sub-section, the first in each of the Articles, refers to the fact that 'all persons shall be equal before the International Tribunal'.[9] This provision has been used as an gateway through which the rights of the accused have come to be bestowed upon the prosecution, the argument being that 'equality' in this sense cannot see one party favoured at the expense of another.[10] However, this strictly literal reading fails to recognise the second element of the general rule on treaty interpretation – the context. The reference to equality is so made under the *chapeau* of 'rights of the accused', indicating that this equality was intended as being between accused persons, as opposed to ensuring that the prosecutor should be treated 'as equally' as the defendants.[11]

Under the *chapeau* of 'rights of the accused', Article 67 of the ICC Statute consists of two sub-sections.[12] The first states that 'the accused shall be entitled to a public hearing ... to a fair hearing conducted impartially' and to a list of nine minimum guarantees 'in full equality', while the second deals with the prosecutorial obligation to disclose exculpatory material to the accused. However, the Court has extended fair trial rights to other actors on a number of occasions, stating that fairness can

---

[6] Ibid.

[7] Statute of the Special Court for Sierra Leone, annexed to the Agreement between the United Nations and the Government of Sierra Leone on the Establishment of the Special Court for Sierra Leone, signed on 16 January 2002 ('SCSL Statute'); Statute of the International Criminal Tribunal for Rwanda, UN Doc S/RES/955, UN Security Council, 1994 ('ICTR Statute'); Statute of the International Criminal Tribunal for the former Yugoslavia, UN Doc S/RES/827, UN Security Council, 1993 ('ICTY Statute').

[8] SCSL Statute, arts 18(2), (3) and (4); ICTR Statute, arts 20(2), (3) and (4); ICTY Statute arts 21(2), (3) and (4) (emphasis added).

[9] SCSL Statute, art 18(1); ICTR Statute, art 20(1); ICTY Statute, art 21(1).

[10] *Prosecutor v Aleksovski* (Decision on Prosecutor's Appeal on Admissibility of Evidence) IT-95-14/1-AR73 (16 February 1999) para 25.

[11] See further on this point, S Vasiliev, 'The Role and Legal Status of the Prosecutor in International Criminal Trials', 25 November 2010, available online at: http://papers.ssrn.com/sol3/papers.cfm?abstract_id=1715465.

[12] Rome Statute of the International Criminal Court, 2187 UNTS 90, 17 July 1998, entered into force 1 July 2002 ('ICC Statute').

also extend to 'other parties, such as the prosecution'[13] and 'should be preserved to the benefit of all participants in the proceedings'.[14]

By far the most fortunate recipient of the international tribunals' extension of the rights of the accused to other actors at trial has been the prosecutor. As early as 1999, the ICTY considered that it would be 'difficult to see how a trial could ever be considered to be fair' where the accused was granted more than a 'strict compliance with' the fundamental guarantees contained in the Statute, at the expense of the prosecution.[15] The extent of this balance between the parties was further clarified in *Milutinović*, where Trial Chamber III considered that the Prosecution was entitled to fairness of opportunity when presenting its case.[16] The ICTR has explicitly stated that the right to a fair trial applies both to the defence and prosecution.[17]

The single greatest enforcement of the prosecutor's 'right' to a fair trial came in 2010, however, when the ICTY Appeals Chamber ordered a partial retrial on the grounds that the Trial Chamber had denied the Prosecutor the opportunity to exhaust all reasonable steps to secure the testimony of two witnesses, who appeared to be unwilling to step forth to testify on the grounds of fear.[18] Whilst not referring explicitly to the Prosecutor's right to a fair trial,[19] the Appeals Chamber considered that the Trial Chamber had not taken sufficient steps to secure the testimony of two witnesses allegedly subject to intimidation.[20] Witness intimidation was described as a grave problem which posed a threat to the integrity of the trial and 'undermined the fairness of the proceedings as guaranteed by the Statute and Rules and resulted in a miscarriage of justice'.[21] The Appeals Chamber did not elaborate on the fact that these guarantees are framed with explicit reference to fairness to the accused.

---

[13] *Situation in Uganda* (Decision on the Prosecution's Application for Leave to Appeal the Decision on Victims' Applications for Participation a/0010/06, a/0064/06 to a/0070/06, a/0081/06 to a/0104/06 and a/0111/06 to a/0127/06) ICC-02/04-01/05 (19 December 2007) para 27.

[14] *Situation in Uganda: Prosecutor v Kony et al* (Decision on the Prosecutor's Application for Leave to Appeal Dated the 15th day of May 2006) ICC-02/04-01/05 (10 July 2006) para 24.

[15] *Prosecutor v Aleksovski* (Decision on Prosecutor's Appeal on Admissibility of Evidence) (n 10) para 25. See further, V Tochilovsky, *Jurisprudence of the International Criminal Courts and the European Court of Human Rights* (Nijhoff, Leiden 2008) 276.

[16] *Prosecutor v Milutinović et al* (Decision on Prosecution's Request for Certification of Rule 73*bis* Issue for Appeal) IT-05-87-T (30 August 2006) para 10.

[17] *Prosecutor v Karemera et al* (Decision on Severance of André Rwamakuba and Amendments to the Indictment) ICTR-98-44-PT (7 December 2004) para 26.

[18] *Prosecutor v Haradinaj et al* (Judgment) IT-04-84-A (19 July 2010) ('*Haradinaj* Appeal Judgment').

[19] It ought to be noted that the original Appeals Chamber decision (n 18) para 46, explicitly stated that the Trial Chamber had placed 'logistical considerations over the Prosecution's right to a fair trial'. In a corrigendum issued on 23 July 2010, this was changed to 'over the Trial Chamber's duty to safeguard the fairness of proceedings'. *Prosecutor v Haradinaj et al* (Corrigendum to Judgement of 19 July 2010) IT-04-84-A (23 July 2010).

[20] *Haradinaj* Appeal Judgment (n 18) para 49.

[21] Ibid.

It would be somewhat far-fetched to suggest that the retrial was ordered in the interest of fairness to the accused, considering the context of the three acquittals. Ramush Haradinaj, Idriz Balaj and Lahi Brahimaj voluntarily surrendered to the Tribunal upon service of the Indictment and were transferred to The Hague on 9 March 2005. The initial indictment against the three accused was amended a number of times, the fourth and final version being confirmed on 15 October 2007. The trial commenced on 5 March 2007 and the evidence of a total of 97 Prosecution witnesses was received; 81 of these witnesses testified *viva voce* and the evidence of the remaining 16 was received in written form pursuant to Rule 92*bis* and *quater* of the Rules of Procedure and Evidence.[22] The three Defence teams left it to the Trial Chamber to determine whether the evidence tendered by the Prosecution was sufficient to sustain a conviction.[23] On 3 April 2008, the Trial Chamber delivered its judgment which found Ramush Haradinaj and Idriz Balaj not guilty of all counts in the indictment, and entered a conviction on two grounds (the war crimes of torture and cruel treatment) against Lahi Brahimaj and sentenced him to six years' imprisonment, with credit for time spent in detention.[24]

The Trial Chamber's judgment acknowledged that there were difficulties securing the testimony of many witnesses,[25] but stressed that:

> the Trial Chamber made use of all its powers under the Rules to facilitate the reception of evidence without stepping beyond its role as an impartial finder of facts. This resulted in the Trial Chamber receiving evidence from more than 90 witnesses.[26]

The measures taken included: protective measures for witnesses;[27] allowing witnesses to testify by video link;[28] and the issuance of subpoenas to testify to 18 Prosecution witnesses,[29] 13 of whom complied with the subpoena and testified before the tribunal, while the written statement of one was issued in lieu of oral testimony.[30] The subpoenas had been requested by the Prosecution on the grounds that the prospect of protective measures did not allay the witnesses' fears.[31] Why the prospect of a fine or short prison sentence from an international tribunal outweighed the alleged fear of death at the hands of the intimidators was not discussed, although it could be argued that the subpoenas allowed witnesses locally to assert that they did not want to testify, but that the Tribunal had left them

---

[22] *Prosecutor v Haradinaj et al* (Judgment) IT-04-84-T (3 April 2008) para 6.
[23] *Prosecutor v Haradinaj et al* (Scheduling Order for Final Trial Briefs and Closing Arguments) IT-04-84-T (30 November 2007).
[24] *Haradinaj* Trial Judgment (n 22) paras 502–505.
[25] Ibid para 6.
[26] Ibid para 28.
[27] Ibid para 22.
[28] Ibid paras 23–28.
[29] Ibid para 22.
[30] Ibid.
[31] Ibid.

with no choice. Of the four subpoenaed individuals who failed to comply, one testified via video link.³² Contempt proceedings were initiated against two, who subsequently decided to testify and the proceedings were dropped. Arrangements were made for the remaining individual to give testimony via video link, due to his ill-health. When he didn't show up, he was arrested by Canadian authorities for his failure to comply with a domestic order to appear.³³ The video-link testimony was scheduled for an alternative date, but he was hospitalised shortly before that date and due to an uncertainty as to when he might be well enough to testify, the Tribunal never received his testimony.³⁴

Two Prosecution witnesses travelled to the seat of the Tribunal, but refused to give evidence when they arrived. On consultation with the Victims and Witnesses Unit, the testimony of one was not pursued.³⁵ Contempt proceedings were issued against the other witness, Shefqet Kabashi, but he returned to the United States before the contempt hearing could commence. Arrangements were made for Kabashi to testify via video link, but again he refused to testify.³⁶

It is submitted that the above contextual framework shows that the Trial Chamber went to great lengths to do everything in its power to secure the testimony of the various Prosecution witnesses. The fact that the threats felt by the witnesses were not serious enough for all but one of them to be willing to face contempt charges says something in itself, but two further points warrant a brief mention. The first concerns the scope of the retrial. The Prosecution has been allowed to address the shortcomings in its original case³⁷ by introducing the testimony of six new witnesses in its pre-trial brief.³⁸ Moreover, when the 'crucial' testimony of

---

32   Ibid para 24.
33   Ibid Appendix A, 'Procedural History', para 24.
34   Ibid para 25.
35   Ibid para 22.
36   *Prosecutor v Haradinaj et al* (Transcript, T. 10939-10941) IT-04-84-T (20 November 2007). Ultimately, Kabashi was transferred to the ICTY in August 2011, and sentenced to two months' imprisonment in September 2011 (*Prosecutor v Kabashi* (Sentencing Judgment) IT-04-84-R77.1 (16 September 2011)). In August 2011, he appeared on the witness stand in the *Haradinaj* retrial as witness for the prosecution, but rather aggressively refused to cooperate, though stressing that he was unable to cooperate, as opposed to being unwilling to do so because of fears of intimidation. He also cast doubts on testimony he had given in the earlier *Limaj* case. Surprisingly, the relevant portion of his testimony in *Limaj* was admitted to the record in *Haradinaj* under Rule 89(C). See further *Prosecutor v Haradinaj et al* (Transcript, T.332-435) IT-04-84*bis*-T (22–24 August 2011), and for a criticism, Y McDermott, 'The Rights and Wrongs of Written Testimony', paper delivered at University College Dublin School of Law conference, *Integrating a Socio-Legal Approach to Evidence in International Criminal Tribunals*, 19 November 2011.
37   See *Prosecutor v Haradinaj et al* (Decision on Whether to Resume Hearing Testimony of Witness 8 and Call Chamber Witness) IT-04-84-T (20 June 2007) on the unreliability of one witness.
38   *Prosecutor v Haradinaj et al* (Appeal Brief on Behalf of Ramush Haradinaj on Scope of Partial Retrial) IT-04-84*bis*-AR73.1 (10 February 2011) para 20; *Prosecutor v Haradinaj et al* (Decision on Haradinaj's Appeal on Scope of Partial Retrial) IT-04-84bis-AR 73.1 (31 May 2011) para 26.

witness Kabashi was ultimately secured at retrial, he was so uncooperative that the Prosecution sought instead to enter the transcript from his testimony in the *Limaj* case under Rule 89(C) as evidence.[39] A reasonable observer might suggest that the Prosecution could have taken this course of action, and introduced the six new witnesses, at the original trial, and thus the implication might be that the Prosecution had been given a second chance to address the shortcomings of its case at trial. The fact remains that, in spite of the two unavailable witnesses at the heart of the Appeals Chamber judgment, more than 90 Prosecution witnesses did testify and were still unable to prove the guilt of the accused on all but the two counts that Brahimaj was convicted of, despite the fact that no Defence witnesses were put forward to counter these witnesses' testimony.

Secondly, the accused Haradinaj was granted provisional release, a somewhat remarkable event in most of the ICTY's practice to date, from June 2005 to February 2007.[40] One of the prerequisites to the award of provisional release is the Tribunal's satisfaction that the accused will not interfere with witnesses.[41] While Haradinaj's application of July 2007 was denied on the grounds that provisional release would add to an atmosphere in which witnesses felt unsafe to give evidence,[42] this ruling did not suggest that he would personally pose a threat to witnesses on release and, furthermore, Haradinaj was granted provisional release on compassionate grounds less than three months later,[43] so the 'unsafe atmosphere' argument cannot have been too overwhelming for the Chamber. Both Brahimaj and Haradinaj were granted provisional release from 21 December 2007 to 4 January 2008. It was considered that the threatening environment felt by witnesses was more a product of a close-knit community network in Kosovo which made anonymity difficult than by any threat deriving directly from any of the accused.[44] This consideration,

---

[39] See n 35 above.

[40] See *Prosecutor v Haradinaj et al* (Decision on Ramush Haradinaj's Motion for Provisional Release) IT-04-84-T (6 June 2005); *Prosecutor v Haradinaj et al* (Decision on Defence Motion on Behalf of Ramush Haradinaj to Request Re-assessment of Conditions of Provisional Release Granted 6 June 2005) IT-04-84-T (12 October 2005) (allowing the accused to carry out certain political activities while on release), and *Prosecutor v Haradinaj et al* (Order recalling Ramush Haradinaj from provisional release) IT-04-84-T (1 February 2007).

[41] Rules of Procedure and Evidence of the International Criminal Tribunal for the former Yugoslavia, UN Doc IT/32/Rev.46 (20 October 2011) ('ICTY RPE'), Rule 65(B).

[42] *Prosecutor v Haradinaj et al* (Decision on Motion on Behalf of Ramush Haradinaj for Provisional Release) IT-04-84-T (20 July 2007).

[43] *Prosecutor v Haradinaj et al* (Decision on Defence Motion on Behalf of Ramush Haradinaj for Urgent Provisional Release) IT-04-84-T (3 October 2007).

[44] *Haradinaj* Trial Judgment (n 22) para 6; *Prosecutor v Haradinaj et al* (Decision on the Admission of a Prosecution Witness Statement under Rule 92*bis* and Prosecution's 17th Motion for Protective Measures) IT-04-84-T (29 October 2007) para 3; *Prosecutor v Haradinaj et al* (Decision on Prosecution's 30th and 31st Motions for Trial-Related Protective Measures) IT-04-84-T (6 November 2007) para 2; *Prosecutor v Haradinaj et al* (Decision on Fourth Batch of 92*bis* Witnesses and Protective Measures for One of These Witnesses) IT-04-84-T (6 November 2007).

combined with the implicit conditions in the granting of provisional release, give rise to questions about the wisdom of subjecting the accused to double jeopardy for circumstances beyond their control.[45]

Thus, we can conclude that the *Haradinaj* Appeals Chamber decision ordering a retrial was fundamentally flawed, and offers a prime example of a trend in recent years to extend the fair trial rights regime to the prosecution, and to elevate the interests of the prosecution to the status of rights. This elevation, in turn, permits the Chamber to place the rights of the accused in a 'balance' with the prosecution's interests, while the rights of the accused properly belong at the apex of any hierarchy of considerations.

In spite of the flawed nature of the notion of the 'prosecutor's right to a fair trial' and the manner in which it has been realised, the fact remains that, rightly or wrongly, the concept has been recognised by almost all of the international criminal tribunals to date. The present author is part of a project which aims to elucidate 'general rules and principles' for international criminal procedure, and the acid test for defining a practice as a 'principle' is that it must be a 'general prescription … shared by all procedural models',[46] while a rule is a more specific standard that gives effect to principles but is not of such a mandatory nature to require uniform adherence.[47] If the prosecutorial right to a fair trial is to be recognised as a rule of international criminal procedure, with the possibility of it moving towards a principle of same, then serious questions need to be addressed as to the scope of operation of that right and its limitations.

## II. The Right to Trial without Undue Delay

On 30 September 2011, almost three years after the close of trial,[48] the ICTR issued its judgment in the case of *Bizimungu, Mugenzi, Bicamumpaka and Mugarineza (Government II)*.[49] Bizimungu was arrested on 11 February 1999, and his three co-defendants were arrested on 6 April 1999.[50] All four remained in the custody of the tribunal from that date until 30 September 2011, when Bizimungu and Bicamumpaka were acquitted of all charges.[51] Mugenzi and Mugarineza were

---

[45] The argument that the Appeals Chamber decision and the scope of the retrial may have the effect of subjecting the accused to double jeopardy is raised by the present author in McDermott (n 2).

[46] 'Introduction' in Hague Institute for the Internationalisation of Law/International Criminal Procedure Expert Framework, *General Rules and Principles of International Criminal Procedure and Recommendations of the International Expert Framework* (HiiL/ICP-EF, The Hague 28 October 2011) 4.

[47] Ibid.

[48] Closing arguments were heard from 1 to 5 December 2008: ibid para 119.

[49] *Prosecutor v Bizimungu et al* (Judgment and Sentence) ICTR-99-50-T (30 September 2011).

[50] Ibid paras 4–17.

[51] Ibid para 1988.

convicted of conspiracy to commit genocide, and convicted of 30 years apiece.[52] In assessing whether there had been a breach in the right to trial without undue delay caused by the failure of the ICTR to prioritise the case,[53] the Trial Chamber referred to the complexity of the case, evidenced by the number of witnesses heard, the number of co-accused and similar factors, without giving any reason as to why it took more than three years from the close of the case to issue the judgment.[54] Mugenzi's allegations were dismissed as ignoring 'the common challenges of trial administration of a multi-accused case with a complicated procedural history',[55] thus disregarding the fact that the length taken to issue a judgment is not a question of 'trial administration' *per se*, but rather one of dedication of judicial time and resources. Judge Short, in a partially dissenting opinion, pointed to these problems and considered that the rights of the accused individuals had been violated and recommended that a reduction in sentence of five years would have been appropriate for Mugenzi and Mugarineza, while the issue of compensation for the acquitted Bizimungu and Bicamumpaka could have been litigated at a later stage.[56]

The Trial Chamber judgment was not the first time that the right to trial without undue delay was litigated in the case. In 2003, Prosper Mugarineza's allegation that this right had been denied by delays resulting from the Prosecution's failure to disclose material pursuant to Rules 66 and 68 was dismissed,[57] with the Trial Chamber holding that there was 'no need to inquire into any role that the Prosecutor might have played about the alleged undue delay'. The Appeals Chamber, quite rightly, noted that the conduct of authorities was one of the key factors to be examined when assessing whether a delay could be considered 'undue',[58] and sent the matter back to the Trial Chamber for determination.[59] On reconsideration, the Trial Chamber held that the burden of proof lay with the accused in proving a

---

[52] Ibid.

[53] This argument had been put forward by the accused Mugenzi.

[54] Ibid paras 66–79. The majority judgment does recognise (para 74) that 'proceedings have been lengthy ... [and] ... the increased workload of the presiding judges more specifically, has contributed to this delay', but this fails to explain in full why they did not get around to issuing a judgment before 2011, and the further inexcusable fact that two of the accused were held to be innocent of all charges. It ought to have been imperative to release these innocent men from detention as a matter of priority as soon as the judges agreed on their acquittal, which doubtless happened before the issuance of the judgment.

[55] Ibid para 79.

[56] *Prosecutor v Bizimungu et al* (Judgment and Sentence) ICTR-99-50-T (30 September 2011) (Partially Dissenting Opinion of Judge Emile Francis Short).

[57] *Prosecutor v Mugiraneza* (Decision on Prosper Mugiraneza's Motion to Dismiss the Indictment for Violation of Article 20(4)(C) of the Statute, Demand for Speedy Trial and for Appropriate Relief) ICTR-99-50-T (2 October 2003).

[58] *Prosecutor v Mugiraneza* (Decision on Prosper Mugaraneza's Interlocutory Appeal from Trial Chamber II Decision of 2 October 2003 Denying the Motion to Dismiss the Indictment, Demand Speedy Trial and for Appropriate Relief) ICTR-99-50-AR73 (27 February 2004) 3.

[59] Ibid.

breach of the right to trial without undue delay and that, given the complexity of the case, the delay was not undue.[60] While the Trial Chamber did confirm that, contrary to the Prosecutor's submissions, the delay was not caused by the 'incessant filing of motions', it added that it was not attributable to the Prosecution, either.[61] Any analysis of the disclosure issue and its impact on the delay caused ended there, which is surprising given that the reason for the Appeals Chamber's referral was the Trial Chamber's lack of inquiry into the role of the Prosecutor. Further motions on undue delay were all dismissed with reference to the complexity of the case, the need to take the totality of the situation into account and the assessment that the length of the delay suffered could not *ipso facto* render a delay undue.[62]

The *Government II* case is illustrative of the often insurmountable barriers faced in the international tribunals when defendants attempt to assert that their right to trial without undue delay has been breached. By contrast, a number of cases have blithely asserted the right to trial without undue delay as a bar to proceeding in a certain manner, often against the will of the accused. In another ICTR case, *Nyiramasuhuko*, only one of the co-accused consented to proceeding with a substitute judge after one of the three trial judges was not re-elected to the Tribunal.[63] Judges Sekule and Ramaroson determined that 'proceedings must not be allowed to drag on endlessly' and that it was in the interests of justice to continue the trial with a substitute judge who would have to confirm that they had familiarised themselves with the trial record, rather than to start anew with three fresh judges.[64] This decision was upheld on appeal,[65] but as Judge Hunt indicated in a very strong dissent, the

---

[60]    *Prosecutor v Bizimungu et al* (Decision on Prosper Mugiraneza's Application for a Hearing or Other Relief on his Motion for Dismissal for Violation of his Right to a Trial without Undue Delay) ICTR-99-50-T (3 November 2004) paras 31–34.

[61]    Ibid para 32. The Chamber did say that it had 'particularly enquired into the conduct of the Prosecutor', but the results of this inquiry remain a mystery.

[62]    See *Prosecutor v Bizimungu et al* (Decision on Prosper Mugiraneza's Second Motion to Dismiss for Deprivation of his Right to Trial without Undue Delay) ICTR-99-50-AR73 (29 May 2007); *Prosecutor v Bizimungu et al* (Decision on Prosper Mugiraneza's Third Motion to Dismiss Indictment for Violation of Right to Trial without Undue Delay) ICTR-99-50-AR73 (10 February 2009); *Prosecutor v Bizimungu et al* (Decision on Prosper Mugiraneza's Fourth Motion to Dismiss Indictment for Violation of Right to Trial without Undue Delay) ICTR-99-50-AR73 (23 June 2010), and *Prosecutor v Bizimungu et al* (Decision on Jérôme-Clément Bicamumpaka's Motion Seeking Permanent Stay of Proceedings) ICTR-99-50-AR73 (27 February 2009). Cf Judge Short's partially dissenting opinion in the Decision on Prosper Mugiraneza's Fourth Motion, where he said (at para 2): 'I consider that the Chamber's failure to deliver its judgement 24 months after close of the evidence in this case is alone sufficient to constitute a violation of Mugiraneza's right to a trial without undue delay', and further criticised the ICTR's policy of commencing new cases while judgments were pending in ongoing ones, and assigning judges to new trials.

[63]    *Prosecutor v Nyiramasuhuko et al* (Decision in the matter of proceedings under Rule 15*bis*(D)) ICTR 98-42-T (15 July 2003).

[64]    Ibid paras 33–34.

[65]    *Prosecutor v Nyiramasuhuko et al* (Decision in the Matter of Proceedings under Rule 15*bis*(D)) ICTR-98-42-A15bis (24 September 2003).

decision failed to take into account the fact that 22 of 23 witnesses were subject to protective measures, and their testimony had not therefore been recorded, making it impossible for the substitute judge to assess their demeanour.[66] Moreover, the non-consenting accused had accepted that a trial anew would impact on their right to an expeditious trial, rendering it even more astounding that this was the primary consideration taken into account by the remaining members of the Trial Chamber.[67] As the conduct of the accused is one of the factors to be taken into account when assessing whether a breach of the right to trial within reasonable time has occurred, the Trial Chamber cannot reasonably have been concerned that a new trial and the extra time it would incur would ultimately result in a need to dismiss the indictment on the grounds of such a breach.

The right to trial without undue delay was again prioritised by the SCSL in a decision relating to evidence from a crime base that was at that time subject to an interlocutory appeal.[68] The Trial Chamber determined that it was 'in the interests of justice and judicial economy' to proceed with hearing that evidence, rather than wait an extra week until the Appeals Chamber had issued its judgment on the interlocutory appeals.[69]

The above examples aim to show that it is immensely difficult for an accused to assert that his or her right trial without undue delay has been violated, but that these difficulties do not seem to arise when the Chamber is convinced that it is in the interest of expedience, and therefore the interests of justice, to continue in a given direction. The placing of expedience to the forefront in limited and inconsistent instances, while adopting a rather relaxed attitude in other circumstances, has continued in the practice of the ICC. In the Kenya situation, counsel for defendants Ruto, Kosgey and Sang applied for an urgent postponement of the deadline for disclosure of material to the Prosecution prior to the confirmation of the charges hearing, and for a resultant postponement of the hearing itself.[70] Their cause for seeking such relief was a number of logistical and practical difficulties which had arisen, including a limitation on the number of witnesses they were allowed to call, meaning that witness statements needed to be taken; a lack of cooperation from Kenyan authorities, the Registry's failure to provide an office for the Defence, the team's need to analyse almost 9,000 pages of disclosed information, and the fact that the Defence team was not familiar with or trained in the court's database for disclosure.[71] They sought a postponement of six weeks, but noted that at the very minimum, they would need an extra week to give full effect to the order of

---

[66] *Nyiramasuhuko* 15*bis* Appeal Decision (n 65) (Dissenting Opinion of Judge David Hunt) para 27.

[67] Ibid para 22.

[68] *Prosecutor v Norman et al* (Decision on Presentation of Witness Testimony on Moyamba Crime Base) SCSL-04-14-T (1 March 2005).

[69] Ibid para 13.

[70] *Situation in the Republic of Kenya: Prosecutor v Ruto, Kosgey and Sang* (Urgent Defence Application for Postponement of the Confirmation Hearing and Extension of Time to Disclose and List Evidence) ICC-01/09-01/11 (11 August 2011).

[71] Ibid para 3.

disclosure.⁷² On 12 August 2011, Judge Trendafilova, acting as Single Judge on behalf of Pre-Trial Chamber II, denied the request, concluding that the Defence team was simply suffering from a 'lack of proper organization',⁷³ and reminding the teams that provision of an office space was not mandatory.⁷⁴ The Judge recalled that 1 September had been set as the 'strict date for the start of the confirmation hearing'⁷⁵ and considered the Defence request for more time to prepare its case 'an abuse of the rights referred to in article 67(1) of the Rome Statute'.⁷⁶ One would take from this decision that the ICC was keen to proceed with the case in the most expeditious fashion, as the Single Judge did not see fit to grant even a week's grace to the Defence team. Later, as a result of further technical difficulties, Kosgey's Defence team sought to extend the 16 August 2011 deadline for disclosure to the Prosecution 'by one day—if and only if the Registry cannot otherwise facilitate the timely processing of the disclosure'.⁷⁷ The Single Judge refused the request, and granted the Defence teams until 23:59 on 16 August 2011 to comply with their disclosure obligations.⁷⁸

The confirmation hearing did take place between 1 and 8 September 2011, wherein parties and participating victims were invited to submit written observations after the close of the hearing.⁷⁹ The last of these observations was submitted on 24 October 2011, and thus the 60-day time limit under Article 61(7), whereby the Chamber has to confirm or decline the charges or to adjourn the hearing, was deemed to run from that date.⁸⁰ However, Single Judge Trendafilova saw fit to postpone this time limit until such a time as the Pre-Trial Chamber in the second case in the Kenya situation issued its decision on the confirmation of the charges, so that both confirmation decisions could be issued on the same date.⁸¹ This was based on the Registrar's assertion that 'whatever is decided in the first case, it is likely that a rise in tension may occur, and speculations or potentially heated public debate might take place, with an expectation of the same result in

---

⁷² Ibid para 2.

⁷³ *Situation in the Republic of Kenya: Prosecutor v Ruto, Kosgey and Sang* (Decision on Urgent Defence Application for Postponement of the Confirmation Hearing and Extension of Time to Disclose and List Evidence) ICC-01/09-01/11 (12 August 2011) para 11.

⁷⁴ Ibid para 13.

⁷⁵ Ibid para 9.

⁷⁶ Ibid para 16.

⁷⁷ *Situation in the Republic of Kenya: Prosecutor v Ruto, Kosgey and Sang* (Henry Kosgey's Contingent Request for Extension of Time Limit for Disclosure in Compliance with the E-Court Protocol with Confidential Annexes 1-3) ICC-01/09-01/11 (15 August 2011) para 13.

⁷⁸ *Situation in the Republic of Kenya: Prosecutor v Ruto, Kosgey and Sang* (Decision on the Defence Requests for Extension of Time Limit for Disclosure in Compliance with the E-Court Protocol) ICC-01/09-01/11 (16 August 2011) para 16.

⁷⁹ See *Situation in the Republic of Kenya: Prosecutor v Ruto, Kosgey and Sang* (Decision on the Issuance of the Decision Pursuant to Article 61(7) of the Rome Statute) ICC-01/09-01/11 (26 October 2011) para 3.

⁸⁰ Ibid para 9.

⁸¹ Ibid para 15.

the second case'.⁸² The indefinite extension granted as a response to the Registrar's undoubtedly hypothetical assessment stands in sharp contrast to the extreme focus on expedition when the Defence team asked for limited extensions of time in advance of the confirmation hearing.

As with the ICTR's decision on substitute judges in *Nyiramasuhuko et al.*, the right to trial without undue delay was used against the interests of the accused in the ICC's Trial Chamber II's decision on admissibility in the *Katanga* case.⁸³ The Chamber, having regard to the *travaux preparatoires* of the ICC Statute, concluded that:

> the provisions of paragraphs 5 to 8 of [article 19 of the ICC Statute] … are clearly aimed at avoiding challenges to admissibility needlessly hindering or delaying the proceedings, which means that they must be brought as soon as possible, preferably during the pre-trial phase.⁸⁴

The Trial Chamber concluded that only admissibility challenges related to *ne bis in idem* could be brought after the confirmation of the charges, while challenges concerning complementarity or gravity must be brought before the end of the pre-trial stage of proceedings.⁸⁵ This determination was based on the consideration that 'it is in the interests of all, and primarily the suspects who have been deprived of their liberty',⁸⁶ that such determinations be made as quickly as possible. As Dov Jacobs has shrewdly noted, the defendant had apparently 'decided not to invoke his right at an earlier stage. It is not necessarily the role of the Trial Chamber to invoke such an interest against the defendant. The justification of the Chamber is based on a fictional assumption of will'.⁸⁷ Where an accused has implicitly recognised that a given right will be jeopardised by the granting of his or her request, it goes against a libertarian notion of human rights to deny the request based on a right which he or she has forfeited in making the request.⁸⁸

The above analysis does not intend to suggest that the right to a speedy trial is always used in a negative fashion; there are a number of instances where it has been asserted in its intended formulation, as simply a right of the accused that must be vindicated. In *Brđanin & Talić*, for example, the Trial Chamber opted to sever the

---

⁸² Ibid para 13.
⁸³ *Situation in the DRC: Prosecutor v Katanga and Chui* (Reasons for the Oral Decision on the Motion Challenging the Admissibility of the Case (Article 19 of the Statute)) ICC-01/04-01/07-1213-tENG (16 June 2009).
⁸⁴ Ibid para 44.
⁸⁵ Ibid para 47.
⁸⁶ Ibid para 45.
⁸⁷ D Jacobs, 'The Importance of Being Earnest: The Timeliness of the Challenge to Admissibility in *Katanga*' (2010) 23(2) *LJIL* 331, 340.
⁸⁸ GP Fletcher has made this point rather eloquently: 'When individuals consent to undergo medical operations, to engage in sexual intercourse, to open their homes to police searches, or to testify against themselves in court, they convert what otherwise would be an invasion of their person or their rights into a harmless or justified activity' (*Basic Concepts of Legal Thought* (OUP, Oxford 1996) 109).

joined trials, as Talić's illness would have interfered with Brđanin's fundamental right to an expeditious trial.[89] This was not before further justification was given, however, on the need to safeguard the witnesses who were prepared to testify, and the impact that a 'stop-start' trial might have on their testimony.[90]

Furthermore, as mentioned at the outset, the right to trial without undue delay is not unique in being asserted even when the accused appears to have forfeited the benefit of that right for other purposes. This point could equally have been illustrated by reference to cases where self-representing accused have had counsel imposed upon them,[91] even though the trade-off between the right to represent oneself and the right to effective assistance of counsel is a clear decision which ought to rest in the hands of the accused, rather than the judges.[92]

# Conclusion

Analyses of international criminal procedure in recent years has typically moved from the 'clash of legal cultures'[93] paradigm originally favoured by commentators to one which recognises the convergence of influences at play in developing a *sui generis* body of law.[94] Commentators are in agreement that international criminal

---

[89] *Prosecutor v Brđanin & Talić* (Decision on the Prosecutor's Oral Request for the Separation of Trials) IT-99-36-T (20 September 2002) para 10.

[90] Ibid paras 25–27.

[91] *Prosecutor v Milošević* (Reasons for Decision on Assignment of Defence Counsel) IT-02-54-T (22 September 2004) para 32 ('In the event that self-representation gives rise to the risk of unfairness to the accused, then steps must be taken, consistent with the provisions of Articles 20 and 21, to secure for an accused a fair trial; otherwise, the purpose of securing for the accused the right to a defence will be nullified. Fundamental to that is ensuring that he has the opportunity and facility to present his defence fully and effectively. However, that does not oblige the Trial Chamber to indulge the wish of an accused to conduct his own defence where his capacity to do so is so impaired that, were he to continue to do so, there would be a material risk that he would not receive a fair trial. The mere assertion on the part of the Accused of his right to defend himself does not ensure an effective defence in circumstances where he is seriously ill and regularly prevented for protracted periods from acting in his own defence').

[92] Other decisions have recognised that by electing to self-represent, a defendant assumes the risk that they might not benefit from as effective a defence as if they were represented by qualified and experienced counsel, e.g. *Prosecutor v Krajišnik* (Decision on Krajišnik Request and on Prosecution Motion) IT-00-39-A (11 September 2007) para 41.

[93] For example, P Carmichael Keen, 'Tempered Adversariality: The Judicial Role and Trial Theory in the International Criminal Tribunals' (2004) 17(4) *LJIL* 767; D Mundis, 'From "Common Law" to "Civil Law": The Evolution of the ICTY Rules of Procedure and Evidence' (2001) 14(2) *LJIL* 367; S Zappalà, *Human Rights in International Criminal Proceedings* (OUP, Oxford 2004); Vasiliev (n 11) 16–17.

[94] DM Amman, 'Harmonic Convergence? Constitutional Criminal Procedure in an International Context' (2000) 75 *Ind. L.J.* 809; Ohlin (n 2); M Bohlander, ''Radbruch Redux:

procedure needs, above all else, to be fair,[95] although some, quite controversially, suggest that a relaxation of certain rights may be a necessary evil of conducting trials in the unique pressure cooker of the international, post-conflict context.[96] Yet, international criminal procedure has enormous potential to lead by example, in setting the highest possible standards for the fair conduct of proceedings domestically. This potential is evidenced by a number of factors, including the principle of complementarity, whereby the ICC must, *inter alia*, determine whether proceedings domestically would be unfairly carried out,[97] and the Rule 11*bis* system of referrals from the *ad hoc* tribunals to national jurisdictions, where one of the considerations in deciding whether to transfer a case is whether the accused would receive a fair trial in the domestic jurisdiction.[98] Implicit in both

---

The Need for Revisiting the Conversation between Common and Civil Law at Root Level at the Example of International Criminal Justice' (2011) 24(2) *LJIL* 393.

[95] K Ambos, 'International Criminal Procedure: "Adversarial", "Inquisitorial" or Mixed?' (2003) 3(1) *ICLR* 1; PL Robinson, 'The Right to a Fair Trial in International Law, with Specific Reference to the Work of the ICTY' (2009) 3 *Berkeley J.L Int'L L. Publicist* 1.

[96] M Damaška, 'Keynote Address prepared for the concluding conference of the International Criminal Procedure Expert Framework', 28 October 2011 (on file with author).

[97] It could be argued from a reading of the Statute and preparatory works that complementarity was intended to relate to the due process of trials only where the intention of such trials was to shield the accused from criminal liability. For an analysis of the need to extend this regime to trials which are procedurally unfair to the accused, see E Carnero Rojo, 'The Role of Fair Trial Considerations in the Complementarity Regime of the International Criminal Court: From "No Peace without Justice" to "No Peace without Victors" Justice'?' (2005) 18(4) *LJIL* 829 and KJ Heller, 'The Shadow Side of Complementarity: The Effect of Article 17 of the Rome Statute on National Due Process' (2006) 17 *CLF* 255, 257. The extension of complementarity to procedural fairness was implicit in the Kenyan government's appeal against the admissibility of the two cases before the ICC, which placed great emphasis on the updated due process protections in the country's constitution: see *Situation in the Republic of Kenya: Prosecutor v Ruto, Kosgey and Sang* and *Prosecutor v Muthaura, Kenyatta and Hussein Ali* (Application on Behalf of the Government of the Republic of Kenya pursuant to Article 19 of the ICC Statute) ICC-01/09-01/11-19 (31 March 2011) paras 1–11. The admissibility challenge failed on the basis that none of the accused individuals were subject to a national investigation for the same conduct at that time. (See, for example, *Situation in the Republic of Kenya: Prosecutor v Muthaura, Kenyatta and Hussein Ali* (Judgment on the appeal of the Republic of Kenya against the decision of Pre-Trial Chamber II of 30 May 2011 entitled 'Decision on the Application by the Government of Kenya Challenging the Admissibility of the Case Pursuant to Article 19(2)(b) of the Statute') ICC-01/09-02/11-274 (30 August 2011)). In 2012, the Libyan government also placed great emphasis on the due process protections afforded to the accused: see *Situation in Libya: Prosecutor v Gaddafi and Al-Senussi* (Application on Behalf of the Government of Libya pursuant to Article 19 of the ICC Statute) ICC-01/11-01/11-130 (1 May 2012) paras 53–67.

[98] Rule 11*bis*(B) ICTY RPE ('The Referral Bench may order such referral … after being satisfied that the accused will receive a fair trial and that the death penalty will not be imposed or carried out'); Rule 11*bis*(C) Rules of Procedure and Evidence, UN Doc ITR/3/Rev.20, International Criminal Tribunal for Rwanda, 1 October 2009 ('the Trial Chamber shall satisfy itself that the accused will receive a fair trial in the courts of the State concerned').

of these provisions is the proviso that domestic criminal trials must be at least as fair as their international counterparts. Moreover, since the rebirth of international criminal justice, clear evidence of its reach has been exemplified in the inclusion of international crimes in domestic penal laws, and the impact of the ICTR's Rule 11*bis* on both the abolition of the death penalty in Rwanda[99] and the domestic law on witness protection within the state.[100]

However, as the above analysis attempted to illustrate, international criminal procedure is at present little more than a local practice which is temporarily acceptable to parties from different legal traditions. There are a number of factors hindering international criminal procedure from reaching its standard-setting potential for the fairness of trials. One is a lack of coherence between decisions, between individual judges and broadly between tribunals. Another is a failure to evince international best practice in achieving the highest standards of fairness. This is evidenced by the number of hurdles which an accused person must jump before motions on his or her rights can succeed, which stands in remarkable contrast to the unfounded extension of rights to other parties at times, and the reverse application of rights in other instances.

---

[99] Organic Law No. 31/2007/OL of 25 July 2007 Relating to the Abolition of the Death Penalty.
[100] Organic Law No 03/2009/OL of 26 May 2009 Modifying and Complementing the Organic Law No 11/2007 of 16/03/2007 Concerning the Transfer of Cases to the Republic of Rwanda from the International Criminal Tribunal for Rwanda and Other States, 26 May 2009.

# Victims' Participation at the International Criminal Court: Benefit or Burden?

Lorraine Smith-van Lin[1]

The participation of victims in proceedings before the International Criminal Court (hereafter, 'ICC' or 'the Court') constitutes a unique phenomenon in the still expanding spectrum of judicial solutions to international crime.[2] Considered one of the major innovations of the Rome Statute, the role and rights ascribed to victims in the ICC's normative texts was a belated attempt to remedy a perceived lacuna at the *ad hoc* International Criminal Tribunals for the former Yugoslavia (ICTY) and Rwanda (ICTR) where victims were treated as mere passive objects within an adversarial judicial context in which prosecution interests and defence rights were considered top priority.[3] Criticised for their failure to adopt an inclusive approach

---

[1] Programme Manager, International Bar Association (IBA) ICC Programme The views expressed herein are those of the author and not the IBA. The author is grateful for the extensive research assistance provided by Rens van der Werf and Maria Radziejowska for this chapter

[2] The victims' rights provisions in the ICC legal texts were influenced by the UN GA, Declaration of Basic Principles of Justice for Victims of Crime and Abuse of Power, UN Doc A/RES/40/34 (29 November 1985) which acknowledged the harm suffered by millions of victims around the world and the necessity of adopting national and international measures to secure the universal and effective respect for their rights.

[3] See D Donat-Cattin, 'Article 68: Protection of Victims and Witnesses and their Participation in the Proceedings' in O Triffterer (ed) *Commentary on the Rome Statute of the International Court* (2nd edn Beck/Hart/Nomos, Berlin 2008) 1277–1278. For an interesting perspective on whether victims experienced secondary traumatisation at the *ad hoc* Tribunals (that is, whether victims were retraumatised for a second time because of their involvement in a judicial process in which they could not actively participate) see C van den Wyngaert, 'Victims before International Criminal Courts, Some Views and Concerns of an ICC Trial Judge', Lecture delivered to Case Western Reserve University, 21 November 2011, http://law.case.edu/journals/JIL/Documents/(22)%20Van%20den%20Wyngaert_Darby.pdf (last accessed January 18, 2013).

to victims and to restore peace in post-conflict societies,[4] the shortcomings of the *ad hoc* Tribunals catalysed a powerful international movement led by civil society,[5] to ensure that victims' right to participate and receive reparations would be firmly entrenched in the ICC Statute.

The Rome Statute affords victims the opportunity to participate in proceedings before the Court in various ways.[6] One significant right is that provided under article 68(3) of the Rome Statute, which permits victims whose personal interests are affected to present their views and concerns at appropriate stages of the proceedings in a manner which is not prejudicial to or inconsistent with the rights of the accused and a fair and impartial trial. However, many of the normative provisions governing the role and procedural rights of victims were not precisely defined and elucidated in the ICC's constitutive documents thus leaving wide discretion to judges to actually shape the victims' participation scheme.[7]

The participation regime is also multi-faceted, requiring interplay of diverse actors and stakeholders, with key roles being played by the judges, the staff of the ICC Registry, legal representatives of victims and the States who fund the Court. While imprecision in the procedural framework has prompted significant and often inconsistent judicial decisions, resource considerations have been the real determinants of the ICC's policy on victims' participation. Unsurprisingly, when States tally the costs associated with funding the ICC, which up to December 2012 had only delivered verdict in two cases, stark fiscal realities prompt strident criticism of a system that was initially lauded and openly embraced. Increasingly, victims' participation at the ICC is being described as 'unsustainable', 'resource intensive', and a 'procedural nightmare'.[8] The scheme has been criticised for

---

[4] See Donat-Cattin (n 3) 1277–1278.

[5] M Glasius, 'How Activists Shaped the Court', *Crimes of War Project* (December 2003) <http://web.archive.org/web/20081205072708/http://www.crimesofwar.org/print/icc/icc-glasius-print.html> last accessed 2 January 2012.

[6] Victims' participation may range from petitioning the Court or volunteering information to applying for participant's status. In accordance with article 15(3) of the Statute, victims may make representations to the Pre-Trial Chamber when the Prosecutor, acting *proprio motu*, submits a request for authorisation of an investigation. Victims may also submit observations, pursuant to article 19(3) of the Rome Statute where there is a challenge to the jurisdiction of the Court or the admissibility of a case. Moreover, in accordance with rule 119 of the ICC Rules of Procedure and Evidence (RPE), the Pre-Trial Chamber has to seek the views of victims before imposing or amending conditions restricting the liberty of the person in the custody of the Court. The Statute and RPE also provide for a specific victim participation scheme with regard to the reparations procedure in Article 75. Additional provisions may also be found in Regulations 86 and 88 of the Regulations of the Court.

[7] E Baumgartner, 'Aspects of Victim Participation in the Proceedings of the International Criminal Court' (2008) 90(870) *Int'l Rev of the Red Cross* 411.

[8] War Crimes Research Office, 'Victims Participation at the Case Stage of Proceedings' (February 2009) <http://www.wcl.american.edu/warcrimes/icc/documents/WCROReportonVictimParticipationattheCaseStageofProceedingsFebruary2009.pdf?rd=1> last accessed 2 January 2012; Y McDermott, 'Victims and International Law:

consuming a significant portion of the Court's resources while delivering 'largely hypothetical rights to victims'.

This chapter will examine some of the challenges currently being faced in the implementation of the victims' participation regime at the ICC. The author argues that perceptions of the victims' participation scheme as 'burdensome and inefficient' are due to three key factors: gaps in the legal texts leading to inconsistent judicial decisions; complex administrative processes struggling to function with limited resources; and a focus on judicial processes more than actual engagement with victims. The author contends that these factors have lead to a system that is unsustainable in its current form and which has not proven itself to be directly beneficial to victims in the manner which was originally intended. The article ends by considering whether victims' expectations should be adjusted to meet the Court's reality, or the Court's practice should be changed to accord with victims' expectations. The ultimate question is whether the ICC's victims' participation scheme can withstand the intense scrutiny and will be able, like a phoenix in rebirth, to emerge from the ashes.

## Burden or benefit

At the tenth session of the Assembly of States Parties Meeting, States Parties to the Rome Statute noted with concern that the Court had continued to experience severe backlogs in processing victims' applications to participate. As such, States recommended that the Court initiate a review of the system of victim participation 'with a view to ensuring its sustainability, effectiveness and efficiency'.[9] The Court was requested to report to the Assembly at its eleventh session concerning the review process.

The concern of States regarding the effectiveness of the ICC victim participation scheme is not an isolated one. Staff within the Court, including ICC Judge Christine van den Wyngaert, as well as external observers have questioned the system's viability in its current form.[10]

Any discussion on victim's participation and an analysis of its viability in the international judicial process will inevitably be fractious. Civil society groups and victims' rights advocates stridently contend that the ICC Statute embodies both retributive as well as restorative justice aims of which the right to meaningful participation is a key component. On the other hand, some commentators argue that extensive victim involvement in criminal trials will inevitably delay trials and

---

Remedies in the Courtroom?' (2009) 4(3) *Hague Justice Journal* 199, 204 (describing victim participation as being 'something of a procedural nightmare' in practice).

[9] ICC-ASP/10/Res.5, 21 December 2011, para 49.
[10] See van den Wyngaert (n 2) and Chung (n 66).

result in adverse fair trial consequences, ultimately denying justice to the accused and the victims.[11]

The Court's approach is that there are key facets to ensuring the sustainability, efficiency and effectiveness of the victim participation system. In their view, the sustainability of the application system refers to its ability to use the necessary resources in a way that does not deplete or permanently damage them; an effective system is one that upholds the rights of victims to meaningful participation, the rights of Defence, and other fair trial guarantees and is reasonably clear and transparent; and an efficient application system allows victim applicants to have their forms duly and timely received and assessed, and is productive without misusing or wasting resources.[12]

Achieving these lofty goals is easier said than done. The Court itself has conceded that given the mass nature of the crimes under the Court's jurisdiction, the current system with the existing resources is unsustainable. The way forward must necessarily include an analysis of the gaps in the legal framework and more consistent judicial decisions, as well as structural and resource changes to facilitate more effective representation. Most importantly, a shift will be required away from judicial processes towards more direct and focused engagement with victims.

## Gaps in the Normative Framework

That victims are central to the ICC's mandate can be seen from the numerous provisions in the Rome Statute, Rules of Procedure and Evidence (RPE) and Regulations dedicated to victims' rights. However, gaps in the statutory framework have created an essentially jurisprudential regime in which judges are tasked almost exclusively with determining the scope and modalities of victims' participation. Article 68(3) governs the victims' right to participate in proceedings. It provides that:

> Where the personal interests of the victims are affected, the Court shall permit their views and concerns to be presented and considered at stages of the proceedings determined to be appropriate by the Court and in a manner which is not prejudicial to or inconsistent with the rights of the accused and a fair and impartial trial. Such views and concerns may be presented by the legal representatives of the victims where the Court considers it appropriate, in accordance with the Rules of Procedure and Evidence.

Vasiliev argues that Article 68 is far from settled and reveals serious controversy on nearly every essential issue relevant to the determination of the prerequisites

---

[11] McDermott (n 8)
[12] Report of the Court on the review of the system for victims to apply to participate in proceedings, ICC-ASP/11/22, 5 November 2012.

to and the scope of victim participation'.[13] For instance, while Article 68(3) refers to 'victim', the term has not been defined in the Statute, but rather in the Rules of Procedure and Evidence (RPE). Rule 85 defines the two categories of victims allowed to participate in the proceedings: 'natural persons who have suffered harm as a result of the commission of a crime within the jurisdiction of the Court'[14] and 'organisations or institutions that have sustained direct harm'[15] to certain types of property. Natural persons are considered victims in the sense of Rule 85 when they have 'suffered harm as a result of the commission of any crime within the jurisdiction of the Statute of the Court'.

Over time the jurisprudence of the Court provided greater clarity concerning the definition of a victim for the purposes of participation: that the victim is a natural person or organisation; the victims' identity has been duly established; that the application relates to a crime within the jurisdiction of the Court and for which the suspect has been charged; and that there is a causal link between the crime and the harm suffered.[16] Judges have further elaborated on key principles for example,

---

[13] S Vasiliev, 'Article 68 (3) and Personal Interests of Victims in the Emerging Practice of the ICC' in C Stahn and G Sluiter (eds) *The Emerging Practice of the International Criminal Court* (Brill, Leiden 2009).

[14] ICC Rules of Procedure and Evidence, ICC-ASP/1/3 (9 September 2002) (ICC RPE).

[15] Rule 85, ICC RPE.

[16] See *Situation in the DRC* (Decision on the applications for Participation in the Proceedings of VPRS 1, VPRS 2, VPRS 3, VPRS 4, VPRS 5 and VPRS 6 (Public redacted Version)) ICC-01/04 (17 January 2006) para 79. See also *Situation in the DRC* (Decision on the Applications for Participation in the Proceedings of a/0001/06, a/0002/06 and a/0003/06 in the case of the Prosecutor v. Thomas Lubanga Dyilo and of the investigation in the Democratic Republic of the Congo) ICC-01/04 (31 July 2006) 7; *Situation in the DRC: Prosecutor v Lubanga* (Decision on the Applications for Participation in the Proceedings of a/0001/06, a/0002/06 and a/0003/06 in the case of the Prosecutor v. Thomas Lubanga Dyilo and of the investigation in the Democratic Republic of the Congo) ICC-01/04-01/06 (28 July 2006) 7; *Situation in the DRC: Prosecutor v Lubanga* (Decision on applications for participation in proceedings a/0004/06 to a/0009/06, a/0016/06, a/0063/06, a/0071/06 to a/0080/06 and a/0105/06 in the case of The Prosecutor v Thomas Lubanga Dyilo) ICC-01/04-01/06 (20 October 2006) 9; *Situation in the DRC* (Decision on the Requests of the Legal Representative of Applicants on application process for victims' participation and legal representation) ICC-01/04 (17 August 2007) para 4; *Situation in the DRC* (Décision sur les demandes de participation à la procédure déposées dans le cadre de l'enquête en République démocratique du Congo par a/0004/06 à a/0009/06, a/0016/06 à a/0063/06, a/0071/06 à a/0080/06 et a/0105/06 à a/0110/06, a/0188/06, a/0128/06 à a/0162/06, a/0199/06, a/0203/06, a/0209/06, a/0214/06, a/0220/06 à a/0222/06, a/0224/06, a/0227/06 à a/0230/06, a/0234/06 à a/0236/06, a/0240/06, a/0225/06, a/0226/06, a/0231/06 à a/0233/06, a/0237/06 à a/0239/06 et a/0241/06 à a/0250/06) ICC-01/04 (31 January 2008) para 36; *Situation in Uganda: Prosecutor v Kony et al* (Decision on victims' applications for participation a/0010/06, a/0064/06 to a/0070/06, a/0081/06, a/0082/06, a/0084/06 to a/0089/06, a/0091/06 to a/0097/06, a/0099/06, a/0100/06, a/0102/06 to a/0104/06, a/0111/06, a/0113/06 to a/0117/06, a/0120/06, a/0121/06 and a/0123/06 to a/0127/06) ICC-02/04-01/05 (14 March 2008) para 8; *Situation in the DRC: Prosecutor v Katanga and Chui* (Decision on the Applications for Participation in the Proceedings of Applicants a/0327/07 to a/0337/07 and a/0001/08)

the term 'natural persons' has generally been interpreted as referring to human beings;[17] and 'organisations or institutions' has been interpreted to include legal persons.[18] The notion of harm has generally been afforded a broad interpretation in the jurisprudence of all the Chambers as including physical, psychological and material harm, and it is now well settled by the Appeals Chamber that both the harm alleged by a victim and the concept of personal interests under Article 68(3) of the Statute must be linked with the charges confirmed against the accused.[19]

The modalities of participation have created some of the greatest challenges. According to rule 89(1) of the *Rules* of Procedure and Evidence, '[t]*he Chamber shall specify the proceedings and manner in which participation* [of victims] *is considered appropriate*', and in general, ICC judges have adopted a positivist approach to the interpretation of victims' rights.[20] There have been areas of general consistency in the jurisprudential interpretation and analysis of Article 68(3) and other key provisions in the RPE concerning (i) the conditions for victims' participation;[21]

---

ICC-01/04-01/07 (2 April 2008) 8. For a criticism of the ICC's broad interpretation of who may participate as a victim, see Y McDermott, 'Some are More Equal than Others: Victim Participation in the ICC' (2008–2009) 5(1) *Eyes on the ICC* 23, 25–33.

[17] H Olasolo and A Kiss, 'The Role of Victims in Criminal Proceedings before the International Criminal Court' (2010) 81(1–2) *Revue Internationale de Droit Penal* 128. See further, *Situation in the DRC* (Decision on the applications for Participation in the Proceedings of VPRS 1, VPRS 2, VPRS 3, VPRS 4, VPRS 5 and VPRS 6 (Public redacted Version)) (n 16) para 80; *Situation in Uganda* (Decision on Victims' Applications for Participation a/0010/06, a/0064/06 to a/0070/06, a/0081/06 to a/0104/06 and a/0111/06 to a/0127/06) ICC-02/04 (10 August 2007).

[18] *Situation in the DRC* (Décision sur les demandes de participation à la procédure déposées dans le cadre de l'enquête en République démocratique du Congo par a/0004/06 à a/0009/06, a/0016/06 à a/0063/06, a/0071/06 à a/0080/06 et a/0105/06 à a/0110/06, a/0188/06, a/0128/06 à a/0162/06, a/0199/06, a/0203/06, a/0209/06, a/0214/06, a/0220/06 à a/0222/06, a/0224/06, a/0227/06 à a/0230/06, a/0234/06 à a/0236/06, a/0240/06, a/0225/06, a/0226/06, a/0231/06 à a/0233/06, a/0237/06 à a/0239/06 et a/0241/06 à a/0250/06) ICC-01/04 (24 December 2007) paras 137 *et seq*.

[19] *Situation in the DRC* (Decision on the applications for Participation in the Proceedings of VPRS 1, VPRS 2, VPRS 3, VPRS 4, VPRS 5 and VPRS 6 (Public redacted Version)) (n 16) paras 94 and 115–117; *Situation in Uganda* (Decision on Victims' Applications for Participation a/0010/06, a/0064/06 to a/0070/06, a/0081/06 to a/0104/06 and a/0111/06 to a/0127/06) (n 17) para 12; *Situation in the DRC: Prosecutor v Lubanga* (Decision on Victims' Participation) ICC-01/04-01/06 (18 January 2008) paras 90–91.

[20] Particularly noticeable in this regard is the decision of Single Judge Sylvia Steiner in *Situation in the DRC: Prosecutor v Katanga and Chui* (Decision on the Set of Procedural Rights Attached to Procedural Status of Victim at the Pre-Trial Stage of the Case) ICC-01/04-01/07 (13 May 2008) in which she mentions in particular the victims' 'right to the truth', 'right to justice', 'right to reparations', 'right to have access', 'right to be notified', 'right to participate', 'right to attend', 'rights to make submissions' and 'to examine ... evidence': see paras 31–44, 127–133, 134, 140, 141–144.

[21] The Appeals Chamber has made it clear that the basic conditions for victims' participation are: (a) that the individual is a 'victim' within the meaning of Rule 85 of the

(ii) the criteria for the granting of victim status; and (iii) the requirements of demonstrating personal interests under Article 68(3) of the Statute. However major inconsistencies remain, resulting in differential treatment of similarly situated victims. For example, the Chambers continue to differ on other key areas including the participation of deceased persons;[22] how to deal with victims previously granted participating status at the pre-trial stage;[23] access by legal representatives to confidential material among other important procedural issues.

This is not surprising. According to Judge René Blattmann, 'the issues pertaining to victims' participation have not been extensively examined through international jurisprudence and the implications of our decisions on the issues are largely untested'.[24] This discretionary legal framework has arguably de-formalised the system of victims' participation. In this context, it is difficult for anyone to have legal certainty, let alone the victims for whom the system was designed. One commentator opines that the decision to invest the Court with an overly broad discretion to shape the victims' participation scheme has endangered the consistency that formal participation schemes should have.[25] Drawing on national experience also did not provide the level of experience that was apposite to the

---

ICC RPE; (b) that the personal interests of the applicant are affected by the legal and factual issues arising in the proceedings; (c) that the applicant's participation is appropriate; and (d) that the manner of participation is not prejudicial to or inconsistent with the rights of the accused and a fair and impartial trial. See *Situation in the DRC: Prosecutor v Lubanga* (Decision, *in limine*, on Victim Participation in the appeals of the Prosecutor and the Defence against Trial Chamber I's Decision entitled 'Decision on Victims' Participation') ICC-01/04-01/06 (16 May 2008) para 36.

[22] *Situation in the DRC: Prosecutor v Lubanga* (Corrigendum to the Decision on the Applications for Participation Filed in Connection with the Investigation in the Democratic Republic of the Congo by a/0004/06 to a/0009/06, a/0016/06 to a/0063/06, a/0071/06 to a/0080/06 and a/0105/06 to a/0110/06, a/0188/06, a/0128/06 to a/0162/06, a/0199/06, a/0203/06, a/0209/06, a/0214/06, a/0220/06 to a/0222/06, a/0224/06, a/0227/06 to a/0230/06, a/0234/06 to a/0236/06, a/0240/06, a/0225/06, a/0226/06, a/0231/06 to a/0233/06, a/0237/06 to a/0239/06 and a/0241/06 to a/0250/06) ICC-01/04 (31 January 2008) 23.

[23] In *Situation in the DRC: Prosecutor v Lubanga* (Decision on Victims' Participation) (n 19) para 112, Trial Chamber I provisionally allowed victims that had been allowed to participate at the pretrial stage of the case to participate at the trial stage pending a new decision on the Chamber on each individual application for participation. By contrast, victims who had been previously granted participatory status in the Katanga and Chui case were authorised to participate in the trial without having to re-register their applications: *Situation in the DRC: Prosecutor v Katanga and Chui* (Decision on the treatment of applications for participation) ICC-01/04-01/07 (26 February 2009) 23.

[24] *Situation in the DRC: Prosecutor v Lubanga* (Decision on the Defence and Prosecution Requests for Leave to Appeal the Decision on Victims' Participation of 18 January 2008) ICC-01/04-01/06 (26 February 2008) 26.

[25] Ibid para 5 and accompanying footnote. See also E Haslam, 'Victim Participation at the International Criminal Court: A Triumph of Hope over Experience?' in D McGoldrick, P Rowe and E Donnelly (eds) *The Permanent International Criminal Court: Legal and Policy Issues* (Hart, Oxford 2004) 315.

context of international criminal trials – which included unique elements such as potentially large numbers of victims from diverse countries and cultures.

The obvious benefit of judge-driven victims' participation regime on the one hand is the existence of a significant body of jurisprudence on an important legal issue and clear evidence to the international legal community of the Court's efforts to effectuate the principles in the Court's legal documents. On the other, the lack of a clear procedural framework has cost significant judicial and administrative time and effort to interpret and devise the scope of an enigmatic scheme, hitherto unheard of in international criminal trials. With the lack of statutory precision, it is difficult to envision how judges will ensure that participation of victims is meaningful rather than purely symbolic. A primarily judge-driven process inevitably results in a casuistic approach to the implementation of victims' rights and is a recipe for inconsistent application of the law, which could result in injustice.

## Impact on the Defence

The participation of victims at the ICC has undoubtedly impacted the rights of the defence. Despite judicial efforts to frame the scope of the participatory rights in language that suggests that the Court is mindful of the rights of the defence, it is difficult even for judges to control the impact of this new regime on a defendant. In fact Zappala is of the view that 'the general situation of uncertainty regarding the overall procedural framework [of victims' participation in the Rome Statute and normative texts] coupled with the lack of clarity as to the specific degree of victims' involvement in the proceedings, has been prejudicial to the first defendants appearing before the ICC. It has entailed delays and complex procedural debates in these initial cases'.[26]

One major challenge has been the time required by the defence to respond to victims' applications to participate. This has been particularly noticeable in the case against Jean-Pierre Bemba which has the largest number of victims' applications to date.[27] Secondly, the Court has granted victims extensive rights in Court particularly during the trial phase. All three Trial Chambers have to varying degrees afforded victims some or all of the following rights: (1) to make opening and closing statements;[28] (2) to attend and participate in hearings; (3) to attend in person and present their views and concerns; (4) to call and question witnesses, experts or the accused; (5) to tender incriminating or potentially exculpatory evidence; (6) to

---

[26] S Zappala, 'The Rights of Victims v. the Rights of the Accused' (2010) 8(1) *JICJ* 137, 143.
[27] See below (n 56).
[28] Under Rule 89(1) of the Rules, victims are explicitly authorised to make opening and closing statements. Chambers have accepted this and to date this has been applied in all the trial proceedings before the ICC. See *Situation in the DRC: Prosecutor v Lubanga* (Decision on Victims' Participation) (n 19) para 117; *Situation in the DRC: Prosecutor v Katanga and Chui* (Directions for the conduct of the proceedings and testimony in accordance with rule 140) ICC-01/04-01/07 (1 December 2009) para 9.

challenge the admissibility of evidence; (7) to obtain evidence on reparation issues; (9) to have access to the case record and to confidential documents – participation in the disclosure process. The Trial Chambers have also had to consider and affirmatively address the nuanced issues associated with victims who have the dual status of also being witnesses in the trial.

The right of victims to lead evidence as to guilt or innocence, has been the most troubling for defence counsel since the judges have not imposed a corresponding disclosure obligation on victims.[29] Notwithstanding the absence of any explicit provision in the ICC's legal texts for such an extensive right the Trial and Appeals Chambers have rationalised their decisions by reference to Article 69(3) of the Statute *viz* 'the authority to request the submission of all evidence that it considers necessary for the determination of the truth'.[30]

Remarkably, the Appeals Chamber has indicated that there is no corresponding burden on victims to disclose potentially exonerating evidence in their possession similar to that which is placed on the Prosecutor by Article 67(2) of the Statute. The legal rationale espoused by the Appeals Chamber is that the Statute places the legal burden of proof on the Prosecutor and no one else and therefore victims are exempted from this obligation. Ironically, this was the very reason that Judges Pikis and Kirsch dissented from the Appeals Chamber judgment in Lubanga on the basis that the role of leading evidence establishing the guilt or innocence of the accused rested with the Prosecution,[31] who is also subject to specific disclosure obligations towards the Defence.[32] Judge Kirsch pointed out that had the drafters intended victims to assume this role, this would have been expressly included in the Rome Statute or the RPE.[33]

It is not to say that judges have given legal representatives carte blanche to intervene on behalf of their clients. If victims wish to testify under oath, the legal

---

[29] *Situation in the DRC: Prosecutor v Lubanga* (Judgment on the appeals of The Prosecutor and The Defence against Trial Chamber I's Decision on Victims' Participation of 18 January 2008) (n 24) paras 93–94; see arts 69(3) and 66(2) of the ICC Statute.

[30] *Situation in the DRC: Prosecutor v Katanga and Chui* (Directions for the conduct of the proceedings and testimony in accordance with rule 140) (n 28) para 81; *Situation in the DRC: Prosecutor v Lubanga* (Judgment on the appeals of The Prosecutor and The Defence against Trial Chamber I's Decision on Victims' Participation of 18 January 2008) (n 24) paras 94–95, 104–105.

[31] *Situation in the DRC: Prosecutor v Lubanga* (Judgment on the appeals of The Prosecutor and The Defence against Trial Chamber I's Decision on Victims' Participation of 18 January 2008) (n 24) Dissenting Opinion of Judge Pikis, paras 7–13, 15; Partly Dissenting Opinion of Judge Kirsch, paras 5–6.

[32] *Situation in the DRC: Prosecutor v Lubanga* (Judgment on the appeals of The Prosecutor and The Defence against Trial Chamber I's Decision on Victims' Participation of 18 January 2008) (n 24) Dissenting Opinion of Judge Pikis, paras 8–11; Partly Dissenting Opinion of Judge Kirsch, paras 7–16.

[33] *Situation in the DRC: Prosecutor v Lubanga* (Judgment on the appeals of The Prosecutor and The Defence against Trial Chamber I's Decision on Victims' Participation of 18 January 2008) (n 24) Partly Dissenting Opinion of Judge Kirsch, paras 4–5, 32.

representative must file a written application with an attached summary of the victim's testimony before the Prosecutor closes its case.[34] Apart from determining the relevance of the purported testimony, the judges will consider if it is repetitive, if it adds anything new to what they have heard and will provide 'a genuine contribution to the ascertainment of truth'. If the victims purport to testify anonymously or the testimony will cause undue delay or transform the victim into auxiliary prosecutor, the application will be rejected.[35] According to the Appeals Chamber, the provisions of Article 68(3) and 69(3–4) of the Statute and rule 91(3) of the RPE determine the procedure and confined limits within which the Court may exercise its authority to permit victims to tender and examine evidence.[36] The determining criteria include: '(i) a discrete application, (ii) notice to the parties, (iii) demonstration of personal interests that are affected by the specific proceedings; (iv) compliance with disclosure obligations and protection orders; (v) determination of appropriateness and (vi) consistency with the rights of the accused and a fair trial.'[37]

The Appeals Chamber in the *Lubanga* case, reaffirming the Trial Chamber's conclusions, determined that victims should also have the possibility of challenging the admissibility and relevance of evidence. The majority of the Judges reasoned that there is no specific reference in Article 69(4) as to who is entitled to submit such a challenge. Article 64(9) on the other hand gives the Chamber discretionary authority to decide upon the relevance and admissibility of evidence on its own motion.[38] The Appeals Chamber concluded that from a clear reading of these provisions with Article 68(3) of the Statute and rules 89 and 91 of the Rules, it cannot be excluded that the Trial Chamber may rule on the admissibility or relevance of evidence upon a victims' submission.[39] This, in their view, would be consistent with the victims' right not to have evidence admitted when its admission would

---

[34] *Situation in the DRC: Prosecutor v Katanga and Chui* (Directions for the conduct of the proceedings and testimony in accordance with rule 140) (n 28) paras 86–93; *Situation in the DRC: Prosecutor v Katanga and Chui* (Directions for the conduct of the proceedings and testimony in accordance with rule 140) ICC-01/04-01/07 (20 November 2009) paras 19–30.

[35] Ibid, decision of 20 November 2009, para 20.

[36] *Prosecutor v Lubanga* (Judgment on the appeals of The Prosecutor and The Defence against Trial Chamber I's Decision on Victims' Participation of 18 January 2008) (n 24) paras 88–95; *Situation in the DRC: Prosecutor v Katanga and Chui* (Directions for the conduct of the proceedings and testimony in accordance with rule 140) (n 28) paras 110–114.

[37] *Situation in the DRC: Prosecutor v Lubanga* (Judgment on the appeals of The Prosecutor and The Defence against Trial Chamber I's Decision on Victims' Participation of 18 January 2008) (n 24) paras 100–104. See dissenting opinions of Judge Pikis (paras 6, 14–15) and Partly Dissenting opinion of Judge Kirsch, paras 19, 33; *Situation in the DRC: Prosecutor v Katanga and Chui* (Directions for the conduct of the proceedings and testimony in accordance with rule 140) (n 28) para 114.

[38] ICC Statute, arts 69(4) and 64(9).

[39] *Prosecutor v Lubanga* (Judgment on the appeals of The Prosecutor and The Defence against Trial Chamber I's Decision on Victims' Participation of 18 January 2008) (n 24) para 101.

affect their personal interests.[40] Judges Kirsch and Pikis also dissented from the majority decision on this issue.[41]

## Dual Status and Anonymous Victims

Furthermore there is an additional challenge with dual status victim/witnesses. Neither the Statute nor the Rules specifically delineate the criteria for dealing with victims who have the dual status of witness. However, there is no express prohibition on the participation of such victims in the proceedings in their dual capacity.[42] According to Trial Chamber I 'a general ban on [victims'] participation in the proceedings if they may be called as witnesses would be contrary to the aim and purpose of article 68(3) of the Statute and the Chamber's obligation to establish the truth'.[43] As further noted by the Chamber, victims with dual status may affect the rights of the defence, therefore when deciding whether or not to allow victims to testify, the Trial Chamber, 'take[s] into consideration the modalities of participation by victims with dual status, the need for their participation and the rights of the accused to a fair and expeditious trial'.[44]

Additionally, the Chambers have consistently upheld the right of victims to participate anonymously in the proceedings, albeit with limited participatory rights. In the *Bemba* case, Trial Chamber III recalled the approach taken in the *Lubanga* and *Katanga* cases in respect of anonymous victims and their participation in the proceedings.[45] In *Lubanga*, Trial Chamber I rejected the submissions that anonymous victims should never be permitted to participate in the proceedings, but at the same time held that their participation in the proceedings requires 'extreme

---

[40] *Prosecutor v Lubanga* (Judgment on the appeals of The Prosecutor and The Defence against Trial Chamber I's Decision on Victims' Participation of 18 January 2008) (n 24) paras 102–103.

[41] *Situation in the DRC: Prosecutor v Lubanga* (Judgment on the appeals of The Prosecutor and The Defence against Trial Chamber I's Decision on Victims' Participation of 18 January 2008) (n 24) Partly Dissenting Opinion of Judge Kirsch, paras 35–36 and Dissenting Opinion of Judge Pikis, para 19.

[42] *Situation in the DRC: Prosecutor v Katanga and Chui* (Directions for the conduct of the proceedings and testimony in accordance with rule 140) (n 28) para 110; See also: *Situation in the DRC: Prosecutor v Lubanga* (Decision on Victims' Participation) (n 19) paras 132–134; *Situation in the DRC: Prosecutor v Lubanga* (Decision on certain practicalities regarding individuals who have the dual status of witness and victim) ICC-01/04-01/06 (5 June 2008).

[43] *Situation in the DRC: Prosecutor v Lubanga* (Decision on Victims' Participation) (n 19) para 133.

[44] Ibid para 134.

[45] *Situation in the Central African Republic: Prosecutor v Bemba* (Corrigendum to Decision on the participation of victims in the trial and on 86 applications by victims to participate in the proceedings) ICC-01/05-01/08 (12 July 2010) paras 65–69.

care' not to 'undermine the fundamental guarantee of a fair trial'.[46] Trial Chamber II in the *Katanga/Chui* case 'did not rule out the possibility of anonymous victims participating in the proceedings'.[47] Nevertheless, the Chamber required that any victim who is called to testify must relinquish their anonymity.[48] These decisions on the matter, although slightly differently phrased, represent a more or less common line taken by all three Chambers to statements given by anonymous victims.

Ultimately, the question of whether victims' participation is beneficial cannot be answered in the abstract. In the context of judicial proceedings, the impact on the accused must be carefully considered. As McDermott opines, 'the most imperative element for victims in the criminal justice system is granting the accused a fair trial, as opposed to the scope and volume of procedural rights which have been painted as necessary to give deference to the victim's suffering in recent years'.[49]

## Administrative Challenges

While there are several legal hurdles to effective participation, the administrative challenges have arguably catalysed the review of the entire process. The individual applications procedure – the means by which victims can directly apply to participate in a situation or a case- has proven on the one hand to be the most direct way of engaging individual victims with the Court, and on the other, the most time and resource intensive means of facilitating participation. Under this system, *each* person or organisation wishing to apply must submit a separate, individual application – a complex and detailed process rarely carried out by victims without assistance.[50] Under the current system, all victims wishing to participate in proceedings before the Court must send applications to the Registry, setting out

---

[46] *Situation in the DRC: Prosecutor v Lubanga* (Decision on Victims' Participation) (n 19) paras 130–131.

[47] *Situation in the DRC: Prosecutor v Katanga and Chui* (Directions for the conduct of the proceedings and testimony in accordance with rule 140) (n 28) paras 92–93.

[48] Ibid.

[49] McDermott(n 8) 199.

[50] Rule 89 of the ICC RPE provides that in order to participate, a victim or organisation shall make a written application setting out why they qualify as a victim to participate, and submit this to the Court along with relevant identifying documents (emphasis added). Regulation 86 of the Regulations of the Court, ICC-BD/01-01-04 (26 May 2004) elaborates further on the necessary criteria which victims must fulfil. In the Court's early days, the victims' application form was a complex 17-page document which required detailed information from the applicant. It was virtually impossible to apply without the assistance of local intermediaries or legal representatives of victims. The application form was amended in early 2011 and has now been reduced to 11 pages. See 'Request for Participation in Proceedings and Reparations at the ICC for Individual Victims' <http://www.icc-cpi.int/NR/rdonlyres/48A75CF0-E38E-48A7-A9E0-026ADD32553D/0/SAFIndividualEng.pdf> last accessed 26 November 2011.

in detail the nature of the harm they suffered, and how their personal interests are affected. The Victims Participation and Reparations Section (VPRS) – the Registry Unit tasked with facilitating victims' participation at the Court – assesses the completeness of applications, and if incomplete, may request additional information pursuant to regulation 86(3) of the Regulations of the Court prior to transmitting the applications and a report to the Chamber.

The individualistic approach to the victims' application procedure has revealed deep fissures in the participation scheme.[51] Processing and ruling on applications to participate has become extremely resource-intensive for the Court.[52] Lack of certainty concerning the criteria for participation in the Court's early years significantly hampered Registry efforts to expedite the processing and submission of complete applications to the Chamber in a timely manner.[53] In November 2008, one victims' rights advocacy group noted that of the 960 victims' applications submitted to the Court for all situations, 770, or approximately 80 per cent, were still awaiting decisions, many since mid-2006.[54] The group pointed out that although the warrant of arrest against Thomas Lubanga had been made public since 17 March 2006 and despite the hundreds of victims applying to participate,

---

[51] Different chambers have required the following information: (i) the identity of the applicant; (ii) the date of the crime(s); (iii) the location of the crime(s); (iv) a description of the harm suffered as a result of the commission of a crime; (v) proof of identity; (vi) if the application is made by a person acting with the consent of the victim, the express consent of that victim; (vii) if the application is made by a person acting on behalf of a victim, in the case of a victim who is a child, proof of kinship or legal guardianship; or, in the case of a victim who is disabled, proof of legal guardianship; (viii) a signature or thumb-print of the Applicant on the document, at the very least, on the last page of the application. See e.g. *Situation in the Central African Republic: Prosecutor v Bemba* (Fourth Decision on Victims' Participation) ICC-01/05-01/08 (12 December 2008) para 81; *Situation in the DRC* (Decision on the Requests of the Legal Representative of Applicants on application process for victims' participation and legal representation) (n 16) para 12; *Situation in the DRC: Prosecutor v Lubanga* (Public Redacted Version of the 'Decision on the 97 Applications for Participation at the Pre-Trial Stage of the Case') ICC-01/04-01/07 (10 June 2008) para 44; *Situation in Darfur, Sudan: Prosecutor v Abu Garda* (Decision on the 34 Applications for Participation at the Pre-Trial Stage of the Case) ICC-02/05-02/09 (29 September 2009) para 7; *Situation in the DRC: Prosecutor v Katanga and Chui* (Decision on the treatment of applications for participation) (n 17) para 28; *Situation in the Central African Republic: Prosecutor v Bemba* (Decision defining the status of 54 victims who participated at the pre-trial stage, and inviting the parties' observations on applications for participation by 86 applicants) ICC-01/05-01/08 (22 February 2010) paras 35–36.

[52] van den Wyngaert (n 3).

[53] See below (n 56). For further commentary on this issue, see Redress, 'Victims and the ICC: Still Room for Improvements', Paper prepared for the 7th Assembly of States Parties (The Hague, 14–22 November 2008) <http://www.redress.org/downloads/publications/ASP%20Paper%20Draft%20Nov08.pdf> last accessed 25 January 2012; War Crimes Research Office Report (n 8).

[54] Redress (n 53) 3.

up to mid-2008 only four victims had been admitted to participate in the case.[55] In general, the need to process and verify individual applications for completeness; for observations by Prosecuting and Defence counsel; and for a decision by the Chambers, have resulted in significant delays in the Court proceedings.

The increasing number of applications has further compounded the issue.[56] Faced with a significant number of applications (783) shortly before the commencement of confirmation of charges hearings in the case of the *Prosecutor v Callixte Mbarushimana*, the VPRS admitted that its inability to meet the Chamber's deadline was primarily due to resource constraints. An alternative approach was proposed.[57] In order not to deprive the remaining victims of any form of participation during the confirmation hearing, the VPRS suggested that the Chamber could nevertheless seek the views of those victims whose applications had not been formally accepted, pursuant to rule 93 of the RPE.[58] The Registry indicated that it would only assess

---

[55]  Ibid.

[56]  According to Registry figures up to October 2011, a total of 9,910 victims applied to participate in proceedings (2,228 for the situation or individual cases in the Democratic Republic of the Congo; 1,028 for Uganda; 209 for Darfur; 3,873 for the Central African Republic and 2,572 for Kenya). 5,639 of these applications were lodged since the beginning of 2011, indicating a steady increase in the number of applications. Of the total number of applicants, only 3,446 had to date been accepted for participation by the relevant Chambers: 127 for the *Lubanga* case; 366 for the *Katanga and Chui* case; 132 for the *Mbarushimana* case; 41 for the *Kony et al* case; 1,937 for the *Bemba* case; 87 for the *Abu Garda* case; six for the *Harun and Kushayb* case; 12 for the *Al Bashir* case; 178 for the *Banda and Jerbo* case; 327 in the *Ruto et al* case; 233 in the *Muthaura et al* case. 6,896 applications for reparations have been received by the Registry (1,160 relating to the DRC; 15 for Uganda; 54 for Darfur; 1,943 for the Central African Republic and 2,857 for Kenya). See Victims' Rights Working Group, 'The Implementation of Victims' Rights before the ICC, Issues and Concerns', paper presented by the Victims' Rights Working Group on the occasion of the 10th Session of the Assembly of States Parties (12–21 December 2011) <http://www.vrwg.org/VRWG_DOC/2011_VRWG_ASP10.pdf> last accessed 24 January 2012, 7 and accompanying footnotes.

[57]  *Situation in the DRC: Prosecutor v Mbarushimana* (Proposal on victim participation in the confirmation hearing) ICC-01/04-01/10 (6 June 2011).

[58]  Ibid paras 10–11. There is precedent for this course of action: see *Situation in the DRC* (Judgment on victim participation in the investigation stage of the proceedings in the appeal of the OPCD against the decision of Pre-Trial Chamber I of 7 December 2007 and in the appeals of the OPCD and the Prosecutor against the decision of Pre-Trial Chamber I) ICC-01/04 (19 December 2008) para 48; *Situation in Darfur, Sudan* (Judgment on victim participation in the investigation stage of the proceedings in the appeal of the OPCD against the decision of Pre-Trial Chamber I of 3 December 2007 and in the appeals of the OPCD and the Prosecutor against the decision of Pre-Trial Chamber I) ICC-02/05 (2 February 2009) para 48; *Situation in Uganda: Prosecutor v Kony et al* (Decision on victims' applications for participation a/0010/06, a/0064/06 to a/0070/06, a/0081/06 to a/0104/06 and a/0111/06 to a/0127/06) ICC-02/04-01/05 (10 August 2007) para 102; *Situation in the DRC: Prosecutor v Lubanga* (Decision on 'Demande de déposition du représentant légales demandeurs des victimes') ICC-01/04-01/06 (25 October 2007) para 3; *Situation in the DRC: Prosecutor v Lubanga* (Decision, *in limine*, on Victim Participation in the appeals of the Prosecutor and the Defence against Trial Chamber I's Decision entitled 'Decision on Victims' Participation') (n 21) paras

preliminarily whether the applications were complete and linked to the case. In their view, this form of participation would provide a limited form of recognition to the applicants in question. The Office of Public Counsel for Victims (OPCV) – an independent Unit at the Court responsible for providing legal support and advice to legal representatives of victims and individual victims – strongly objected to this proposal. The OPCV argued that the proposed approach would create two categories of victims – first and second class of participants, the latter having an 'observer status', which would only serve to undermine the meaningful role of victims and their substantial impact in the proceedings.[59] In the case of Jean-Pierre Bemba Gombo, despite almost 1,900 applications approved for participation prior to the commencement of the trial, the Registrar notified the Chamber, while the trial was underway, that an additional 2,830 applications had been filed.[60] In order to manage the process, the VPRS proposed a timeline for the transfer of these applications in nine different sets of 200 to 350 applications per set.

The Court is clearly unable to cope with the increasing number of victims' applications within the scope of existing resources. According to Court documents, 'the number of victims applying to the Court has increased as a natural consequence of the proliferation of proceedings. The rate at which the Court received applications has increased by 300 per cent, from 187 applications received on average per month in 2010, to 564 in 2011. As at the end of April 2012, 19,422 applications for participation and for reparations have been submitted, and 4,107 victims have been accepted to participate in proceedings before the Court'.[61] The most concerning conclusion from the empirical analysis of victim applications is the discrepancy between the number of applications made to the Registry and the number of victims ultimately accepted to participate in proceedings. The balance has clearly not been found between the interest of victims to participate in ICC proceedings and the resources necessary to effectuate the participation scheme.

It is clear that the individualised approach to victims' participation envisioned in the RPE is not sustainable. As one ICC Judge noted:

---

9–11; *Situation in Darfur, Sudan: Prosecutor v al Bashir* (Decision on the Second Application by Victims a/0443/09 to a/0450/09 to Participate in the Appeal against the 'Decision on the Prosecution's Application for a Warrant of Arrest against Omar Hassan Ahmad Al Bashir') ICC-02/05-01/09 (28 January 2010) para 4; *Situation in the Central African Republic: Prosecutor v Bemba* (Decision on the legal representation of victim applicants at trial) ICC-01/05-01/08 (19 November 2010) paras 22–23.

[59] *Situation in the DRC: Prosecutor v Mbarushimana* (Request to access documents in the case record in relation to the Defence Challenge to the Jurisdiction of the Court) ICC-01/04-01/10 (19 June 2011).

[60] Email of 26 August 2011 from the Chief of the Victims Representation and Participation Section to the Assistant Legal Officer, Trial Division (referred to in *Situation in the Central African Republic: Prosecutor v Bemba* (Decision setting a timeline for the filing of observations on pending victims' applications) ICC-01/05-01/08 (9 September 2011) para 3).

[61] Report of the Court on the review of the system for victims to apply to participate in proceedings, ICC-ASP/11/22, para 5.

> This individualized approach to victim participation may work in a national proceeding, where there are only a few victims in each case. At the ICC, however, the number of victims is becoming overwhelming. The judges had to go through this entire process for each of the nearly 10.000 applications received, and more applications continue to arrive, now that the Court is investigating the Libya and Ivory Coast situations. The Court may soon reach the point where this individual case by case approach becomes unsustainable. It may well have to consider replacing individual applications with collective applications. This would, of course, require amendments to the applicable texts.[62]

Most significantly, it appears to have had an adverse effect on participating victims. The Victims' Rights Working Group argues that victims are paying the consequences for the Court's shortcomings; that the current system is not working satisfactorily and victims are 'losing out'.[63] The group claims that high numbers of applications are a positive indication that victims and wider communities wish to engage with the Court. As such, it is the Court's responsibility to effectively and efficiently manage this engagement through adequate staffing, resources and improved procedures.[64] In 2008, Christine Chung noted that:

> The considerable effort expended by the judges and the participants in attempting to define and provide meaningful victims' participation, however, has not yielded a coherent or workable system of providing concrete participation. The progression of decisions of the Pre-Trial and Trial Chambers reflects an evolution from conviction that broad participation can be conferred, to uncertainty in the first standards chosen, to hope that the Appeals Chamber will find solutions from among the disparate, potentially controversial, and burdensome standards implemented by the lower Chambers.[65]

At that time, only 509 applications had been received by the Registry, a fraction of the numbers today.

While lack of resources may be one cause of the current challenges, the Court will in all likelihood continue to face resource constraints. The current procedural framework does not place a limit on the number of victims who may potentially apply; thus if hundreds of thousands of victims wish to participate they may conceivably do so. If the Court must assess each individual application submitted, proceedings will

---

[62] van den Wyngaert (n 3).
[63] Victims' Rights Working Group (n 56) 8.
[64] Ibid.
[65] CH Chung, 'Victims' Participation at the International Criminal Court: Are Concessions of the Court Clouding the Promise?' (2008) 6(3) *Northwestern University J of Int'l Human Rights* 459, 497.

grind to a halt and victims will continue to be frustrated. The individualised approach appears to be a waste of precious time and resources and there is no evidence that this approach ensures the meaningful (as opposed to symbolic) participation of victims. Furthermore, under the current system, individual victims rarely directly address the Court and to date only a handful of victims have applied to directly attend Court to present their views and concerns or testify on their own behalf (not as prosecution witnesses), and this is likely to continue.[66]

The Court has tentatively begun to explore the feasibility of the system of collective applications (partial and full). At the request of the Pre-Trial Chamber in the case of *Laurent Gbagbo*, the Registry implemented a partly collective approach to victim applications. Each applicant completed an individual declaration (confirming their wish to participate in proceedings and detailing their harm suffered), but information relating to the crime/incident and other elements common to the group was recorded in a collective form. Victims' applications were determined individually and, if accepted, they participated individually. However, the Court noted that in relation to resources, whilst the partly collective application process was less time consuming for processing of applications, it would require *more* resources for several Registry sections in the field (VPRS, Public Information and Documentation Section (PIDS), Victims and Witnesses Unit and legal representatives of victims. Several disadvantages were also noted for the fully collective applications, which allow a group of applicants to present information and to participate on a collective basis. In this system, applications could be accepted from a representative of a community on behalf of a community, and/or on behalf of a recognised association. The Court noted that this option would among others create several legal and administrative obstacles with the establishment of an association and would require an amendment to the existing legal texts of the Court.[67]

It would be naïve to suggest that a system of collective applications to participate could be implemented without a major change in both the perceptions concerning the scope of participatory rights, the expectations of victims (and victims' advocates) and effective measures to safeguard the rights of the accused. If collective applications are encouraged, the scope of the rights would be very limited and essentially theoretical since neither prosecution, defence nor indeed the Court would have had the opportunity to rigorously scrutinise the basis on which such persons purport to be victims within the meaning of the Rome Statute. While victims are entitled to several rights within the Rome Statute framework, the time is fast approaching where the Court (or the Assembly of States Parties) may need to determine which rights should be considered paramount.

---

[66] See, e.g., *Situation in the DRC: Prosecutor v Lubanga* (Order issuing public redacted version of the Decision on the request by victims a/ 0225/06, a/0229/06 and a/0270/07 to express their views and concerns in person and to present evidence during the trial) ICC-01/04-01/06 (26 June 2009).

[67] Report of the Court on the Review of the System for Victims to Apply to Participate in Proceedings (n 12).

## More external focus

Realistically, given the limitations of the criminal justice process, including the limited nature of charges, length of proceedings and the need to safeguard the rights of accused persons, the time has come to examine whether active participation in the ICC pre-trial and trial process is in fact achieving the goal of ensuring the victims' right to justice. The movement towards a collective application system and an increased push for a more streamlined process to ensure procedural efficiency at the pre-trial and trial phase, could result in a gradual erosion of the actual participation of victims in ICC proceedings. This does not have to translate to a diminution of victims' rights at the Court but is an opportunity to foster even greater engagement with the victim community to ensure that a wider range of their needs are met. Targeted and sustained engagement will be critical to ensuring that the Court does not lose confidence and support within the victim community. The Court has admitted to exceeding difficultly in communicating effectively with victims in remote and/or hard to reach locations. In other areas, security or lack of resources – both human and financial – have made it challenging to reach out to victims living in certain regions of situation countries.[68] Nevertheless, going forward, emphasis will have to be placed on fostering engagement with victims and affected communities through outreach and supporting legal representatives in fulfilling their functions.

- Encourage and empower legal representatives of victims

One important means of fostering this engagement is through legal representatives of victims. The ICC's normative texts are mindful that a significant number of participating victims could adversely affect the proceedings and the fair trial rights of defendants before the Court. Thus, while the victims' right to participate is not *per se* contingent on being represented by counsel,[69] given the jurisdictional scope

---

[68] Report of the Court on the Review of the System for Victims to Apply to Participate in Proceedings (n 12).

[69] The ICC's legal texts do not require victims to participate through counsel. Rule 90(1) provides that victims shall be free to choose a legal representative, which suggests that they may opt not to choose one. In relevant part, Rule 92(2) provides for notification to *either* victims *or* their legal representatives concerning the decision of the Prosecutor not to initiate an investigation or not to prosecute pursuant to art 53 of the ICC Statute. Rule 92(3) further provides that in a manner consistent with the ruling made under Rules 89–91, *victims or their legal representatives* participating in proceedings shall, in respect of those proceedings, be notified by the Registrar in a timely manner of (a) Proceedings before the Court, including the date of hearings, any postponements and the date of delivery of the decision; (b) Requests, submissions, motions and other relevant documents. Victims or their legal representatives who have participated in a certain stage of the proceedings should be notified as soon as possible of the decisions of the Court in those proceedings (Rule 90(6)). Additionally, Rule 93 enables the Chamber to seek the views of *either* victims *or* their legal representative participating in proceedings pursuant to Rules 89–91. However,

of the ICC, and the likelihood of large numbers of victims applying to participate in trials, victims *are encouraged* to appoint legal representatives in order to make the exercise of the rights conferred upon them more effective as well as to avoid undue delay in the proceedings.[70] Ironically, notwithstanding the individualised approach to the applications process, to further facilitate the participation of large numbers of victims, the RPE contemplates the implementation of the system of common legal representation through which a common legal representative represents all or the majority of victims in pre-trial or trial proceedings (provided that there is no conflict of interest).[71]

In the Court's earlier days, common legal representation was organised at a later stage of the proceedings with continuity of legal representation being the key deciding factor in the selection of a common legal representative. This was done either by enabling the existing legal representatives to form teams and work together,[72] or by choosing one or more of the counsel already involved in a case to act as a common legal representative.[73] While this ensured continuity in representation and enabled the relationships of trust formed between victims and their lawyers to be continued throughout the proceedings, no formal evaluation of the quality of legal representation being afforded to victims had been carried out.[74]

---

it does appear from the legal texts however that the procedural rights to participate for unrepresented victims are more limited. As such, a Chamber may opt to appoint a legal representative in the interest of justice pursuant to Regulation 80 of the Regulations of the Court. For additional discussion on this issue, see Office of Public Counsel for Victims, *Representing Victims before the International Criminal Court: A Manual for Legal Representatives* (International Criminal Court, The Hague 2010) <http://www.icc-cpi.int/iccdocs/PIDS/tmp/Representing%20Victims%20before%20ICC.PDF> last accessed 26 January 2011, 103.

[70] See also International Federation for Human Rights, 'Chapter V: Legal Representation', *Victims' Rights before the ICC* (FIDH, Paris 2010) <http://www.fidh.org/IMG/pdf/8-CH-V_Legal_Representation.pdf> last accessed 26 January 2012, 5.

[71] Ibid 4.

[72] *Situation in the DRC: Prosecutor v Lubanga* (Transcript) ICC-01/04-01/06-T-105-ENG, 12–13.

[73] *Situation in the DRC: Prosecutor v Katanga and Chui* (Report of the Registry on the organization of the common legal representation of victims) ICC-01/04-01/07 (14 August 2009); *Situation in the Republic of Kenya: Prosecutor v Ruto et al* (Proposal for the common legal representation of victims (including annexes)) ICC-01/09-01/11 (1 August 2011); *Situation in the Central African Republic: Prosecutor v Bemba* (Désignation d'un représentant légal commun pour les victimes autorisées à participer à la procédure dans l'affaire Le Procureur c. Jean-Pierre Bemba) ICC-01/05-01/08 (5 January 2009); *Situation in the Central African Republic: Prosecutor v Bemba* (Decision on common legal representation of victims for the purpose of trial) ICC-01/05-01/08 (10 November 2010); *Situation in the Central African Republic: Prosecutor v Bemba* (Notification of designation of common legal representatives) ICC-01/05-01/08 (22 November 2010).

[74] *Situation in the Republic of Kenya: Prosecutor v Ruto et al* (Proposal for the common legal representation of victims (including annexes)) (n 74) para 8; *Situation in the Republic of Kenya: Prosecutor v Muthaura et al* (Proposal for the common legal representation of victims (including annexes)) ICC-01/09-02/11 (5 August 2011) para 8; see also *Situation in Darfur,*

On 1 August 2011, the ICC Registry implemented a new framework for arranging common legal representation at the Court. The new policy was implemented in the cases of *The Prosecutor v Ruto, Kosgey and Sang* (Kenya 1); *The Prosecutor v Muthuara, Kenyatta and Hussein Ali* (Kenya 2) and *The Prosecutor v Banda and Jerbo* (Darfur).[75] According to the Registry, the new approach was consistent with its general mandate under rule 16(1)(b) of the RPE to assist victims with the organisation of their legal representation; and was aimed at developing an open, transparent and objective system for ensuring meaningful participation of victims in proceedings through the highest quality legal representation, without prejudice to the rights of the defence or the expediency of the proceedings.[76]

The main features of the new policy include organisation of common legal representation at an earlier stage in the proceedings; departure from a presumption in favour of extending the mandate/s of the existing legal representatives; formal evaluation of the suitability of counsel; and limiting the number of victim groups providing that the rights of victims are not infringed upon (such as where there are conflicting interests).[77] The Registry's approach to grouping victims under this policy is based on the assumption that a smaller number of victims' groups and corresponding legal teams will bring significant advantages, including more efficient proceedings.[78] Additional benefits include the coherence of a common victim strategy, and the reduction of cost due to the expense associated with each lead counsel; which is consistent with the resource limitations of the legal aid scheme.[79] Designated groupings were to be reviewed throughout the proceedings in the event of a conflict at a later stage.[80] In implementing the new policy and whilst underscoring the importance of previous engagement, continuity of representation and a relationship of trust between the former legal representatives and their victim clients, the Registry stressed that based on their experience with other cases at the Court, there were other equally important criteria to be taken into account in appointing a common legal representative, including the level of

---

*Sudan: Prosecutor v Banda and Jerbo* (Proposal for the common legal representation of victims) ICC-02/05-03/09 (25 August 2011) para 8.

[75] *Situation in Darfur, Sudan: Prosecutor v Banda and Jerbo* (Proposal for the common legal representation of victims) (n 75).

[76] Ibid 10.

[77] Ibid.

[78] Ibid 9; *Situation in Darfur, Sudan: Prosecutor v Banda and Jerbo* (Report on the implementation of the Chamber's Order instructing the Registry to start consultations on the organization of common legal representation) ICC-02/05-03/09 (21 June 2011); *Situation in the Republic of Kenya: Prosecutor v Muthaura et al* (Proposal for the common legal representation of victims (including annexes)) (n 50) 9.

[79] *Situation in the Republic of Kenya: Prosecutor v Ruto et al* (Proposal for the common legal representation of victims (including annexes)) (n 49) 9.

[80] *Situation in Darfur, Sudan: Prosecutor v Banda and Jerbo* (Proposal for the common legal representation of victims) (n 50) para 31.

familiarity of the former legal representatives with the victim client and the Court proceedings generally.[81]

However, the implementation of the new policy was marred by problems. Victims' legal representatives complained that there was a general absence of consultation by the Registry prior to the implementation of the new policy; that their former clients were excluded from the procedure for the appointment of the common legal representative; that their views were not taken into account by the Registry; and that they were given no meaningful opportunity to organise themselves before a decision on common legal representation was taken.[82] The Registry has admitted that its failure to consult was due to temporal and logistical constraints.[83] This has negatively impacted the smooth transition between the former and current legal representatives and has led to significant litigation.

The ICC's legal framework provides little guidance concerning consultations with victims and legal representatives. The judges in the *Banda and Jerbo* case held that consultation regarding common legal representation 'shall be conducted in the presence of the legal representatives currently representing the victims in the case'.[84] However, the Registry has expressed marked reluctance to consult with victims in the presence of their existing legal representatives for fear that this will affect victims' ability to, among other things, frankly and freely express possible concerns about the effectiveness of the legal representation to date.[85]

---

[81] The Registry submitted that although continuity of representation is an important factor, other criteria must also be taken into account when appointing a common legal representative under Rule 90(3) including: 1) Relationship of trust with the victims; 2) Demonstrated commitment to working with vulnerable persons; 3) Familiarity/connection with the situation country; 4) Sufficient availability; 5) Relevant litigation expertise/experience; 6) and information and technology skills: see *Situation in Darfur, Sudan: Prosecutor v Banda and Jerbo* (Report on the implementation of the Chamber's Order instructing the Registry to start consultations on the organization of common legal representation) (n 79). One of the current legal representatives indicated on 7 July that the Registry's report contained many material inaccuracies, see *Situation in Darfur, Sudan: Prosecutor v Banda and Jerbo* (Submissions on behalf of victims ... in response to the Interim Report of the Registrar regarding the issue of common legal representation of victims participating in the case) ICC-02/05-03/09 (7 July 2011).

[82] Ibid para 13.

[83] Concerns regarding the importance of considering the preferences of victims were also communicated in a letter to Registrar Silvana Arbia in August 2011 by the Victims' Right Working Group: Victims' Right Working Group, Letter to the ICC Registrar on its approach to the Common Legal Representation of Victims <http://www.vrwg.org/VRWG_DOC/2011_08_17_VRWGLetter.PDF> last accessed 26 January 2012.

[84] *Situation in Darfur, Sudan: Prosecutor v Banda and Jerbo* (Order instructing the Registry to start consultations on the organisation of common legal representation) ICC-02/05-03/09 (21 June 2011) para 7.

[85] *Situation in the Republic of Kenya: Prosecutor v Ruto et al* (Proposal for the common legal representation of victims (including annexes)) (n 74) para 7; *Situation in Darfur, Sudan: Prosecutor v Banda and Jerbo* (Report recommending a decision concerning the common legal representation of victims participating in the case) (n 37) ICC-02/05-03/09 (15 April 2011).

Ideally, a clear framework for consulting with and obtaining the choice of victims for organising common legal representation needs to be set out by the Court. In this regard, the approach adopted by the judges in the *Banda and Jerbo* case would be preferable (consultation in the presence of the legal representative). However, in circumstances where there are clear reasons to depart from this practice (such as where specific concerns have been communicated confidentially by the victims), the Registry should nevertheless seek the permission of the legal representative concerned and if this is denied, seek the leave of the Chamber.

The ICC's legal texts do not expressly prescribe the procedure for ensuring a smooth transition between the former legal representative and the current common legal representative, particularly in circumstances where the appointment of the latter is disputed. The former legal representative does however have certain clear obligations under the ICC Code of Professional Conduct for Counsel (the Code). For example, Article 15(2) provides that when counsel is discharged from or terminates the representation agreement, he or she shall convey as promptly as possible to the former client or replacement counsel any communication received relating to the representation, without prejudice to the duties which subsist after the end of the representation. Similarly under Article 18 of the Code, counsel is mandated to convey to replacement counsel the entire case file, including any material or document relating to it. It should be noted that, in some instances, the Code does not take into account the specific circumstances of legal representatives for victims. The provision was drafted with defence counsel in mind and envisages an individual lawyer–client relationship, when it is conceivable that legal representatives of hundreds of victims may not necessarily directly consult and take instruction from each individual victim on every separate legal issue about which they wish to intervene before the Chamber.

The fact is that common legal representatives of victims face their own resource and logistical challenges. The assignment of counsel to large groups of victims, some of whom may reside in different countries, undoubtedly places a strain on counsel's ability to effectively fulfil their mandate. Furthermore, legal aid is not available to victims' legal representatives to assist with the applications phase, and is only granted once participation status has been granted. The Committee on Budget and Finance (CBF) – a subsidiary body of the ICC Assembly of States Parties, the Court's governing body – has consistently referred to legal aid for both victims and accused as a major cost-driver. The CBF recommended that the Assembly seriously reconsider the option of the OPCV[86] being exclusively responsible for legal representation of victims. The CBF recommendations are

---

[86] The Office of Public Counsel for Victims was established to provide assistance and support to the legal representatives of victims and victims. The Office of Public Counsel for Victims functions independently and is attached to the Registry only for administrative purposes. In cases where the Chamber deems it necessary and in the interests of justice, the Office of Public Counsel for Victims may be appointed to represent unrepresented victims. To date, the Office has assisted 39 legal representatives and more than 2,300 participating victims.

likely to be concerning to the legal representatives of victims, particularly in relation to the suggested internalisation of legal representation exclusively within the OPCV. Expanding the mandate of the OPCV to include full responsibility for legal representation of victims at the ICC requires careful thought and consultation, particularly with respect to weighing the benefits of maintaining external counsel and lawyers from situation countries. Furthermore, the office would need to be provided with sufficient resources to fulfil this mandate. Several considerations first need to be explored, such as whether counsel should be attached to the office on a temporary contractual basis, thus entitling counsel to some staff benefits; and whether there should be a standing requirement that mandates the recruitment of counsel from situation countries. Irrespective of the decision, external counsel, particularly those with relevant experience from the field, should not be sidelined because of financial reasons.

- More sustained outreach and public information to victims

Apart from the VPRS, the Office of the Prosecutor and legal representatives of victims, the PIDS of the Registry and local intermediaries are the most important sources of information for victims. Again, resource challenges have constrained the scope of possible engagement. Mindful of this gap, the Court has committed in its revised strategy in relation to victims to 'strengthen its two-way dialogue with victims and affected communities and to further optimise and adapt outreach activities to the needs of victims'.[87] This is a lofty goal which must be resourced in order to be realised. States have been consistently reluctant to increase the Court's outreach budget, referring to Outreach as a non-core activity that is not central to the judicial processes.[88] A decision will have to be made concerning whether the Court will be able to pursue purely symbolic or actual engagement with victims and affected communities. As Redress puts it:

> 'Given the remoteness of the Court to victims and the challenges facing most victims of crimes coming within its jurisdiction, field presence and related work on the ground are vital to ensure that victims receive sufficient information about the Court and its processes. Thus, ensuring sufficient budget for the outreach capacity of field offices is important to maximise the effectiveness of outreach to victims and affected communities.'[89]

---

[87] eport of the Court on the Review of the System for Victims to Apply to Participate in Proceedings (n 12), para. 20..
[88] Report of the Committee on Budget and Finance on the work of its 17th session ('CBF 17th Session Report'), ICC-ASP/10/15, 18 November 2011, para. 25
[89] Redress, The Participation of Victims in International Criminal Court Proceedings: A Review of the Practice and Consideration of Options for the Future, http://www.redress.org/downloads/publications/121030participation_report.pdf (last accessed January 19, 2012).

## Conclusion

The right of victims to participate in proceedings at the ICC is an important, innovative legal concept. The right of victims to access justice, to obtain the truth, to be heard and to obtain reparations for the harm suffered are among those fully recognised by the international legal community and codified by the ICC Statute and legal texts. However, the scope of this right must be considered against other equally weighty considerations, including resource constraints and the rights of accused persons. The current individualised procedure for victims' applications to participate is urgently in need of review. However, finding the most feasible solution is difficult as granting large numbers of victims procedural rights *simpliciter* does have other grave legal and resource implications for the Court.

It does appear that in many ways participation of victims has become a burden, albeit an important and necessary one. The recurring complaints from Registry staff concerning lack of resources to process applications; the concerns of defence and prosecuting counsel regarding the scope of participatory rights and the legal obligations to make observations and respond to filings; and the extent of judicial time taken by filings and decisions on this issue leads to questions about the scheme's viability. By contrast, it remains unclear what clear benefits victims, many of whom have waited for years for applications to be determined, have received. Whether participation as it has currently evolved at the ICC provides actual as opposed to perceived benefits to victim communities remains an open question. The process of review that has been initiated by the Court is timely but may require some tough decisions that do not satisfy all stakeholders. Going forward, while concrete steps are taken to ensure judicial consistency in the decision making process to streamline gaps in the procedural framework and to strengthen administrative processes, a more difficult task will be to foster sustained engagement with victim communities in order to realign their expectations with the Court's realities. Although it is currently burdensome, the current system should no means be seen as a failure given its unprecedented recognition of the suffering of thousands of victims. Any future decision taken on the victim participation scheme at the ICC must continue to place value on the important role of victims but should not undermine the fairness and effectiveness of the judicial process and the rights of the accused.

# A Shifting Scale of Power: Who is in Charge of the Charges at the International Criminal Court?

Dov Jacobs

One issue that has come to the fore in the early practice of the International Criminal Court (ICC) is the question of who determines the content of the charges against an accused individual and the scope and timing of any amendments that are to be made. The importance of this issue is threefold. First, having a clear framework for the amendment of charges is important from the point of view of the accused. If he or she is to have adequate time for the preparation of the defence,[1] it is important that there be some certainty as to the charges resting against him or her, without running the risk of multiple amendments. Second, the issues are illustrative of the more general concern in the ICC Statute to achieve a balance between legal certainty and judicial efficiency. The former requires that as few amendments as possible be allowed the more advanced the proceedings are, whereas the latter opens to door to some flexibility to avoid acquittals based on a faulty determination of the charges. Third, as will be illustrated in the course of the chapter, it more generally highlights the difficult balance of power to be struck between various organs of the Court, not just between the Prosecutor and the Chambers, but also between the Pre-Trial Chamber and the Appeals Chamber, and begs the question as to whether the judges of the ICC ought to have the final say in matters that might seem to relate more to a legislative rather than judicial function.

This chapter will address these questions in three sections. Section I considers the pre-trial proceedings, where control over the charges essentially rests on the Prosecutor, with the final decision as to their confirmation given to the Pre-Trial Chamber. Section II examines the trial phase. In that phase, the Statute is silent

---

[1] Rome Statute of the International Criminal Court, 2187 UNTS 90, 17 July 1998, entered into force 1 July 2002 ('ICC Statute'), art 67(1)(b).

on any possible amendments to the charges, but the Trial Chamber is granted the power under the Regulations of the Court to legally re-characterise the facts described in the charges, thus raising the question of the legality and opportunity of such a procedure. Finally, Section III looks at the framework relating to charges as a whole, and addresses some difficulties in its operation, its interaction with other provisions of the Statute, such as *ne bis in idem* and complementarity, and with the balance of power within the Court.

## I. Amending the Charges at the Pre-Trial Phase

### A. The Meaning of a 'Charge'

As is widely known, pre-trial decisions relating to investigations and prosecutions are largely left to the Prosecutor, who will decide whether to open an investigation based on information received, irrespective of whether the situation has been referred to him by a State Party,[2] by the United Nations Security Council,[3] or whether he is exercising his *proprio motu* powers,[4] even if some of these initial decisions will be subject to judicial control.[5] In the same way, it is the Prosecutor's decision whether or not to proceed with a prosecution in a given situation.[6]

In relation to the charges, it is equally left to the Prosecutor to initially determine their content. It is interesting to note in this respect that the ICC Statute itself does not use the 'indictment' terminology, as is the case in other international tribunals,[7] but rather refers to a 'document containing the charges'.[8] However, this document does not seem to be given any real formal legal value, as evidenced by the fact that any discussions of amendments in the Statute concern 'the charges', rather than 'the document containing the charges', compared to other tribunals which

---

[2] Ibid art 12(a).
[3] Ibid art 12(b).
[4] Ibid art 12(c).
[5] For example, the decision to open an investigation *proprio motu* requires authorisation by the Pre-Trial Chamber (ibid art 15) and the decision not to open an investigation in the 'interests of justice' (ibid art 53(1)(c)) needs to be confirmed by the Pre-Trial Chamber (ibid art 53(3)(b)).
[6] Subject to the same possibility for the Pre-Trial Chamber to review the decision (ibid art 53(3)(b)).
[7] See for example, ibid arts 18 and 19; STL Statute, art 18.
[8] ICC Statute, art 61(3)(a). The consequences of this change have not fully been explored. It might be that it makes no difference. It could, however, have consequences later on in the procedure in relation to rules of notification and possible amendment of the charges, as well as on the possibility for the ICC to 'import' rules elaborated at other tribunals on the 'curing' of the indictment.

consider changes to the indictment, as a formal document.⁹ This means that in order to discuss questions of 'amendments to the charges' it is logically necessary to identify what exactly a 'charge' is.¹⁰

Surprisingly, given the importance of such a notion in the proceedings, neither the Statute of the ICC nor its Rules of Procedure and Evidence offers such a definition. However, the content of the document containing the charges is specified in the Regulations of the Court which provides that the full name of the person charged and any other relevant identifying information, a statement of the facts 'which provides a sufficient legal and factual basis to bring the person or persons to trial' and a legal characterisation of the facts as well as the precise form of participation alleged should be included.¹¹

This Regulation is in line with the definition of an indictment in the ICTY Rules which provide that 'the indictment shall set forth the name and particulars of the suspect and a concise statement of the facts of the case and of the crime with which the suspect is charged'.¹² This is not necessarily a definition of a charge itself. One interpretation posits that a charge is composed of two elements, a *factual description* of the crimes and a *legal characterisation* of the facts. Under this interpretation, the legal characterisation covers both the definition of the crimes and the form of participation. It would therefore follow that any change to any of these elements, be it to the facts, legal characterisation of the crimes, or the form of participation, would qualify as an amendment to the charges.

A second interpretation could be that not all the elements mentioned are actually part of the charge *stricto sensu*, which would mean that a change to one element would not necessarily imply an amendment to the charge itself. In practice, as will be seen, the ICC apparently prefers the first interpretation; decisions on the confirmation of the charges confirm both the factual elements underlying the crime, and the legal characterisation of those facts.¹³ This interpretation has also been favoured by the UN Human Rights Committee.¹⁴

---

⁹ Rules of Procedure and Evidence of the International Criminal Tribunal for the former Yugoslavia, UN Doc IT/32/Rev46 (20 October 2011) ('ICTY RPE'), Rule 50.

¹⁰ This will be particularly relevant for the discussion of ICC Regulation 55, which allows the Trial Chamber to change the legal characterisation of the facts; see Section II below.

¹¹ International Criminal Court, Regulations of the Court, ICC-BD/01-01-04 (26 May 2004) ('ICC Regulations'), Regulation 52.

¹² ICTY RPE, Rule 47(C).

¹³ See for example *Situation in the Democratic Republic of the Congo: Prosecutor v Lubanga* (Decision on the Confirmation of Charges) ICC-01/04-01/06 (29 January 2007).

¹⁴ WA Schabas, *The International Criminal Court: A Commentary on the Rome Statute* (OUP, Oxford 2010) 802–803.

## B. Amendment of the Charges

Prior to the confirmation of charges, 'the Prosecutor may continue the investigation and may amend or withdraw the charges'.[15] Reasonable notice must be given to the person who is the object of the charges in case of amendment or withdrawal. Moreover, any withdrawal must be notified to the Pre-Trial Chamber, with reasons given.[16] The confirmation of charges hearing must provide the Pre-Trial Chamber with 'sufficient evidence to establish substantial grounds to believe that the person committed each of the crimes charged'.[17] The Pre-Trial Chamber is given a series of options in this regard. It shall confirm the charges for which there is sufficient evidence,[18] decline to confirm charges for which there is insufficient evidence,[19] or it can adjourn the hearing in order to request from the Prosecutor that he either provide further evidence in relation to a particular charge[20] or amend a charge if the 'evidence submitted appears to establish a different crime within the jurisdiction of the Court'.[21] After the confirmation hearing, 'the Prosecutor may, with the permission of the Pre-Trial Chamber and after notice of the accused, amend the charges'.[22] If the purpose of the change is to add more charges, or substitute more serious ones,[23] a new confirmation hearing must be held.[24]

This procedure has several notable features. First of all, the distribution of tasks between the Prosecutor and the Pre-Trial Chamber is clearly defined, with the Prosecutor being the primary organ responsible for determining the content of the charges and their amendment, whereas the Pre-Trial Chamber exercises control over the procedure, without having itself any powers in relation to the

---

[15] ICC Statute, art 61(4).
[16] Ibid.
[17] Ibid art 61(7).
[18] Ibid art 61(7)(a).
[19] Ibid art 61(7)(b).
[20] Ibid art 61(7)(c)(i).
[21] Ibid art 61(7)(c)(ii).
[22] Ibid art 61(9). International Criminal Court, Rules of Procedure and Evidence, ICC-ASP/1/3 (Part.II-A), 9 September 2002 ('ICC RPE'), Rule 128 further provides that it is the Chamber's function to notify the accused following a written request by the Prosecutor. Moreover, the determination of whether a new confirmation hearing is necessary is the duty of the Chamber.
[23] The concept of 'more serious charges' could be problematic given the fact that the ICC Statute does not provide for a hierarchy of crimes within the jurisdiction of the Court, all of them being considered as 'the most serious crimes of international concern' (ICC Statute, art 1). This is also evidenced in the absence of differentiated sentences for specific crimes (ICC Statute, art 77). This discussion finds an echo in the difficulty of applying the gravity threshold for admissibility under ICC Statute, art 17(1)(d) of the Statute. On this see WA Schabas, 'Prosecutorial Discretion and Gravity' in C Stahn and G Sluiter (eds) *The Emerging Practice of the International Criminal Court* (Martinus Nijhoff, Leiden 2009) 229–246 and D Jacobs, 'Commentary on Arrest Warrants and Admissibility' in G Sluiter and A Klip (eds) *Annotated Cases in International Criminal Law: Volume 23* (Intersentia, Antwerp 2010) 118.
[24] ICC Statute, art 61(9).

actual content of the charges. More particularly, should the evidence indicate that another crime than the one charged be more appropriate, the Pre-Trial Chamber can invite the Prosecutor to amend the charges, but it cannot do so *proprio motu*. There is a shifting balance between the Prosecutor's discretion and the authority of the Pre-Trial Chamber, whereby the Prosecutor's discretion in relation to the content of the charges diminishes the closer the procedure moves towards the actual trial. Finally, the procedure takes into account the rights of the defence. Not only must the person be provided within a reasonable time before the hearing with a copy of the document containing the charges and be informed of the Prosecutor's evidence,[25] but any subsequent changes to the charges must be notified, both before the confirmation hearing and after.[26]

## C. Case-Law in Relation to the Powers of the Pre-Trial Chamber

The confirmation of charges decisions in the *Lubanga* and *Bemba* cases provide some additional information on the scope of the role of the Pre-Trial Chamber in relation to the reclassification of charges. The question of the requalification of the facts came up in the first confirmation of charges at the ICC in the *Lubanga* case.[27] More particularly, the issue arose in relation to the nature of the armed conflict in Ituri.

The Prosecutor had initially charged[28] Lubanga with three counts of war crimes under Article 8(2)(e)(vii), which relates to the crime of 'conscripting or enlisting children under the age of fifteen years into armed forces or groups or using them to participate actively in hostilities' as a serious violation of the 'laws and customs applicable in armed conflicts not of an international character'.[29] This latter allegation on the nature of the armed conflict was laconically made at the very beginning of the document containing the charges,[30] without any particular supporting argumentation in the rest of the Prosecutor's reasoning.

Following challenges by both the defence and the victims' representatives,[31] the Pre-Trial Chamber found that there were in fact two phases in the timeframe of the indictment. In the first one, from July 2002 to June 2003, the presence of Uganda as

---

[25] Ibid art 61(3).

[26] ICC RPE, Rule 128(3). In relation to this, see *Situation in the Democratic Republic of the Congo: Prosecutor v Mbarushimana* (Decision on the Defence request to exclude the Prosecution's amended document containing the charges and amended list of evidence) ICC-01/04-01/10 (22 July 2011), in which the Single Judge chastises the Prosecutor for having amended the charges and the supporting evidence too close to the actual confirmation of charges hearing, under the guise of 'correcting' mistakes in the originally filed document.

[27] *Prosecutor v Lubanga* (Decision on the Confirmation of Charges) (n 13).

[28] *Situation in the Democratic Republic of the Congo: Prosecutor v Lubanga* (Document Containing the Charges) ICC-01/04-01/06 (28 August 2006).

[29] ICC Statute, art 8(2)(e).

[30] *Prosecutor v Lubanga* (Document Containing the Charges) (n 28) para 7.

[31] *Prosecutor v Lubanga* (Decision on the Confirmation of Charges) (n 13) para 200.

an occupying power allowed for a characterisation of the conflict as international.[32] After Uganda's withdrawal, on 2 June 2003, the conflict was best characterised as non-international.[33] As a consequence, whereas the counts under Article 8(2)(e)(vii) were confirmed for the second phase, Lubanga was charged under Article 8(2)(b)(xxvi), the equivalent provision on child soldiers, but in relation to international armed conflicts, for the first phase[34]. Two points need to be highlighted in relation to this reclassification of charges.

First, it is notable that the Pre-Trial Chamber decided against following the procedure for the amendment of charges as laid down by the Statute whereby the hearing should be adjourned to give the Prosecutor a chance to amend the charges if the evidence submitted establishes a different crime.[35] Instead, the judges apparently adopted a teleological reading of Article 61(7)(c)(ii), and found that such a provision was meant as a safeguard of the rights of the defence. More specifically, it was designed to avoid that the chamber commit 'a person for trials for crimes which would be materially different from those set out in the document containing the charges and for which the defence would not have had the opportunity to submit observations at the confirmation hearing'.[36] In light of this, the Pre-Trial Chamber found that because both articles under consideration, 8(2)(e)(vii) and 8(2)(b)(xxvi), criminalise the same conduct, irrespective of the nature of the armed conflict, it was 'not necessary to adjourn the hearing and request the Prosecutor to amend the charges'.[37] While this position might be understandable from the point of view of the judges, it faces one major challenge: it is not permitted by the Statute, as it does not fit into any of the three options open to the Pre-Trial Chamber at the confirmation of the charges stage, as discussed above. Further, the Pre-Trial Chamber's assertion of the purpose of the provision is not substantiated in the decision, either by reference to the Statute itself, or by recourse to the *travaux préparatoires*. Moreover, in spite of great similarities between the original and the amended charges (both provisions are essentially identical), the fact remains that, technically, these are two distinct crimes. In effect, the Pre-Trial Chamber, by giving itself the power to amend the charges directly, changed the distribution of competences foreseen by the drafters. The policy consequences are important and the decision suggests that the judges at the ICC are willing, as their colleagues at the ICTY, to adopt a flexible approach to the interpretation of the Statute.

---

[32] Ibid para 220.

[33] Ibid paras 227–237.

[34] It should however be noted that in the final Judgment, the Trial Chamber actually recharacterised the facts in application of Regulation 55 of the Regulations of the Court, and found that the conflict was of a non-international character for the duration of the period covered by the charges (*Situation in the Democratic Republic of the Congo: Prosecutor v Lubanga* (Judgment pursuant to Article 74 of the Statute) ICC-01/04-01/06 (14 March 2012) § 566).

[35] ICC Statute, art 61(7)(c)(ii).

[36] *Prosecutor v Lubanga* (Decision on the Confirmation of Charges) (n 13) para 203. It is notable that ICC Statute, art 67(7)(c) is silent as to the issue of the rights of the defense and only mentions the prosecutor as the 'beneficiary' of the adjournment.

[37] Ibid para 204.

It has been suggested that:

> the Pre-Trial Chamber has no subsequent control over the Prosecutor, and it would seem that he cannot be under an obligation to investigate and prove certain charges simply because the confirmation decision has added them.[38]

This is technically true, but practically speaking, to the extent that the person is committed to trial on the confirmed charges, should the Prosecutor 'choose' not to investigate and prove the substituted charges, the person would simply be acquitted, which would be against the Prosecutor's interest. In effect, although there is no subsequent control of the Pre-Trial Chamber over the Prosecutor, he or she remains bound by the charges confirmed.[39] In this author's view, however, there is one benefit to the Pre-Trial Chamber's decision, insofar as it illustrates the irrelevance of defining a conflict as 'internal' or 'international' where the same crime exists in both situations. Had the ICC Statute recognised that there is no need for such a distinction where the same crime exists in both, and that in these occurrences the dichotomies imported from International Humanitarian Law are essentially irrelevant, this kind of debate on the *Lubanga* confirmation of the charges decision could have been avoided.

The confirmation proceedings in the *Bemba* case gave further scope to examine the role of the Pre-Trial Chamber in relation to the charges. In that case, it appeared during the hearings that although the Prosecutor had argued that Bemba was directly liable under Article 25(3) of the Statute, the evidence showed that charging him under command responsibility (Article 28) would have been more appropriate. The Pre-Trial Chamber therefore decided to exercise its power to adjourn the hearing and request that the Prosecutor consider an amendment of the document containing the charges addressing Article 28 as a possible mode of liability.[40] In so doing, the Pre-Trial Chamber took the opportunity to interpret the conditions of operation of the adjournment provisions in Article 61(7)(c)(ii).

The judges stressed the difference between this provision, and sub-paragraphs (a) and (b) of Article 61(7), which concern the actual decision to confirm (or not) the charges,[41] and sub-paragraph (c), under which the Pre-Trial Chamber does not take a decision on the merits of the case, but rather decides to adjourn proceedings to allow the Prosecutor to overcome deficiencies in the evidence or legal characterisation presented.[42] As a consequence of this difference, the standard of proof is not the same as for the confirmation of charges. Instead of the standard of 'substantial grounds to believe that the person committed each of the crimes

---

[38] Schabas (n 14) 743.
[39] This has been confirmed by the Trial Chamber and is discussed further below.
[40] *Situation in the Central African Republic: Prosecutor v Bemba* (Decision Adjourning the Hearing Pursuant to Article 61(7)(c)(ii) of the Rome Statute) ICC-01/05-01/08 (3 March 2009).
[41] See Section I above.
[42] *Prosecutor v Bemba* (Decision Adjourning the Hearing) (n 40) para 14.

charged',[43] the standard of proof under Article 67(c)(ii) is rather that 'the evidence submitted appears to establish a different crime'. In this sense, it 'is a *lex specialis* that establishes a lower threshold and accordingly requires a specific approach to the evidence as well as a different kind of determination to be made by the Chamber'.[44] The Pre-Trial Chamber also took the opportunity to explain what was meant by a 'different crime', and interpreted it to include both the crime and the mode of participation, in light of the close correlation between the two.[45] This interpretation was also justified in the interests of fairness, because if the mode of liability were excluded from the purview of Article 61(7)(c)(ii), it would deprive the defence of its right to be informed promptly of the nature, cause and content of the charge, as provided for by Article 67(1)(a).[46]

## II. Reclassifying the Charges at the Trial Phase

### A. The Statutory Framework

The confirmation of the charges marks the end of the pre-trial procedure and triggers the constitution of the Trial Chamber by the Presidency.[47] In relation to the charges, the Statute provides for a limited number of situations where any modification is possible. After the confirmation and 'before the trial has begun', the Prosecutor can ask for an amendment to the charges with the permission of the Pre-Trial Chamber.[48] Further, 'after the commencement of the trial, the Prosecutor may, with permission of the Trial Chamber, withdraw the charges'.[49] The Trial Chamber has found that the 'commencement of trial' is the 'true opening of the trial when opening statements, if any, are made prior to the calling of witnesses'.[50] Apart from this last possibility for the Prosecutor to withdraw the charges once the trial has begun, neither the Statute nor the RPE provide for any discretion, either on the part

---

[43] ICC Statute, art 61(7).
[44] *Prosecutor v Bemba* (Decision Adjourning the Hearing) (n 40) para 18.
[45] Ibid para 25.
[46] Ibid para 28.
[47] ICC Statute, art 61(11).
[48] Ibid art 61(9).
[49] Ibid.
[50] *Situation in the Democratic Republic of the Congo: Prosecutor v Lubanga* (Decision on the status before the Trial Chamber of the evidence heard by the Pre-Trial Chamber and the decisions of the Pre-Trial Chamber in trial proceedings, and the manner in which evidence shall be submitted) ICC-01/04-01/06(13 December 2007). For a general discussion on the notion of the 'beginning of the trial' in the ICC Statute, see D Jacobs, 'The Importance of Being Earnest: The Timeliness of the Challenge to Admissibility in Katanga' (2010) 23(2) *LJIL* 331–342.

of the Prosecutor or the Trial Chamber, to amend the charges after the confirmation has taken place.

It has been argued, however, that the Trial Chamber would have an inherent power to contest the legal characterisation given by the Pre-Trial Chamber in the confirmation of charges decision. This argument was put forward by the Prosecution in the *Lubanga* case, who argued this based on the role of the Trial Chamber to 'ensure that the trial is fair and expeditious'[51] and on the fact that it can rule on 'any other relevant matter'.[52] This was strongly rejected by the Trial Chamber, recalling that 'the power to frame the charges'[53] was a key function of the Pre-Trial Chamber and the result was binding on the Trial Chamber.[54] In the Trial Chamber's reasoning, because the exercise of functions under Article 61(11) is 'subject to paragraph 9', that power afforded to the Pre-Trial Chamber as regards the charges remains with it, at least in the 'preparation phase of the trial'.[55] Although not clearly indicated by the Trial Chamber, one can only assume that the reasoning holds equally once the trial has begun.[56]

In light of the above, it appears that the framework provided for in the Statute and the RPE in relation to possible amendments, re-characterisation and withdrawal of the charges clearly distinguishes between the pre-trial phase and the trial. Prior to the trial, the content of the charges is determined by the Prosecutor, with the ultimate decision resting with the Pre-Trial Chamber, whereas once the trial has begun, the Prosecutor may only withdraw charges, and neither him nor the Trial Chamber have any power to modify them. It remains to be seen whether this clear statutory framework is challenged by the adoption by the judges of Regulation 55 in the Regulations of the Court.

## B. Regulation 55 and the Power to Legally Re-Characterise the Facts

In May 2004, the judges of the ICC adopted the Regulations of the Court in application of Article 52 of the Rome Statute.[57] These Regulations are meant to be 'necessary for its routine functioning'.[58] They are adopted by a majority of

---

[51] ICC Statute, art 64(2).
[52] Ibid art 64(6)(f).
[53] *Prosecutor v Lubanga* (Decision on the Status of Evidence) (n 50) para 39.
[54] Ibid para 43.
[55] Ibid para 40.
[56] For a contrary interpretation, see O Triffterer, 'Article 74' in O Triffterer (ed) *Commentary on the Rome Statute of the International Criminal Court* (2nd edn CH Beck, Baden-Baden 2008) 1396, suggesting that because the Statute authorises the Trial Chamber to exercise all functions of the Pre-Trial Chamber, art 61(9) can also be applied during the Trial.
[57] On art 52 see Schabas (n 14) 650–652 and H-J Behrens and C Staker, 'Article 52' in O Triffterer (ed) *Commentary on the Rome Statute of the International Criminal Court* (2nd edn CH Beck, Baden-Baden 2008) 1053–1063.
[58] ICC Statute, art 52(1).

the judges, and are subject to the approval of the State Parties.⁵⁹ Among those Regulations, Regulation 55 grants the Trial Chamber authority to modify the legal characterisation of facts, under certain circumstances. The Regulation concerns two different stages of the proceedings. The first sub-regulation complements the operation of Article 74 which relates to the final judgment of the Trial Chamber. More particularly, it applies in relation to Article 74(2) according to which 'the Trial Chamber's decision shall be based on its evaluation of the evidence and the entire proceedings. The decision shall not exceed the facts and circumstances described in the charges and any amendments to the charges'. The Regulation therefore allows the Chamber in its decision, and within the boundaries of the facts, to legally re-characterise them in relation to the crimes or the forms of participation. On the other hand, the following sub-regulation allows the Court, in the course of the trial, to put the participants on notice that the legal characterisation of the facts might be subject to change. Regulation 55(3) provides that particular attention to the rights of the accused shall be paid in the exercise of this function.

The *Lubanga* case provided the Judges with an opportunity to interpret this Regulation more specifically. In May 2009, the legal representatives of the victims filed a joint request⁶⁰ pursuant to Regulation 55 to ask the Trial Chamber to consider a legal re-characterisation of the facts. According to this request, the evidence presented during the trial suggested that serious crimes falling under the jurisdiction of the court where being committed during the period of the case which could be 'characterized in a different manner from that chosen by the Prosecution'.⁶¹ More specifically, the victims contended that there was evidence of inhuman treatment, cruel treatment and sexual slavery as war crimes, and sexual slavery as a crime against humanity.⁶² Trial Chamber I issued its Decision on 14 July 2009.⁶³ In a fairly short decision, the majority of the Chamber, Judge Fulford dissenting,⁶⁴ found that, in application of the requirements of Regulation 55(2), and in light of the evidence heard and the submissions of the legal representatives of the victims, the 'legal characterization of the facts may be subject to change' and 'accordingly, the parties and participants have a right to receive early notice'.⁶⁵ In relation to the scope of application of Regulation 55(2) it was considered by the majority that the requirement that the change in the legal characterisation of facts not exceed the facts and circumstances described in the charges as contained in

---

⁵⁹ Ibid art 52(3).
⁶⁰ *Situation in the Democratic Republic of the Congo: Prosecutor v Lubanga* (Joint Application of the Legal Representatives of the Victims for the Implementation of the Procedure under Regulation 55 of the Regulations of the Court) ICC-01/04-01/06 (22 May 2009).
⁶¹ Ibid para 15.
⁶² Ibid para 17.
⁶³ *Situation in the Democratic Republic of the Congo: Prosecutor v Lubanga* (Decision giving notice to the parties and participants that the legal characterization of the facts may be subject to change in accordance with Regulation 55(2) of the Regulations of the Court) ICC-01/04-01/06 (14 July 2009).
⁶⁴ Ibid (Dissenting Opinion of Judge Adrian Fulford).
⁶⁵ *Prosecutor v Lubanga* (Regulation 55 Decision) (n 63) para 33.

Regulation 55(1) did not apply in this situation. The two paragraphs of Regulation 55 were interpreted as applying to two different stages of the proceedings, which justified that different conditions apply, most notably the possibility to recall a witness that has already testified or call a new witness.[66]

The Appeals Chamber rejected this interpretation of the Regulation,[67] holding that it would lead it to be in contradiction with the wording of Article 74, which provides that 'the decision shall not exceed the facts and circumstances described in the charges and any amendments to the charges'.[68] According to the Appeals Chamber, 'the purpose of the provision was to bind the Chamber to the factual allegations on the charges. The Trial Chamber's interpretation of Regulation would be inconsistent with that purpose'.[69] With this conclusion, the Appeals Chamber agreed with the Minority Opinion of Judge Fulford, who had tried to demonstrate at length that all the paragraphs of the Regulation should be read together,[70] and that therefore, Regulation 55 was 'a singular and indivisible provision'.[71] Despite the policy considerations that would justify the existence of this power granted to the Trial Chamber, discussed in some detail below, there is some doubt regarding the legality of Regulation 55, even in the narrower interpretation given by the Appeals Chamber. In light of the absence of any provision relating to an amendment of the charge after the commencement of trial,[72] it is difficult to imagine how Regulation 55 can in fact be reconciled with the Statute as it stands.

It has been argued that the change of the legal characterisation of facts does not necessarily amend the charges, because it only changes one component of Regulation 52.[73] If this position is perfectly tenable on principle, it seems to be at odds with any common sense idea of what 'change' means, under which it seems difficult to argue that a modification of the crime being prosecuted is not an amendment to the charge itself.[74] Moreover, under this approach, what would

---

[66] ICC Regulations, Regulation 55(3)(b).

[67] *Situation in the Democratic Republic of the Congo: Prosecutor v Lubanga* (Judgment on the appeals of Mr Lubanga Dyilo and the Prosecutor against the Decision of Trial Chamber I of 14 July 2009 entitled 'Decision giving notice to the parties and participants that the legal characterization of the facts may be subject to change in accordance with Regulation 55(2) of the Regulations of the Court') ICC-01/04-01/06 (8 December 2009).

[68] ICC Statute, art 74(2).

[69] *Prosecutor v Lubanga* (Appeals Chamber Decision on Recharacterization) (n 67) para 91.

[70] *Prosecutor v Lubanga* (Regulation 55 Decision) (n 63) paras 21–30.

[71] Ibid para 27.

[72] ICC Statute, art 61(9).

[73] C Stahn, 'Modification of the Legal Characterization of Facts in the ICC System: a Portrayal of Regulation 55' (2005) 16 *CLF* 1–31 at 17. See also GM Pikis, *The Rome Statute of the International Criminal Court* (Martinus Nijhoff, Leiden 2010) at 141–142 (arguing that because Regulation 55 relates to the legal characterisation of facts, 'this is not equivalent to the amendment of a charge, importing the commission of a crime other than the one charged').

[74] See Schabas (n 14) 779.

prevent a Trial Chamber to add new facts to the case, while still keeping the same legal characterisation? This would not be an amendment because it would only modify one component of Regulation 52.[75] Finally, this 'decoupled' approach to the elements of the charge runs contrary to the case-law which has clearly said that a change to the legal characterisation requires an amendment of the charges.[76]

One general argument put forward to justify the legality of Regulation 55 is that the drafters of the ICC Statute left the question of the legal re-characterisation of facts open, through the operation of the nebulous concept of 'constructive ambiguity'.[77] This was essentially the position taken by the Appeals Chamber in the *Lubanga* case when considering whether Regulation 55 was in contradiction with Article 61(9). According to the appellate judges, '[Article 61(9)] does not exclude the possibility that a Trial Chamber modifies the legal characterization of the facts on its own motion once the trial has commenced'.[78] The Appeals Chamber therefore concluded that 'Article 61(9) of the Statute and Regulation 55 address different powers of different entities at different stages of the procedure, and the two provisions are not inherently incompatible'.[79] The general idea is therefore that because Article 61(9) does not explicitly exclude the powers of Regulation 55, there is room to interpret the Statute as allowing the practice of legal re-characterisation. This also informs the position taken in relation to Article 74(2). According to the Appeals Chamber, 'this latter provision binds the Trial Chamber only to the facts and circumstances described in the charges or any amendment thereto, but does not make reference to the legal characterization of these facts and circumstances'.[80]

This kind of approach is debatable. It is one thing to acknowledge that there was disagreement on the issue of legal re-characterisation of facts in the drafting process,[81] but it is altogether another to decide that the Statute is ambiguous as a result. A treaty, as any contract, is always the result of a negotiating process and only contains what was agreed on by the parties. It is a slightly puzzling argument to say that what did not make it into the Statute because of a disagreement can be subsequently read into it by another entity. The Statute clearly lays down the situations and conditions under which the charges can be amended and there is no language in the Statute to suggest that there is any discretion to add new facets to those applicable circumstances. In light of this, there does not seem any room to apply the concept of 'constructive ambiguity' to the present issue.[82] In addition,

---

[75] See Section I above.
[76] *Prosecutor v Bemba* (Decision Adjourning the Hearing) (n 40).
[77] Stahn (n 73) 4. See also G Bitti, 'Two Bones of Contention Between Civil and Common Law: The Record of the Proceedings and the Treatment of Concursus Delictorum' in H Fischer, C Kress and S Rolf Lüder (eds) *International and National Prosecution of Crimes Under International Law* (Spitz, Berlin 2001) 272, 284–286.
[78] *Prosecutor v Lubanga* (Appeals Chamber Decision on Recharacterization) (n 67) 77.
[79] Ibid.
[80] Ibid para 93. See also Stahn (n 73) 17.
[81] For an overview of proposals see Stahn (n 73) 10–11.
[82] This relates more generally to the idea that the absence of a provision in a Statute is due to a lacuna by the drafters. The Appeals Chamber has had the opportunity to express

the reasoning of the Appeals Chamber is all the more surprising given its own interpretation of Regulation 55 as not allowing the Trial Chamber to go beyond the facts alleged by the Prosecutor, because it 'would be contrary to the distribution of powers under the Statute'.[83] How does that not apply also to the legal characterisation of facts, which is also left, according to the Statute, to the Prosecutor?

In spite of these very serious questions surrounding the legality of Regulation 55, a number of justifications have been put forward to justify its inclusion. One argument, which mirrors what has been put forward in relation to the legality of the Regulation, is that it fills a gap of something that was not settled in the founding documents of the Court.[84] This is however once again a biased way of presenting the situation, because it presumes that if something is not explicitly in the Statute, it is missing from it. But, in the absence of a specific provision, the Statute as it stands does provide an answer to the above-raised question: if the elements of the charges, as confirmed by the Pre-Trial Chamber, have not been proven, then the person is acquitted. There is nothing ambiguous or unclear about this textual application of the Statute. This relates to another justification for Regulation 55 which is often advanced: that is, to avoid an 'impunity gap', whereby an accused person could be acquitted, even though it had clearly been demonstrated that he or she committed a crime within the jurisdiction of the Court.[85]

One can wonder whether this broad teleological *policy* approach can be an adequate *legal* justification for a statutory provision. Indeed, this could, for example, be the basis for allowing the judges to take into account new facts during the trial, for not having a charging document at all, for allowing any type of evidence, irrespective of its credibility, or allowing torture as a mode of interrogation. This would certainly increase the likelihood of a conviction and close the 'accountability gap', but would obviously be odious to those who propose the impunity argument as justification for Regulation 55. The question, therefore, ought not to be whether a provision is in conformity with the objectives of the Statute, but rather whether those objectives allow for its creation. In this sense, it is unlikely that such a polymorphous and indeterminate notion as 'the end of impunity' can specifically justify the creation of any new legal provision. A further argument put forward to justify Regulation 55 is to avoid prosecutorial charging

---

themselves on this point in the past. See *Situation in the Democratic Republic of the Congo* (Judgment on the Prosecutor's Application for Extraordinary Review of Pre-Trial Chamber I's 31 March 2006 Decision Denying Leave to Appeal) ICC-01/04-168 (13 July 2006) para 41, rejecting the Prosecutor's assertion that the drafters had 'forgotten' a ground for appeal against a Pre-Trial Chamber decision on the basis that the absence of such a ground for appeal was to be considered as the intent of the drafters.

[83] *Prosecutor v Lubanga* (Appeals Chamber Decision on Recharacterization) (n 67) para 94.

[84] Stahn (n 73) 3.

[85] Ibid; *Prosecutor v Lubanga* (Appeals Chamber Decision on Recharacterization) (n 67) para 77; Bitti (n 77) 287 (arguing, before the adoption of Regulation 55, that it would be in contradiction with the primary goal of the Court, namely to end impunity, if the Trial Chamber were not able to change the legal characterisation of facts).

strategies whereby the Prosecutor 'burden[s] the Chambers with an overload of alternative or cumulative charges in order to avoid the risk of acquittal'.[86] This argument is equally unconvincing on a number of levels.

First, it is not obvious how Regulation 55 directly responds to the concern of an 'overload' of charges. It relates to the power of the Trial Chamber when reaching its decision, and does not directly circumscribe the Prosecutor's discretion in the charging policy. Neither is it clear how it encourages 'a *precise* charging practice from the very beginning of the proceedings'.[87] On the contrary, the Prosecutor could rely on the fact that Regulation 55 might be used as a justification for imprecision in his charging policy, because any 'mistake' in the legal characterisation could be 'corrected' at trial. Second, it creates a sense that there is a necessary link between streamlining the process with focused charges and the power of the Trial Chamber to legally re-characterise the facts. But these issues need not be automatically related. Indeed, it is perfectly possible to imagine that rules be provided compelling the Prosecutor to adopt a minimalist charging policy, as an objective in and of itself, independently of whether the Trial Chamber has the power to change the chosen and confirmed legal classification during the trial. Third, the link that is drawn between both issues ignores the complex policy considerations that underscore the Prosecutor's charging decisions. Indeed, in the pre-trial phase, some time before the actual trial, it is just as likely that questions of availability of evidence and opportunity guide the choice of charges, rather than the far-away prospect that the Trial Chamber might see fit to adopt a different legal characterisation. Further, such an argument ignores the current procedural framework of the Statute, which requires that the Prosecutor put forward specific evidence for specific charges to be confirmed by the Pre-Trial Chamber. If one accepts the idea that the legal characterisation of facts is indeed an element of the charge, there is in fact no room for the Prosecutor to take into account the possibility of Regulation 55 being applied, because a flexible charging policy in the pre-trial phase would not meet the requirements of the confirmation of charges proceedings.

Finally, it is rather unfortunate for the proponents of the idea that Regulation 55 could streamline the procedure that the only practical application of the provision so far has taken place in the *Lubanga* case, where the Prosecutor had in fact adopted an extremely limited set of charges and where the use of the Regulation by the Trial Chamber was aimed at adding new charges.

## III. Shifting Balances at the ICC

The practice of the ICC chambers in relation to charges, both in the pre-trial phase and the trial phase therefore partially departs from the actual statutory framework

---

[86] Stahn (n 73) 3; HP Kaul, 'Construction Site For More Justice: The International Criminal Court After Two Years' (2005) 99 *AJIL* 370–384.

[87] Stahn (n 72) 30 (emphasis added).

as drafted in Rome. Beyond the previous discussion of the content of this practice, this final section will highlight how it shifts a number of balances at the ICC. First of all, this practice, especially the adoption of Regulation 55, essentially shifts the balance away from an adversarial approach to an inquisitorial approach to international criminal procedure. Indeed, in the adversarial approach, the judge 'is an observer and an umpire',[88] and the Prosecutor has the burden of correctly preparing his case and bears the full responsibility for the results of the choices made in the charges, therefore leading to the result that any mistake in that respect profits the accused. This is the position taken by the Statute of the Court. In the inquisitorial approach, on the other hand, the judge is the ultimate guarantor of the trial achieving objectified goals of truth and justice.[89] In this second approach, the judge has a 'managerial role'[90] and a corrective power over the elements of the trial, therefore relieving the Prosecutor of some of his obligations and increasing the likelihood of conviction for the accused. In this sense, one could say that now the risk of an inadequate legal characterisation rests with the accused, which is the consequence of the adoption of Regulation 55.[91]

It should be noted, however, that the case-law does not always favour the prosecution over the accused in this balance. As indicated by the Pre-Trial Chamber in the *Mbarushimana* case, which struck down the Prosecutor's attempt to amend the charges without following the provided procedure: 'the errors, internal inconsistencies and omissions which appear in the document containing the charges and the list of evidence are the responsibility of the Prosecutor and that any prejudice resulting therefrom must be borne by the Prosecutor and cannot be shifted to the Defence.'[92] Second of all, the choice of charges not only affects the conduct of the actual trial of the accused. It also affects the operation of other provisions of the Statute. Two of those can be mentioned briefly. First, under the principle of complementarity, a case might be inadmissible before the Court if it 'is being investigated or prosecuted by a State which has jurisdiction over it'.[93] This provision has been interpreted in a narrow way, and held to apply not only to the same person, but also if the national proceedings relate to the same conduct, which includes the legal characterisation of that conduct.[94]

---

[88] S De Smet, 'A Structural Analysis of the Role of the Pre-Trial Chamber in the Fact-Finding Process of the ICC' in Stahn and Sluiter (n 23) 409.

[89] R Heinsch, 'How to Achieve Fair and Expeditious Trial Proceedings before the ICC: Is it Time for a More Judge-Dominated Approach?' in Stahn and Sluiter (n 23) 490.

[90] De Smet (n 88) 410.

[91] For a discussion on the common law and civil law approaches to the legal recharacterization of facts, see Stahn (n 73) 4–6; *Prosecutor v Kupreškić et al* (Judgment) IT-95-16-T (14 January 2000) paras 728–733.

[92] *Situation in the Democratic Republic of the Congo: Prosecutor v Mbarushimana* (Decision on the Defence request to exclude the Prosecution's amended document containing the charges and amended list of evidence) ICC-01/04-01/10 (22 July 2011) 6.

[93] ICC Statute, art 17(1)(a).

[94] See *Situation in the Democratic Republic of the Congo: Prosecutor v Lubanga* (Decision on the Prosecutor's Application for an Arrest Warrant, Article 58) ICC-01/04-01/06 (10 February

This approach means that the legal characterisation of the facts is crucial to the question of applying the criteria of complementarity: for the accused to be able to challenge admissibility on this ground, he must be fully aware, at the time that this challenge is possible,[95] what he is being prosecuted for. Further, the possibility that the Trial Chamber could change the legal characterisation of the facts up until the judgment, through the operation of Regulation 55, raises the question of whether this could not be deemed to be a way to circumvent the requirements of complementarity, therefore violating the rights of the defence, because a challenge on this ground is no longer possible after the commencement of trial.[96] A second challenge which can only be raised at the start of trial could also be affected by the current framework on the legal re-characterisation of facts: that is, *ne bis in idem*.[97] Under this well-known rule, a person cannot be prosecuted twice for the same crime. In the Statute of the ICC, it applies both to national proceedings in relation to the Court,[98] and to the Court in relation to national proceedings.[99] This second situation is particularly interesting for the purposes of our discussion. Article 20(3), in its reference to 'the same conduct' clearly implies that the legal characterisation of facts is a key element in mounting a challenge to admissibility based on the *ne bis in idem* principle.[100] It therefore follows that a subsequent change in the legal characterisation during the course of the trial might pave the way for a challenge to admissibility based on a prior conviction relying on that specific new crime.

These two examples of how the current framework on charges might affect other provisions of the Statute illustrates the fact that any changes made to the balance struck by the Statute, as is the case with Regulation 55, may ultimately have unforeseen, and probably undesired, consequences. Indeed, it has already been shown that Regulation 55 was used, not to streamline the procedure, as its defenders argue, but to burden it with new charges. The examples of complementarity and *ne bis in idem* show that recourse to that Regulation could further slow down proceedings by creating new opportunities for procedural delays due to late challenges to admissibility. Finally, the current framework on the amendment of charges should be seen in the broader context of the constant shifts of power between the organs of the Court, notably the Chambers and the Prosecutor. Indeed, the early case-law of the Court discussed in this chapter shows that both the Pre-Trial Chamber in the confirmation of charges and the Trial Chamber, with the use of Regulation 55, have increased their control over the charges beyond what was initially envisioned by the Statute. This echoes the

---

2006), §37–39. The 'same person, same conduct' approach has been consistently following in subsequent practice. See most recently *Situation In The Republic Of Kenya: Prosecutor v Ruto et al* (Decision on the Admissibility Challenge) ICC 01/09-01/11 (30 May 2011).

[95] That is, at the commencement of trial, pursuant to ICC Statute, art 19(2).
[96] Ibid art 19(4).
[97] Ibid art 20.
[98] Ibid art 20(2).
[99] Ibid art 20(3).
[100] Ibid art 17(1)(d).

practice of the Pre-Trial Chamber which has on a number of occasions encroached upon the autonomy of the Prosecutor over the conduct of investigations by, *inter alia*, calling for a 'progress report' on the evaluation of a situation,[101] and inviting *amicus* briefs on issues of witness protection and evidence preservation.[102]

## Conclusion: International Criminal Judges as Lawmakers

It is beyond the scope of this chapter to discuss the issue of the lawmaking powers of the international judges. It is however interesting to note how the framework on the amendment of charges informs this crucial question. Indeed, what the previous analysis shows is that, despite the notable differences between the ICC and the *ad hoc* tribunals, in terms of the specificity of the Statute, and the margin of appreciation left to the judges, ICC Chambers have shown the same general tendency as their counterparts at the *ad hoc* tribunals to use all available means at their disposal to expand their powers, even in the absence of any clear textual support. These means include the rules of interpretation, as illustrated by the Pre-Trial Chamber's decision to re-characterise the nature of the armed conflict in the *Lubanga* case without requesting that the Prosecutor amend the charges. Another illustration of this is the use of the 'lacuna argument', whereby the absence of an explicit prohibition in the Statute on a certain issue is interpreted as being an implicit authorisation. This echoes the *Lotus* approach to international law, whereby what is not prohibited is allowed.[103] Also available to the judges of the Court, despite having lost control over the RPE, is the possibility to enact what could be described as 'secondary legislation', through the drafting of the Regulations of the Court, thus enabling them, as illustrated by Regulation 55, to grant themselves powers that were not envisioned in the Statute.[104]

This tendency for judicial lawmaking, and more generally for judicial creativity, is a permanent feature of international tribunals, and more specifically of international

---

[101] *Situation in the Central African Republic* (Decision Requesting Information on the Status of the Preliminary Examination of the Situation in the Central African Republic) ICC-01/05 (30 November 2006).

[102] *Situation in Darfur, Sudan* (Decision inviting Observations in Application of Rule 103 of the Rules of Procedure and Evidence) ICC-02/05 (24 July 2006). In other occurrences, the Chambers have on the contrary afforded too much discretion on the Prosecution. See Jacobs (n 23) (arguing that the Chambers have failed in exercising their judicial function properly by refusing to define gravity in the admissibility phase and therefore not adequately reviewing the Prosecutor's determination of the gravity of a case).

[103] *SS Lotus case* (France v Turkey) (1927) PCIJ Rep (Ser A No 10) 28.

[104] For a contrary interpretation see C Stahn, 'Modification of the Legal Characterization of Facts in the ICC System: a Portrayal of Regulation 55' (2005) 16 *CLF* 1, 31 (arguing that because Regulation 55 only refines a power 'implanted' in Article 74(2), 'the case for a change in practice was conveyed in a quiet fashion in the ICC system, namely by legal interpretation rather than judicial lawmaking').

criminal tribunals.[105] In this latter context, it raises specific difficulties, in light of the application of traditional criminal law concepts such as the principle of legality and the protection of the rights of the defence[106]. It is therefore troublesome that, despite the increasing codification of international criminal law and international criminal procedure, international judges still resort to quasi-legislative powers that confuse their role as a judicial organ and continue to affect their authority, due to the perceived arbitrariness of the methodology employed.

Therefore, the real question raised by this chapter, beyond the discussion of the modalities of amendment of the charges, and the policy considerations that justify or not the adoption of certain rules, is whether the judges should be left to decide on these complex issues. I would argue that the legitimacy of the international criminal law system rests on a clear separation of roles between those who create the rules and those who apply them. Arguments that invoke the efficiency of such a method, in the light of the reality of the slow legislative process at the international level, are short-sighted, because the international legal order, if it is to achieve its objectives to abide by the rule of law, will not forever be able to escape the necessary self-reflection on the separation of powers that all modern legal systems have gone through. In the words of Montesquieu, one of the forefathers of this foundational question:

> there is no liberty, if the judiciary power be not separated from the legislative and executive. Were it joined with the legislative, the life and liberty of the subject would be exposed to arbitrary control; for the judge would be then the legislator. Were it joined to the executive power, the judge might behave with violence and oppression. There would be an end of everything, were the same man or the same body, whether of the nobles or of the people, to exercise those three powers, that of enacting laws, that of executing the public resolutions, and of trying the causes of individuals.[107]

---

[105] S Darcy and J Powderly (eds), *Judicial Creativity at the International Criminal Tribunals* (OUP, Oxford 2010) 19.

[106] On the scope of the principle of legality in International Criminal Law, see D Jacobs, 'Positivism and International Criminal Law: The Principle of Legality as a Rule of Conflict of Theories', in J d'Aspremont and J Kammerhofer (eds), *International Legal Positivism in a Postmodern World* (CUP, Forthcoming) Available at SSRN: http://ssrn.com/abstract=2046311.

[107] C De Montesquieu, *The Spirits of Laws* (Hafner Press, New York 1949) 152.

# Distinguishing Creativity from Activism: International Criminal Law and the 'Legitimacy' of Judicial Development of the Law

Joseph Powderly

A lot of ins, a lot of outs, a lot of what-have-yous.[1]

To those with even a passing interest in the revival of international criminal law as a healthy limb of the international legal order, the suggestion that its progressive development has been predominantly the product of concerted creative judicial interpretation and not the conventional, consensual legislative acts of states would most likely elicit little more than a knowing nod and a retort to the effect

---

[1]  J Coen and E Coen, *The Big Lebowski* (Polygram Filmed Entertainment, Hollywood 1998). Before going any further it seems only fair to provide some semblance of rationale for the not-so-subtle and frequent allusions this chapter makes to the Coen Brothers' cult existential masterpiece *The Big Lebowski*. The plot proceeds from an apparently straightforward set of events. The hero, Jeffrey 'The Dude' Lebowski has been the victim of an unfortunate case of mistaken identity ultimately resulting in, *inter alia*, assault and the soiling and theft of a beloved Persian rug. Thus victimised, The Dude has but one goal: reparation for the much-mourned rug. However, despite the modest intentions of his quest, The Dude soon finds himself mired in a series of unforeseen events from a fake kidnapping and blackmail to an encounter with nihilist extremists and a predatory female modern artist. Needless to say, The Dude never receives reparation for his rug, but he has learned a lot about himself and the world around him along the way. In many ways, judges who engage in judicial creativity often find themselves in similar circumstances to The Dude. Their goal, like The Dude's, is often a modest one, namely, the filling of a gap or *lacunae* in the law in order to discharge justice. However, if sufficient care is not observed, the attempted attainment of a modest goal can lead to some fairly extreme results and unforeseen consequences. In the end, many creative judges may feel that the outcome may not have been worth the effort. Granted, the allusion is perhaps a little tenuous, but nevertheless The Dude abides.

of 'and your point is ...?'. To the domestic criminal lawyer of a typically positivist persuasion, such blasé regard for the sanctity and integrity of enumerated rules would certainly have the potential for a major falling out, and would perhaps even result in the institution of vexatious disciplinary proceedings before the relevant Bar Association for reckless disregard for the rich heritage of black letter law and the doctrine of the separation of powers. However, it would seem to be an obvious and unavoidable fact, stretching back to the relative Eden of Nuremberg that international criminal law and positivism were not destined for a formal union and could hope at best for a strained, long distance friendship with modest highs and frequent lows.[2] The vast majority of scholars and practitioners of contemporary international criminal law have been required to accept – without endorsement necessarily – that, given the inchoate nature of the international legal order, responsibility for the evolution of international criminal law as a body of law lies, in reality, with its diversely constituted bench[3] and not with the states footing the bill and attempting to set the agenda.

Such acceptance necessitated a large degree of faith, or at least agnosticism, in the capacity of the bench to undertake this role in a manner consistent with both the principle of legality (*nullum crimen sine lege*) and established rules of customary international law.[4] However, the preservation of this faith, and the integrity of the international criminal justice enterprise as a whole, was dependent on the benches' ability to issue decisions and judgments which were beyond reproach in terms of their objective legitimacy. On the face of it, recourse to a concept such as legitimacy, whose opacity rivals that of 'justice', 'human dignity' and the 'rule of law', would

---

[2] See for example, *Trials of the Major War Criminals before the International Military Tribunal, Nuremberg, 14 November 1945 – 1 October 1946* Vol 1, Judgment (International Military Tribunal, Nuremberg 1947–1949) 221; *United States of America v Alstötter et al* ('the *Justice* case') Judgment (4 December 1947), in *Trials of War Criminals before the Nuremberg Military Tribunals under Control Council Law No. 10*, Vol III, 974–975 – '[i]nternational law is not the product of a statute. Its content is not static. The absence from the world of any governmental body authorized to enact substantive rules of international law has not prevented the progressive development of the law. After the manner of the English common law, it has grown to meet the exigencies of changing conditions'; D Hunt, 'The International Criminal Court: High Hopes, "Creative Ambiguity" and an Unfortunate Mistrust in International Judges' (2004) 2 *JICJ* 56, 58: 'There was no Moses to produce on slabs of stone a code of commandments which were intended to be all-encompassing for all time.'

[3] Diverse in the sense not only of nationality, but also of legal culture and expertise.

[4] As explicitly mandated by Secretary-General Boutros Boutros-Ghali in his interpretative commentary on the Statute of the International Criminal Tribunal for the former Yugoslavia: 'Report of the Secretary-General Pursuant to Paragraph 2 of Security Council Resolution 808 (1993)', UN Doc S/25704 (3 May 1993) para 34: 'In the view of the Secretary-General, the application of the principle *nullum crimen sine lege* requires that the international tribunal should apply rules of international humanitarian law which are beyond any doubt part of customary law so that the problem of adherence of some but not all States to specific conventions does not arise. This would appear to be particularly important in the context of an international tribunal prosecuting persons responsible for serious violations of international humanitarian law.'

seem to be an ambitious, not to say labourious, academic enterprise. Indeed, the phrase 'objective legitimacy' could be persuasively argued to be a contradiction in terms. However, in discussing the progressive and increasingly fragmented development of international law, particularly in a post-Cold War context, the recent scholarly trajectory places considerable emphasis on delimiting the possible contours of legitimate rule creation. In the present context, it is necessary at the very outset to acknowledge that considering the legitimacy of a rule and the manner of its creation is understood to be entirely distinct from questions relating to the very legitimacy of the establishment of the array of courts and tribunals charged with the interpretation and application of such rules in defined circumstances. In this sense, this chapter is not overly concerned with institutional legitimacy as such, but seeks rather to hone in on issues pertaining to the measurement or evaluation of decisional legitimacy.

There is no one single test which will indicate the legitimacy or otherwise of a judicial decision; it is rather 'a product of substance and perception that shows itself in the people's acceptance of the judiciary as fit to determine what the ... law means and to declare what it demands'.[5] It is generally accepted that in discussing the legitimacy of a decision we are talking about the legitimacy of that decision as viewed by the relevant interpretive community,[6] in other words, the community of individuals who read and digest judicial opinions.[7] In perhaps an overly simplistic formulation, the legitimacy of a judicial decision is not to be measured exclusively in terms of the ultimate outcome of that decision, but rather on the reasoned route undertaken. Legitimacy, as Ronald Dworkin might put it, is to be measured not by result, but rather by the coherence of the method.[8] Admittedly, the argument can be made that any discussion of the legitimacy of judicial decisions or rules in general will ultimately reside in the province of hermeneutics rather than epistemology. Nevertheless, it is proposed that in the context of international criminal law, if a bench arrives at a broadly creative legal determination following clearly illustrated, exhaustive reasoning which is evidently compatible with the

---

[5] MD Daneker, 'Moral Reasoning and the Quest of Legitimacy' (1993–1994) 43 *Am U L Rev* 49, 50, quoting US Supreme Court Justices O'Connor, Souter and Kennedy. See A Cassese, 'The Legitimacy of International Criminal Tribunals and the Current Prospects of International Criminal Justice' (2012) 25 *LJIL* 491.

[6] See S Fish, *Is There a Text in this Class* (Boston, Harvard University Press 1980) 147–174.

[7] As Michael Daneker has illustrated, '[w]ith some exceptions, judges use opinions to persuade the interpretative community. The judges, in turn, rely on the interpretive community to persuade the general public'; Daneker (n 5) 51. It is far from easy to exhaustively characterise the make-up of the interpretive community of international criminal law beyond to say that it is comprised of academics, practitioners, inter-governmental and non-governmental organisations, states and crucially other international courts and tribunals with related competences.

[8] R Badinter and S Breyer (eds), *Judges in Contemporary Democracy: An International Conversation* (New York, New York University Press 2004), 243–244. See generally, R Dworkin, *Law's Empire* (Oregon, Hart Publishing 1986).

principle of legality and customary international law, then that decision will enjoy at least *prima facie* legitimacy amongst the interpretive community, that is, amongst international criminal law scholars, practitioners and observers. In short, the legitimacy of judicial creativity (at least in the context of international criminal law) is measured in terms of the transparency and exhaustive nature of the reasoning undertaken and the broad basis of the result in existing rules, be they conventional or customary in nature.

In the early, sparse, years of the *ad hoc* Tribunals for the former Yugoslavia (ICTY) and Rwanda (ICTR), it was certainly possible to observe a keenness amongst the bench to adhere to this conception of decisional legitimacy. Decisions such as the *Tadić* Jurisdiction Decision[9] and the *Erdemović* Sentencing Appeals Judgment[10] were seminal, creative and exceptional from the perspective of exhaustive reasoning. Their creative impart was initially challenged academically, but have come to be entirely accepted and vindicated by the interpretive community.[11] However, with the acceleration in the activities of these institutions and the related emergence of additional international criminal institutions such as, amongst others, the Special Court for Sierra Leone (SCSL), the International Criminal Court (ICC) and the Special Tribunal for Lebanon (STL), there has been a resultant depreciation in the rigour with which the interpretive community have tested the legitimacy of creative judicial decision-making. This increase in competition for the attentions of the interpretive community, coupled with a vastly expanded case load has, perhaps unsurprisingly, resulted in a commensurate depreciation in the quality of judicial reasoning and hence an undermining of decisional legitimacy in international criminal law. A related and extremely alarming consequence of this atrophied reasoning is the emergence of a more fluid conception of the principle

---

[9] *Prosecutor v Tadić* (Appeals Chamber Decision on the Defence Motion for Interlocutory Appeal on Jurisdiction) IT-94-1-AR72 (2 October 1995).

[10] *Prosecutor v Erdemović* (Sentencing Appeal Judgment) IT-96-22-A (7 October 1997).

[11] See for example, C Greenwood, 'International Humanitarian Law and the *Tadić* Case' (1996) 7 *EJIL* 265; C Warbrick, 'The International Criminal Tribunal for Yugoslavia: The Decision of the Appeals Chamber on the Interlocutory Appeal on Jurisdiction in the *Tadić* Case' (1996) 45 *ICLQ* 691; GH Aldrich, 'Jurisdiction of the International Criminal Tribunal for the former Yugoslavia' (1996) 90 *AJIL* 64; LG Maresca, 'Case Analysis: *The Prosecutor v Tadić* The Appellate Decision of the ICTY and Internal Violations of Humanitarian Law as International Crimes' (1996) 9 *LJIL* 219; WJ Fenrick, 'The Development of the Law of Armed Conflict Through the Jurisprudence of the International Criminal Tribunal for the former Yugoslavia' (1998) 3 *J Armed Conflict L* 197; IG Corey, 'The Fine Line Between Policy and Custom: *Prosecutor v Tadić* and the Customary International Law of Internal Armed Conflict' (2000) 166 *Mil L Rev* 145; S Yee, 'The *Erdemović* Sentencing Judgment: A Questionable Milestone for the International Criminal Tribunal for the former Yugoslavia' (1997) 26 *Geo J Int'l Comp L* 263; R Cryer, 'One Appeal, Two Philosophies, Four Opinions and a Remittal: The Erdemović Case at the ICTY Appeals Chamber' (1997) 2 *J Armed Conflict L* 193; D Turns, 'The International Criminal Tribunal for the former Yugoslavia: *The Erdemović* Case' (1998) 47 *ICLQ* 461; SC Newman, 'Duress as a Defense to War Crimes and Crimes Against Humanity – *Prosecutor v Drazen Erdemović*' (2000) 166 *Mil L Rev* 158.

of legality, but more specifically, of a speculative approach to customary rule identification. As the vigilance of the interpretive community has waned, the international criminal bench – in its broadest sense – has frequently seen fit to pronounce on numerous issues, which at least would seem *prima facie* to be beyond their competence, such as for instance the 'discovery' of a customary definition of international terrorism,[12] the *de facto* outlawing of the waging of war[13] and the removal of head of state immunity with respect to the prosecution of all crimes within the jurisdiction of international courts and tribunals.[14] In the absence of a legislative body with powers of review over the activities of international courts and tribunals, the interpretive community must assume an additional monitoring function, which is capable of bringing these institutions to task with respect to the legitimacy of their decision-making.[15] The accusation, however, is that with the proliferation of international criminal jurisdictions, the interpretive community is increasingly incapable of effectively executing this responsibility.

Taking this admittedly bold claim as a hypothesis, this chapter aims to: first, further lay out the groundwork for the identification of the legitimate exercise of judicial creativity, as viewed from both domestic legal and international legal traditions, while also briefly alluding to the centrality of judicial creativity in the continuing evolution of core aspects of substantive and procedural international criminal law (Section II); second, to illustrate the gradual depreciation of the legitimacy of contemporary judicial creativity by looking at two recent, controversial decisions from the ICTY and the STL (Section III); and finally, with this achieved, to ruminate on some concluding remarks.

---

[12] See *Interlocutory Decision on the Applicable Law: Terrorism, Conspiracy, Homicide, Perpetration, Cumulative Charging*, STL-11-01/I/AC/R176bis (18 February 2011) [hereinafter, STL Appeals Chamber Decision].

[13] See *Prosecutor v Perišić* (Trial Chamber Judgment) IT-04-81-T (6 September 2011).

[14] See *Situation in Darfur, Sudan: Prosecutor v al Bashir* (Decision Pursuant to Article 87(7) of the Rome Statute on the Failure by the Republic of Malawi to Comply with the Cooperation Requests Issued by the Court with Respect to the Arrest and Surrender of Omar Hassan Ahmad al Bashir) ICC-02/05-01/09 (12 December 2011; *Situation in Darfur, Sudan: Prosecutor v al Bashir* (Decision Pursuant to Article 87(7) of the Rome Statute on the Failure by the Republic of Chad to Comply with the Cooperation Requests Issued by the Court with Respect to the Arrest and Surrender of Omar Hassan Ahmad al Bashir) ICC-02/05-01/09 (13 December 2011).

[15] See L Arbour, 'Stefan A Riesenfeld Award Lecture – Crimes Against Women Under International Law' (2003) 21 *Berk J Int'l L* 196. See also J Stone, '*Non Liquet* and the Function of Law in the International Community' (1959) 35 *Brit Y B Int'l L* 124, 152: 'How much *law-creating* responsibility can we sensibly place on international courts in a world as changeful as ours, and in the absence of any organ for correction of judicial errors' [emphasis in the original].

# I. The Contours of Judicial Creativity and its Affinity with International Criminal Law

## A. The Broader Picture: Creativity, Activism and the Completeness of Legal Orders

> This is not Nam, this is bowling. There are rules.[16]

It is no doubt trite to remark that judicial creativity is and has been – at least since Blackstone's era – a deeply polarising subject amongst the political and legal establishments of both common and civil jurisdictions. It is safe to say that should a lawyer find himself at a particularly dull lunch with colleagues[17] (heaven forbid), the safest topic to raise in an effort to liven the conversation up a little is the issue of the merits or otherwise of a liberally legislating bench. As you might imagine – since it is glaringly obvious – common law lawyers are likely to be either resigned to its spectral existence or to endorse its utilisation in the interests of justice and as an inherent feature of the judicial function. As Judge Benjamin Cardozo famously remarked, for the common law lawyer, judicial law-making must be regarded as 'one of the existing realities of life'[18] which lies at the heart of the progressive development of the law, irrespective of the activities or protestations of the legislature. While the civil law tradition sanctifies the position of the legislature, the principle of *jurisprudence constante* affords the bench the ability to adopt a creative approach, safe in the knowledge that such an approach is not binding on lower courts without subsequent legislative amendment.[19] Despite their diverging rationales, both systems acknowledge that the primary responsibility of the bench is to apply the will of the legislator as enacted in law and only to encroach on this primary responsibility where a gap or *lacuna* demands creative action. The commentary of Lord Steyn on this point is particularly useful:

> In construing statutes the courts have no law-making role. On the other hand, in the exposition of the common law, the courts have a creative role. If this statement causes surprise in some quarters, one need only point to the fact that the whole common law is judge made law. On the

---

[16] *The Big Lebowski* (n 1).
[17] As frequently experienced by the unfortunate Horace Rumpole.
[18] B Cardozo, *The Nature of the Judicial Process* (New Haven, Yale University Press 1921) 10. See also CE Clark and DM Trubeck, 'The Creative Role of the Judge: Restraint and Freedom in the Common Law Tradition' (1961–1962) 71 *YLJ* 255.
[19] For an excellent and brief summation of these distinct, but complementary, approaches, see M Shahabuddeen, 'Judicial Creativity and Joint Criminal Enterprise' in S Darcy and J Powderly (eds) *Judicial Creativity at the International Criminal Tribunals* (Oxford, Oxford University Press 2011).

other hand, it is necessary for courts, when developing the common law, to proceed with caution lest they undermine confidence in their judgments. The courts are therefore constrained when Parliament has spoken. But in general courts are not so constrained when Parliament has not spoken since Parliament's silence and inaction is usually ambiguous. The courts do not have the last word. Parliament may reverse any decision unacceptable to it.[20]

At this juncture it is essential to distinguish judicial creativity from the value laden and righteous label of 'judicial activism'. The term judicial activism has assumed, especially in the context of US constitutional law scholarship, an inherently negative connotation, and is presumed to imply an entirely arbitrary excursion into judge-made law on the basis of personal predilections rather than from a firm basis in pre-existing positive law.[21] It is argued that while the distinction between creativity and activism may boil down to a semantic argument or a purely subjective analysis, the fundamental distinction for the purposes of this chapter is quite straightforward. Judicial creativity implies the filling of *lacunae* on the basis of the reasoned development of acknowledged pre-existing legal principles, which takes into account both the teleological underpinnings of the law in question and issues of public policy affecting its application.[22] On the other hand, judicial activism implies arbitrary rule creation which has no foundation in pre-existing principles or rules and is based not on teleology, but rather on the subjective desires of the bench. This characterisation applies with equal validity in the context of international jurisprudence. As Sir Hersh Lauterpacht states in his seminal work *The Development of International Law by the International Court*, '[j]udicial legislation, so long as it does not assume the form of deliberate disregard of existing law, is a phenomenon both healthy and unavoidable'.[23] Mohamed Shahabuddeen has commented that judges liable to be criticised as activist 'are likely to be old, male, rich, upper class – people

---

[20] Lord Steyn, 'Deference: A Tangled Story', Judicial Studies Board Lecture, Belfast (25 November 2004) 4, quoted approvingly in Shahabuddeen (n 19) 185.

[21] See AT Mason, 'Judicial Activism: Old and New' (1969) 55 *Virg L Rev* 385; BC Canon, 'Defining the Dimensions of Judicial Activism' (1982–1983) 66 *Judicature* 66; KD Kmiec, 'The Origin and Current Meanings of "Judicial Activism"' (2004) 92 *Cal L Rev* 1441.

[22] It is worth referring to the words of Judge Cardozo in this respect: 'The judge, even when he is free, is not wholly free. He is not to innovate at pleasure. He is not a knight-errant roaming at will in pursuit of his own ideal of beauty or of goodness. He is to draw his inspiration from consecrated principles. He is not to yield to spasmodic sentiment, to vague and unregulated benevolence. He is to exercise a discretion informed by tradition, methodized by analogy, disciplined by system, and subordinated to "primordial necessity or order in the social life". Wide enough in all conscience is the field of discretion that remains'. Cardozo (n 18) 141.

[23] H Lauterpacht, *The Development of International Law by the International Court* (London, Stevens and Sons 1958) 156.

who mechanically reflect the outlook of their kind without concerning themselves with the interests of the wider society'.[24]

This broad acceptance, that it is inherent in the nature of the judicial function that judges should be afforded the authority to legitimately address apparent *lacunae* in the interests of justice, presupposes the completeness of the legal order. Any discussion of the completeness of the legal order (international or otherwise), takes us down the road of discussing diverging conceptions of the theory of 'gaps'. As tempting a proposition as this undoubtedly is, this is perhaps not the most appropriate time for such a tangential discussion, but a brief note is certainly acceptable.

In the context of international law, conflicting theories with respect to its completeness as a legal order has given rise to a rich body of scholarship and numerous fascinating exchanges. The most famous exchange pitted Sir Hersh Lauterpacht[25] and Lucien Siorat[26] against Julius Stone[27] on the question of the prohibition of an international court issuing a finding of *non liquet* or 'no applicable law' when faced with a *lacuna* in the law. For Lauterpacht and Siorat, the principle of completeness implied that 'in regard to contentious proceedings, a legal tribunal is – and must always be – in the position to determine whether a claim is justified in law and whether judgment must therefore be given for the plaintiff or the defendant'.[28] In other words, 'the judge is bound to give a decision on the dispute before him'.[29] As a natural law thinker, Lauterpacht rejected the proposition that there were insurmountable 'gaps' in the law, preferring to describe such 'gaps' as 'only *primae impressionis* difficulties to decide cases'.[30] Lauterpacht was not unaware, however, of the counter-argument (advanced by cautious positivists such as Stone) that the principle of the completeness of the legal order was a convenient fiction which facilitated unrestrained judicial law-making. He rebutted such propositions in terms which are worth producing in full:

> Notwithstanding the admitted peculiarities and comprehensiveness of its gaps, international law, like any other system of law, is complete from the point of view of its adequacy to deal with any dispute brought before an international judicial tribunal. At the same time it has been shown that, like any other system of law, international law contains gaps from the point of view of the approximation of its rules

---

[24] Shahabuddeen (n 19) 185.

[25] See H Lauterpacht, 'Some Observations on the Prohibition of *Non Liquet* and the Completeness of the Legal Order' (1958) *Symbolae Verzijl* 196.

[26] See L Siorat, *Le Probléme des lacunes en droit international* (Paris, Librairie Générale de Droit 1959).

[27] See J Stone, '*Non Liquet* and the Function of Law in the International Community' (1959) 35 *Brit Y B Int'l L* 129.

[28] Ibid 128.

[29] H Lauterpacht, *The Function of Law in the International Community* (Oxford, Oxford Clarendon Press 1933) 135.

[30] M Koskenniemi, 'The Function of Law in the International Community: 75 Years After' (2009) 85 *Brit Y B Int'l L* 353, 359.

to the essential purposes of international law and to the requirements of international justice. To disregard this fact, in deference to a purely mechanical conception of the completeness of international law, is to thwart the judicial activity of international tribunals in a manner contrary to the spirit of international law. The juxtaposition of these apparently contradictory submissions, namely, that in one sense there exist gaps and that in another sense there cannot be a question of gaps, is apt to prove confusing. But the confusion must disappear when the significance of the double meaning of the term 'gap' is fully realized. According to one meaning, which has gained currency in international law, it connotes the inability of the law to give any decision at all in a given case; according to the other it connotes the inability to a give a decision consistent with the social purpose of the law and with the requirement of unity within the law. The analysis here undertaken has revealed that *ultimately* there are no gaps in the law either from the jurisdictional (i.e. formal) or the material point of view. From the jurisdictional point of view there are no gaps, inasmuch as it is axiomatic that the judge is bound to give a decision in the dispute before him. *From the point of view of the material adequacy of the existing law, such gaps as undoubtedly occur to the judicial mind are merely provisional. They are ultimately either filled by the legislative process of developing the existing legal materials* or eliminated, however, reluctantly, from the purview of judicial, as distinguished from legislative cognizance.[31]

Therefore, for Lauterpacht, to assume the completeness of the legal order is to acknowledge that *lacunae* are merely provisional, ephemeral obstacles that must be negotiated, in the interests of justice and the spirit of the law, via the creative judicial development of existing positive law. In this sense, the principle of the completeness of the legal order is tied up not only with the prohibition of *non liquet*, but also with the necessity of judicial creativity with respect to the interpretation of existing or discoverable sources of law undertaken in pursuit of the principle of the effectiveness of law or *ut res magis valeat quam pereat*. To channel Goethe for a moment, this theoretical approach screams, '[m]ighty is the law, but mightier still is necessity'.[32]

## B. Judicial Creativity and International Criminal Law: A Long-Lasting Love Affair

This rather summary discussion of the *a priori* completeness of all legal orders which mandates the bench to respond to *lacunae* in a creative, developmental way

---

[31] Lauterpacht (n 29) 134–135 [emphasis added].
[32] JW von Goethe, *Faust*, Part I, Act 1.

has proven especially useful in the context of international criminal law. Following the establishment of the ICTY and the ICTR in 1993 and 1994 respectively, the unfortunate original cohort of judges (depending on your viewpoint) did not have the task of applying a body of pre-existing law as much as discovering that law, both from the bare bones statute before them and from a laissez-faire approach to customary law identification. As former member of the ICTY bench, Patricia Wald, has remarked:

> make no mistake: judicial creativity was the mantra of the new courts ... [t]he role of judicial creativity at the ICTY ... in identifying and articulating its law, was indisputable but it had to be performed in a cautious and carefully crafted way. The ICTY's baptismal papers – its Statute and the Secretary-General's Report – sought to reassure states and skeptics that this new court could not make up its own law, but rather administer that elusive body of 'customary international law'.[33]

As the first President of the ICTY, the late Antonio Cassese appeared to revel in the humanising potential of creative judicial development of international criminal law.[34] For him the function of the international criminal judiciary was subtly distinguishable from that of colleagues sitting on related courts and tribunals:

> The issue is that international criminal courts in a way have to play a role that goes beyond the traditional role of the judge (the application and interpretation of existing law). Why is it so? Because international criminal law is extremely rudimentary, the precedents are very poor. If you read the Nuremberg judgment, you realize that it is really a very poor judgment.[35]

Judge Cassese was refreshingly forthcoming in describing the practical implementation of this creative function as it played out in the *Tadić* Appeal Judgment's controversial formulation of the extended form of the joint criminal enterprise doctrine:[36]

> Today, international criminal courts are faced with areas of law that are full of gaps. *Out of nothing – very few cases – you have to create a new law, and you have to say something new.* So, again the role of judges is

---

[33] P Wald, 'Note from the Bench' in Darcy and Powderly (n 19) xxxvi.
[34] See T Hoffmann, 'The Gentle Humanizer of Humanitarian Law – Antonio Cassese and the Creation of the Customary Law of Non-International Armed Conflict' in C Stahn and L van den Herik (eds), *Future Perspectives on International Criminal Justice* (The Hague, TMC Asser Press 2010) 58.
[35] Badinter and Breyer (n 8) 212–213.
[36] See Chapter 6 in this volume for an exploration of some of the more troubling aspects of the current state of the law on this mode of liability.

increasingly important, particularly in the area of criminal law, where we normally tend to stick to the principle of *nullum crimen sine lege*, but sometimes, you have to find a new principle. For instance, we had the *Tadić* case, where Tadić was acquitted by a trial chamber on a particular count because there was no evidence that he had taken part in the killing of five Muslims in a particular village. He was a member of a group, and there was no evidence that he had participated in the killing or that there was a criminal agreement with respect to the killing of those people. So he was acquitted because there was no evidence of direct responsibility. Then, at the appellate level, the court relied on the common law notion of 'common purpose' – which is to some extent unknown to our countries – where one should have reasonably expected, as a member of a sort of criminal gang, that some members of the gang may kill somebody, although the individual has not agreed on the killing and has no direct responsibility. The adoption of his principle, and the resulting category of crime, was a very important development. We were doubtful at the time. May we, in criminal law, use notions and new principles? Does this practice infringe on the rights of the defendant? The defendant should know in advance under which category of crime he may be convicted so that he may adequately prepare.[37]

The *Tadić* Appeals Judgment stands out as a perfect, if very obvious, example of what might affectionately be referred to as the 'Cassese Approach to Creative Rule Development', which quickly took root in the judicial practice of both the ICTY and the ICTR and several years later was to be adopted by the STL during his time as President. This approach essentially mandates that most, if not all, statutory *lacunae* can be addressed via careful, consistent interpretation of the object and purpose (i.e. a teleological approach which draws on key elements of international public policy) of the constituent statute, coupled with the excavation of previously undetected rules of customary international law and a principled appreciation of the open texture of legal rules. In this way, the Appeals Chamber of the ICTY under the leadership of Cassese insulated the acknowledged need for the creative development of substantive international criminal law from accusations of naked judicial activism by deliberately couching such creativity in the panacea of custom and accepted rules of statutory and treaty interpretation.

Our key concern as members of the interpretive community is whether we can objectively accept the legitimacy of the Appeals Chamber's approach. To make such a determination, our primary concern, as outlined above, is with the argumentative method by which the Chamber arrived at its decision and not exclusively with the end result. The reading of joint criminal enterprise liability into the text of Article 7(1) of the Statute proceeded on a basis of a logically reasoned argument, constructed in the following way:

---

[37] Badinter and Breyer (n 8) 214 [emphasis added].

1. *Identification and statement of the 'gap' or ambiguity*: 'whether the acts of one person can give rise to the criminal culpability of another where both participate in the execution of a common criminal plan'.[38]
2. *Statement of the applicable law*: Article 7(1) – 'A person who planned, instigated, ordered, committed or otherwise aided and abetted in the planning, preparation or execution of a crime referred to in Articles 2 to 5 of the present Statute, shall be individually responsible for the crime'.
3. *Reference to the understanding attaching to the impugned provision, as laid out in the Secretary-General's Report, as an indication of the 'drafters'' original intent*: 'An important element in relation to the competence *ratione personae* (personal jurisdiction) of the International Tribunal is the principle of individual criminal responsibility. As noted above, the Security Council has reaffirmed in a number of resolutions that persons committing serious violations of international humanitarian law in the former Yugoslavia are individually responsible for such violations'.[39]
4. *Filling of the 'gap' via the adoption of an object and purpose interpretation of Article 7(1), as deduced from the context of the Statute and indications of original intent contained in the Report of the Secretary-General*: 'An interpretation of the Statute based on its object and purpose leads to the conclusion that the Statute intends to extend the jurisdiction of the International Tribunal to *all* those "responsible for serious violations of international humanitarian law" committed in the former Yugoslavia (Article 1). As is apparent from the wording of both Article 7(1) and the provisions setting forth the crimes over which the International Tribunal has jurisdiction (Articles 2 to 5), such responsibility for serious violations of international humanitarian law is not limited merely to those who actually carry out the *actus reus* of the enumerated crimes but appears to extend also to other offenders'.[40]
5. *Allusion to the principle of effectiveness as an additional justification for the filling of the 'gap'*: 'The above interpretation is not only dictated by the object and purpose of the Statute but is also warranted by the very nature of many international crimes which are committed most commonly in wartime situations … This interpretation, based on the Statute and the inherent characteristics of many crimes perpetrated in wartime, warrants the conclusion that international criminal responsibility embraces actions perpetrated by a collectivity of persons in furtherance of a common criminal design'.[41]
6. *Establishment of the consistency of the interpretation adopted with customary international law standards and the ascertainment of the applicable objective and subjective elements*: 'It may also be noted that … international criminal rules on common purpose are substantially rooted in, and to a large extent reflect, the position taken by many States of the world in their national systems …

---

[38] *Prosecutor v Tadić* (Appeals Judgment) IT-94-1-A (15 July 1999) para 185.
[39] Ibid para 186, quoting Secretary-General's Report (n 4) para 53.
[40] Ibid para 189.
[41] Ibid paras 191 and 193.

the Tribunal's Statute does not specify (either expressly or by implication) the objective and subjective elements (*actus reus* and *mens rea*) of this category of collective criminality. To identify these elements one must turn to customary international law. Customary rules on this matter are discernible on the basis of various elements: chiefly case law and a few instances of international legislation'.[42]

7. *Conclusion: gap filled* – 'In sum, the Appeals Chamber holds the view that the notion of common design as a form of accomplice liability is firmly established in customary international law and in addition is upheld, albeit implicitly, in the Statute of the International Tribunal'.[43]

This clearly illustrates the Appeals Chamber's cognizance of the obligation to develop the law not in an arbitrary and declarative way, but rather by means of reasoned argumentation. Throughout the first decade of the *ad hoc* tribunals' activities, this method was identifiable in the majority of decisions dealing with statutory *lacunae* of one kind or another.[44] However, it is nevertheless obvious that without the tribunals' 'modern' approach to customary international law identification, the creative capacity of the bench would have been greatly curtailed.[45]

The *ad hoc* tribunals' distortion of the traditional means of customary rule identification – based on the formula of state practice with supporting *opinio juris* – has been the subject of extensive criticism over the years.[46] It is certainly true that, in the context of international criminal law, the identification of customary norms requires consideration of additional sources of state practice, such as domestic

---

[42] Ibid paras 193–194. Discussion of the customary basis for joint criminal enterprise liability runs from para 195 to 229.

[43] Ibid para 220.

[44] See for example, amongst many others that in the interest of space are not included here, *Prosecutor v Erdemović* Sentencing Appeal Judgment (n 10) (permissibility of the defence of duress); *Prosecutor v Furundžija* (Trial Judgment) IT-95-17/1-T (10 December 1998) (definition of rape and aiding and abetting); *Prosecutor v Delalić et al* (Trial Judgment) IT-96-21-T (16 November 1998) (re applicability of common article three); *Prosecutor v Jelisić* (Trial Judgment) IT-95-10-T (14 December 1999) (sole perpetration of genocide); *Prosecutor v Galić* (Trial Judgment) IT-98-29-T (5 December 2003) (war crime of terror); *Prosecutor v Krstić* (Trial Judgment) IT-98-33-T (2 August 2001) (aiding and abetting genocide).

[45] See AE Roberts, 'Traditional and Modern Approaches to Customary International Law: A Reconciliation' (2001) 95 *AJIL* 757.

[46] See J Powderly, 'Judicial Interpretation at the Ad Hoc Tribunals: Method from Chaos?' in Darcy and Powderly (n 19) 17; L van den Herik, 'Using Custom to Reconceptualize Crimes Against Humanity' in Darcy and Powderly (n 19) 80; A Nolkaepmer, 'The Legitimacy of International Law in the Case Law of the International Criminal Tribunal for the former Yugoslavia' in T Vandamme and J Reestman (eds) *Ambiguity in the Rule of Law: The Interface Between National and International Legal Systems* (Groningen, Europa Law Publishing 2001); I Bantekas, 'Reflections on Some Sources and Methods of International Criminal and Humanitarian Law' (2006) 6 *ICLR* 121; G Sluiter and A Zahar, *International Criminal Law: A Critical Introduction* (Oxford, Oxford University Press 2008); cf T Meron, 'The Revival of Customary Humanitarian Law' (2005) 99 *AJIL* 817.

criminal law, for which there will be no supporting *opinio juris*, as well as soft law sources such as General Assembly Resolutions and resolutions of various other multilateral forums.[47] Such a modern approach to customary international law identification is not *per se* objectionable, and is indeed observable in the practice of other international courts and tribunals.[48] However, issues do arise with respect to the consistency of the approach adopted. In the understandable eagerness to underpin the basis for the creative development of the law in observable norms of customary international law, there has been a tendency to treat this source of law as a panacea for all the interpretative woes facing the bench. In their attempt to identify new norms based on state practice and *opinio juris*, significant reliance has been placed on post-Second World War military tribunal jurisprudence as well as obscure case-law from a handful of jurisdictions, the relevance of which is often very difficult to determine[49] (in fact, the jurisdictions relied upon in this regard will most likely conform with the backgrounds of the bench and no doubt that of their legal officers).

There is a definite danger then that the convenient selectiveness of established and newly identified customary rules is being used as a fail-safe mechanism when compliance with the principle of legality is brought into question as a consequence. Some critical scholars might even go as far as to say that, before the international criminal tribunals, customary international law is to be considered inherently malleable and capable of saying whatever you want it to say.[50] This is perhaps excessively cynical and certainly only attaches to a minority of cases; however, the critique is not without some merit. Cassese was without doubt keenly aware of the creative potential of custom:

> At least, in my area in international law, lawmakers very often are utterly impotent. Lawmakers often cannot make a decision, and the judges have to step in and decide, in lieu of lawmakers ... We have all made judgments. *We know that we are prone to manipulation. We manipulate laws, standards, political principles, and principles of interpretation.* Very often in a criminal case, I sense that the defendant is guilty, and common sense leads me to believe that we should come to a particular conclusion. Then I say, 'alright, let us now build sound reasoning to support that conclusion'.[51]

---

[47] See *Military and Paramilitary Activities in and against Nicaragua* (1986) ICJ Reports 14, para 186.

[48] The International Court of Justice has been far from consistent with respect to the method of identification and has on occasion lapsed into the realm of declarative identification. See *Case Concerning Military and Paramilitary Activities in and against Nicaragua (Nicaragua v United States)* ibid para 218.

[49] See Sluiter and Zahar (n 46).

[50] See ibid 92–105.

[51] Badinter and Breyer (n 8) 33 [emphasis added].

There is therefore a legitimate concern that recourse to 'new' norms of customary international law, identified on the basis of questionable evidence of state practice and *opinio juris*, may be used as a means of concealing the arbitrary development of the law and its fraught relationship with the principle of legality. It is the responsibility of the interpretive community to remain vigilant of the possibility of such arbitrary development, by constantly testing the grounds upon which creative interpretation is based and raising the alarm-bells when compliance with the principle of legality is called into question. Should the interpretive community shirk this responsibility, we may face the prospect that core aspects of the progressive development of international criminal law will be based not on rigorously extracted norms of customary international law, but rather on a series of fictions. It must be borne in mind that 'the elasticity of legal rules in not unlimited' and, as Morris Cohen has eloquently cautioned,

> [W]hen the new wine can no longer be poured into the old bottles courts resort to fictions, whereby the new vessels are adopted as old possessions of the legal household. Legal fiction is the mask which progress must wear to pass the faithful but blear-eyed watchers of our ancient legal treasures. But though legal fictions are useful in thus mitigating or absorbing the shock of innovation, they work havoc in the form of intellectual confusion. The least that can be said is that they tend to make us all ignore the magnitude and character of the actual changes wrought by them. The mask shuts off a great deal of needed light.[52]

While there is absolutely no question of the centrality of judicial creativity in the development of contemporary international criminal law, the foregoing has illustrated that, irrespective of the forum, certain rules or boundaries must be respected if judicial creativity is not to descend into the realm of judicial activism. The following section will highlight a number of instances in which activism has held sway over exhaustive reasoning in order to prioritise the *lex ferenda* over the *lex lata*.

---

[52] M R Cohen, 'The Process of Judicial Legislation' (1914) 48 *Am L Rev* 161, 175.

## II. Evolving International Criminal Law and the Slide towards Compromised Legitimacy

This is what happens Larry …[53]

With the proliferation of new international criminal courts and tribunals over the course of the last decade and the consequent explosion in case law, there has been an appreciable decline in the quality and exhaustiveness of judicial reasoning with respect to customary international law. To a certain extent this is linked to the institution of the *de facto* observance of *stare decisis* and the need for the expeditious conduct of proceedings.[54] The practical import of this trend is seen in the tendency of the bench to rely on contentious customary rules that have been identified in previous cases, often without question or independent inquiry.[55] Given our discussion of the apparent malleability of custom and its frequently fraught relationship with the principle of legality, this certainly gives cause for concern. It would seem that logically reasoned arguments constructed with comparable care to that forwarded in the *Tadić* Appeal Judgment are increasingly set aside in favour of a more summary or declarative approach to decision-making. In recent times, instances of particularly questionable reasoning have gone hand-in-hand with judicial pronouncements on issues which are of significant importance to international public policy such as head of state immunity[56] and the *de facto*

---

[53] *The Big Lebowski* (n 1).

[54] See *Prosecutor v Aleksovski* (Appeal Judgment) IT-95-14/1-A (24 March 2000) paras 112–113; *Prosecutor v Erdemović* (Sentencing Appeal Judgment) IT-96-22-A (7 October 1997) paras 41–45; *Tadić* Appeal Judgment (n 38 above) paras 255–270; *Prosecutor v Milošević* (Decision on Preliminary Motions) IT-02-54-PT (8 November 2001) paras 32–33.

[55] Some examples amongst many include: *Prosecutor v Delalić et al* (Trial Judgment) IT-96-21-T (16 November 1998) (re applicability of common article three); *Prosecutor v Kupreškić* (Trial Judgment) IT-95-16-T (14 January 2000) (re customary prohibition of reprisals – referencing the Martens Clause); *Prosecutor v Kunarac et al* (Appeals Chamber Judgment) IT-96-23 and IT-96-23/1-A (12 June 2002) (re customary status of policy element of crimes against humanity); *Prosecutor v Hadžihasanović* (Decision on Joint Challenge to Jurisdiction) IT-01-47-PT (16 July 2003) (command responsibility); *Prosecutor v Blaškić* (Appeal Judgment) IT-95-14-A (29 July 2004) (re plunder as an element of persecution); *Prosecutor v Kordić and Čerkez* (Appeal Judgment) IT-95-14/2-A (17 December 2004) (re customary status of certain provisions of Additional Protocol I); *Situation in the DRC: Prosecutor v Lubanga* (Decision on the Confirmation of Charges) ICC-01/04-01/06 (29 January 2007) (re customary nature of prohibition of use an recruitment of child soldiers); *Situation in Darfur, Sudan: Prosecutor v al Bashir* (Decision Pursuant to Article 87(7) of the Rome Statute on the Failure by the Republic of Malawi to Comply with the Cooperation Requests Issued by the Court with Respect to the Arrest and Surrender of Omar Hassan Ahmad al Bashir) ICC-02/05-01/09 (12 December 2011) (re head of state immunity).

[56] See for example *Situation in Darfur, Sudan: Prosecutor v al Bashir* (Decision Pursuant to Article 87(7) of the Rome Statute on the Failure by the Republic of Malawi to Comply with the Cooperation Requests Issued by the Court with Respect to the Arrest and Surrender of

criminalisation of the waging of war.[57] If the legitimacy of judicial creativity is to be measured, as this chapter argues, in terms of the transparency and exhaustive nature of the reasoning undertaken and the broad basis of the result in existing rules, then it is submitted that the legitimacy of judicial development of international criminal law may be in danger of entering into gradual decline.

It is entirely beyond the scope of this chapter to do anything other than merely touch the surface of some of the issues that have come to the fore with respect to the legitimacy of more recent examples of judicial creativity in the context of international criminal law. The intention is not to impugn the competence or capabilities of the entire international criminal judiciary, far from it. Rather the objective is to illustrate indications of a depreciating standard of reasoning via recourse to a couple of recent troubling decisions. In the interests of brevity just two decisions have been selected for this purpose: (i) the February 2011 decision of the STL Appeals Chamber on the applicable law;[58] and (ii) the September 2011 ICTY Trial Judgment in the *Perišić* case.[59]

## A. The Applicable Law Before the STL: Terrorism, Custom and the Absence of Judicial Restraint

The STL Appeals Chamber's 'Interlocutory Decision on the Applicable Law'[60] is a prime example of when a bench crosses the line separating good faith creative interpretation from naked judicial activism. Setting the curious circumstances and chronology of the proceedings leading to the decision to one side (they have, however, been expertly dealt with by Ben Saul in Chapter 4 in this volume and elsewhere[61]), the actual content of the decision is breathtaking from a number of perspectives. On 21 January 2011, Pre-Trial Judge Daniel Fransen, acting pursuant to Rule 68 (G) of the Rules of Procedure and Evidence[62] requested the Appeals Chamber to respond *in limine litus* and *in abstracto* to 15 questions pertaining to

---

Omar Hassan Ahmad al Bashir) ICC-02/05-01/09 (12 December 2011); *Situation in Darfur, Sudan*: *Prosecutor v al Bashir* (Decision Pursuant to Article 87(7) of the Rome Statute on the Failure by the Republic of Chad to Comply with the Cooperation Requests Issued by the Court with Respect to the Arrest and Surrender of Omar Hassan Ahmad al Bashir) ICC-02/05-01/09 (13 December 2011).

[57] See discussion of *Perišić* trial judgment below.
[58] See STL Appeals Chamber Decision (n 12).
[59] See *Perišić* Trial Judgment (n 13).
[60] STL Appeals Chamber Decision (n 12).
[61] See further B Saul, 'Legislating from a Radical Hague: The United Nations Special Tribunal for Lebanon Invents an International Crime of Transnational Terrorism' (2011) 24 *LJIL* 677; B Saul, 'Amicus Curiae Brief on the Notion of Terrorist Acts Submitted to the Appeals Chamber of the Special Tribunal for Lebanon Pursuant to Rule 131 of the Rules of Procedure and Evidence' (2011) 22 *CLF* 365.
[62] Special Tribunal for Lebanon, Rules of Procedure and Evidence, Rule 68(G): 'The Pre-Trial Judge may submit to the Appeals Chamber any preliminary question, on the

the applicable law before the Tribunal. These 15 questions can be grouped under five core headings: (i) the appropriate means of interpretation of the STL Statute; (ii) the notion and definition of terrorism to be applied by the Tribunal; (iii) the applicable law with respect to the plurality of offences within the jurisdiction of the STL; (iv) the modes of individual criminal responsibility to be applied; and (v) the permissibility of cumulative charging.[63] While each of the five categories provoked a host of often curious determinations from the Chamber,[64] the findings with respect to categories (i) and (ii) gave rise to the greatest concern from the perspective of legitimate judicial creativity.

It is fair to say that the STL does not sit altogether comfortably in the community of international criminal justice institutions. Established pursuant to UN Security Council Resolution 1757,[65] the STL is a treaty based court of an international or internationalised character which is to operate on the basis of 'the highest international standards of criminal justice'.[66] However, in his Report on its establishment, Secretary-General Ban Ki Moon was quite explicit in remarking that while the STL has various characteristics of an international tribunal, 'its subject matter jurisdiction or the applicable law remain national in character'.[67] Indeed, read in accordance with its ordinary meaning, the text of Article 2(a) of the constituent Statute would seem to leave remarkably little ambiguity on the matter – the internationalised bench of the tribunal is to apply '[t]he provisions of the Lebanese Criminal Code'[68] and not the potentially relevant provisions of international law, customary or otherwise.

---

interpretation of the Agreement, Statute and Rules regarding the applicable law, that he deems necessary in order to examine and rule on the indictment.'

[63] See Order on Preliminary Questions Addressed to the Judges of the Appeals Chamber pursuant to Rule 68, paragraph (G) of the Rules of Procedure and Evidence, STL-11-01/I/AC-R176*bis* (21 January 2011) para 1.

[64] See K Ambos, 'Amicus Curiae Brief Submitted to the Appeals Chamber of the Special Tribunal for Lebanon on the Question of the Applicable Terrorism Offence with a Particular Focus on "Special" Special Intent and/or A Special Motive as Additional Subjective Requirements – Introductory Remarks' (2011) 22 *CLF* 389; S Sácouto and K Cleary, 'Amicus Curiae Brief on the Practice of Cumulative Charging Before International Criminal Bodies Submitted to the Appeals Chamber of the Special Tribunal for Lebanon Pursuant to Rule 131 of the Rules of Procedure and Evidence – Introductory Remarks' (2011) 22 *CLF* 409.

[65] UN SC Res. 1757 (30 May 2007).

[66] 'Report of the Secretary-General on the Establishment of a Special Tribunal for Lebanon' S/2006/893 (15 November 2006) para 7.

[67] Ibid: 'The legal basis for the establishment of the special tribunal is an international agreement between the United Nations and a Member State; its composition is mixed with a substantial international component; its standards of justice, including principles of due process of law, are those applicable in all international or United Nations-based criminal jurisdictions; its rules of procedure and evidence are to be inspired, in part, by reference materials reflecting the highest standards of international criminal procedure; and its success may rely considerably on the cooperation of third States.'

[68] Statute of the Special Tribunal for Lebanon, annexed to UN SC Res. 1757 (n 65).

Accepting that the Lebanese Criminal Code was the primary applicable law, with respect to category (i) on the appropriate means of interpretation of the Statute, President Cassese formulated the issue as boiling down to a question of 'whether the Tribunal can call upon international law, not to determine whether or not an offence has been committed or to determine the material elements of the crime, but rather to interpret Lebanese Law?'.[69] Responding to this question in oral submissions, Prosecutor Daniel Bellemare stated quite bluntly that '[t]here are no gaps or *lacuna* that need to be filled by reverting to international law',[70] a view that was fully endorsed by Head of the Defence Office, François Roux.[71] The alternative argument forwarded by both parties proposed that when faced with a *lacuna* the bench should first revert to general principles of Lebanese criminal law and should only invoke international law as an interpretative aid when 'relevant Lebanese jurisprudence is uncertain or divided or based on a manifestly incorrect interpretation of Lebanese law'.[72] According to the Defence Office, the Tribunal was not 'jurisdictionally enabled to import into the interpretative process methods or means of interpretation that are not recognized as applicable to the interpretation of Lebanese criminal law in the Lebanese legal order'.[73] There could be no doubt that the parties were united in their scepticism of the relevance of international law, particularly customary international law, in the interpretation of the Lebanese Criminal Code.

In the introductory paragraphs to the decision, the Chamber loftily invokes Lauterpacht, stating:

> 'the function of the judge to pronounce in each case *quid est juris* [what is the law?] is pre-eminently a practical one. He is neither compelled nor permitted to resign himself to the *ignorabimus* [it shall be ignored] which besets the perennial quest of the philosopher and the investigator in the domain of natural science'. It is the responsibility of the Appeals Chamber to accomplish this task by stating the applicable law in the clearest and most coherent way possible.[74]

The decision then embarks on a 24-paragraph exegesis on the general principles of statutory and treaty interpretation that the Tribunal may draw upon in applying the Statute. It is without question an academically useful discussion touching on issues such as: *in claris non fit interpretatio* (when a text is clear there is no need

---

[69] STL Transcript – 7 February 2011, 83. The Decision itself formulates the question as amounting to 'when and whether international law, based on the international nature and mandate of this Tribunal, should inform the Tribunal's application of Lebanese criminal law' – STL Appeals Chamber Decision (n 12) para 16.

[70] STL Transcript – 7 February 2011, 11.

[71] Ibid 55.

[72] Prosecution Submission para 5-12. See STL Appeal Chamber Decision (n 12), para 17 for a summary of prosecution arguments on this point.

[73] Defence Submission para 59.

[74] STL Appeal Chamber Decision (n 12) para 11.

for interpretation);⁷⁵ the importance of internal and external context, commenting that '[c]ontext must embrace all legitimate aids to interpretation. Important among them are the international obligations undertaken by Lebanon with which, in the absence of very clear language, it is presumed any legislation complies';⁷⁶ the relevance of drafters' intent;⁷⁷ the prohibition of *non liquet*;⁷⁸ the applicability of Articles 31 to 33 of the Vienna Convention on the Law of Treaties with respect to the interpretation of the Statute;⁷⁹ the primacy of the application of the principle of teleological interpretation;⁸⁰ the irrelevance of the principle of *in dubio mitius* (in case of doubt, the more favourable construction should be chosen);⁸¹ the principle of effectiveness;⁸² the principle of *favor rei* or *in dubio pro reo* (in case of conflicting interpretations, the understanding that best favours the accused should be adopted).⁸³

This is all very interesting, especially to those (like the present author) who have a keen interest in interpretative issues, but the remarkable fact is that despite the section having been labelled 'General Principles on the Interpretation of the Lebanese Criminal Law and the STL Statute' and itself containing a subsection entitled 'Principles on the Interpretation of Lebanese Law', this exegesis references the Lebanese Criminal Code only once (on the issue of *non liquet*)⁸⁴ and contains absolutely no reference to primary or secondary materials discussing interpretation in the specific context of the Lebanese legal tradition.⁸⁵ The overwhelming majority of sources cited pertain to either common law case law (there is no reference to civil law jurisprudence) or the case law of other international courts and tribunals (most frequently the International Court of Justice and the ICTY) with the same applying to the secondary source material referenced. It is somewhat astonishing that, having acknowledged that the Lebanese Criminal Code constituted the principle body of applicable law, the Tribunal paid absolutely no heed to the Lebanese legal order in determining the applicable rules of interpretation attaching to this body of law. It was ignored, in fact, with the basic impart of this determination being that because the issue arose in a (partially) internationally constituted institution, the general principles of interpretation that are typically applied before international courts and tribunals trumped any principles derived from domestic Lebanese practice.

It is unsurprising therefore, that in reiterating its commitment to apply and interpret Lebanese law as applied by Lebanese courts (without any discussion of the means and methods inherent in such an approach), the Chamber must

---

⁷⁵ Ibid para 19.
⁷⁶ Ibid para 20.
⁷⁷ Ibid paras 22 and 27.
⁷⁸ Ibid para 23.
⁷⁹ Ibid para 26.
⁸⁰ Ibid paras 28–29.
⁸¹ Ibid para 29.
⁸² Ibid para 30
⁸³ Ibid para 32.
⁸⁴ Ibid para 23, footnote 38.
⁸⁵ Ibid, see paras 17–24.

nevertheless interpret the Lebanese Criminal Code in light of international rules that are binding on Lebanon, since international law 'is part of the legal context in which its legislation is construed'.[86] So while international rules are not directly applicable before the Tribunal, the applicable law is to be interpreted in light of the international rules, and in particular customary international rules, binding on Lebanon. The import of this subtle distinction between interpretation and application effectively allowed the Appeals Chamber to entirely reconstruct the plain meaning of Article 2 of the Statute and to install principles of international law into the Statute via the back door.

As we saw in our discussion of the methodology followed by the ICTY Appeals Chamber in the *Tadić* case, legitimate judicial creativity proceeds on the basis of the identification of a gap or ambiguity in the law that must be resolved in the interests of justice. However, in this instance there was agreement amongst the parties that there was no ambiguity in Article 2 of the Statute as to the applicability of the international law. This was supported both by the drafting history and the Report of the Secretary-General. What's more, the opinion of the Chamber did not proceed on the basis of existing Lebanese law and practice but rather on the basis of reified *lex ferenda*. In this instance, the clear methodology extolled by the ICTY Appeals Chamber under the stewardship of Cassese was not followed by the STL. In short, the conclusion must be drawn that this was not judicial creativity, but rather judicial activism.

This activist ruling on the applicable law formed the basis for the Chamber's analysis in relation to category (ii) on the notion and definition of terrorism to be applied by the Tribunal. By determining that Article 2 of the Lebanese Criminal Code was to be interpreted in light of those rules of international law (customary and conventional) binding on Lebanon, the Chamber embarked on an investigation into the existence of an applicable customary definition of the crime of transnational terrorism. As Ben Saul details in Chapter 4, the manner in which this 'rule' was identified sharply illustrates the dangers of a malleable approach to custom identification highlighted in the previous section, and reinforces the plainly activist motivations behind this decision. This designation has been fully endorsed by various members of the interpretive community and the criticisms voiced are not likely to abate any time soon.[87] In attempting to discover a customary definition of the crime of terrorism by throwing all sense of judicial restraint out of the room, the Appeals Chamber may perhaps have been attempting to achieve a utopian ideal of the law, but without dwelling sufficiently on the reasons why utopias tend to be unattainable.

---

[86] Ibid paras 40–41.
[87] See for example M Gillett and M Schuster, 'Fast-track Justice: The Special Tribunal for Lebanon Defines Terrorism' (2011) 9 *JICJ* 989; S Kirsch and A Oehmichen, 'Judges Gone Astray: The Fabrication of Terrorism as an International Crime by the Special Tribunal for Lebanon' (2011) 1 *Durham L Rev* 32.

## B. The Perišić Case: Aiding and Abetting, Strict Liability, the De Facto Prohibition of the Waging of War and Curtailing the Responsibility to Protect[88]

The judicial utopianism that characterised the decision of the STL Appeals Chamber is also observable in the ICTY Trial Chamber Judgment in the *Perišić* case. The indictment against Momčilo Perišić charged him with, *inter alia*: aiding and abetting (pursuant to Article 7(1) of the Statute) a military campaign of artillery and mortar shelling and sniping of civilian areas of Sarajevo and upon its civilian population, killing and wounding thousands of civilians, and aiding and abetting crimes committed against the Bosnian Muslim population of Srebrenica.[89] It was alleged that, as Chief of the General Staff of the Yugoslav Army (VJ), Perišić knowingly aided and abetted the criminal acts committed in Sarajevo and Srebrenica by providing substantial assistance to the Army of the Republica Srpska (VRS). This substantial assistance was alleged to have taken the form of supplies of weapons and ammunitions and secondment of personnel, as well as the payment of salaries and benefits to top officers of the VRS, including the VRS Commander, General Ratko Mladić.[90] The prosecution argument essentially centred on the assertion that the assistance offered to the VRS by the VJ under Perišić's command had a substantial effect on the commission of well documented crimes in Sarajevo and Srebrenica. A Majority of the Trial Chamber, Presiding Judge Moloto dissenting, found him guilty on these grounds. The main issue for our purposes is the manner in which the Majority interpreted the objective and subjective elements of aiding and abetting as a mode of individual criminal responsibility, the import of which was to introduce a *de facto* strict liability standard into Article 7(1) of the Statute.

The Trial Chamber Majority construed the objective elements of aiding and abetting as consisting of 'acts or omissions directed at providing practical assistance, encouragement or moral support to the perpetration of the crime, which have a substantial effect on the perpetration of the crime'.[91] The Chamber added (relying entirely on the Appeals Chamber Judgment in *Prosecutor v Blagojević and Jokić*),[92] that '"specific direction" is not a requisite element of the *actus reus* of aiding

---

[88] The author is extremely grateful to Gregor Guy-Smith for his comments, guidance and assistance on this section. Similar arguments on these issues were raised on appeal.

[89] See *Prosecutor v Perišić* (Prosecution Filing of Revised Second Amended Indictment with Annex A) IT-04-81-PT (5 February 2008). See in particular Counts 1–4 and 9–12.

[90] Ibid. See also *Prosecutor v Perišić* (Summary of the Judgment in the Case of *Prosecutor v Momčilo Perišić*) IT-04-81-T (6 September 2011) <http://www.icty.org/x/cases/perisic/tjug/en/110906_summary.pdf> last accessed 10 January 2012.

[91] *Perišić* Trial Judgment (n 13) para 126.

[92] See *Prosecutor v Blagojević and Jokić* (Appeal Judgment) IT-02-60-A (9 May 2007) para 182. Contrary to the Trial Chamber's *prima facie* absolutist interpretation, the Appeals Chamber's determination on this point was more nuanced. While acknowledging that 'specific direction' was '*not always*' [emphasis added] considered as an additional express element of the *actus reus* of aiding and abetting, its relevance and validity as a determining

and abetting'.[93] In elaborating on the understanding to be given to 'substantial effect', the Majority determined that this element does not 'require that an accused provided the specific weapon used by the perpetrator [as it] may be established by numerous other forms of practical assistance ... which substantially facilitated the perpetrators' crimes'.[94] Furthermore, the Majority considered that there 'is neither a requirement of a cause-effect relationship between Perišić's conduct as an aider and abettor and the commission of the crimes, nor a requirement that his actions served as a condition precedent to the commission of the crimes, nor a requirement that his actions have been the cause *sine quo non* of the crimes'.[95]

Turning to the requisite subjective element of aiding and abetting, the Majority concluded that the applicable standard was 'knowledge that the acts performed assist the commission of the specific crime of the perpetrator'.[96] Included within this knowledge standard is an awareness on the part of the accused 'of the "essential elements" of the crime committed by the principal perpetrator, including the state of mind of the principal perpetrator'.[97] However, it is not required that the aider and abettor share the *mens rea* necessary for the commission of the crime in question. Indeed, relying on the *Furundžija* Trial Judgment, the Majority endorsed the interpretation that 'it is not necessary that the aider and abettor knows either the precise crime that was intended or the one that was, in the event, committed. If he is aware that one of a number of crimes will probably be committed, and one of those crimes was in fact committed, he has intended to facilitate the commission of that crime'.[98]

The major difficulty with this interpretation of Article 7(1) is that, by conveniently disregarding the centrality of the 'specifically directed' component of 'substantial effect' and by instituting a *mens rea* standard of basic knowledge or foreseeability,[99] the Majority were establishing a standard which placed unrealistic and arbitrary constraints on the waging of war and on the potentiality of states to intervene militarily in circumstances where the responsibility to protect comes into play. The assertion of the Majority was that, since the VRS were significantly dependent on the assistance offered by the VJ for their continued participation in hostilities, this was enough to infer substantial effect. An important clarification of this point is that its impact is specific to individuals in positions of high command in national armed forces who will frequently find themselves required to lend assistance in a variety of forms to the armed forces of a second state or indeed, and perhaps more likely, to non-state armed groups. Given the state of contemporary international

---

factor was 'implicit in the finding that the accused has provided practical assistance to the principal perpetrator which had a substantial effect on the commission of the crime'.

[93] *Perišić* Trial Judgment (n 13) para 126.
[94] Ibid para 1624.
[95] Ibid para 1626.
[96] Ibid para 129.
[97] Ibid para 129.
[98] Ibid para 130, citing *Prosecutor v Furundžija* (Trial Judgment) IT-95-17/1-T (10 December 1998) para 246.
[99] Ibid para 1646.

relations, this is a simple and unavoidable reality. Indeed, that very point was at the centre of Judge Molotov's dissenting opinion:

> If we are to accept the Majority's conclusion based solely on the finding of dependence, as it is *in case*, without requiring that such assistance be specifically directed to the assistance of crimes, then all military and political leaders, who on the basis of circumstantial evidence are found to provide logistical assistance to a foreign army dependent on such assistance, can meet the objective element of aiding and abetting. I respectfully hold that such an approach is manifestly inconsistent with the law.[100]

For Moloto, a distinction must be drawn 'between aiding and abetting in the present case and cases which have previously been decided by the Appeals Chamber, where the aider and abettor was either at, or proximate to, the crime scene. I contend that in cases of remoteness, the notion of specific direction must form an integral and *explicit* component of the objective element of aiding and abetting'.[101]

In ignoring the 'specifically directed' element of aiding and abetting – not on the basis of a customary international law interpretation, but rather on the basis of a qualified statement of the Appeals Chamber in *Blagojevic and Jokić*[102] – and by failing to read in a lesser standard of 'for the purposes of facilitating', as found in Article 25(3)(c) of the Rome Statute of the ICC, the Majority set in place a threshold approaching that of strict liability. This emergence of a strict liability standard is afforded further credence by the manner in which the Majority evaluated evidence relating to knowledge and substantial effect. In the absence of concrete evidence, the Majority relied on circumstantial evidence and drew inferences from Perišić's alleged knowledge of the criminal objectives of the VRS. Indeed, the approach of the Majority was such as to designate the VRS as a *de facto* criminal organisation. With this designation, for the Majority, any assistance offered to the VRS was of necessity to aid and abet in their criminal acts; in other words, to assist the VRS in the waging of war in the knowledge that a certain proportion of VRS staff were, had been or were likely to commit violations of international humanitarian law was to aid and abet those violations. As Judge Moloto argues:

> [t]he provision of assistance by Perišić to the VRS is too remote from the crimes committed during the war to qualify as aiding and abetting such crimes. To conclude otherwise, as the Majority has done, is to criminalize the waging of war, which is not a crime according to the Statute of the Tribunal. In addition, it raises the question: where is the cut-off line?[103]

---

[100] Ibid paras 32–33.
[101] Ibid para 10.
[102] See *Blagojević and Jokić* Appeal Judgment (n 92).
[103] *Perišić* Trial Judgment, dissenting opinion of Judge Moloto (n 13) para 3.

While the determination of the Majority might appear on its face to be solidly grounded and legitimate with respect to Perišić's actions, it is its implications for the future development of international criminal law that we are primarily concerned with. Were this standard to be adopted by the ICC – a not entirely inconceivable scenario – the consequences have the potential to be quite severe. Taking the recent Libyan conflict as a possible example, we can see how this might play out in practice. The facts of the 2011 Libyan conflict are common knowledge by this stage. In the context of international law, it will forever be associated with UN Security Council Resolution 1973's invocation of the emerging doctrine of the responsibility to protect as set out in the following terms:

> [The Security Council] *Authorizes* Member States that have notified the Secretary-General, acting nationally or through regional organizations or arrangements, and acting in cooperation with the Secretary-General, to take all necessary measures … to protect civilians and civilian populated areas under threat of attack in the Libyan Arab Jamihirya.[104]

As we can see the Security Council authorised states 'to take all necessary measures' to enforce the responsibility to protect and resulted in a the formation of a coalition of states (including, *inter alia*, the UK, France, United States and Canada) who were prepared to participate in an air campaign – in consultation and with the support of anti-Gaddafi armed forces – aimed at reducing the capacity of Gaddafi's forces to target and attack civilians. In addition to air support, it is now known that at least two states, France and the UK, offered additional assistance to rebel forces in the form of equipment, ammunition and training.[105]

By assisting in this way, states made the determination that the best way to enforce the responsibility to protect was to actively assist the rebel forces of the National Transitional Council (NTC) in their armed struggle against pro-Gaddafi forces. States made this determination in the knowledge that the NTC constituted an irregular non-state armed group which lacked a formalised chain of command and training in the proper conduct of hostilities. It was therefore foreseeable that

---

[104] UNSC Res 1973 (17 March 2011) para 4.

[105] See M Birnbaum, 'France Sent Arms to Libyan Rebels', *Washington Post* (30 June 2011) <http://www.washingtonpost.com/world/france-sent-arms-to-libyan-rebels/2011/06/29/AGcBxkqH_story.html> last accessed 10 January 2012; L Charbonneau and H Hassan, 'France Defends Arms Airlift to Libyan Rebels', *Reuters* (29 June 2011) <http://www.reuters.com/article/2011/06/29/us-libya-idUSTRE7270JP20110629> last accessed 10 January 2012; 'Libya Conflict: France Air-Dropped Arms to Rebels', *BBC News* (29 June 2011) <http://www.bbc.co.uk/news/world-africa-13955751> last accessed 10 January 2012; M Urban, 'Inside Story of the UK's Secret Mission to Beat Gaddafi', *BBC News, Newsnight* (19 January 2012) <http://www.bbc.co.uk/news/magazine-16573516> and video report here: <http://www.bbc.co.uk/news/world-africa-16624401> last accessed 20 January 2012; T Harding et al, 'Libya: SAS Leads Hunt for Gaddafi', *The Daily Telegraph* (24 August 2011) <http://www.telegraph.co.uk/news/worldnews/africaandindianocean/libya/8721291/Libya-SAS-leads-hunt-for-Gaddafi.html> last accessed 10 December 2011.

assistance offered to an armed group of this nature – namely one lacking in formal instruction with respect to the applicable rules of international humanitarian law – would likely contribute to, or have a substantial effect on, the potential future commission of war crimes and crimes against humanity.

Applying the standard adopted by the Majority to this scenario, if states provided assistance to the NTC with knowledge that that assistance may in some way be used to contribute to the commission of crimes, and such crimes were subsequently committed, then the military and political high command with authority to offer and provide such assistance would be subject to criminal sanction for aiding and abetting in the commission of crimes. This, regrettably, is not merely a hypothetical scenario, since it is now widely acknowledged that rebel forces under the command of the NTC frequently committed violations of international humanitarian and human rights law of such gravity as to warrant investigation by the Office of the Prosecutor of the ICC who became seized of the situation pursuant to UN Security Council Resolution 1970.[106] The implication, therefore, is that were the standard adopted by the Majority to be relied upon in subsequent prosecutions of NTC crimes, then there would certainly be reasonable grounds for instituting proceedings against the military and civilian high command of assisting states such as the UK and France. This potentiality serves to illustrate the absurd, uncertain and logically incoherent nature of the Majority's reasoning.

The facts surrounding the Libyan conflict are far from unique and it is certainly foreseeable that the international community will be called upon to make similar decisions with respect to the enforcement of the responsibility to protect in non-international armed conflicts. The practical reality is that should the

---

[106]  See for example Human Rights Watch (HRW), 'Libya: Protect Civilians in Sirte Fighting' (12 October 2011) <http://www.hrw.org/news/2011/10/12/libya-protect-civilians-sirte-fighting> last accessed 10 December 2011; HRW, 'Libya: Militias Terrorizing Residents of "Loyalist" Town' (30 October 2011) <http://www.hrw.org/news/2011/10/30/libya-militias-terrorizing-residents-loyalist-town> last accessed 10 December 2011; HRW, 'The Murder Brigades of Misrata' (28 October 2011) <http://www.hrw.org/news/2011/10/28/murder-brigades-misrata> last accessed 10 December 2011; HRW, 'Libya: Apparent Execution of 53 Gaddafi Supporters' (23 October 2011) <http://www.hrw.org/news/2011/10/24/libya-apparent-execution-53-gaddafi-supporters> last accessed 10 December 2011; HRW, 'Libya: Investigate Deaths of Gaddafi and Son' (22 October 2011) <http://www.hrw.org/news/2011/10/22/libya-investigate-deaths-gaddafi-and-son> last accessed 10 December 2011; HRW, 'Libya: Cease Arbitrary Arrests, Abuse of Detainees' (30 September 2011) <http://www.hrw.org/news/2011/09/30/libya-cease-arbitrary-arrests-abuse-detainees> last accessed 10 December 2011; Amnesty International (AI), 'Libya Urged to Investigate Whether Al-Gaddafi Death was a War Crime' (21 October 2011) <http://www.amnesty.org/en/for-media/press-releases/libya-urged-investigate-whether-al-gaddafi-death-was-war-crime-2011-10-21> last accessed 10 December 2011; AI, 'Libya Detention Abuses Staining the New Libya' (13 October 2011) <http://www.amnesty.org/en/library/info/MDE19/036/2011/en> last accessed 10 December 2011; AI, 'The Battle for Libya: Killings, Disappearances and Torture' (13 September 2011), specifically chapter 5 'Abuses by Opposition Forces' <http://www.amnesty.org/en/library/asset/MDE19/025/2011/en/8f2e1c49-8f43-46d3-917d-383c17d36377/mde190252011en.pdf> last accessed 10 December 2011.

Majority interpretation be adopted beyond the confines of the *Perišić* case, states will increasingly have to decide between the lesser of two potential evils when intervention is deemed absolutely necessary for the protection of civilians; either support and assist a party to a conflict fighting oppression who is known to be engaged in criminal acts, and risk criminal sanction for aiding and abetting, or ignore the moral and humanitarian imperative to intervene.

It is conceded that the activist import of the Majority's reasoning in this decision is not immediately obvious; however, on closer inspection it is clear that there are several significant deficiencies in the reasoning of the Majority to warrant significant cause for concern. In the absence of concrete evidence establishing the specifically directed nature of the assistance offered by Perišić, the Majority chose to ignore it as an element of substantial effect. In other words, the Majority compromised the integrity of the law to get the desired result, namely a conviction. The fact that their reasoning had the potential to undermine the certainty and predictability of the law relating to aiding and abetting was far from their thinking. It is difficult to avoid the sense that the reasoning of the Majority was undertaken not with a view to filling a perceived gap in the law, but rather to paper over the failings of the prosecution case which, from an objective viewpoint, should have sought to find Perišić liable for aiding and abetting a joint criminal enterprise and not as a aider and abettor to the principle perpetrators of the crimes. In so doing, the Majority distorted the law to the extent that it gave rise to the absurd conclusion that, should the standard adopted be taken up by other international courts and tribunals, the willingness of states to militarily intervene in support of a non-state armed group which may foreseeably commit crimes with the assistance offered will be significantly curtailed. We may dream of a day when the international community prohibits the waging of war. However, at this present moment the best we have are constraints on the conduct of hostilities. Unfortunately, the Majority's reasoning is at odds with this very clear reality.

# Conclusion

[I]t really tied the room together.[107]

This chapter set itself the profoundly ambitious task of not only delineating the boundaries of legitimate judicial creativity in the realm of international criminal law but also of pointing to indicators of a gradual decline in the quality of reasoning before international criminal courts and tribunals. Evidently, the former has been more successful than the latter; however, it is nevertheless maintained that indicators are there both in jurisprudence and doctrine[108] to support this contention. As has been discussed, international criminal law has been entangled in a long

---

[107] *The Big Lebowski* (n 1).
[108] To which this volume is a valuable addition.

running love affair with judicial creativity, the ultimate fruit of which has been the institution of a continuously evolving body of law. The question is how much longer we can expect this relationship to last before the spectre of judicial activism prises them apart. The answer lies in the interpretive community's commitment to the pillars of legality and the consistent and coherent identification of applicable norms of customary international law. It has been proposed that legitimacy is measured by method rather than exclusively by result. In the absence of a method couched in exhaustive reasoning and fidelity to legality and custom, the perception of legitimacy will not be maintained. This chapter discussed just two instances in which the line was clearly crossed from creativity to activism, but regrettably they are far from unique. The international criminal judiciary must continue to grapple with and contribute to what is a rapidly evolving legal order, however, in so doing they must not lose sight of the fact that the legitimate transformation of the 'ought' to the 'is' is entirely dependent on the quality and coherence of the reasoning they forward. There is no doubt that this can be achieved, all that is required is vigilance and a renewed commitment to the integrity and coherence of the judicial function.

# Equality of Arms in International Criminal Law: Continuing Challenges

## Charles Chernor Jalloh and Amy DiBella

Equality of arms is a key principle of the international criminal justice system. It encompasses many other procedural promises of a trial, such as the right to public hearings and the right of the defence to examine witnesses under the same conditions as those for prosecution. It is part of the overarching concern for fair trial which weighs into nearly every critical decision. Despite multiple judgments, decisions, briefs and scholarly articles stating the theoretical importance of equality of arms, its practical implementation is left in want. A vast disparity in resources between defence and prosecution has been well-documented in each of the ad hoc tribunals as well as in the permanent International Criminal Court (ICC).[1] With the exception of the Special Tribunal for Lebanon (STL), the structural position of the defence has been subordinated to the prosecution, as well as to Chambers and the Registry, in each of these courts.[2] The lobby outside of the ICC courtrooms bears symbolic testimony to this in the framed pictures of the Judges, the Registrar and Deputy Registrar alongside those of the Prosecutor and Deputy Prosecutor. The ICC does not appear to be exceptional in this as the ICTR lobby is similarly adorned with photographs of its principals without the defence.

Like the ICC and ICTR lobbies, international organisations such as the United Nations (UN) and many non-governmental organisations give the prosecution centre stage. Those groups offer additional support; they are on the ground liaising with victims and witnesses, in the media calling for an end to impunity, and often,

---

[1] See for example E Groulx, '"Equality of Arms": Challenges Confronting the Legal Profession in the Emerging International Criminal Justice System' (2006) 3 *Oxford University Comparative Law Forum* <http://ouclf.iuscomp.org/articles/groulx.shtml> last accessed 11 December 2011; JT Tuinstra, *Defence Counsel in International Criminal Law* (TMC Asser Press, The Hague 2009); RJ Wilson, '"Emaciated" Defense or a Trend to Independence and Equality of Arms in Internationalized Criminal Tribunals?' (2008) 15 *Human Rights Brief* 6.

[2] Groulx (n 1) (discussing the 'basic concept' of a third pillar).

prematurely pronouncing the guilt of the accused. At times, one wonders whether we need to subsequently hold trials at all.[3] In the words of the ICC Office of the Prosecutor, these groups and individuals, the so-called intermediaries, 'fulfill a critical role during investigations, they are individuals who facilitate contact between the Prosecution and a witness or any other source of information'.[4] These largely unregulated investigators further supplement the disparity of arms.

This chapter aims to evaluate certain aspects of the implementation of equality of arms in international criminal justice to date. After introducing and better defining the concept, the chapter delves into a discussion of one of the well-documented inequalities, that of investigative resources. Section II critically assesses the significance of the resource disparity in light of the prosecution's burden of proof. It also assesses the jurisprudence on the issue, bringing to light the courts' mechanisms or attempts for reframing the right to avoid violations. Section III considers whether the inequality of investigative resources is offset by the obligation that prosecutors investigate and disclose both incriminating and exculpatory evidence to the defence.

The rationale for making these two issues – investigative resources and disclosure obligations – the centre of an equality of arms analysis is twofold. First, framing the discussion in this way allows us to look at unique, misunderstood and often overlooked aspects of equality of arms. For instance, can disclosure obligations balance out the prosecutor's ability – and the defence's general inability – to secure state cooperation, procure witnesses, make statements to the international community and be represented in various international, national and NGO forums? The jurisprudence on the issue demonstrates how judges have redefined the concept of equality of arms to fit the unique circumstances of international criminal law.

Second, this focus provides a foundation for further discussion about seemingly simple mechanisms for maintaining, or perhaps more appropriately re-establishing, equality. By better enforcing disclosure obligations, for instance, international criminal courts may better discharge their responsibilities to give credible justice, ultimately providing greater protection for the fairness of the international criminal justice process and the rights of the accused.

## I. The Significance of Equality of Arms

According to the preamble to the Rome Statute, the State Parties thereto are determined 'to put an end to impunity for the perpetrators of these [most serious

---

[3] For other authors expressing similar sentiments, see for example, M Damaška, 'What is the Point of International Criminal Justice?' (2008) 83 *Chicago-Kent L Rev* 329, 356 (asserting that the 'silent assumption of guilt lurking under the surface' avoids embarrassing acquittals): '[I]t is only a short step from [this unspoken assumption] to a criminal justice system programmed to convict.'

[4] *Situation in the DRC: Prosecutor v Lubanga* (Prosecution Proposed Procedure for Dealing with Intermediaries) ICC-01/04-01/06 (19 March 2010) 3.

crimes of concern to the international community] and thus to contribute to the prevention of these crimes'.[5] The prosecution investigates crimes which are committed by powerful persons 'who heretofore have avoided justice by threats and intimidation and in territories where there are still significant tensions and difficulties to control violence'.[6] Thus, international criminal law aims to prosecute and convict those most responsible, in the hope of checking widespread impunity.[7]

However important the convictions may be to ending impunity, international law requires that fairness be at the foundation of prosecutions and trials. Since the Nuremberg Trials, it has been recognised that the defendants were entitled to ask for one thing: that they 'receive a fair trial on the facts and law'.[8] The Special Court for Sierra Leone (SCSL) mandate, as envisaged both by the Sierra Leonean government and the UN Security Council, was 'premised on the completion of fair trials in accordance with international standards of justice'.[9] The Rome Statute guarantees this fairness through its provisions that an accused is entitled to a public and fair hearing conducted impartially. It also promises a number of minimum guarantees, including the right to be informed promptly of the nature and cause of the charges, the right to adequate time and facilities for the defence, the right to be tried without undue delay, and the right to counsel.[10] Thus, in reaching its decisions and judgments, the ICC applies the Rome Statute and Rules of Procedure and Evidence[11] in a manner consistent with 'internationally recognized human rights'.[12]

If it were ever in doubt, scholars and practitioners also recognise fairness as central to justice. As Damaška suggests, one of the main purposes of international criminal law is to spread the human rights gospel,[13] not only in terms of adjudicating over

---

[5] Rome Statute of the International Criminal Court, 2187 UNTS 90, 17 July 1998, entered into force 1 July 2002, preambular paras 4–5 ('ICC Statute').

[6] *Lubanga* Prosecution Proposed Procedure for Dealing with Intermediaries (n 4) 3.

[7] HH Jeschek, 'International Criminal Law Set Out in Nuremberg, as Mirrored in the ICC Statute' (2004) 2 *JICJ* 38, 54; see also UN Secretary General, 'Activities of Secretary-General in Italy' (15 April 2002) Press Release SG/T/2320 (quoting the UN Secretary-General as stating that through the creation of the International Criminal Court, 'impunity has been dealt a decisive blow').

[8] Jeschek (n 7) 39–40 (citing 'Judgment of the International Military Tribunal (Nuremberg)' (1947) 41 *AJIL (supplement)* 172).

[9] W Jordash, 'Due Process and Fair Trial Rights at the Special Court: How the Desire for Accountability Outweighed the Demands of Justice at the Special Court for Sierra Leone' (2010) 23 *LJIL* 585, 585 and CC Jalloh, 'Special Court for Sierra Leone: Achieving Justice?' (2011) 32 *Michigan J Int'l L* 395, 400–444.

[10] ICC Statute art 67(1) (a)–(d).

[11] Ibid art 21(1)(a): 'The Court shall apply: In the first place, the Statute, Elements of Crimes and its Rules of Procedure and Evidence.'

[12] Ibid art 21(3): 'The application and interpretation of law pursuant to this article must be consistent with internationally recognized human rights, and be without any adverse distinction.' See also art 69(7).

[13] JT Tuinstra, 'The Role of Defence Counsel in International Criminal Trials; Defending the Defenders' (2010) 8 *JICJ* 463, 486 (citing M Damaška, 'Discussion' (2009) 7 *JICJ* 97, 105).

mass human rights violations, but also in securing the defendant's fair trial rights.[14] Zappalà underscores that safeguarding the rights of the accused is essential to the criminal trial.[15] He makes a compelling argument that respect for defence rights is necessary and central to justice:

> Respecting the rules to establish the truth requires full consistency with rights of the accused; these must be seen as an essential component of accurate and truthful fact finding on which punishment is premised ... there is no truth that can be reached without full respect of the rights of the accused.[16]

As affirmed by the Rome Statute and as restated by scholars,[17] the criminal tribunals must respect the international human rights standards, both in order to spread human rights, and to guarantee their legitimacy.

In accordance with international human rights standards, the Rome Statute enshrines guarantees of a fair investigation. For instance, Articles 69(4) and 69(7) of the Statute protect the accuracy and reliability of fact-finding.[18] According to Trial Chamber II, the seventh paragraph of Article 69 specifically safeguards the moral integrity and legitimacy of the proceedings by requiring a fair process of investigation.[19] Otherwise, as Prosecutor Jackson warned with regard to fairness at Nuremberg, 'to pass a poisoned chalice to the lips of the defendants is to pass it to our own'.[20]

Equality of arms is a central human rights norm, seen as a 'fundamental principle of the law',[21] and recognised by the UN Human Rights Committee as an implicit

---

[14] Damaška (n 3) 355 ('It would indeed be a disheartening irony if a justice system, designed to contribute to the protection of human rights, could properly function only by disregarding humanistic values rooted, *inter alia*, in the presumption of innocence').

[15] S Zappalà, 'Rights of the Accused' in A Cassese and others, *The Rome Statute of the International Criminal Court: A Commentary: Vol. II* (OUP, Oxford 2002) 1319.

[16] S Zappalà, 'The Rights of Victims v The Rights of the Accused' (2010) 8 *JICJ* 137, 135. The author also emphasised that the rights of the accused, whether termed minimum guarantees or not, are also crucial constitutive fact finding elements for a credible criminal justice system: 'If only one of these rights is violated, in only one aspect, in only one instance, the whole process loses credibility and is likely to fail in its objective of properly establishing the truth and of imposing just punishment. There is no truth outside the process.'

[17] In addition to previous quotes, see also, WA Schabas, 'Article 67' in O Triffterer (ed) *Commentary on the Rome Statute of the International Criminal Court: Observers' Notes, Article by Article* (2nd edn Hart, Oxford 2008) 1249 especially n 8.

[18] *Situation in the DRC: Prosecutor v Katanga and Chui* (Decision on the Prosecutor's Bar Table Motions) ICC-01/04-01/07 (17 December 2010) para 39.

[19] Ibid.

[20] Opening Statement of Justice Jackson, Chief Prosecutor for the United States, International Military Tribunal, Second Day, 21 November 1945.

[21] *Situation in the DRC: Prosecutor v Lubanga* (Decision on the Prosecutor's 'Application for Leave to Reply to "Conclusions de la défense en réponse au mémoire d'appel du Procureur"') ICC-01/04-01/06 (12 September 2006) para 6.

guarantee of the International Covenant on Civil and Political Rights (ICCPR).[22] Although most international criminal tribunals are not bound in their founding documents to guarantee equality of arms, the doctrine having been developed through case law, most have reaffirmed its pre-eminence.[23] According to the ICC Appeals Chamber, the principle is an indivisible element of fairness, an 'indispensable requisite of an adversarial trial' that 'permeates the entire judicial process'.[24] Scholars, too, emphasise equality of arms as a central tenet of international criminal law.[25] Despite the widespread agreement as to its centrality, somewhat surprisingly, there is no unified definition of what it means to guarantee a defendant equality of arms with the prosecution.

Perhaps partly as a result of its unclear meaning, equality of arms has long been a critical issue with which the courts constantly wrestle in order to ensure the fairest trial possible. Defendants rely on this principle in demanding new counsel, requesting additional resources and in many other circumstances. For instance, in the early stages of his trial, former Liberian President Charles Taylor invoked equality of arms in the SCSL:

> Justice is blind, justice pursues truth, justice is fair, justice is immune to politics. It is not justice to preordain convictions or emaciate my defence to the extent that I'm unable to launch an effective defence ... The Special Court's administration has been so dilatory that I have only one counsel to appear on my behalf, one counsel against a Prosecution team fully composed of nine lawyers. This is neither fair nor just ... It is therefore with great regret that I must decline to attend any further hearings in this case until adequate time and facilities are provided for my Defence team.[26]

---

[22] K Vanderpuye, 'Traditions in Conflict: The Internationalization of Confrontation' (2010) 43 *Cornell Intl L J* 513, 539 (listing UN Human Rights Committee Communications which affirm that under Article 14(1) of the ICCPR the guarantee of fair trial includes, as 'an indispensable aspect' and 'at a minimum', equality of arms).

[23] Tuinstra (n 1) 145 (noting, although the principle 'is not incorporated as such in the Statutes of international criminal courts or in international human rights treaties, it is widely acknowledged to be an element of the overall right to a fair trial'); see also *Lubanga* Decision on the Prosecutor's 'Application for Leave to Reply to "Conclusions de la défense en réponse au mémoire d'appel du Procureur"' (n 21) para 6 (noting equality of arms as having been 'repeatedly acknowledged and proclaimed by international courts and institutions established to monitor the application of human rights').

[24] *Lubanga* Decision on the Prosecutor's 'Application for Leave to Reply to "Conclusions de la défense en réponse au mémoire d'appel du Procureur"' (n 21) para 6.

[25] C Safferling, 'Equality of Arms' in A Cassese (ed) *The Oxford Companion to International Criminal Justice* (OUP, Oxford 2009) 311. Vanderpuye (n 22) 575.

[26] For example Wilson (n 1).

Faced with defence claims of inadequate resources as well as other budgetary challenges,[27] the courts are pressured to guarantee equality of arms in creative ways. In order to understand and analyse the judicial responses to such pressures, it is first necessary to appreciate the underlying purpose and possible meanings of the principle. As already noted, our discussion here considers equality of arms with regard to investigative resources. It considers the issue exclusively from the defence perspective, although it seems that the general jurisprudential position in international criminal law, at least as at now, is that the prosecution may also have claims to equality of arms.[28]

## II. Discerning the Meaning of Equality of Arms

Though it does not contain a definition of the phrase 'equality of arms', *Black's Law Dictionary* defines 'equality' as 'the quality or state of being equal; esp., likeness in power or political status'.[29] This definition is sufficient to capture the sense in which we use it here which is that equality of arms is deemed as a way to uphold the adversarial nature of criminal trials.[30] With the pictures hung in the lobbies, the hierarchy in the ICC, like that of the ICTR, ICTY and SCSL, appears to be established, and the achievement of a fair match between two apparently adversarial parties seems near impossible. In the midst of the structural inequality, the principle has devolved into a certain term of art, seemingly detached from its original definition and implying new things entirely.

For one thing, the concept evokes a broad consideration of fairness. Thus, rather than add meaning to the term, courts have largely removed from equality its substantive content or sense of likeness in power or status[31] and reverted to a more

---

[27] See S Bibas and WW Burke-White, 'International Idealism meets Domestic-Criminal-Procedure Realism' (2010) 59 *Duke L J* 637, 676–678 for an elaborate overview of funding difficulties at the international tribunals. See also 'US Embassy Cables: The Protracted Case against Charles Taylor' *The Guardian* (London 17 December 2010) <http://www.guardian.co.uk/world/us-embassy-cables-documents/202468> last accessed 11 December 2011 (citing to document of US embassy in The Hague 000247, 15 April 2009) (the summary: 'SCSL meets a key milestone, but faces uncertainty in terms of timing, finances, and completion issues' draws attention to the issue described with regard to the Taylor trial: 'Timing may be particularly important given expected funding shortfalls and the possible loss of courtroom space').

[28] See e.g. Tuinstra (n 1).

[29] 'Equality', *Black's Law Dictionary* (7th edn West, Minneapolis 1999).

[30] Tuinstra (n 1); see also *Lubanga* Decision on the Prosecutor's 'Application for Leave to Reply to "Conclusions de la défense en réponse au mémoire d'appel du Procureur"' (n 21) para 6.

[31] *Black's Law Dictionary* (n 29).

general, abstract promise of overall fairness.³² The ICTY Appeals Chamber noted it as 'only one feature of the wider concept of a fair trial'.³³ In that sense, equality of arms is not unlike the vague common law notion of due process.³⁴ As Schabas explains, the fundamentally important aspect of equality 'is that the parties, prosecution and defence, be treated equally and that the trial be fundamentally fair'.³⁵

This concept of fairness also defines equality as a 'procedural parity'³⁶ or 'procedural equality'.³⁷ As used here, the adjective 'procedural' is not intended to suggest that the promise is not substantive. On the contrary, such a distinction between procedural and substantive fairness confuses the meaning of the principle.³⁸ The SCSL thus clearly rejected the idea that equality of arms was merely a procedural right as it seems to be understood in international human rights law.³⁹ In international criminal procedure,

---

³² See, e.g., *Prosecutor v Gbao* (Decision on the Prosecution Motion for Immediate Protective Measures for Witnesses and Victims and for Non-Public Disclosure) SCSL-2003-09-PT (10 October 2003) para 48 (holding that, while equality of arms in international criminal law and at the SCSL is more than a mere procedural guarantee, it does not entail a 'strict equality in terms of means and resources' between the Prosecution and Defence).

³³ *Prosecutor v Kordić and Čerkez* (Decision on application by Mario Čerkez for extension of time to file his respondent's brief) IT-95-14/2-A (11 September 2011) para 5.

³⁴ The comparison is made in: MC Bassiouni, 'Human Rights in the Context of Criminal Justice: Identifying International Procedural Protections and Equivalent Protections in National Constitutions' (1993) 3 *Duke J of Comparative and Int'l L* 235, 278; M Fedorova, S Verhoeven and J Wouters, 'Safeguarding the Rights of Suspects and Accused Persons in International Criminal Proceedings' *Leuven Centre for Global Governance Studies* Working Paper No. 27 (June 2009) 17 (referring to equality of arms as 'an inherent element of due process').

³⁵ Schabas (n 17) 1265; this may be the same sentiment of the Prosecution team, nine-strong, facing the single defence attorney, at the early stages of the Taylor trial (see Wilson (n 1) 6).

³⁶ Vanderpuye (n 22) 513.

³⁷ See ibid at n 202 (citing *B. d. B. et al. v Netherlands* (1989) UN Doc Supp No. 40 (A/44/40) (30 March 1989)).

³⁸ See *Garza v United States*, Inter-American Commission of Human Rights, Report No. 52/01, Case 12.243 (4 April 2001) para 53. In that case, the US government argued that 'equality of arms protects procedural rather than substantive equality, and therefore the fact that the State may have more resources than a defendant-which, the State notes, it almost invariably does-cannot found a claim that a particular proceeding was not fair'. See also for similar arguments, ibid paras 56–57. To come to this conclusion, the United States relied on ICTY and UN Human Rights Committee case law, both of which include substantive rights, such as adequate time and facilities for a defence, within their conceptions of equality of arms.

³⁹ *Gbao* Decision on the Prosecution Motion for Immediate Protective Measures for Witnesses and Victims and for Non-Public Disclosure (n 32) para 49 (the SCSL 'is of the opinion that equality of arms before international criminal tribunals is more than a mere procedural equality, like it is for international human rights law').

procedural parity is fundamental to the adversarial battle[40] or *procedure contradictoire*.[41] Equality of arms, in this sense, means that parties enjoy rights of participation and equal access to the court.[42] The courtroom is a playing field, and the defendant and prosecution, teams entitled to both a fair match and the appearance of a fair match.[43] Though perhaps not surprising given that modern international criminal law is still a relatively new phenomenon, and therefore a somewhat primitive legal system, the record of the tribunals is stronger on the latter more than the former.

Like the phrase 'equality of arms', the concept of procedural parity lacks specificity; thus, the ICC and ad hoc tribunals attach a number of meanings to the terms.[44] Interestingly, some national constitutions include equality of arms and specifically incorporate within that right, 'a cluster of rights'.[45] In the first place, the defendant must receive information on both the charges and evidence against him.[46] Second, the defendant must have access to the procedural mechanisms which enable him to challenge the prosecution. That is, a defendant must know the charges, have access to the evidence and information used against him, as well as access to and an ability to call witnesses on his behalf.[47] The defendant's right also encompasses the disclosure regimes under which the prosecution must investigate and share with defence both exonerating and incriminatory evidence.[48] Third, the defendant must enjoy certain structural assets in conducting the investigation. For instance, defence counsel must

---

[40] Bassiouni (n 34) 275 (stating that equality of arms is 'fundamental to the adversarial nature of modern criminal proceedings').

[41] Vanderpuye (n 22) 513.

[42] Bassiouni (n 34) 277; Vanderpuye (n 22) 513.

[43] Tuinstra (n 1) 148.

[44] The Appeals Chamber at the ICTR affirmed that equality of arms includes the accused's entitlement to a 'fair and public hearing' as well as the 'minimum guarantees in full equality' (under Statute of the International Criminal Tribunal for Rwanda, UN Doc S/RES/955, UN Security Council, 1994 ('ICTR Statute'), art 20(4)) such as the right to a legal counsel and the right to have adequate time and facilities to prepare his or her defence. *Prosecutor v Kayishema and Ruzindana* (Appeals Chamber Judgment) ICTR-95-1-A (1 June 2001) para 67.

[45] Bassiouni (n 34) 278.

[46] Statute of the International Criminal Tribunal for the former Yugoslavia, UN Doc S/RES/827, UN Security Council, 1993 ('ICTY Statute') arts 20(2) and 21(4)(a); ICTR Statute, arts 19(2) and 20(4)(a); ICC Statute, arts 61(3)(a)–(b) and 67(1)(a); Statute of the Special Court for Sierra Leone, annexed to the Agreement between the United Nations and the Government of Sierra Leone on the Establishment of the Special Court for Sierra Leone, signed on 16 January 2002 ('SCSL Statute') art 17(4)(a); Statute of the Special Tribunal for Lebanon, UN Doc S/RES/1757, UN Security Council, 2007 ('STL Statute') arts 15(a) and 16(4)(a).

[47] ICTY Statute art 21(4)(e); ICTR Statute art 20(4)(e); ICC Statute art 67(1)(e); SCSL Statute art 17(4)(e); STL Statute art 16(4)(e).

[48] Rules of Procedure and Evidence of the International Criminal Tribunal for the former Yugoslavia, UN Doc IT/32/Rev.46 (20 October 2011) ('ICTY RPE') Rules 66–68; Rules of Procedure and Evidence of the International Criminal Tribunal for Rwanda, UN Doc ITR/3/Rev.20 (1 October 2009) ('ICTR RPE') Rules 66–68; Rules of Procedure and Evidence of the Special Court for Sierra Leone, as amended (28 May 2010) ('SCSL RPE') Rules 66–

have certain privileges and immunities that enable them to effectively perform their functions in defending their clients.[49]

Rather than elaborate on this long list of rights,[50] this discussion aims to distil aspects relevant to the considerations of investigative resources. Firstly, none of the above-listed rights is an absolute guarantee. Although the defendant's right to secure witnesses is an essential element of the equality principle,[51] the defendant does not have an absolute right to the attendance of a witness, but only the right to secure the attendance of a witness under the same conditions as witnesses against him.[52] Secondly, equality of arms seems to be a lofty goal that is applied feebly. Its terms suggest a just match-up, a likeness between the parties, as the ICC hopefully stated, a 'balance'.[53] As compared to the definition of equality given in *Black's Law Dictionary*, the meaning afforded to the term by its constitutive parts seems less solid and almost lackadaisical. The specific requirement of equality of arms seems to be that the defence has sufficient, adequate facilities and faces no 'substantive disadvantage'.[54] Accordingly, equality of arms 'requires that no substantial disadvantage exist between

---

68; Rules of Procedure and Evidence of the Special Tribunal for Lebanon, as amended (10 November 2010) ('STL RPE') Rules 110–113; ICC Statute arts 54(1)(a) and 67(2).

[49] ICTY Statute art 30; ICTR Statute art 29; SCSL Statute arts 12–14; STL Statute arts 10–13; ICC Statute art 48.

[50] Tuinstra (n 1) 154, provides the following list of guarantees which fall under equality of arms: 'that the accused is informed promptly of the charges against him, has adequate time and facilities to prepare his defence, has access to and is able to comment on the evidence against him, and has the right to secure "the attendance and examination of witnesses on his behalf under the same conditions as witnesses against him."' Bassiouni (n 34) 235, 278 also includes additional, or at least, differently worded, rights in stating that major human rights documents 'express equality of arms in conjunction with the rights of confrontation and compulsory process'. See also Vanderpuye (n 22) for support that confrontation is an aspect of equality of arms.

[51] W Schomburg, 'The Role of International Criminal Tribunals in Promoting Respect for Fair Trials' (2009) 8(1) *Northwestern J of Int'l Human Rights* 1, 62; see also Vanderpuye (n 22) 571 ('[Equality of arms] frames the right to examine as conferred by virtually all modern regional and multilateral treaties subscribing to fair trial rights').

[52] ICTY Statute art 21(4)(e); ICTR Statute art 20(4)(e); ICC Statute art 67(1)(e); SCSL Statute art 17(4)(e); STL Statute art 16(4)(e).

[53] *Situation in Uganda: Prosecutor v Kony et al* (Decision on Prosecutor's Application for Leave to Appeal in part Pre-Trial Chamber II's Decision on the Prosecutor's Applications for Warrants of Arrest under Article 58) ICC-02/04-01/05 (19 August 2005) para 30; see also *Situation in the DRC: Prosecutor v Lubanga* (Décision sur la demande d'autorisation d'appel de la Défense relative à la transmission des Demandes de Participation des Victimes) ICC-01/04-01/06 (6 November 2006) 6 (noting, 'ATTENDU par ailleurs, que les critères d'appréciation de l'égalité des armes tiennent aux circonstances de l'affaire et à la situation de fait à l'origine de la saisine de la Chambre').

[54] Tuinstra (n 13) 466 (noting 'that a defence lawyer has sufficient and adequate facilities to do so and will not be at a substantive disadvantage in the proceedings vis-à-vis the prosecution. He should be able to present his case to the judges on an equal basis as the prosecution').

one party and another when presenting his or her case in court'.⁵⁵ Thus, equality is in a way construed as a negative, rather than a positive right, a sort of floor that implies that there is a minimal guarantee of adequate and sufficient time and resources to present one's defence.

The ICC Pre-Trial Chamber II enunciated this view when it explained equality as the right of a 'party to a proceeding to *adequately* make its case, with a view to influencing the outcome of the proceedings in its favor'.⁵⁶ In giving meaning to the guarantee, another Chamber considered that 'an effective and meaningful application of the principle of *audi alteram partem* requires that the responding party has *sufficient* time to prepare its response'.⁵⁷ Although it is termed a guarantee of procedural 'equality' in the courtroom, this principle is often reduced to something less. It is a promise that neither party will be significantly unequal.

Thirdly, many of these rights address the guarantee of a public trial. Since Nuremberg,⁵⁸ the trial has come to serve as the 'centrepiece' of the international criminal proceedings.⁵⁹ Defence counsel at the ICC, as others elsewhere, have emphasised the importance of public trials as part of the equality of arms discussions.⁶⁰ They find support in the work of human rights bodies. For instance, according to the UN Human Rights Committee, equality of arms must be understood as an aspect of the right to be heard; it is 'one of the features of the wider concept of a fair trial' under which 'each party must be afforded a reasonable opportunity to present his case under conditions that do not place him at a disadvantage vis-à-vis his opponent'.⁶¹ Thus, in discussing

---

[55] K Yesberg, 'Accessing Justice through Victim Participation at the Khmer Rouge Tribunal' (2009) 40 *Victoria University of Wellington L Rev* 555, 575–577.

[56] *Kony* Decision on Prosecutor's Application for leave to Appeal in part Pre-Trial Chamber II's Decision on the Prosecutor's Applications for Warrants of Arrest under Article 58 (n 53) (emphasis added). See also, *Lubanga* Décision sur la demande d'autorisation d'appel de la Défense relative à la transmission des Demandes de Participation des Victimes (n 53) 6.

[57] *Situation in the DRC: Prosecutor v Katanga and Chui* (Decision on the 'Prosecution's Application Concerning Disclosure Pursuant to Rules 78 and 79(4)') ICC-01/04-01/07 (14 September 2010) para 37 (emphasis added).

[58] O Pannenbecker, 'The Nuremberg War-Crimes Trial' (1965) 14 *DePaul L Rev* 348, 352 ('for clarifying important questions of the trial, it was necessary for the witnesses to appear personally before the court so that they could be cross-examined by the opposite party').

[59] On the preference for orality, see K Ambos, 'International Criminal Procedure: "Adversarial", "Inquisitorial" or Mixed?' (2003) 3 *ICLR* 1, 3; Vanderpuye (n 22) 549; S Kendall and M Staggs, 'Interim Report on the Special Court for Sierra Leone' *Berkeley War Crimes Center* (April 2005) 30; E O'Sullivan and D Montgomery, 'The Erosion of the Right to Confrontation under the Cloak of Fairness at the ICTY' (2010) 8 *JICJ* 511, 514; Tuinstra (n 1) 172.

[60] XJ Keïta and C Fourçans, 'Article 67 (1)- Droits de l'accusé' in S Sur and E Decaux (eds) *Commentaire critique du statut de Rome de la Cour pénale internationale* (Pedone, Paris 2011) 2 (citing *Situation in the DRC: Prosecutor v Lubanga* (Transcript) ICC-01/04-01/06-T-109-FRA (27 January 2009) 20 and *Situation in the DRC: Prosecutor v Katanga and Chui* (Defence Request with Regard to Private Session Hearings) 01/04-01/07 (1 June 2010)).

[61] Vanderpuye (n 22) 539 footnote 200 (citing *Bulut v Austria* (App No 17358/90) 5 EHRR 169 para 47).

equality of arms, courts and scholars generally agree that equality of arms is closely linked to the rights attendant to an impartial and public trial.

The final relevant aspect of these promises is that the equality of arms is not only a trial right but also a more expansive entitlement within the structure of the criminal justice system. Numerous debates in international criminal law[62] have led to the conclusion that the protection of equality of arms can be achieved only through offering the defence institutional or structural independence within the Court.[63] According to a report of the Secretary-General, 'the need for a defence office to protect the rights of suspects and accused ... has evolved in the practice of the UN-based tribunals as part of the need to ensure "equality of arms"'.[64] An International Criminal Defence Attorneys Association proposal to include a defence office in the Rome Statute was apparently ignored.[65] It was not until later, with the support of influential states, that the need for an office was recognised and, thus, incorporated via the Regulations of the Court.[66] Such offices are becoming more common, as several of the tribunals, especially the newer ones such as the SCSL, are providing offices[67] and in one instance, an organ, on equal footing with the prosecution,[68] dedicated to safeguarding defence rights throughout the proceedings.[69] The recognition of this 'right', if followed by the routine inclusion of a defence organ in the tribunals and

---

[62] The Rome conference debate over the creation of a defence office was not fruitful: Groulx (n 1) n 35 and accompanying text.

[63] For an overview of the debate and the need for supporting the defence office, see Fedorova et al (n 34) 14–15; VO Nmehielle, Position Paper on the Independence of the Office of the Principal Defender at the Special Court for Sierra Leone (on file with the authors) (submitted to the Management Committee of the SCSL by Vincent O. Nmehielle, Principal Defender) and Jalloh (n 9) 438–439 (arguing that the Defence Office could have enhanced the realisation of the rights of the accused in the SCSL if it enjoyed full independence and autonomy from the Registrar).

[64] UN SC, *Report of the Secretary-General on the Establishment of a Special Tribunal for Lebanon*, UN Doc S/2006/893 (15 November 2006) para 30.

[65] Groulx (n 1) Section III: 'History and involvement of the legal profession in the institution-building process'.

[66] Ibid; ICC, 'Regulations of the Court' ICC-BD/01-01-04 (26 May 2004) Regulation 77 provides, *inter alia*, that the Registrar shall establish the OPCD and that its responsibility 'shall include representing and protecting the rights of the defence during the initial stages of the investigation', and also 'provid[ing] support and assistance to defence counsel and to the person entitled to legal assistance, including where appropriate: (a) [l]egal research and advice; and (b) [a]ppearing before a Chamber in respect of specific issues'.

[67] See SCSL RPE Rule 45 which created the Office of the Principal Defender and ICC Regulations of the Court (n 66) Regulation 77.

[68] UN SC (n 64) para 30; STL Statute art 7 (under which the Defence Office is listed as one of the organs of the Special Tribunal).

[69] See Vanderpuye (n 22) 572; Groulx (n 1) Section IV: 'ICC Legal Community as Part of Institution-Building' for elaboration of the type of institutional support and coordination provided by independent defence bodies. Although this section does not elaborate specific functions of the defence offices at the tribunals, its discussion of the criminal bar's role in assisting defence teams is indicative.

backed up with sufficient resources, is a significant institutional advancement in the protection of equality of arms over the past decade.[70]

Through the establishment of defence offices, international criminal law has recognised a key structural or institutional aspect of equality of arms. To date, as already observed, the substantive meaning of equality appears to be removed from the principle, as courts revert to basic concepts of fairness and guarantees of sufficient or adequate resources rather than offer actual parity with the prosecution. The general expectation appears to be that by obtaining representation at the institutional table, such offices may in turn contribute to rebalancing the substantive trial inequalities that currently exist.[71] Through coordinated campaigns to restore the adversarial confrontation or fair match in the courtroom, the defence offices may further the development of the cluster of procedural promises. Besides putting the Defence on the map within and outside the tribunals, the defence offices' 'institutional memory' becomes an invaluable resource to defence teams as contracting counsel comes and goes.[72] They provide a platform for defence advocacy which could spur progress towards a more substantive meaning to the equality of arms and the spread of the gospel of human rights.

The next part of this chapter attempts to locate the precise injustices arising out of inequalities in investigative resources. A review of the relevant jurisprudence will critically analyse whether modern international criminal procedure guarantees equality or adequacy, parity or sufficiency.[73] Ultimately, by clarifying the roots of the

---

[70] Recall that in the ICTY and ICTR, defence and prosecution are structurally imbalanced as defence counsel does not benefit from centralised offices: Groulx (n 1) text to n 32–36. Note also that the development of this right has been gradual. At the ICC, before the Regulations of the Court were adopted to create the Office of Public Counsel for the Defence, the Rules of Procedure and Evidence were adopted to recognise the importance of structural independence of defence counsel: ICC RPE Rules 20–22. See also CC Jalloh, 'The Contribution of the Special Court for Sierra Leone to the Development of International Law' (2007) 15 *African J Int'l and Comparative L* 165, 180 and Jalloh (n 9) 444. Cf *Prosecutor v Brima et al* (Decision on Brima-Kamara Defence Appeal Motion against Trial Chamber II Majority Decision on Extremely Urgent Confidential Joint Motion for the Re-Appointment of Kevin Metzger and Wilbert Harris as Lead Counsel for Alex Tamba Brima and Brima Bazzy Kamara) SCSL-2004-16-AR73 (8 December 2005) paras 82–84 (inferring that no organ carries responsibility for ensuring the rights of the Accused, but rather, it must be 'a common duty shared by the three organs').

[71] See Kendall and Staggs (n 59) 15 (noting that ensuring equality of arms and fair trials are the main functions of the Defence Office at the SCSL).

[72] ICC, 'Office of Public Counsel for the Defence' (11 April 2011) <http://www.icc-cpi.int/menus/icc/structure%20of%20the%20court/defence/office%20of%20public%20counsel%20for%20the%20defence/the%20office%20of%20public%20counsel%20for%20the%20defence?lan=en-GB> last accessed 14 December 2011.

[73] See Bassiouni (n 34) 253 ('the only way to determine the extent to which each of the articulated rights is actually protected is to scrutinize the actual practices of criminal law enforcement on the streets, police stations, jails, and courts of a given country, and the degree of judicial control over transgressions').

imbalanced investigative resources, we hope to shed light on often overlooked and basic legal remedies for such injustices based on the principle of equality of arms.

## III. Inequality of Resources

This chapter starts from the premise that equality of arms often devolves into an issue of resources. Our discussion focuses primarily on *investigative resources*, which we define as *assets which improve the functioning capacity to search for, find and procure information and sources relating to the criminal charges against this defendant*. Better funding, for instance, might improve the ability of the defence to hire a well-trained team of lawyers, legal assistants, case managers, investigators and translators who are better able to find information related to a particular defendant's trial.

Money is the asset most often at the centre of the discussion. But this definition also includes other unique assets which cannot, at least ethically, be secured by more funds. Subpoena powers,[74] the attention and support of the UN Security Council,[75] support from NGOs,[76] and cooperation from local governments[77] are just

---

[74] See *Garza v United States* (n 38) para 55 (in which the defendant argued that he, unlike the State, lacked power to subpoena witnesses located in Mexico; the State responded that it did have a treaty with Mexico which does enhance its ability to collect evidence, but 'in no way restrains the defense from challenging that evidence or presenting his own').

[75] Consider for instance the lectures at the 19th diplomatic briefing of the ICC; the President, Prosecutor and Registrar each gave statements. As compared to the Prosecutor who was given the floor to address its own needs and concerns, the Registrar advocated for defence concerns. Her interests are undoubtedly conflicted as she must also use the platform to advocate for victims and state cooperation. L Moreno-Ocampo, 'Statement at the 19th Diplomatic Briefing' (3 November 2010) and S Arbia, 'Remarks to the 19th Diplomatic Briefing' (3 November 2010). Consider also that the Prosecutor is in regular communication with the Security Council, providing briefings on situations and asking for support. UN General Assembly, *Report of the International Criminal Court* UN Doc A/65/313 (19 August 2010) paras 96–97.

[76] In considering the role of NGOs supporting the work of the ICC, informed discussions revolve around cooperation particularly with regard to the Prosecutor. Human Rights First, 'The Role of Human Rights NGOs in Relation to ICC Investigations', Discussion Paper (September 2004) <http://www.amicc.org/docs/Human%20Rights%20First%20NGO_Role_Discussion_Paper.pdf> last accessed 11 April 2011. *See also Prosecutor v Hadžihasanović and Kabura* (Decision on joint defence application for certification of decision on access to EUMM archives of 12 September 2003) IT-01-47-PT (25 September 2003) as cited in Tuinstra (n 1) 170 (commenting that international organisations have denied defence proper access to documents in the ICTY).

[77] *Prosecutor v Kayishema and Ruzindana* (Appeals Judgment) (n 44) para 72 (in which the defendant challenged equality of arms on the basis that Defence Counsel could not investigate on the ground to verify the technical and material data asserted by the Prosecution. In that instance, the Appeals Chamber upheld the Trial Chamber's findings that Defence Counsel failed to demonstrate that he was *unable* to visit Rwanda, especially in

a few examples. Some of these resources are outside the control of tribunal judges.[78] And some are inherent virtues of the Prosecutor's attractive position as the court's 'public face'.[79] Regardless of where the blame lies for inequalities in these types of resources, the gospel of human rights might require courts to provide remedies in order to guarantee fair matches.[80]

Moreover, the court may be implicated by the inequality. For instance, the court itself does not give the Prosecutor the UN Security Council audience. Rather, states give the Prosecutor this asset. In the case of the twin ad hoc tribunals, ICTY/R, the UN is the very body which established the courts and their jurisdiction. In that sense, it may not be the courts giving these resources to the prosecution but the (state or institutional) founders of the courts themselves. The UN Prosecutors have legitimate reasons for being granted this audience, for instance, their institutional functions such as reporting on the tribunal's activities and requesting state cooperation and support for arrests and investigations. However, insofar as the prosecutors have this institutional role, which in some respects becomes an advertising tool at their disposal, defence offices are generally overlooked. The defence could enjoy such a forum to make pleas for provisional release and acquittal arrangements and to (tactfully) publicise persistent non-cooperation by certain states with the defence teams. But they do not have such status. That said, the point should not be overstated as this again is at least partly a function of their roles in the system of international criminal justice as independent contractors working only to advance the interests of their clients.

We assert here that, in addition to being fundamental to the adversarial process inside the courtroom, equality of arms is particularly important – and must be guarded more fervently – at the investigative stages of the justice process. The unfairness of this resource inequality has been heavily debated. We will analyse the underlying arguments about the legitimacy of the prosecution's overwhelming resources, in particular in light of the prosecution's burden. Perhaps the Prosecution's burden to prove a case beyond a reasonable doubt necessarily contemplates that it will enjoy greater resources. This would, in general, not be

---

light of the fact that investigators, paid for by the ICTR, were at the disposal of the Defence and Trial Chamber).

[78] Ibid para 73. ('The Appeals Chamber concurs with ICTY Appeals Chamber's position expressed in *Tadić*, that the principle of equality of arms does not apply to "conditions, outside the control of a court," that prevented a party from securing the attendance of certain witnesses. Consequently, the Appeals Chamber dismisses Kayishema's claim that problems encountered in locating and contacting potential witnesses allegedly constitutes an error in fact and in law under Article 20 of the Statute'.)

[79] S Cviic, 'Profile: Luis Moreno Ocampo' *BBC News* (London 21 April 2003) <http://news.bbc.co.uk/2/hi/2965263.stm> last accessed 12 December 2012 (referring to Luis Moreno Ocampo as the 'ICC's public face').

[80] One author suggests that judges could compensate the defence for state non-cooperation by excluding prosecution evidence gained through state cooperation. That author predicts that the ICC is prepared to offer compensation to defence when authorities refuse to cooperate. Tuinstra (n 1) 167-171.

different from mature criminal justice systems at the national level wherein prosecutors generally have better investigative resources compared to public defenders. As will be demonstrated, despite the court's lack of direct responsibility for some of these imbalances, it may still hold responsibility for providing defence remedies for inequalities – especially where those affect the substantive fairness of the trials and ultimate outcome of the proceedings.

## A. Structural and Resource Inequalities Exist

To begin, the prosecution and defence at international courts do generally enjoy very different investigative resources. Despite theoretical promises of parity, '[p]ractice, particularly at the ad hoc tribunals, has taught that the reality of international trials, like their domestic counterparts, do not always live up to normative notions of equality'.[81] It is not just a slight inequality but a significant difference in the investigative resources available that lead defence lawyers to complain of the 'inequality in strength' between the parties.[82] The inequality is historically rooted, and goes back to the disparities between the prosecution and defence at the Nuremberg trials. One of the two defence spokespersons at those trials, Otto Kranzbühler, drew attention to the historical tradition of equality and how it was failed at the military tribunals.[83] Kranzbühler stated that the Anglo-American procedure was particularly well-suited for political trials, subject to the requirement of equality of arms.[84] He argued that this 'was not the case at Nuremberg'.[85]

In his view, the scales of justice at Nuremberg were tipped in favour of the Prosecution. For example, whereas the prosecution had multiple investigators to search through the German archives for documentary evidence for use in the trials, defence counsel were barred from the archives and could search through only those documents which the prosecution introduced into evidence.[86] During the investigation stages, defence counsel were barred from accessing the archives which would form the foundation of the prosecution case and were thus unable to investigate.[87] According to Kranzbühler, investigations are always pertinent for the defence, and particularly so in historical trials.[88] Unfortunately, such concerns remain a mystery in the private archives of that tribunal as many important procedural matters were discussed *in camera*, and thus, are not on any public court record.[89]

---

[81] Vanderpuye (n 22) 572.
[82] *Prosecutor v Milošević* (Decision in relation to severance, extension of time and rest) IT-02-54-T (12 December 2005) para 13.
[83] O Kranzbühler, 'Nuremberg Eighteen Years Afterwards' (1965) 14 *DePaul L Rev* 333, 345.
[84] Ibid 333, 336.
[85] Ibid.
[86] Ibid.
[87] Ibid.
[88] Ibid.
[89] Ibid 345.

International criminal law continues to be a field of historical and political trials; thus the concern for defence resources at the early stages remains pertinent. The historically rooted issues reflect the type of unequal attention and support offered to the parties from different international actors in modern international criminal law. Consider the structural and resource inequality at the East Timor war crimes panels: the UN directly funded the tribunal's prosecutor, while the 'impoverished'[90] local government had to fund the defence.[91] Or consider the hybrid chamber in the national courts of Bosnia, where the defence received payment only for in-court hours, and absolutely no remuneration for investigation.[92] Shortcomings in defence resources at the SCSL are apparently a reflection of the general insufficiency of donor funding.[93] However, this excuse does not adequately explain why, with the notable exception of the *Taylor* case, the Defence appears to have received such disproportionately lower means and resources than the Prosecution.[94] Indeed, although it cannot be said that they did not face their share of challenges, it may be a testament of the significance of having access to better investigative resources that the legal team defending the former Liberian president mounted probably the best courtroom defence ever seen in the history of the Sierra Leone tribunal's trials.

These disparities in prosecution and defence funding are problematic, and often lead to 'significant disparities'.[95] In the East Timor tribunal, where the 'impoverished East Timorese government funded the defence'[96] as noted above, Bibas and Burke-White claim that inadequate funding partially explains why defence counsel in that court did not call any witnesses during the first two years of trials.[97] Indeed, there were only six public defenders to cover cases during most of 2001; and in regards to the available resources, they were allocated such that one defence lawyer would be assigned to multiple defendants in the same trial.[98]

These are budgetary issues for indigent defendants, defendants who depend on the courts to protect their rights and interests. By comparing the resources of private versus court-funded defence cases, the actual discrepancy between what is

---

[90] Bibas and Burke-White (n 27) 679.

[91] See UNSC Res 1272 (25 October 1999) UN Doc S/RES/1272; ibid, and see also WW Burke-White, 'A Community of Courts: Toward A System of International Criminal Law Enforcement' (2003) 24 *Mich J Int'l L* 1, 70 (explaining that the actual UN mandate offered in Security Council Resolution 1272 provided for this funding structure).

[92] Bibas and Burke-White (n 27) 679.

[93] Human Rights Watch, 'Bringing Justice: The Special Court for Sierra Leone; Accomplishments, Shortcomings, and Needed Support' (2004) 6 <http://www.hrw.org/en/reports/2004/09/07/bringing-justice-special-court-sierra-leone> last accessed 11 December 2011.

[94] See ibid for descriptions of material inequalities which result from the lack of donor funding (noting that 'the extent of disproportionate allocation of such resources at the Special Court could contribute to a perception that trials are unfair and that equality of arms is not upheld').

[95] Burke-White (n 91) 70.

[96] Bibas and Burke-White (n 27) 679.

[97] Ibid.

[98] Burke-White (n 91) 70.

needed and provided to each side is revealed. Based on the filings of one privately funded defence team at the ICTY, it appears that a defendant apparently used four defence lawyers on his team.[99] On the other hand, Sesay's counsel, Wayne Jordash, at the SCSL, was only assisted by one co-counsel.[100] The inequality in the courtroom was stark; according to Jordash, he was facing about seven Prosecution lawyers at a time.[101]

Admittedly, comparing the number of lawyers on a case is perhaps only a loose indicator of inequality. However, it is a visible means by which the public may perceive the differing arms of the sides. It further raises concerns given the reality that the lawyers assigned to the case work essentially to either prosecute or defend against the same charges covering the same crime bases, and often, the same or similar numbers of witnesses in addition to evidentiary material. It may not therefore be a stretch to conclude that, with less hands on deck to wade through disclosure, to prepare written motions, present oral arguments in court and oversee defence investigators in relation to the criminal charges, qualified and competent defence counsel may, through no fault of their own, prove to be relatively less effective in presenting their cases than their (adversarial) counterparts in the prosecution.

In light of the high number of persons employed by the Prosecutor's investigation division at the ICTR (120),[102] it is no surprise that defence counsel at that tribunal have complained of similar inequalities. One defence team submitted a motion for full equality in the form of the number of assistants to the prosecution and defence.[103] The motion requested the court to 'order the disclosure of the number of lawyers, consultants, assistants and investigators that had been at the disposal of the Prosecution since the beginning of the case'.[104] The team requested the Chamber 'to restrict the number of assistants utilised by the Prosecution during trial to the same number as those authorised for the Defence'.[105]

---

[99] *Prosecutor v Haradinaj et al* (Decision on Prosecution's Urgent Application for Authorisation to Exceed Page Limit for Responses) IT-04-84-PT (5 May 2005).

[100] *Prosecutor v Sesay et al* (Decision on the Sesay Defence Team's Application for Judicial Review of the Registrar's Refusal to Provide Additional Funds for an Additional Counsel as Part of the Implementation of the Arbitration Agreement of the 26th of April 2007) SCSL-04-15-T (12 February 2008) para 37.

[101] Ibid.

[102] UNGA and UNSC, 'Sixth Annual Report of the International Criminal Tribunal for the Prosecution of Persons Responsible for Genocide and Other Serious Violations of International Humanitarian Law Committed in the Territory of Rwanda and Rwandan Citizens Responsible for Genocide and Other Such Violations Committed in the Territory of Neighbouring States between 1 January and 31 December 1994, For the Period of 1 July 2000 to 30 June 2001' UN Doc A/56/351 and UN Doc S/2001/863 (14 September 2001) para 104; see also Tuinstra (n 1) 154.

[103] *Prosecutor v Kayishema and Ruzindana* (Trial Chamber Judgment and Sentence) ICTR-95-1-T (21 May 1999) para 56.

[104] Ibid.

[105] Ibid.

The inequality of arms is striking in courtroom processes as well, and may reflect the inequality of investigative resources. Before the Appeals Chamber decision on the issue, the ICTY Trial Chamber in *Orić* limited the defence to 30 witnesses, as compared to the prosecution's 50.[106] There have been some disputes about the number of witnesses and the amount of time allotted to defence at the tribunals. All of them appear to draw attention to the defence perception that it faces a significant disadvantage vis-à-vis the prosecution.[107] At the ICTR, defendant Kanyabashi compared himself to the Prosecution on his case, which, according to his account, had never been forced to reduce the number of its witnesses and reserved its right to review the witness list throughout trial.[108] His repeated arguments for equality of arms understood as the ability to call more witnesses were unsuccessful.[109] The number of witnesses allowed to each side may be an indication of inequality, although depending on the chamber and group of judges involved, it appears that the tribunals have over time improved their records by guaranteeing a certain proportionality of witnesses and time to ensure a general level of fair play as between the two sides.[110]

Structural inequality may be engrained in the international criminal justice structure. One author argues that 'great institutional disparity' is an inherent feature of the ICC 'distribution of power contemplated by the respective organic statutes of international courts'.[111] Amidst the courts' adversarial systems, it may be that the Statute and the Rules of Procedure and Evidence fail to offer the necessary tools

---

[106] *Prosecutor v Orić* (Interlocutory decision on length of defence case) IT-03-68-AR73.2 (20 July 2005) para 9 (stating the question as whether 'the amount of time and the number of witnesses allocated to Orić's defense are reasonably proportionally to the Prosecution's allocation and sufficient to permit Orić a fair opportunity to present his case' and finding that 'Given the complexity of the issues at stake, particularly regarding military necessity, such disproportion cannot be justified').

[107] *Prosecutor v Milosević* (Decision in relation to severance, extension of time and rest) (n 82) paras 19, 24; UN Human Rights Committee, *Larranaga v The Phillipines* UN Doc CCPR/C/87/D/1421/2005 (14 September 2006) para 7.7 (noting defendant's cross-examination of main prosecution witness was repeatedly cut short to avoid the possibility of harm to the witness, and that the trial judge refused to hear a number of defence witnesses without substantial justification as the judge merely noted time constraints and that the evidence was 'irrelevant and immaterial'. The Committee stated that in light of the seriousness of the charges, the trial court's refusal to hear the remaining defence witnesses, while not similarly restricting the number of prosecution witnesses, violated article 14 of the ICCPR); *Prosecutor v Orić* (Interlocutory decision on length of defence case) (n 106) para 9.

[108] *Prosecutor v Ndayambaje et al* (Decision on Joseph Kanyabashi's Appeal against the Decision of Trial Chamber II of 21 March 2007 concerning the Dismissal of Motions to Vary his Witness List) ICTR-98-42-AR73 (21 August 2007) para 25.

[109] Ibid para 26 (finding that the Appellant 'failed to demonstrate any infringement of the principle of equality of arms in his case' and accordingly dismissed his contention).

[110] *Prosecutor v Orić* (Interlocutory decision on length of defence case) (n 106) para 9.

[111] Vanderpuye (n 22) 572.

and rights to effectively gather evidence.[112] The defence complaints and requests for longer witness lists may reflect that the defence has greater difficulty than the prosecution in obtaining evidence.[113] Thus, the seemingly innocuous courtroom disparities may in fact reflect disparities in investigative resources, inequalities engrained in the very organic structure of the courts.

Similarly, the defence's ability to enter countries to obtain witnesses and evidence was obscured at the start in some of these courts. Some defence counsel, at the ICTR for example, have been denied entry to Rwanda, and after receiving visas, were subsequently harassed, arrested and jailed by Rwandan authorities. It took the intervention of the ICTR Appeals Chamber to secure their release. Regrettably, the original documents of ICTY, ICTR and ICC neglected to accord defence lawyers the same privileges and immunities to allow counsel to investigate in the country at issue.[114] The ICC has supplemented its system by adopting an agreement on privileges and immunities.[115] One scholar suggests immunities at the UN tribunals could protect the Prosecution from being sent to disciplinary proceedings in front of national ethics boards;[116] practice has shown that defence enjoy no such immunity.[117]

Structural inequalities may be exacerbated by the political nature of the situation and the politicisation of the charges against the accused. A failure of states to cooperate may hinder either party's attempts to secure witnesses and evidence within its territory.[118] Especially in sensitive political situations, states might have an interest in assisting or hindering the work of a tribunal.[119] The tribunal practice whereby some governments send experienced police investigators, and sometimes even lawyers, to assist tribunal counterparts suggests that this type of

---

[112] Tuinstra (n 1) (citing KN Calvo-Goller, *The Trial Proceedings of the International Criminal Court, ICTY and ICTR Precedents* (Martinus Nijhoff Publishers, Leiden and Boston 2006) 50).

[113] Tuinstra (n 1) 146.

[114] See ICTR Statute, art 29; ICTY Statute, art 30 and ICC Statute, art 40; see also Tuinstra (n 1) 151.

[115] Agreement on the Privileges and Immunities of the International Criminal Court (signed 9 September 2002) <http://untreaty.un.org/cod/icc/index.html> last accessed 12 April 2011. For more on the issue at the ICC, see KS Gallant, 'The Role and Powers of Defence Counsel in the Rome Statute of the International Criminal Court' (2000) 34 *Int'l Lawyer* 21, 31.

[116] F Mégret, 'International Prosecutors: Accountability and Ethics', *Leuven Centre for Global Governance Studies Working Paper No. 18*, 22 (December 2008).

[117] See for instance, *Prosecutor v Karemera et al.* (Minutes of Proceedings, Trial Day 307) ICTR-98-44-T (8 June 2010) (noting that the 'Chamber issued a warning against Peter Robinson and instructed the Registry to communicate it to his Bar Association').

[118] R Byrne, 'The New Public International Lawyer and the Hidden art of International Criminal Trial Practice' (2010) 25 *Connecticut J Int'l L* 243, 251 ('The reliance by international tribunals on state cooperation in obtaining evidence renders international courts less able to presume a level playing field in the conduct of proceedings').

[119] Ibid 251 ('Depending upon the implications of the indictments for the state, either the prosecution or the defence may face considerable barriers in accessing evidence and witnesses').

gratis support is overwhelmingly given in favour of the Prosecution instead of the Defence. The scales of equality between the two adversarial parties are thus, perhaps unwittingly, further tipped on behalf of the former against the latter.

While the Courts have attempted to protect defence rights from self-interested states, such attempts bring to light the general judicial inability to rebalance the parties at trial. During the *Mulitinović* case, for instance, defendants requested documentation from certain states under Article 29 of the ICTY Statute, which obliges states to cooperate with the tribunal, and Rule 54 *bis* which lays out the requirements on a party seeking an order to oblige the United States to produce documents or information.[120] The Court reviewed the defendant's request and the US response which limited its search in relation to exculpatory material:

> A State cannot arrogate to itself the right to limit the request of an applicant to material that it considers to be favorable to the Applicant's case. If a specific request is made for the production of material relevant to an issue in the case, then the primary obligation of a State is to cooperate with the Applicant by searching for any material falling within the terms of the Request. It is for the Applicant to determine which documents, if any, of those produced should be used in his case.[121]

The Court's critique of the United States' unwillingness to fulfil the entirety of the request demonstrates a telling aspect of equality of arms. The judges recognised the necessity of state cooperation for investigation by both parties. States' attempts to limit and control the extent of their cooperation may thus interfere with evidence gathering, and ultimately, the fairness of tribunal trials which could potentially lead to a miscarriage of justice.[122] Sometimes, tension between a particular government and the court could even threaten to derail the work of an entire tribunal.[123] As the

---

[120] *Prosecutor v Milutinović et al* (Decision on second application of Dragoljub Ojdanić for binding orders pursuant to Rule 54bis) IT-05-87-PT (17 November 2005) paras 17–18.

[121] Ibid para 23.

[122] Bibas and Burke-White (n 27) 697–698 (offering the following example: 'only days after the ICTY convicted a Bosnian Croat general of atrocities, Croatia turned over thousands of pages of potentially exculpatory evidence, leading the Appeals Chamber to overturn sixteen of his nineteen convictions'). For more on that complex ICTY trial, see *Prosecutor v Blaškić* (Appeals Judgment) IT-95-14-A (29 July 2004).

[123] The Rwandan Government's decided not to cooperate with the ICTR to signal its displeasure after the ICTR Appeals Chamber ordered the defendant's release after dismissing the Prosecutor's indictment, with prejudice, due to unduly lengthy pre-trial detention. The Prosecutor successfully, if controversially, sought a reconsideration of that decision in *Prosecutor v Barayagwiza* (Decision on Prosecutor's Request for Review or Reconsideration) ICTR-97-19-AR72 (31 March 2000). For a dramatic account of the *Barayagwiza* saga, from the chief prosecutor's perspective, see Carla del Ponte and Chuck Sudetic, *Madame Prosecutor: Confrontations with Humanity's Worst Criminals and the Culture of Impunity: A Memoir* (Other

analysis brings to light, this common investigative problem, the general unwillingness of states to offer exculpatory information, causes defendants to suffer.[124]

Although the Court may attempt to help the defendant, and sometimes does so successfully, the reality is that state cooperation issues often leave the defence in want of basic investigative resources. The defence may be unable to enter territories in which the crimes were allegedly committed for lack of permission from the government.[125] States and other bodies may be willing to cooperate with prosecution's fishing expeditions, and at the same time, reluctant to fulfil defence requests for access to that same information.[126] In addition to the lack of cooperation from governments, defence teams appear to experience greater difficulty in their ability to investigate and proffer witnesses. The first ground of appeal from the final judgment in *Tadić*, though perhaps not surprising for a maiden tribunal case, was 'inequality of arms leading to denial of fair trial'.[127] The defence team complained that issues such as witness intimidation impaired the presentation of its case.[128] Despite the Trial Chamber's willingness to assist defence applications to Serbia for cooperation,[129] the defence claimed that 'counsel might have been unaware of the degree of obstruction by the Bosnian Serb authorities in preventing the discovery of witnesses helpful to the Defence case'.[130]

Unlike disadvantages stemming from asymmetry in state cooperation, an issue ostensibly outside of the Court's control and a bigger problem for international criminal tribunals more generally, burdens resulting from disproportionate

---

Press, New York 2008) 84. That dispute was probably the lowest point in the relationship between Kigali and Arusha.

[124] The Court later goes on to describe the types of excuses offered by the States for not cooperating fully with defendants' requests. As grounds for security concerns, Canada asserted that it was difficult to assess whether national security issues were engaged; the United States argued that production could reveal the nature and extent of US intelligence-gathering capabilities. These arguments are easy to make. To these authors, such arguments may be valid but are beside the point as they could be used to hide a general unwillingness to cooperate simply to avoid assisting tribunal defendants. Indeed, as the Court helpfully clarified in response to this argument: 'The applicant has no interest in the techniques the States use to gather information, but only wants the information relevant to his request that they possess.' Ibid paras 33–34.

[125] *Prosecutor v Kayishema and Ruzindana* (Appeals Judgment) (n 44) paras 64–65 (noting defendant's submission that Rwanda's lack of permission for Counsel to visit sites of the indictment as impairing defence's ability to verify facts, and locate and contact witnesses).

[126] *Prosecutor v Hadžihasanović and Kabura* (Decision on defence access to EUMM archives) IT-07-47-PT (12 September 2003) and *Prosecutor v Hadžihasanović and Kabura* (Decision on joint defence application for certification of decision on access to EUMM archives of 12 September 2003) (n 76).

[127] *Prosecutor v Tadić* (Appeals Judgment) IT-04-1-A (15 July 1999) paras 32–34 (noting that the Appeals Chamber recognised defence witnesses had been intimidated into not appearing).

[128] Ibid.
[129] Ibid para 54.
[130] Ibid para 36.

financial resources might be alleviated by restructuring budgets. The Chamber may be better positioned to allay concerns of inequality by responding to the common complaints that resources are insufficient for counsel to adequately defend their clients.[131] However, the judges relinquish responsibility for finances as well.[132] While they do not have the direct responsibility for dispensing legal aid, their role as the ultimate guarantors of fair trials demand that they order the Registrar to find the resources necessary for justice. The inequality of investigative resources, in the form of financial support and state cooperation assets, is clearly great. Defence counsel thus turns to the Court seeking relief. The changed position of the *Taylor* Defence at the SCSL, following a serious gamble on the part of the accused to terminate counsel and boycott the proceedings at the opening of his trial, illustrates a trial chamber's capacity to require tribunal administrators to ensure better realisation of equality of arms. This next section considers the judicial responses to such complaints, and analyses the jurisprudence on equality of arms to consider the possible remedies for defence team's disproportionate inability to investigate.

## B. Jurisprudence on Structural and Resource Inequality

Rather than attempting to rectify inequalities in resources, courts appear to have instead reconstructed the concept of equality of arms. As one scholar despondently reports, 'it is not surprising that the Appeals Chamber adapts the principle of equality of arms to account for the disequilibrium between the parties in international justice'.[133] Courts reference layers of argument which, more or less, can combat nearly any defence claim of inequality. First, courts explain that equality of arms is not equality of resources. The Appeals Chambers at the ICTR and ICTY, for instance, have stated that equality of arms should not be confused with equality of resources.[134] Rather than comparing defence and prosecution resources, the courts suggest a review of the sufficiency of defence resources without regard to parity or equality with the prosecution. This approach protects the apparent secrecy of the

---

[131] *Prosecutor v Hadžihasanović and Kabura* (Decision on urgent motion for ex parte oral hearing on allocation of resources to the defence and consequences thereof for the rights of the accused to a fair trial) IT-07-47-PT (17 June 2003); *Prosecutor v Sesay et al* (Decision on Sesay Defence Application I—Logistical Resources) SCSL-04-15-T (24 January 2007); *Situation in the DRC: Prosecutor v Lubanga* (Decision of the Presidency upon the document entitled 'Clarification' filed by Thomas Lubanga Dyilo on 3 April 2007, the requests of the Registrar of 5 April 2007 and the requests of Thomas Lubanga Dyilo of 17 April 2007) ICC-01/04-01/06 (2 May 2007) para 6.

[132] *Prosecutor v Hadžihasanović and Kabura* (Decision on urgent motion for ex parte oral hearing on allocation of resources to the defence and consequences thereof for the rights of the accused to a fair trial) IT-07-47-PT (17 June 2003) (noting that the 'legal aid payment system is a primary responsibility for the Registrar').

[133] Byrne (n 118) 251.

[134] *Prosecutor v Kayishema and Ruzindana* (Appeals Judgment) (n 44) paras 63–64.

prosecutorial practice and counsels restraint in reviewing the investigations of the prosecution.[135] It becomes a way for the tribunal to move the conversation away from an inquiry that is bound to lead to the conclusion that there is in fact actual disparity between the two sides.

Second, courts often assess whether the defence is at a *severe* disadvantage vis-à-vis the prosecution. Although this approach compares the two sides, it finds a violation only when the disparity is deemed to be great. Through this type of argumentation the courts overlook the basic meaning of equality. We assert that equality of arms is a guarantee promised to the defendant throughout the pre-trial and trial phases. To comply with this principle, the courts must do more than assure that defence was not severely disadvantaged by decisions and judgments; they must assure that the defence was not placed on unequal footing during investigations and the procedures leading up to those decisions and judgments.

Third, courts sometimes consider whether the defence was put at a disadvantage *by the court*, or whether external factors justify the court relinquishing responsibility for the inequality. Of course, as a matter of principle, there is nothing wrong with this approach. The question does, however, arise as to whether in instances where other factors, or better yet third entities, affect the balance of equilibrium against the defendant, whose responsibility it would be to correct that resource disequilibrium.

These three judicial approaches obscure the clarity and strength of the principle, and thus contribute to the defence perception that equality of arms seems impossible in the international criminal justice system – at least, as it is currently structured and run. At the ad hoc tribunals, defence attorneys have argued that resource inequality is impermissible under equality of arms. For instance, the defence arguments in the ICTR case *Kayishema* offer that perspective. Counsel for Kayishema had filed a Motion requesting what the court referred to as 'full equality of arms ... that is, both parties must be afforded the same means and resources'.[136] The First Annual Report of the President at the SCSL reveals similar aspirations to provide full equality.[137] That Court has been applauded for its attempt to equalise

---

[135] See, e.g., *Prosecutor v Sesay et al* (Decision on the Sesay Defence Team's Application for Judicial Review of the Registrar's Refusal to Provide Additional Funds for an Additional Counsel as Part of the Implementation of the Arbitration Agreement of the 26th of April 2007) (n 100) para 38 (reminding defence counsel 'that the Prosecution is an independent Statutory Organ') and *Prosecutor v Kayishema and Ruzindana* (Trial Chamber Judgment and Sentence) (n 103) para 57 (noting, without disagreeing, that 'the Prosecution submitted that the information requested by the Defence was not public and was intrinsically linked to the exercise of the Prosecutor's mandate, in accordance with Article 15 of the Statute').

[136] *Prosecutor v Kayishema and Ruzindana* (Appeals Judgment) (n 44) para 63.

[137] The President of the SCSL, *First Annual Report of the President of the Special Court for Sierra Leone* (1 December 2003) 16 (discussing defence at the SCSL, how the creation of the Defence Office 'is an innovation in the structure of international courts. It ensures the rights of suspects and accused persons, providing a counterbalance to the Prosecution. The Office has implemented measures to attract only experienced, competent and honest counsel, so as to comply with the human rights principle that adversarial trials should manifest an "equality of arms" (i.e., reasonable equivalence in ability and resources of the Prosecution and Defence)').

assets.¹³⁸ According to the Appeals Chamber at the ICTY, the legal aid system is designed to 'secure equality of arms with the Prosecution'.¹³⁹

Despite applauding efforts for full equality, one scholar goes on to offer a list of the basic requirements to ensure effective defence and refers only to 'sufficient resources and reasonable facilities'.¹⁴⁰ Within that list, the author apparently provides realistic, short-term goals. As demonstrated by the contrast between that author's applauding the SCSL efforts and the conservative list of requirements, it may be too soon to expect courts to grant full equality to the defence. Similarly, the Trial Chamber in *Kayishema* explicitly rejected the Defence request for full equality,¹⁴¹ and the Appeals Chamber affirmed that position. The judges emphasised the 'sound' legal finding that: 'the rights of the accused and equality between the parties should not be confused with the equality of means and resources.'¹⁴² Courts thus reject claims for equality of investigative means by stating that such resources are not contemplated by the principle.

It is not just the Appeals and Trial Chamber at the ICTR, but also many other sources which adopt the view that equality is not about having the same finances and resources. One article discussing 'emaciated' defence in the SCSL noted, '[w]hile that guarantee does not mean dollar-for-dollar parity with prosecution funding, the defense must be provided with resources—time, space, library, staff, and compensation—sufficient for the task'.¹⁴³ Moreover, reputable commentaries assert the same.¹⁴⁴ As with the courts' rejection of resource parity, these rejections may reflect a concern for the realistic expectations, as opposed to principles or ideals, for defence. The principle of equality of arms has, at a basic level, been interpreted to excuse or justify the prosecutor's greater resources. That is, resource allocation is seen as responsive to the prosecutor's higher burden of proof and is therefore contemplated as a form of permissible inequality between two adversarial sides. This idea has been endorsed by many judges at the different tribunals. At the ICTY, the judges explained that:

> The Prosecution has the burden of telling an entire story, of putting together a coherent narrative and proving every necessary element of the crimes charged beyond a reasonable doubt. Defence strategy, by contrast, often focuses on poking specifically targeted holes in the Prosecution's case, *an endeavor which may require less time and fewer witnesses.* This is sufficient reason to explain why a principle of basic proportionality, rather than a strict principle of mathematical equality,

---

[138] Human Rights Watch (n 93) 6; see also Tuinstra (n 13) 483.
[139] *Prosecutor v Milutinović et al* (Decision on interlocutory appeal on motion for additional funds) IT-99-37-AR73.2 (13 November 2003) para 3.
[140] Tuinstra (n 13) 483.
[141] *Prosecutor v Kayishema and Ruzindana* (Appeals Judgment) (n 44) para 63.
[142] Ibid paras 63–64.
[143] Wilson (n 1) 7–8.
[144] Schabas (n 17) 1254; see also Human Rights Watch (n 93) 6.

generally governs the relationship between the time and witnesses allocated to the two sides.¹⁴⁵

We do not contest that, in a criminal trial, it is the prosecution that bears the burden to prove the charges against the accused beyond a reasonable doubt. That is settled ground. However, in our view, the foregoing reasoning cannot by itself suffice to justify disparate resources, even if it is self-evident that the judges attempted to qualify their answer (as shown by the italicized sentence). The judges, in describing defence strategy as 'only' poking targeted holes, define their own ideas of what the defence strategy ought to be. They seemingly substitute their opinions for the interests and wishes of the accused and overlook the reality that defence teams may, and do, take other approaches demanded by their clients.¹⁴⁶ Moreover, as the parties are increasingly encouraged to stipulate to agreed-upon facts,¹⁴⁷ as a way of promoting efficiency in the trials, the prosecution's burden may, in some instances, be reduced to proving the issues of contention, the same amount of information as the defence's 'specifically targeted holes'.¹⁴⁸ The SCSL judges have endorsed this ICTY logic. In response to defence counsel's requests for greater resources, the Court determined that the Prosecutor:

> bears the burden of proving beyond a reasonable doubt every count and essential element of those counts, while the Defence only needs to raise a reasonable doubt in order to secure the acquittal of the Accused. This reality, we consider, might justify the attribution of more resources and more time to enable the Prosecution to accomplish this very heavy and delicate task.¹⁴⁹

Again, by using qualified instead of definitive language, it seems apparent that the Court recognized that it was treading on dangerous territory that may be more the responsibility of the defendant and his counsel. Still, when put in this way, the logic here oversimplifies the reality of international criminal charges. It suggests that the prosecutor must undertake investigation to prove each element of the offence and

---

¹⁴⁵ *Prosecutor v Orić* (Interlocutory decision on length of defence case) (n 106) para 7.

¹⁴⁶ See for instance, the defence abuse of process application in the *Lubanga* trial which cannot be said to merely poke holes and cannot be said to require less time. *Situation in the DRC: Prosecutor v Lubanga* (Transcript) ICC-01/04-01/06-T-236-Red-ENG (27 January 2010) 20–25.

¹⁴⁷ See, e.g., *Situation in the Central African Republic: Prosecutor v Bemba* (Transcript) ICC-01/05-01/08-T-30-ENG (21 October 2010) 9–12.

¹⁴⁸ *Prosecutor v Orić* (Interlocutory decision on length of defence case) (n 106) para 7.

¹⁴⁹ *Prosecutor v Sesay et al* (Decision on the Sesay Defence Team's Application for Judicial Review of the Registrar's Refusal to Provide Additional Funds for an Additional Counsel as Part of the Implementation of the Arbitration Agreement of the 26th of April 2007) (n 100) para 39; see also *Prosecutor v Sesay et al* (Written Decision on Sesay Defence Application for a Week's Adjournment—Insufficient Resources in Violation of Article 17(4)(b) of the Statute of the Special Court) SCSL-04-15-T (5 March 2008) para 61.

the defence, on the other hand, need disprove only one element to be successful. However, defendants facing complex crimes like crimes against humanity with relatively more expansive modes of liability such as command responsibility and joint criminal enterprise vis-à-vis domestic criminal trials can hardly succeed by launching one smoking bullet through the prosecutor's arguments. As long as the Prosecutor has the option of amending the charges,[150] even after the start of trial, active and conscientious defence teams will likely be striving to develop a strategy which applies against both the actual and the foreseeable charges against the accused. In that sense, the defence might perceive that it is better placed if it targets and discredits the prosecution's entire narrative in addition to poking specific holes in both the present and prospective indictment.[151]

The preceding type of judicial reasoning suggests that the defence *might* only undertake to investigate one element of the offence. However, this type of reasoning suffers from various flaws. First, the defence needs to investigate the whole of the prosecution's case to understand the charges and situation. Second, to find holes and weak points, counsel must look into each of the elements. Third, and perhaps more fundamentally, if the prosecutor receives support proportionate to his burden – i.e. 'the attribution of more resources and more time'[152] – then claims of parity between the parties become meaningless. It seems that it is the latter that poses the greatest brain twister to tribunal judges.

Equality of arms is one of multiple fair trial guarantees. The fairness of the trial and justice of the verdict depends on each of these guarantees properly functioning to protect the rights of the accused and the interests of justice. From these judgments arises a question: is the presumption of innocence an 'arm' of the defence? Is the increased burden of proof a handicap on the prosecution to equalise arms with defence? Or is it, as the courts suggest, a handicap on the prosecution which may be compensated by offering the defence less resources? Consider the opposite. If there were a completely equal adversarial game between the prosecution and defence, if the defendant were to have the same investigative resources as the prosecution, would he no longer be entitled to the presumption of innocence? This theoretical debate could go on for a long time. Rather than expand on the theory, we turn to

---

[150] Rule 128, ICC RPE allows the Prosecutor to apply to amend the charges even after the start of the trial.

[151] Although the Chamber did not ultimately use JCE when it convicted Taylor in April 2012, in an earlier decision, it had effectively implied that it wanted to retain the option to do so. See *Prosecutor v Taylor* (Decision on 'Defence Notice of Appeal and Submissions Regarding the Majority Decision Concerning the Pleading of JCE in the Second Amended Indictment') SCSL-03-1-T (1 May 2009) paras 4; 24–27 (holding that despite defence arguments of insufficient notice of the material facts in the indictment, the original indictment's explanation of the specific objective of the JCE was sufficiently clear to put the defendant on notice).

[152] *Prosecutor v Sesay et al* (Decision on the Sesay Defence Team's Application for Judicial Review of the Registrar's Refusal to Provide Additional Funds for an Additional Counsel as Part of the Implementation of the Arbitration Agreement of the 26th of April 2007) (n 100) para 39.

the judgments for more thorough considerations of the weighing that goes into the equality of arms jurisprudence.

This first statement of courts, that equality of arms is not a guarantee of resources, but rather a question of sufficiency or adequacy of resources[153] serves to undo a number of defence requests. For instance, the *Kayishema* Trial Chamber provided the following contestable reasoning. It first noted that the provision on indigent defendants provided that the costs and expenses of legal representation 'necessarily and reasonably incurred shall be covered by the Tribunal to the extent that such expenses cannot be borne by the suspect or the accused because of his financial situation'.[154] The Chamber said that the rule should be read together with Article 20(4)(d) of the Statute which says legal assistance shall be provided by the tribunal for defendants without sufficient means.[155] Reading those together, the Chamber felt that:

> the rights of the accused should not be interpreted to mean that the Defence is entitled to the same means and resources as the Prosecution. Any other position would be contrary to the status quo that exists within jurisdictions throughout the world and *would clearly not reflect the intentions of the drafters of this Tribunal's Statute*.[156]

It seems apparent that such an interpretation might run counter to the ICTR Statute, given the fact that it never explicitly included equality of arms in the first place. Perhaps more fundamentally, this is the same statute that explicitly omitted provisions for a defence office or other mechanisms to guarantee accused rights thereby, arguably, contributing to a situation of prosecutorial–defence inequality. In this context, although it may be that the Court had in mind the fair trial rights of the accused spelled out in the constitutive documents of the tribunal, it seems difficult to accept the proposition that the intention of the drafters should be the compelling justification behind any interpretation of the jurisprudentially developed concept of equality of arms. Indeed, because of the substantive provision incorporated by the drafters of the ICTR Statute enshrining the right to fair trial, one might argue exactly the opposite position to that of the judges: that it is more in line with the

---

[153] *Situation in Uganda: Prosecutor v Kony* (Decision on Prosecutor's Application for leave to Appeal in Part Pre-Trial Chamber II's Decision on the Prosecutor's Applications for Warrants of Arrest under Article 58) (n 53) para 30 (describing equality as the right of a 'party to a proceeding to adequately make its case, with a view to influencing the outcome of the proceedings in its favor' (emphasis added)). See also *Situation in the DRC: Prosecutor v Lubanga* (Decision sur la demande d'autorisation d'appel de la Défense relative à la transmission des Demandes de participation des victimes) (n 53) 6 (noting, 'ATTENDU par ailleurs, que les critères d'appréciation de l'égalité des armes tiennent aux circonstances de l'affaire et à la situation de fait à l'origine de la saisine de la Chambre').

[154] *Prosecutor v Kayishema and Ruzindana* (Trial Chamber Judgment and Sentence) (n 103) para 59.

[155] Ibid para 60.

[156] Ibid (emphasis added).

spirit of the drafter's intent to ensure a substantive realisation of the rights of the accused, especially in the face of persistent defence complaints about inequality of arms in essentially all the tribunals. It may thus be better to reason that the status quo in other jurisdictions does not mandate that equality of arms translate into an equality of resources between the defence and the prosecution. That said, we may then question whether the status quo, which itself is unsatisfactory, is the proper yardstick by which to measure the extent of realisation of the sacrosanct rights of the accused. This is all the more so when we consider that it is the international courts, rather than the domestic jurisdictions, that are supposed to be setting the higher standards for emulation as to how justice ought to be administered in criminal trials involving the most heinous crimes known to law.

As for the Chamber's other rationale, regarding the limitations imposed by legal aid, its reasoning also appears problematic. An indigent defendant is bootstrapped to the court's determination of what expenses are 'reasonably and necessarily incurred'. Unlike defendants who pay for their own defence and might thus be represented by their chosen number of lawyers,[157] an indigent defendant is limited to that which the court deems reasonable and necessary. While the defendants reliant on the public purse will necessarily be limited in the resources that they receive, as is the norm in most national legal aid systems, this view could have encroached on the quality of defence at the ICTR as well.[158]

The Appeals Chamber in *Kayishema* endorsed the Trial Chamber position that equality of arms is not about equality of means and resources.[159] Rather than focus on the reasonableness of the resources requested, the Appeals Chamber noted the reasoning of the ICTY which looks more to the second layer of interpretation, that of disadvantage. The Appeals Chamber opined on the 'scope of equality of arms': '[i]n deciding on the scope of the principle of equality of arms, ICTY Appeals Chamber in *Tadić* held that "equality of arms obligates a judicial body to ensure that neither party is put at a disadvantage when presenting its case."'[160] As mentioned above, the requirement of equality of arms is often phrased as a protection or refuge from 'substantive disadvantage.'[161]

As has already been shown, courts frequently interpret the principle to require 'that no substantial disadvantage exist between one party and another when presenting his or her case in court'.[162] The SCSL Appeals Chamber in the *Brima* case

---

[157] *Prosecutor v Haradinaj et al* (Decision on Prosecution's Urgent Application for Authorisation to Exceed Page Limit for Responses) (n 99).

[158] Tuinstra (n 1) 154 ('At the ICTR, having to hand in meticulous accounts of their professional activities to the Registry, the defence could be deprived of remuneration for activities that were deemed necessary').

[159] *Prosecutor v Kayishema and Ruzindana* (Appeals Judgment) (n 44) para 63.

[160] Ibid para 69.

[161] Tuinstra (n 13) 483 (arguing 'that a defence lawyer has sufficient and adequate facilities to do so and will not be at a substantive disadvantage in the proceedings vis-à-vis the prosecution. He should be able to present his case to the judges on an equal basis as the prosecution').

[162] Yesberg (n 55) footnotes 119–120 and accompanying text.

has faced claims of inequality of arms. That court has been accused of 'summarily' dismissing arguments about the important doctrinal issue of equality of arms.[163] The judges agreed with the prosecutor that Brima's complaint had failed to provide specific instances of violations of the right.[164] The judges rejected the claims on the ground that the defence failed to support his assertion of inequality with a 'specific claim as to how greater resources would have put him on more level footing, or what investigations were not undertaken due to the purported lack of time or resources'.[165] Thus, the Court provides requirements for future defence lawyers that they must lay-out the cognisable disadvantage at trial that resulted from discrepancies in order to demonstrate the prejudice that arises from the inequality of arms with prosecutors when the issue goes on appeal.

Though this issue arose in the context of an appeal, and it is common ground that a party making a claim bears the burden of proving it, the courts' interpretations requiring a cognizable disadvantage may have gone too far and could have been addressed differently by requesting the defendant's substantiating evidence of inequality during the course of the appeals hearing rather than waiting till the end of the appeal to simply dismiss it. In any case, the European Court of Human Rights, for instance, has held that importance attaches to the appearance of fairness and equality, not just when prejudice results.[166] The Court explained, even though it was admittedly speaking only about party submissions, that 'the principle of equality of arms does not depend on further, quantifiable unfairness flowing from a procedural inequality. It is a matter for the defence to assess whether a submission deserves a reaction. It is therefore unfair for the prosecution to make submissions to a court without the knowledge of the defence'.[167]

This second factor, whether the defence is at a severe disadvantage, is used often in response to different concerns that defence lawyers have less access to evidence or witnesses due to state non-cooperation. One may assume based on the Statutes and Rules that the defence and prosecution have the same capacity to subpoena witnesses, to request visas and entry into countries, and to approach witnesses. As the argument goes, state non-cooperation (or difficulty in securing witnesses and other related issues) theoretically *can* hurt both sides and it therefore 'conforms to the principle' as neither party is put at a severe disadvantage.[168]

State non-cooperation is also a recurring theme in courts' analyses of the third layer of equality of arms. That is, when courts consider whether the defence was put at a disadvantage *by the court* they often assert that external factors – in the

---

[163] CC Jalloh and J Osei-Tutu, '*Prosecutor v Brima, Kamara and Kanu*: First Judgment from the Appeals Chamber of the Special Court for Sierra Leone' (20 May 2008) 12 *ASIL Insights*, Issue 10.

[164] Ibid.

[165] *Prosecutor v Brima et al* (Appeals Judgment) SCSL-2004-16-A (22 February 2008) paras 222–224.

[166] *Bulut v Austria* (Judgment) App No 17358/90 (22 February 1996) para 47.

[167] Ibid para 48.

[168] G Sluiter, '"I beg you, please come testify": The Problematic Absence of Subpoena Powers at the ICC' (2009) 12 *New Crim L Rev* 590.

form of State non-cooperation – justify the court relinquishing responsibility for the inequality. Courts often blame State non-cooperation as the culprit responsible for disadvantaged defence investigations. Typically, the argument is that the prosecutor too faces external factors and difficulties of state cooperation. This is fair because it is true, to some extent. The difference is that the Prosecutor, for instance, at the ICC, is often the beneficiary of state self-referrals which are predicates to his conduct of formal investigations. For these, as in the Democratic Republic of Congo and the Central African Republic, he expects and usually receives state cooperation. This means that he typically can rely on greater cooperation, from that particular state or other third states, to support his investigative efforts of that particular situation. Even if the situation is an external imposition in the form of a Security Council referral, such as in Darfur and more recently Libya, the Prosecutor can turn to and rely on, at least in principle, the Security Council to compel state compliance with his investigations requests. No such mechanism is available to the Defence, though there is nothing in principle prohibiting counsel from seeking a finding of non-compliance and for the ICC judges to ask the president of the tribunal to report a recalcitrant state to the Security Council for a failure to comply with defence requests for investigative assistance.

At the ICTR, defendant Kayishema challenged consistency with the equality of arms doctrine on the basis that his counsel had been unable to travel to Rwandan sites referred to in the indictment to verify factual allegations, while the Prosecutor was able to make such site visits.[169] The Trial and Appeals Chamber were able to easily dismiss suggestions of 'impossibility to verify the technical and material data about Kibuye *prefecture* submitted by the Prosecution'.[170] The Appeals Chamber examined the defendant's appeal, noting that 'the mere fact of not being able to travel to Rwanda is not sufficient to establish inequality of arms between the Prosecution and the Defence'.[171] Apparently the defence counsel had investigators at her disposal, and had a budget which she could decide how to spend. The Appeals Chamber restated the original holding: '*The Trial Chamber is satisfied that all the necessary provisions for the preparation of a comprehensive defence were available,* and were afforded to all Defence Counsel in this case. The utilisation of those resources is not a matter for the Trial Chamber.'[172] In the end, the ability and option of travelling to investigate may have existed, but choosing whether or not to exercise it is a different matter. In dismissing Kayishema's appeal, the Appeals Chamber reiterated equality of arms does not apply to conditions outside of the court's control.[173]

This reasoning seems logical. The difficulty was that, according to the defence, Kayishema's counsel had not been given permission by Rwanda to visit the crime

---

[169] *Prosecutor v Kayishema and Ruzindana* (Appeals Judgment) (n 44).
[170] Ibid para 72.
[171] Ibid.
[172] Ibid (emphasis in original).
[173] Ibid para 73.

bases referred to in the Indictment.[174] Thus, the issue was not about funding, but about permission from the government in Kigali in the pre-trial stage in relation to counsel's intention to visit the *locus delicti*. The Chamber's response, which focuses on the investigators put at counsel's disposal,[175] turns the attention away from the Defence complaint that the Prosecutor could go there and the lead counsel for defence could not.

The United States submitted similar arguments, that the court is not responsible for external conditions of state cooperation, before the Inter-American Court of Human Rights. Similar to the ICTR Chambers' reflections on Kayishema's access to resources, the US government argued that the 'issue' of inability to investigate and access certain evidence is not within the purview of equality of arms concerns. In that case, defendant Garza was unable to access evidence in Mexico, while the prosecution was able to do so, aided by the mechanisms enshrined in a mutual assistance treaty between the United States and Mexico. The United States argued that 'this treaty merely enhances the State's ability to collect evidence against the accused and in no way restrains the defense from challenging that evidence or presenting his own evidence'.[176] Thus, in line with the second layer, the State asserted that the defence could not have been said to be severely disadvantaged. The State asserted the following to disclaim any responsibility for state non-cooperation:

> Further, the State argues that neither the existence of the MLAT between the U.S. and Mexico nor the decision by the U.S. and Mexico not to apply the Inter-American Convention on Letters Rogatory to criminal matters affect the ability of a litigant, civil or criminal, from obtaining evidence through letters rogatory, as this process is rooted in custom between countries regardless of their treaty relations.[177]

The US government submitted that which had been offered in *Tadić* and *Kayishema*: equality of arms does not apply to conditions outside of the court's control.[178] Finally, the State pointed to one interesting mechanism at appellant's disposal, that is, 'the fact that the U.S. Constitution requires the prosecution to turn over to the accused before trial all aggravating or mitigating evidence'.[179] It is interesting that in the ICC, but not in the ad hoc tribunal context, the Prosecutor is required to investigate and turn over such evidence to the defence. This is one of the critical differences in the role of prosecutors at the permanent penal tribunal – which is obviously seen and mandated by states to play a broader minister of justice role rather than just the type of role expected of a purely adversarial party. Assuming that the ICC Prosecution abides by this statutory edict, in good faith, this may well

---

[174] Ibid para 64.
[175] Ibid para 72.
[176] *Garza v United States* (n 38) para 55.
[177] Ibid.
[178] *Prosecutor v Kayishema and Ruzindana* (Appeals Judgment) (n 44) para 73.
[179] *Garza v United States* (n 38) para 55.

serve to mitigate the differently situated parties in relation to this argument. The practice of the Office of the Prosecutor so far suggests that the opposite is true.

State non-cooperation is an unfortunate and persistent problem for the tribunals[180] without a clear solution. Given the principle of state sovereignty as it currently prevails, the state-centric international legal system lacks mechanisms sufficient to compel states to disclose documents, arrest defendants or grant permission to defence counsel to enter the regions of investigation.[181] Courts, insufficiently armed to compel States to offer support when they are not interested in doing so of their own accord, thus appear justified in shirking themselves of blame for inequalities caused by such non-cooperation. However, this is not to suggest that we should be complacent. Sluiter rightly differentiates between differing types of non-cooperation, and in doing so, points out certain instances in which certain officers of the Court may be responsible for problems otherwise falling under the heading of non-cooperation. In differentiating between lack of subpoena powers and disclosure failures he notes the 'culpability' of the court: 'Of course, a vital difference is that contrary to the Lubanga disclosure situation, the Prosecutor cannot be blamed in any way for the lack of subpoena powers and is likely to suffer from it as well.'[182] If the Court is to phrase the argument in terms of external vs. internal guarantees of equality of arms, it must take responsibility – and thus offer a remedy – for those inequalities resulting from disclosure failures.

On the other hand, insofar as the Court is free from blame for the inequalities, it may still fall on the institution to provide a remedy in order to protect the fundamental rights of the accused and the integrity of the court's processes.[183] The reality is that, for the most part, states seem to give the tribunals the type of support that they need to carry out their work – even when they do not appear to directly gain from the relevant prosecutions. But, perhaps partly because of their inability to force unwilling states to particular results, international courts seem generally hesitant to issue harsh binding orders against national authorities that, when unimplemented, would undermine the soft authority of the courts as judicial institutions.

---

[180] Byrne (n 118) 251 ('The reliance by international tribunals on state cooperation in obtaining evidence renders international courts less able to presume a level playing field in the conduct of proceedings').

[181] The fact that the Courts are unable, in actuality, to compel cooperation is depicted by Byrne using the following metaphor: 'While international law formally addresses the issue of state cooperation through the core legal instruments of international criminal law, trial practice is informally marked by the invisible state actor in the public gallery.' Ibid 297.

[182] Sluiter (n 168) text following footnote 35.

[183] Tuinstra (n 1) 168.

## IV. Disclosure

Unequal allocation of investigation resources need not necessarily result in a fundamentally disadvantaged defence investigation. At the ICC, unlike the ICTY, ICTR and the SCSL, the prosecution has the obligation to investigate and disclose both incriminatory and exculpatory evidence to the defence.[184] In that sense, the prosecution must investigate for the defence; in essence, the statute envision systems under which the resources given to the prosecution are, at least to an extent, shared between the parties. Disclosure is at the heart of the fair trial. Disclosure has roots in the adversarial system but, as Ambos notes, is also reflected in the inquisitorial concept of 'case dossier'.[185] It is a key, unique mechanism by which defence may counterbalance the prosecutor's resources to achieve some kind of equality of arms.[186] It is also essential for transparency and to facilitate monitoring of the proceedings.[187]

Disclosure obligations of parties are significantly different based on roles at trial: the prosecution has the burden of proof and has to investigate incriminating and exonerating circumstances under Article 51(1)(a) of the Statute, whereas the defence has a mainly reactive role.[188] The Rome Statute and Rules oblige the prosecutor to make disclosure in order that the accused has time to adequately prepare her defence.[189] Disclosure poses problems. One author refers to the issue as a problem of 'fragmented authority' over the investigation.[190] There are insufficient evidentiary, ethical and procedural limitations on investigation techniques, allowing for the prosecution to delegate much of his powers of investigation. At the same time, the prosecution ostensibly fails to delegate his responsibility over the techniques, in particular, the obligation to investigate and disclose exculpatory evidence.

At the ICTY, the prosecution's duty to turn over exculpating or mitigating evidence 'extends only to information that the prosecutor *actually knows* about and possesses or controls' [emphasis added].[191] For instance, when the prosecutor's investigation depends on a state, he may not know about evidence within a state's

---

[184] ICTR RPE, Rules 66–68; ICTY RPE, Rules 66–68; SCSL RPE Rules 66–68; STL RPE, Rules 110–113; ICC Statute, arts 54(1)(a) and 67(2).

[185] K Ambos, 'Confidential Investigations (Article 54(3)(E) ICC Statute) vs. Disclosure Obligations: The Lubanga Case and National Law' (2009) 12 New Crim. L. Rev. 543, footnotes 159–160 and accompanying text.

[186] Ibid.

[187] Yesberg (n 55) 578.

[188] *Situation in the DRC: Prosecutor v Katanga and Chui* (Decision on the 'Prosecution's Application Concerning Disclosure Pursuant to Rules 78 and 79(4)') (n 57) para 36.

[189] Ibid.

[190] Bibas and Burke-White (n 27) 696.

[191] Ibid (citing ICTY RPE, rule 68 and *Prosecutor v Blaškić* (Decision on the Production of Discovery Materials) IT-95-14-T (27 January 1997) paras 41–49).

hands.¹⁹² And, in those instances, he has no explicit obligation to seek it for the purposes of turning it over to the defence. Even more complicated problems arise when states release information to the prosecution on the condition that it not be disclosed to the defence.¹⁹³

At the ICC, Article 67(2) of the Statute provides the standard that the Prosecutor shall disclose evidence 'in the Prosecutor's possession or control which he or she believes shows or tends to show the innocence of the accused, or to mitigate the guilt of the accused or which may affect the credibility of prosecution evidence. In case of doubt ... the Court shall decide'.¹⁹⁴ The Prosecutor's obligation needs to be clearly explained and should be stricter than a subjective test of actual knowledge. As the standard in the United States reveals, it is not just about what he actually knows, but also what the prosecutor should know.¹⁹⁵

Disclosure law is complex due to conflicting interests of defence rights and public or private security.¹⁹⁶ The responsibility to pursue a neutral investigation may be overshadowed by the prosecutor's concern for protecting sources.¹⁹⁷ The *Lubanga* trial provides the most obvious example of the difficulties that ensue. In that case, the ICC Prosecution focused on using confidential information from third parties which appeared to provide quick investigative results.¹⁹⁸ Amidst the insufficient evidentiary, ethical and procedural limitations on investigation techniques, the prosecution began presenting its case arguably without having carried out a complete or 'proper' investigation, and certainly, without respecting the fundamental disclosure obligations which relate so closely to the rights of the accused.¹⁹⁹ Not just ICC case law, but also developments at the ad hoc tribunals demonstrate the Court's willingness to subjugate defence interests in exculpatory materials. The ICTY Rules of Procedure and Evidence, for instance, were amended in 2003 to qualify the right to such materials, 'subject to the provisions of Rule 70' on confidential state materials.²⁰⁰

---

¹⁹²  Bibas and Burke-White (n 27) 697–698 (offering the following example: 'only days after the ICTY convicted a Bosnian Croat general of atrocities, Croatia turned over thousands of pages of potentially exculpatory evidence, leading the Appeals Chamber to overturn sixteen of his nineteen convictions'). For more on that complex ICTY trial, see *Prosecutor v Blaškić* (Appeals Chamber Judgment) (n 122).
¹⁹³  Bibas and Burke-White (n 27) 698.
¹⁹⁴  ICC Statute, art 67(2).
¹⁹⁵  Bibas and Burke-White (n 27) 698 (proposing the following: 'At the very least, international prosecutors should face the same standard, bearing a burden to investigate what they should know instead of hiding behind lack of actual knowledge').
¹⁹⁶  Ambos (n 185 ) footnote 161 and accompanying text.
¹⁹⁷  Ibid footnotes 162–167.
¹⁹⁸  Ibid text accompanying footnote 168 (noting that the 'prosecution strove for quick but not sustainable success by seeking "to obtain a wide range of materials under the cloak of confidentiality"').
¹⁹⁹  Ibid.
²⁰⁰  O'Sullivan and Montgomery (n 59) 529–530 (noting the unfair implications of this amendment, that the Prosecutor need not inform anyone of the existence of exculpatory

There is room for improvement of the disclosure regimes within the Rome Statute and Rules of Procedure and Evidence, for instance, which do not offer clear well-delineated procedures for alternative disclosure with confidential information dealing with state security concerns.[201] In addition to the procedural rules, ethical rules would also be helpful to enforce the prosecutor's disclosure obligations. Failure to disclose evidence in some national jurisdictions can lead to ethical sanctions.[202] Unlike those national jurisdictions,[203] the ICC system does not have a code of ethics for the prosecution. Initial ICDAA proposals to subject the Prosecution's trial attorneys to the same code of conduct as defence counsel failed.[204] The ICTY's record for assessing attorney misconduct is limited to sanctions on defence counsel, and fails to keep the prosecution in check.[205]

The SCSL was more progressive in adopting a single and common code for both prosecution and defence, seemingly the first in international criminal tribunals.[206] In comparison, the UN tribunals' written ethics rules seem to apply solely to the defence. The ICC system includes a Code of Professional Conduct, applying to the Defence Counsel and Legal Representatives of victims;[207] alongside a Code of Judicial Ethics for judges. According to Mégret, the OTP at the ICTY and ICTR did not seek to establish accountability standards, but instead, viewed ethics 'at best as an internal affair'.[208] It appears that Prosecutor Louise Arbour developed her

---

materials in the absence of the provider's consent).

[201] L Korecki, 'Procedural Tools for Ensuring Cooperation of States with the Special Tribunal for Lebanon' (2009) 7 *JICJ* 927, 944.

[202] American Bar Association, *Model Rules of Professional Conduct*, Rule 3.8 Special Roles of a Prosecutor, 'The prosecutor in a criminal case shall ... (d) make timely disclosure to the defense of all evidence or information known to the prosecutor that tends to negate the guilt of the accused or mitigates the offense, and, in connection with sentencing, disclose to the defense and to the tribunal all unprivileged mitigating information known to the prosecutor, except when the prosecutor is relieved of this responsibility by a protective order of the tribunal.'

[203] For instance, in the United States, '[a]ll jurisdictions ... have rules that address ethical responsibilities of prosecutors'. P Krug, 'Section V Prosecutorial Discretion and its Limits' (2002) 50 *American J Comparative L* 643, 651.

[204] M Bohlander, 'International Criminal Defence Ethics: The Law of Professional Conduct for Defence Counsel Appearing before International Criminal Tribunals' (2000) 1 *San Diego Int'l L J* 75, 98.

[205] CA Rogers, 'Lawyers Without Borders' (2009) 30 *U Penn J Int'l L* 1035, 1084 (arguing that the power to resolve important international and transnational legal issues must be accompanied by a power to control and regulate the attorneys who participate in those proceedings).

[206] 'Code of Professional Conduct for Counsel with the Right of Audience before the Special Court for Sierra Leone' in CC Jalloh (ed) *Consolidated Legal Texts for the Special Court for Sierra Leone* (Martinus Nijhoff, Dordrecht 2007) 167.

[207] ICC Code of Professional Conduct (adopted 2 December 2005, entry into force 1 January 2006) <http://www.icc-cpi.int/Menus/ICC/Legal+Texts+and+Tools/Official+Journal/Code+of+Professional+Conduct+for+counsel+_.htm> last accessed 13 December 2011.

[208] Mégret (n 116) 11.

own regulations for prosecution lawyers, as a form of soft self-regulation.[209] As the discussion of disclosure demonstrates, the equality of arms interests relate not just to the immediate trial, but also to bigger issues such as investigation procedures and ethics regulations. Disparity of resources becomes a more pressing concern when defence is given inadequate and questionable disclosure.

## Conclusion

When courts relinquish responsibility for the investigative inequalities outside of the courtroom, they do a disservice to the legitimacy of the courts and the quality of justice that may be rendered. Earlier we discussed how state cooperation can create fundamental disadvantages as states are often interested in helping one side of the case rather than another;[210] this inequality undoubtedly creates an unequal playing field.[211] As Byrne asserts, it is 'not surprising' that the courts have adapted equality of arms 'to account for the disequilibrium between the parties in international justice'.[212] She explains that the court's failure to consider the principle in relation to the unique realities of international criminal law has led to 'pragmatic and skeletal' legal analysis.[213]

To conclude, we review the legitimacy of 'full' equality versus the three layered weaker protections. In civil law systems, 'the principle of equality of arms does not necessarily require proportionality in terms of resources between the prosecution and the defence for conducting investigations'.[214] That is because the parties are not

---

[209] Ibid 11–12.
[210] Bibas and Burke-White (n 27) 697–698 ('The fragmentation of investigative and enforcement authority across different states and international organizations, however, means that the prosecutor may not actually know about or control evidence in a state's hands. For example, only days after the ICTY convicted a Bosnian Croat general of atrocities, Croatia turned over thousands of pages of potentially exculpatory evidence, leading the Appeals Chamber to overturn sixteen of his nineteen convictions'). For more on that ICTY case, see *Prosecutor v Blaškić* (Appeals Chamber Judgment) (n 122).
[211] Byrne (n 118) 251 ('The reliance by international tribunals on state cooperation in obtaining evidence renders international courts less able to presume a level playing field in the conduct of proceedings. The most crucial state cooperation required by international courts is that of ruling regimes in the jurisdictions where the crimes at issue were committed; evidence of international crimes within these fragile jurisdictions is often politically sensitive. Depending upon the implications of the indictments for the state, either the prosecution or the defense may face considerable barriers in accessing evidence and witnesses. Where this is the case for defense counsel, this obstacle to effective representation is compounded by the considerable inequity in the resources provided by the international tribunals to defense counsel, as compared to the Office of the Prosecutor').
[212] Ibid.
[213] Ibid.
[214] Tuinstra (n 13) 466.

responsible for the investigation. Instead, it is typically the investigating judge who looks for both incriminating and exculpatory evidence.

This is where the problem begins. International courts attempt to blend both systems together, and they attempt to do so while maintaining the important principles of each. However, the compromise demanded by such a blending also leads to a compromise in values, the human rights values, such as equality of arms. This calls back to the idea that equality of arms is being adapted to fit the needs of modern international criminal justice. One article expresses this concern: 'Our argument is not that a pure adversarial or inquisitorial system is preferable. Our fear is that the mishmash of the two systems has abandoned some distinctive checks on which each system depends.'[215] On the other hand, equality of arms is a principle of international human rights law; although it may originally derive from the adversarial procedure, it is not limited to common law systems.

Regardless of the legitimacy of full versus watered-down equality of arms, what remains clear is that 'the mishmash of systems obscures how to allocate resources'.[216] And as stated above, one of the main foundations, if not goals, of international criminal law, is that it will champion human rights law.[217] It would be ironic if a system, whose basic rationale is in many ways predicated on the idea of ensuring a dignified way of dealing with humanity's worst atrocities, itself countenances oppression of individual human rights guarantees all the while shrouding itself in the language and legitimacy of law. As Bibas and Burke-White caution, 'Ultimately, the legitimacy of international criminal law depends on zealous defence. That in turn requires compensation for full and effective—but not dilatory—litigation and common budget constraints for the prosecutor and the defence.'[218]

In closing, this chapter also discussed disclosure regimes in order to shed light on one possible mechanism to compensate for inequality of arms. Overall, if the general conclusion from this study is that the defence arm is the Achilles heel of modern international criminal justice, the conclusion seems inescapable that there is a strong imperative for a clearer and more consistent approach to the principle and practice of equality of arms, which is one of the most important jurisprudentially developed doctrines, employed to ensure fairness remain within international criminal law.

---

[215] Bibas and Burke-White (n 27) 695.

[216] Ibid 695–696 ('Because an adversarial system is based on two relatively equal parties contesting facts and evidence, each side needs roughly equal, adequate resources in order to investigate. American experience teaches that in an adversarial system, parity of funding for the two sides is crucial. But when inquisitorial judges carry the burden of investigating for both sides, the parties need fewer resources and the judges need more resources').

[217] See Section I. A. above, 'The Significance of Equality of Arms'.

[218] Bibas and Burke-White (n 27) 679.

# Protecting the Rights of the Accused in International Criminal Proceedings: Lip Service or Affirmative Action?

Colleen Rohan[1]

> A vigorous, un-intimidated, knowledgeable defense is the sine qua non of a fair trial.[2]

The newest incarnation of the practice of international criminal law is still a developing, dynamic legal process. It is comprised of judges, prosecutors and defence counsel from countries around the world who are the products of different cultures and legal traditions. It is made up of disparate courts which do not share the same system of substantive or procedural law. It has also been in existence for less than 20 years; relative infancy as compared to countries with legal philosophies and traditions that are centuries old.[3] The assumption that this developing legal process is already a fair and essentially stable system is as premature as speculation that the system will never be a truly viable one. It is just too early to tell.

There are trends in the system which can be identified, however, particularly now that the ICTY and ICTR, which are nearing the close of their mandates, have

---

[1] The author wishes to thank Legal Assistant Sofie Breslau for her assistance with this chapter.

[2] Judge Patricia Wald, International Criminal Tribunal for the former Yugoslavia. See PM Wald, 'The International Criminal Tribunal for the Former Yugoslavia Comes of Age: Some Observations on Day-to-Day Dilemmas of an International Court' (2001) 5 *J of L and Policy* 87, 102.

[3] The International Criminal Tribunal for the Former Yugoslavia (ICTY) was established by UNSC Res 827 (25 May 1993), UN Doc S/RES/827. The International Criminal Tribunal for Rwanda (ICTR) was established by UNSC Res 955 (8 November 1994), UN Doc S/RES/955.

an historical record which can be assessed. Some trends are disquieting to lawyers charged with representing the accused in international criminal trials as they appear to represent a gradual and growing retreat from a principled enforcement of the established rights of those accused of international crimes. This chapter briefly discusses two areas which reflect the close to unanimous concern of defence attorneys in international cases that the current procedural rules are moving in a direction which, though it may result in quicker trials, will do so at the expense of providing fair trials.

## I. Right to Adequate Time and Facilities to Prepare a Defence

All the international conventions and statutes which address the topic of the rights of an individual accused of crime provide that the accused is presumed to be innocent,[4] is entitled to a fair and public trial,[5] without undue delay,[6] the assistance of counsel,[7] the right to confront and cross-examine the witnesses called against him or her at trial,[8] and 'adequate time and facilities' to prepare a defence.[9] Given that all accused are presumed innocent unless and until the prosecution proves otherwise beyond a reasonable doubt,[10] adequate time and facilities to prepare a 'defence' refers not just to the preparation of an affirmative defence case, but also to adequate time and facilities with which to investigate and prepare to meet the prosecution's evidence at trial. The prosecution bears the burden of proof at trial; a burden which never shifts to the accused.[11] The accused has no burden to present

---

[4]   Statute of the International Criminal Tribunal for the former Yugoslavia, UN Doc S/RES/827 (ICTY Statute), art 21(3); Statute of the International Criminal Tribunal for Rwanda, UN Doc S/RES/955 (ICTR Statute), art 20(3); ICC Statute of the International Criminal Court, 2187 UNTS 90 (17 July 1998, entered into force 1 July 2002) (ICC statute), art 66; International Covenant on Civil and Political Rights 999 UNTS 171 (adopted 16 December 1966, entered into force 23 March 1976) (ICCPR), art 14(2); European Convention for the Protection of Human Rights and Fundamental Freedoms, 213 UNTS 222 (entered into force 3 September 1953) (ECHR), art 6(2).

[5]   ICTY Statute, art 21(2); ICTR Statute, art 20(2); ICC Statute, art 67(1); ICCPR, art 14(1); ECHR, art 6(1).

[6]   ICTY Statute, art 21(4)(c); ICTR Statute, art 20(4)(c); ICC Statute, art 67(1); ICCPR, art 14(3)(c); ECHR, art 6(1) (trial must be 'within a reasonable time').

[7]   ICTY Statute, art 21(4)(b); ICTR Statute, art 20(4)(b); ICC Statute, art 67(1)(b); ICCPR, art 14(3)(b); ECHR, art 6(3)(c).

[8]   ICTY Statute, art 21(4)(e); ICTR Statute, art 20(4)(e); ICC Statute, art 67(1)(e); ICCPR, art 14(3)(e); ECHR, art 6(3)(d).

[9]   ICTY Statute, art 21(4)(b); ICTR Statute, art 20(4)(b); ICC Statute, art 67(1)(b); ICCPR, art 14(3)(b); ECHR, art 6(3)(b).

[10]  See for example *Prosecutor v Limaj et al* (Trial Judgment) IT-03-66-T (30 November 2005), para 10.

[11]  Ibid. See further *Prosecutor v Naletilic and Martinovic* (Trial Judgment) IT-98-34-T (31 March 2003).

an affirmative defence case and may rest on the strength, or lack thereof, of the prosecution evidence standing on its own.[12]

In order to prepare a case for trial counsel for the accused must have timely access to the substance of the prosecution case; the disclosure which will comprise the prosecution evidence at trial. In fact and in practice:

> The disclosure process is arguably the most important mechanism for ensuring that an accused receives a fair trial. This is predominantly due to the fact that prosecutors have resources for investigations far in excess of that of defendants. Requiring the disclosure of evidence obtained during the course of prosecution investigations seeks to redress this imbalance.[13]

A number of rules governing disclosure of prosecution evidence have been put in place at the *ad hoc* tribunals and at the ICC. There are reasons for these rules. Timely disclosure of prosecution evidence is the sole means for affording the accused adequate time and facilities in which to investigate that evidence and prepare to meet it at trial. The near-universal view of defence counsel is that these rules are honoured as much in their breach as in their observance.[14]

## A. The Rules at Issue

The Rules of Procedure and Evidence (RPE) developed by the *ad hoc* tribunals and at the ICC represent a *sui generis* mix of legal concepts taken from Western civil and common law traditions. They do not constitute the transposition of any specific national legal system, be it of civil or common law origin, onto the international legal stage.[15] These rules must also be assessed in the context in which they are

---

[12] See for example *Prosecutor v Haradinaj et al* (Trial Judgment) IT-04-84-T (3 April 2008), acquitting two of three accused of all 37 counts in the Indictment after all accused rested on the Prosecution evidence; *Prosecutor v Limaj* (Trial Judgment) (n 9), in which one of the three accused rested on the state of the evidence and was acquitted of all charges. In *Haradinaj et al* the Appeals Chamber subsequently reversed six of the acquittals and ordered a re-trial on those counts—the first such re-trial, after acquittals, in the international courts. At the re-trial all three accused were acquitted of all 6 counts; again after presenting no affirmative defence. *Prosecutor v Haradinaj et al* (Trial Judgement) IT-04-84*bis*-T (29 November 2012). The Prosecutor has not appealed these second acquittals.

[13] K Gibson and C Lussiaa-Berdou, 'Disclosure of Evidence' in K Kahn, C Buisman and C Gosnell (eds) *Principles of Evidence in International Criminal Justice* (OUP, Oxford 2010) 306.

[14] See for example JI Turner, 'Defence Perspectives on Law and Politics in International Criminal Trials' (2008) 48(3) *Virginia J of Int'l Law* 529, 557–558 (containing survey results on this topic from defence counsel practising at the ICTY).

[15] *Prosecutor v Blaškić* (Decision on the Standing Objection of the Defence to the Admission of Hearsay With No Inquiry as to its Reliability) IT-95-14-T (21 January 1998), para 5; see further C Schuon, *International Criminal Procedure: A Clash of Legal Cultures* (TMC

applied. The approach to the admission of evidence in international trials is very liberal.[16] With rare exceptions, almost all evidence, even multiple hearsay, is admissible if it has some probative value and some indicia of reliability.[17] Similar to the civil law tradition, the judges who sit at trial are charged with the responsibility of assigning what weight they deem appropriate to the evidence produced.[18] Given this liberal approach to the admission of evidence, one recognised 'safeguard' to ensure the fair trial rights of the accused are respected are the rules requiring timely and comprehensive disclosure of prosecution evidence.[19]

## B. The Need to Effectively Enforce Disclosure Rules

The accused at the *ad hoc* tribunals are provided, as a general matter, with all materials filed in support of the Indictment within 30 days of their initial appearance in court.[20] That disclosure usually consists of several hundred to several thousand pages of documents; however, these materials are usually just the tip of the disclosure iceberg. The RPE at the *ad hoc* tribunals and the ICC describe in detail the prosecution's obligation to provide the defence with *timely* disclosure of all remaining relevant materials which will be used by the prosecution at trial.[21] At the ICTY, for example, within a time period set by the Pre-Trial or Trial Chamber, the prosecution must serve the accused with copies of all statements of all witnesses it intends to call at trial, copies of all exhibits it intends to put into evidence at trial, and copies of statements from any additional trial witnesses as of the time the decision is made to call those witnesses.[22]

---

Asser Press, The Hague 2010), containing an in-depth comparison of the many variations in procedural rules between civil and common law jurisdictions, the RPE at the ICTY and the RPE at the ICC.

[16] Schuon (n 15) 136; C Gosnell, 'Admissibility of Evidence' in Kahn et al (n 13) 375.

[17] Rules of Procedure and Evidence of the International Criminal Tribunal for the former Yugoslavia, UN Doc IT/32/Rev46 (20 October 2011) (ICTY RPE), Rule 89; Rules of Procedure and Evidence of the International Criminal Tribunal for Rwanda, UN Doc ITR/3/Rev20 (1 October 2009) (ICTR RPE), Rule 89; International Criminal Court, Rules of Procedure and Evidence, ICC-ASP/1/3 (Part.II-A) (9 September 2002) (ICC RPE), Rule 63.

[18] There are no juries in the international courts. Trials at the *ad hoc* tribunals and the ICC take place in front of a panel of three judges. An accused can be convicted or acquitted by majority vote.

[19] R May and M Wierda, 'Trends in International Criminal Evidence: Nuremberg, Tokyo, The Hague, and Arusha' (1999) 37 *Colum J Transnat'l L* 725, 753.

[20] ICTY RPE, Rule 66(A)(i); ICTR RPE, Rule 66(A)(i).

[21] ICTY RPE, Rules 65*ter* and 66; ICTR RPE, Rules 66 and 67; ICC RPE, Rules 76, 77, 78, 84 (Rule 76 requires that the names and prior statements of prosecution trial witnesses must be disclosed to the accused 'sufficiently in advance to enable the adequate preparation of the defence').

[22] ICTY RPE, Rule 66(A)(ii).

The amount of this disclosure will, of course, vary from case to case. There are some cases at the ICTR and ICC which involve relatively small amounts of pre-trial disclosure. It is not unusual at the ICTY, on the other hand, for disclosure, particularly in multi-defendant cases, and cases involving broadly charged joint criminal enterprise theories and/or command responsibility, to exceed hundreds of thousands of pages. The *Karadžić* case, currently on trial at the ICTY, includes approximately two million pages of disclosure to date. Despite the deadlines imposed by the relevant disclosure rules, prosecution disclosure at the ICTY routinely continues throughout the trial proceedings.[23] It frequently includes witness statements, archival documents and other materials which have been in the possession of the prosecution for months or years prior to the beginning of trial. It can occur on the eve of trial, mid-trial, or only one or two days prior to the testimony of the witness to whom it relates, leaving the accused without the time and resources to investigate the facts much less integrate them into a coherent overview of how to go about meeting the evidence through informed, effective cross-examination.[24] As put by one defence practitioner:

> Just imagine being served with hundreds or even thousands of pages of new disclosure material, in the form of witness statements or documents, right before trial, or in the middle of trial, or just before closing argument, or even while the appeal is pending after the submission of the briefs ... More often than not the defence does not have the funds to react to the situation completely.[25]

It is equally true that more often than not the defence team does not have the time to react to the situation completely.[26]

All practitioners are aware and accept that items of disclosure may be inadvertently overlooked during preparation of the Prosecutor's case pre-trial. All practitioners also know that new items of evidence, not previously in the possession of the Prosecutor, may become available for the first time only during the course of trial. The accused's fundamental rights are undermined, however, when late disclosure is allowed without adequate explanation for its untimely revelation

---

[23] In the *Karadžić* case, the Prosecution has been required to file disclosure reports on a monthly basis listing the disclosure provided to the accused. See for example *Prosecutor v Karadžić* (Prosecution Periodic Disclosure Report with Confidential Appendices A, B and C) IT-95-5/18-T (15 April 2010) and those filed thereafter. The monthly reports reflect that thousands of pages of disclosure were produced only after trial testimony began in April 2010; significant quantities of which were in the possession of the Prosecution before trial began.

[24] See Turner (n 14) 557.

[25] Ibid, noting similar responses to a questionnaire sent to defence attorneys at the ICTY and ICTR on the topic of disclosure.

[26] Ibid 558. The survey revealed that the problem of late disclosure is so endemic that some defence attorneys believe delayed disclosure is an intentional prosecution tactic, designed to overwhelm the Defence and exhaust its resources.

and without any sanction being imposed on the offending party as a means to deter continued violation of disclosure rules. When this occurs, it is no answer that the accused can always investigate the evidence later and perhaps confront or rebut it during the defence case. The accused does not have the burden of proof. Requiring the accused, due to late disclosure of prosecution evidence, to put on an affirmative defence improperly shifts the burden of proof to the accused at least as to the evidence in question. Likewise, focusing on what the accused might do to ameliorate a problem created by the prosecution, as a means of finding the accused suffered no prejudice due to the late disclosure, allows an offending prosecutor, be the behaviour intentional or repeatedly negligent, to function with impunity.[27]

The undermining of the fair trial rights of the accused is exacerbated when late disclosure includes exculpatory or potentially exculpatory evidence. The *ad hoc* tribunals as well as the ICC[28] provide that the Prosecutor shall, as soon as practicable, disclose to the defence any materials which may suggest the innocence or mitigate the guilt of the accused or affect the credibility of prosecution evidence.[29] The Prosecutor's duty to disclose exculpatory evidence is an ongoing one throughout the course of the trial and appeal process.[30] The Prosecutor also has the duty to be diligent in identifying and disclosing exculpatory materials. Negligent performance of this critical obligation, due to the late disclosure of exculpatory material, does not equate and should not be seen as equating with compliance with the rules.[31] The late provision of exculpatory materials is an ongoing problem for the accused at the ICTY and ICTR even though the prosecution's obligation to disclose exculpatory evidence is essential to providing the accused with adequate time and facilities to prepare a defence. Timely disclosure of exculpatory evidence

---

[27] See Gibson and Lussiaa-Berdou (n 13) 313, noting that 'while the chambers of [the *ad hoc*] tribunals regularly recall the importance of disclosure as a fundamental component of fair trials, even repeated violations of disclosure obligations by the prosecution fail to elicit sanctions, and the remedy for late or non-disclosure is regularly limited to postponement of the testimony or cross-examination of the relevant witness, rather than the more stringent remedies of exclusion of evidence, dismissal of charges which rely on the evidence, or a stay of proceedings'.

[28] ICTY RPE, Rule 68; ICTR RPE, Rule 68; ICC Statute, art 67(2).

[29] At the ICC, unlike the ICTY and ICTR, the procedural framework provides that in 'case of a doubt' as to whether evidence is exculpatory 'the Court shall decide' (a process which will occur *in camera*). See ICC Statute, art 67(2).

[30] See for example *Prosecutor v Brđanin* (Decision on Appellant's Motion for Disclosure Pursuant to Rule 68 and Motion for an order to the Registrar to Disclose Certain Materials) IT-99-36-A (7 December 2004), 2; *Prosecutor v Blaškić* (Decision on the Appellant's Motion for the Production of Materials, Suspension or Extension of Briefing Schedule and Additional Filings) IT-95-14-A (26 September 2000), para 42.

[31] See *Prosecutor v Krstić* (Appeals Judgment) IT-98-33-A (19 April 2004), paras 197–198, noting that while the Prosecution argument that the Defence had enough time to 'consider' late Rule 68 disclosure may allay allegations of prejudice to the Defence case, it did not address the fact that the Prosecution breached Rule 68 by not providing the disclosure at issue as soon as practicable. As the *Krstić* Appeals Chamber put it (at para 197): 'It is not for the Prosecution to determine the amount of time the Defence requires to conduct its case.'

is also, as an ethical matter, prerequisite to the prosecution discharging its duty to assist the Trial Chamber in arriving at the truth and to providing 'justice for the international community, victims and the accused'.[32]

Nonetheless, the procedural rules do not provide for any specific sanction for late disclosure of exculpatory materials.[33] At the ICTY a prosecutor was recently publicly and personally reprimanded, under Rule 68*bis*, for his continued violation of Rule 68; a rare sanction in that Tribunal's jurisprudence.[34] The Office of the Prosecutor sought reconsideration of the individual reprimand, arguing that a personal reprimand of the individual prosecutor who engaged in the disclosure violations was beyond the power of the Chambers under Rule 68*bis* and that the Chamber was restricted to reprimanding 'the Prosecutor as a party to the proceedings, or the Prosecutor.'[35]

By majority vote the Trial Chamber adopted this argument, and vacated the personal reprimand of the individual, offending prosecutor.[36] The dissent, however, properly emphasized that the power to reprimand an individual attorney under Rule 68*bis* 'is a necessary option to hold attorneys accountable for grave disclosure violations' and the failure to do so 'may foster a climate of impunity by sending attorneys the message that they cannot be held accountable for misconduct unless the Chamber takes the extraordinary step of applying Rule 46[37] [which empowers a Trial Chamber, after 'due warning' to refuse individual counsel audience or report him or her to bar authorities]. As the Dissent noted, an individual sanction pursuant to Rule 68*bis* is intended to enforce the fair trial rights of the accused, not to impact on the individual prosecutor's rights of audience.[38]

Individual Trial Chambers at the ICTY and ICTR have, on infrequent occasion, exercised their discretion to create case-related sanctions based on the circumstances in the case before them; such as drawing reasonable inferences in favour of the accused regarding the evidence to which the late disclosure relates

---

[32] ICTY, Standards of Professional Conduct for Prosecution Counsel, Prosecutor's Regulation No 2 (1999), 2(a).

[33] ICTY RPE, Rule 68*bis*, providing that sanctions may be imposed, but not providing what those sanctions might include. A similar rule does not exist at the ICTR. See also *Krstić* (Appeals Judgment) (n 31), para 200, finding the Prosecution violated Rule 68 in that case and opining that the 'consequences are governed by Rule 46 (Misconduct of Counsel) and Rule 68*bis*'.

[34] See *Prosecutor v Haradinaj et al* (Decision on Joint Defence Motion for Relief From Rule 68 Violations by the Prosecution and for Sanctions Pursuant to Rule 68Bis) IT-04-84*bis* (12 October 2011), para 71(e).

[35] *Prosecutor v Haradinaj et al* (Motion for Reconsideration of Relief Ordered Pursuant to Rule 68*BIS*) IT-04-84*bis*-T (25 October 2011), paras 6-8; 20.

[36] *Prosecutor v Haradinaj et al* (Decision on Prosecutor's Motion for Reconsideration of Relief Ordered Pursuant to Rule 68*BIS* With Partially Dissenting Opinion of Judge Hall) IT-04-84*bis*-T (27 March 2012),

[37] Ibid (Partially Dissenting Opinion by Judge Hall), paras 1-4; ICTY RPE, Rule 46.

[38] Ibid (Partially Dissenting Opinion by Judge Hall), paras 4; 6.

or affording less weight to that evidence.³⁹ Trial Chambers have also considered the cumulative prejudice arising from repeated late disclosure.⁴⁰ Suffice it to say, however, that rulings, such as that in the *Haradinaj et al* case contribute to a climate of impunity regarding disclosure violations. Rule 46 proceedings relate only to the gravest forms of misconduct. The Prosecutor's duty to timely disclose potentially exculpatory evidence, nonetheless, is 'key to ensuring a fair trial' for the accused.⁴¹

The ICC, on the other hand, imposed case-related sanctions on the prosecution for the late disclosure of exculpatory evidence in the very first case brought before it. Shortly before the beginning of the trial in the *Lubanga* case, the Trial Chamber issued a stay of the proceedings due to its finding of a 'wholesale and serious abuse' of the prosecutor's obligation to disclose exculpatory evidence to the accused.⁴² Lubanga was ordered to be released because, as the Trial Chamber held, a 'fair trial is not possible and the entire justification for his detention has been removed'.⁴³ The order for Lubanga's release was ultimately overturned on appeal after prosecutors took steps to comply with their disclosure obligations.⁴⁴ The case-related sanction, in short, resulted in the Prosecution finally fulfilling its disclosure obligations. This has not solved the problem of late disclosure or non-disclosure at the ICC.⁴⁵ It does illustrate the need for and the efficacy of case-related sanctions, under appropriate

---

³⁹ See for example *Prosecutor v Orić* (Decision on Ongoing Complaints About Prosecutor's Non-Compliance with Rule 68 of the Rules) IT-03-68-T (13 December 2005), paras 32–35.

⁴⁰ See for example *Prosecutor v Karadžić* (Decision on Accused's Twenty-Second, Twenty-Fourth and Twenty-Sixth Disclosure Violation Motions) IT-95-5-18-T (11 November 2010), paras 40–41, noting the 'significant number of violations by the Prosecution of its disclosure obligations under Rules 66(A)(ii) and 68 of the Rules which have been found to date in this case'.

⁴¹ *Prosecutor v Haradinaj et al* (Decision on Prosecutor's Motion for Reconsideration of Relief Ordered Pursuant to Rule 68*BIS* With Partially Dissenting Opinion of Judge Hall) IT-04-84-T (27 March 2012), (Partially Dissenting Opinion by Judge Hall), para 4; citing *Prosecutor v Krstic* (Appeals Judgement), IT-98-33-A (19 April 2004), para 180.

⁴² *Situation in the Democratic Republic of the Congo: Prosecutor v Lubanga* (Decision on the consequences of the non-disclosure of exculpatory materials covered by Article 54(3)(e) agreements and the application to stay the proceedings of the accused, together with certain other issues raised at the Status Conference on 10 June 2008) ICC-01/04/01/06 (13 June 2008), para 73.

⁴³ *Situation in the Democratic Republic of the Congo: Prosecutor v Lubanga* (Decision on the Release of Thomas Lubanga Dyilo) ICC-01/04-01/06 (2 July 2008), para 34.

⁴⁴ See Gibson and Lussiaa-Berdou (n 13) 350–351 (containing discussion of the procedures in *Lubanga* and comparing the ICC disclosure regime with that of the ICTY and ICTR).

⁴⁵ *Situation in the Democratic Republic of the Congo: Prosecutor v Katanga* (Decision on Article 54(3) Documents Identified as Potentially Exculpatory or Otherwise Material for the Defence's Preparation for the Confirmation Hearing) ICC-01/04-01/07 (20 June 2008), paras 123–124 (finding abuse of prosecution disclosure obligations though no stay of proceedings was entered).

circumstances, when disclosure obligations are violated, as an essential means for protecting the accused right to a fair trial.

International criminal law, if it intends to create a legacy of reliable verdicts which are acceptable to the community at large, must effectively address and minimise the problem of late prosecution disclosure by developing a consistent system of case-related sanctions in those instances when late disclosure is the result of intentional conduct or repeated negligence. Slapping the wrists of an offending party with 'warnings'[46] and without imposition of any real sanctions has historically not worked as an effective deterrent. Most importantly, it does not 'safeguard' the accused's right to adequate time and facilities to prepare a defence, to the effective assistance of counsel or, in some cases, to the right to effectively confront and cross-examine the witnesses against him or her at trial.

## II. Right to Confront and Cross-Examine Witnesses

When the ICTY first came into being the Rules of Procedure and Evidence expressed a preference for witnesses to appear in person at trial and provide *viva voce* testimony.[47] The ICTR procedural rules continue to contain that preference.[48] It has been removed from the ICTY rules, however, and there has been an increasing reliance on written witness statements and resultant amendments to the ICTY RPE to allow for their expanded use ever since.[49] The trend to supplant *viva voce* testimony, which can be cross-examined, with written witness statements, which cannot, is another instance in which form is placed over substance regarding the fundamental rights of the accused.

### A. Rule 92bis

Rule 92*bis*, adopted at both the ICTY and ICTR, allows for the admission of written witness statements if the statements do not go to the acts and conduct of the accused.[50] The idea underlying enactment of these rules is to 'facilitate the

---

[46] See for example *Prosecutor v Karemera* (Decision on Prosecutor's Rule 66(D) Application and Joseph Nzirorera's 12th Notice of Rule 68 Violation) ICTR-98-44-T (26 March 2009), in which the Trial Chamber 'warned' the prosecutor to comply with the applicable disclosure rules.

[47] *Prosecutor v Kordić and Čerkez* (Decision on Appeal Regarding Statement of a Deceased Witness) IT-95-14/2-AR73.5 (21 July 2000), para 19; *Prosecutor v Blagojević and Jokić* (Trial Judgment) IT-02-60-T (17 January 2005), para 21.

[48] ICTR RPE, Rule 90(A).

[49] ICTY RPE, Rules 92*ter* (adopted 13 September 2006); 92*quater* (adopted 13 September 2006); 92*quinquies* (adopted 10 December 2009).

[50] ICTY RPE, Rule 92*bis*(A); ICTR RPE, Rule 92*bis*(A). A fuller and more specific comparison of the variations between these two rules can be found in Gosnell (n 16) 395–413.

admission by way of written statements of peripheral or background evidence in order to expedite proceedings while protecting the rights of the accused under the Statute'.[51] The credibility and/or reliability of this written 'evidence' is not subject to testing by cross-examination.[52]

Since the adoption of Rule 92*bis*, there has been an increasing reliance on written statements at trial. In the *Krajišnik* case at the ICTY, for example, more witness statements were admitted under Rule 92*bis* (168) than statements given by *viva voce* witnesses (101).[53] There has also been a proliferation of litigation regarding which statements fall within the Rule's provisions and which do not. The litigation has frequently resulted in a relatively lenient assessment as to those statements which qualify for admission under the rule; a foreseeable event given the political pressure placed on the *ad hoc* tribunals to complete the cases before them within a specific period of time.[54]

## B. Rule 92quater

In September of 2006, Rules 92*ter* and 92*quater* were adopted at the ICTY. Prior to the enactment of Rule 92*quater*, Rule 92*bis*(A) and (C) provided that the written statement of a witness who was deceased by the time of trial, missing or unable to testify due to bodily or mental condition could *not* be admitted if the statement went to the acts and conduct of the accused.[55] Rule 92*quater* did away with that limitation. It provides that the written statement or transcript of testimony from a witness is admissible without cross-examination if (1) the Trial Chamber is satisfied the witness is unavailable under the conditions listed in the Rule, and (2) finds from the circumstances in which 'the statement was made and recorded' that it is 'reliable'. The fact that a statement goes to the acts and conduct of the accused 'as charged in the indictment' is treated as a factor which only weighs against, but

---

[51] Eighth Annual Report of the ICTY, UN Doc A/56/352 and UN Doc S/2001/865.

[52] ICTY RPE, Rule 92*bis* lists as potential 'peripheral' issues: evidence relating to historical, political or military background; statistical analysis of ethnic populations; the impact of crimes upon victims; the character of the accused; and factors to be taken into account in sentencing. One need only look at Indictments filed in the 161 cases at the ICTY to see that in any number of cases these are not peripheral issues. Hence the rule has resulted in a significant amount of litigation regarding admission of such statements.

[53] *Prosecutor v Krajišnik* (Decision on Prosecution Motions for Judicial Notice of Adjudicated Facts and for Admission of Written Statements of Witnesses Pursuant to Rule 92*bis*) IT-00-39-T (28 February 2003), para 26; discussed further in Gosnell (n 16) 396.

[54] See MA Fairlie, 'Due Process Erosion: The Diminution of Live Testimony at the ICTY' (2003) 34 *Cal W Int'l L J* 47.

[55] ICTY RPE, Rules 92(A) and (C) (as adopted in December 2000). The ICTR has not adopted a rule similar to the ICTY's Rule 92*quater*. Under ICTR RPE, Rule 92*bis* statements from unavailable witnesses which go to the acts and conduct of the accused remain inadmissible even when the prior statement is sworn testimony previously given before the Tribunal; see ICTR RPE 92*bis*(D).

does not prevent, admission of the statement.⁵⁶ Ironically, unlike written witness statements offered under Rule 92*bis* which may *not* go to the acts or conduct of the accused and which require, as a prerequisite to admission in evidence, a formal declaration from the witness under penalty of perjury that the statement is true,⁵⁷ 92*quater* statements, which *may* go to the acts and conduct of the accused maybe admitted at the ICTY without a similar formal attestation.⁵⁸

In the international courts pre-trial written witness statements are gathered by prosecution investigators or prosecution attorneys as part of the prosecution's partisan investigation of its own case. No neutral party is involved in the process. With extremely rare exception, no one representing the interests of the accused is present at the time such statements are obtained.⁵⁹ The 'statements' are also *summaries* of what the witness said; summaries prepared by prosecutors or the investigators working on prosecution teams. There is no rule requiring that witness statements must be tape recorded. Verbatim transcripts of such statements are rarely available. Serious questions have been raised, at least at the ICC, as to the process by which some of these statements have been obtained. As recently emphasized by the Confirmation Chamber in the *Mbarushimana* case:

> . . . the Chamber wishes to highlight its concern at the technique followed in several instances by some Prosecution investigators, which seems utterly inappropriate when viewed in light of the objective, set out in article 54(1)(a) of the Statute, to establish the truth by 'investigating incriminating and exonerating circumstances equally.' The reader of the transcripts of interviews is repeatedly left with the impression that the investigator is so attached to his or her theory or assumption that he or she does not refrain from putting questions in leading terms and from showing resentment, impatience or disappointment whenever the witness replies in terms which are not entirely in line with his or her expectations. Suggesting that the witness may not be 'really remembering exactly what was said,' complaining about having 'to milk out' from the witness details which are of relevance to the investigation, lamenting that the witness does not 'really understand what is important' to the investigators

---

⁵⁶ ICTY RPE, Rule 92*quater*(B).
⁵⁷ ICTY RPE, Rule 92*bis*(B)(ii)(c).
⁵⁸ Witnesses who testify orally must also make a solemn declaration to tell the truth, with the exception of young children who may testify without the oath if they understand the duty to tell the truth. ICTY RPE, Rule 90(A); ICTR RPE, Rule 90(A); ICC RPE, Rule 66. Witnesses who testify orally, of course, are available for cross-examination by the opposing party and questioning by the Trial Chambers.
⁵⁹ *Prosecutor v Kordić and Čerkez* (n 47), para 27. See further *Prosecutor v Naletilić and Martinović* (Decision on the Prosecutor's Request for Public Version of Trial Chambers 'Decision on the Motion to Admit Statement of Deceased Witness [...]' of 22 January 2002) IT-98-34-T (27 February 2002), para 7, listing a number of factors as cause for concern regarding 'the general reliability of witness statements given to investigators of the Prosecution'.

in the case, or hinting at the fact that the witness may be 'trying to cover' for the Suspect, seem hardly reconcilable with a professional and impartial technique of witness questioning. Accordingly, the Chamber cannot refrain from deprecating such techniques and from highlighting that, as a consequence, the probative value of evidence obtained by these means may be significantly weakened.[60]

In addition to the concerns just addressed, no matter how well intentioned, ethical and meticulous prosecution lawyers and investigators may be, there is no doubt that critical information can be overlooked or lost in the process of creating written summaries of whatever it was the witness actually said. The majority of the statements also require translation, a process itself fraught with the possibility – indeed probability – that translation errors will occur. The production of new information and/or corrections to prior written statements, almost routinely offered from prosecution witnesses during *viva voce* testimony at trial or after 'proofing' sessions conducted immediately before a witness is called to testify,[61] itself strongly suggests that the pre-trial written witness statements are not entirely reliable, even assuming the witness is credible.[62]

A comment made by Judge Bonomy in the *Milutinović* case at the ICTY dramatically illustrates this latter point. There a complaint was raised regarding the prosecution practice to disclose new information obtained during proofing sessions so late that the Defence had little to no opportunity to investigate the new information before the witness appeared in court. In response to that concern, the Prosecution explained that it had initially intended to submit several witnesses' statements under Rule 92*bis* without cross-examination, which would have avoided any problems arising from the late 'proofing' of witnesses. The Chambers responded:

> Judge Bonomy: Well, can I say that the first reason strikes me as extraordinarily naïve because one thing that's absolutely clear from

---

[60] See *Situation in the Democratic Republic of Congo in the Case of Prosecutor v Callixte Mbarushimana* (Decision on the confirmation of charges) ICC-01/04-01/10 16 (December 2011), para 51.

[61] 'Witness proofing' generally refers to a meeting held between a party to the proceedings and a witness shortly before the witness is to testify in court, the purpose of which is to prepare and familiarise the witness with courtroom procedures and to review the witness' prior statements. See 'Trial Management – Proofing of Witnesses' in *ICTY Manual on Developed Practices* (UNICRI, Turin 2009), 83–84; *Prosecutor v Haradinaj et al* (Decision on Defence Request for Audio-Recording of Prosecution Witness Proofing Sessions) IT-04-84-T (23 May 2007).

[62] The process of witness proofing is controversial. It is allowed at the ICTY and ICTR, but is not permitted at the ICC except for purposes of familiarising the witness with courtroom procedures. For a discussion of the practice and controversy surrounding its use, see W Jordash 'The Practice of "Witness Proofing" in International Criminal Tribunals: Why the International Criminal Court Should Prohibit the Practice' (2009) 22 *Leiden J of Int'l L* 501.

the way in which this case has been conducted so far is that there could have been the grossest miscarriage of justice if these witnesses had not been available for cross-examination.

Prosecutor: Your Honour, I understand your point. But I indicate to you it's not naïve on my part based on the experience in the other case that I worked on in the Tribunal.

Judge Bonomy: Well, all that's happened through – well, one thing that's become clear through cross-examination is that it was necessary. I shudder to think what might have happened without that opportunity being available.[63]

## C. Rule 92ter

Rule 92*ter* at the ICTY allows for admission of the written statement of a witness which does go to the acts and conduct of the accused, if the witness is present in court, is available for cross-examination, and the witness attests that the written statement or transcript offered in lieu of his or her direct testimony is what the witness would say if examined orally on the same issues in court.[64] The rule can save time in court as the party offering a '92*ter* witness' need only elicit testimony from the witness that the prior written statement is still true and correct. After that the statement is given an exhibit number and admitted in evidence. Then cross-examination begins.[65] The ramifications of this rule can also potentially undermine the rights of the accused, in this instance to a public trial.

The procedure may result in the only oral evidence heard in court being the cross-examination of the witness by the opposing party. There will be 'no opportunity for the Judges to make their own impression of the credibility of the witness from the evidence-in-chief; they would have to take that from the statement itself'.[66] Rule 92*ter* statements are also increasingly used as vehicles to introduce dozens of written exhibits as matters 'associated' with the *prior* statements or testimony which constitute the 92*ter* statement. The 'associated' exhibits may or may not ever be mentioned, discussed or be the subject of examination in open court. In fact, the exact content of the 92*ter* statement itself – which is the witness's testimony in the

---

[63] *Prosecutor v Milutinović et al* (Trial Proceedings) IT-05-87-T (31 August 2006), 2675–2676.

[64] See *Prosecutor v Milošević* (Decision on Interlocutory Appeal on the Admissibility of Evidence-in-Chief in the Form of Written Statements) IT-02-54-AR73.4 (30 September 2003), interpreting the then extant ICTY RPE Rule 89(c) as allowing for this process. ICTY RPE, Rule 92*ter* now codifies the same procedure. The ICTR does not have a comparable rule.

[65] In practice this does not always occur. Witnesses can be offered as a 'partial 92*ter* witness' meaning that the 92*ter* statement will be admitted and the party will supplement it with some additional oral testimony.

[66] S Kay 'The Move From Oral Evidence to Written Evidence' (2004) 2 *JICJ* 495, 500.

case-in-chief – is never revealed in open court. Instead, a very short, generalised summary is read into the record by the party offering the witness.

The international community has a continuing interest in the content of the evidence in international war crimes trials, including witness testimony. The extensive use of the 92*ter* process, however, can serve to undermine the accused right to a public trial by hindering the access of the international community to the evidence produced at trial.[67]

## D. Rule 92quinquies

ICTY Rule 92*quinquies* is the latest and hopefully the last of the rules permitting written witness statements in evidence at the expense of the accused right to cross-examination and to a fair trial. Rule 92*quinquies* provides, in essence, that a prior written statement of a witness may be admitted in lieu of that witness's oral testimony if the failure to testify has been, *inter alia*, 'materially influenced by improper interference including threats, intimidation, injury, bribery, or coercion'.[68] Rule 92*quinquies* specifically provides that written statements admitted under the rule '*may* include evidence that goes to proof of the acts and conduct of the accused as charged in the indictment'.[69] The rule was enacted in late 2009. There are no rulings or cases construing its provisions as yet. Its enactment at this late stage in ICTY history is extremely troublesome regarding attitudes underlying the development of a fair and consistent system of international criminal law which respects and protects the rights of the accused.

The rule provides that statements can be admitted pursuant to its provisions 'in the interests of justice', but contains no standards regarding whether the interference, threats, intimidation or coercion is to be judged by an objective, reasonable person standard or by the entirely subjective perceptions of the witness at issue. The rule does provide that, in determining whether to admit a written statement, 'the interests of justice' include an assessment of the reliability of the statement or transcript [of the witness] having regard to the circumstances in which it was made and recorded,[70] the apparent role of a party or someone acting on behalf of a party to the proceedings in the improper interference,[71] and whether the statement or transcript goes to proof of the acts and conduct of the accused as charged in the indictment.[72]

---

[67] It is possible to read the 92*ter* statements which are kept in the court archives of its trial records. What is highly questionable is whether anyone who has not worked at one of the tribunals knows that fact or knows how to get access to those records.
[68] ICTY RPE, Rule 92*quinquies* (enacted 10 December 2009).
[69] ICTY RPE, Rule 92*quinquies*(B)(iii).
[70] ICTY RPE 92*quinquies*(B)(ii)(a)
[71] Ibid at (B)(ii)(b)
[72] Ibid at (B)(ii)(c). In this sense the fact a statement goes to the acts and conduct of the accused might be a factor weighing against admission of the statement but it is not cause to prevent its admission.

However, subsection (C) of the rule provides that the 'Trial Chamber may have regard to any relevant evidence, including written evidence, for the purpose of applying this Rule'. This provision is certainly subject to more than one interpretation, but it suggests that a Trial Chamber may rely on written 'evidence' for purposes of determining whether the predicate fact which triggers the rule – the existence of a threat, intimidation, interference, coercion or bribery – ever occurred. If the accused has no means to cross-examine regarding the reliability and/or credibility of written 'evidence' as to those predicate facts, 92*quinquies* potentially represents a two-step denial of an accused's right to confront the witnesses against him or her.

The adoption of these rules expanding the circumstances under which un-cross-examined, written statements can be admitted at trial in lieu of oral testimony may expedite trials. The same rules also increasingly undermine the accused's right to confront and cross-examine the witnesses against him or her at trial. This is particularly true when written witness statements, going to the acts and conduct of the accused as charged in the indictment, are admitted in evidence. In those instances the accused may be simply foreclosed from challenging the evidence at all; a circumstance wholly inconsistent with the requirement that an accused is entitled to a fair trial.[73]

## E. The Rome Statute

The Rome Statute reflects a welcome return to the principle that witnesses should testify in person, in court. Article 69(2) states that: '[t]he testimony of a witness at trial shall be given in person, except to the extent provided by the measures set forth in Article 68 or in the Rules of Procedure and Evidence.' The ICC procedural rules 'authorize the admission of testimony in written form in two circumstances: (i) in the form of a deposition (ICC, Rule 68(a)), or (ii) if the person appears before the chamber as a witness, agrees to its admission, and is ready to be cross-examined thereon (ICC Rule 68(b))'.[74] The Rome Statute and the ICC Rules permit, under specified circumstances, the presentation of testimony by video or audio technology,[75] but that testimony must take place under circumstances which 'permit(s) the witness to be examined by the Prosecutor, the Defence, and by the Chamber itself, *at the time that the witness so testifies*'. The admission of prior written

---

[73] For a broader discussion of the increasing curtailment of the accused's right to cross examination due to various other procedural rules, in addition to the admission of written witness statements, see E O'Sullivan and D Montgomery, 'The Erosion of the Right to Confrontation Under the Cloak of Fairness at the ICTY' (2010) 8 *JICJ* 511.

[74] Gosnell (n 16) 379 (containing a detailed comparison of the ICTY, ICTR and ICC rules on this point). Section (ii) of this particular rule is essentially identical to the ICTY's RPE 92*ter*.

[75] ICC Statute, art 69(2) [emphasis added]. The ICTY also permits video link testimony upon request of a party or *proprio motu* by the Trial Chamber if it is in the interests of justice; see ICTY RPE, Rule 81*bis*.

testimony or statements of a witness at the ICC, at least thus far, is permitted only under limited circumstances, far more proscribed than the regime which has been in place at the ICTY.[76] On the other hand, the Special Tribunal for Lebanon, organised after the adoption of the Rome Statute, has incorporated the substance of the ICTY's RPE 92*bis, ter* and *quater* in essentially identical form into its RPE.[77] Indeed, the STL has added provisions for the use of anonymous witnesses and trials in absentia.[78]

There is no doubt that, particularly given the high media profile of international criminal trials and the heinous nature of the crimes at issue, it is a rare witness who looks forward to appearing in court to give evidence about painful, horrific events. The argument exists that reliance on written witness statements obviates the need to bring witnesses to court and saves time and money. It also denies the accused his or her fundamental right to confront and cross-examine the witnesses brought against him or her at trial; an internationally recognised right which should not be outweighed by political or economic pressures in a system which seeks to both create and enforce the rule of law.

## III. The Defence Function and the Right to Counsel

All accused in the international courts have the right to counsel. This right has been consistently enforced at the *ad hoc* tribunals and at the ICC. The *ad hoc* tribunals[79] as well as the ICC[80] have compiled lists of defence counsel who are required to possess sufficient professional education and/or experience to represent accused in the factually and legally complex cases which comprise the docket in the international courts. Those lists are made available to any accused who needs assistance in selecting counsel.[81] An accused is also free to hire counsel of his or her own choosing. Accused who lack the funds to hire counsel can receive legal aid assistance. A secondary

---

[76] See for example *Situation in the Democratic Republic of the Congo: Prosecutor v Lubanga* (Decision on the prosecution's application for the admission of prior recorded statements of two witnesses) ICC-01/04-01/06 (15 January 2009).

[77] Rules of Procedure and Evidence of the Special Tribunal for Lebanon, STL/BD/2009/01/Rev.3 (10 November 2010) (STL RPE), Rule 155 (adopting provisions of ICTY RPE 92*bis*); STL RPE, Rule 156 (adopting ICTY RPE 92*ter*); STL RPE, Rule 158 (adopting ICTY RPE 92*quater*).

[78] STL RPE, Rules 106–109 (procedures applicable to trials in absentia); 93 (questioning of anonymous witnesses by pre-trial judge); 159 (providing a conviction may not be based solely or in 'decisive' part on a statement from an anonymous witness).

[79] ICTY RPE, Rules 44 and 45; ICTR RPE, Rules 44 and 45.

[80] ICC RPE, Rule 22.

[81] See for example 'Legal Aid and Defence Counsel Issues' in *ICTY Manual on Developed Practices* (n 61), 205–219 (summarising procedures for determining the qualifications of counsel, legal aid for the accused, and other matters related to the provision of counsel) and ICC RPE, Rule 20 (outlining the duty of the ICC Registry to, among other matters, assist

issue, however, is the context in which the Defence, as an institution, is viewed by the international community, including the courts, and what implications that may have regarding the continued protection of the rights of individual accused as well as counsel's ability to effectively represent individual accused.

The *ad hoc* tribunals and the ICC do not recognise the defence as comprising one of the organs of those institutions,[82] despite the essential role defence counsel play in the fair and efficient functioning of trials conducted in the international courts. Defence counsel's primary obligation is to represent the accused and to protect the rights of the accused. In doing so the international defence community has contributed to and will continue to contribute to the challenge of creating a fair and balanced system of international criminal justice as well as an historical record. Nonetheless, the defence at the *ad hoc* tribunals has been historically marginalised. In the early years at the ICTY, for example, defence counsel, unlike individuals working in the Registry, Chambers or Office of the Prosecution, had no effective, collective voice in the development of policies which directly impacted on the rights of the accused and the role of defence counsel, such as the sufficiency of defence funding, changes in the Rules of Procedure and Evidence, disclosure policies, trial scheduling and the like.

In late 2002, the Association of Defence Counsel Practicing Before the ICTY (ADC-ICTY) was established in conjunction with a rule change by the judges requiring that all defence counsel practising at that tribunal be a member of an officially recognised association of counsel. The organisation of defence counsel eventually precipitated, in a number of ways, an institutional change of view regarding the participation of defence counsel in the day-to-day business of the tribunal. Members of the ADC-ICTY now participate in the Rules Committee of the ICTY in which proposed changes to the Rules of Procedure and Evidence are debated. ADC-ICTY attorneys are delegated as ADC representatives to the ICTY Disciplinary Board and Disciplinary Panel where cases regarding misconduct or other improprieties, brought against tribunal personnel, are heard and decided. The ADC has its own, self-regulating Disciplinary Council which has participated as *amicus curiae* in cases pending before the ICTY,[83] as has the Amicus Committee of the ADC-ICTY on substantive issues of law.[84] ADC members have also been privileged to address the Judicial Plenary of the ICTY regarding defence issues.

---

arrested persons, suspects and the accused in obtaining legal advice and the assistance of legal counsel).

[82] ICTY Statute, art 11 'Organisation of the International Tribunal', stating that the ICTY shall 'consist of' the Chambers, Prosecutor and Registry; ICTR Statute, art 10 'Organisation of the International Tribunal for Rwanda' (same provision); ICC Statute, art 34 (same provision); Statute of the Special Court for Sierra Leone, 2178 UNTS 138, art 11 (same provision).

[83] *Prosecutor v Prlić et al* (Advisory Opinion of Amicus Curiae Disciplinary Council of the Association of Defence Counsel of the ICTY) IT-04-74-T (10 August 2009).

[84] *Prosecutor v Brđanin* (Amicus Brief of Association of Defence Counsel-ICTY) IT-99-36-A (5 July 2005), on the question of the extent of liability under the theory of joint criminal enterprise.

The ICC, the Special Court for Sierra Leone and the Special Tribunal for Lebanon established defence offices on the premises of those institutions which are available to provide direct legal advice to counsel in individual cases and have provided training for defence counsel who qualify to practice before those institutions. The need to provide training for defence counsel is critical as the developing system of international criminal practice includes procedural rules, various forms of database storage and research platforms, and courtroom skills which may be new to even the most experienced of counsel.

Whatever the reasons for the isolation of the defence from the remainder of the ICTY during its early years, developments since that time at the ICTY as well as other international courts reflect a growing appreciation of the importance of including the defence in those aspects of the courts' daily business which impact on the defence function. Although there still remains room for improvement, the increasing acceptance of defence participation in this regard is a positive and encouraging change.

## Conclusion

There are issues which this chapter has not addressed, raised in the jurisprudence at the ICC, which are potentially of significant concern regarding the continued protection of the rights of the accused, including, for example, the extent of the role of victims' representatives during trial[85] and the use of 'intermediaries' in the identification of witnesses and/or collection of witness statements. As of the date of this writing, the ICC has only completed two trials and no appeals from trial judgements. It is still too early to discern a 'trend' in these areas or to predict what will happen. What is evident is that there are numerous inconsistencies in the procedures put in place thus far at the various international courts, and although the rights of the accused have certainly been afforded far more care than mere 'lip service', vigilant 'affirmative action' on the part of the international legal community is essential to ensure those rights are effectively enforced in future international criminal trials.

---

[85] *Situation in the Democratic Republic of the Congo: Prosecutor v Lubanga* (Judgment on the Appeals of the Prosecutor and the Defence against Trial Chamber I's Decision on Victim's Participation of 18 January 2008) ICC-01/04-01/06 (11 July 2008).

# Reconciliation and Sentencing in the Practice of the *ad hoc* Tribunals

Silvia D'Ascoli[1]

Reconciliation and justice are evocative and multi-faceted concepts, whose definition is difficult to capture in a formula. In the context of war or political violence resulting in mass atrocities, reconciliation often represents a bridge between the past and the future of the affected communities, and is usually linked to justice and peace.[2] If justice and peace are mutually reinforcing when pursued together, there is also a belief that prosecution and criminal trials can contribute to reconciliation through the process of retributive justice, and that justice is thus a precondition for reconciliation.[3] Whether justice after mass atrocities can lead to peace and reconciliation is a contentious issue that has attracted much debate and different schools of thought.[4]

---

[1] The views expressed herein are those of the author alone and do not necessarily reflect the views of the International Tribunal or the United Nations in general.

[2] On the concept of 'reconciliation', and its various definitions and interpretations, see e.g. T Govier and W Verwoerd, 'Trust and the Problem of National Reconciliation' (2002) 32(2) *Philosophy of Social Sciences* 178 and E Stover, *The Witnesses: War Crimes and the Promise of Justice in The Hague* (University of Pennsylvania Press, Philadelphia 2007).

[3] See e.g. WA Schabas, 'Penalties' in F Lattanzi (ed) *The International Criminal Court: Comments on the Draft Statute* (Editoriale Scientifica, Napoli 1998) 281–284; P Akhavan, 'Justice in The Hague, Peace in the former Yugoslavia?' (1998) 20 *HRQ* 737.

[4] See e.g. Akhavan (n 3); M Minow, *Between Vengeance and Forgiveness* (Beacon Press, Boston 1998); A Fatić, *Reconciliation via the War Crimes Tribunal?* (Ashgate, Aldershot 2000); JE Stromseth (ed) *Accountability for Atrocities* (Transnational Publishers, New York 2003) 57–59, 77–81; D Zolo, 'Peace through Criminal Law?' (2004) 2(3) *JICJ* 727; E Hughes, WA Schabas and R Thakur (eds) *Atrocities and International Accountability: Beyond Transitional Justice* (United Nations University Press, Tokyo 2007), 23–40; R Hodžić, 'A Long Road Yet to Reconciliation: The Impact of the ICTY on Reconciliation and Victims' Perceptions of Criminal Justice' in RH Steinberg (ed) *Assessing the Legacy of the ICTY* (Martinus Nijhoff Publishers, Leiden and Boston 2011) 115.

Supporters of retributive justice and international prosecutions argue that 'holding individuals accountable for these acts alleviates collective guilt by differentiating between the perpetrators and innocent bystanders, thus promoting reconciliation'.[5] Retributive justice – which emphasises individualisation of the crime and punishment – would thus promote reconciliation by holding individuals accountable for the atrocities committed, refocusing blame and guilt from the entire community to the specific individuals bearing responsibility for the crimes occurred, and thus lifting the stigma of criminality from the collective and the community. However, the quest of extending the role of courts and criminal trials beyond their traditional mission of justice and prosecution of crimes to include the reconciliation of the affected communities has proved to be challenging. The International Criminal Tribunal for the former Yugoslavia (ICTY) and the International Criminal Tribunal for Rwanda (ICTR) offer an invaluable opportunity to analyse the purported linkage between justice and reconciliation.

In the specific case of the *ad hoc* Tribunals, the Security Council was convinced that the punishment of perpetrators of crimes committed in the regions of the former Yugoslavia and Rwanda would contribute to the process of national reconciliation and restoration and maintenance of peace in those regions. The founding documents of the *ad hoc* Tribunals, as well as the sentences meted out, refer to 'reconciliation' as one of the aims of the establishment of the Tribunals and as one of the objectives of punishment. Has this objective been achieved? Has the sentencing practice of the *ad hoc* Tribunals helped achieving reconciliation? If not, what lessons can be learned?

This chapter intends to analyse the linkage between reconciliation and justice in the sentencing practice of the *ad hoc* Tribunals, to discuss how the objective of reconciliation has been implemented and which impact, if any, the reconciliation ideology has had on sentencing and thus on the final outcomes of criminal proceedings: the judgments pronounced. For this purpose, this chapter will first outline the linkage between reconciliation and sentencing established in the founding documents of the *ad hoc* Tribunals, as well as in their case-law. It will then discuss how some specific aspects of the ICTY and ICTR sentencing practice have not been conducive to the reconciliation purpose, but have actually undermined it. In particular, the leniency of sentences, and guilty plea and plea-bargaining procedures will be analysed in light of the reconciliation purpose.

As the ICTY and ICTR approach the end of their mandate, evaluating their achievements becomes increasingly important. By December 2012 2011, the ICTY

---

[5] LE Fletcher and HM Weinstein, 'Violence and Social Repair: Rethinking the Contribution of Justice to Reconciliation' (2002) 24 *HRQ* 573, 598. See also *First Annual Report of the International Criminal Tribunal for the Former Yugoslavia*, 29 August 1994, UN Doc A/49/342–S/1994/1007, para 16: 'If responsibility for the appalling crimes perpetrated in the former Yugoslavia is not attributed to individuals, then whole ethnic and religious groups will be held accountable for these crimes and branded as criminal.'

has concluded proceedings for 130 defendants;[6] the ICTR for 72 defendants.[7] The Tribunals have produced to date a considerable amount of case-law, and their sentencing practice offers an unprecedented example to evaluate their efforts in achieving the objectives set at the time of their establishment.

Reconciliation and peace are certainly long-term objectives whose achievement is difficult to assess in the short term. Empirical analysis will be needed in the future, after the completion of the Tribunals' mandate, in order to verify the impact of their work in the countries of the former Yugoslavia and Rwanda. Although it is clear from the outset that the ICTY and the ICTR could not be the panacea for solving all political and internal issues in the afflicted communities of the former Yugoslavia and Rwanda, an evaluation of the Tribunals in terms of their effectiveness in fostering their purported objectives, including reconciliation, will nonetheless be necessary and useful.

# I. The Link between Reconciliation and Sentencing in the System of the *ad hoc* Tribunals

The establishment of the *ad hoc* Tribunals, and their subsequent practice, has brought growing attention to international sentencing. In less than a decade, these international tribunals went from being an abstract idea to an actual reality and have greatly contributed to the development of international criminal procedure. In particular, they can be considered the main source of international sentencing practice.

Sentencing constitutes an essential phase of international criminal proceedings. International trials serve, *inter alia*, the purpose of demonstrating the seriousness, with which the international community regards violations of its laws, condemns transgressions and metes out penalties for the commission of crimes of international concern. It is thus self-evident that a verdict at the end of a public trial, and the imposition of a penalty on the perpetrator(s) of crimes, is one of the most important contributions of criminal proceedings to the repression and possible prevention of violations of legally protected values. Judgments, and thus sentencing, can be considered as 'the symbolic keystone of the criminal justice system'.[8] As justice

---

[6] See the ICTY website for full details on ongoing and concluded proceedings: <http://www.icty.org/sections/TheCases/KeyFigures> last accessed 12 December 2012.

[7] See the ICTR website for full details on ongoing and concluded proceedings: <http://www.unictr.org/Cases/StatusofCases/tabid/204/Default.aspx> last accessed 12 December 2012.

[8] See A Blumstein, J Cohen, SE Martin and M Tonry, *Research on Sentencing: The Search for Reform*, Vols 1–2 (National Academy Press, Washington DC 1983) 1.

should not only be done but also 'seen to be done',[9] sentencing is the phase through which the general public becomes familiar with the 'outcome' of the criminal process.

Although important, the sentencing process has remained unregulated in many aspects in the Statutes and Rules of Procedure and Evidence (RPE) of the *ad hoc* Tribunals. Especially when considering the law of sentencing at the domestic level, the lack of exact norms and pre-defined principles in international sentencing is even more striking. In fact, as to normative provisions, the ICTY and ICTR can only avail themselves of a few norms on the application of penalties, and do not rely on detailed sentencing principles and rules.[10] This implies that – in meting out penalties – international judges are called upon to use a high degree of discretion, much greater than is normal for cases at the national level. This leaves open numerous possibilities of interpretation for judges when imposing penalties, may favour inconsistencies in sentencing between similar cases, and does not foster the development of a unite policy of international sentencing.

In particular, several areas were left undeveloped by the founding instruments of the *ad hoc* Tribunals: purposes of punishment; ranges of penalties for the various crimes under the jurisdiction of the Tribunals; individual circumstances of the accused (aggravating and mitigating factors) and consequent increases or reductions in penalties; impact of modes of liability on sentencing; and impact of guilty pleas on sentencing.[11] The scarcity of theoretical reflection on key issues such as the meaning,

---

[9] See *R v Sussex Justices, Ex parte McCarthy* [1923] All ER Rep 233: 'Not only should justice be done; it should also be seen to be done.'

[10] Statute of the International Criminal Tribunal for the former Yugoslavia, UN Doc S/RES/827, UN Security Council, 1993 ('ICTY Statute'), art 24; Statute of the International Criminal Tribunal for Rwanda, UN Doc S/RES/955, UN Security Council, 1994 ('ICTR Statute'), art 23; Rules of Procedure and Evidence of the International Criminal Tribunal for the former Yugoslavia, UN Doc IT/32/Rev.46 (20 October 2011) ('ICTY RPE'), Rule 101.

[11] The limited scope of this chapter does not allow for a more extensive analysis of these problematic areas of sentencing. For a more detailed discussion of sentencing in international criminal law, and the sentencing practice of the *ad hoc* Tribunals, see e.g. WA Schabas, 'International Sentencing: From Leipzig (1923) to Arusha (1996)' in MC Bassiouni (ed) *International Criminal Law Vol III* (2nd edn Transnational Publishers, New York 1999) 171–193; JC Nemitz, 'Sentencing in the Jurisprudence of the International Criminal Tribunals for the former Yugoslavia and Rwanda' in H Fischer and C Kress (eds) *International and National Prosecution of Crimes under International Law – Current Developments* (Verlag, Berlin 2001) 605; FNM Mumba, 'Topics within the Sphere of Sentencing in International Criminal Law' in L Vohrah and F Pocar (eds) *Man's Inhumanity to Man – Essays on International Law in Honour of Antonio Cassese* (Kluwer Law International, The Hague 2003) 567; M Findlay and R Henham, *Transforming International Criminal Justice – Retributive and Restorative Justice in the Trial Process* (Willan Publishing, Devon 2005); R Henham, *Punishment and Process in International Criminal Trials* (Ashgate, Aldershot 2005); O Olusanya, *Sentencing War Crimes and Crimes Against Humanity under the International Criminal Tribunal for the Former Yugoslavia* (Europa Law Publishing, Groningen 2005); R Haveman and O Olusanya, *Sentencing and Sanctioning in Supranational Criminal Law* (Intersentia, Antwerp 2006); MA Drumbl, *Atrocity, Punishment and International Law* (CUP, Cambridge 2007); S D'Ascoli, *Sentencing in International Criminal Law: the UN ad hoc Tribunals and Future Perspectives for the ICC* (Hart, Oxford 2011).

quality and severity of punishment, when international crimes are concerned, may lead to uncertainty and inconsistency in the practice of international criminal courts and tribunals. This is evident in the practice of the *ad hoc* Tribunals insofar as sentencing and the implementation of the purported objectives of the Tribunals' mandate are concerned. In fact, it is through sentencing that one can also evaluate whether the objectives of criminal adjudication have been achieved or not. As discussed in the following section, one of the Tribunals' objectives was reconciliation.

## A. The Objectives of the UN Security Council in Establishing the ICTY and ICTR

The ICTY and ICTR were established by the Security Council as a response, and to provide a judicial solution, to the large-scale and systematic violations of international humanitarian law occurring in the regions of the former Yugoslavia and Rwanda. The Tribunals' core mandate was to try those most responsible for the heinous acts of genocide, crimes against humanity and war crimes perpetrated. However, in the context of war and post-conflict societies, justice in the strict sense of punishing the perpetrators of crimes is certainly a fundamental goal, but not the only one. When establishing the *ad hoc* Tribunals, 'reconciliation' of the concerned regions upset by civil wars also came into play.

In the wording of the relevant SC Resolutions[12] and the two Reports of the Secretary-General on the establishment of the ICTY and ICTR,[13] clear elements indicated that establishing the Tribunals had the aim of halting the atrocities being committed in the former Yugoslavia and Rwanda, bringing to justice the perpetrators of such offences, and thus contributing to the process of national reconciliation and restoration and maintenance of peace.[14] For the ICTR, we find mention of the purpose of reconciliation directly in the SC Resolution 955(1994), establishing the Tribunal, where the Security Council declared itself convinced that 'the prosecution of persons responsible for serious violations of international humanitarian law ...

---

[12] See, for the ICTY: UN SC Res 808, UN Doc S/Res/808 (22 February 1993) preamble; UN SC Res 827, UN Doc S/Res/827 (25 May 1993) preamble. For the ICTR, see: UN SC Res 955, UN Doc S/Res/955 (8 November 1994) preamble.

[13] Report of the Secretary-General pursuant to paragraph 2 of Security Council Resolution 808(1993) UN Doc S/25704 (3 May 1993); Report of the Secretary-General pursuant to paragraph 5 of Security Council Resolution 955(1994) UN Doc S/1995/134 (13 February 1995).

[14] The founders of the ICTY also hoped that the establishment of the Tribunal, which was set up while the war in the countries of the former Yugoslavia was still ongoing, could have a deterrent effect on the rest of the conflict and prevent further massacres. They proved to be wrong. The Srebrenica massacre happened in July 1995 when the ICTY was fully operational, and Radovan Karadžić and Ratko Mladić had already been indicted. The existence of the ICTY did not either prevent the outbreak of the conflict in Kosovo and the crimes there occurred in 1998/1999.

would contribute to the process of national reconciliation'.[15] For the ICTY, it is in the Tribunal's First Annual Report that its first President, Antonio Cassese, recalled that the Tribunal was meant to be 'a tool for promoting reconciliation and restoring true peace'.[16]

In all the above-mentioned documents, it is possible to appreciate an expressed link between justice and peace. It is the axiom well expressed by Kelsen's 'peace through criminal law'.[17] Judges of the *ad hoc* Tribunals subsequently restated the linkage between the Tribunals' work and the objective of reconciliation through the case-law.

## B. The Purposes of Sentencing Recognised in the ICTY and ICTR Case-Law

In the very first sentence imposed by the ICTY, judges acknowledged that:

> Neither the Statute nor the Report of the Secretary-General nor the Rules elaborate on the objectives sought by imposing such a sentence. Accordingly, in order to identify them, the focus must be on the International Tribunal's very object and purpose, as perceived by the Member States of the Security Council of the United Nations and by the International Tribunal itself.[18]

In the absence of any guidance in their founding Statutes, Chambers of the *ad hoc* Tribunals examined the purposes of penalties in light of the aims identified in the Security Council Resolutions (namely, retribution, deterrence, national reconciliation and restoration of peace), and took those objectives into account also for sentencing purposes.

Although a handful of various goals of punishment were taken into account, *retribution* and *deterrence* were deemed the most important objectives, both by ICTY[19]

---

[15] UN SC Res 955, UN Doc S/Res/955 (8 November 1994) preamble.

[16] First Annual Report of the International Criminal Tribunal for the Former Yugoslavia, UN Doc A/49/342–S/1994/1007 (29 August 1994) para 16. See also para 17: 'Thus the establishment of the Tribunal should undoubtedly be regarded as a measure designed to promote peace by meting out justice in a manner conducive to the full establishment of *healthy and cooperative relations* among the various national and ethnic groups in the former Yugoslavia' (emphasis added).

[17] H Kelsen, *Peace through Law* (Garland Publishers, New York 1973) (first published 1944).

[18] *Prosecutor v Erdemović* (Sentencing Judgment) IT-96-22-T (29 November 1996) para 57.

[19] See e.g. *Prosecutor v Tadić* (Sentencing Judgment) IT-94-1-T*bis*-R117 (11 November 1999) paras 7–9; *Prosecutor v Kupreskić* (Trial Judgment) IT-95-16-T (14 January 2000) para 848; *Prosecutor v Aleksovski* (Appeal Judgment) IT-95-14/1-A (24 March 2000) para 185; *Prosecutor v Delalić et al* (Appeal Judgment) IT-96-21-A (20 February 2001) para 806; *Prosecutor v Kunarac* (Trial Judgment) IT-96-23-T (22 February 2001) para 838; *Prosecutor v Stakić* (Trial Judgment) IT-97-24-T (31 July 2003) paras 900–902; *Prosecutor v Deronjić* (Sentencing Judgment) IT-02-61-S

and ICTR[20] Chambers. Through their judgments, the Tribunals also reaffirmed the link between reconciliation, sentencing and justice.[21]

In the *Erdemović* sentencing judgments, for instance, judges of the ICTY restated that one of the Tribunal's objectives was to contribute to *collective* reconciliation,[22] and that the exercise of the Tribunal's judicial functions would contribute to accountability, reconciliation and the establishment of truth.[23] Similarly, in the *Muvunyi* case, ICTR judges recalled the 'objectives of justice, deterrence, reconciliation and the restoration and maintenance of peace' in SC Resolution 955(1994), and thus found:

> These objectives largely reflect the goals of sentencing in criminal law which are retribution, deterrence, rehabilitation, and societal protection. In determining the appropriate sentence to impose on the Accused in respect of the crimes for which he has been found guilty, the Chamber will be guided by these goals, as well as the provisions of the Statute and Rules relevant to sentencing.[24]

A critical remark about the way in which Chambers of the *ad hoc* Tribunals addressed not only reconciliatory aims, but the objectives of punishment in general, is that no attempt was made to define the recognised purposes or to try and explain their meaning. Judges did not exhaustively tackle sentencing aims, nor did they fully explore their specific meaning in the international trial context.

The justifications of punishment adopted remained abstract and vague: the purported aims are only 'mentioned', listed, but not discussed. There is no final systematisation of the rationales of punishment in international criminal adjudication,

---

(30 March 2004) paras 142–150; *Prosecutor v Strugar* (Trial Judgment) IT-01-42-T (31 January 2005) para 458; *Prosecutor v Krajišnik* (Trial Judgment) IT-00-39&40-T (27 September 2006) para 1134; *Prosecutor v Zelenović* (Sentencing Judgment) IT-96-23/2-S (4 April 2007) para 31.

[20] *Prosecutor v Kayishema and Ruzindana* (Judgment and Sentence) ICTR-95-1-T (21 May 1999) para 2; *Prosecutor v Akayesu* (Trial Judgment) ICTR-96-4-T (2 September 1998) paras 2–19; *Prosecutor v Kambanda* (Judgment and Sentence) ICTR-97-23-S (4 September 1998) paras 28, 58–59; *Prosecutor v Ruggiu* (Trial Judgment) ICTR-97-32-I (1 June 2000) para 33; *Prosecutor v Ntakirutimana* (Trial Judgment) ICTR-96-10 and ICTR-96-17-T (21 February 2003) para 882; *Prosecutor v Rugambarara* (Sentencing Judgment) ICTR-00-59-T (16 November 2007) para 11.

[21] See e.g. *Prosecutor v Erdemović* (Sentencing Judgment) (n 18) para 58; *Prosecutor v Kayishema and Ruzindana* (Trial Judgment) (n 20) para 1; *Prosecutor v Semanza* (Judgment and Sentence) ICTR-97-20-T (15 May 2003) para 554; *Prosecutor v Obrenović* (Sentencing Judgment) IT-02-60/2-S (10 December 2003) paras 45–46; *Prosecutor v Nikolić* (Sentencing Judgment) IT-94-2-S (18 December 2003) para 245; *Prosecutor v Kamuhanda* (Trial Judgment) ICTR-95-54A-T (22 January 2004) para 753; *Prosecutor v Nzabirinda* (Trial Judgment) ICTR-2001-77-T (23 February 2007) para 49.

[22] *Prosecutor v Erdemović* (Sentencing Judgment) (n 18) para 58.

[23] *Prosecutor v Erdemović* (Sentencing Judgment) IT-96-22-T*bis* (5 March 1998) para 21: 'Discovering the truth is the cornerstone of the rule of law and a fundamental step on the way to reconciliation: for it is the truth that cleanses the ethnic and religious hatreds and begins the healing process.'

[24] *Prosecutor v Muvunyi* (Trial Judgment) ICTR-2000-55A-T (12 September 2006) para 532.

no attempt to develop any consistent theory, and no explanation of how particular objectives affect the sentence meted out.[25] Ultimately, the *ad hoc* Tribunals have probably missed an opportunity to elaborate and bring forward an organic theory of the purposes of punishment in international criminal proceedings, and of the overall objectives of international criminal justice.[26] This is evident with regard to the objective of reconciliation, here in discussion. It seems that, despite the clear mandate of the Tribunals, reconciliation remained an abstract concept in the judgments of the ICTY and ICTR. A simple *mention* of the objective of reconciliation, without further elaboration, and especially without any discussion devoted to how this objective would be fostered in the specific circumstances of the case at hand, highlights the difficulty for Trial Chambers to effectively integrate this concept into their sentencing practice.

## II. A Critical Analysis of Sentencing in Light of the Reconciliation Purpose

### A. Leniency, Retribution and Reconciliation

Sentencing practice at the ICTY and ICTR has been criticised for its overall inconsistency and/or lack of proportionality.[27] The sentencing part of judgments has been considered little more than an 'afterthought';[28] the sentences imposed seemed to reflect more the

---

[25] Chambers of both Tribunals seem to have addressed the purposes of sentencing by merely 'listing' them, without an exhaustive analysis which could justify their adoption in the international trial context. See e.g. *Prosecutor v Rutaganda* (Judgment and Sentence) ICTR-96-3-T (6 December 1999) para 456; *Prosecutor v Ruggiu* (Trial Judgment) (n 20) para 33; *Prosecutor v Todorović* (Sentencing Judgment) IT-95-9/1-S (31 July 2001) paras 28–30. In the *Blagojević and Jokić* case, the Trial Chamber recognised its duty to discern 'the underlying principles and rationales for punishment that respond to both the needs of the society of the former Yugoslavia and the international community', but once again this statement did not translate in a more detailed or principled analysis (see *Prosecutor v Blagojević and Jokić* (Trial Judgment) IT-02-60-T (17 January 2005) paras 816, 820).

[26] For a more detailed discussion of the purposes of the international justice system versus those of international sentencing, see D'Ascoli (n 11) 294–303. See also Conclusion, below.

[27] With regard to the issue of proportionality in sentencing and its importance in the context of the ICTY, J Meernik and K King observed that, 'it is crucial that the sentences meted out be generally viewed as proportionate, fair and understandable. If, at the end of the day, these punishments are perceived as inconsistent or biased and thus, inexplicable ... the verdict on the ICTY will be flawed' (J Meernik and K King, 'The Sentencing Determinants of the International Criminal Tribunal for the Former Yugoslavia: An Empirical and Doctrinal Analysis' (2003) 16 *LJIL* 717, 718).

[28] WA Schabas, 'International Sentencing: From Leipzig (1923) to Arusha (1996)' in MC Bassiouni (ed) *International Criminal Law: Vol III* (2nd edn Transnational Publishers, New York

personal views of judges than an attempt to establish a coherent sentencing policy or framework.[29] The character of punishment imposed by the *ad hoc* Tribunals – and *within* each Tribunal – has varied from case to case. Inconsistencies have regarded the application of mitigating and aggravating factors, the use of guilty pleas, and the length of sentences.[30] Different rationales of punishment have been emphasised, at times also with significant effects on the severity of the penalties imposed.[31]

With regard to the length of sentences of the two Tribunals, there is an appreciable disparity between the sentences pronounced by the ICTY and those pronounced by the ICTR. Despite the seriousness of the crimes dealt with, the ICTY has imposed life imprisonment only in a few instances,[32] with the majority of the defendants sentenced to less than 25 years' imprisonment;[33] on the other hand, the ICTR has imposed life

---

1999) 171. See also RD Sloane, 'Sentencing for the "Crime of Crimes" – The Evolving "Common Law" of Sentencing of the International Criminal Tribunal for Rwanda' (2007) 5(3) *JICJ* 713, 716.

[29] See J Jones and S Powles, *International Criminal Practice* (3rd edn OUP, Oxford 2003) 778; Drumbl (n 11) 59.

[30] D'Ascoli (n 11) 186–198.

[31] See e.g. *Prosecutor v Blaškić* (Trial Judgment) IT-95-14-T (3 March 2000) para 761 (where the Trial Chamber considered the deterrent function of punishment as 'the most important factor in the assessment of appropriate sentences for violations of humanitarian law'); *Prosecutor v Delalić et al* (Trial Judgment) IT-96-21-T (16 November 1998) para 1234 (where the Trial Chamber also considered deterrence as the most important factor in the assessment of an appropriate sentence); and *Prosecutor v Tadić* (Sentencing Judgment) IT-94-1A*bis* (26 January 2000) para 56 (where the Appeals Chamber found that deterrence is a factor which 'must not be accorded undue prominence in the overall assessment of the sentences to be imposed'). The *Aleksovski* Appeals Chamber concurred with this finding (*Prosecutor v Aleksovski* (Appeal Judgment) (n 19) para 185).

[32] By December 2012, at the ICTY life imprisonment has been imposed at trial on: Milomir Stakić, whose life sentence was then annulled on appeal and replaced with 40 years' imprisonment (*Prosecutor v Stakić* (Appeal Judgment) IT-97-24-A (22 March 2006)); Milan Lukić (*Prosecutor v Lukić & Lukić* (Trial Judgment) IT-98-32/1-T (20 July 2009) & (Appeal Judgment) IT-98-32/1-A (4 December 2012)); Vujadin Popović and Ljubisa Beara (*Prosecutor v Popović et al* (Trial Judgment) IT-05-88-T (10 June 2010)), whose sentences are currently on appeal; and Zdravko Tolimir (*Prosecutor v Tolimir* (Trial Judgment) IT-05-88/2-T (12 December 2012) On appeal, life imprisonment was imposed on Stanislav Galić, who had been sentenced to 20 years of imprisonment at trial (*Prosecutor v Galić* (Appeal Judgment) IT-98-29-A (30 November 2006)).

[33] D'Ascoli (n 11) 215–219.

sentences more frequently[34] and harsher sentences in general.[35] There are a number of cases that could be used as examples of the leniency in sentencing at the ICTY.[36]

For instance, Zlatko Aleksovski, the commander of a prison camp (Kaonik) in central Bosnia and Herzegovina, was sentenced to two years and six months' imprisonment for violations of the laws and customs of war (outrages upon personal dignity).[37] While commander of the Kaonik prison, Aleksovski subjected hundreds of prisoners to physical and psychological maltreatment; he participated in the selection of detainees to be used as human shields and trench diggers; he encouraged his subordinates to commit maltreatments and similar acts; finally, as a superior in the camp, he failed to take any steps either to prevent his subordinates from committing crimes or to punish them for such commission.[38] The Prosecution appealed the lenient sentence on the basis that, *inter alia*, such sentence was *manifestly disproportionate* to the crimes committed and, accordingly, outside the limits of a fairly exercised discretion.[39] The Appeals Chamber accepted the Prosecution arguments and held that the Trial Chamber erred in not having had sufficient regard to the gravity of Aleksovski's conduct, which – for its seriousness – should have resulted in a longer sentence.[40] The sentence imposed by the Trial Chamber was considered manifestly inadequate and was adjusted to seven years'

---

[34] See e.g. *Prosecutor v Kambanda* (Trial Judgment) (n 20) (life imprisonment also confirmed on appeal); *Prosecutor v Akayesu* (Trial Judgment) (n 20) (life imprisonment also confirmed on appeal); *Prosecutor v Kayishema and Ruzindana* (Trial Judgment) (n 20), imposing on Clement Kayishema a life sentence (also confirmed on appeal); *Prosecutor v Rutaganda* (Trial Judgment) (n 25) (life imprisonment also confirmed on appeal); *Prosecutor v Musema* (Judgment and Sentence) ICTR-96-13-T (27 January 2000) (life imprisonment also confirmed on appeal); *Prosecutor v Kamuhanda* (Trial Judgment) (n 21) (life imprisonment also confirmed on appeal); *Prosecutor v Niyitegeka* (Judgment and Sentence) ICTR-96-14-T (16 May 2003) (life imprisonment also confirmed on appeal); *Prosecutor v Kajelijeli* (Judgment and Sentence) ICTR-98-44A-T (1 December 2003) (reduced to 45 years imprisonment by the Appeals Chamber, due to the violation at the trial stage of the defendant's rights in relation to his arrest and detention: see *Prosecutor v Kajelijeli* (Appeal Judgment) ICTR-98-44A-A (23 May 2005)); *Prosecutor v Nahimana et al* (Judgment and Sentence) ICTR-99-52-T (3 December 2003) (Ngeze and Nahimana sentenced to life imprisonment; on appeal their sentences were reduced to respectively 35 and 30 years' imprisonment); *Prosecutor v Ndindabahizi* (Trial Judgment) ICTR-2001-71-I (15 January 2004) (life imprisonment also confirmed on appeal); *Prosecutor v Muhimana* (Judgment and Sentence) ICTR-95-1B-T (28 April 2005) (life imprisonment also confirmed on appeal); *Karera* Trial Judgment (life imprisonment also confirmed on appeal).

[35] D'Ascoli (n 11) 216–219.

[36] As discussed in the following section, leniency has mostly characterised also guilty plea cases.

[37] *Prosecutor v Aleksovski* (Trial Judgment) IT-95-14/1-T (25 June 1999) 89, 'Disposition'.

[38] See ibid paras 211–229.

[39] *Prosecutor v Aleksovski* (Appeal Judgment) (n 19) para 179.

[40] Ibid paras 183, 186.

imprisonment.⁴¹ This is still a lenient sentence, and still lighter than those that would typically be imposed by national courts for similar conducts.

In the *Delalić et al.* case, the Prosecution appealed Zdravko Mucić's sentence as 'manifestly inadequate'.⁴² Mucić, a commander of the Čelebići prison-camp in central Bosnia and Herzegovina, had been sentenced to seven years' imprisonment on eight counts of grave breaches of the Geneva Conventions (including wilful killings and torture), and seven counts of violations of the laws and customs of war (including murders and cruel treatment).⁴³ The Appeals Chamber concurred with the Prosecution that the Trial Chamber did not have sufficient regard to the gravity of Mucić's offences and imposed a sentence which did not adequately reflect his overall criminal conduct.⁴⁴ The Appeals Chamber thus remitted to the Trial Chamber the imposition of an appropriate revised sentence for Mucić, with the suggestion to impose a sentence of around 10 years' imprisonment.⁴⁵

Overall, the ICTY has appeared to victims' eyes as meting out 'justice' inadequately. This criticism is linked either to the lack of a uniform sentencing policy, to the leniency of sentences, or to the early releases of the convicted perpetrators.⁴⁶ Sentences imposed by the ICTY have generally been regarded by the public and the victims of crimes as inadequate and inconsistent with the stated purposes of the Tribunal.⁴⁷ Further, Serbs have often expressed their dissatisfaction with regard to the justice delivered by the ICTY, mostly because they have considered it 'selective' and 'lenient', and have perceived the Tribunal as being biased against the Serbs.⁴⁸

More generally, critics of the sentencing practice of the *ad hoc* Tribunals have questioned whether the sentences imposed were proportionate to the gravity of the crimes committed. How can offenders found guilty of the murder of hundreds of people receive sentences of five, 10 or 20 years' imprisonment, whereas at the national level similar perpetrators might receive a higher punishment for a single murder alone? Are 'extraordinary crimes' adjudicated through an 'ordinary process', and mainly with 'ordinary sentences' and 'ordinary punishment'?⁴⁹ Is this conducive to reconciliation of the local communities? The disapproval concerning excessive leniency has been stronger with regard to ICTY judgments, given that, conversely, at the ICTR lenient penalties have mostly concerned guilty plea cases,

---

⁴¹ Ibid para 191.
⁴² *Prosecutor v Delalić et al* (Appeal Judgment) (n 19) paras 726–729.
⁴³ *Prosecutor v Delalić et al* (Trial Judgment) (n 31) para 1285.
⁴⁴ *Prosecutor v Delalić et al* (Appeal Judgment) (n 19) para 851.
⁴⁵ Mucić received a final sentence of nine years imprisonment. See *Prosecutor v Delalić et al* (Sentencing Judgment) IT-96-21-T*bis* (9 October 2001).
⁴⁶ See E Ramulić, 'Victims' Perspectives' in RH Steinberg (ed) *Assessing the Legacy of the ICTY* (Martinus Nijhoff Publishers, Leiden 2011) 103, 104.
⁴⁷ See Hodžić (n 4) 118.
⁴⁸ See e.g. V Petrović (ed), *Human Rights in Serbia and Montenegro 2005: Legal Provisions, Practice and Awareness in the State Union of Serbia and Montenegro compared to International Human Rights Standards* (Belgrade Centre for Human Rights, Belgrade 2006).
⁴⁹ For the use of these dichotomies, see: Drumbl (n 11) 1; MB Harmon and F Gaynor, 'Ordinary Sentences for Extraordinary Crimes' (2007) 5(3) *JICJ* 683.

and sentences for life imprisonment have more frequently been imposed by ICTR judges.[50] As discussed in the following section, judges at the Rwanda Tribunal imposed life imprisonment even in a case of guilty plea.[51]

With regard to the ICTR, it is interesting to make reference to the *Kamuhanda* case, where the Appeals Chamber dismissed Kamuhanda's ground of appeal that the sentence of life imprisonment imposed in his case was irreconcilable with the Tribunal's declared objective of national reconciliation and restoration of peace.[52] The Appeals Chamber recognised the 'harms to both general deterrence and national reconciliation that would be created by a lenient sentence that was not perceived to reflect the gravity of the crimes committed'.[53] This is a consideration that Chambers of the *ad hoc* Tribunals should have been aware of when meting out penalties; to the contrary, this standard was considered only a few times.[54]

If the international community is seriously committed to prosecute persons responsible for international crimes and bases its action on international principles and international customary law, sentences meted out should not apply different theories of punishment and impose inconsistent or inadequate penalties, but should strive for proportionality and consistency.[55] Inconsistency and lack of proportionality in sentencing, besides infringing the principle of equal treatment for accused persons,[56] also undermine the public perception of the Tribunals' work and the very objectives of their creation. Public perception is important and does matter. Although punishment should not have an *exemplary* function *per se*, the retributive character of sentences must be maintained. A disproportionately lenient sentence that does not reflect the gravity of the crimes committed not only undermines fundamental principles of sentencing (like the principle of proportionality) and the very norms that it intends to reinforce, but is also open to criticism because it weakens the pursuit of other objectives that the system is meant to achieve, like reconciliation. Although reconciliation was articulated as a

---

[50] As of December 2012, 16 defendants have received life sentences which are final (i.e. confirmed on appeal). See 'Status of ICTR Detainees' <http://www.unictr.org/cases/tabid/202/Default.aspx> last accessed 12 December 2012.

[51] This is the case of Jean Kambanda, Prime Minister of the Interim Government during the genocidal campaign in 1994, who received a life sentence after pleading guilty to six counts including genocide and crimes against humanity. See *Prosecutor v Kambanda* (Trial Judgment) (n 20) 27–28.

[52] *Kamuhanda v Prosecutor* (Appeals Judgment) ICTR-99-54A-A (19 September 2005) para 350.

[53] Ibid para 351.

[54] Besides the *Kamuhanda* case at the ICTR, See also the *Lukić & Lukić* case at the ICTY, where the Trial Chamber did not agree that for Milan Lukić 'a shorter prison term than is otherwise warranted, given the gravity of the crimes, the aggravating factors and the mitigating factors, will assist in community reconciliation' (*Prosecutor v Lukić & Lukić* (Trial Judgment) (n 32) para 1083).

[55] See e.g. M Penrose, 'Lest We Fail: The Importance of Enforcement in International Criminal Law' (2000) 15(2) *American University Int'l L Rev* 321, 380 *et seq*.

[56] ICTY Statute, art 21(1).

sentencing objective, through leniency and lack of proportionality of the sentences imposed the *ad hoc* Tribunals seem to have undermined their ambitious goal to contribute to the national reconciliation of the affected communities in the former Yugoslavia and Rwanda.

## B. Reconciliation and Guilty Pleas/Plea-Bargaining

The objective of reconciliation finds a more frequent occurrence, and at times a more in-depth elaboration, in sentencing judgments resulting from guilty pleas and plea-bargaining. In these judgments, reconciliation has been used to justify the use of guilty pleas and plea-bargaining, and the imposition of lenient sentences: judges have argued that guilty pleas would represent, *inter alia*, an important contribution to reconciliation, and would thus further one of the goals of the Tribunals.[57] To date, there have been 20 cases of guilty pleas at the ICTY,[58] the majority of which also implied plea-bargaining; and nine cases at the ICTR.[59] The use that the two Tribunals have made of guilty pleas and plea-bargaining, and the value attributed to them, has differed from case to case.

Although guilty pleas and plea-bargaining procedures by the *ad hoc* Tribunals have provoked controversy and concerns, and have been analysed and discussed under various points of view,[60] this section is only concerned with how the ICTY

---

[57] See e.g. *Prosecutor v Simić* (Sentencing Judgment) IT-95-9/2-S (17 October 2002) para 83 ('This Trial Chamber is of the view that an accused's admission of guilt and acceptance of the facts as related by victim-witnesses provides a unique and unquestionable fact-finding tool that greatly contributes to peace-building and reconciliation among the affected communities'); *Prosecutor v Plavšić* (Sentencing Judgment) IT-00-39&40/1-S (27 February 2003) paras 70, 73, 79–80; *Prosecutor v Obrenović* (Sentencing Judgment) (n 21) para 111; *Prosecutor v Nikolić* (Sentencing Judgment) (n 21) paras 245–252; *Prosecutor v Deronjić* (Sentencing Judgment) (n 19) paras 134, 236; *Prosecutor v Bralo* (Sentencing Judgment) IT-95-17-S (7 December 2005) para 71; *Prosecutor v Rajić* (Sentencing Judgment) IT-95-12-S (8 May 2006) paras 145–146; *Prosecutor v Serugendo* (Judgment and Sentence) ICTR-2005-84-I (12 June 2006) paras 32, 52, 57, 59, 89; *Prosecutor v Nzabirinda* (Trial Judgment) (n 21) paras 68, 71.

[58] These are: Milan Babić, Predrag Banović, Miroslav Bralo, Ranko Češić, Miroslav Deronjić, Damir Došen, Dražen Erdemović, Miodrag Jokić, Goran Jelisić, Dragan Kolundžija, Darko Mrđa, Dragan Nikolić, Momir Nikolić, Dragan Obrenović, Biljana Plavšić, Ivica Rajić, Duško Sikirica, Milan Simić, Stevan Todorović, Dragan Zelenović.

[59] These are: Michel Bagaragaza, Paul Bisengimana, Jean Kambanda, Joseph Nzabirinda, Juvénal Rugambarara, Georges Ruggiu, Vincent Rutaganira, Joseph Serugendo, Omar Serushago.

[60] See e.g. NA Combs, 'Copping a Plea to Genocide: The Plea Bargaining of International Crimes' (2002) 151(1) *U Penn L Rev* 1; NA Combs, 'Prosecutor v Plavšić' (2003) 97 *AJIL* 929; M Damaška, 'Negotiated Justice in International Criminal Courts' (2004) 2(4) *JICJ* 1018; M Scharf, 'Trading Justice for Efficiency: Plea-Bargaining and International Tribunals' (2004) 2 *JICJ* 1070; JA Cook, 'Plea Bargaining at The Hague' (2005) 30(2) *Yale J Int'l L* 473; A Tieger, 'Plea Agreements in the ICTY' (2005) 3(3) *JICJ* 666; R Dixon, 'Advising Defendants about Guilty

and ICTR have used guilty pleas to reinforce or express the link between their work and the objective of reconciliation.

*i. The evolving relation between reconciliation and guilty pleas in the ICTY and ICTR case-law*

The very first ICTY judgment was also the first guilty plea opportunity for the Tribunal: Dražen Erdemović, a soldier in the 10th Sabotage Detachment of the Bosnian Serb Army operating in the Zvornik Municipality of Bosnia and Herzegovina, was the first defendant to plead guilty at the ICTY. Erdemović voluntary confessed to his involvement in the murder of hundreds of Bosnian-Muslim men from Srebrenica who were executed at the Pilica collective farm in the Zvornik municipality.[61] He was sentenced to five years' imprisonment.[62]

In this early case, reconciliation hardly had any influence on Erdemović's sentence, also considering that very little thought or elaboration had been devoted until then to sentencing issues or the underlying philosophy of international punishment. Judges acknowledged the importance of reconciliation as one of the objectives of the establishment of the Tribunal,[63] but there was no attempt to integrate reconciliation into the context of Erdemović's guilty plea or to link it to the scope of his sentence. Reconciliation thus did not seem to have any particular influence on the length of Erdemović's penalty.

Reconciliation did not play any role either in another early guilty plea case, this time before the ICTR. Jean Kambanda, Prime Minister of the Interim Government of Rwanda from 8 April 1994 to 17 July 1994, received a sentence of life imprisonment despite his guilty plea. He pleaded guilty to six counts of genocide and crimes against humanity.[64] The Trial Chamber justified the imposition of the highest penalty available in consideration of Kambanda's role and position, and the intrinsic gravity of the crime of genocide.[65] The Chamber was of the opinion that 'the aggravating circumstances surrounding the crimes committed by Jean Kambanda negate the mitigating circumstances, especially since Jean Kambanda occupied a high ministerial post, at the time he committed the said crimes'.[66]

---

Pleas before International Courts' (2005) 3(3) *JICJ* 680; R Henham, 'Plea Bargaining at the International Criminal Tribunal for the Former Yugoslavia' (2005) 16(1) *CLF* 33; R Henham, 'Plea Bargaining and the Legitimacy of International Trial Justice: some Observations on the Dragan Nikolić Sentencing Judgment of the ICTY' (2005) 5(4) *ICLR* 601; NA Combs, *Guilty Pleas in International Criminal Law – Constructing a Restorative Justice Approach* (Stanford University Press, Palo Alto 2007).

[61] *Prosecutor v Erdemović* (Sentencing Judgment) (n 23) paras 1–8.
[62] Ibid para 23.
[63] See *Prosecutor v Erdemović* (Sentencing Judgment) (n 18) para 58; *Prosecutor v Erdemović* (Sentencing Judgment) (n 23) para 21.
[64] *Prosecutor v Kambanda* (Trial Judgment) (n 20) paras 3, 5–7.
[65] Ibid paras 61–62.
[66] Ibid para 62.

Further, the Chamber noted that, despite his guilty plea, Kambanda 'has offered no explanation for his voluntary participation in the genocide; nor has he expressed contrition, regret or sympathy for the victims in Rwanda, even when given the opportunity to do so by the Chamber'.[67] This was the only case before the *ad hoc* Tribunals where life imprisonment was imposed in a guilty plea case. Although the Tribunal's objective to foster national reconciliation and peace in Rwanda was recalled by both parties and by the Chamber,[68] it was not considered as having any impact on the imposition of the appropriate sentence.

The third and last example of this early jurisprudence of the Tribunals where reconciliation had little, if any, impact on sentencing is the case of Goran Jelisić. The world 'reconciliation' does not even appear once in the judgment. The Trial Chamber accorded only little weight to Jelisić's guilty plea, and sentenced him to 40 years' imprisonment, due to the seriousness of the crimes committed[69] and the fact that the Chamber did not recognise as sincere his plea and remorse.[70]

The *Plavšić* case seems to offer a completely different evaluation of the reconciliatory objective, and seems to start a different phase in the ICTY jurisprudence – the 'age of reconciliation'. In this case, reconciliation exercised a significant influence as a mitigating factor on Plavšić's sentence, with the consequence that her sentence resulted in a very lenient one, despite the seriousness of the crimes committed, her degree of responsibility and participation in them, and her high-ranking role. Biljana Plavšić, a member of the Bosnian Serb Presidency,[71] pleaded guilty to persecutions as a crime against humanity and, despite the prominent role she played and her involvement in a campaign of ethnic separation which resulted in the death of thousands and the expulsion of thousands more, she received a sentence of 11 years' imprisonment.[72]

Both the Prosecution and the Defence emphasised the importance and the particular significance of Plavšić's guilty plea for reconciliation purposes.[73] The Trial

---

[67] Ibid para 51.

[68] See ibid paras 50, 59–60.

[69] Jelisić pleaded guilty to a total of 31 charges of crimes against humanity and violations of the laws or customs of war. The Prosecution refused to dismiss the charge of genocide, which was brought to trial but did not succeed: *Prosecutor v Jelisić* (Trial Judgment) IT-95-10-T (14 December 1999) paras 4–17, 138.

[70] Ibid para 127. Jelisić appealed the judgment on the point that the Trial Chamber failed to give him any credit for his guilty plea, but the Appeals Chamber found that Jelisić did not demonstrate that the Trial Chamber erred in exercising its discretion on the weight to accord to the guilty plea. See *Prosecutor v Jelisić* (Appeal Judgment) IT-95-10-A (5 July 2001) paras 119–123.

[71] Plavšić was a leading Bosnian-Serb political figure from 1990 until the end of the war, having held the following positions: member of the collective Presidency of Bosnia and Herzegovina; member of the three-member Presidency of the Serbian Republic; member of the Supreme Command of the armed forces of the Serbian Republic. On the *Plavšić* case, see Combs, 'Prosecutor v Plavšić' (n 60).

[72] *Prosecutor v Plavšić* (Sentencing Judgment) (n 57) para 134.

[73] Ibid paras 66–70.

Chamber discussed in detail the importance of reconciliation in the case at hand, and how Plavšić's plea represented an important contribution to the reconciliatory process in the region.[74] It thus concluded:

> The Trial Chamber accepts that acknowledgement and full disclosure of serious crimes are very important when establishing the truth in relation to such crimes. This, together with acceptance of responsibility for the committed wrongs, *will promote reconciliation*. In this respect, the Trial Chamber concludes that the guilty plea of Mrs. Plavšić and her acknowledgement of responsibility, particularly in the light of her former position as President of Republika Srpska, *should promote reconciliation* in Bosnia and Herzegovina and the region as a whole.[75]

However, despite the parties' submissions and the Trial Chamber's findings, the *Plavšić* case seems to undermine the objective of reconciliation for at least two reasons:

1. in exchange for Plavšić's guilty plea to one count of persecutions as a crime against humanity, the Prosecution dropped the charge of genocide, without explaining the reasons for dismissing such serious charges;
2. Plavšić was sentenced to a penalty (11 years' imprisonment) that did not reflect the gravity of her crimes and her responsibilities in their commission.

In the author's view, the lack of transparency in the acceptance and negotiation of Plavšić's guilty plea, and the leniency of her sentence mainly motivated by the use of reconciliation as a mitigating factor, cannot be said to be conducive to reconciliation. To the contrary, a penalty that appears unjust because too lenient hinders both the achievement of the primary objectives of sentencing (retribution and deterrence), and of broader objectives of the system such as reconciliation and maintenance of peace. Plavšić's victims harshly condemned both the withdrawal of the genocide charges and the lenient 11-year sentence.[76]

A lack of transparency in plea-bargaining also characterised the process leading to the 'highly disputed sentencing judgment'[77] in the case of Miroslav Deronjić. Deronjić, former President of the Bratunac Municipal Board of the Serbian Democratic Party (SDS) of Bosnia and Herzegovina, also President of the Bratunac Crisis Staff and member of the Main Board of the SDS, was sentenced to 10 years' imprisonment, having pleaded guilty to persecutions as a crime against

---

[74] Ibid paras 73–81. The word 'reconciliation' appears 27 times in the 41-page long sentencing judgment.
[75] Ibid para 80 (emphasis added).
[76] Combs, 'Prosecutor v Plavšić' (n 60) 936.
[77] The judgment was so defined by the Presiding Judge: see *Prosecutor v Deronjić* (Transcript) IT-02-61-T (30 March 2004) 341.

humanity.[78] Deronjić accepted responsibility for having ordered the Bratunac Territorial Defence forces and police forces to attack the village of Glogova (in eastern Bosnia and Herzegovina). As a result of his order, 64 Muslim civilians from the village were killed, Bosnian Muslim homes, private property, and the mosque were destroyed, and a substantial part of Glogova was razed to the ground.[79]

In his strongly worded dissenting opinion, Judge Schomburg observed that, given the gravity of the crimes committed, Deronjić deserved a sentence of no less than 20 years,[80] and that the sentence imposed, recommended by the OTP, was not within the mandate and spirit of the ICTY.[81] Judge Schomburg harshly criticised what he considered to be the 'arbitrary' selection of charges and facts in the indictment against Deronjić and the fact that the judges eventually decided upon a 'clinically clean compilation of selected facts by the Prosecutor'.[82] Conversely, Judge Mumba, in her separate opinion supporting the decision of the majority, stressed the importance of guilty plea as a sign of rehabilitation of the offender and an important step towards reconciliation of the offended community.[83]

When discussing sentencing, the *Deronjić* Trial Chamber recalled the link between justice and reconciliation, and found that guilty pleas contribute to the reconciliation process through the defendant's acknowledgement of responsibility for his actions and by protecting victims from having to relive their experiences and re-open old wounds.[84] However, if guilty pleas may provide a degree of closure to victims, and if victims may feel relieved because the perpetrator admits his guilt, guilty pleas are not necessarily conducive to reconciliation when they result in excessively lenient sentences. Victims also expect that a just and proportionate penalty be imposed. The link between a just and adequate punishment and reconciliatory objectives was apparent in the words of some Prosecution witnesses who expressed their opinion regarding Deronjić's guilty plea. One of the witnesses stated:

> I saw Miroslav Deronjić plead guilty on the television. The Bosnian Muslims in the community that I have spoken to, felt relieved because he admitted his guilt. This is a positive thing and can heal the wounds of the community provided that he is *punished adequately*. A mild punishment however would not serve any purpose; he does not deserve any compassion as he did not show any, not only to people of Glogova but also to the other Muslim Bosnians of Bratunac and Srebrenica.[85]

---

[78] *Prosecutor v Deronjić* (Sentencing Judgment) (n 19) para 48, and 'Disposition'.
[79] Ibid para 44.
[80] Ibid Dissenting Opinion of Judge Schomburg, para 2: 'The sentence is not proportional to the crimes it is based on and amounts to a singing from the wrong hymn sheet. The Accused deserves a sentence of no less than twenty years of imprisonment.'
[81] Ibid para 3.
[82] Ibid paras 9(c)–10.
[83] Ibid Separate Opinion of Judge Florence Mumba, paras 2–3.
[84] Ibid paras 133–134, 238–239.
[85] Ibid para 238 (emphasis added).

In the words of another witness:

> I saw Miroslav Deronjić plead guilty and I felt glad that he admitted his guilt. I do not however understand how is it possible to give him any lenient term of imprisonment after what he himself has confessed.[86]

The Chamber's response to these concerns was to accept the Defence's submissions that 'a sentence is a relative category because ... there is no sentence that can give the victims full satisfaction for their losses',[87] and thus to sentence Deronjić to 10 years' imprisonment.

Obviously, no penalty or term of imprisonment will ever be sufficient to remedy to the loss of human life. However, this does not mean that sentences imposed by international tribunals should not strive as much as possible to hand out a proportionate punishment that reflects the gravity of the crimes committed and the responsibilities of their perpetrators. In numerous cases the reconciliatory objective was used to justify plea-bargaining and the request and imposition of lenient sentences.[88] Also at the ICTR, with the exception of the *Kambanda* case, sentences imposed in guilty plea cases have been rather lenient.[89]

---

[86] Ibid para 239.

[87] Ibid para 240. This argument was made also in the *Plavšić* case: *Prosecutor v Plavšić* (Sentencing Judgment) (n 57) para 132.

[88] See e.g. ibid para 83: 'This Trial Chamber is of the view that an accused's admission of guilt and acceptance of the facts as related by victim-witnesses provides a unique and unquestionable fact-finding tool that greatly contributes to peace-building and reconciliation among the affected communities.' See *Prosecutor v Banović* (Sentencing Judgment) IT-02-65/1-S (28 October 2003) para 69: 'The Accused added that he felt sorry for all the victims and wished that his plea and expressed remorse will be "understood as a balm for those wounds and as a contribution to the reconciliation of all people in Prijedor and the restoration of the situation that existed before the war".' See further *Prosecutor v Nikolić* (Sentencing Judgment) (n 21) para 274, where the Trial Chamber, also on the basis of the reconciliatory goal, accorded a substantial reduction of the penalty that would otherwise be imposed: 'Considering all the above-mentioned mitigating circumstances together and giving particular importance to such factors as the guilty plea, expression of remorse, *reconciliation* and the disclosing of additional information to the Prosecution, the Trial Chamber is convinced that a *substantial reduction* of the sentence is warranted' (emphasis added).

[89] For example, Michel Bagaragaza pleaded guilty to complicity in genocide and was sentenced to eight years' imprisonment (*Prosecutor v Bagaragaza* (Sentencing Judgment) ICTR-05-86-S (17 November 2009) para 15 and 'Verdict'). Georges Ruggiu was sentenced to 12 years' imprisonment, having pleaded guilty to the two counts against him, namely direct and public incitement to commit genocide, and persecutions as a crime against humanity (*Prosecutor v Ruggiu* (Trial Judgment) (n 20) paras 4, 10 and 'Verdict'). Joseph Serugendo, who pleaded guilty to direct and public incitement to commit genocide and persecutions as a crime against humanity, was sentenced to six years' imprisonment (see *Prosecutor v Serugendo* (Sentencing Judgment) (n 57) paras 1–14, and 'Disposition'). Omar Serushago was sentenced to 15 years' imprisonment having pleaded guilty to four counts: genocide, and murder, extermination and torture as crimes against humanity (*Prosecutor v Serushago*

The link instituted between reconciliation and guilty pleas/plea-bargaining procedures is problematic for at least two reasons:

1. the lack of transparency in the bargaining process that often leads to a substantial reduction of the charges included in the initial indictment;[90] and
2. the leniency of the sentences imposed, which are ultimately disproportionate to the gravity of the crimes and the responsibilities of the perpetrators.

Probably as a reaction to the dissent caused among judges by the *Deronjić* case, and to the leniency of penalties in guilty plea cases, in the following guilty plea case before the ICTY, judges did not follow the Prosecution's recommendations on sentencing. In fact, Milan Babić was sentenced to 13 years' imprisonment despite a maximum penalty of 11 years recommended by the Prosecution.[91] At the same time, the Trial Chamber recognised that 'by his guilty plea and his account of the events, Babić has contributed significantly to the reconciliation process in the territory of the former Yugoslavia, in particular in Croatia and Bosnia-Herzegovina'.[92]

It is not only leniency in sentencing, when not proportional to the gravity of the crimes and the responsibility of the perpetrator, that undermines the objectives of reconciliation, but also the fact that this leniency has been applied inconsistently by the *ad hoc* Tribunals – so that certain defendants have received greater discount than others. This undermines the objectives and the credibility of punishment imposed by the Tribunals. There are for example a number of cases where low-level perpetrators who pleaded guilty were not accorded the same degree of mitigation in sentencing than high-level perpetrators. This can be appreciated when considering the guilty plea cases of Biljana Plavšić, Miroslav Bralo and Dragan Nikolić.

---

(Sentencing Judgment) ICTR-98-39-T (5 February 1999) para 4, and 'Verdict'. The 15-year sentence was upheld on appeal).

[90] E.g. the indictment against Stevan Todorović initially charged him with 27 counts related to crimes against humanity (persecutions on political, racial and religious grounds; deportation; murder; inhumane acts; rape and torture); grave breaches of the Geneva Conventions (unlawful deportation or transfer; wilful killing; wilfully causing great suffering and torture or inhuman treatment); and violations of the laws or customs of war (murder; cruel treatment; humiliating and degrading treatment and torture). See *Prosecutor v Simić et al* (Second Amended Indictment) IT-95-9 (19 November 1998). As a result of the plea-bargaining, all charges were dropped and only the main one of persecutions as a crime against humanity (Count 1), to which Todorović pleaded guilty, was maintained and formed part of the agreement (*Prosecutor v Todorović* (Sentencing Judgment) (n 25) paras 1–17). In the case of Momir Nikolić, the Prosecution agreed to drop the charges of genocide and to maintain only that of persecutions as a crime against humanity (*Prosecutor v Nikolić* (Sentencing Judgment) IT-02-60/1-S (2 December 2003) paras 3–16). Substantial charges were dropped also in the *Deronjić* case (see *Prosecutor v Deronjić* (Sentencing Judgment) (n 19) paras 14–28; Dissenting Opinion of Judge Schomburg, paras 6–12).

[91] *Prosecutor v Babić* (Sentencing Judgment) IT-03-72-S (29 June 2004) paras 101–102.

[92] Ibid para 69.

By comparing the nature and extent of Plavšić's and Bralo's guilty pleas, one can easily notice that, while Plavšić accepted responsibility for only a part of the crimes charged and benefited of a substantial reduction of the charges (which were divested of the genocide charge), Bralo fully accepted his responsibilities and the new charges of persecutions as a crime against humanity that were added to his indictment (which initially comprised only charges of war crimes).[93] Nikolić also fully acknowledged his criminal responsibility, expressed sincere remorse, and fully cooperated with the Prosecution (all factors lacking in the Plavšić's case).[94] However, despite their guilty pleas being more substantial and less opportunistic, Bralo and Nikolić did not receive as much mitigation as Plavšić did for having contributed to reconciliation through their guilty pleas.[95] The role and hierarchical level of the three defendants was also very different. Plavšić's role during the war has been recalled before. Miroslav Bralo was a member of the 'Jokers', the anti-terrorist platoon of the 4th Military Police Battalion of the Croatian Defence Council (HVO), which operated primarily in the Lašva Valley region in central Bosnia and Herzegovina; Dragan Nikolić was the Commander of the Sušica Detention Camp in the municipality of Vlasenica (eastern Bosnia and Herzegovina). Bralo and Nikolić were definitely not as high-level perpetrators as Plavšić was; still they received higher sentences.

An inconsistent approach in sentencing not only undermines the objectives of punishment and the principle of equality before the law at the eyes of the public, but also misinterprets the reconciliation aim as it fails to properly reflect the individual culpability of high-level perpetrators.

*ii. Evaluating the link between reconciliation and sentencing cases of guilty pleas*
In sum, it seems that in many cases the *ad hoc* Tribunals, particularly the ICTY, have relied upon the objective of reconciliation to justify the practice of lenient sentences for guilty plea cases.

However, as discussed above, the use of reconciliation as a (mitigating) factor to validate lenient sentences has proved questionable for at least two reasons. A guilty plea that is rewarded with a substantial plea-bargaining and with an excessively lenient sentence is more likely to hinder the process of reconciliation than to favour it. Disproportionately lenient sentences have left many victims, who are essential to the reconciliation process, believing that justice has not been

---

[93] *Prosecutor v Bralo* (Sentencing Judgment) (n 57) paras 1–6.
[94] *Prosecutor v Nikolić* (Sentencing Judgment) (n 21) paras 235–260.
[95] Bralo was sentenced to 20 years' imprisonment (*Prosecutor v Bralo* (Sentencing Judgment) (n 57) para 97; *Prosecutor v Bralo* (Judgment on Sentencing Appeal) IT-95-17-A (2 April 2007) 44, 'Disposition'). Dragan Nikolić was initially sentenced to 23 years imprisonment (*Prosecutor v Nikolić* (Sentencing Judgment) (n 19) 'Disposition'), term reduced to 20 years' imprisonment on appeal (*Prosecutor v Nikolić* (Judgment on Sentencing Appeal) IT-94-2-A (4 February 2005) 44, 'Disposition').

done.⁹⁶ Full accountability of perpetrators and transparency in the prosecutorial choices are essential to the perception that the public has of the judicial process in international criminal law.

The achievement of goals such as reconciliation and maintenance of peace may easily be jeopardised by an improper or unprincipled use of guilty plea and plea-bargaining procedures. In particular, the elements that render guilty pleas defective with regard to reconciliation, and unlikely to foster such objective, can be summarised as follows:

- The process of negotiating charges and sentence may be contrary to the interest of justice and the establishment of truth, if this bargaining is not transparent and if it is not motivated or explained to the public.
- When a defendant pleads guilty, the absence of a normal trial with presentation of evidence and witness testimony may impede witnesses to come forward to tell their stories and go through a cathartic process. In fact, some witnesses might find the process of giving testimony useful.
- Defendants who plead guilty are not always genuinely remorseful for their deeds, but may only be motivated by the convenience of the guilty plea procedure and the prospect of a discounted sentence. If in these cases the guilty plea of the defendant is wrongly characterised as genuine and conducive to reconciliation, and is thus attributed undue weight, this might undermine the victims' and public perception of justice 'been done' and 'seen to be done'.⁹⁷
- The lenient penalties imposed in guilty plea cases may not be well accepted or understood by victims. Victims' dissatisfaction regarding lenient penalties can thus have a negative impact on the process of reconciliation.

In truth, it is not a guilty plea *per se* which automatically makes a contribution to the process of reconciliation and peace-building. Rather, what is relevant is the quality of the factors comprising the guilty plea, i.e. the genuineness of the defendant's plea and of the statements underlying the plea; the degree of acceptance of responsibility; the type and quality of the information provided; the degree of cooperation in other/related trials; whether the guilty plea is also accompanied by

---

⁹⁶ Stover (n 2) 142.

⁹⁷ The *Plavšić* case can be brought once more as an example of this misrepresentation. In 2009, Biljana Plavšić gave an interview to a Swedish newspaper in which she retracted her confession and revealed the true motives of her guilty plea. The article reported that, 'She now claims to have pleaded guilty in an attempt to have the remaining charges against her, including those of genocide, dropped. "I sacrificed myself. I have done nothing wrong. I pleaded guilty to crimes against humanity so I could bargain for the other charges. If I hadn't, the trial would have lasted three, three and-a-half years. Considering my age that wasn't an option", the now 79-year-old Plavšić told *Vi* magazine' (D Uggelberg Goldberg, 'Plavšić Retracts War-Crimes Confession' (Stockholm 4 February 2009) <http://www.bosnia.org.uk/news/news_body.cfm?newsid=2544> last accessed 2 January 2012.

sincere remorse. If these elements are not ensured or are not genuine, no advantage should be expected in terms of reconciliation.

In the author's view, the mitigating value of guilty pleas has been misinterpreted by Chambers of the *ad hoc* Tribunals; the weight to accord to guilty pleas should have been assessed more carefully. Considering that the ICTY and ICTR have jurisdiction over the most serious crimes of international concern, a guilty plea should not detract from the gravity of these crimes and the responsibilities of their perpetrators, and should not warrant disproportionately lenient sentences, especially not in light of reconciliation. Thus it seems that, ironically, while the Tribunals 'attempt to use the guilty plea's potential to promote reconciliation as a justification for rewarding it with sentencing concessions', in fact 'rewarding it with sentencing concessions undermines its potential to promote reconciliation'.[98]

# Conclusion

Criminal trials represent only one of a possible number of responses available to the international community to heal the wounds of society after a conflict. There are certainly limits to what can be achieved through law and trial proceedings; the sentencing practice of the *ad hoc* Tribunals offers a number of examples of these limits in light of the alleged reconciliatory function of justice. The question that has animated this chapter is how reconciliation, one of the declared objectives for the establishment of the *ad hoc* Tribunals, has been interpreted and applied through their sentencing practice. Some aspects of the Tribunals' sentencing practice show that these institutions had difficulties in performing that function of reconciliation and promotion of peace.

On the one hand, the lack of a principled and systematic elaboration of the reconciliatory rationale has either caused confusion with regard to its scope of application, or has resulted in a vague and ineffective 'mention' of such rationale with no real implications in the international trial context. Reconciliation and promotion of peace have lacked sufficient theoretical elaboration and empirical underpinning in the system of the *ad hoc* Tribunals, and have thus resulted rather ineffective in their implementation. On the other hand, the challenge of achieving reconciliation through sentencing has led to results often in opposition with the very objective of reconciliation: unjustified leniency in sentencing or inconsistent sentencing outcomes, and an improper or contradictory use of guilty plea and plea-bargaining procedures.

If international tribunals and courts link too strongly reconciliation and penalties in their sentencing process with the result of imposing disproportionately lenient sentences under the reconciliatory umbrella, they risk frustrating the very achievement of their principal aim: justice. Further, if justice handed out by international tribunals and courts is unpredictable and incomplete, or inconsistent

---

[98] Combs (n 60) 151.

and unjust, part of their broader objectives, for example contributing to the reconciliation of the affected communities, will undoubtedly be undermined. The difficulty in balancing the reconciliatory rationale with the traditional purposes of punishment when meting out sentences has also been favoured by the lack of a proper sentencing policy in international criminal justice and by the fact that many areas of sentencing were still undeveloped when the Tribunals started functioning.[99]

When the elaboration of fundamental issues like those concerning sentencing is underdeveloped or even inconsistent across their practice, the outcome might be represented by inconsistent or inadequate sentences that are unsuitable to either the goals of the international criminal justice system and the goals of punishment generally speaking, or to the objectives specifically envisaged for the institutions concerned (for example, in the case of the *ad hoc* Tribunals, the specific objectives for which they were established, including reconciliation). Incidentally, the tension between reconciliation and sentencing, and the difficulties highlighted above in achieving reconciliation *through* sentencing, brings the attention to the unsolved issue of identifying, on the one hand, the objectives of the international criminal justice system overall considered, and on the other hand the more specific purposes of punishment in international criminal proceedings.

The main objectives of international justice and of each specific stage of international criminal proceedings should thus be identified with more specificity. Different objectives might be appropriate for each different stage of the proceedings. These different objectives should then be balanced differently in the various phases of the process of international criminal adjudication. While the objectives of the whole system of international criminal justice are by their nature more directed to the entire international community as a whole, the purposes of international sentencing – namely punishment when meted out by international courts or tribunals – are more related to individual criminal responsibility and the appropriate penalty to impose to individual offenders. Reconciliation is a laudable goal for the international criminal justice system, but not a realistic *direct* objective for international criminal proceedings and in particular for sentencing, where other rationales such as retribution, individual deterrence, incapacitation and rehabilitation are at stake.

The system of international criminal justice is characterised in particular by its attention to the reconciliatory, restorative and historical paradigm. Fight against impunity, general deterrence, reconciliation and maintenance of peace are thus amongst the primary objectives of the international criminal justice system, and they should be pursued in various ways.

International criminal tribunals are certainly an important part of the reconciliatory and peace-building process in post-conflict societies. However, the 'justice' they deliver might not always be the most effective means to secure reconciliation. Justice on its own is not sufficient if it is not aided by other means and by the commitment of the affected communities. While international criminal trials can bring much to post-war communities and societies in transition, they

---

[99] See Section I above.

are certainly not the only answer to the commission of atrocities. At the end of a civil war, and in a situation of post-war transition, much more is needed.[100] The more articulated and multi-dimensioned the response and intervention of the international community is, the more likely the chances of success in the goal of promoting peace and reconciliation.

To conclude, the general questions of whether justice and reconciliation are truly linked, whether trials can generally serve as an effective tool to promote reconciliation, and whether justice can effectively contribute to reconcile post-conflict societies, are probably bound to remain unanswered for the time being, also due to the lack of enough empirical research that could give a pragmatic basis to any evaluation or analysis, and thus measure the contribution of trials to reconciliation and social reconstruction.[101] However, as the *ad hoc* Tribunals represent an interesting case-study with regard to the impact of the reconciliatory objective on sentencing practice, some lessons can be learned from their practice.

'Reconciliation is not the goal of criminal trials except in the most abstract sense'.[102] Thus, reconciliation should not unduly influence the penalty imposed, and international judges should carefully evaluate the influence of reconciliation on sentencing. Further, the Appeals Chamber of the *ad hoc* Tribunals should have encouraged a careful approach towards using the 'contribution towards reconciliation' as a significant mitigating factor in sentencing, thus bringing significant sentencing discount. As the Appeals Chamber has in some instances called upon a careful use of other specific purposes of punishment, such as rehabilitation, when not properly balanced with the main purposes of sentencing like retribution and deterrence,[103] and discouraged an 'unduly influence' of these

---

[100] UN SC, 'Report of the Secretary-General: The Rule of Law and Transitional Justice in Conflict and Post-Conflict Societies' UN Doc S/2004/616 (23 August 2004), para 25: 'The international community must see transitional justice in a way that extends well beyond courts and tribunals. The challenges of post-conflict environments necessitate an approach that balances a variety of goals, including the pursuit of accountability, truth and reparation, the preservation of peace and the building of democracy and the rule of law.'

[101] See e.g. Fletcher and Weinstein (n 5) 585; R Byrne, 'Promises of Peace and Reconciliation: Previewing the Legacy of the International Criminal Tribunal for Rwanda' (2006) 14(4) *European Review* 485, 493.

[102] M Minow, *Between Vengeance and Forgiveness* (Beacon Press, Boston 1998) 26.

[103] See *Prosecutor v Delalić et al* (Appeal Judgment) (n 19) para 806, where the Appeals Chamber acknowledged the significance of rehabilitation but, at the same time, stressed the fact that 'rehabilitation' should not 'play a predominant role' in the decision-making process and must be subordinated to deterrence and retribution as the main purposes of sentencing within the system of the *ad hoc* Tribunals. Similarly, the Appeals Chamber in the *Media* case, where one of the Appellants, Barayagwiza, maintained that the Trial Chamber, in determining the final penalty, failed to give importance to the objectives of national reconciliation and rehabilitation. The Appeals Chamber recognised the primary importance of retribution and deterrence in sentencing, and stressed that the objective of rehabilitation of the accused should not play a major role in the determination of penalty (*Prosecutor v Nahimana et al* (Appeal Judgment) ICTR-99-52-A (28 November 2007) paras 1056–1057).

factors on the penalty imposed, similarly it should have warned against a similar use of the reconciliation rationale.

In order not to dilute the reconciliatory objective that international criminal tribunals might have, international criminal justice needs to avail itself of a more developed and principled system of international sentencing, in particular: a statement of purposes and principles for international sentencing; procedural norms to provide guidance and ensure consistency and fairness in the sentencing process; a range of penalties for the underlying acts of international crimes; a better defined system of aggravating and mitigating circumstances.

# PART III
# Complementarity and Sentencing: A Discussion

# 14

# A Sentence-Based Theory of Complementarity

## Kevin Jon Heller[1]

Scholars generally agree that nothing in the Rome Statute prohibits states from prosecuting international crimes as ordinary crimes.[2] They have yet to identify a complementarity heuristic, however, that is capable of reliably distinguishing between acceptable and unacceptable national prosecutions. In this chapter, I propose a heuristic that focuses exclusively on sentence. More specifically, I argue that the Court should deem inadmissible *any* national prosecution of an ordinary crime that results in a sentence equal to, or longer than, the sentence the perpetrator would receive from the ICC, regardless of the gravity of the crime or whether it is based on different conduct than the international crime.

## I. Current Doctrine

Although the ICC itself has not yet taken a definitive position on the relationship between complementarity and ordinary crimes, the Appeals Chamber has held that, at a minimum, a national prosecution must 'cover the same person and substantially the same conduct as alleged in the proceedings before the Court'.[3]

---

[1] A longer version of this chapter was published as KJ Heller, 'A Sentence-Based Theory of Complementarity' (2012) 53 *Harvard Int'l L J* 201.

[2] See e.g. JK Kleffner, 'The Impact of Complementarity on National Implementation of Substantive Criminal Law' (2003) 1 *JICJ* 86, 99; B Broomhall, 'The International Criminal Court: A Checklist for National Implementation' (1999) 13*quater Nouvelles Etudes Penales* 113, 149; G Werle, *Principles of International Criminal Law* (TMC Asser Press: The Hague 2005) 77.

[3] See *Situation in the Republic of Kenya: Prosecutor v Muthaura, Kenyatta and Ali* (Judgment on Defence Appeal Challenging Admissibility of Case) ICC-01/09-02/11 (30 August 2011) para 39; *Situation in Darfur, Sudan: Prosecutor v Harun and Kushayb* (Decision on the Prosecution Application Under Article 58(7) of the Statute) ICC-02/05-01/07 (27 April 2007) para 24; *Situation in the DRC: Prosecutor v Lubanga* (Decision on the Prosecutor's Application for a Warrant of Arrest, Article 58) ICC-01/04-01/06 (10 February 2006) para 37.

That holding is not surprising; the 'same conduct' language was specifically added to the chapeaux of Article 20(3) during the Rome Conference to make clear that a national prosecution of a crime – international or ordinary – did not prohibit ICC retrial for charges based on different conduct. Moreover, two other Articles in the Rome Statute also indicate that the complementarity requirements in Article 17 are limited to national prosecutions involving the same conduct as the ICC prosecution. Article 89 specifically addresses situations in which the ICC requests surrender of a suspect who 'is being proceeded against or is serving a sentence in the requested State for a crime different from that for which surrender to the Court is sought'.[4] In such situations, the conflict is resolved not by applying Article 17, but through consultation between the ICC and the state.[5] Similarly, Article 94 provides that '[i]f the immediate execution of a request [for surrender] would interfere with an ongoing investigation or prosecution of a case different from that to which the request relates, the requested State may postpone the execution of the request for a period of time agreed upon with the Court'.[6]

The 'same-conduct test' determines whether a state is 'inactive' with regard to an ICC prosecution; it says nothing about whether a state satisfies Article 17(1)'s willingness requirement.[7] Scholars have thus encouraged the Court to supplement the same-conduct test by adopting a view of unwillingness that limits states to charging defendants with 'serious' ordinary crimes. Bruce Broomhall argues that a national prosecution should be deemed inadmissible only if 'the conduct is treated with an appropriate amount of gravity.'[8] Markus Benzing agrees, noting that if 'the charge chosen by national authorities does not reflect and adequately capture the severity of the perpetrator's conduct ... this may be seen as conflicting with an intent to bring the perpetrator to justice'.[9] And Linda Carter argues that 'if the national prosecution was for a minor crime, such as assault, in a context in which the conduct should be charged as genocide, then the sham trial exception should

---

[4] Rome Statute of the International Criminal Court, 2187 UNTS 90, 17 July 1998, entered into force 1 July 2002, art 89(4) ('ICC Statute').

[5] Ibid art 89(4).

[6] Ibid art 94(1).

[7] See, e.g., R Rastan, 'What is a "Case" for the Purpose of the Rome Statute?' (2008) 19 CLF 435, 438; D Robinson, 'The Mysterious Mysteriousness of Complementarity' (2010) 21 CLF 67, 85.

[8] Broomhall (n 2) 149.

[9] M Benzing, 'The Complementarity Regime of the International Criminal Court: International Criminal Justice Between State Sovereignty and the Fight Against Impunity' (2003) 7 *Max Planck Ybk UN L* 591, 616.

apply'.¹⁰ Genocide as assault is a particularly common example of unwillingness,¹¹ as is prosecuting the war crime of pillage as theft.¹²

## II. The Sentence-Based Alternative

Scholars who emphasise conduct and gravity do not deny that sentence should play a role in complementarity analysis. On the contrary, most accept that an inadequate sentence can also justify the ICC pre-empting a national prosecution of an ordinary crime.¹³ No scholar to date, however, has suggested that the *ex post* imposition of a lengthy sentence can compensate for the *ex ante* decision to charge an ordinary crime that is not sufficiently serious. Moreover, only Sharon Williams and William A. Schabas have questioned whether the same-conduct requirement is consistent with the goals of complementarity.¹⁴

I argue, by contrast, that the Court should focus *exclusively* on sentence when determining whether a national prosecution of an ordinary crime is admissible. As long as a national prosecution results in a sentence no less severe than the defendant would receive in the ICC prosecution, the case should be inadmissible regardless of the gravity of the crime or whether it is based on the same conduct.

Here is how the sentence-based heuristic would work. Pursuant to Article 17, a state can challenge the admissibility of a case in two different situations: (1) when it is currently investigating or prosecuting the case itself;¹⁵ or (2) when it has already

---

[10] LE Carter, 'The Principle of Complementarity and the International Criminal Court: The Role of *Ne Bis in Idem*' (2010) 8 *Santa Clara J Int'l L* 165, 194; see also Office of the Prosecutor, International Criminal Court, *Informal Expert Paper: The Principle of Complementarity in Practice* <http://www.icc-cpi.int/iccdocs/doc/doc654724.pdf> last accessed 2 December 2011, 30 (describing '[a]dequacy of charge ... vis-à-vis the gravity and evidence' as an indicator of willingness); D Robinson, 'The Rome Statute and its Impact on National Law' in A Cassese et al (eds) *The Rome Statute of the International Criminal Court: A Commentary* (OUP, Oxford 2002) 1864 (arguing that if the 'stigma attached to a certain national offence do[es] not reflect the grave seriousness of the crime in international law, then this might contribute to a finding of unwillingness or inability to genuinely prosecute').

[11] Carter (n 10) 194; see also International Centre for Criminal Law Reform and Criminal Justice Policy, *International Criminal Court: Manual for the Ratification and Implementation of the Rome Statute* (3rd edn International Centre for Criminal Law Reform and Criminal Justice Policy, Vancouver 2008) 66 (hereinafter, 'Ratification Manual').

[12] See, e.g., Kleffner (n 2) 97; Ratification Manual (n 11) 84.

[13] They are divided, however, over whether an inadequate sentence represents unwillingness or inability. Broomhall (n 2) 153 and the *Informal Expert Paper* (n 10) 31 fall in the former category, while Benzing (n 9) 617 and Kleffner (n 2) 97 are in the latter.

[14] SA Williams and WA Schabas, 'Article 17' in O Triffterer (ed) *Commentary on the Rome Statute of the International Criminal Court: Observers' Notes, Article by Article* (2nd edn Hart, Oxford 2008) 617. Rastan has also raised the issue, but he did not take a firm position on it. See Rastan (n 7) 440.

[15] ICC Statute, art 17(1)(a).

prosecuted the perpetrator and either convicted or acquitted him.[16] If a state challenged admissibility pre-conviction, the Court would compare the average sentence for the international crime charged by the ICC with the average sentence for the ordinary crime being investigated or prosecuted by the state. As long as the national average was equal to or greater than the ICC average, the case would be inadmissible. The Court could then revisit the admissibility challenge after the national prosecution concluded, retrying the defendant under Article 20(3) if the defendant was acquitted after a sham trial or received an inadequate sentence.

The comparison would be even more straightforward if a state challenged admissibility post-conviction. In that situation, the Court would simply compare the actual sentence the defendant received for the ordinary crime with the average sentence for the international crime charged by the ICC. As long as the actual sentence was equal to or greater than the ICC maximum – or perhaps slightly below it, permitting states a certain 'margin of appreciation'[17] – the case would be inadmissible.[18]

This heuristic is, of course, open to an important objection: because the ICC ha completed only one trial, it is impossible to know what the 'average' sentence will be for the international crimes within its jurisdiction. That problem should decrease over time, as the Court develops its sentencing jurisprudence. In the interim, two solutions are possible. To begin with, when faced with an admissibility challenge, the Court could determine the applicable statutory maximum for the international crime – 30 years if the crime was neither extremely grave nor the defendant particularly heinous,[19] life otherwise[20] – and use that as its baseline for comparison. Alternatively, the Court could apply the average sentence for the international

---

[16] Ibid art 17(1)(c).

[17] Both Broomhall and Kleffner have suggested that states should be entitled to such a margin when the Court judges the adequacy of a sentence for an ordinary crime. See B Broomhall, *International Justice and the International Criminal Court: Between Sovereignty and the Rule of Law* (OUP, Oxford 2004) 92–93; JK Kleffner, *Complementarity in the Rome Statute and National Jurisdictions* (OUP, Oxford 2008) 72, 137.

[18] A situation could arise in which a convicted defendant who received an adequate sentence served an inadequate amount of time in prison because of pardon or parole. In such a situation – which affects any complementarity heuristic – art 20(3)(a) would permit the Court to retry the defendant, assuming that the circumstances of his release reflected an intention to 'shield[] the person concerned from criminal responsibility'. MM El Zeidy, *The Principle of Complementarity in International Criminal Law: Origin, Development and Practice* (Martinus Nijhoff, The Hague 2008) 297–298.

[19] ICC Statute, art 77(1)(a).

[20] Ibid art 77(1)(b).

crime at the ICTY and ICTR,[21] which have sentenced more than 100 defendants for a variety of international crimes.[22]

## III. A Taxonomy of Ordinary Crime Prosecutions

To understand why a sentence-based heuristic is superior to a heuristic based on conduct and gravity, it is helpful to create a taxonomy of scenarios in which a state charges a defendant with an ordinary crime instead of an international crime. Three factors are particularly relevant: (1) whether the ordinary crime and the international crime are based on the same conduct or different conduct; (2) whether the ordinary crime is serious or minor; and (3) whether the ordinary crime carries a severe or light sentence. Those factors generate the following taxonomy:

| Scenario | Conduct | Crime | Sentence |
|---|---|---|---|
| 1 | Same | Serious | Severe |
| 2 | Same | Serious | Lenient |
| 3 | Same | Minor | Severe |
| 4 | Same | Minor | Lenient |
| 5 | Different | Serious | Severe |
| 6 | Different | Serious | Lenient |
| 7 | Different | Minor | Severe |
| 8 | Different | Minor | Lenient |

Although a degree of subjectivity inheres in all three factors, it is not difficult to identify a prototypical example of each scenario. Scenarios 1–4 involve ordinary crimes that are based on the same conduct as the international crime charged by the ICC:

---

[21] The ICC, of course, is not bound by the sentencing jurisprudence of the *ad hoc* tribunals. Moreover, as discussed below (see text accompanying notes 49–58), there is reason to believe that the ICTY and (to a lesser extent) the ICTR have imposed sentences that are relatively lenient relative to the gravity of convicted defendants' crimes. Those sentences nevertheless remain the primary source of data concerning 'appropriate' international sentences.

[22] The ICC would need to use the average sentence for a particular crime, because individual sentences are affected by the presence of aggravating and mitigating factors that differ between defendants. See, e.g., MB Harmon and F Gaynor, 'Ordinary Sentences for Extraordinary Crimes' (2007) 5 *JICJ* 683, 688–689 (discussing the impact of those factors in the context of ICTY sentences).

> **Scenario 1**: a defendant charged with murder as a crime against humanity is convicted of ordinary murder and sentenced to death.
> **Scenario 2**: a defendant charged with the crime against humanity of rape is convicted of ordinary rape and sentenced to five years in prison.
> **Scenario 3**: a defendant charged with the crime against humanity of murder is convicted of assault and sentenced to 30 years in prison.
> **Scenario 4**: a defendant charged with the crime against humanity of rape is convicted of indecent assault and sentenced to three years in prison.

Scenarios 5–8, by contrast, involve situations in which a state ignores the conduct underlying the ICC prosecution and prosecutes the defendant for an unrelated ordinary crime.

> **Scenario 5**: a defendant charged with the crime against humanity of rape is convicted of murder and sentenced to death.
> **Scenario 6**: a defendant charged with the crime against humanity of murder is convicted of ordinary rape and sentenced to five years in prison.
> **Scenario 7**: a defendant charged with the crime against humanity of rape is convicted of theft and sentenced to thirty years in prison.
> **Scenario 8**: a defendant charged with the crime against humanity of murder is convicted of theft and sentenced to three years in prison.

## A. Applying the Heuristics

We can now apply the heuristics to the scenarios in the taxonomy. Scenarios 1–4 each satisfy the 'same conduct' requirement, so the most important factor under the traditional heuristic would be gravity. Scenario 1 would clearly be inadmissible, because murder is the most serious ordinary crime. Scenario 2 is not as clear-cut as Scenario 1, but would likely be admissible: although rape is a serious ordinary crime, a five-year sentence seems manifestly inadequate relative to the crime against humanity of rape, and even scholars who emphasise gravity agree that an inadequate sentence can manifest a state's unwillingness to genuinely prosecute.[23] Scenario 4, by contrast, would almost certainly be admissible, given that a conviction for assault does not reflect the gravity of rape.

The most difficult 'same conduct' situation is Scenario 3, where a defendant charged by the ICC with the crime against humanity of murder is convicted of assault and given a 30-year sentence. Here the gravity and sentence factors point in different directions: an assault conviction does not reflect the gravity of murder, but 30 years in prison is far longer than the defendant would likely receive if he were convicted by the ICC of murder as a crime against humanity – the average

---

[23] See, e.g., Broomhall (n 2) 153; *Informal Expert Paper* (n 10) 31; Benzing (n 9) 617; Kleffner (n 2) 97.

sentence for that crime at the ICTR is 12–20 years,[24] and the ICTR is generally far more punitive than the ICTY.[25] Most scholars would nevertheless deem Scenario 3 admissible, given their consistent emphasis on gravity and the fact that no scholar who emphasises gravity has ever suggested that a lengthy sentence can offset the choice of an inadequate ordinary crime.

Because the Appeals Chamber has adopted the same-conduct requirement, Scenarios 5–8 would each be admissible on the ground that the state was 'inactive' in relation to the ICC proceeding. In the absence of the same-conduct requirement, the analysis would be similar to the analysis of Scenarios 1–4. Scenario 5 would be inadmissible, because murder is at least as serious as rape. Scenario 6 would likely be admissible even though rape is a serious crime because of the manifestly inadequate sentence. Scenario 7 would likely be admissible because the severe sentence does not compensate for the difference in gravity between the international and ordinary crime. Finally, Scenario 8 would clearly be inadmissible because murder is a far more serious crime than theft.

The traditional complementarity heuristic, in short, leads to a very ICC-centric approach to the prosecution of ordinary crimes. Indeed, given the same-conduct requirement, the traditional heuristic would deem only one of the eight scenarios inadmissible: Scenario 1. A sentence-based complementarity heuristic, by contrast, leads to a much more state-centric approach to the prosecution of ordinary crimes. It would deem four scenarios inadmissible, because each involves an adequate sentence vis-à-vis the ICC proceeding. Scenarios 1 and 5 would be inadmissible because the death penalty is more severe than the most severe sentence (life) that the ICC can impose. Scenario 3 would be inadmissible, despite involving the 'minor' crime of assault, because a 30-year sentence is well above the average sentence for the crime against humanity of murder. Scenario 7 would also be inadmissible, despite involving the 'minor' crime of theft, because a 30-year sentence is far longer than the defendant would likely receive if he was convicted by the ICC of rape as a crime against humanity – the average sentence for that crime at the ICTR is 12–15 years.[26]

## IV. The Advantages of a Sentence-Based Theory of Complementarity

The differences between the traditional conduct-and-gravity heuristic and the sentence-based heuristic thus centre on Scenarios 3, 5 and 7. All three are admissible under the former but not the latter: Scenario 3 because the ordinary crime is not considered grave enough; Scenario 5 because the underlying conduct is different; Scenario 7 because of both factors. In all three scenarios, however, a successful

---

[24] See *Prosecutor v Semanza* (Judgment and Sentence) ICTR-97-20-T (15 May 2003) para 564.
[25] MA Drumbl, *Atrocity, Punishment, and International Law* (CUP, Cambridge 2007) 56.
[26] *Semanza* Judgment (n 24) para 564.

ICC prosecution for the international crime would result in a sentence that is no more severe than the national prosecution for the ordinary crime. What justifies that ostensible waste of the ICC's limited resources?

This chapter's answer is straightforward: nothing. There *is* no justification for the ICC to admit a national prosecution of an ordinary crime that results in an adequate sentence simply because the ordinary crime does not capture the gravity of the international crime charged by the ICC or is based on a different conduct. On the contrary, adopting a complementarity heuristic that focuses exclusively on sentence would not only be more administrable than the current approach, it would also better promote the goals of what Burke-White has called the 'Rome System of Justice' – the 'tiered system of prosecutorial authority' created by the Rome Statute's relationship between the ICC and national criminal-justice systems.[27]

## A. Administrability

The administrability issue focuses on Scenarios 3 and 7, in which admissibility is predicated on a state's choice of an *inadequate* ordinary crime. The problem with a gravity-centred complementarity heuristic is that it fails to answer a critical question: how should the Court determine whether an ordinary crime is so minor that the Court should infer that the state is attempting to 'shield the person concerned from criminal responsibility'? International tribunals have struggled to determine the relative gravity of *categories* of international crimes;[28] they have not even attempted to rank specific international crimes. Is there any reason to believe that it is possible to reliably compare the gravity of international crimes and ordinary crimes? The drafters of Article 20 did not believe such comparisons were possible; as noted earlier, that is precisely why they eliminated the ICTY and ICTR's 'ordinary crimes' exception to the *ne bis in idem* bar.[29]

The drafters' scepticism was warranted. By definition, there will be *some* gravity deficit in a national prosecution for an ordinary crime, because the element of collective perpetration or collective victimisation that distinguishes international

---

[27] WW Burke-White, 'Proactive Complementarity: The International Criminal Court and National Courts in the Rome System of International Justice' (2008) 49 *Harvard Int'l L J* 53, 57.

[28] In *Erdemović*, for example, Judges McDonald and Vohrah argued that crimes against humanity were more serious than war crimes: *Prosecutor v Erdemović* (Appeal of Sentencing Judgment, Joint Separate Opinion of Judges McDonald and Vohrah) IT-96-22-T*bis* (7 October 1997) para 24, while Judge Li took precisely the opposite position: *Prosecutor v Erdemović* (Appeal of Sentencing Judgment, Separate and Dissenting Opinion of Judge Li) IT-96-22-T*bis* (7 October 1997) para 22.

[29] JT Holmes, 'The Principle of Complementarity' in RS Lee (ed) *The International Criminal Court, the Making of the Rome Statute: Issues, Negotiations, Results* (Transnational, Ardsley, NY 1999) 41, 57.

crimes from ordinary ones will necessarily be lacking.[30] So when does a gravity deficit become an unacceptable gravity deficit? Some situations may be obvious, such as Carter's example of where genocide is charged as assault[31] or – to use a non-hypothetical example – the Sudanese government's decision to charge two intelligence officers suspected of involvement in a mass killing with looting instead of murder.[32] Those situations will be the exception, however, not the rule. What about the more difficult ones? If the ICC charges an international crime involving intentional murder, does a state's decision to charge any lesser included offence – reckless murder, manslaughter, assault with intent to cause grievous bodily harm – automatically make the case admissible? If not, where should the line be drawn? Alternatively, consider Jann Kleffner's example of pillage being charged as theft.[33] He accepts that a state does not have to charge pillage as pillage to satisfy complementarity. So what does a state have to charge? Must it charge multiple counts of theft? How many counts are equivalent to pillage – two, 10, 50?

A sentence-based heuristic, by contrast, avoids these problems. It determines whether a national prosecution of an ordinary crime is adequate by comparing two factors that can be empirically determined: on the international side, the ICC sentence maximum and/or the average sentence imposed by international tribunals; on the national side, average sentences and/or the actual sentence imposed in the case in question. The need to make difficult and inherently subjective assessments of the gravity of the ordinary crime disappears; as long as the sentence for the ordinary crime is equal to the sentence for the international crime, the nature of the ordinary crime is irrelevant.

Some proponents of the gravity approach, including Kleffner, recognise that it is difficult to compare the gravity of international and ordinary crimes. His explanation of what demonstrates that an international crime is more serious than an ordinary crime, however, is revealing: '[t]he latter crime will normally entail a far lower maximum sentence than for crimes considered to be the most severe.'[34] But if that is the case – if the primary concern with 'minor' ordinary crimes is that they are not punished severely enough in comparison to an ICC prosecution – what is the justification for admitting a national prosecution involving a minor crime that *does* result in an adequate sentence?

A sentence-based heuristic also helps address two other situations in which a gravity-based approach has difficulty determining whether a national prosecution of an ordinary crime should be admissible. The first is where a state charges a

---

[30] See AM Danner, 'Constructing a Hierarchy of Crimes in International Criminal Law Sentencing' (2001) 85 *Virginia L Rev* 415, 470 ('The *mens rea* element of the chapeau provisions of each of the three categories of crimes within the Tribunals' jurisdiction ... provides a proxy for accounting for secondary harms because it incorporates notions of collective perpetration and collective victimization absent from the enumerated acts').
[31] See text accompanying n 10 above.
[32] See Human Rights Watch, Briefing Paper, *Lack of Conviction: The Special Criminal Court on the Events in Darfur* (HRW, New York 2006) 13–14.
[33] See text accompanying n 11 above.
[34] Kleffner (n 2) 97.

serious ordinary crime, but attempts to connect the defendant to that crime through an inadequate mode of participation. Broomhall, for example, claims that 'were national law to provide a markedly narrower scope of responsibility' than the Rome Statute, 'the ICC could, in appropriate circumstances, admit the case'.[35] Two scenarios are possible here. To begin with, the state might charge a mode of participation that is narrower than the Rome Statute equivalent. Broomhall cites a national definition of command responsibility that makes it more difficult to convict a military superior[36] – for example, by requiring the superior to have knowledge of his subordinates' crimes.[37] The other scenario includes situations in which a mode of participation arguably understates the perpetrator's culpability, such as a prosecution in a state that treats command responsibility as a form of dereliction of duty (like Canada[38]) instead of as a mode of participation,[39] or a national prosecution that charges the defendant as an aider-and-abettor (accessorial liability) instead of as a co-perpetrator or perpetrator-by-means (principal liability).

The problem with a gravity-based heuristic is that it does not help us determine *when* such deviations from the Rome Statute should render a national prosecution admissible. At best, it supports a categorical rule that any deviation is unacceptable. But that result is overbroad, as the three scenarios indicate. It is indeed problematic if a narrow definition of command responsibility results in an acquittal. (If it does, retrial by the ICC is the obvious solution.) But why should the ICC be concerned about the narrowness of the definition if the defendant is convicted and receives an adequate sentence? Similarly, why should the ICC be concerned whether a state like Canada treats command responsibility as a form of dereliction of duty if it punishes such derelictions just as severely as the Court punishes commanders convicted of their subordinates' crimes? Or that a state charges a defendant as an accessory instead of as a principal if the punishment is the same?[40]

---

[35] Broomhall (n 17) 92; Robinson (n 10) 1864 ('If a State wants to be sure of meeting the complementarity test, then it would be prudent to review the grounds of responsibility in the Rome Statute, and to ensure that the national law is at least as broad'); *Informal Expert Paper* (n 10) 30.

[36] Broomhall (n 17) 92.

[37] The ICC Statute, art 28(a)(i) provides that negligence satisfies the *mens rea* of command responsibility for military superiors ('That military commander or person either knew or, owing to the circumstances at the time, should have known that the forces were committing or about to commit such crimes').

[38] R Cryer et al, *An Introduction to International Criminal Law and Procedure* (CUP, Cambridge 2007) 238.

[39] See, e.g., ICC Statute, art 28(a) (holding a military superior responsible 'for crimes within the jurisdiction of the Court committed by forces under his or her effective command and control').

[40] A study of sentencing practice in 22 states found that most states do not require lesser sentences for accessories. Thirteen of the 22 states (60 per cent) permitted accessories and principals to be punished equally, and a number of the others – such as Chile and Spain – punished accessories nearly as severely as principals. See U Sieber, *The Punishment*

The other difficult situation is where a state 'overprotects' a defendant charged with an ordinary crime by providing defences that are considerably broader than the grounds for excluding criminal responsibility in the Rome Statute. A number of scholars agree with Benzing that, like the failure to charge an equally serious crime, such overprotection 'may be seen as conflicting with an intent to bring the perpetrator to justice'.[41] It remains to be seen, for example, how the ICC will treat civil-law states that treat unavoidable mistakes of law as exculpatory and avoidable mistakes of fact as reducing the perpetrator's culpability;[42] that approach is considerably more expansive than Article 32 of the Rome Statute, which only recognises mistakes that negate the perpetrator's *mens rea*.[43] Another difficult situation involves states that consider mistake of law to be a mitigating factor, such as Japan;[44] it is unclear whether the ICC will take a similar approach.[45]

As with narrower modes of participation, a gravity-based complementarity heuristic cannot tell us when the Court should consider a national prosecution involving an 'overprotective' defence admissible; the only possibility is a categorical rule that national and international defences must be equivalent.[46] Such a rule, however, is not only inconsistent with Article 31 of the Rome Statute – which permits the Court to apply defences that are not specifically enumerated in the Statute[47] – it is also overbroad. As long as the national prosecution results in an adequate sentence, it should not matter whether an overprotective defence led to reduced culpability or was treated at sentencing as a mitigating factor.

---

*of Serious Crimes: A Comparative Analysis of Sentencing Law and Practice* (Max Planck Institute for Foreign and International Criminal Law, Freiburg 2003) 81.

[41] Benzing (n 9) 616; cf Robinson (n 10) 1865 ('if the defences available under national law are dramatically broader than those available under the Rome Statute, then it is conceivable that a State could find itself unable to secure a conviction of a person who would clearly be liable under the Rome Statute').

[42] See T Weigend, 'Germany' in KJ Heller and MD Dubber (eds) *Handbook of Comparative Criminal Law* (Stanford Law Books, Stanford 2011) 272 (discussing the German approach to mistake).

[43] ICC Statute, art 32 (recognising a mistake only when it 'negates the mental element required ... by a crime').

[44] JO Haley, 'Japan' in Heller and Dubber (n 42) 405.

[45] Rule 145(2)(a) of the Rules of Procedure and Evidence, International Criminal Court, ICC-ASP/1/3 (Part.II-A) (9 September 2002), entitles the Court to take into account mitigating factors such as 'circumstances falling short of constituting grounds for exclusion of criminal responsibility'. Art 32's insistence on limiting mistakes of law to those that negate *mens rea* makes it unlikely, however, that the Court will recognise other mistakes as mitigating.

[46] Kleffner (n 2) 103 (noting, with regard to defences, that 'States can reasonably be expected to bring their laws into conformity with the decisions of the ICC in order to avoid cases being declared admissible in future').

[47] ICC Statute, art 31(3).

## B. Promoting the Rome System of International Justice

Even if a gravity-based heuristic was administrable, it would still be an open question whether deeming Scenarios 3 and 7 admissible would promote the goals of complementarity. Moreover, although the Appeals Chamber's 'same conduct' requirement is clearly consistent with the text of the Rome Statute, neither the Court nor scholars have ever explained why the ICC should spend its limited resources prosecuting a defendant who is either facing a prison sentence equivalent to what the Court would impose or who has already received such a sentence – the situations in Scenarios 5 and 7.

In fact, it makes little sense for the Court to exclude Scenarios 3, 5 and 7 from the category of admissible cases. On the contrary, deeming such scenarios inadmissible on the ground that they involve adequate sentences would have a number of important practical benefits for the Rome system of international justice.

### i. Minimising the ICC's burden

The most important benefit of adopting a sentence-based complementarity heuristic is that, because it provides states with greater flexibility to prosecute international crimes as ordinary crimes than the conduct-and-gravity heuristic, it would significantly decrease the number of national prosecutions that the Court would have to either pre-empt (prior to conviction) or re-try (after conviction), thereby conserving the ICC's limited resources. The Office of the Prosecutor (OTP) has estimated that, at most, it can prepare six to 10 cases for prosecution over a three-year period.[48] The Court thus has to be exceptionally careful to avoid admitting cases in which the state is not, in fact, attempting to shield the perpetrator from criminal responsibility. Even a small number of errors could quite literally be catastrophic for the Court.

The primary objection to a sentence-based heuristic seems to be the concern that, to recall Kleffner, ordinary crimes 'will normally entail a far lower maximum sentence' than international crimes.[49] That is an empirical claim, and testing it would require a study far more comprehensive than any scholar has conducted to date. The data that are available, however, indicate that in fact the opposite is true: we should be far more concerned about *international* sentences being excessively lenient. The sentencing practice of the ICTY, for example, is anything but harsh. As of 2007, 84 per cent of the defendants convicted at the ICTY had been sentenced to less than 20 years in prison, with 35 per cent receiving less than 10 years.[50] Other studies have found that the average final sentence at the ICTY is 14.3 years,[51]

---

[48] ICC OTP, *Report on Prosecutorial Strategy* (The Hague 14 September 2006) <http://www.icc-cpi.int/NR/rdonlyres/D673DD8C-D427-4547-BC69-2D363E07274B/143708/ProsecutorialStrategy20060914_English.pdf> last accessed 13 December 2011, 7.
[49] Kleffner (n 2) 97.
[50] Harmon and Gaynor (n 22) 684.
[51] Drumbl (n 25) 56.

with average sentences of 15.7 and 10.9 years for crimes against humanity and war crimes, respectively.[52] Some specific sentences also seem remarkably lenient, such as Dražen Erdemović's 10-year sentence for personally executing 70 Bosnian civilians[53] and Miroslav Kvočka's seven-year sentence for co-perpetrating the war crimes of murder and torture and the crime against humanity of persecution.[54]

Nor is the ICTY's record anomalous. The ICTR is more punitive than the ICTY – which is not surprising, given the scale of the genocide in Rwanda – yet the sentences still seem, as one scholar puts it, 'incongruously lenient'.[55] As of 2007, little more than one-third of the defendants convicted by the ICTR had been sentenced to life imprisonment,[56] even though nearly all of the convictions were for genocide or crimes against humanity.[57] Indeed, an almost equal number of defendants had been sentenced to less than 20 years, and 11 per cent had been sentenced to less than 10 years.[58] The average sentence for the crimes against humanity of rape, torture and murder were 12–15, 5–12 and 12–20 years, respectively.[59]

By contrast, there is evidence that states impose quite significant sentences when they prosecute international crimes as ordinary crimes. In a ground-breaking 2003 study commissioned by the ICTY,[60] Ulrich Sieber examined how 22 non-Balkan states[61] would punish a variety of scenarios involving crimes against humanity if they charged the underlying conduct as an ordinary crime. Three scenarios tested the crimes against humanity of rape, torture and murder – the crimes for which we have average sentence ranges at the ICTR, the more punitive of the two *ad hoc*

---

[52] JM Meernik and K King, 'The Sentencing Determinants of the International Criminal Tribunal for the Former Yugoslavia: An Empirical and Doctrinal Analysis' (2003) 16 *LJIL* 717, 735.

[53] See *Erdemović* Case Information Sheet <www.icty.org/case/erdemovic/> last accessed 2 December 2011.

[54] See *Kvočka* Case Information Sheet <www.icty.org/case/kvocka/> last accessed 2 December 2011.

[55] R Sloane, 'The Expressive Capacity of International Punishment: The Limits of the National Law Analogy and the Potential of International Criminal Law' (2007) 43 *Stanford J Int'l L* 39, 69. Joseph Serugendo received a six-year sentence after pleading guilty to direct and public incitement to genocide and persecution as a crime against humanity: *Prosecutor v Serugendo* (Judgment and Sentence) ICTR-2005-84-I (12 June 2006). Elizaphan Ntakirutimana received a 10-year sentence after being convicted for aiding and abetting genocide: *Prosecutor v Ntakirutimana* (Appeals Judgment) ICTR-96-17-A (13 December 2004).

[56] Harmon and Gaynor (n 22) 685.

[57] Drumbl (n 25) 56.

[58] Harmon and Gaynor (n 22) 685.

[59] *Semanza* Judgment (n 24) 36.

[60] Sieber (n 40).

[61] Argentina, Austria, Belgium, Brazil, Canada, Chile, China, England, Finland, France, Germany, Greece, Italy, Ivory Coast, Mexico, Poland, Russia, South Africa, Spain, Sweden, Turkey and the United States.

tribunals. Here is a table of the maximum national sentences for each crime against humanity when prosecuted as an equivalent[62] ordinary crime:

| Country | Rape[a] | Torture[b] | Murder[c] |
|---|---|---|---|
| Argentina | 25 years | 25 years | Life |
| Austria | Life | 5 years | Life |
| Belgium | 22 years | 5 years | 30 years |
| Brazil | 20 years | 8 years | 30 years |
| Canada | Life | 14 years | Life |
| Chile | Life | 15 years | Life |
| China | Death | 3 years | Death |
| England | Life | Life | Life |
| Finland | 10 years | 10 years | Life |
| France | Life | 15 years | Life |
| Germany | 15 years | 5 years | Life |
| Greece | 20 years | 20 years | Life |
| Italy | 12 years | 5.4 years | Life |
| Cote D'Ivoire | 20 years | Life | Life |
| Mexico | 14 years | 13.5 years | 50 years |
| Poland | 10 years | 10 years | Life |
| Russia | 14 years | 18 years | Death |
| South Africa | Life | Unknown | Life |
| Spain | 19 years | 6 years | 25 years |
| Sweden | 10 years | 10 years | Life |
| Turkey | 18 years | 12 years | Life |
| United States | 9 years | 20 years | Death |

Notes: [a] Sieber (n 40) 109; [b] Ibid 105; [c] Ibid 94.

[62] States would not always charge the same ordinary crimes. Torture, for example, would be charged as 'threat to death' in France, as 'moral mistreatment' in Poland, and as 'abuse of authority with the use of violence' in Russia: Sieber (n 40) 9. The specific crime, however, is less important than the maximum punishment that crime could entail. Indeed, the point of the sentence-based complementarity heuristic is to de-emphasise the nature of the charged crime in favour of an emphasis on sentence.

As the table indicates, national courts are almost always able to punish ordinary equivalents of international crimes just as harshly as international tribunals punish the international crimes themselves. Only five of the 22 maximum sentences for rape equivalents are beneath the ICTR's average sentence range for the crime against humanity of rape: England, Finland, Poland, Sweden and the United States. Only one of the 22 maximum sentences for torture equivalents are beneath the ICTR's average sentence range for the crime against humanity of torture: China. And none of the 22 maximum sentences for murder are beneath the ICTR's average sentence range for the crime against humanity of murder.

To be sure, the table does not indicate what sentence convicted defendants would actually receive in the 22 states. Studies of the ICTY and ICTR indicate, however, that national sentences for ordinary crimes are rarely more lenient than international sentences for international crimes. As of 2007, for example, the sentence breakdown at the ICTR was as follows: 37 per cent life imprisonment; 33 per cent 20 years or more; 19 per cent 10–20 years; 11 per cent less than 10 years.[63] That breakdown is not dramatically different than the breakdown of sentences imposed as of 2006 by Rwanda's genocide courts, which prosecuted ordinary crimes: 15 per cent death; 30 per cent life imprisonment; 55 per cent a term of years, with an average sentence of 15.25 years.[64] A comparison of ICTY sentences to sentences imposed by courts in the former Yugoslavia leads to similar results.[65]

Although these actual-sentence statistics are informative, it is important to note that they are only indirectly relevant to whether the sentence-based heuristic provides a workable alternative to the traditional conduct-and-gravity heuristic. The sentence-based heuristic would be problematic only if states are *unable* to impose adequate sentences for ordinary crimes. As long as their sentencing regimes are adequate, there is no reason why the ICC could not adopt a complementarity heuristic that required them to impose sentences for ordinary crimes no less severe than their (relatively lenient) international counterparts. National prosecutors could easily determine the minimum sentence necessary to avoid an admissibility finding and adjust their charging decisions accordingly.

### ii. Avoiding impunity gaps

The sentence-based heuristic also addresses the problem of 'impunity gaps' much better than the conduct-and-gravity heuristic. Scholars are right to be concerned with situations in which deficiencies in national criminal law – the absence of an ordinary equivalent to an international crime, inadequate modes of participation, or overly broad defences – prevent a state from effectively prosecuting an individual who has committed an international crime.[66] Such gaps are unavoidable, however,

---

[63] Harmon and Gaynor (n 22) 685. Twenty-six per cent of the sentences to date were under appeal at the time of writing.
[64] Drumbl (n 25) 77.
[65] See Meernik and King (n 52) 727.
[66] See notes accompanying above table.

unless the Court *requires* states to fully incorporate the Rome Statute, which it has yet to do. In the absence of such a requirement, it seems prudent for the Court to adopt a complementarity heuristic that at least *minimises* the likelihood that impunity gaps will require it to pre-empt a national prosecution of an ordinary crime. The conduct-and-gravity heuristic is inconsistent with that goal, because it limits the kinds of ordinary crimes that a state can charge in lieu of the international crime and prevents a state from responding to an impunity gap by prosecuting different conduct that might be easier to prove. The sentence-based heuristic, by contrast, permits a state to respond to an impunity gap by charging any crime and prosecuting any conduct that will result in a conviction and adequate sentence.

Consider, for example, a particularly common impunity gap: a situation in which the absence of command responsibility prevents a state from prosecuting a powerful military or civilian superior for failing to prevent his subordinates from committing serious crimes.[67] That gap will always be fatal to a national prosecution under the conduct-and-gravity heuristic, because the state will not have the option of prosecuting the superior for an ordinary crime based on different conduct. Under the sentence-based heuristic, in contrast, the state would not be so limited: it would have the option of compensating for its failure to criminalise command responsibility by relying on a different mode of participation to convict the superior of a different ordinary crime. If such an alternative prosecution was possible and would result in an adequate sentence, the Court would defer to the national prosecution. If not – and it may well be the case that, for certain military and civilian superiors, it will indeed be command responsibility or nothing – the Court would prosecute the superior itself. Either way, the Court would intervene only when it was absolutely necessary, efficiently allocating its scarce resources.

*iii. Avoiding primacy*
The arbitrary limitations imposed on states by the same-conduct requirement indicate another advantage of the sentence-based complementarity heuristic: it is far more consistent with the idea that the ICC should defer to national prosecutions whenever possible.[68] Throughout the drafting of the Rome Statute, states consistently emphasised that – in the words of the Informal Expert Paper – '[t]he standard for assessing "genuineness" should reflect appropriate deference to national systems as well as the fact that the ICC is not an international court of

---

[67] Sudanese criminal law is an example. A number of NGOs have singled out the absence of command responsibility as one of the primary reasons that a Sudanese challenge to the arrest warrants against Haroun, Kushayb, or Bashir would fail. See, e.g., Human Rights Watch (n 32) 16.

[68] See, e.g., Holmes (n 29) 675; cf Kleffner (n 17) 96 (noting that, in developing complementarity, 'States were much more concerned about safeguarding their sovereign prerogative to punish these perpetrators than they were in the context of ad hoc international criminal tribunals').

appeal'.⁶⁹ The sentence-based heuristic reflects the drafters' desire to protect state sovereignty, because it gives national prosecutors complete discretion to select the conduct and ordinary crime they believe will be the easiest to prove, subject only to the requirement that the selected crime carry an appropriate sentence. The same-conduct requirement, by contrast, privileges the ICC instead of states, because it limits national prosecutors to charging ordinary crimes that involve the specific conduct that the ICC is investigating, even if those crimes will be more difficult to prosecute.⁷⁰ Indeed, given that a diligent state will often begin investigating conduct amounting to an international crime *before* the ICC begins its investigation, the same-conduct requirement expects states to be mind-readers: if they do not accurately anticipate the precise conduct that will draw the ICC's attention – no small task, given the 'universe of criminality in atrocity-crime situations'⁷¹ – they will be deemed 'inactive' with regard to the international proceedings and the Court will admit the case.⁷²

*iv. Promoting ratification*

A sentence-based complementarity heuristic would also provide non-member states with a greater incentive to join the ICC than the traditional heuristic. The willingness of a non-member state to ratify the Rome Statute depends, in large part, on its perceived ability to prevent its nationals from being prosecuted by the ICC. The sentence-based heuristic provides states with maximum flexibility to prosecute their nationals for ordinary crimes without being found unwilling to prosecute; it thus maximises the incentive to ratify. The traditional heuristic, by contrast, undermines that incentive by limiting both the conduct a state can investigate and the kinds of crimes a state can charge. Indeed, the same-conduct requirement is particularly problematic from a ratification standpoint: as noted above, the requirement redistributes authority to determine how an international crime will be investigated and prosecuted from states to the ICC, effectively transforming complementarity into primacy.

The sentence-based heuristic would also blunt one of the United States' primary criticisms of the principle of complementarity: that 'the ICC has the final word on what counts as a "genuine" investigation based on its judgment whether the domestic proceedings are "inconsistent with an intent to bring the person concerned to justice"'.⁷³ Focusing complementarity exclusively on sentencing would not

---

⁶⁹ *Informal Expert Paper* (n 10) 16.

⁷⁰ Cf Robinson (n 7) 101 (noting that '[t]he more narrowly "case" is defined, the harder it becomes for a State to show that it is acting in relation to that same "case", and the easier for the ICC to assert admissibility').

⁷¹ Rastan (n 7) 439.

⁷² This is precisely what happened in the *Lubanga* case: see Decision on the Prosecutor's Application for a Warrant of Arrest (n 3) paras 33–38.

⁷³ J Goldsmith, 'The Self-Defeating International Criminal Court' (2003) 70 *University of Chicago L Rev* 89, 95 (quoting ICC Statute, art 17(2)(b)).

reallocate the 'final word' to states, but it would free the Court from making difficult – and inherently subjective – judgments concerning the gravity of crimes, modes of participation and defences. States could thus join the ICC knowing that although the Court itself would ultimately determine whether a national prosecution was admissible, it would do so through a relatively mechanical comparison of national sentences to international norms.

## C. Promoting the Rationales of Punishment

All of these practical benefits would be meaningless, of course, if a sentence-based heuristic was inconsistent with either of the ICC's primary rationales for punishment, retribution and deterrence.[74] In practice, however, such a heuristic would promote both rationales *better* than the traditional conduct-and-gravity heuristic.

*i. Retribution*
As Mark Drumbl has pointed out, because 'sentence constitutes the central— and, basically, only—measurement device that liberal legalist institutions avail themselves of when it comes to operationalising punishment in extant sentencing frameworks', the 'length of a prison term is ... a meter for retributive value'.[75] By definition, therefore, the sentence-based heuristic is no less retributive than the conduct-and-gravity heuristic: the sentence-based heuristic only expands the category of inadmissible national prosecutions to include prosecutions that result in a sentence no less severe than the equivalent ICC sentence – namely, Scenarios 3, 5 and 7.

In fact, because the sentence-based heuristic makes it easier for states to prosecute international crimes as ordinary crimes than the conduct-and-gravity heuristic, its retributive value is likely to be considerably greater. In many cases, national sentences for ordinary crimes are *more* severe than international sentences for international crimes. Consider, for example, murder. The average sentence for murder as a crime against humanity at the ICTR, the most punitive *ad hoc* tribunal, is 12–20 years. By contrast, the ICTY Trial Chamber concluded in *Nikolić* that 'in most countries, a single act of murder attracts life imprisonment or the death penalty, as either an optional or mandatory sanction'.[76] Sieber's study supports that conclusion: of the 22 states in the study, 12 (55 per cent) required a *minimum* 20-year sentence for murder as an ordinary crime, with 10 of those states requiring life.[77] From a retributive standpoint, therefore, a national conviction for murder as

---

[74] See ICC Statute, preambular paras 4 and 5.
[75] Drumbl (n 25) 155.
[76] *Prosecutor v Nikolić* (Sentencing Judgment) IT-94-2-S (18 December 2003) para 172.
[77] Argentina, Canada, England, Finland, Germany, Greece, South Africa, Turkey, the United States, Belgium (20 years) and Italy (21 years) imposed a term of years instead. Sieber (n 40) 94.

an ordinary crime will often be more desirable than an international conviction for murder as an international crime.

*ii. Deterrence*
The deterrent value of a criminal-justice system – international or national – is a function of three factors: the likelihood that a perpetrator will be prosecuted; the likelihood that a prosecuted perpetrator will be convicted; and the severity of the sentence that a convicted perpetrator will receive.[78] All three factors indicate that the deterrent value of a sentence-based heuristic will be greater than the deterrent value of the conduct-and-gravity heuristic. First, the likelihood that a perpetrator will be prosecuted is intimately connected to the number of prosecutions that states are capable of pursuing. Because prosecutions of international crimes are so legally complicated and resource-intensive, prosecutions for ordinary crimes will normally take far less time and cost far less to complete.[79] States that prosecute international crimes as ordinary crimes can thus be expected, *ceteris paribus*, to prosecute more defendants than states that prosecute international crimes as international crimes. Second, national prosecutions are far more likely to result in conviction when prosecutors are not artificially limited in terms of the conduct they can investigate and the ordinary crimes they can charge. Third, national sentences for ordinary crimes are normally longer than international sentences for international crimes.

## V. Implementing the Heuristic

Nothing in the Rome Statute would prevent the Court from applying a sentence-based complementarity heuristic instead of a heuristic based on gravity. Article 17(2)(a) simply prohibits States from conducting prosecutions that are designed to shield perpetrators from criminal responsibility; it does not explain what kinds of prosecutions exhibit that prohibited intent, much less equate willingness with the prosecution of serious ordinary crimes. The Court thus remains free to adopt an understanding of willingness that focuses on sentence instead.

The 'same conduct' requirement, by contrast, poses a more formidable challenge. The Court could simply not ignore the requirement when applying Article 17, because it has a strong foundation in the text and history of Article 20(3)'s upward *ne bis in idem* provision (which Article 17(1)(c) incorporates by reference), and is supported by the two articles in the Rome Statute that concern the obligation of

---

[78] See, e.g., RH Speier and others, *Nonproliferation Sanctions* (RAND, Santa Monica 2001) 55.

[79] Cf NA Combs, *Guilty Pleas in International Criminal Law: Constructing a Restorative Justice Approach* (Stanford University Press, Stanford 2006) 41 (noting that '[d]omestic prosecutions can reduce trial time by charging domestic crimes, such as murder, in lieu of international crimes').

states to surrender suspects to the Court. The first is Article 89(4), which provides that 'if the person sought is being proceeded against or is serving a sentence in the requested State for *a crime different from that for which surrender to the Court is sought*, the requested State, after making its decision to grant the request, shall consult with the Court'.[80] The second is Article 94(1), which provides, in relevant part, that '[i]f the immediate execution of a request would interfere with an ongoing investigation or prosecution of *a case different from that to which the request relates*, the requested State may postpone the execution of the request for a period of time agreed upon with the Court'.[81]

The best way to eliminate the same-conduct requirement, therefore, would be to amend those three Articles to make clear that a sufficiently punitive national prosecution of an ordinary crime is inadmissible even if it involves different conduct than the ICC prosecution.

Needless to say, the ASP is unlikely to make the necessary changes anytime soon. The Rome Statute is very difficult to amend: two-thirds of States Parties must approve an amendment, and an approved amendment does not enter into force until seven-eighths ratify it.[82] The more practical solution, therefore, would be for the Court to rely on the same articles in the Rome Statute that make clear Article 17's presumption of inadmissibility does not apply to prosecutions – for international or for ordinary crimes – that are based on different conduct than the ICC prosecution. Although Articles 89(4) and 94(1) are not the picture of clarity,[83] neither expressly *requires* the Court to pre-empt a national investigation, prosecution or sentence that involves a different crime. Indeed, most scholars believe – to quote Hans-Peter Kaul and Claus Kress – that although 'the requested state may not refuse the execution of the request ... execution may be postponed for a period of time as agreed upon with the Court'.[84] The Court could thus decide, as a matter of policy, to apply the sentence-based heuristic to national prosecutions and sentences falling under Articles 89(4) and 94(1), permitting states whose national prosecutions and sentences satisfy the heuristic to 'delay' surrendering the perpetrator until *after* he served the duration of his national sentence.

Applying the sentence-based heuristic, in short, would require the Court to proceed along two parallel tracks. If a national prosecution involved the same

---

[80] ICC Statute, art 89(4) (emphasis added).
[81] Ibid art 94(1) (emphasis added).
[82] Ibid arts 121(3) and 121(4).
[83] See, e.g., *Report of the Commonwealth Expert Group on Implementing Legislation for the Rome Statute of the International Criminal Court* (London 7–9 July 2004) <http://www.thecommonwealth.org/shared_asp_files/uploadedfiles/%7BF3BC7D68-4922-4B35-A14E-ED26AECA86F5%7D_FINAL%20REPORT-%20london%20ICC.pdf> last accessed 12 December 2011, para 93 ('The Rome Statute does not resolve what happens if a person sought by the Court is serving a sentence domestically or being prosecuted'); H-P Kaul and C Kress, 'Jurisdiction and Cooperation in the Statute of the International Criminal Court: Principles and Compromises' (1999) 2 *Ybk Int'l Humanitarian L* 143, 166 (noting the 'constructive ambiguity' in the two articles).
[84] Kaul and Kress (n 83) 166.

conduct as the ICC prosecution, thus triggering Article 17's complementarity provisions, the Court would apply the heuristic as the best method for determining whether a state is genuinely willing to prosecute. If the national prosecution involved different conduct, thus falling within the ambit of Articles 89(4) and 94(1), the Court would apply the heuristic as a matter of surrender policy. Such a bifurcated approach to complementarity would be less than ideal, but it would be better than continuing to apply a gravity-and-conduct heuristic that undermines instead of promotes the fight against impunity.

## Conclusion

This chapter has defended a complementarity heuristic that determines whether a state is genuinely willing to prosecute solely by reference to sentence, an approach that is not based on the Appeals Chamber's arbitrary 'same conduct' requirement and that does not require the ICC to make difficult and contestable judgments concerning the relative gravity of ordinary crimes. There is no question that the need for such a heuristic reflects contingent material limitations on the Court and on national criminal-justice systems. The day may yet come when the ICC is so well staffed and amply funded that nothing will be lost by encouraging – or even requiring – states to prosecute international crimes as international crimes. Until then, however, the traditional conduct-and-gravity heuristic will remain a luxury that the neither the Court nor states can afford.

# 'Sentencing Horror' or 'Sentencing Heuristic'? A Reply to Heller's 'Sentence-Based' Theory of Complementarity

Carsten Stahn[1]

Kevin Heller's chapter on a 'sentenced-based theory of complementarity' marks a significant contribution to the growing scholarship on the International Criminal Court (ICC) and complementarity. His proposed re-thinking of the complementarity regime is original and helpful in highlighting existing policy dilemmas of ICC practice. A '"sentence-based" heuristic' is appealing in its clarity and its objective to facilitate effective repression. Nevertheless, I share some hesitation regarding the central claim of this theory. In my view, the argument that the ICC should focus 'exclusively on sentencing' when determining whether an 'ordinary' crime prosecution is admissible before the ICC is neither desirable nor manageable in all cases. I will focus on three aspects: the assumptions underlying the central claim, the desirability of a new methodology, and its manageability.

---

[1] This comment is part of a *Harvard International Law Journal/Opinio Juris* symposium on Kevin Heller's 'A Sentence-Based Theory of Complementarity'. A previous version was published in *Harvard International Law Journal*, Print Responses. It forms part of research on complementarity, carried out under the umbrella of the 'Post-Conflict Justice and Local Ownership' project, funded by the Netherlands Organization of Scientific Research (NWO). I wish to thank Dov Jacobs and Jennifer Easterday for their helpful input on this comment.

## I. Underlying Assumptions

Heller's case for a deviation from existing approaches relies on four basic premises: (i) the claim that the ICC admissibility test[2] creates undue pressure to charge international crimes under an international label; (ii) the alleged disadvantages of domestic prosecution of international crimes; (iii) the advantages of a 'sentencing' heuristic over threat-based compliance; and (iv) the assumption that 'higher' sentences might create 'better' justice. All four key assumptions merit further critical reflection.

### A. What the ICC 'Imposes', What International Law Says and What National Law Suggests

Heller challenges existing theories (i.e. the '"hard" and the "soft" mirror' thesis), based on the premise that the complementarity regime 'pressures states to prosecute international crimes under an international label'. This starting point is partly misleading and might overstretch the role of the ICC. Complementarity provides primarily a tool for the ICC to determine its competence. It is largely based on incentives rather than a desire to 'restructure national criminal justice systems in the ICC's image'. It organises 'shared obligations' based on a scheme that has typically been agreed by choice, i.e. by ratification. Under Article 17(3) of the Rome Statute (the 'Statute'), a state might be found to be partially unavailable if its domestic legal system does not contain a legal basis for prosecution of crimes within the jurisdiction of the ICC.[3] But the Statute does not *per se* oblige states to investigate and prosecute under an 'international crimes' label. Nor is it directly meant to serve as a standard-setting instrument. If an obligation to use an international crime label might exist, it might flow from pre-existing treaty obligations or customary law. Yet, even international law appears to leave states flexibility to comply with their duty to punish international crimes (e.g. war crimes, crimes against humanity) as 'ordinary' crimes, or sometimes even as a different 'international crime'.[4] The general duty to penalise under treaty law or customary law does not necessarily coincide with a duty to prosecute a specific

---

[2] For a survey, see C Stahn and M El Zeidy (eds), *The International Criminal Court and Complementarity: From Theory to Practice* (CUP, Cambridge 2011). For an in-depth study, see also D Robinson, 'The Mysterious Mysteriousness of Complementarity' (2010) 21 *CLF* 67.

[3] See Rome Statute of the International Criminal Court, 2187 UNTS 90, 17 July 1998, entered into force 1 July 2002 ('ICC Statute'), art 17(3) ('the Court shall consider whether, due to ... *unavailability of its national judicial system,* the State is unable to obtain the accused or the necessary evidence and testimony *or otherwise unable to carry out its proceedings'*). Emphasis added.

[4] For a study, see W Ferdinandusse, *Direct Application of International Criminal Law in Domestic Courts* (TMC Asser Press, The Hague 2006), 18–21, 205; W Ferdinandusse, 'The Prosecution of Grave Breaches in National Courts' (2009) 7 *JICJ* 723–741.

crime under the respective label.⁵ An 'ordinary' crime label might not be ideal since domestic law might not reflect all specific aspects of international crimes, capture their specific 'gravity' or provide 'effective penalties' that take into account their contextual elements. But the obligation to use a specific 'international crime' label results mostly from domestic provisions, such as prosecutorial duties to pursue the most 'serious' charges or charges that reflect the context and characteristics of the crime most suitably. This principle is largely independent of Western or non-Western cultures. It is thus somewhat artificial to 'blame' the ICC admissibility system for introducing a pull towards an 'equivalence' rule that is hard to comply with, or to associate this trend with a 'Western' bias. This prerogative is often of domestic origin, and might be subject to less international proscription than Heller assumes.

## B. Cost–Benefit Analysis of 'Ordinary' Crime Prosecution

Heller supports his criticism of the 'equivalence' principle by a generalised preference for ordinary crime prosecution. He seeks to encourage states to prosecute international crimes as 'ordinary' crimes and argues that 'national prosecutions of ordinary crimes are far more likely to succeed than national prosecutions of international crimes'. This claim is based on a slippery dichotomy. To present these two options as two diametrically opposed schemes is artificial. While 'international crimes' may be more difficult to investigate or prosecute, they also offer certain advantages which must be brought into the equation. An 'international crime' label might offer a broader basis for jurisdiction (i.e. prosecution of extraterritorial acts), curtail the applicability of statutes of limitation or extend the prospects for cooperation and judicial assistance. Some studies indicate that implementation of the ICC Statute has led to an increase of national prosecutions for international

---

⁵ See *Prosecutor v Hadzihasanovic* (Trial Judgment) IT-01-47-T (15 March 2006) para 260 ('there is no rule, either in customary or in positive law, which obliges States to prosecute acts which can be characterized as war crimes solely in the basis of international humanitarian law, completely setting aside any characterizations of their national criminal law'). Note that the ICC Pre-Trial Chamber set a high threshold in the context of the Libyan admissibility challenge under Article 19. It 'directed' Libya to clarify 'whether and how Libyan laws capture' the crime of persecution 'which is defined, under article 7(2) (g) of the Statute, as "the intentional and severe deprivation of fundamental rights contrary to international law by reason of the identity of the group or collectivity'. See ICC, Pre-Trial Chamber I, Decision requesting further submissions on issues related to the admissibility of the case against Saif Al-Islam Gaddafi, 7 December 2012, ICC-01/11-01/11, para, 37. The Chamber also inquired 'whether Mr Gaddafi would qualify as a public officer within the Libyan legal system, given that a number of crimes referred to by Libya seem to apply only to acts committed by public officers, such as torture of prisoners, abuse of power against individuals, arrest of people without cause and restraint of personal liberty without justification.'

crimes.[6] Surveys on the exercise universal jurisdiction suggest that it remains an 'important tool that should be considered and used alongside other local, regional, and international remedies' – despite its obvious difficulties.[7] Supporters point, in particular, to the fact that an 'international crime' label might draw greater attention to atrocity crimes among governments, the press and the general public.[8] Moreover, in practice, domestic and international crime labels are *de facto* often interrelated in a domestic setting. Many jurisdictions rely on a mix of 'international' and 'ordinary crime' definitions in order to try offences, or adjust modes of liability to capture the conduct in question.[9] These factors are not taken into account in Heller's 'cost–benefit' analysis. Paradoxically, in existing practice, 'ordinary crime' prosecutions (e.g. war crimes) are often criticised since they result in lower sentences. To reduce incentives for international crimes prosecution is thus partially counter-productive and disregards the existing inter-connections. The proposed generic preference for 'ordinary crime' prosecution might in fact reduce the options for prosecution overall which runs to Heller's overall objective of increasing effectiveness.

## C. Checks and Balances v. 'Sentencing' Heuristic

Heller's justification for the turn to a 'sentencing heuristic' is that a sentence-based assessment of admissibility is better suited to address accountability gaps than a 'conduct' and 'gravity'-based logic. This argument is founded on the overall assumption that even greater flexibility for states to investigate and prosecute might create better compliance rates. This logic is open to challenge. It is questionable whether greater freedom to use an 'ordinary' crime label might encourage more investigation and prosecution. This argument seems to overstretch the reach of the law. More often than not, other factors than the choice of the 'crime label' may be more determinate causes of action or inaction. This choice is heavily influenced by contextual factors, such as the nature of the conflict, internal political factors (i.e. regime change) or general attention to atrocities.

According to the drafters, complementarity was designed as an incentive-based system of checks and balances, with multiple layers of scrutiny, partly in order to promote greater transparency and monitoring. Heller's attempt to reduce the

---

[6] See J Rikhof, 'Fewer Places to Hide? The Impact of Domestic War Crimes Prosecutions on International Impunity' (2009) 20 *CLF* 1.

[7] See W Kaleck, 'From Pinochet to Rumsfeld: Universal Jurisdiction in Europe' (2009) 30 *Michigan J Int'l L* 928, 980; C Ryngaert, 'Applying the Rome Statute's Complementarity Principle: Drawing Lessons from the Prosecution of Core Crimes by States Acting under the Universality Principle' (2008) 19 *CLF* 153.

[8] See CK Hall, 'The Role of Universal Jurisdiction in the International Criminal Court Complementarity System' in M Bergsmo (ed) *Complementarity and the Exercise of Universal Jurisdiction for Core International Crimes* (Torkel Opsahl Academic, Oslo 2010) 201, 231.

[9] See, e.g., Dutch District Court, The Hague, *Judgment against Frans Van Anraat*, Public Prosecutor's Office number 09/751003-04 (23 December 2005) <http://www.haguejusticeportal.net/eCache/DEF/4/497.html> last accessed 31 January 2012.

interpretative space offered to the ICC (e.g. through a more flexible 'conduct' test and greater deference to 'ordinary crime prosecution') may effectively limit the scope of accountability. The existing architecture of the complementarity regime foresees a nuanced system of checks and balances: compliance by threat (including the ICC's power as ultimate arbiter over disputes) and consensual burden-sharing.[10] In practice, Heller's test leads to a more determinate 'all-or-nothing' choice. According to the application of the 'sentencing' logic, either the ICC or a domestic jurisdiction assumes 'ownership' over the case. This leaves little space for burden-sharing or parallel action which might sometimes be an asset from a compliance point of view. Given the limited number of atrocity trials overall, it might be premature to abandon this structure at this moment in time.

### D. 'Higher Sentence' Equals 'Better Justice'

Heller's theory operates on the assumption that a justice system based on 'higher sentences' provides better and more efficient justice than a system with potentially lower sentences. This vision reduces the rationales of the admissibility assessment to considerations of retribution and alleged effectiveness. This approach privileges 'outcome' over 'process'. It might sideline other systematic factors that are inherent in the system of forum allocation under the Statute, such as judicial independence, fairness or sustainability.[11] Most fundamentally, Heller's claim implies that a 'higher sentence' provides 'better' justice. This argument appears to go against the very rationales of sentencing which typically preserves a great degree of flexibility in order to pay adequate tribute to individual interests. It is ill-suited to provide an appropriate logic for forum choices in situations in which sentence and penalties may be of lesser importance in achieving justice, such as transitional justice scenarios. Heller's test curtails flexibility in such contexts.

## II. Is a Change of Methodology Desirable?

Legally, the 'soft mirror' approach is not expressly required by the core provisions on 'unwillingness' and 'inability' under Article 17. *A priori*, the ICC's admissibility system might offer greater flexibility than the Rule 11*bis* deferral mechanism of the *ad hoc* tribunals and the strict scrutiny exercised by the International Criminal

---

[10] See R Rastan, 'Complementarity: Contest or Collaboration' in M Bergsmo (ed) *Complementarity and the Exercise of Universal Jurisdiction for Core International Crimes* (Torkel Opsahl Academic, Oslo 2010) 83.

[11] For a study of (meta-)principles underlying complementarity, see C Stahn, 'Taking Complementarity Seriously' in C Stahn and M El Zeidy (eds) *The International Criminal Court and Complementarity: From Theory to Practice* (CUP, Cambridge 2011) 233, 244–248; 274–281.

Tribunal for Rwanda (ICTR) in *Bagaragaza*[12] since the ICC does not enjoy primacy of jurisdiction. In the ICC context, the symmetry argument is mostly a consequence of the interpretation of the notion of the 'case'[13] for jurisdictional purposes under the Statute, and an assurance to domestic authorities that the ICC might not conduct proceedings under the *ne bis in idem* clause under Article 20(3) (which does not contain a strict symmetry requirement itself).[14]

## A. Merits of the 'Same Conduct' Test

It is questionable whether this framework requires adjustment. The existing methodology has some merit. The 'same conduct' test is based on a consistent application of the notion of the 'case' under the admissibility regime (namely Article 17(1)(a) and (b), and Article 17(1)(c) in conjunction with Article 20(3)),[15] and the distinction between 'same conduct' and 'other conduct' in the cooperation regime (in particular Article 90).[16] It determines admissibility considerations primarily on the basis of a factual qualification (i.e. domestic investigation or prosecution of 'conduct'). It leaves states flexibility since it does not *per se* require identity in the legal qualification of the criminal conduct.[17] Its application has further largely

---

[12] See *Prosecutor v Bagaragaza* (Decision on Rule 11*bis* Appeal) ICTR-05-86-Ar11*bis* (30 August 2006) paras 16 and 17. The Chamber held that art 8 of the ICTR Statute 'delimits the Tribunal's authority, allowing it only to refer cases where the state will charge and convict for those international crimes listed in its Statute'. It further noted that according to art 9, 'the Tribunal may still try a person who has been tried before a national court for "acts constituting serious violations of international humanitarian law" if the acts for which he or she was tried were "categorized as an ordinary crime"'.

[13] In *Lubanga*, the Pre-Trial Chamber held that: '[I]t is a *condition sine qua non* for a case arising from the investigation of a situation to be inadmissible that national proceedings encompass both the person and the conduct which is the subject of the case before the Court.' See *Situation in the DRC: Prosecutor v Lubanga* (Decision on the Prosecutor's Application for a Warrant of Arrest) ICC-01/04-01/06-8-Corr (24 February 2006) paras 39–30. See also *Situation in the Republic of Kenya: Prosecutor v Ruto et al* (Decision on the Application of the Government of Kenya challenging the Admissibility of the Case Pursuant to Article 19(2)(b) of the Statute) ICC-01/09-01/11-101 (30 May 2011) para 55 ('So far, the Court's jurisprudence has been consistent on this issue').

[14] See article 20(3), which refers to 'conduct *also* proscribed under articles 6, 7 or 8'. Emphasis added. For a discussion, see M El Zeidy, *The Principle of Complementarity in International Criminal Law* (Martinus Nijhoff, Leiden 2008) 287–293.

[15] Art 19(5) contains a value judgment that conflicts be sorted as early as possible. In this light, it would be strange if a more 'lenient' test was allowed prior under art 17, and a more strict test (strict scrutiny) under the *ne bis in idem* clause.

[16] See R Rastan, 'Situation and Case: Defining the Parameters' in C Stahn and M El Zeidy (eds) *The International Criminal Court and Complementarity: From Theory to Practice* (CUP, Cambridge 2011) 419, 444–445.

[17] For a detailed inquiry into domestic laws and procedures under the 'same conduct' test, see Pre-Trial Chamber, (n 5) paras. 13-40.

detached the method of forum allocation under the Statute from the stigma of 'failure' associated with the applicability of the 'unwillingness' and 'inability' criteria.

## B. Relevance of the 'Sentencing Heuristic'

Given the existing *status quo*, it might not be necessary to introduce a new 'heuristic'. Due to the large number of perpetrators and crimes committed under ICC jurisdiction, conflicts over the prioritisation of 'ordinary' v. 'international crime' prosecution are a relatively rare exception. In many existing ICC situations (Democratic Republic of Congo, Uganda, Central African Republic), states have entrusted the ICC with the mandate to investigate and prosecute. In these circumstances, it would be largely unfeasible to force the ICC to encourage the exercise of domestic jurisdiction, based on the consideration that the domestic system might potentially impose a higher sentence. The Court cannot compel states to exercise jurisdiction, nor should it required to suspend its own proceedings, based on the speculation that domestic authorities might act – be it under an 'ordinary' or an 'international' crime label.[18]

Potential conflicts might arise in cases of competing proceedings involving the 'same conduct', and specifically in cases where domestic investigations or prosecutions cover the same 'incident'. Such conflicts can be avoided though prosecutorial selection practice and appropriate charging strategy. A 'sentencing' heuristic is not strictly necessary to save ICC resources. In many instances, the same result may be achieved through other constraints (e.g. budgetary (self-)restriction) and the proper exercise of prosecutorial discretion. In circumstances, where there is overlap, there is a range of different options. The Prosecutor might on his/her own motion decide not to proceed further, e.g. based on 'new facts or information' under Article 53(4). The respective state might seek to convince the Prosecutor to 'withdraw the charges'.[19] Moreover, ICC may defer to domestic jurisdictions if investigations or prosecutions are genuine. In the first two cases, the application of the 'sentencing' logic is not required. In the last case, it is doubtful whether the estimated gravity of the 'sentence' should be the 'exclusive criterion' to make this admissibility judgment.

## C. 'Hard' Cases

Heller mentions two examples where the existing regime might produce unsatisfactory results because it might complicate 'ordinary crime' prosecution.

---

[18] See in this sense *Situation in the DRC: Prosecutor v Katanga and Chui* (Judgment on the Appeal of Mr Germain Katanga against the Oral Decision of Trial Chamber II of 12 June 2009 on the Admissibility of the Case) ICC-01/04-01/07-1497 (25 September 2009) paras 79 and 86.

[19] See art 61(9).

The first is the charging of an 'inadequate mode of participation', and the second is an 'overprotective' use of domestic defences. Both examples are less clear-cut than suggested, and might not necessarily require exclusive application of the 'sentencing heuristic'. Even Rule 11*bis* jurisprudence before the *ad hoc* tribunals has left domestic authorities some flexibility in relation to the adjudication of modes of liability.[20] Curiously, in some cases, domestic authorities (rather than international courts) have pushed to 'give preference to the bounds of international liability instead of national liability'.[21] The second scenario might often be resolved through application of the traditional admissibility criteria under Article 17(2) (i.e. 'purpose of shielding', 'intent to bring the person to justice'), or 17(3), which already allow the Court to take sentencing consideration into account.[22]

The most difficult scenarios are 'borderline' cases that relate to context. The resolution of such cases might deserve a more nuanced consideration than 'sentencing'. For instance, there might be a legitimate interest for the ICC to consider the broader context of charges if a perpetrator is charged as an isolated actor, i.e. irrespective of a link to a state or organisational policy, to an armed conflict or the widespread or systematic commission of crimes. As noted by Rod Rastan, this finding might arguably provide a reason not to defer, if such a strategy ultimately limits responsibility to low-level perpetrators and prevents proceedings at a higher echelon.[23]

## D. Alternative 'Conduct' Definition?

A more radical alternative to achieve greater leeway for the exercise of domestic jurisdiction in the context of competing proceedings would be the adoption of a broader notion of 'conduct'. Such a proposal has been made in *Katanga* where the Defence proposed the application of a 'comprehensive conduct test' based on a comparison of the intended gravity or factual scope of the case at the ICC and the national level.[24] This approach might indeed provide greater possibility to challenge

---

[20] See with respect to command responsibility, *Prosecutor v Ademi and Norac* (Decision for Referral to the Authorities of the Republic of Croatia pursuant to Rule 11*bis*) IT-04-78-PT (14 September 2005) para 46 ('On the basis of these considerations, the Referral Bench is not persuaded that it should exclude referral for the reason only that there may well be found to be a limited difference between the law applied by the Tribunal and the Croatian Court. Should this case be referred, it will be for the incumbent County Court in Croatia to determine the law applicable to each of the alleged criminal acts of the Accused').

[21] See with respect to *mens rea*, *Van Anraat* (n 9) para 6.3. For a discussion, see H van der Wilt, 'Genocide, Complicity in Genocide and International v. Domestic Jurisdiction' (2006) 4 *JICJ* 239; H van der Wilt, 'Genocide v. War Crimes in the *Van Anraat* Appeal' (2008) 9 *JICJ* 557.

[22] For a study, see H Olasolo, 'Complementarity Analysis of National Sentencing' in H Olasolo, *Essays on International Criminal Justice* (Hart, Oxford 2012) 74.

[23] See Rastan (n 16) 452, footnote 88.

[24] See *Situation in the DRC: Prosecutor v Katanga and Chui* (Motion Challenging the Admissibility of the Case by the Defence of Germain Katanga, pursuant to Article 19(2)(a) of

admissibility. But it also causes new problems, both legally and conceptually. To incorporate 'gravity' considerations into the 'conduct' requirement shifts interpretational dilemmas from Article 17(1)(d) into the definition of the 'case'. It introduces 'normative' concepts (i.e. a 'gravity'-based comparator) into a primarily 'factual' notion. Moreover, it makes the distinction between the 'international' and the 'domestic' case' difficult to operate. This might increase disputes over the scope of exercise of jurisdiction, rather than facilitate effective investigation and prosecution.

### E. Other Side-Effects of the 'Sentencing' Heuristic

The 'sentencing heuristic' might be a lesser evil. But even in its 'moderate' form, it produces some side-effects that are not necessarily desirable. It pays little attention to the interests of defendants. It might require the Prosecutor or Judges to make a 'sentencing' hypothesis even prior to the 'confirmation of charges', or the closure of the investigation.

Moreover, it would implicitly encourage a 'race to top' in terms of penalties, both at the ICC and the domestic level. Such a prioritisation of 'higher' penalties through ICC procedure is not necessarily in the spirit of the Statute. The Statute is neutral in this respect as confirmed by the wording of Article 80.[25]

The debate on admissibility in relation to Libya[26] illustrates some of the difficulties of Heller's position. Taken to the extreme, Heller's argument might be understood as an incentive for states to extend the death penalty for conduct underlying 'core crimes'. This poses problems on several levels. The ICC is not a forum or appellate body mandated to remedy general human rights violations to the disadvantage of the person occurring in domestic criminal proceedings (i.e. akin to a human rights Court).[27] But in some cases, considerations related to the 'proportionality' of the domestic penalty might have to be assessed. Moreover, Heller's logic would ultimately force the Prosecutor or Judges to justify a forum choice and deferral to

---

the Statute) ICC-01/04-01/07-949 (11 March 2009) paras 39–52.

[25] It states: 'Nothing in this Part affects the application by States of penalties prescribed by their national law, nor the law of States which do not provide for penalties in this Part.'

[26] For a discussion, see e.g., JD Ohlin, 'Libya & The Death Penalty: Can the ICC Complain About Too Much Punishment?' Lieber Code Blog (28 November 2011) <http://www.liebercode.org/2011/11/libya-death-penalty-can-icc-complain.html> last accessed 1 February 2012; C Stahn,. Libya, the ICC and Complementarity: A Test for 'shared responsibility', (2012) 10 *JICJ* 325-351.

[27] Violation of fair trial principles is not *per se* a principle of case selection. Admissibility is rather tied to circumstances in which these violations reflect an intent not to bring a person to justice. See E Carnero Rojo, 'The Role of Fair Trial Considerations in the Complementarity Regime of the International Criminal Court: From "No Peace without Justice" to "No Peace without Victor's Justice"?' (2005) 18 *LJIL* 829, 840–856. For a different view, see F Gioia, 'Comments on Chapter 3 of Jann Kleffner' in J Kleffner and G Kor (eds) *Complementary views on Complementarity* (CUP, Cambridge 2006) 112.

domestic jurisdiction because that domestic system recognises capital punishment as the main sentence. This positive endorsement of the potential application of the death penalty might be difficult to reconcile with the Statute and Rule 11*bis* practice.[28] Ultimately, the ICC might not be prohibited from deferring a case to a state applying capital punishment, if one takes the view that admissibility assessment should not involve consideration of potential violations to the detriment of the defendant. But even if one adopts that view, Heller's proposal is not appealing from a 'policy' perspective. The problem with Heller's 'sentencing heuristic' is that it places the ICC in the uncomfortable position of making that choice in the first place. By natural instinct, Court officials will be inclined to avoid entering into such determinations. This makes this test very hard to apply in practice.

Finally, Heller's theory would ultimately treat states that reject the death penalty less 'favourably' in terms of deference than states who apply it. This inequality will be hard to defend.

## III. Is a Change of Methodology Manageable?

This leads to the last question treated by Heller, namely the issue as to whether this new approach would be manageable. Heller gives in-depth consideration to the question whether the 'sentencing heuristic' would be manageable in light of the absence of internationally agreed sentencing standards. The problem may not only lie in the determination of an anticipated international penalty, but in the prediction of a domestic sentence by the ICC. This determination exercise involves a great degree of uncertainty, and certain risks.

### A. 'Domestic' Sentence Assessment

Heller's proposal might require not only Judges, but also the Prosecutor to determine an estimated 'average' sentence for respective crimes. Such a determination may be difficult at the early stages of the proceedings (i.e. at pre-trial), where investigations continue and the scope of the 'case' and charges are still undefined.

Heller's test would further require the ICC to carry out in-depth analysis of domestic law in order to determine an estimated 'average' sentence. This would pose significant problems. Sentencing criteria typically contain a large number of

---

[28] The ICC Statute does not include the death penalty in its sentencing regime. Art 21(3) provides the applicable law of the ICC must be interpreted and applied consistently 'with internationally recognized human rights'. Rule 11*bis* of the Rules of Procedure and Evidence, UN Doc ITR/3/Rev.20, International Criminal Tribunal for Rwanda, 1 October 2009 and Evidence specified specifically that a case shall only be referred back by a Trial Chamber if the accused will receive a fair trial and if 'the death penalty will not be imposed or carried out'.

individualised discretionary elements, i.e. due to the discrepancy between minimum and maximum penalty. To properly understand the specificities of the domestic system, ICC Judges or the Prosecutor might have engaged deeply with applicable domestic law and jurisprudence. It is questionable whether the ICC would be properly equipped to carry out such an assessment. Any calculation might entail a great degree of uncertainty and risk of misinterpretation. Further complications might arise if the ICC might have to address factors such as cumulative charging, plea bargaining or applicable mitigating circumstances under domestic law. If a party (e.g. the defendant) would appeal the initial admissibility decision under Article 82(1)(a),[29] the ICC might be involved more with the correct interpretation of national law, rather than its core business: to investigate and prosecute cases.

## B. The 'Lower' Sentence Dilemma

Finally, there is an inherent flaw in the design of the model. In some cases, the ICC might wish to give preference to proceedings at the domestic level, although such proceedings might actually lead to the imposition of a lower sentence. Such cases might in particular arise in contexts where mitigated or alternative sentences are part of a 'transitional justice' strategy (e.g. Colombia).[30] Heller's model might have to be adjusted in order to take into account such specificities.

# Conclusion

As it stands, Heller's approach is thus still more a creative thought experiment than a fully manageable model. Heller argues that 'the sentence-based heuristic is the worst complementarity heuristic – except for all the others'.[31] I would argue that a case-by-case assessment, which makes best use of the existing flexibility under the Statute and takes into account 'sentencing' criteria as part of the admissibility criteria under Article 17, might in the end present a more nuanced and suitable approach.

---

[29] This appeal would not require 'leave to appeal' by the Pre-Trial Chamber.

[30] For a discussion of the Colombian example, see K Ambos, 'The Colombian Peace Process (Law 975 of 2005) and the ICC's Principle of Complementarity' in C Stahn and M El Zeidy (eds) *The International Criminal Court and Complementarity: From Theory to Practice* (CUP, Cambridge 2011) 1071; J Easterday, 'Deciding the Fate of Complementarity: A Colombian Case Study' (2009) 26 *Arizona J Int'l and Comparative L* 49.

[31] See KJ Heller's reply on the *Opinio Juris* Symposium <http://opiniojuris.org/2012/01/24/hilj_heller-response-to-robinson-and-stahn/> last accessed 31 January 2012.

# Three Theories of Complementarity: Charge, Sentence or Process? A Comment on Kevin Heller's Sentence-Based Theory of Complementarity

Darryl Robinson[1]

The principle of complementarity, which governs the International Criminal Court (ICC), will inevitably require some difficult determinations about whether a national proceeding warrants deference. One may discern in the literature three major theories about what the ICC should scrutinise when it assesses a national proceeding: the nature of the *charges* laid, the severity of the *sentence* imposed, or the quality of the *process* adopted. These three approaches are not necessarily mutually exclusive; they can be combined in different ways and with different emphases into plausible schemas.

Kevin Jon Heller's chapter in this edited volume, 'A Sentence-Based Theory of Complementarity', makes some valuable contributions to the discussion on complementarity.[2] He advances an important and convincing critique of *charge-based* approaches, i.e. approaches that would focus on the domestic or international nature of the charges, or on the serious or minor gravity of the charges. He proposes to replace such approaches with one focused on the sentence. While Professor Heller may be successful in showing that a *sentence-based* approach is superior to a charge-based approach, I will argue that a sentence-based approach also raises some quite serious difficulties that have not been addressed. The clarity with which

---

[1] This contribution was part of a *Harvard International Law Journal/Opinio Juris* symposium on Kevin Heller's 'A Sentence-Based Theory of Complementarity'. A previous version of this work was published in *Harvard International Law Journal*, Print Responses. This research was supported by the Social Sciences and Humanities Research Council of Canada.
[2] KJ Heller, 'A Sentence-Based Theory of Complementarity' (2012) 53 *Harvard Int'l L J* 201.

Heller has laid out the charge-based and sentence-based approaches leads me to suggest a third option, a *process-based* approach. I believe that a process-based approach is not only the best fit with the Statute (the positive law); it is also the most elegant theory. A process-based approach can refer to charges and sentences as *indicia*, insofar as they shed light on the genuineness of the process.

While I have reservations about the more radical proposal to adopt a new approach to complementarity that focuses exclusively or even primarily on sentence severity, 'A Sentence-Based Theory of Complementarity' (Chapter 14, this volume) offers two important insights. The first demonstrates the very limited role that should be accorded to 'charges'. The second demonstrates the potentially important role that can, in some circumstances, be accorded to 'sentences'. I would absorb these insights into a process-based theory.

Heller also raises concerns about the 'same conduct' test adopted by the ICC. Similar concerns have been raised in other recent thoughtful scholarship, so it is valuable to inspect the concerns here. While I agree that some flexibility is needed, I hope to show that the problem is actually much narrower than it is often perceived in the literature. The Statute already provides solutions to the scenario where a state wishes to prosecute a person for a *different crime*. In my view, stretching the admissibility regime to cover such scenarios is not only unnecessary but would generate incoherencies. Thus, while I partly agree with the concerns raised by Heller and others, I will argue for a much narrower solution.

All references to 'admissibility' in this comment concern the complementarity aspects (Article 17(1)(a)–(c)) and not the distinct issue of 'gravity' (Article 17(1)(d)).

# I. Charge-Based Approaches: The Hard Mirror and the Soft Mirror

The first two sections of Heller's chapter advance an informative critique of two approaches that would focus on the charges laid at the national level. One approach is the '"hard" mirror thesis',[3] which is the view that prosecuting an international crime by using 'ordinary' criminal offences (e.g. murder, assault) will not satisfy the principle of complementarity.[4] Heller convincingly demonstrates that the 'hard

---

[3] The term 'mirror thesis' is adapted from Frédéric Mégret, who used the term in the context of legislative implementation of ICC obligations, to describe the view that a state should or must establish offences matching those of the ICC Statute. Heller helpfully divides this into two variations. F Mégret, 'Too Much of a Good Thing? ICC Implementation and the Uses of Complementarity' in C Stahn and M El Zeidy (eds) *The International Criminal Court and Complementarity: From Theory to Practice* (CUP, Cambridge 2011) 363, 372.

[4] Heller (n 2) 204.

mirror thesis' is not supported by the Statute,[5] and that it would have negative effects such as creating a disincentive and formidable barrier to implementing and ratifying the ICC Statute as well as to prosecution.[6]

The other approach is the '"soft" mirror thesis', which acknowledges that states are not *obliged* to use ICC definitions, but argues more modestly that it is *preferable* for states to do so.[7] Because the soft mirror thesis is more plausible and attractive, Heller's critique is all the more eye-opening and thought-provoking. He shows that a position favouring the use of international definitions may have the undesirable effect of promoting impunity. Prosecution of international crimes requires experience with international legal jurisprudence as well as the investigative burden of collecting contextual evidence.[8] Using international definitions will render proceedings much more difficult and perilous and may lead to failures of investigations or prosecutions.[9] This is particularly a concern and a disproportionate burden for developing countries. Heller convincingly shows that the expressive value of using international definitions is outweighed by the costs and consequences of such an approach.[10]

The critique is valuable because some well-meaning scholars and advocates have advanced hard and soft versions of the mirror thesis in order to encourage wide-reaching reforms and use of international definitions, and the implications of such claims must be inspected.[11] However, charge-based approaches may not be quite as ubiquitous as Heller indicates, and thus his position is not as lonely and contrarian as it may seem. Whereas Heller refers to a 'nearly uniform insistence among scholars' that international definitions be used,[12] I think the literature is more nuanced. From the initial commentary by John Holmes onwards, it seems a clear theme in much of the commentary that the admissibility regime does not require international

---

[5] Indeed, whereas the ICTY and ICTR Statutes allow international prosecutions of a person who has been tried for an 'ordinary' rather than 'international crime', the ICC drafters specifically considered and rejected that language and instead refer to prosecutions for 'conduct also proscribed under article 6, 7 or 8': Rome Statute of the International Criminal Court, 2187 UNTS 90, 17 July 1998, entered into force 1 July 2002 ('ICC Statute'), art 20(3). See also JT Holmes, 'The Principle of Complementarity' in RS Lee, *The International Criminal Court: The Making of the Rome Statute* (Transnational Publishers, New York 1999) 41, 57–58.

[6] Heller (n 2) 212–213.

[7] Ibid 213.

[8] International crimes require proof of the actus reus as well as 'contextual elements', i.e. the surrounding context that justifies international jurisdiction. For example, in crimes against humanity, the crimes must be part of a widespread or systematic attack directed against a civilian population: ICC Statute, art 7.

[9] Heller (n 2) 216–223.

[10] Ibid 246–247.

[11] See also the discussion in Mégret (n 3).

[12] See Kevin Heller's reply on the *Opinio Juris* Symposium <http://opiniojuris.org/2012/01/24/hilj_heller-response-to-robinson-and-stahn/>. See also Heller (n 2) 203 ('traditional'), 212 (view that international charges are better is held 'almost without exception'), 248 ('orthodoxy' ... 'almost never questioned').

charges.¹³ For example, Heller cites the experts group on complementarity as an example of the soft mirror approach, but the cited passage merely says that effective implementing legislation should be encouraged, which is quite unobjectionable and says nothing at all about preferring or requiring international definitions.¹⁴

Several authors cited by Heller propose that states should incorporate international crimes into domestic law, not because international definitions are *per se* better, but because it is desirable to ensure that domestic law is at least co-extensive with ICC definitions.¹⁵ These passages do not suggest that the admissibility regime requires or favours international charges; they simply indicate that availability of international definitions is a prudent way to avoid a scenario where a crime occurs that is not covered under national law.¹⁶ Otherwise, the state would not be in a position to bring a national prosecution at all and thus could not resist admissibility of the case before the ICC.¹⁷ That proposition, which is about options during implementation, remains accurate.¹⁸

Another type of charge-based theory would focus not on the national or international nature of the charges, but rather on whether the charge is for a serious or minor crime. Heller convincingly shows that admissibility cannot focus entirely

---

13   Holmes (n 4) 57–58.
14   Heller (n 2) 213.
15   Ibid 212–214.
16   As Heller rightly acknowledges ((n 1) 213–214).
17   Note that I am not speaking of the state being deemed to be 'unable', which is a term of art in ICC Statute, art 17(3). I mean that the state literally cannot do a prosecution because it has no law for the crime, and hence there would be no proceeding. Thus the case would be admissible before the ICC, because the explicit proceedings requirement in art 17(1)(a), (b) and (c) would not be met. For those unfamiliar with the explicit proceedings requirement in art 17(1), this is demonstrated in D Robinson, 'The Mysterious Mysteriousness of Complementarity' (2010) 21 *CLF* 67.
18   I agree of course with the critiques by Heller (n 2) and Mégret (n 3) of commentators who misstate this implementation option as a duty. Heller's partial answer to the co-extensiveness problem is that the state can simply charge the person for a different crime, using some offence that is on the books: Heller (n 2) 240. However, this solution is not viable if the accused is not guilty of any other offences. For example, if the person has committed only one type of crime, such as declaring that no quarter shall be given or recruiting child soldiers (art 8(2)(b)(xii) or (xxvi)), and domestic law does not cover that conduct, then there is no legal possibility to proceed against him. Thus, the proposition survives unaltered that, if a state wishes to be sure that it can exercise jurisdiction over crimes by its nationals or on its territory, it remains prudent to ensure that its criminal laws are at least as broad as the subject matter jurisdiction of the ICC. Heller rightly warns that the adoption of international crimes legislation may create an expectation that the state will use it to deal with international crimes, rather than proceeding with domestic charges that cover the same subject matter (Heller (n 2) 215–216). The point is sound, and thus, to avoid falling back into the problem of requiring difficult proceedings that are less likely to succeed, it must be that we cannot favour 'international' charges over 'ordinary' charges in an admissibility determination, even where a state has relevant legislation.

on the gravity of the charge.[19] I would again simply note that some of the works cited by Heller as examples of approaches focused on the gravity of the charge are amenable to a more subtle and generous reading. Rather than suggesting that the gravity of the charge should be *determinative* (which would be problematic), they seem to have simply been noting that in some circumstances trivial charges may be one *indicator* of a non-genuine process.[20] This is a more subtle position that I will explore below.

The point of the last few paragraphs is that the postulated preference for international charges is not as monolithic as it may seem. Nonetheless, charge-based theories are certainly advanced in the literature and thus Heller's careful critique is valuable. His critique of the 'soft' mirror thesis is particularly insightful and important.

## II. The Sentence-Based Theory

The second, more radical step in 'A Sentence-Based Theory' is to suggest a sentence-based approach as an 'exclusive' test (at least where the state uses ordinary criminal charges).[21] On this approach, to assess the national proceeding, the Court would examine the sentence imposed and require it to be at least equivalently stringent (with a modest margin of appreciation) with the *average* imposed by the ICC for the corresponding international crime.[22] Heller anticipates some of the possible objections to this approach, including *inter alia* that the ICC does not yet have any convictions and hence does not have any 'average' sentences. To address such objections, he introduces various work-arounds, such as incorporating ICTY and ICTR averages as well as Statute sentence maxima.[23]

I believe that the chapter advances insightful observations about the role of sentences in the admissibility determination (as I will discuss below). However, I would suggest that a sentence-based approach cannot be the exclusive or even primary test, because it would generate some significant difficulties that have not yet been addressed.

The first problem is that the sentence theory cannot cope with acquittals. Where an accused is acquitted, there is no sentence; it is therefore impossible to compare the sentence to international averages. Acquittals can, of course, be a perfectly appropriate outcome. For example, an acquittal does not and should not generate

---

[19] Heller (n 2) 227–232. In Heller's (sentence-based) account, this is because the minor charge might still produce a serious sentence. On my (process-based) account, this is because a minor charge might still be part of a genuine process.

[20] See Heller (n 2) 225.

[21] Ibid 225; see also ibid 248 (determination of willingness should be made 'solely' by reference to sentence).

[22] Ibid 225.

[23] Ibid 226–227.

ICC admissibility if the accused is innocent of the crime. Or, it may be that guilt cannot be established beyond a reasonable doubt on the diligently collected and presented evidence. Alternatively, a state could legitimately grant a stay of proceedings where necessary to uphold fundamental values. The problem of being unequipped to evaluate acquittals is alone sufficient to preclude a sentence-based approach from being an exclusive test.

A second problem with a sentence approach is that one must wait until the end of the proceeding to assess the outcome. Heller offers a partial interim solution, by suggesting that the Court do its comparison with the state's average sentences to date for that crime.[24] However, the state's historic average sentence for routine cases for a given offence is a somewhat peripheral datum that may tell us rather little about whether the particular case is being handled genuinely.[25] By contrast, a process-based theory focuses on the particular proceeding and is able to intervene as soon as there is sufficient evidence that the process is not genuine.

Third, several challenges arise from an insurmountable tension between (i) the crudeness of aggregate data and (ii) the problems of exceeding the nature of an admissibility hearing. In looking at average sentences, we either take into account the specific facts, or we do not. Let us assume first that we do *not* look at the specific facts. If we do not take into account the wildly different factual circumstances that can arise, aggregate data on sentences for a particular charge is too crude to be meaningful. The accused may face a serious-sounding charge but have played a very minor role, or there may be extensive mitigating circumstances.[26] Thus, a proceeding may produce a sentence dramatically below the 'average' sentence without in any way being improper or warranting ICC action. General comparisons with average sentences tell us relatively little about the genuineness of a particular proceeding.

To avoid those problems, it therefore seems we have no choice but to take the alternate route of looking at the facts of the particular case. However, once we take that route, we no longer have the reassurance of a scientific-sounding approach based on average sentences. We also immediately encounter two problems. First, to have any sense of the appropriate sentence, we would have to know what atrocities

---

[24] Ibid 226.

[25] For example, a state may have a track record of truly harsh offences for 'ordinary' criminals while also having a track record of shielding state officials. This is why the analysis must be much more subtle. Sentence may play a *role* in that analysis. For example, if prosecutors faced with evidence of serious transgressions select a trivial charge with a mild maximum sentence, this may be an indicium of non-genuineness.

[26] As an example of the latter, the *Erdemović* case, in which the accused voluntarily came forward and testified against himself and others, included an extreme situation of duress (so extreme that many jurists thought he should have been acquitted rather than convicted at all). See, e.g., A Fichtelberg, 'Liberal Values in International Criminal Law: A Critique of Erdemović' (2008) 6 *JICJ* 3; V Epps, 'The Soldier's Obligation to Die When Ordered to Shoot Civilians or Face Death Himself' (2003) 37 *New England L Rev* 987; LE Chiesa, 'Duress, Demanding Heroism and Proportionality: The Erdemović Case and Beyond' (2008) 41 *Vanderbilt J Transnat'l L* 741.

were committed, how many incidents occurred, and what aggravating factors (e.g. cruelty, leadership role) or mitigating factors (e.g. duress) were present. In other words, we would need a trial. Thus the approach would transform an admissibility hearing into a criminal trial (or re-trial or pre-trial). Second, a decision as to what range of sentence is appropriate logically necessitates a conclusion of guilt.[27] This generates complications with the presumption of innocence. An explicit or implicit determination of guilt would be necessitated in a pre-trial proceeding, after which one could *start* the trial. Of course the trial would be conducted by a different chamber, but something still seems amiss if guilt must be shown in order to establish admissibility and start the trial. It was for reasons like that this that the Experts Group report on complementarity warned that the admissibility determination had to focus on the *process*, not the *outcome*.[28]

There are still other difficulties for the sentence theory. For example, one concern expressed about complementarity is the danger that it will lead to a homogenisation of national processes.[29] A sentence-based approach would impose an even more severe form of homogenisation. The ICC would effectively be inviting the state to conduct a trial in accordance with national laws and procedures, with a rather hefty caveat such as 'by the way, if it does not result in a conviction for 15.7 years or more of imprisonment, we will do it all over again at the ICC'. Further, if the ICC seizes cases *because* the national sentence is below average, it would become difficult for the ICC judges to then issue a below-average sentence where justice required it. Another strange effect of the approach would be that, year after year, as each state has to meet or exceed the international average sentence for each offence in order to retain carriage of cases, the average sentences would continuously be driven upwards. Additional concerns are noted by Carsten Stahn in Chapter 15 of the present volume.

## III. A Process-Based Approach

For the foregoing reasons, I would hesitate about the more sweeping proposal to embrace the sentence-based methodology. Nonetheless, Heller advances important insights about the role of charges and the role of sentences that should be absorbed into any theory of complementarity.

---

[27] One cannot ruminate about appropriate sentences unless one is first satisfied that the accused is culpable, and indeed one would need a sense of the crimes for which he is culpable.

[28] Experts Group, *The Principle of Complementarity in Practice* (2003) <http://www.icc-cpi.int/iccdocs/doc/doc654724.pdf> last accessed 22 January 2012, para 46.

[29] See Mégret (n 3) 388–389 and MA Drumbl, 'Policy through Complementarity: The Atrocity Trial as Justice' in C Stahn and M El Zeidy (eds) *The International Criminal Court and Complementarity: From Theory to Practice* (CUP, Cambridge 2011) 197.

The admissibility determination cannot centre on the *charges* (as Heller has shown); nor can it centre on *sentences* (as I hope I have shown). Admissibility should centre on the *process*, and more specifically the genuineness of the process. I believe that this is not only most compatible with Article 17 as a matter of positive law; it is also normatively superior to alternatives. Once it is shown that a state is carrying out or has carried out its own proceedings in relation to a case,[30] the question is whether the state is carrying out (or has carried out) those proceedings 'genuinely'.[31] There are two major ways to show that proceedings are not genuine: the state is *unwilling* to carry out proceedings genuinely (e.g. a lack of intent to bring the persons concerned to justice) or *unable* to carry out the proceedings genuinely (collapse or unavailability).[32] Thus, interpreting 'genuinely' using the context of Articles 17(2) and (3), we find two aspects: one about the sincerity of the effort and one requiring a very rudimentary level of capacity.[33] Process is the master theory; we can look at charges and sentences insofar as they reveal something about genuineness of the process.[34]

The charge laid may be an *indicator* in assessing genuineness of the process. For the reasons presented by Heller, the choice of an 'international' or an 'ordinary' offence (e.g. war crime of murder versus murder *simpliciter*) should likely be given zero weight. As Heller has shown, the use of international definitions may have expressive value, but we cannot require their use, and doing so may have the undesirable effect of encouraging unsuccessful proceedings.[35]

By contrast, the decision to charge the accused with a 'serious' offence versus a 'minor' offence *can* properly be an indicator. It is not determinative, for the reasons shown by Heller: a 'minor' charge might still culminate in a serious sentence and a serious process, which would address our complementarity concerns.[36] However, on a process theory, the charge can nonetheless be a significant indicator in assessing genuineness, by indicating whether the state is attempting to minimise and whitewash the crime by focusing on a trivial charge that ignores the gravamen of the available evidence.

Similarly, sentence can be an *indicator* in assessing genuineness. For example, an extremely mild sentence that is mismatched with the available evidence may

---

[30] See the first condition stated in each of arts 17(1)(a), (b) and (c).

[31] Art 17(1)(a) and (b) (the terms following 'unless'); see also art 20.

[32] Art 17(1), (2) and (3).

[33] Experts Group (n 28) para 22–23; JT Holmes, 'Complementarity: National Courts versus the ICC' in A Cassese et al (eds) *The Rome Statute of the International Criminal Court: A Commentary* (OUP, Oxford 2002) 667, 674.

[34] As was mentioned above, admissibility determinations should centre on process not outcomes. One may look at outcomes and procedural developments as a factor, not because the outcome is by definition problematic but rather insofar as it is indication that the process was not genuine. Thus, a light sentence cannot *per se* be a reason for admissibility. A light sentence may however, in conjunction with other factors, help to indicate a non-genuine process that does not warrant deference.

[35] Section II above.

[36] Heller (n 2) 227–229.

suggest that the process had a flawed, sham character.[37] Alternatively, if the maximum available sentence is mild, this may arguably go to unavailability of legal system for that serious international crime.[38] I would say that *lenient* sentences may be only a modest indicator, useful only in conjunction with other indicators, because lenient sentences are not *per se* evidence of non-genuineness.

Conversely, a most intriguing point convincingly advanced by Heller is that sentence can work in the other direction in a very dramatic fashion. As Heller notes, where the sentence is stringent enough, we may not need to worry about the nature and seriousness of the charge, or the details of the proceedings, because the impunity-avoidance aim of the complementarity regime has been satisfied.[39] The person has been brought to justice. Interestingly, then, while *lenient* sentences are only a modest indicator (useful only in conjunction with other factors), *severe* sentences may be much more conclusive evidence of genuineness, ending the need for a further search for evidence of non-genuineness.[40]

This proposition is potentially subject to at least one[41] caveat: a stern sentence may not foreclose the need for further analysis *if* the Court adopts an approach to complementarity that is concerned with draconian national processes. When I have referred in this comment to a 'process' approach, I am archetypally speaking of the inquiry whether a process is not genuine because it is *too lenient*. However, some have argued that the ICC should be able to take a case where the national proceedings are *too repressive*, i.e. they do not provide due process.[42] Heller has addressed such arguments elsewhere,[43] and he has put forward powerful arguments, rooted in the text and drafting history, that complementarity is concerned only with proceedings that are too lenient or ineffective, and not proceedings that are too stringent. I personally lean in the same direction as Heller, but ultimately my position is

---

[37] See e.g. Experts Group (n 28) Annex 4 (listing indicators).

[38] Views plausibly differ on the meaning of 'unavailability' in art 17(3). See e.g. Experts Group (n 28) para 49, suggesting a broad interpretation to promote coherence with the rest of the provision.

[39] Heller (n 2) 225–229.

[40] This may at first glance seem contradictory. However, it is not contradictory once one recalls the burden of proof. Once one is within the unwilling/unable exception, the burden is to prove unwillingness or inability. A lenient sentence by itself is not sufficient to meet the burden, so one must go on to consider other indicia. Conversely, a severe sentence might be strongly persuasive that the burden is *not* met, ending the need for further search for evidence of non-genuineness.

[41] Another caveat arises where a stern sentence is swiftly followed by an executive pardon, which can raise suspicions about the genuineness of the process from the start.

[42] See e.g. F Gioia, 'State Sovereignty, Jurisdiction and "Modern" International Law: The Principle of Complementarity in the International Criminal Court' (2006) 19 *LJIL* 1095, 1110–1113; M Politi, 'The Establishment on International Criminal Court at the Crossroads: Issues and Prospects after the First Session of the Preparatory Committee' (1999) 13 *Nouvelles Études Pénales* 115.

[43] KJ Heller, 'The Shadow Side of Complementarity: The Effect of Article 17 of the Rome Statute on National Due Process' (2006) 17 *CLF* 255.

agnostic: it is one of those issues where arguments that are at least plausible can be made on either side, so the Court could defensibly take either interpretation.[44] I would therefore simply note that if the ICC reaches the interpretation that excessively repressive national proceedings can trigger admissibility, then a harsh sentence will not forestall further inquiry into genuineness, and it will still be necessary to look at all factors.

## IV. A Defence of the 'Same Conduct' Test: Why Admissibility is Rightly About 'The Case'

Finally, Heller raises important concerns about the 'same conduct' test, which is the test employed by ICC chambers to determine if a state is proceeding with the same 'case'. This concern has been raised in recent thoughtful scholarship,[45] so it is timely and valuable to examine the question here. While I agree that an overly rigid application of the same-conduct test would be unfortunate, I will try to demonstrate that the problem is actually much narrower than it is widely perceived. I want to show that admissibility is quite fundamentally about *the case*, and whether the case has been genuinely addressed.[46] The scenario where a state wishes to prosecute the same person for a *different case* is not an admissibility issue. Nor is it a lacuna

---

[44] During the drafting of art 17, most delegates were concerned with sham or ineffective proceedings, and thought that the problem of overly-harsh national proceedings is one that could be taken up with a human rights body (which protects rights), not the ICC (which is about preventing impunity). Other delegates, including Mauro Politi of Italy (later a judge at the ICC) were of a different view, and secured an ambiguous but potentially significant reference to 'due process' in art 17. Accordingly, it is at least arguable that art 17 requires national proceedings that are not only effective but also fair. On this view the requirement of bringing a person 'to justice' would emphasise that 'justice' entails some due process. See e.g. Gioia (n 42). Heller is also somewhat ambivalent; he feels that *legally* the ICC cannot declare cases admissible because national proceedings were in violation of due process (too stringent), but that *normatively* it would be a good idea: see Heller (n 43).

[45] See also e.g. NN Jurdi, 'Some Lessons on Complementarity for the International Criminal Court Review Conference' (2009) 34 *South African Ybk of Int'l L* 28; SA Williams and WA Schabas, 'Article 17' in O Triffterer (ed) *Commentary on the Rome Statute of the International Criminal Court* (2nd edn Nomos, Berlin 2008) 605, 616; S Sacouto and K Cleary, 'The *Katanga* Complementarity Decisions: Sound Law but Flawed Policy' (2003) 23 *LJIL* 363. Sacouto and Cleary express understandable concerns about compatibility with the *policy* of positive complementarity; for a partial explanation of how these are reconciled see Robinson (n 17) 92–101 and C Stahn, 'Taking Complementarity Seriously' in C Stahn and M El Zeidy (eds), *The International Criminal Court and Complementarity: From Theory to Practice* (CUP, Cambridge 2011) 233.

[46] As noted in the introduction, by 'admissibility', I refer only to the complementarity aspects of admissibility and not the separate issue of 'gravity' (art 17(1)(d)).

of the Statute: I will show that the scenario is addressed by other provisions of the Statute, and they address it better than Article 17 could.

To appreciate the significance of the same-conduct test, one must discern that Article 17 provides a two-step test for admissibility. Heller and I are on the same page in recognising the two-step structure of Article 17. (There has been a remarkably widespread and persistent tendency in ICL discourse to fixate exclusively only on the 'unwilling or unable' exception in Article 17 and to treat that exception as if it were the *entire test*, which has generated a lot of confusion and misplaced accusations against the Court for departing from the Statute. I explore this curious phenomenon in ICC discourse elsewhere.[47]) The first step of the admissibility test asks whether there are or have been national proceedings with respect to the case, i.e. 'the case is being investigated or prosecuted' (Article 17(1)(a)) or 'the case has been investigated ... and the State has decided not to prosecute' (Article 17(1)(b)).[48] If and only if there are such proceedings, one reaches the exception, and must assess whether the State is unwilling or unable to *genuinely* carry out that proceeding. This means that the scope of the term 'case' has a very important role in the admissibility determination. ICC jurisprudence uses the 'same conduct' test as part of its determination whether a national proceeding concerns the same case.

Like many scholars in recent literature,[49] Heller expresses concern that the same-conduct test is too stringent. The concern is that same-conduct test 'privileges the ICC instead of states' because it requires national authorities to investigate the specific conduct that the ICC is investigating.[50] It is argued that the test requires governments to be 'mind readers' because they have to anticipate ICC cases.[51] If the state selects a different case, then the Court would be 'required to preempt national proceedings'[52] and 'would be powerless to refuse to admit the case'.[53] Thus, 'because of the same-conduct requirement, [states] cannot charge crimes—including serious ones—that involve conduct the ICC is not investigating, even if prosecuting different conduct would be far more likely to result in a conviction'.[54] Heller argues that there is 'no justification' for a case to be admissible just because

---

[47] Robinson (n 17). The fixation on the unwilling/unable test is accompanied by a curious but persistent tendency to overlook the 55 words of art 17 which explicitly, unambiguously and deliberately require that there be national proceedings in relation to the case. Surprisingly, many commentators overlook the words and then condemn the Court for 'inventing' new requirements; this puzzling disconnect is the 'mysterious mysteriousness' of complementarity.

[48] Art 17(1)(c) addresses the third alternative, when a national trial has been completed. Some commentators treat *ne bis in idem* as part of complementarity and others treat it as separate but closely related; that possible difference is not of concern here.

[49] See above (n 45).
[50] Heller (n 1) 241.
[51] Ibid 241.
[52] Ibid 224.
[53] Ibid 242.
[54] Ibid 239.

national proceeding is based on different conduct;[55] the ICC case should be rendered inadmissible if a different case pursued by a state is a serious one.[56]

While I agree that a margin of flexibility is indeed needed in identifying the 'case', the scope of the problem is considerably narrower than it is generally perceived. I would like to contribute five points to the discourse about the supposed lacuna where a state wishes to prosecute the same person for a different but serious matter.

First, Article 17 does not exhaust the principle of complementarity. Article 17 is an important but technical admissibility rule, which renders a case inadmissible before the ICC if it is genuinely addressed by a state. Article 17 is certainly a centrepiece of complementarity, and it is understandable that it is often the focus of complementarity discussion. However, insofar as 'complementarity' refers to the broader interplay and division of labour between national jurisdictions and the ICC, it is woven through many other articles of the Statute,[57] and in many more profound respects remains to be fleshed out by policies of the Court.[58]

In this vein, I would highlight that the 'different case' scenario is actually contemplated and addressed in Part 9 of the Statute, which deals with cooperation. Articles 89(4) and 94(1) provide for consultation between the state and the Court where the Court's request (for assistance in general or for surrender specifically) would interfere with the state's investigation or prosecution of a different case or the serving of the person's sentence.[59] Both provisions are linked to the general consultation provision (Article 97). Heller's article is an advance on many other works, because it acknowledges Articles 89/94.[60] However, it does so only briefly, without fully assimilating the implications of Articles 89/94 for the critique of the same-conduct test or the scope of admissibility. My aim is to press a little further in exploring those implications.

Second, there is not a lacuna in the Statute requiring repair. It is simply not true that the Court would be 'powerless to refuse to admit the case' or 'required to preempt the national proceedings'. The Statute provides the Court with *two* distinct ways to defer its case. One, as was just mentioned, the consultation mechanism expressly allows the Court to defer in this exact scenario. While the policies to be employed by the Court in that mechanism remain to be determined, as I will discuss in a moment, they would undoubtedly entail deference to effective national investigations for equally or more serious atrocities. Furthermore, there is also a

---

[55] Ibid 230; see also ibid 234 ('makes little sense') and ibid 240 ('arbitrary limitation').

[56] Ibid 229. On a sentence-based theory, this would entail that the national case culminated in a severe sentence.

[57] Including arts 1, 17, 18, 19, 20, 89(4), 90, 93(10) and 94 of the ICC Statute.

[58] The most important and impressive work on this question is Stahn (n 45). See also Robinson (n 17); Experts Group (n 28).

[59] Art 89(4) ICC Statute: 'If the person sought is being proceeded against or is serving a sentence in the requested state for a crime different from that for which surrender to the Court is sought, the requested state, after making its decision to grant the request, shall consult the Court.'

[60] Heller (n 2) 224 and 245–246.

second mechanism, the 'interests of justice' test.[61] If the ICC deferred under Part 9 of the Statute and the person was punished for different crimes, the ICC could decide it is no longer in the interests of justice to invest resources prosecuting an aged defendant who has already been punished for different but related crimes.[62]

Third, there is no question of the ICC 'requiring' states to prosecute any case, nor of 'prohibiting' or 'limiting' them from prosecuting other cases, nor of 'nullifying' national proceedings over other cases.[63] The state is free to initiate any cases it wishes. The ICC has concurrent jurisdiction, and exercises it subject to the rules of the Statute. If the state proceeds against a case also pursued by the ICC, then the state can argue that the ICC case is inadmissible. If the state proceeds against a person sought by the ICC but for a different case, the state can invoke the consultation mechanism (and/or the interests of justice test).

Fourth, to address the 'different case' scenario through admissibility is not only unnecessary[64] and legally unavailable:[65] it is also *normatively undesirable*. Under the existing Statute regime, wherein competing claims are resolved through the consultation mechanism, the issue is one of *sequencing*, i.e. which jurisdiction does its case first. If, however, we stretch the admissibility regime, we create a problem, because a genuine proceeding renders a case *forever inadmissible*.[66] Assume that we follow the suggestion of scholars, so that case X can be rendered inadmissible because case Y is being investigated and prosecuted. The case is rendered inadmissible not only during ongoing genuine national proceedings (Article 17(1)(a)), it also *remains* inadmissible once the state carries out the proceedings to a genuine conclusion (Articles 17(1)(b) and (c)). It makes sense that the successful handling of case Y renders case Y inadmissible; it does not make sense for it to render cases X or Z inadmissible.[67] A conviction for one crime (e.g. fraud in Las Vegas) does not and should not legally insulate a person from future proceedings for a completely different crime (e.g. murder in Los Angeles).

---

[61] Art 53(2)(c).

[62] Art 53(2)(c) ICC Statute. Suppose for example that the ICC wanted to prosecute the accused for crimes A, B and C, but deferred (under Part 9) to national proceedings for crimes D, E and F. After the accused served his sentence for crimes D, E and F, the ICC case for crimes A, B and C would still be admissible, because the case has never been addressed. However, the ICC could decide it is no longer in the interests of justice to prosecute the person further. Or, at earlier stages, the ICC could decide it is not in the interests of justice to press forward with a case that would disrupt effective national efforts concerning different but important crimes.

[63] Heller (n 2) 224, 239, 241, 249.

[64] Since the Statute already addresses it, as explained in the preceding paragraphs.

[65] Since art 17 asks whether 'the case' has been addressed.

[66] In the same vein, see R Rastan, 'Situation and Case: Defining the Parameters' in C Stahn and M El Zeidy (eds) *The International Criminal Court and Complementarity: From Theory to Practice* (CUP, Cambridge 2011) 419, 443–445.

[67] One could try to graft on additional creative 'work-arounds' to ameliorate the resulting problems, but each work-around generates new incoherencies; the incoherencies arise because of the departure from the immanent structure of admissibility.

Which brings me to my fifth point: admissibility is about the *case*, not just as a matter of positive law or a happenstance of drafting, but as a matter of fundamental structure. The *case* remains admissible before the ICC for a very good reason: because no jurisdiction on earth has dealt with the case. There may be reasons *other than admissibility* for the Court not to deal with the case. The Court may defer to a national prosecution of a different case as a cooperation matter, or the Court may conclude it is not in the 'interests of justice' to pursue further a person who has already been extensively punished. The limit on how much we might pass one person around to face justice for his or her diverse crimes is the 'interests of justice', not admissibility.[68]

Having laid down those parameters, I still partially agree with the concern. We simply need to clarify its boundaries. Inspired by Heller's lead in presenting scenarios that helpfully clarified a proposition, I would outline four scenarios. The state may be pursuing (1) the identical case, (2) a significantly overlapping case, (3) a different case within the overall 'situation' and (4) a completely unconnected case (e.g. embezzlement).

Scenario 1 poses no problem: it meets the same-conduct test. Scenario 4 is also straightforward; for the reasons I have just advanced, it raises no admissibility issue at all. It is in scenario 2 (overlapping case) that we must argue for a 'margin of appreciation' in the state's identification of its 'case'. It should not be required that the state has selected, for example, the identical offences and incidents. A 'perfect incident-specific mapping' is unlikely.[69] A significant overlap in the gravamen of the case should be enough to engage the admissibility regime.[70] Scenario 3 raises some subtleties of admissibility which I am unable to explore here in the present space,[71] but it can generally be addressed by the consultation mechanism, which

---

[68] For example, General Noriega was prosecuted in the United States, extradited to France to face prosecution for other crimes, and then extradited to Panama to face prosecution for other crimes.

[69] R Rastan, 'What is a "Case" for the Purpose of the Rome Statute?' (2008) 19 *CLF* 435, 439.

[70] The ICC Appeals Chamber has arguably addressed this concern as well, requiring 'substantially' the same conduct: *Situation in the Republic of Kenya: Prosecutor v Muthaura, Kenyatta and Ali* (Judgment on Defence Appeal Challenging Admissibility of Case) ICC-01/09-02/11 (30 August 2011).

[71] As one example, scenario 3 would have a different complexion during preliminary examination, when the decision is whether to initiate an investigation of the *situation*. Admissibility is about cases, but at the preliminary examination stage there are not yet defined cases, and thus the Court must consider the universe of likely case (presumably focusing on persons most responsible for the most serious crimes). That approach is now endorsed and confirmed *inter alia* by the ICC Appeals Chamber, ibid para 38. I would argue that, at the situation stage, the state must be accorded a significant margin to select cases, and to identify persons most responsible for most serious crimes, even if ICC analysts would have selected one or two different perpetrators and some different crimes or incidents.

should be applied generously to a state acting in good faith to contend with a mass crimes situation.

Two counterpoints can be made to my argument. First, in our online symposium, Heller has made some excellent counter-arguments about the limits of the consultation regime.[72] The strongest of these is that, in order to invoke Article 89(4), the state must first declare its readiness to surrender the suspect. I agree with Heller that this provision sends an unfortunate signal which seems to tilt the balance in favour of ICC proceedings.[73] I would suggest that states and the ICC could use the general consultation provision of Article 97 to moderate that problem. However, to try to solve the perceived problem in Part 9 by distorting the admissibility regime would cause even greater problems, including the problem of permanent inadmissibility (as discussed above), instead of the more nimble 'sequencing' solution already established in the Statute.

Second, one could argue that reliance on the consultation regime is unsatisfying, because it leaves too much discretion to the Court.[74] One could argue, in the name of precision and certainty, that there should be a juridified process in which the state is entitled to bring a formal legal challenge based on its pursuit of a different but important case. This argument would have merits, given the importance of clarifying the interplay between national and international jurisdictions. An ambitious option would be to amend the Statute to allow challenges by states pursuing the same person for different crimes, but this is unlikely given the Statute amendment formula.[75] More plausibly, the Assembly of States Parties could amend the Rules of Procedure and Evidence, to establish guidelines for consultation and sequencing decisions.[76] Relevant factors might include the comparative seriousness of the conduct in the different cases, prospects for a genuine proceeding, the

---

[72] See KJ Heller's reply on the *Opinio Juris* Symposium <http://opiniojuris.org/2012/01/24/hilj_heller-response-to-robinson-and-stahn/> last accessed 31 January 2012.

[73] Art 89(4) ICC Statute. Heller also raises a concern about art 94: that it only allows postponement during investigation and prosecution but not during the serving of sentence, so that the state might be obliged to surrender the person once the trial is complete. This concern can be addressed, however, because art 94 only applies to requests for assistance; a request for surrender would be governed by art 89(4), which expressly allows postponement during the serving of sentence. Heller also makes an excellent point that the interests of justice test lies in the first instance in the hands of the Prosecutor, with only limited reviewability. This is an important point, and is linked to complex questions about the optimal locus, scope and reviewability of decisions, and whether the scope to raise 'interests of justice' arguments should be expanded.

[74] See e.g. Heller (n 2) 246 (noting that the regime is 'not the picture of clarity').

[75] Art 121 ICC Statute. It would also require careful thought about when, why and for how long a national proceeding of case Y should render case X inadmissible. Again, the regime already provided in Part 9 addresses the 'different case' scenario most elegantly, because it allows for a simple prioritisation and sequencing.

[76] Art 51 ICC Statute. Some guidance is arguably already embedded in art 90 (competing requests).

desirability of national proceedings, and so on.[77] At this early stage, however, it is not clear that we need to codify any such rule. The ICC has never rejected, nor has it ever received, a request for postponement from a state wishing to pursue a suspect for a different case. It may be preferable to let the Court develop its practice on the issue in light of experience. If problems emerge, such as the ICC proving to be too 'ICC-centric', then the Assembly of States Parties is free to act by developing a rule.

## Conclusion

In 'A Sentence-Based Theory', Kevin Heller makes an important contribution to the complementarity discussion. I have advanced two points of disagreement. First, I would not replace existing approaches with an entirely new sentence-based methodology. I would however absorb his important observations about charges and sentences into a process-based approach. Second, I think the same-conduct test is not as problematic as it seems. I do agree that it needs flexibility at the margins. The most valuable insights of his article concern (1) the very limited role that can be ascribed to 'charges', and particularly the eye-opening critique of the 'soft mirror' thesis, and (2) the potentially significant role that can be played by sentences, most particularly the proposition that a clearly adequate sentence may forestall the need for further inquiry.

---

[77] See Robinson (n 17) 97–99 and 101; Stahn (n 45).

# PART IV
International Criminal Justice in Context

# 17

**ASHGATE RESEARCH COMPANION**

# The Short Arm of International Criminal Law

## William A. Schabas

Imagine a domestic criminal justice system where the prosecuting authorities respond to only a tiny handful of complaints. They confine their attention to a few, carefully selected communities and neglect everything else. When asked to explain the apparent arbitrariness of their choices, those in charge of the system answer that they are selecting only the 'the most serious' matters for prosecution. It is apparent that while the situations they select are certainly serious, many equally serious ones are ignored. The vast majority of the victims of such crimes, who generally believe that their own circumstances are 'the most serious', will never see justice done. Although constantly told that the process is being conducted in their name, they remain profoundly dissatisfied (aside from the tiny minority for whom justice is delivered). As victims of serious crimes against the person, the fact that their own communities are entirely overlooked while others attract the attention of the authorities is incomprehensible.

But even in the rare communities to which the justice system turns its attention, not all perpetrators of serious crimes are brought to justice. Once again, the prosecutors insist that they target 'the most serious' offenders. Sometimes, they explain that they are going after the leaders. But the leaders are not always easy to prosecute because they have powerful networks of protection. Sometimes, the prosecutors seem to tackle the low-hanging fruit, that is to say, opportunistic cases of suspects who seem to stumble carelessly onto their radar. These people meet the criterion of 'seriousness' in an abstract sense, but they are indistinguishable from so many other possible defendants. Sometimes, the choices are justified on the basis of quantitative and qualitative factors, such as the number of victims, or the fact that the victims have some special role within the community.

The prosecutors can't do more, because they have a minuscule budget for investigation given the number of crimes committed. In any case, there are only two courtrooms and a small number of judges. The judicial procedure is clumsy, repetitive and time-consuming. Judges take an inordinate amount of time dealing with even a single case, often years of hearings punctuated by interlocutory appeals on matters that do not always seem essential.

Professionals, especially academics, who attempt to understand and analyse this system generally confine themselves to technical questions such as the procedural issues. Criminologists cannot understand how it works. It seems that this scheme of criminal justice is premised entirely on general deterrence, which is to say preventing crime and protecting society by example. Whether the criminals are deterred by a jail with a dozen people in custody and fewer actually on trial, and perhaps one conviction every decade, is debatable. In any event, performance is impossible to measure because those who are actually deterred cannot readily be identified.

The progress, if that is the word for it, seems slow compared with other accomplishments of the same society: impressive technological advances, breakthroughs in medicine, the fine arts, and so on. By comparison, criminal justice looks primitive and amateurish. In its defence, it is said that these are 'early days'. But those who work within it do not seem to have a vision of the future. They cannot tell the victims whether their suffering will eventually be addressed because the system will increasingly be able to deal with all cases and situations comprehensively, an unlikely prospect given the scale of things. Nor are they at all convinced that the paltry number of prosecutions will actually achieve the putative goal of general deterrence, thereby indirectly responding to the needs of the victims in communities where the short arm of the law does not reach.

# I. Prosecutorial Discretion at the International Criminal Court

This is the enigma of the International Criminal Court. The project is a brilliant one. It has fascinated international lawyers for nearly a century. A first generation of temporary institutions, at Nuremberg and The Hague, was followed 50 years later by a second phase that featured the United Nations international criminal tribunals for the former Yugoslavia, Rwanda and Sierra Leone. Each one of these bodies ultimately accomplished the tasks that were set for it when the institution was established, confirming the viability of the model albeit at a cost in time and money that had not been anticipated at the outset. The great dream of a permanent, universal institution remained elusive until the 1990s. Then, rather more quickly than most had expected, the United Nations provided the framework for the adoption of the Rome Statute. An exhilarating pace of ratification brought that instrument into force within less than four years. The International Criminal Court was created. By June 2003, all of its pieces were in place and it was ready to begin operations.

The Court was to build upon the successes of the *ad hoc* tribunals. It could draw on an increasingly rich experience in both substantive and procedural matters. There was also a large cohort of experienced lawyers and other professionals to operate the new institution, something that could not be said at the time that its predecessors were launched.

There were great expectations. They have not been fulfilled. In 2004, when presenting the proposed budget for his Office to the Assembly of States Parties, the Prosecutor said that '[i]n 2005, the Office plans to conduct one full trial, begin a second and carry out two new investigations'.[1] A flow chart derived from the Prosecutor's forecasts indicated that the first trial before the Court would be completed by August 2005.[2] He became somewhat less ambitious in 2006, when a three-year strategic plan proclaimed the expectation that the Court would *complete* two 'expeditious trials by 2009, and ... conduct four to six new investigations'.[3] In other words, the Prosecutor expected that by the time it had been fully operational for six years, the Court would have completed two 'expeditious trials'. This was not very much by comparison with what had gone before. Six years after their operations began, the Yugoslavia, Rwanda and Sierra Leone tribunals had already finished many trials, several of them at the appeals stage.

However, the Court did not even come close to realising the Prosecutor's modest plans. By 2012, it had failed to complete a single trial. A cohort of judges of the Appeals Chamber retired in March 2012 after finishing a nine-year term, most of it in full-time service at the seat of the Court, but without ever hearing an appeal from a conviction which was, after all, the *raison d'être* for a five-member Appeals Chamber. By comparison, when the Yugoslavia Tribunal was the same age, it had completed 12 trials, six of them to the appeals stage, involving 27 defendants.

Of course it wasn't only the Prosecutor who had such high hopes for the new International Criminal Court. But what were these hopes? Probably many thought that a permanent institution, with an aspiration of universality and a membership that soon comprised more than half of the Member States of the United Nations, would bring an end to the piecemeal approach of *ad hoc* tribunals. A selective approach to justice was inevitable with the Security Council in control of the agenda. Many believed that the permanent Court would provide a more comprehensive, consistent and thorough mechanism. But such an aspiration, however laudable, was patently unrealistic. Perhaps many enthusiasts had not given much thought to the practical aspects of a Court with such a broad jurisdictional reach; they were focussed on particular issues or regions of the world, and would measure success by whether their particular area of concern was being addressed: women, child soldiers, Darfur, Palestine, Afghanistan, Mexico and so on. Some more prudently may have expected the Court to operate as a permanent *ad hoc* tribunal, obviating the need to establish a new institution for each crisis and ensuring that the decision

---

[1] International Criminal Court, Draft Programme Budget for 2005, ICC-ASP/3/2 <http://www.icc-cpi.int/iccdocs/asp_docs/library/asp/ICC-ASP3-2_budget_English.pdf> last accessed 20 December 2011, para 159.

[2] Ibid 49.

[3] Office of the Prosecutor, International Criminal Court, Report on Prosecutorial Strategy <http://www.icc-cpi.int/NR/rdonlyres/D673DD8C-D427-4547BC692D363E07274B/143708/ProsecutorialStrategy20060914_English.pdf> last accessed 20 December 2011, 3.

to proceed lay with a body enjoying greater legitimacy than the United Nations Security Council. Can any of these rather different visions or expectations have been even remotely satisfied? Why is it possible to establish a functional international criminal tribunal on an *ad hoc* basis, one that meets the targets that have been set, while the permanent institution that was initially envisaged as a great improvement on the temporary bodies struggles to find its way?

The fanciful scenario presented at the start of this chapter suggests an analogy with national justice. At the domestic level, we expect all serious crimes against the person to be investigated and prosecuted. This is central to the rule of law. International human rights tribunals have held that justice is also an entitlement of victims.[4] There is no place for impunity, whether it be for so-called international offences like crimes against humanity or for ordinary ones like murder and rape. International justice is premised on the notion that when domestic courts fail to fulfil their responsibilities, the state in question forfeits its claim that such matters are reserved to its sovereign jurisdiction, immune from external scrutiny.

When the Security Council established the *ad hoc* tribunals, it predicated international intervention on powers derived from the Charter of the United Nations relating to the maintenance of international peace and security. Many states – they now number more than 120 – have solemnly acknowledged the authority of international criminal law by ratifying the Rome Statute. Yet when national institutions fail and international justice institutions step in to address impunity, they are unable to replace the national courts. At their best, they can target the leaders of a campaign of persecution, violence and oppression, as they did in the former Yugoslavia or Rwanda, or perhaps a representative sample, as in Sierra Leone, Nuremberg or Tokyo.

The Rome Statute distinguishes between a 'situation' and a 'case'. Examples of situations of concern to the Court include Darfur, northern Uganda, Libya and Côte d'Ivoire. Only after the situation has been determined does the Court proceed to identify individual cases: Bashir, Lubanga, Gaddafi and so on. By contrast, the *ad hoc* tribunals never really concerned themselves with identifying a 'situation'. That task was already fulfilled at the time of their creation. It resulted from a decision by a political body, be it the four-power London Conference that set up the Nuremberg Tribunal, or the United Nations Security Council in the case of the Yugoslavia and Rwanda Tribunals.

The authority of the Security Council to identify situations for prosecution, something about which there was some debate in the early 1990s, is now beyond much question. Since the Yugoslavia Tribunal was established, there have been incessant calls for the Security Council to create new and similar bodies. For Rwanda and Sierra Leone, there was a positive response, while elsewhere, in place like Burundi, Sri Lanka and Burma, there has been nothing but inertia. How can these choices be explained? The obvious answer is that they reflect the political

---

[4] *Case of 97 Members of the Gldani Congregation of Jehovah's Witnesses and 4 Others v Georgia*, (Judgment) App No 71156/01 (3 May 2007) para 97.

priorities and concerns of the members of the Security Council, and especially those of the five permanent members.

Within the narrow remit, which is to say within the 'situation' assigned to them, the prosecutors of the *ad hoc* tribunals are relatively unconstrained when they identify appropriate cases for prosecution. At the Special Court for Sierra Leone, the Prosecutor's choice of defendants is limited by the Statute to 'those who bear the greatest responsibility', which has been held to impose a jurisdictional requirement rather than mere 'guidance' for the exercise of prosecutorial discretion, as was originally suggested by the Secretary-General.[5] In the latter years of the International Criminal Tribunal for the former Yugoslavia, judges trimmed the discretion of the Prosecutor by enacting an amendment to the Rules of Procedure and Evidence so as to require that a proposed indictment concentrate 'on one or more of the most senior leaders suspected of being most responsible for crimes within the jurisdiction of the Tribunal'.[6] They considered that they were empowered to adopt such a measure by virtue of a Security Council resolution.[7] Judges at the International Criminal Tribunal for Rwanda never enacted anything similar, apparently believing that this would encroach upon the Prosecutor's discretion. In a formal sense, and within these limits, the prosecutors of the *ad hoc* tribunals are free to take decisions about proceeding with cases that may not be popular with the Security Council or with certain of its members. They cannot, however, decide on situations other than those assigned to them by their creators. The choice of the situation is not a judicial matter.

The independence of the prosecutors of the *ad hoc* tribunals is also constrained in other ways. For example, it is not secured by adequate legal provisions. Prosecutors at all of the *ad hoc* tribunals have been subject to relatively short-term contracts, of three or four years. The contracts may be renewed, but that can only happen if the Security Council is satisfied with prior performance. Moreover, the grounds and procedures for their dismissal are nowhere set out, although this has never been tested in removal proceedings. By contrast, the Prosecutor of the International Criminal Court enjoys much greater security. The term of office is nine years, more than double that of any previous international tribunal. Discipline and removal of the Prosecutor of the International Criminal Court is governed by detailed legislation,[8] providing a further degree of protection for the office-holder.

---

[5] *Prosecutor v Fofana* (Decision on the Preliminary Defence Motion on the Lack of Personal Jurisdiction Filed on Behalf of the Accused Fofana) SCSL-2004-14-PT (3 March 2004), paras 27, 39.

[6] Rules of Procedure and Evidence of the International Criminal Tribunal for the former Yugoslavia, UN Doc IT/32/Rev.46 (20 October 2011) ('ICTY RPE'), Rule 28(A).

[7] UNSC Res 1534 (2004) UN Doc S/RES/1534 (26 March 2004). See further Statement by the President of the Security Council UN Doc S/PRST/2002/21 (23 July 2002); UNSC Res 1503 (2003) UN Doc S/RES/1503 (28 August 2003), preamble.

[8] Rome Statute of the International Criminal Court, 2187 UNTS 90, 17 July 1998, entered into force 1 July 2002, arts 46, 47 ('ICC Statute'); International Criminal Court, Rules of Procedure and Evidence, Rules 24 *et seq*.

The most fundamental innovation of the International Criminal Court, by contrast with the *ad hoc* tribunals, is the freedom of the Prosecutor to select situations. This manifests itself in two ways. First, the Prosecutor may decide to initiate investigations into a situation, subject only to confirmation by a three-judge Pre-Trial Chamber.[9] In the case of proceedings where the crime of aggression is charged, authorisation of the entire Chamber is required; the relevant provision is not yet in force.[10] Second, the Prosecutor may decline to proceed when a situation has been referred or 'triggered' by either the Security Council or by a State Party. Such triggering is similar to what prevails at the *ad hoc* tribunals, with the important distinction that the Prosecutor at the *ad hoc* tribunals has no freedom to decline to proceed. Willingness to pursue cases within the situation assigned to an *ad hoc* tribunal is simply part of the Prosecutor's job description. Should he or she decline to invitation, he or she might as well look for a new job.

At the International Criminal Court, the Prosecutor's decision not to proceed, like the decision to proceed, is subject to a degree of judicial review by the Pre-Trial Chamber.[11] The nature of the judicial review over decisions by the Prosecutor respecting the choice of situations, be they to proceed with an investigation or to decline to proceed, remains a subject of some uncertainty. To date, the Prosecutor has not declined to proceed when a situation has been referred by a State Party or by the Security Council, so the nature of the intervention remains speculative. There have been two decisions that deal with authorisation to proceed with an investigation, both of them favourable to the position of the Prosecutor. Given the positive outcome, there has been no appeal.

## II. Judicial Authorisation for an Investigation

The first authorisation decision by a Pre-Trial Chamber of the International Criminal Court concerned the investigation into post-electoral violence in Kenya. The Court may exercise jurisdiction over the territory of Kenya in accordance with Article 12(2) because Kenya is a State Party to the Rome Statute. In its ruling, Pre-Trial Chamber II described Article 15 as 'one of the most delicate provisions of the Statute'.[12] Noting that it was 'the product of extensive debates and division of views throughout the drafting process and until the end of the Rome Conference', the Chamber explained that '[t]he main point of controversy was whether the

---

[9] ICC Statute, art 15(3).
[10] International Criminal Court, Assembly of States Parties, Resolution RC/Res.6 on the Crime of Aggression <http://www.icc-cpi.int/iccdocs/asp_docs/Resolutions/RC-Res.6-ENG.pdf> last accessed 20 December 2011, Annex I, art 15*bis*(8).
[11] ICC Statute, art 53.
[12] *Situation in the Republic of Kenya* (Decision Pursuant to Article 15 of the Rome Statute on the Authorization of an Investigation into the Situation in the Republic of Kenya) ICC-01/09 (31 March 2010) para 17.

Prosecutor should be empowered to trigger the jurisdiction of the Court, of his own motion, in the absence of a referral from a State Party or the Security Council'.[13] The Pre-Trial Chamber noted that there were concerns about 'the risk of politicizing the Court',[14] and said that this was addressed by the procedure set out in Article 15, which imposes the requirement of judicial authorisation. The Chamber said it would conduct its examination 'taking into consideration the sensitive nature and specific purpose of this procedure'.[15] The Chamber noted that the test it was to impose was identical to the one set out in Article 53, which applies when the Prosecutor opts not to proceed, thereby confirming the close relationship between the two provisions. Indeed, it is 'one and the same standard'.[16] The Pre-Trial Chamber said that the purpose of the judicial authorisation required by the Rome Statute was 'to prevent the Court from proceeding with unwarranted, frivolous, or politically motivated investigations that could have a negative effect on its credibility'.[17]

Relating Article 15 to Article 53 enabled the Chamber to rely upon the rather more detailed language of the latter provision in applying the former. Article 15 says that the Pre-Trial Chamber must confirm or reject the Prosecutor's assessment that there is a reasonable basis to proceed with an investigation, but offers no guidance as to the grounds for its analysis. Article 53, on the other hand, sets out three factors that are to be assessed by the Prosecutor in making a determination to proceed with an investigation. First, there must be jurisdiction. Second, the situation must be admissible. Here the two issues identified in Article 17 are brought to bear: complementarity and gravity. The familiar complementarity analysis involves examining whether the relevant national justice system is unwilling or unable to proceed. The reference 'to the insufficiency of gravity is actually an additional safeguard, which prevents the Court from investigating, prosecuting and trying peripheral cases'.[18] The Chamber did not speak of the gravity of the situation but rather it said that 'gravity should be examined against the backdrop of the likely set of cases or "potential case(s)" that would arise from investigating the situation'.[19] In this way, it seemed to blur the distinction between situations and cases. Judge Hans-Peter Kaul dissented from the majority on the issue of jurisdiction. He did not consider that the Prosecutor's submission adequately demonstrated that crimes within the jurisdiction of the Court had been committed.[20]

Of the three main dimensions of the analysis, two lend themselves to a relatively objective assessment. Determining whether the Court has jurisdiction over possible cases and whether the national authorities are active or inactive is not really a

---

[13] Ibid.
[14] Ibid para 18.
[15] Ibid.
[16] Ibid para 23.
[17] Ibid para 32.
[18] Ibid para 56.
[19] Ibid para 58.
[20] *Situation in the Republic of Kenya* (Decision Pursuant to Article 15 of the Rome Statute on the Authorization of an Investigation into the Situation in the Republic of Kenya – Dissenting Opinion of Judge Hans-Peter Kaul) ICC-01/09 (31 March 2010).

matter of degree or nuance. Whether negative or affirmative, there is a clear answer to these two questions, even if reasonable people may disagree on what it is, as indeed was the case with the three judges of the Pre-Trial Chamber. The gravity issue, on the other hand, suggests much more subjectivity. In particular, it lends itself to a comparative perspective. An observer, concerned about the focus of the Court and the use of its precious resources, would want to know not only whether the Situation in Kenya was of sufficient gravity, but also how this compared with other situations crying out for prosecution.

Whether or not something can be judged to be 'serious' is generally determined by setting it alongside matters that are 'less serious' or 'more serious'. But, in the Kenya decision, the Pre-Trial Chamber did not assess whether the Prosecutor had neglected other more important situations that might better meet the text of gravity. In a sense, it attempted to make the gravity determination as objective as possible. But doing so in isolation and without comparison with other situations is far more challenging than looking at jurisdiction and complementarity, both of which can be examined without reference to other situations and without involving policy considerations. Really, in order to determine whether the Situation in Kenya was serious, the judges would have to compare it with other situations elsewhere in the world. But this would involve an examination of the policy of the Office of the Prosecutor, and it was something they were not prepared to undertake.

The second decision on authorisation was issued on 3 October 2011. It concerned the Situation in Côte d'Ivoire. Like the Situation in Kenya, it was related to post-election violence. Jurisdiction of the Court was the result of a declaration formulated by Côte d'Ivoire dated 18 April 2003 pursuant to Article 12(3) of the Statute, a provision that may be invoked by a non-State Party. Côte d'Ivoire has yet to ratify the Rome Statute. The bulk of the decision of Pre-Trial Chamber III was devoted to a rather fastidious study of the elements of the crimes that were charged and the evidence in support, drawing largely upon reports from non-governmental organisations and United Nations monitors. The Chamber concluded that there were 'reasonable grounds' to believe that crimes against humanity and war crimes had been committed during the relevant period. Other jurisdictional matters, such as temporal jurisdiction, were considered more summarily. The same was true for the complementarity issue. As for gravity, the Chamber devoted only a few perfunctory paragraphs in this 86-page ruling to the subject. That criterion was satisfactory answered, according to the Chamber, because of the Prosecutor's plan to charge 'high-ranking political and military figures who allegedly played a role in the violence'.[21]

Presiding Judge Silvia Fernandez issued a separate and partially dissenting opinion.[22] She said she agreed with the majority that authorisation to the Prosecutor

---

[21] *Situation in the Republic of Côte d'Ivoire* (Decision Pursuant to Article 15 of the Rome Statute on the Authorisation of an Investigation into the Situation in the Republic of Côte d'Ivoire) ICC-02/11 (3 October 2011) para 205.

[22] *Situation in the Republic of Côte d'Ivoire* (Judge Fernandez de Gurmendi's Separate and Partially Dissenting Opinion to the Decision Pursuant to Article 15 of the Rome Statute

should be granted, but felt that the bar may have been set too high. According to Judge Fernandez, the decision exceeded the supervisory role granted to the Chamber under Article 15 of the Statute and 'the Chamber's proper (and limited) function in relation to the commencement of an investigation and case selection within a situation'.[23] She invoked the words of Pre-Trial Chamber II in the Kenya decision about Article 15 being 'one of the most delicate provisions of the Statute', adding that 'until the end of the Rome Conference, the main point of controversy was whether the Prosecutor should be empowered to trigger the jurisdiction of the Court on its own motion'.[24] Judge Fernandez was herself a delegate to the Rome Conference; indeed, she served as one of three vice-presidents of the Committee of the Whole and chaired the Working Group on Procedural Matters.[25]

According to Judge Fernandez:

> By the end of the negotiations, there was growing recognition that there were some real risks of abuse of power and that some checks and balances were needed, both in order to prevent arbitrary decisions taken in a solitary fashion by the Prosecutor, and to help insulate the Prosecutor from external pressure. In the last session of the Preparatory Committee held in April 1998, Argentina and Germany proposed a system of judicial control, to be exercised by the Pre-trial Chamber, over the Prosecutor's decision to open an investigation. With minor changes introduced during the last days of the Rome Conference, the proposal became the current form of Article 15 of the Statute.[26]

Judge Fernandez was a member of the delegation of Argentina at the Rome Conference and in prior sessions of the Preparatory Committee. She continued:

> It is clear from the negotiating history that the drafters wanted to grant a supervisory role to the Pre-trial Chamber solely over the intention of the Prosecutor to initiate an investigation. This supervisory role was intended to provide judicial 'internal' safeguards for the Prosecutor's decision and compensate for the absence of a referral from external actors.[27]

---

on the Authorisation of an Investigation into the Situation in the Republic of Côte d'Ivoire) ICC-02/11 (3 October 2011).

[23] Ibid para 5.
[24] Ibid para 7.
[25] Final Act of the United Nations Diplomatic Conference of Plenipotentiaries on the Establishment of an International Criminal Court, A/CONF.183/13 (Vol I), 67 para 19.
[26] *Situation in the Republic of Côte d'Ivoire* (Judge Fernandez de Gurmendi's Separate and Partially Dissenting Opinion to the Decision Pursuant to Article 15 of the Rome Statute on the Authorisation of an Investigation into the Situation in the Republic of Côte d'Ivoire) ICC-02/11 (3 October 2011) para 8.
[27] Ibid para 9.

She recalled that the judicial review of the Prosecutor's determination had a 'limited purpose' that should be 'guided by the underlying purpose of providing a judicial safeguard against frivolous or politically-motivated charges'.[28] It is confined 'to ascertain[ing] the accuracy of the statement of facts and reasons of law advanced by the Prosecutor with regard to crimes and incidents identified in his own request and determin[ing], on this basis, whether the requirements of Article 53 of the Statute are met'.[29]

Judge Fernandez's views apparently did not rally her two colleagues, and perhaps they represent an extremely narrow interpretation of Article 15 that is not shared by other judges of the Court. Be that as it may, even the apparently broader construction of the scope of judicial review taken by the majorities in both the Côte d'Ivoire and Kenya authorisation decisions confirms that the Prosecutor's discretion in this respect is quite vast. The supervisory role of the Chambers does not address the policy considerations upon which the Prosecutor has acted. How could they, given that the Chambers do not have either the information or the expertise to assess this dimension? The two decisions of the Pre-Trial Chambers simply confirm that the wisdom of proceeding in one situation or another remains the sole prerogative of the Prosecutor and is not subject to any real form of judicial oversight. Essentially, they mimic the discussion that takes place when Pre-Trial Chambers consider applications for the issuance of arrest warrants, except that the evidentiary standard is arguably lower. Article 15 requires the Prosecutor to show a 'reasonable basis' whereas Article 58 speaks of 'reasonable grounds'. In practice, the two notions are virtually indistinguishable; the best anyone can do is say the former is slightly lower than the latter, and vice versa.

## III. A Bulwark Against 'Politicisation'

Both Pre-Trial Chambers invoked the bugbear of 'politicisation'. The prevailing view, it seems, is that the purpose of the judicial review of the Prosecutor's application for authorisation to proceed with an investigation is to avoid, reduce or minimise 'politicisation'. Yet, neither Pre-Trial Chamber gave any consideration to what the Prosecutor's policy might be. The judges did not inquire at all into the possibility that the Prosecutor might be pursuing a policy and then consider whether it might discredit the Court. Their view seemed to be that the task is purely judicial. But if that is the case, how can this judicial review actually determine whether or not there is any 'politicisation'?

Nevertheless, the complaint that the Prosecutor is 'politicised' has come from other quarters. For example, the Prosecutor's policies have been questioned by

---

[28] Ibid para 16.
[29] Ibid para 28.

the African Union and by several individual African states.[30] Concern has been expressed that the Prosecutor is unfairly focussing attention on African states. It is a fact that the only investigations, arrest warrants and prosecutions undertaken by the Court in its first decade of operations concern central and northern Africa. Seven African States are object of prosecutions, yet there are none on any other continent. At first blush, this looks like a policy. It is hardly unreasonable for the African Union to express its concern about 'politicisation'. There may well be a good and reasonable explanation, of course. But if the role of the Pre-Trial Chamber is to act as a bulwark against 'politicisation', perhaps it should consider the possibility that there is a policy, and an inappropriate one, that targets African States? There is a paradox in the reasoning of the Pre-Trial Chambers. On the one hand, they purport to conduct an exercise aimed at preventing 'politicisation' but in reality they fail to consider the issue at all, confining their examination to a superficial analysis of the definitions of crimes, the sufficiency of the evidence, the inadequacy of domestic prosecutions and the importance of the potential suspects.

Despite the indications of the Pre-Trial Chambers, nothing in the text of Article 15 of the Rome Statute suggests that they are to address the issue of 'politicisation'. The framework of judicial review is described in this manner:

> If the Pre-Trial Chamber, upon examination of the request and the supporting material, considers that there is a reasonable basis to proceed with an investigation, and that the case appears to fall within the jurisdiction of the Court, it shall authorize the commencement of the investigation, without prejudice to subsequent determinations by the Court with regard to the jurisdiction and admissibility of a case.[31]

The notion that this is about 'politicization' is not derived from a textual or even a teleological method of interpretation. Such interpretative approaches would actually suggest that the judicial review is essentially analogous to that conducted at the stage of review of an arrest warrant and confirmation of the document containing the charges. The idea that Article 15(4) is designed to address 'politicisation' is based exclusively on the *travaux préparatoires* of the Rome Statute, generously enriched of course by the memories of those who were present at the 1998 Conference. It is not insignificant that both of the Pre-Trial Chambers, in Kenya and Côte d'Ivoire, included judges who had, in earlier diplomatic careers, participated in the negotiations at the Rome Conference. Indeed, the decisive amendment to draft article 15 to which Judge Fernandez made reference in her separate and dissenting opinion was proposed jointly by Germany and Argentina. Judge Hans-Peter Kaul of Pre-Trial Chamber II was a member of the German delegation to the Rome Conference, while Judge Silvia Fernandez of Pre-Trial Chamber III was a member of the Argentinean delegation.

---

[30] See for example African Union, *Decision on the Implementation of the Assembly Decisions on the International Criminal Court*, Doc EX.CL/670(XIX), Assembly/AU/Dec.366 (XVII), para 6.

[31] ICC Statute, art 15(4).

Probably, Germany and Argentina would have preferred to have no judicial review of the Prosecutor's determination. Article 15(4) was a concession that they introduced to make the idea of a *proprio motu* Prosecutor more palatable to staunch adversaries of the entire concept, such as the United States. This explains the minimalist approach of Judge Fernandez to the construction of Article 15(4). It is perhaps of interest to recall the early discussions on the issue, which took place during sessions of the Preparatory Committee in 1996. The idea of an independent or *proprio motu* prosecutor had begun to emerge. It was a radical innovation, a departure from anything that had previously been present in international criminal justice. No such thing had been contemplated by the International Law Commission in the draft statute it proposed to the General Assembly in 1994. The report of the Preparatory Committee explains:

> Some delegations found the role of the Prosecutor, under article 25, too restricted. In their view, States or the Security Council, for a variety of political reasons, would be unlikely to lodge a complaint. The Prosecutor should therefore be empowered to initiate investigations ex officio or on the basis of information obtained from any source. It was noted that the Prosecutors of the two existing *ad hoc* tribunals were granted such rights; there was no reason to deny the same power to the Prosecutor of this Court. Hence the suggestion to add a new paragraph to article 25 along the lines of article 18(1) of the Statute of the Tribunal for the former Yugoslavia and article 17(1) of the Statute of the Tribunal for Rwanda. Under this system, therefore, individuals would also be able to lodge complaints.
>
> In order to prevent any abuse of the process by any of the triggering parties, a procedure was proposed requiring that in case a complaint was lodged by a State or an individual or initiated by the Prosecutor, the Prosecutor would first have to satisfy himself or herself that a *prima facie* case against an individual obtained and the requirements of admissibility had been satisfied. The Prosecutor would then have to present the matter to a chamber of the Court (which would not ultimately try the case) and inform all interested States so that they would have the opportunity to participate in the proceedings. In this respect the indictment chamber was considered as the appropriate chamber. The chamber, upon a hearing, would decide whether the matter should be pursued by the Prosecutor or the case should be dropped. Up to this point, the procedure would be in camera and confidential, thus preventing any publicity about the case and protecting the interest of the States.[32]

---

[32] Report of the Preparatory Committee on the Establishment of an International Criminal Court, Volume I (Proceedings of the Preparatory Committee during March–April and August 1996), UN Doc A/51/22, paras 149–150.

These paragraphs in the 1996 Report point to the genesis of Article 15(4). Its objective was to prevent 'abuse of process by any of the triggering parties'.

If indeed the purpose of Article 15(4) is to provide a check on politicisation, all that can be said is that it does not provide a very adequate framework. In national courts, where judicial review allows for consideration of improper exercise of discretion, the inquiry is generally much broader. To begin with, it is hard to imagine how this can be done in an *ex parte* framework, where the alleged victim of such abuse is not present and cannot submit evidence to make out the argument. In a domestic setting, judicial review addressing prosecutorial abuse will be at the initiative of the defendant. It can hardly be expected that, at the authorisation stage, the Prosecutor will provide the Pre-Trial Chamber with evidence to show that his or her intentions are abusive, vexatious or improper. Furthermore, it is surely possible for a prosecution to be 'politicised' yet at the same time respond to the mechanistic criteria of jurisdiction and admissibility. The formalist inquiry of the Pre-Trial Chamber is not really able to fulfil the task that it is claimed was intended by the drafters at Rome when they established this mechanism of judicial review.

The fable at the beginning of this chapter was meant to encourage reflection on the inevitability of politicisation when a judicial mechanism with extremely limited resources is forced to choose from an enormous number of potential situations and cases for prosecution. It cannot be otherwise. Ineluctably, the Prosecutor must select some situations for attention and, consequently, put others to the side. The first ICC Prosecutor has very occasionally spoken of situations where he has chosen not to proceed. Perhaps he chose not to proceed in other situations, such as Gaza, but found it expedient to proclaim that he had not yet made up his mind.

In 2005, after arrest warrants for five Ugandan rebel leaders were issued, he explained why he had not sought to prosecute government military leaders as well. The Prosecutor was answering criticism from international non-governmental organisations that he was addressing only one side in the conflict.[33] In a speech to legal advisors of Ministries of Foreign Affairs, delivered in New York on 24 October 2005, the Prosecutor said:

> In Uganda, the criterion for selection of the first case was gravity. We analysed the gravity of all crimes in Northern Uganda committed by all groups – the LRA, the UPDF and other forces. Our investigations indicated that the crimes committed by the LRA were of dramatically higher gravity. We therefore started with an investigation of the LRA. At the same time, we have continued to collect information on allegations concerning all other groups, to determine whether other

---

[33] See for example Amnesty International, *Uganda: First ever arrest warrants by International Criminal Court – A First Step Towards Addressing Impunity*, 14 October 2005, AI Index: AFR 59/008/2005 <http://www.iccnow.org/documents/AI_ugandaarrests_14oct05.pdf> last accessed 20 December 2011; Human Rights Watch, *ICC Takes Decisive Step for Justice in Uganda*, 14 October 2005 <http://iccnow.org/documents/HRW_Ugandaarrests_14octr05.pdf> last accessed 20 December 2011.

crimes meet the stringent thresholds of the Statute and our policy are met.³⁴

A month later, in his address to the Assembly of States Parties, the Prosecutor stated:

> In Uganda, we examined information concerning all groups that had committed crimes in the region. We selected our first case based on gravity. Between July 2002 and June 2004, the Lord's Resistance Army (LRA) was allegedly responsible for at least 2200 killings and 3200 abductions in over 850 attacks. It was clear that we must start with the LRA.³⁵

The Prosecutor returned to this quantitative approach in February 2006, when he issued a public letter explaining his decision not to proceed against British nationals for war crimes committed in Iraq. The Prosecutor explained that during his analysis of the Situation in Iraq following the invasion by the United Kingdom and the United States,

> allegations came to light in the media concerning incidents of mistreatment of detainees and wilful killing of civilians. General allegations included brutality against persons upon capture and initial custody, causing death or serious injury. In addition, there were incidents in which civilians were killed during policing operations in the occupation phase. After analyzing all the available information, it was concluded that there was a reasonable basis to believe that crimes within the jurisdiction of the Court had been committed, namely wilful killing and inhuman treatment. The information available at this time supports a reasonable basis for an estimated 4 to 12 victims of wilful killing and a limited number of victims of inhuman treatment, totalling in all less than 20 persons.³⁶

---

³⁴ International Criminal Court, Statement by Luis Moreno-Ocampo, Prosecutor of the International Criminal Court, Informal meeting of Legal Advisors of Ministries of Foreign Affairs (New York 24 October 2005)

<http://212.159.242.181/iccdocs/asp_docs/library/organs/otp/speeches/LMO_20051024_English.pdf> last accessed 20 December 2011, 7.

³⁵ International Criminal Court, Statement by Luis Moreno-Ocampo, Prosecutor of the International Criminal Court, Fourth Session of the Assembly of States Parties, 28 November – 3 December 2005 (The Hague 28 November 2005)

<http://www.iccnow.org/documents/ProsecutorMorenoOcampo_Opening_28Nov05.pdf> last accessed 20 December 2011, 2.

³⁶ International Criminal Court, Office of the Prosecutor, Letter of the Prosecutor dated 9 February 2006 <http://www.icc-cpi.int/NR/rdonlyres/04D143C8-19FB-466C-AB77-4CDB2FDEBEF7/143682/OTP_letter_to_senders_re_Iraq_9_February_2006.pdf> last accessed 20 December 2011, 7–8.

The Prosecutor went on to consider the 'gravity' dimension of the admissibility determination.

> The Office considers various factors in assessing gravity. A key consideration is the number of victims of particularly serious crimes, such as wilful killing or rape. The number of potential victims of crimes within the jurisdiction of the Court in this situation – 4 to 12 victims of wilful killing and a limited number of victims of inhuman treatment – was of a different order than the number of victims found in other situations under investigation or analysis by the Office. It is worth bearing in mind that the OTP is currently investigating three situations involving long-running conflicts in Northern Uganda, the Democratic Republic of Congo and Darfur. Each of the three situations under investigation involves thousands of wilful killings as well as intentional and large-scale sexual violence and abductions. Collectively, they have resulted in the displacement of more than 5 million people. Other situations under analysis also feature hundreds or thousands of such crimes. Taking into account all the considerations, the situation did not appear to meet the required threshold of the Statute.[37]

Although his analysis did not hinge upon this point, the Prosecutor also pointed out that 'national proceedings had been initiated with respect to each of the relevant incidents',[38] thus answering the other prong of the admissibility assessment. It is worth noting, however, that even if British courts were proceeding on these complaints at the time of the Prosecutor's letter, they do not appear to have been effective and have not resulted in convictions.[39] British atrocities in Iraq have led to important rulings of the European Court of Human Rights that confirm the inadequacies of the national justice system.[40]

The Prosecutor's reduction of the gravity debate to a strictly quantitative matter was never particularly convincing. Later, the Prosecutor decided to proceed in situations where the numbers were low and, indeed, comparable in magnitude to those he had invoked with respect to Iraq. Thus, in 2008 he initiated a prosecution against two rebel leaders in Darfur charging them with responsibility for the deaths of 12 African Union peacekeepers and causing serious injury to another eight. Conscious of the inconsistency, he explained, in his application for issuance of a summons to appear, that intentional attacks on peacekeepers were 'exceptional [sic] serious offences which "strike at the very heart of the international legal system established for the purpose of maintaining international peace and security"'.[41]

---

[37] Ibid 8–9.
[38] Ibid 10.
[39] See for example M Evans, 'Case Collapses' *The Times* (London 15 February 2007).
[40] *Al-Skeini et al v United Kingdom* (Judgment) App No 55721/07 (7 July 2011).
[41] *Situation in Darfur, Sudan* (Summary of the Prosecutor's Application under Article 58) ICC-02/05 (20 November 2008) para 7, citing the Commentary of the International Law

Fair enough, but couldn't one say the same thing about wilful killing and inhuman treatment of civilians, especially when the crimes are perpetrated in the context of a war of aggression? Although at the time somewhat inchoate in its formulation, even in 2003 the crime of aggression came within the jurisdiction of the International Criminal Court, pursuant to Article 5(1) of the Rome Statute.

## IV. Codifying the Gravity Assessment

The Rome Statute provides little if any guidance here. It probably would have been impossible for States Parties to reach agreement on the criteria to be employed. A subsequent instrument negotiated by the States Parties, the Rules of Procedure and Evidence, does nothing to fill the void. Even before Luis Moreno-Ocampo took office as the first Prosecutor of the International Criminal Court, the employees of his Office prepared draft Regulations of the Office of the Prosecutor that attempted to codify the process by which 'situations' were to be selected among the many deserving possibilities.[42] These draft regulations naïvely approached the matter of selection of situations in a manner that suggested the Prosecutor would proceed with everything that was admissible. There was a complex procedure, involving 'evaluation teams' and a 'draft investigation plan', leading to a decision by the Prosecutor. Nothing indicated the grounds on which the Prosecutor would make the determination, although there was an intriguing reference to his or her 'inherent powers'. But the Prosecutor did not adopt the draft. Years later, he proclaimed a new and much streamlined version of the Regulations that vaguely referred to the 'seriousness of the information', 'jurisdiction, admissibility (including gravity), as well as the interests of justice'. These were the factors to be assessed in identifying the 'situations' that the Prosecutor would target. It said that in assessing gravity, 'various factors including their scale, nature, manner of commission, and impact' were to be taken into account.[43]

The word gravity was used only once in the 2003 draft regulations. Probably at the time nobody in the Office of the Prosecutor thought that the concept of 'gravity' was very significant in the selection of situations or of cases. The term 'gravity', which appears in the Statute in two places relevant to the selection of cases and situations, did not figure in any significant manner in the early pronouncements

---

Commission to Article 19 of the Final Draft Code of Crimes Against the Peace and Security of Mankind (UN Doc A/51/10).

[42] International Criminal Court, Office of the Prosecutor, Draft Regulations of the Office of the Prosecutor (3 June 2003) <http://www.jura.uni-muenchen.de/fakultaet/lehrstuehle/satzger/materialien/istghdrre.pdf> last accessed 20 December 2011.

[43] International Criminal Court, Office of the Prosecutor, Regulations of the Office of the Prosecutor, ICC-BD/05-01-09 <http://www.icc-cpi.int/NR/rdonlyres/FFF97111-ECD6-40B5-9CDA-792BCBE1E695/280253/ICCBD050109ENG.pdf> last accessed 20 December 2011, Regulation 29.

of the Office of the Prosecutor. Up to that time, academic writers on the Rome Statute had generally failed to view the concept of 'gravity' as being particularly relevant to the exercise of prosecutorial discretion. For example, the authoritative two-volume commentary on the *Rome Statute*, edited by Antonio Cassese, Paola Gaeta and John Jones, is essentially silent on the issue. The word 'gravity' does not even appear in the index to the commentary, in striking contrast with the word 'complementarity', which takes the best part of a page in the index.[44] There is no reference to 'gravity' within the sub-index to admissibility.[45] The chapters in the commentary on admissibility consider the concept as if was synonymous with complementarity.[46] Neglect of the gravity criterion changed in late 2005, when the Prosecutor invoked it in order to explain his decision to proceed against the leaders of the Lord's Resistance Army in Uganda rather than against those of the government forces. He returned to the theme in early 2006 so as to justify a decision not to proceed against British nationals with respect to the conflict in Iraq.

The reasoning with respect to Iraq, cited above, remains unconvincing. Any reasonable observer knows that since the invasion by the United Kingdom and the United States in 2003, and largely as a consequence, Iraq has been the scene of massive human rights violations. At a minimum tens of thousands of innocent civilians have been killed and perhaps millions have been displaced. By setting specific acts attributable to British troops of which he had evidence, rather than the war as a whole, alongside general reports of victimisation in other conflicts in central Africa, the Prosecutor was comparing apples and oranges. The fallacy of the comparison between Iraq and central Africa became clear within a matter of days, when Moreno-Ocampo announced the arrest of the Court's first prisoner, Thomas Lubanga. A Congolese warlord, Lubanga was not charged with the murders, abductions and sexual violence that the Prosecutor had invoked in his comparison with the British conduct in Iraq. Lubanga was accused only with the recruitment of child soldiers within the context of a civil war. Was that more serious than the murder and ill-treatment of civilians by British soldiers engaged in a war of aggression?

Many suspected that Moreno-Ocampo was actually trying to steer clear of a confrontation with one or two major powers. Sometimes, people around the Court would mutter such excuses under their breath, as if it was an embarrassing secret. Perhaps they hadn't suspected that much of the world is familiar with double-standards by which the South is judged differently than the North. All that the Prosecutor's decision did was confirm suspicions that the Court was not the politically neutral body its proponents had bragged about. In addition to being an influential member of the Court, the United Kingdom is also a permanent member of the Security Council. In contrast, the Democratic Republic of the Congo was a soft target for the Court's activities. It was also a willing one, in a sense, to the

---

[44] A Cassese, P Gaeta and JRWD Jones (eds) *The Rome Statute of the International Criminal Court: A Commentary* (OUP, Oxford 2002) 1946.
[45] Ibid 1939.
[46] Ibid 667–731.

extent that the Prosecutor appeared to be interested only in rebel groups rather than government forces, much as he had been in neighbouring Uganda.

The contrived reasoning about gravity also kept the Prosecutor sweet with the Americans, who would not have been keen about prosecutions relating to the behaviour of their principal military ally in the Iraq invasion. Indeed, it was about this time that the United States began to warm to the International Criminal Court. Years later, the Wikileaks website published a revealing confidential document, written in July 2003, from an American diplomat assessing the Prosecutor's attitude towards Iraq. 'Ocampo has said that he was looking at the actions of British forces in Iraq -- which ... led a British ICTY prosecutor nearly to fall off his chair', said the dispatch. 'Privately, Ocampo has said that he wishes to dispose of Iraq issues (i.e. not to investigate them).'[47]

## Conclusion: The Inevitability of 'Politicisation'

In a domestic criminal justice system where all serious crimes against the person are investigated and prosecuted, the charge that situations, cases, crimes and suspects are politically selected will be difficult to sustain. But when criminal justice, be it national or international, can only deal with a handful of cases over which the courts have jurisdiction and which are admissible, questions necessarily arise about the basis upon which the targets for prosecution are selected. It is rarely a challenge to explain that the cases selected for prosecution are 'serious'. But it is often not at all obvious why they are *more* serious than other cases which are effectively ignored.

How then can the decisions of the Prosecutor over the first nine years of activity of the Court be explained? Undoubtedly the situations and cases selected are serious, but so are those where there has been no interest or activity. Surely a policy of sorts must be at work. In this sense, prosecution is 'politicised'. But it is hard to determine the policy when the Prosecutor denies that one exists and the Pre-Trial Chambers decline to examine if this really is the case. Whatever the agenda may be, it certainly is hidden.

As an experiment, ask every individual in a room full of people to write the single 'situation' that they think is most deserving of international justice. Inevitably, the responses will vary greatly. If victims of atrocities are present, they will almost invariably select the situations that concern them. Understandably, victims cannot easily make such choices with objectivity. But even those who are more detached will usually indicate the countries, regions and types of crime that, for one reason or another, often related to their personal interests and experiences, are their greatest concern: Iraq, Gaza, Sri Lanka, Colombia, child soldiers, sexual violence,

---

[47] Quoted in A Hirsch, 'Wikileaks Cables Lay Bare US Hostility to International Criminal Court' *The Guardian* (London 17 December 2010) <http://www.guardian.co.uk/law/2010/dec/17/wikileaks-us-international-criminal-court> last accessed 20 December 2011.

cluster munitions, hate propaganda. Each situation has its merits, each manifests gravity, and each has a legitimate claim to be at the top of the list. But why is the individual determination made by the Prosecutor of the International Criminal Court any more legitimate than that of one of the individuals in this casual survey?

Perhaps the reason why the *ad hoc* tribunals have been so productive and effective is the relative transparency of the policy that underpins them. They were created by a political body and given a political task, to bring peace to a troubled land. There was never any indulgence in a pretence that their creation resulted from the impartial evaluation of objective factors. Albeit somewhat lacking at the moment of their establishment, gradually a consensus grew around their importance. When senior officials like Milošević were captured and brought before the Yugoslavia Tribunal, there was broad agreement in the region concerned that this was a desirable outcome. In other words, far from undermining success, 'politicisation' contributed to it.

As it enters its second decade, the International Criminal Court is still searching for the correct path. It may be that the architects of the Rome Statute, who campaigned for an independent prosecutor immunised against political factors, had a dream that was unrealistic, or at any rate premature. Their model works when the system can ensure that all deserving cases are brought to justice. But it struggles when the system can only address a very limited number of such cases. As long as the Court pretends that such decisions are divorced from policy considerations, its effectiveness is weak and relatively inconsequential. This becomes apparent when it is compared with overtly politicised bodies – the *ad hoc* tribunals – whose impressive success cannot be gainsaid.

To conclude, perhaps the medicine for the ailing International Criminal Court is not less politics but more. Once the inevitability of 'politicisation' is acknowledged, it can address the choices that must be made in a more transparent and therefore more credible manner. The consensus that will result from commitment to the policy objectives of a Prosecutor will strengthen international justice, not weaken it.

# Palestine and the Politics of International Criminal Justice

Michael Kearney and John Reynolds

On 3 April 2012, the Office of the Prosecutor of the International Criminal Court issued a statement declining jurisdiction over Palestine.[1] The decision referred to the continued lack of clarity over the status of Palestine on the international legal stage. Although long contested in terms of rhetoric and politics, Palestine's status had lain dormant from the perspective of international law since the United Nations' 1947 Partition Resolution;[2] some significant attention following the Palestinian Declaration of Independence in 1988 notwithstanding.[3] From 2002, the primary vehicle for the resolution of the status of the Palestinian territory occupied by Israel since 1967 became the 'Quartet', comprised of the United States, the European Union, Russia and the UN. Working with the respective authorities representing Israelis and Palestinians, their shared goal was the resolution of the conflict through the establishment and recognition of 'an independent, viable, sovereign Palestinian state, living in peace and security alongside Israel'.[4]

The mechanisms of the Quartet revolved around the facilitation of negotiations between the Palestinian Authority and Israel, and were for all intents and purposes entirely detached from the rule or framework of international law. Respect for human rights and commitments to the purposes and principles of the UN were a recurring refrain when addressing the preconditions to be met by the Palestinian side, yet there was no indication of intent to bring an end to conflict or occupation by reference to the legal rights and obligations accruing to Israel, Palestine, third states or international organisations. International law was – as during previous rounds of

---

[1] International Criminal Court (Office of the Prosecutor) 'Situation in Palestine' (3 April 2012).
[2] UNGA Res 181(II) (29 November 1947), UN Doc A/RES/181(II).
[3] Palestine National Council, Declaration of Independence (15 November 1988), UN Doc A/43/827-S/20278 (18 November 1988).
[4] UN Security Council, Letter dated 7 May 2003 from the Secretary-General Addressed to the President of the Security Council, 'A Performance-Based Roadmap to a Permanent Two-State Solution to the Israeli-Palestinian Conflict' (30 April 2003), UN Doc S/2003/529.

negotiations throughout the 1990s – conspicuous by its absence. Political coercion, compromise and deferral of hard 'decisions' on final status issues remained the order of the day. Following the outbreak of the Palestinian uprising known as the al-Aqsa *intifada* in 2000, Israel's occupation became ever more entrenched. As their disenfranchisement deepened, Palestinians turned increasingly to international law as an alternative means for asserting their rights.

With the potential role of the International Criminal Court in Palestine and Israel in mind, this chapter seeks to reflect on how Palestinian efforts at engaging with the international legal framework have to date been repeatedly stymied. The first section will consider various efforts of the Palestine Liberation Organisation (PLO) to accede to international treaties and to participate in the activities of the UN, as well as the response of various states to initiatives such as the 2003 request for an advisory opinion from the International Court of Justice on the legal consequences of Israel's construction of the Wall in the occupied West Bank. This will demonstrate that, at least on the part of those states generally considered as apologists for Israel's occupation of Palestinian territory, there has been a sustained effort towards excluding the application of legal norms when it comes to Palestinian rights and Israeli obligations. The second and third parts of the chapter discuss how this tendency, whereby the politics of compromise trump the rights of Palestinians as set forth in international law, has played out around the issue of Palestine's efforts at granting jurisdiction over its territory to the International Criminal Court.

Underlying any discussion of Palestine is the question of its status: whether Palestine is a state or not determines the extent to which it can engage with international law, both as a subject and as an instigator. This remains the case irrespective of whether Palestinian self-determination is achieved; that is to say, if Palestine is recognised as a state, yet Palestinian territory remains subject to Israeli occupation, its lack of independence will necessarily colour but not preclude Palestine's rights and duties under the international legal framework. Indeed, recognition as a state will allow full and proper recourse by Palestinians to the organs of the UN, the International Court of Justice and the International Criminal Court. Even short of formal acceptance into the international community of states, nascent Palestinian engagement with international law has been identified as a major cause for concern by Israel. As noted in January 2010 by Israel's Deputy Foreign Minister Danny Ayalon, confronting Palestinian engagement with the framework of international law should be one of Israel's foreign policy priorities 'over the coming decade'.[5] Referring to past attacks against Israel, he claimed that while military, economic and terrorist threats since the 1960s had all failed, 'now we see the brunt, which is political warfare – political and legal warfare … Today the trenches are in Geneva in the Council of Human Rights, or in New York in the

---

[5] D Ayalon, 'Challenges for Israeli Foreign Policy' (Address by Deputy Foreign Minister Danny Ayalon at the Israel Council on Foreign Relations, Jerusalem, 6 January 2010) <http://www.mfa.gov.il/MFA/About+the+Ministry/Deputy_Foreign_Minister/Speeches/DepFM_Ayalon_Challenges_Israeli_Foreign_Policy_6-Jan-2010.htm> last accessed 15 May 2012.

General Assembly, or in the Security Council, or in the Hague, the ICJ'.⁶ Keeping this sentiment in mind, it is essential to again note that considering the question of Palestine through the prism of international law and legal institutions inevitably requires consideration of the political. Few today suggest that any simple law/politics binary of distinction exists within the international legal framework.

## I. Towards Legitimacy: Palestinian Engagement with International Law

Since the establishment of the Palestinian Authority (PA) in the wake of negotiations between the PLO and Israel in the early 1990s, the international community has operated along the lines that the PA is the representative body of a Palestinian 'state in waiting'. No longer dismissed as merely the front for a terrorist organisation following the PLO's recognition of Israel in 1988, engagement in institution-building in the occupied Palestinian territory, and close diplomatic and security cooperation with the European Union and the United States, as well as with Israel, resulted in Palestine emerging as an international actor without significant controversy, and in many respects acting as a *de facto* state entity. Palestine was admitted into the International Olympic Committee in 1995 and added as a member of the Fédération Internationale de Football Association (FIFA) in 1998. The Internet Corporation for Assigned Names and Numbers (ICANN) provided Palestine with an Internet suffix and Palestinian phones received a national prefix. Palestinian Authority-issued passports are accepted internationally, while taxation and trading regimes were formalised by the PA in agreements with the EU and in bilateral agreements with individual states.

Concomitantly, as it appeared to be developing as a legal personality on the international stage, Palestine was itself increasingly fragmented politically and geographically. From the inception of the PLO–Israel negotiations in Madrid in 1991, expansionist Israeli settlement activity was increasingly promoted and funded by successive Israeli governments, keen to gain control over as much West Bank territory as possible beneath the convenient veil of a stuttering peace process. From a settler population of 227,600 in 1991, the number of Israelis living in the West Bank, including East Jerusalem, almost doubled to 443,303 by 2005.⁷ Palestine's elevated status on the international stage was in stark contrast to the conditions of Palestinians on the ground, and an initial enthusiasm for peace negotiations turned to despair at deteriorating human rights standards and increased Israeli military, civilian and administrative presence in the West Bank and Jerusalem.

---

⁶ Ibid.
⁷ Foundation for Middle East Peace, *Statistics and Tables: Comprehensive Settlement Population 1972–2009* <http://www.fmep.org/settlement_info/settlement-info-and-tables/stats-data/comprehensive-settlement-population-1972-2006> last accessed 15 May 2012.

Parliamentary elections for the Palestinian Legislative Council in January 2006 saw Hamas win out over rivals Fateh, an outcome that was swiftly punished by the international community. External funding for its civil service and institutions, upon which the PA is reliant, was suspended, while Israel withheld customs revenues that it collected on behalf of the Palestinians. The western world effectively subjected the Palestinian Authority to a diplomatic boycott and economic sanctions, demanding that Hamas either abandon the policies on which it had campaigned and fulfil imposed preconditions, or watch as Palestine's burgeoning international legitimacy was dismantled. The compromise offered to the international community by the creation of a national unity government in February 2007 failed to return the Palestinians from the diplomatic cold, amid growing humanitarian and political crises. The shock to Fateh of losing its position of dominance, and the animosity shown by external donors towards Hamas, added fuel to the fire of previously existing tensions and led to a low-intensity but deeply significant internal conflict. The outcome was the further territorial and societal fragmentation of Palestine that left Hamas as the *de facto* authority within the Gaza Strip, while Fateh, assisted by Israeli military action against Hamas political leaders and bolstered by US training of its security forces,[8] retained control of Palestinian urban areas in the West Bank.

With Hamas excluded and Fateh regaining command of the Palestinian Authority, the international community moved ahead with the aim of securing a Palestinian state that could join the United Nations. The PA was instructed to clean up corruption, train and discipline its police and security forces, practice 'good governance', and continue the process of institution-building. By keeping a tight line on Hamas and continuing to negotiate with Israel, the Fateh-controlled PA was assured that the international community would stand by them and ensure that, with certain compromises, an independent Palestinian state would be recognised and supported by the international community. While the preference of the western powers for a pliable political process rather than one impelled by law is clear, another layer of the state-building methodology pursued within that process reveals itself through the ostracism of Hamas and the reinforcement of the clout

---

[8] US security assistance has been extended to the Palestinian Authority since its inception, initially on a covert and ad hoc basis, but openly through direct financial, personnel and training support since 2005. See for example: T Weiner, 'CIA Officers, With Israel's Knowledge, Teach Palestinians the Tricks of the Trade' *New York Times* (New York, 5 March 1998); International Institute for Strategic Studies, 'The Palestinian Authority and the CIA' (Vol 4(10), December 1998) <http://www.iiss.org/EasySiteWeb/getresource.axd?AssetID=264&type=full&servicetype=Attachment> last accessed 15 May 2012; S Erlanger, 'US Offers Plan to Strengthen Abbas' *International Herald Tribune* (New York 4 October 2006); B Lia, *Building Arafat's Police: International Police Assistance in the Palestinian Territories after Oslo* (Ithaca Press, London 2007); J Zanotti, 'US Security Assistance to the Palestinian Authority' (Congressional Research Service, Report R40664, 8 January 2010) <http://www.fas.org/sgp/crs/mideast/R40664.pdf> last accessed 15 May 2012; N Thrall, 'Our Man in Palestine' *New York Review of Books* (New York 14 October 2010).

of a Fateh-led PA security force; that is, the preference of a militarised political process over a democratic one.[9]

One thing that the international community could not or would not guarantee to the Palestinians was that Israel would follow through on the deal to which it was assumed to have agreed. Former Israeli Prime Minister Ehud Olmert frequently asserted his government's commitment to an independent Palestinian state, citing the fear of an anti-apartheid-style civil rights movement developing throughout historic Palestine[10] if a state within the 1967 territories were not to be facilitated.[11] Despite this, the status quo that characterised the conflict at the onset of the al-Aqsa *intifada* has remained unchanged, with the exception that the levels of violence to which Palestinians have been subjected and the scale of Israeli settlements have steadily increased. One notable and ongoing development that has emerged, however haphazard, has been the endeavour to penetrate the political deadlock and satisfy Palestinian aspirations of statehood by recourse to the international legal framework.

A prominent manifestation of such attempts was the Palestinian attempt to accept the jurisdiction of the International Criminal Court in January 2009. This came on the back of Israel's 'Operation Cast Lead' assault on Gaza, in a broader context in which evidence of the commission of war crimes and crimes against humanity, amidst a climate of total impunity, has long been overwhelming. Having been held in a sort of legal purgatory on the doorstep of the Court for more than three years, the Palestinians were turned away in April 2012. Before moving to discuss the various arguments – political and legal – that were raised either advocating for the ICC's acceptance of jurisdiction over Palestine or disputing such a move, it is useful to consider how Palestinian engagement with the international legal framework has fared over the years. In the first instance, it should be recalled that the international community, now represented by the United Nations, bears a special responsibility with respect to Palestine. This was initially a result of the League of Nations Mandate[12] and the UN Partition Resolution,[13] and is now evident in the role the UN has assumed within the Quartet and, more broadly, as the trustee of the international legal framework for the maintenance of international peace and security and the protection and promotion of human rights. The role of the UN with regard to the question of Palestine has been described by the General Assembly as 'a permanent responsibility ... until the question is resolved in all its

---

[9] For further elaboration of this point, see A Crooke, 'Permanent Temporariness' 33(5) *London Review of Books* (London 3 March 2011).

[10] 'Historic Palestine' refers to the territory covered by the League of Nations Mandate for Palestine, encompassing the land over which Israeli statehood was declared in 1948, as well as the remaining Palestinian territory occupied by Israel since 1967.

[11] R McCarthy, 'Israel Risks Apartheid-Like Struggle if Two-State Solution Fails, says Olmert' *Guardian* (London 30 November 2007); see also R McCarthy, 'Barak: Make Peace with Palestinians or Face Apartheid' *Guardian* (London 3 February 2010).

[12] League of Nations, *Mandate for Palestine*, C529 M314 VI (12 August 1922).

[13] UNGA Res 181(II) (29 November 1947), UN Doc A/RES/181(II).

aspects in a satisfactory manner in accordance with international legitimacy'.[14] In the *Wall* Advisory Opinion, the International Court of Justice noted its duty:

> to draw the attention of the General Assembly, to which the present Opinion is addressed, to the need for these efforts to be encouraged with a view to achieving as soon as possible, on the basis of international law, a negotiated solution to the outstanding problems and the establishment of a Palestinian State, existing side by side with Israel and its other neighbours, with peace and security for all in the region.[15]

At the core of Palestinian engagement with an international legal framework that remains essentially state-centric lies the question of Palestinian statehood. The UN in its capacity as a political institution acknowledged this in 1974 by inviting the PLO to participate as an observer at the General Assembly.[16] Given the centrality of the question of Palestine to so much of the work of the General Assembly, it was seen as necessary that the Palestinians themselves have some opportunity to participate and plead their case. Opposition to Palestinian exercise of the right to self-determination prevailed, however, and full UN membership was, and remains, denied. In 1988, the General Assembly decided that the designation 'Palestine' would replace 'PLO' at the UN.[17] This was partly in response to the PLO's compromise, whereby it recognised the state of Israel on the territory held by Israel before the 1967 war, signalling its acceptance that any Palestinian state would be limited to the remaining 22 per cent of historic Palestine occupied by Israel in 1967. The Security Council admitted the Palestinian delegation to sessions of concern to Palestine,[18] prompting some to argue that it thereby 'treated Palestine as a state'.[19] Such an invitation has not been extended in more recent years, however.

Attempting to seize the opportunity to assert Palestinian rights and duties by sharing in the obligations adhering to all states, in June 1989, the PLO made its first significant move of engagement with international law, submitting ratification documents for the Geneva Conventions and their Additional Protocols to Switzerland as the depository state of the Geneva Conventions. This attempted accession was stalled when the Swiss government noted that it was not in a position to decide whether the Palestinian submission could be accepted as an instrument of accession 'due to the incertainty [*sic*] within the international community as to the

---

[14] UNGA Res 57/107 (3 December 2002), UN Doc A/RES/57/107.

[15] Legal Consequences of the Construction of a Wall in the Occupied Palestinian Territories (Advisory Opinion), [2004] ICJ Rep 136, para 162.

[16] UNGA Res 3237 (XXIX) (22 November 1974), UN Doc A/RES/3237/XXIX.

[17] UNGA Res 43/177 (15 December 1988), UN Doc A/RES/43/177.

[18] UNSC (44th Session, 2841st meeting) Official Record (11 January 1989), UN Doc S/PV.2841.

[19] J Quigley, 'The Israel PLO Agreements: Are They Treaties?' (1997) 30 *Cornell Int'l L J* 717, 722. According to the Security Council's rules of procedure, only states are permitted to participate in such session. See UNSC, *Provisional Rules of Procedure*, UN Doc. S/96/Rev.4 (1946), Rule 14.

existence or the non-existence of a State of Palestine'.[20] The strategy of attempting to accede to international treaties was accompanied by a move to elicit membership of UN specialised agencies. Thus, the PLO also applied for membership of the World Health Organization and UNESCO at this time, both of whom similarly deferred decisions on the basis that the status of Palestine as a state remained unclear.[21]

Throughout the following decade or so of political negotiations, compromises and Palestinian institution-building, international law, despite the advocacy of civil society, remained sidelined as Palestine was 'schooled' for independence. By 2003, with the region scarred by violence and impunity, the PLO once again sought to move on the international legal playing field in response to Israel's unilateral construction of a Wall within the occupied West Bank that was further restricting the space for Palestine to exist. Following the submission to the International Court of Justice of the question of the legality of the Wall by the General Assembly, the Court held that Israel's construction of the Wall on Palestinian territory was unlawful, and that Israel is legally obliged to terminate its breaches of international law, to dismantle the Wall, and to make reparation for all damage caused by its construction.[22] The Court further asserted that all states are under an obligation not to recognise, aid or assist the illegal situation resulting from the construction of the Wall and its associated regime, while stressing that the High Contracting Parties to the Fourth Geneva Convention 'are under an obligation, while respecting the United Nations Charter and international law, to ensure compliance by Israel with international humanitarian law as embodied in that Convention'.[23]

Israel considered it inappropriate for the Court to take a decision 'that accords "Palestine" a status that has been highly contentious amongst UN Members for many years', claiming that to allow Palestine to participate in the Court's proceedings reinforced Israel's wider concerns, since 'the Order itself is already being viewed as an additional substantive factor in the political debate about Palestinian statehood'.[24] The referral to the Court had been opposed by the UK, the United States, the EU,[25] and the Quartet amongst others, on the basis that to allow the rule of international law to impinge on the political process that they

---

[20] Swiss Federal Council, Note of Information sent to States Parties to the Convention and Protocol (13 September 1989).

[21] See World Health Organisation (Tenth Plenary Meeting of the 42nd World Health Assembly) 'Request of Palestine for Admission as a Member of the World Health Organisation' (12 May 1989) A42/VR/10 and UNESCO (General Conference, 25th Session) 'Request for the Admission of Palestine to UNESCO' (29 September 1989) 132 EX/31 respectively.

[22] International Court of Justice, *Wall* Advisory Opinion (n 15) paras 147–153.

[23] Ibid paras 154–160.

[24] Israeli Ministry of Foreign Affairs, Written Statement of the Government of Israel on Jurisdiction and Propriety (30 January 2004) <http://www.icj-cij.org/docket/files/131/1579.pdf> last accessed 15 May 2012, para 2.16.

[25] Irish Ministry of Foreign Affairs, Statement of Ireland on behalf of the European Union (29 January 2004) <http://www.icj-cij.org/docket/files/131/1615.pdf> last accessed 15 May 2012. It should be noted that, independent of the EU, Ireland favoured the referral of the question to the Court by the General Assembly.

favoured would serve to undermine opportunities for peace. According to Britain, 'the United Kingdom and the other States involved in the Quartet have made it clear that they consider that for the Court to give an opinion on this matter would be likely to hinder, rather than assist, the peace process'.[26] Switzerland similarly opposed the referral on the basis that: 'We do not judge it to be appropriate in the current circumstances to bring before a legal body a subject in which highly political implications predominate.'[27]

The approach to the Palestinian engagement with the ICJ can be contrasted with the response to the Court's Advisory Opinion on Kosovo's Unilateral Declaration of Independence. Although many western states were wary of the Court engaging in the dispute between Serbia and Kosovo, they nonetheless seized upon the Opinion to assert for recognition of an independent state of Kosovo, while absolutely failing to realise the obligations that the Court had affirmed were owed by all states to assisting Palestine's self-determination. A similar attitude was visible in the response of the international community to the Report of the UN Fact-Finding Mission on the Gaza Conflict, commonly referred to as the 'Goldstone Report'. Published in September 2009, the Report found evidence that all parties to the conflict had committed war crimes and possibly crimes against humanity. In relation to Israel's assault on Gaza, the Report concluded that 'what occurred in just over three weeks at the end of 2008 and the beginning of 2009 was a deliberately disproportionate attack designed to punish, humiliate and terrorize a civilian population, radically diminish its local economic capacity both to work and to provide for itself, and to force upon it an ever increasing sense of dependency and vulnerability'.[28] The Report asserted that '[w]hatever violations of international humanitarian and human rights law may have been committed, the systematic and deliberate nature of the activities described in this report leave the Mission in no doubt that responsibility lies in the first place with those who designed, planned, ordered and oversaw the operations'.[29]

With its emphasis on the necessity of identifying those most responsible for the crimes committed in Gaza, the Report stressed the role which the International Criminal Court should play in the international community's responsibility for ensuring accountability for the victims of Operation Cast Lead. The Fact-Finding Mission recommended that the United Nations Human Rights Council formally submit the Report to the Prosecutor of the International Criminal Court, and that in the absence of good faith investigations by the parties to the conflict, the UN

---

[26] Written Statement of the United Kingdom of Great Britain and Northern Ireland (29 January 2004) <http://www.icj-cij.org/docket/files/131/1605.pdf> last accessed 15 May 2012, para 1.6.

[27] Written statement addressed to the International Court of Justice by the Swiss Confederation pursuant to the Order of the Court of 19 December 2003 <http://www.icj-cij.org/docket/files/131/1577.pdf> last accessed 15 May 2012, para 7.

[28] UN Human Rights Council (12th Session) Report of the United Nations Fact-Finding Mission on the Gaza Conflict (15 September 2009) UN Doc A/HRC/12/48, para 1690.

[29] Ibid para 1692.

Security Council, acting under Chapter VII of the Charter of the United Nations, should refer the situation in Gaza to the Prosecutor of the International Criminal Court pursuant to Article 13 (b) of the Rome Statute.[30] While the Report was endorsed by both the Human Rights Council and the General Assembly, neither of these recommendations has been implemented. Addressing the Prosecutor of the International Criminal Court directly, the Report also recommended that:

> With reference to the declaration under article 12 (3) received by the Office of the Prosecutor of the ICC from the Government of Palestine, the Mission considers that accountability for victims and the interests of peace and justice in the region require that the legal determination should be made by the Prosecutor as expeditiously as possible.[31]

Despite a broad welcome for the findings of the Report from Palestinian authorities, armed groups and civil society, on 1 October 2009, the Human Rights Council deferred consideration of the Report until March 2010 at the request of the Palestinian Authority. This decision, taken the evening before a scheduled vote on a draft resolution endorsing the Report, was the result of diplomatic pressure exerted by the United States on the Palestinian leadership in the West Bank.[32] The news caused an outcry from Palestinians that forced the PA to backtrack and to subsequently request the convening of a special session of the Council, which, only days later, endorsed the Report and submitted it for discussion at the General Assembly. At this stage, Palestinian NGOs criticised the PLO's negotiating strategy at the General Assembly on the basis that '[t]oo often have the rights of Palestinians been negotiated away in order to provide the appearance of political progress, and too often has progress manifested itself as mere maintenance of the status quo, which for decades has denied Palestinians their fundamental rights'.[33] The Report of the Fact-Finding Mission was adopted by a majority vote, calling upon the parties to the conflict to conduct proper investigations and calling on Switzerland to reconvene the Conference of High Contracting Parties to the Fourth Geneva Convention on measures to enforce the Convention in the occupied Palestinian territory, and requesting the Secretary-General to report to the General Assembly within a period of three months on the implementation of the resolution

---

[30] Ibid paras 1765–1766.

[31] Ibid paras 1692, 1765–1767.

[32] N Mozgovaya and B Ravid, 'Source: Palestinians Drop Endorsement of Goldstone Report' *Ha'aretz* (Tel Aviv 1 October 2009).

[33] Joint Press Release: Adalah – Legal Center for Arab Minority Rights in Israel; Addameer; Al Dameer Association for Human Rights; Al-Haq; Al Mezan Centre for Human Rights; Arab Association for Human Rights; Badil Resource Center for Palestinian Residency and Refugee Rights; Defence for Children International-Palestine Section; Ensan Center for Human Rights and Democracy; Jerusalem Legal Aid Center; Palestinian Centre for Human Rights; Ramallah Center for Human Rights Studies; Women's Center for Legal Aid and Counselling, 'The Goldstone Report at the UN General Assembly: States Must Ensure Victim's Rights and Not Compromise the Rule of Law' (4 November 2009).

with a view to considering further action.³⁴ The resolution made no reference to international criminal law, and to date little if any action has been taken at any level to implement what recommendations were made.

The opposition of the United States, Canada, Australia and the majority of European states to the pursuit of accountability through law was again highlighted by their lack of support for the General Assembly's endorsement of the Report at the General Assembly.³⁵ Here, a palpable contrast to the response to the Report of the International Commission on Darfur in 2005 – which similarly recommended Security Council referral of the situation to the International Criminal Court, a recommendation that was promptly implemented³⁶ – reveals itself. The predominant position of western states on the Report of the Fact-Finding Mission on the Gaza Conflict was reflected in a resolution of the US House of Representatives declaring it 'irredeemably biased and unworthy of further consideration or legitimacy'.³⁷ Pursuant to this position, the United States had led the charge against accountability for crimes allegedly committed during Operation Cast Lead. US ambassador to the UN Susan Rice met with Israel's Deputy Foreign Minister Danny Ayalon the day after the publication of the Report of the Fact-Finding Mission. She advised that the Report would be 'more easily managed' if there was any indication of progress on the peace process, and reassured Ayalon that 'she could not foresee a scenario in which the Security Council referred the case to the ICC'.³⁸ The following month, Rice reported to Israeli Foreign Minister Lieberman on 'positive U.S. engagement with the Israeli Missions in New York and Geneva to blunt the effects of the Goldstone report in those fora'.³⁹ She further noted that the United States had the

---

³⁴ UNGA (64th Session, Report of the Human Rights Council, Draft Resolution) 'Follow-up to the Report of the United Nations Fact-Finding Mission on the Gaza Conflict' (2 November 2009) UN Doc A/64/L.11.

³⁵ UNGA (64th Session, 38th and 39th Meetings, Press Release) 'By Recorded Vote, General Assembly Urges Israel, Palestinians to Conduct Credible, Independent Investigations into Alleged War Crimes in Gaza' (5 November 2009) UN Doc GA/10883. Only a handful of peripheral EU states – Cyprus, Ireland, Malta, Portugal, Slovenia – voted in favour of endorsing the Report.

³⁶ UNSC Res 1593 (31 March 2005), UN Doc S/RES/1593.

³⁷ US House of Representatives (111th Congress, 1st Session) 'Resolution Calling on the President and the Secretary of State to Oppose Unequivocally Any Endorsement or Further Consideration of the "Report of the United Nations Fact-Finding Mission on the Gaza Conflict" in Multilateral Fora' H Res 867 (3 November 2009).

³⁸ Wikileaks (Classified Memo from the US Mission to the UN to the US Secretary of State) 'Ambassador Rice's September 16 Meeting with Israeli Deputy Foreign Minister Ayalon and Secretary-General's Comments at Security Council Lunch on Goldstone Report' (17 September 2009) <http://www.scoop.co.nz/stories/WL0909/S00268.htm> last accessed 15 May 2012.

³⁹ Ibid.

capacity 'to build a blocking coalition' at the Security Council if necessary to ensure that no action would be taken on the Report at that level.[40]

As indicated above, the United States also brought pressure to bear on the Palestinian leadership in this context. By January 2010, Palestinian President Mahmoud Abbas had admitted having given the directive to change the Palestinian stance at the Human Rights Council following a meeting with US and Arab officials, the explanation being one of internal communication failures. This was found to have been the case by an internal PA commission of inquiry, which confirmed that on 28 September 2009, President Abbas attended General Assembly meetings where he was told he should deal with the Report very carefully because of the way it dealt with Palestinian resistance groups and due to 'larger issues with the international standing of the report'.[41] The inquiry found that, on 1 October 2009, the US representative to the PA spoke with Palestinian Prime Minister Salam Fayyad and asked him to delay the vote. Fayyad testified that he refused the request but, nonetheless, Abbas gave the directive that evening. The Commission found near universal astonishment within the PA at the magnitude of the fallout over the act: 'According to the Commission chairman, and PA legislator Azmi Shu'aybi, none of the Palestinian officials involved properly estimated the reaction of Palestinians to the postponement. The only thing on the minds of the leaders influencing the decision, the Commission found, were the final days in Geneva and Ramallah when the United States began applying pressure on the issue.'[42] A *Ha'aretz* report claimed that the decision came after Shin Bet[43] chief Yuval Diskin threatened that unless Abbas deferred the vote, Israel would revoke promises to lift movement restrictions, withdraw the operational capacity for a second Palestinian mobile phone network, and turn the West Bank into a 'second Gaza'.[44]

The position of Israel and its allies on the role of international law in the Palestinian context was reinforced by the response to an April 2011 newspaper opinion piece in which the chair of the UN Fact-Finding Mission, Justice Richard Goldstone (who following the Report had been subjected to a relentless campaign of attacks on his character and invasion of his private life by pro-Israel pressure groups), stated that '[i]f I had known then what I know now, the Goldstone Report would have been

---

[40] Wikileaks (Classified Memo from the US Mission to the UN to the US Secretary of State) 'Ambassador Rice's October 21st Meeting with Israeli Foreign Minister Lieberman' (27 October 2009) <http://www.jewishvirtuallibrary.org/jsource/US-Israel/wikiUScable8.html> last accessed 15 May 2012.

[41] 'Abbas Takes Blame for Goldstone Delay, Commission Says', *Ma'an News Agency* (Bethlehem, 9 January 2010) <http://www.maannews.net/eng/ViewDetails.aspx?ID=253025> last accessed 15 May 2012.

[42] Ibid.

[43] Israel's internal security agency.

[44] A Eldar, 'Diskin to Abbas: Defer UN Vote on Goldstone or Face "Second Gaza"' *Ha'aretz* (Tel Aviv 17 January 2010). See further S Farhan Mustafa, 'PA Stonewalled the Goldstone Vote' *Al-Jazeera* (26 January 2011).

a different document'.⁴⁵ Goldstone raised a question mark over only one aspect of the Fact-Finding Mission's 575-page report – that the Israeli military had a policy of deliberately targeting civilians – and did not present any information that would rebut its findings.⁴⁶ The other three members of the Mission responded in order to 'to dispel any impression that subsequent developments have rendered any part of the mission's report unsubstantiated, erroneous or inaccurate'.⁴⁷ Despite this, the United States seized upon and distorted Goldstone's comments, with Ambassador Rice telling the Security Council that Justice Goldstone had now 'reached the same conclusion' that her government had advanced all along regarding the flaws of the report's findings, and called for measures to be taken accordingly: 'The United States urges the United Nations to end, once and for all, its actions in relation to the Goldstone Report.'⁴⁸ The US Senate unanimously passed a resolution calling on the UN Human Rights Council 'to reflect the author's repudiation of the Goldstone report's central findings, rescind the report, and reconsider further Council actions with respect to the report's findings', and on the Secretary-General 'to do all in his power to redress the damage to Israel's reputation caused by the Goldstone report' and 'to prevent any further United Nations action on the report's findings'.⁴⁹ The rhetorical and unfounded nature of this call is evident in a failure on the part of any US authority to provide any factual information or legal argument to challenge or invalidate the Report's meticulous documentation and analysis.

## II. Towards Accountability: Palestine and the International Criminal Court

It is clear that the policy preference of the hegemonic powers elucidated above – that international law be excluded from the Palestinian realm – was firmly entrenched by the time Israel launched Operation Cast Lead in late December 2008. The most

---

⁴⁵ R Goldstone, 'Reconsidering the Goldstone Report on Israel and War Crimes' *The Washington Post* (Washington, 1 April 2011).

⁴⁶ For further analysis, see for example J Dugard, 'Where Now for the Goldstone Report?' *New Statesman* (London 6 April 2011); W Schabas, 'Richard Goldstone Did Not Retract the Report' (PhD Studies in Human Rights, 4 April 2011) <http://humanrightsdoctorate.blogspot.com/2011/04/richard-goldstone-did-not-retract.html> last accessed 15 May 2012.

⁴⁷ H Jilani, C Chinkin and D Travers, 'Goldstone Report: Statement Issued by Members of UN Mission on Gaza War' *Guardian* (London 14 April 2011).

⁴⁸ US Mission to the UN, 'Remarks by Ambassador Susan E. Rice, U.S. Permanent Representative to the United Nations, at a Security Council Debate on the Middle East' (21 April 2011) <http://usun.state.gov/briefing/statements/2011/161438.htm> last accessed 15 May 2012.

⁴⁹ US Senate (112th Congress, 1st Session) 'Resolution Calling on the United Nations to Rescind the Goldstone Report, and for Other Purposes' S Res 138 (14 April 2011) <http://www.govtrack.us/congress/billtext.xpd?bill=sr112-138> last accessed 15 May 2012.

extensive assault on the Gaza Strip since the Six-Day War of 1967 came on the back of a period of relative calm.[50] Despite this, upon the initiation of Operation Cast Lead, western government officials immediately slipped into auto-response mode and parroted a common mantra about Israel's right to defend itself.[51] The legal propriety or otherwise of Israel's invocation of Article 51 of the UN Charter[52] was paid little regard by states outside the global South. While a host of such states from Chile[53] to Namibia[54] to Malaysia[55] implicitly disputed the self-defence claim by accusing Israel of aggression in its attack on Gaza, the Security Council failed to give the matter any consideration. In relation to alleged international crimes committed by both Palestinian armed groups and the Israeli military forces, the

---

[50] While the eyes of the world converged on the US presidential election on 4 November 2008, Israel transgressed an existing six-month ceasefire agreement with an air strike on Gaza that killed six and injured seven Palestinians. See UN Office for the Coordination of Humanitarian Affairs (OCHA), *Protection of Civilians Weekly Report No. 284* (29 October – 4 November 2008) <http://unispal.un.org/UNISPAL.NSF/0/CA96747799276A1C85257 4F900701113> last accessed 15 May 2012. For research showing that from the initiation of the ceasefire on 19 June until 4 November 2008, 'the rate of rocket and mortar fire from Gaza dropped to almost zero', see N Kanwisher, H Haushofer and A Biletzski, 'Reigniting Violence: How Do Ceasefires End?' *The Huffington Post* (6 January 2009). See further UNGA (Human Rights Council, 10th Session) 'Report of the Special Rapporteur on the Situation of Human Rights in the Palestinian Territories Occupied Since 1967, Richard Falk' (11 February 2009), UN Doc A/HRC/10/20, para 28.

[51] Even after being forced to retract a particularly hawkish statement in support of Israel's decision to launch Operation Cast Lead, the European Union Presidency issued a revised statement which continued to imply that Israel's invocation of self-defence was valid, although it would not allow actions disproportionately affecting civilians. See D Cronin, 'Israel's Czech Mate' *Guardian* (London 10 January 2009) <http://www.guardian.co.uk/commentisfree/2009/jan/10/czech-republic-israel-european-union-palestine> last accessed 15 May 2012. Even the Goldstone Report failed to challenge the Israeli claim to self-defence under the UN Charter; see J Reynolds, 'The Use of Force in a Colonial Present and the Goldstone Report's Blind Spot' (2010) 16 *Palestine Ybk Int'l L* 55.

[52] UNSC, 'Identical Letters dated 27 December 2008 from the Permanent Representative of Israel to the United Nations Addressed to the Secretary-General and to the President of the Security Council' (27 December 2008), UN Doc S/2008/816.

[53] UNGA (Tenth Emergency Special Session, 34th and 35th Meetings) 'General Assembly Demands Full Respect for Security Council Resolution 1860 Calling for Immediate Gaza Ceasefire, as Emergency Session Concludes' (16 January 2009), UN Doc GA/10809/Rev.1, Statement of the Chilean Representative to the UN General Assembly. See also the statements of Libya, Jordan, Nicaragua, Kuwait, Oman, Tunisia, Ecuador, Bolivia, Pakistan, the Maldives, Mauritania, Lebanon, Cuba and Iran referring to Israel's actions as aggression.

[54] Namibian Ministry of Foreign Affairs Press Release, quoted in 'Gaza Carnage Must Stop' *The Namibian* (Windhoek 9 January 2009).

[55] UNGA (Tenth Emergency Special Session) 'Letter Dated 14 January 2009 from the Permanent Representative of Malaysia to the United Nations Addressed to the President of the General Assembly' (16 January 2009), UN Doc A/ES-10/444.

Security Council response to Operation Cast Lead also remained notably silent on questions of accountability and impunity.[56]

Conversely, the response of the Palestinian authorities in the West Bank was reflective of the ongoing strategy of engagement with international law, ultimately aimed towards recognition as a legitimate actor on the international stage. Within days of Operation Cast Lead drawing to a halt, the Palestinian Authority[57] submitted a declaration to the Registrar of the International Criminal Court accepting the jurisdiction of the Court over international crimes committed in Palestine since 1 July 2002, the date the Court came into operation.[58] In itself this was a quite surprising move, the PA acting unilaterally in the international arena without prior approval from its sponsors in Europe or the United States. With neither Israel nor Palestine being a State Party to the Rome Statute, the declaration submitted by Minister of Justice Ali Khashan thus based itself on Article 12(3) of the Statute:

> In conformity with Article 12, paragraph 3 of the Statute of the International Criminal Court, the Government of Palestine hereby recognizes the jurisdiction of the Court for the purpose of identifying, prosecuting and judging the authors and accomplices of acts committed on the territory of Palestine since 1 July 2002.[59]

The implication arising from such an attempted transfer of jurisdiction – through a process intended to apply to the situation of 'a State which is not a Party to this Statute' – is that Palestine does possess statehood in some shape or form. The decision of the Security Council not to refer the situation in Palestine to the International Criminal Court, as it has done with Darfur previously[60] and Libya subsequently[61] – a decision which can only be described as politically motivated – meant that short of full Palestinian accession to the Rome Statute, the Article

---

[56] UNSC Res 1860 (8 January 2009), UN Doc S/RES/1860.

[57] The 'Palestinian Interim Self-Government Authority' was established under Article 1 of the Declaration of Principles on Interim Self-Government Arrangements, signed by representatives of the Palestine Liberation Organisation and the Government of Israel on 13 September 1993.

[58] International Criminal Court (Press Release) 'Visit of the Minister of Justice of the Palestinian National Authority, Mr. Ali Khashan, to the ICC' (22 January 2009) <http://www.icc-cpi.int/NR/rdonlyres/979C2995-9D3A-4E0D-8192-105395DC6F9A/280603/ICCOTP20090122Palestinerev1.pdf> last accessed 15 May 2012. The transfer of jurisdiction dating back to 2002 would grant the Court the potential to investigate the situation in the West Bank and Gaza on a broader temporal and geographic scale than solely the crimes committed during Operation Cast Lead.

[59] Palestinian National Authority (Ministry of Justice) 'Declaration Recognizing the Jurisdiction of the International Criminal Court' (21 January 2009) <http://www.icc-cpi.int/NR/rdonlyres/74EEE201-0FED-4481-95D4-C8071087102C/279777/20090122PalestinianDeclaration2.pdf> last accessed 15 May 2012.

[60] UNSC Res 1593 (31 March 2005), UN Doc S/RES/1593.

[61] UNSC Res 1973 (17 March 2011), UN Doc S/RES/1973.

12(3) declaration represented the key path to The Hague for those responsible for the commission of war crimes and crimes against humanity in Palestine.[62] Determination of jurisdiction appeared to rest on another essentially politically contingent decision by the Court as to whether Palestine constitutes a state for the purposes of Article 12(3).

The process following the lodging of the declaration involved meetings and correspondence between the Office of the Prosecutor and representatives of the Palestinian Authority and the League of Arab States, consultation with relevant human rights organisations by the Prosecutor, and a host of submissions by interested parties detailing legal arguments both for and against the acceptance of jurisdiction.[63] By October 2010, the line being presented by the Office of the Prosecutor was that while it was still receiving submissions, it had the primary legal arguments before it and was close to having all necessary information to make an assessment of the declaration.[64]

The arguments submitted to the Prosecutor were marked by a broad dichotomy in approach, the essence of which is a distinction between an orthodox and functional interpretation of the question of statehood in the context of the Rome Statute. A number of the submissions relied on classical notions of how a state is defined, based on rigid applications of the 1933 Montevideo Convention, to conclude that Palestine is not a state and by consequence must be precluded from engaging with

---

[62] The domestic context is one of ongoing impunity. See for example Human Rights Watch, *Promoting Impunity – The Israeli Military's Failure to Investigate Wrongdoing*, June 2005 <http://www.hrw.org/sites/default/files/reports/iopt0605.pdf> last accessed 15 May 2012. Israel has shown itself unwilling to investigate and prosecute alleged crimes committed by its forces, and has actively sought to undermine civil society efforts to invoke universal jurisdiction over Israeli officials in third states as politically motivated 'lawfare'. See further M Kearney, 'Lawfare, Legitimacy & Resistance: The Weak and the Law' (2010) 16 *Palestine Ybk Int'l L* 79.

[63] These submissions, which are referred to individually below, are accessible on the website of the International Criminal Court <http://www.icc-cpi.int/menus/icc/structure%20 of%20the%20court/office%20of%20the%20
Prosecutor/comm%20and%20ref/palestine/summary%20of%20submissions%20on%20 whether%20the%20declaration%20lodged%20by%20the%20palestinian%20national%20 authority%20meets> last accessed 15 May 2012. A summary covering the initial batch of submissions made is also accessible: International Criminal Court (Office of the Prosecutor) 'Situation in Palestine: Summary of Submissions on whether the Declaration Lodged by the Palestinian National Authority Meets Statutory Requirements' (3 May 2010) <http:// www.icc-cpi.int/NR/rdonlyres/D3C77FA6-9DEE-45B1-ACC0-B41706BB41E5/282852/ PALESTINEFINAL201010272.pdf> last accessed 15 May 2012. The information submitted by the Palestinian Authority has not been made publicly available by the Office of the Prosecutor.

[64] Jennifer Schense (representative of the Office of the Prosecutor, International Criminal Court) 'Roundtable Discussion: The Palestine Declaration to the ICC' (Comments made at the Palestinian Red Crescent Society, Ramallah, 24 October 2010).

the International Criminal Court.⁶⁵ The possibility that statehood for the purposes of the Rome Statute may be construed independently of its supposed traditional meaning in international law and relations was either ignored or rejected. Such a rudimentary approach may be contested by reference to the outdated nature of the formula represented in the Montevideo Convention – now considered unfit for modern purpose⁶⁶ – as well as by reference to the fact that the Rome Statute neither refers to the Montevideo Convention nor defines 'State' for the purposes of the statute. Here it must be borne in mind that the foremost authority on the subject, James Crawford, has concluded that there has long been no generally accepted and satisfactory legal definition of statehood.⁶⁷

Without direct reference to the Montevideo Convention, Yael Ronen posited a similarly orthodox position rooted in traditional conceptions of statehood, repeating the debatable contention that the Palestinians themselves do not assert such statehood, and rejecting any purposive interpretation of Article 12(3) that might admit declarations from 'quasi-states'.⁶⁸ Ronen articulated the standard policy arguments against a flexible approach to jurisdiction – that it would open the floodgates for non-state entities to advance various subversive goals through the Court, that it would politicise the functions of the Prosecutor's office and entangle the Court in political conflicts – while at the same time admitting that the international judicial mechanism cannot be fully impervious to political forces.⁶⁹ The reality is that the situation raised by the Palestinian Authority's declaration was one not explicitly provided for in the Rome Statute, and cannot be adequately resolved by a simplistic approach based on Westphalian constructs of statehood.

---

⁶⁵ European Centre for Law and Justice, 'Legal Memorandum Opposing Accession to ICC Jurisdiction by Non-State Entities' (9 September 2009) <http://www.icc-cpi.int/NR/rdonlyres/D3C77FA6-9DEE-45B1-ACC0-B41706BB41E5/281869/OTPlegalmemorandum1.pdf> last accessed 15 May 2012; International Association of Jewish Lawyers and Jurists, 'Opinion in the Matter of the Jurisdiction of the ICC with Regard to the Declaration of the Palestinian Authority' (9 September 2009) <http://www.icc-cpi.int/NR/rdonlyres/D3C77FA6-9DEE-45B1-ACC0B41706BB41E5/283640/OTP2009000036046InformationreceivedfromInternation.pdf> last accessed 15 May 2012; D Davenport et al, 'The Palestinian Declaration and ICC Jurisdiction' (19 November 2009) <http://www.icc-cpi.int/NR/rdonlyres/D3C77FA6-9DEE-45B1-ACC0-B41706BB41E5/281873/Paldeclandiccjurisd1.pdf> last accessed 15 May 2012; D Benoliel and R Perry, 'Israel, Palestine and the ICC' (5 November 2009) <http://www.icc-cpi.int/NR/rdonlyres/D3C77FA6-9DEE-45B1-ACC0-B41706BB41E5/281910/BPIsraelPalestineandtheICCMay2011.pdf> last accessed 15 May 2012.

⁶⁶ See J Crawford, *The Creation of States in International Law* (2nd edn OUP, Oxford 2007) 437, describing the Montevideo definition of statehood as 'hackneyed'.

⁶⁷ Ibid 37.

⁶⁸ Y Ronen, 'ICC Jurisdiction over Acts Committed in the Gaza Strip: Article 12(3) of the ICC Statute and Non-state Entities' (2010) 8 *JICJ* 3 (submitted to the Office of the Prosecutor October 2010).

⁶⁹ Ibid 24–27.

At the other end of the spectrum, John Quigley and Errol Mendes argued for the existence of a Palestinian state based on widespread recognition[70] and Palestinian capacity to enter into foreign relations, combined with an interpretation of traditional statehood criteria that avoids a simple mechanical approach and has reference to the Palestinian right to self-determination and exclusive claim to sovereignty over the West Bank and Gaza.[71] Mendes goes on to consider whether the relevance of international legal personality, as opposed to ostensibly 'well-established' criteria of statehood under international law, should be the gauge by which to measure the validity of the Palestinian declaration. His conclusion was that, at the very least, Palestine enjoys adequate international legal personality to be regarded as a state for the purposes of Article 12(3).

This comports with a functional or teleological approach to the Prosecutor's dilemma, also advanced by the submissions of Alain Pellet and Al-Haq.[72] Such a perspective suggests that the term 'State' in Article 12(3) should be examined in the specific context of the Rome Statute and its object and purpose. Given that the term is subject to variable defining characteristics under public international law, the

---

[70] Following recognition by Uruguay on 15 March 2011, 118 states have recognised the state of Palestine, of which 99 have established full diplomatic relations with the PLO.

[71] J Quigley, 'Memo to the Prosecutor' (23 March 2009) <http://www.icc-cpi.int/NR/rdonlyres/D3C77FA6-9DEE-45B1-ACC0-B41706BB41E5/281879/JohnQuigleyiccmemoPNADeclaration3.pdf> last accessed 15 May 2012; J Quigley, 'The Palestine Declaration to the International Criminal Court: The Statehood Issue' (19 May 2009) <http://www.icc-cpi.int/NR/rdonlyres/D3C77FA6-9DEE-45B1-ACC0-B41706BB41E5/281882/QuigleyPalestinedeclarationandtheICC1.pdf> last accessed 15 May 2012; J Quigley, 'Additional Memo: Posted Submissions in Regard to Palestine Declaration' (20 May 2010) <http://www.icc-cpi.int/NR/rdonlyres/D3C77FA6-9DEE-45B1-ACC0-B41706BB41E5/281978/Quigleyadditionalsubmission1.pdf> last accessed 15 May 2012; E Mendes. 'Statehood and Palestine for the Purposes of Article 12(3) of the ICC Statute: A Contrary Perspective' (30 March 2010) <http://www.icc-cpi.int/NR/rdonlyres/D3C77FA6-9DEE-45B1-ACC0-B41706BB41E5/281876/OTPErrolMendesNewSTATEHOODANDPALESTINEFORTHEPURPOS.pdf> last accessed 15 May 2012.

[72] Al-Haq, 'Position Paper on Issues Arising from the Palestinian Authority's Submission of a Declaration to the Prosecutor of the International Criminal Court under Article 12(3) of the Rome Statute' (14 December 2009) <http://www.icc-cpi.int/NR/rdonlyres/D3C77FA6-9DEE-45B1-ACC0-B41706BB41E5/281874/OTPAlHaqposi tionpapericc14December20091.pdf> last accessed 15 May 2012; A Pellet, 'Effects of Palestinian Recognition of the Jurisdiction of the I.C.C.' (14 February 2010) <http://www.icc-cpi.int/NR/rdonlyres/D3C77FA6-9DEE-45B1-ACC0-B41706BB41E5/281927/PelletENGCLEAN1.pdf> last accessed 15 May 2012 [original in French]. Functional approaches have also been suggested elsewhere by, among others, J Reynolds, 'Sovereignty, Colonialism and the "State" of Palestine under International Law' (Human Sciences Research Council, Cape Town, 13 June 2009) <http://papers.ssrn.com/sol3/papers.cfm?abstract_id=1682636> last accessed 15 May 2012; J Dugard, 'Take the Case' *New York Times* (New York 22 July 2009); M Kearney, 'Palestine and the International Criminal Court: Asking the Right Question' (2010) 1 *UCLA Human Rights & Int'l Crim L Online Forum* <http://papers.ssrn.com/sol3/papers.cfm?abstract_id=1633975> last accessed 15 May 2012.

question for the Prosecutor and ultimately the Court ought not to have been one of pronouncing *in abstracto* whether Palestine is a state for all intents and purposes. Rather, it should have involved a determination of whether Palestine is an entity with the capacity to enter into relations with states and international organisations that holds jurisdiction over the crimes set forth in the Rome Statute, which it has the capacity to validly transfer to the International Criminal Court. If so, it may be considered as a state for the purposes of Article 12(3) of the Statute.

Such an approach is broadly consistent with the advice proffered to the Palestinian leadership by its Negotiations Support Unit, as per a March 2009 memo leaked by Al-Jazeera as part of the 'Palestine Papers' document dump. In considering various legal avenues for the Palestinian Authority to pursue in its representations to the International Criminal Court, its advisors come down in favour of the position that short of actual statehood, Palestine enjoys functional statehood for the purposes of applying and implementing international humanitarian law, and prosecuting war crimes:

> This approach is based on the premise that, short of actual statehood, Palestine is a 'state' for the purpose of Article 12 of the Rome Statute because it is 'sufficiently an international entity for the prohibition of armed attack on others to be applicable.' In other words, if Palestine is enough of an international entity to be bound by IHL, and bound by international law prohibitions on the use of force, in the same way that it would be if it were a recognized state, then Palestine should also be treated as a 'state' by the court that is responsible for the enforcement of IHL and the punishment of war crimes.[73]

Adopting a functional approach to such a complex and politically loaded question is an established feature of international legal practice.[74] In relation to Kosovo, for instance, the question put by the General Assembly to the International Court of Justice for an advisory opinion did not ask whether Kosovo is a state *per se*, but rather was both asked and answered within the much narrower rubric of whether Kosovo's unilateral declaration of independence conforms with international law.[75] In the same vein, Pellet suggested, 'the ICC is not called upon to "recognize" the State of Palestine but only to make sure that the conditions necessary for the exercise of its jurisdiction are fulfilled'.[76]

---

[73] Palestine Liberation Organisation (Negotiations Support Unit, Confidential Memorandum) 'Legal Approaches to be Advanced at the ICC in Order to Protect Overall Palestinian Strategy and Realize Palestinian Rights and Interests' (25 March 2009) <http://www.ajtransparency.com/en/document/4494> last accessed 15 May 2012.

[74] Pellet (n 72) paras 9–15.

[75] UNGA Res 63/3 (8 October 2008), UN Doc A/RES/63/3; Accordance with International Law of the Unilateral Declaration of Independence in Respect of Kosovo (Advisory Opinion), [2010] ICJ Rep.

[76] Pellet (n 72) para 7.

Interpreting the provisions of a statute by recourse to its object and purpose is of course a common and prescribed practice of international law.[77] The object and purpose of the Rome Statute generally is to address impunity and promote accountability; within that the object and purpose arising from Article 12(3) is to facilitate the exercise of jurisdiction. A conservative reading of the statute that interprets 'State' as denoting a United Nations member state, for example, would arguably run contrary to the interests of justice and to pertinent legal developments. It bears noting that the Court's jurisdiction in general is not contingent on statehood (its exercise of jurisdiction over a territorial area other than the state in Darfur being a case in point). Were the Security Council to refer the situation in Palestine to the Court, it would certainly not hesitate to exercise jurisdiction on the basis of a lack of statehood.

In the realm of international criminal law, recourse to the 'object and purpose' of the foundational statutes or their provisions has frequently been made to underpin progressive applications of the law.[78] Similarly, liberal approaches to the jurisdiction of international criminal tribunals have been taken in the interests of ensuring that a wide net of accountability is cast. In bestowing expansive subject-matter jurisdiction upon the International Criminal Tribunal for Rwanda, for example, to apply conventional humanitarian law instruments addressing non-international armed conflict which were not beyond doubt customary in nature, the Security Council 'appears to have broken the golden rule of fidelity to customary law' in order to further the object and purpose of international criminal justice.[79]

Although the Office of the Prosecutor remained relatively aloof while conducting its preliminary assessment of the Article 12(3) declaration, the specific follow-up questions on which it requested information from the Palestinian Authority did suggest that it may have been leaning towards a purposive, non-classical approach to statehood in the context of Article 12; that is, one based on criminal jurisdiction and capacity to transfer it to the International Criminal Court. Those questions related to the capacity of the Palestinian Authority to enter into foreign relations, its capacity to try Palestinians on criminal charges, and its capacity to try Israelis on criminal charges.[80]

Contrary to arguments that a purposive, teleological interpretation of Article 12(3) would constitute an overly politicised corruption of the judicial functions of the Court, adopting such a functional approach would have provided the Court with an escape route from having to make a determination on the thorny issue of Palestinian statehood. Where a rigid or orthodox approach to this jurisdictional quandary effectively entails the International Criminal Court taking a definitive position that Palestine *is* or *is not* a state, a functional approach allows the Prosecutor

---

[77] Vienna Convention on the Law of Treaties (1979) 1155 UNTS 331, art 31.
[78] See generally S Darcy and J Powderly (eds), *Judicial Creativity at the International Criminal Tribunals* (OUP, Oxford 2010).
[79] J Powderly, 'Judicial Interpretation at the Ad Hoc Tribunals: Method from Chaos?' in Darcy and Powderly (n 78) 24–26.
[80] For a discussion of these questions, see Al-Haq (n 72) paras 25–38.

and the Court to separate the criminal law aspects of a situation from its more contested diplomatic elements.

## III. Deferring the Decision, Deference to the Security Council

As it transpired, in April 2012 the Prosecutor issued a stilted statement, suggesting that for his office to define the term 'state' in the context of the Palestinian declaration would be *ultra vires*.[81] Amnesty International decried this as a 'dangerous decision' that 'opens the ICC to accusations of political bias': rather than allowing the Court's Pre-Trial Chamber to review the Palestinian declaration as required by the Rome Statute, the Prosecutor had instead chosen to dodge the question, 'passing it to other political bodies'.[82] The statement of the Prosecutor, while quite short and confused, demonstrated an explicit bias in favour of the status quo and the desires of the European and North American powers – and thus against the Palestinians – in its treatment of the recognition of the state of Palestine.

In the first instance, the Prosecutor noted that his Office had been informed that 'Palestine has been recognized as a State in bilateral relations by more than 130 governments and by certain international organisations'.[83] No weight is attached to this fact, however, despite it demonstrating that a clear majority of states perceive Palestine as a sovereign equal.

The statement goes on to acknowledge that recognition of Palestinian statehood has also been granted by 'United Nation [sic] bodies'.[84] This alludes to the October 2011 admission of Palestine as a member state of UNESCO. The membership vote was carried by a majority of UNESCO's members to the order of 107 to 14,[85] with UNESCO's Director-General noting that '[t]he admission of a new Member State is a mark of respect and confidence'.[86] On the day, three of the Security Council's permanent members voted in favour of admitting the state of Palestine: France,

---

[81] International Criminal Court (n 1).

[82] Amnesty International, 'ICC Prosecutor Statement: Fears Over Justice for Gaza Victims' (4 April 2012). See also Amnesty International, 'Questions and Answers: Amnesty International's Response to the ICC Office of the Prosecutor's Statement that it Cannot Investigate Crimes Committed during the Gaza Conflict' AI Index MDE 15/018/2012 (4 April 2012).

[83] International Criminal Court (n 1) para 7.

[84] Ibid.

[85] UNESCO (Press Release) 'General Conference admits Palestine as UNESCO Member' (31 October 2011) <http://unispal.un.org/UNISPAL.nsf/47D4E277B48D9D3685256DDC00612265/F32B83B0D5E6D75A8525793A004C8312> last accessed 15 May 2012. The vote was carried by 107 votes in favour of admission and 14 against, with 52 abstentions.

[86] UN News Centre, 'UNESCO Votes to Admit Palestine as Full Member' (31 October 2011) <http://www.un.org/apps/news/story.asp?NewsID=40253> last accessed 15 May 2012.

Russia and China. The UK abstained, as is its wont, leaving the United States as the sole permanent member to oppose.

This striking development, signalling convincing evidence of the international community's recognition of Palestinian statehood, prompted several commentators to conclude that Palestine must now be considered as a state should it seek to accede to international treaties, including the Rome Statute. According to the Summary of Practice of the Secretary-General as Depositary of Multilateral Treaties, the membership of UN specialised agencies is considered as 'fully representative of the international community'. Admission to such agencies therefore provides guidance to the Secretary-General where the status of an entity is unclear, and is to be taken as evidence of the international community having 'duly decided in the affirmative' on the concerned entity's statehood and capacity to ratify international treaties.[87] As such, the Treaty Section of the UN Office of Legal Affairs counsels that no doubt arises for the Secretary-General in accepting ratifications from entities 'falling within the "Vienna formula", i.e. States that are Members of the United Nations or members of the specialized agencies, or Parties to the Statute of the International Court of Justice'.[88] Membership of UNESCO brings Palestine under the umbrella of the 'Vienna formula'; it provides grounds for Palestine to accede to the Rome Statute itself. As William Schabas pointed out, if UNESCO membership is sufficient for the Secretary-General in terms of accession to the Statute as whole, then it must be sufficient for the Prosecutor in terms of the application of Article 12(3).[89]

Nonetheless, the Prosecutor chose to ignore the ramifications of the UNESCO decision, the multitude of bilateral recognitions, and the possibility of placing the correctness of accepting the declaration before the Pre-Trial Chamber. It was explained instead that since the Security Council had yet to decide on the formal application for UN membership submitted by Palestine in September 2011,[90] and that Palestine did not have 'non-member state' observer status, the Prosecutor could not make a decision on the declaration. The decisive paragraph of the Prosecutor's statement concluded with the somewhat muddled assertion that the Palestinian application for full UN membership has 'no direct link' with the Palestinian declaration, but nonetheless 'informs the current legal status of Palestine for the interpretation and application of article 12'.[91] Considering the guidance of the Summary of Practice of the Secretary-General as Depositary of Multilateral Treaties, the absence of a veto-induced democratic deficit in the voting system, and

---

[87] UN Office of Legal Affairs (Treaty Section) 'Summary of Practice of the Secretary-General as Depositary of Multilateral Treaties', UN Doc ST/LEG/7/Rev.1, para 86.

[88] Ibid para 81.

[89] WA Schabas, 'Relevant Depositary Practice of the Secretary-General and its Bearing on Palestinian Accession to the Rome Statute' (PhD Studies in Human Rights, 3 November 2011) <http://humanrightsdoctorate.blogspot.com/2011/11/relevant-depositary-practice-of.html> last accessed 15 May 2012.

[90] UNGA, UNSC (66th Session, Admission of New Members to the United Nations) 'Application of Palestine for Admission to Membership in the United Nations' (23 September 2011), UN Doc A/66/317 and UN Doc S/2011/592.

[91] International Criminal Court (n 1) para 7.

the conclusiveness of the process, it appears that Palestine's completed accession to UNESCO should have been given greater weight than a UN membership procedure that remains in progress.

The elaborate consultation process undertaken by the Office of the Prosecutor – in which it organised roundtables with NGOs and practitioners, pursued extensive and substantive engagement with the Palestinian legal team and instigated an academic dialogue with experts and scholars (resulting in the investment of huge amounts of time and resources from all parties on the understanding that this was a genuine and serious process of discovery) – lasted for more than three years. It seems absurd that the sum result of this process is two perfunctory paragraphs holding that the Office of the Prosecutor has no authority to decide on Palestine's competency to grant jurisdiction under Article 12(3). This dubious repudiation of responsibility could surely have come in 2009 without the need for a protracted deliberations, rather than in the middle of a period in which Palestine's status at the UN is undergoing a review that the Prosecutor's office itself holds up as determinative. While the ultimate pandering to the Security Council is clear, it appears impossible on the face of it to locate the logic – legally or politically – in the timing of the decision, given that the Prosecutor had happily dragged his feet on it for two and a half years prior to Palestine's UN initiative. We suggest, however, that if any method is to be found in Prosecutor Moreno-Ocampo's apparent madness, it is rooted in the desire to present a front of performing a purely technical role; to elide the inherently political nature of international criminal law. Rumours aside, the influence of the PA, Israel, or any other actor on the timing or content of the decision remains decidedly uncertain.

## Conclusion: The Politics of International Justice

> [O]ne should note the hegemonic trends within the spectacular rise of international criminal law ... The important point is that criminal law itself always consolidates some hegemonic narrative, some understanding of the political conflict which is a part of that conflict itself.[92]

Given the role of the dominant powers at the UN in maintaining a status quo whereby Israel has been permitted to continue to consolidate its occupation of Palestinian territory to the point of annexation, and the consistent fudging around Palestinian efforts to engage with international law and legal institutions, it is clear that the question of the existence or non-existence of a state of Palestine has served as a smokescreen by which the international community can continue to deny Palestinians the full protections of the law. The compromises demanded from the Palestinians by the international community – over Jerusalem, settlements and

---

[92] M Koskenniemi, 'International Law and Hegemony: A Reconfiguration' (2004) 17(2) *Cambridge Rev Int'l Affairs* 197, 210.

refugees – clash with Palestinian rights; indeed, demand the negation of Palestinian rights. Similarly, the absence of a Palestinian state ensures that Israelis liable for prosecution for international crimes remain confident in their impunity. In reflecting upon this we may understand why the exclusion of Palestinians from the international legal framework has remained such a priority over decades of occupation.

Whether Palestinian statehood will be recognised in the form of full UN membership as opposed to merely 'observer state' status – and whether any such move will serve to correct the untenable situation that prevails in the region – remains to be seen. Recognition at the UN would not, of course, end the occupation of the West Bank and Gaza in itself, and in this regard caution must be exercised. If not based at least on the 1967 borders with a feasible plan for dismantlement of the existing infrastructure of occupation, such a determination may be at risk of perpetuating a 'Bantustan' type state.[93] Similarly, Palestinian accession to UNESCO, while significant, will not induce any restless nights for alleged Israeli or Palestinian war criminals. Had the Prosecutor accepted the Article 12(3) declaration, the story might have been different. French support for Palestinian membership may have tipped the voting equilibrium of the Permanent Five to a slightly more sympathetic calibration than normal, but such support in respect of a primarily cultural organisation is unlikely to translate to the more contentious realm of international criminal justice. Either way, the US stance remains intransigent.

The indeterminacy of international law rarely works in favour of the peoples of the global South. Ambiguities and uncertainties are invariably resolved by resort to broader legal principles, policy goals or social contexts that have most often been shaped by colonial views of the world and the conceptual apparatuses that support such views.[94] The glimmer of hope presented in the wake of Third World decolonisation by an international law that seemed to offer the prospect of a realignment of the global balance of power and the possibility of a new international economic order has long been extinguished. Despite this, the nations that were on the wrong side of imperial history remain unwilling to depart the arena of international law, retaining a belief in its transformative potential and in the ideal of law as a means of constraining, if not subverting, the hegemony of empire. The promise of the International Criminal Court in this regard lies in its truly global potential. By virtue of its mere existence, the Court alters the dynamics of international relations and sounds a warning signal that no Colonel, Comrade or Commander-in-Chief remains impervious.

---

[93] Nor would the establishment of a fully sovereign Palestinian state provide a silver bullet cure. While sovereignty entails numerous benefits (see, for example, M Koskenniemi, 'What Use for Sovereignty Today?' (2010) *Asian J Int'l L* 1), it also brings obvious pitfalls, not least for a postcolonial state entering a hegemonic international system.

[94] A Anghie and BS Chimni, 'Third World Approaches to International Law and Individual Responsibility in Internal Conflicts' (2003) *Chinese J Int'l L* 77, 101.

At the same time, the reality is that all international legal institutions are 'intensely political actors'.[95] The International Criminal Court is no different. As Koskenniemi suggests, it can be understood as a site of meta-conflict, where conflict over the nature of a given conflict plays out, and inevitably some particular narrative is endorsed and consolidated at the expense of others. What that narrative will be often depends less on the law than on the socio-political context. The premise that international criminal justice can fully transcend international politics is a false one – it is inherently political. The International Criminal Court in both its constitution (its relationship with the Security Council, for example) and its functioning (the Prosecutor's exercise of discretion, for example) essentially serves to implement a form of foreign policy.[96]

The Office of the Prosecutor's decision to eschew a functional approach to Article 12(3) and decline jurisdiction over alleged international crimes committed in Palestine is read in this light. Despite the clearly political nature of his position, Moreno-Ocampo persisted with the mantra that his sole function was to apply the law. The lengthy masquerade of engagement with Palestinian legal advisors and fostering of legal debate around some the nuances of statehood, sovereignty and jurisdiction ultimately appears to have been merely for the purpose of simulating a technical, legalistic, apolitical role. When, in fact, the political decision to avoid taking any sort of progressive stance on Palestinian personality was most likely sewn up from the outset.

This will not help in restoring the faith of the subaltern populations of the world in an international legal system that remains tainted by its colonial origins; a system in which the imperial powers developed a legal-normative framework that reified themselves as sovereign while concomitantly denying sovereignty to the indigenous peoples of the lands they colonised, thus facilitating the legal acquisition of territory and exploitation of resources.[97] Nineteenth-century positivist jurisprudence reinforced international law as the body of rules prevailing 'between states',[98] and consolidated a framework which prevented non-sovereign, non-European peoples from asserting any legal personality. The legacy of this genesis lingers unmistakeably, its stamp firmly imprinted on contemporary international law, with the primacy of 'State Parties' continuing to operate as the basic organising premise of the international legal system, even within the human rights paradigm that has emerged. The result is a lacuna whereby nations and peoples that are evidently entitled to independence have been left on the wrong

---

[95] KW Abbott, 'International Relations Theory, International Law and the Regime Governing Atrocities in Internal Conflicts' (1999) 93 *AJIL* 361, 377.

[96] For further elaboration of this point, see F Megret, 'La Cour Pénale Internationale: Objet Politique' (23 April 2010) <http://ssrn.com/abstract=1594794> last accessed 15 May 2012.

[97] See generally A Anghie, *Imperialism, Sovereignty and the Making of International Law* (CUP, Cambridge 2005).

[98] J Westlake, *Chapters on the Principles of International Law* (CUP, Cambridge 1894), 1.

side of 'the murky line between statehood and non-statehood'[99] for the purposes of political expediency, and denied the full protection of the law.

After the Palestinian strategy to seek recognition at the UN was announced in the spring of 2011, the Prosecutor capitalised on this new mask behind which to hide his continuing inertia on the Palestinian Article 12(3) declaration, implying that his office would defer any decision pending developments at the UN. If anything, Palestine's admission to UNESCO should have sealed the matter in favour of accepting the declaration. At the time of writing, the Palestinian effort to secure UN membership remains stalled at the Security Council, with the United States having affirmed its intention to veto any effort to consider permitting Palestine's admission. The manner by which the Office of the Prosecutor deferred to the Security Council in rejecting the Palestine declaration, failing to give regard to the UNESCO vote, can only suggest that a political decision was taken to acquiesce to the US position.

The General Assembly vote on collective recognition of Palestinian statehood as a non-member 'observer state' in November 2012 secured an even more decisive majority (138 in favour, 9 against) than that attained at UNESCO. Diplomatic manoeuvring suggests that the significance of UN recognition – short of UN membership blocked at the Security Council – may be muffled by the retention of limitations on the ability of Palestine to secure independent investigation by the ICC of international crimes committed on its territory. A proposal by representatives of the EU suggested that European states would recognise Palestine but only on a conditional basis, subject to the imposition of 'a quiet understanding with the Palestinians that they would not pursue I.C.C. jurisdiction for a significant period'.[100] Any such understanding would leave Palestine in the unique and rather absurd position whereby it is recognised as a state, held to the obligations of a state, but deprived the full rights of a state. As in the case of the Oslo Accords under which the Palestinian para-state was denied the protection of international law from Israel's burgeoning settlement project, Europe's string-pulling regarding the ICC seeks to ensure that any Palestinian state will continue to be excluded from relevant international legal institutions.

Here we must consider why Palestine approached the International Criminal Court in the first instance. It does not appear to have been a unilateral step aimed solely at eliciting recognition of the state of Palestine. On endorsing the Report of the Fact-Finding Mission on the Gaza Conflict, the General Assembly declared that the Palestinian authorities should investigate and prosecute anyone responsible for grave violations of the Geneva Conventions. This capacity and jurisdiction to investigate and prosecute, and the duty to do so, adheres only to states. Thus, Palestine has been held to share in the obligations of states under international law, yet remains denied recognition of the concomitant rights. During Operation Cast Lead, the Palestinian Authority in the West Bank was unable and unwilling to

---

[99] J Quigley, 'The Israel PLO Agreements: Are They Treaties?' (1997) 30 *Cornell Int'l L J* 717, 717.

[100] M Ahtisaari and J Solana, 'Ten Reasons for a European "Yes"' *International Herald Tribune* (New York 16 September 2011).

take any effective action to defend Palestinians in Gaza that were being subjected to a ferocious military onslaught, leaving it marooned politically; a mere observer, lacking not only a popular mandate to govern but any ability to protect its citizens. In this context, it made sense to approach an institution whose very purpose is to independently investigate and prosecute those responsible for the crimes that were unfolding. Given the Palestinian people's recent history of dispossession, disenfranchisement and exclusion, a history punctured with violence and characterised by impunity for those responsible, turning to the ICC by transferring the jurisdiction held by the Palestinians as the sole sovereign over the West Bank and Gaza appears a prudent political move.[101] Why then has there been such a glaring absence of support from the international community in response to Palestine's efforts at engaging with the celebrated liberal project that is the International Criminal Court? And why has the Palestinian political leadership since failed to display any vigour in following through on those initial efforts? It is likely that the answers to these questions are very much related.

In his 2010 address to Israel's Council on Foreign Relations, Deputy Foreign Minister Ayalon stated that increased application of international law to the conflict 'directly damages our relations with the Palestinians and any possibility of a smooth and viable political process with the Palestinians, because it doesn't build too much credibility or trust with us'.[102] This reflects the dominant view that has long been shared by Israel and its allies, who persist in telling the Palestinians to know their place, to strive to earn the trust of the occupier and of the powers that ensure the perpetuation of the occupation. It is inconceivable that the Palestinian Authority sought 'permission' from any of its international backers before submitting the Article 12(3) declaration to the International Criminal Court, for it would have been promptly ordered to refrain from such a move.[103] Having taken that step, however, the limbo into which Palestine as an entity and the Palestinians as a people have been cast is reinforced. It now appears that, as with the efforts led by the United States to bury the Report of the Fact-Finding Mission on the Gaza Conflict, silence with respect to the acceptance or otherwise of the Article 12(3) declaration was adopted as policy. It bears noting that in a meeting with the President of the International Criminal Court in 2009, US ambassador to the UN Susan Rice issued a thinly veiled warning that any investigations into alleged crimes in Gaza could harm the Court's standing with the United States, just as the Obama administration was beginning to foster a relationship with it: 'how the ICC handles issues concerning the Goldstone

---

[101] On the use of international criminal justice as 'a weapon in political struggles' and the importance of acknowledging the International Criminal Court's political dimensions, see S Nouwen and W Werner, 'Doing Justice to the Political: The International Criminal Court in Uganda and Sudan' (2010) 21 *European J Int'l Law* 941.

[102] Address by Deputy Foreign Minister Danny Ayalon (n 5).

[103] US dissatisfaction as expressed to the Palestinians regarding the strategy of engaging the ICC can be seen, for example, in the minutes of a meeting between George Mitchell and Saeb Erakat on 21 October 2009 <http://www.ajtransparency.com/files/4899.pdf> last accessed 15 May 2012.

Report will be perceived by many in the US as a test for the ICC, as this is a very sensitive matter'.[104] Such obstructionism on the part of a veto-wielding Security Council power, that is not a member of the Court itself, provided all the more grounds for the Article 12(3) declaration to be supported.

The failure of the International Criminal Court to accept the transfer of jurisdiction and to investigate the alleged war crimes and crimes against humanity that have occurred in Palestine suggests that the Court, as a political-legal institution, has, for now, failed to distinguish itself as a progressive actor.

---

[104] Wikileaks (Unclassified Memo from the US Mission to the UN to the US Secretary of State) 'Ambassador Rice Meeting with ICC President Song' (3 November 2009) <http://www.washingtonpost.com/wp-srv/special/world/wikileaks/cable21.html> last accessed 15 May 2012.

# Lions and Tigers and Deterrence, Oh My: Evaluating Expectations of International Criminal Justice

Kate Cronin-Furman and Amanda Taub

There is no shortage of claims regarding the anticipated benefits of international criminal trials. Transitional justice enthusiasts argue that, in addition to punishing the guilty, trials for war crimes and crimes against humanity can produce a range of other effects. They will provide accountability, give voice to the victims and create a historical record. In addition, it has increasingly been argued in recent years, they will serve as a powerful deterrent mechanism, which will diminish the occurrence of future war crimes and crimes against humanity.

However, these predictions remain speculative. Claims about the impact of international justice mechanisms are largely unproven; the study of international criminal law is characterised by a 'paucity of empirical evidence to substantiate claims about how well criminal trials achieve the goals ascribed to them'.[1] In part, this absence of evidence is due to the difficulty of testing these claims. However, it is also due to a lack of clarity about what, precisely, these expectations are, and how they are derived.

In this chapter, we look specifically at claims about deterrence, and attempt to first tease out the logic underpinning expectations for a reduction in the commission of mass atrocity and then consider the reasonableness of these predictions. We are of the opinion that claims about deterrence in the international legal literature actually break down into two separate arguments. The first – which we classify as a 'traditional deterrence' narrative – is rooted in the classical conception of deterrence through the risk of punishment. The second is focused less on the deterrent value of punishment itself, and more on the secondary stigmatising effects of the punishment. We call this idea 'expressive' deterrence.

Because we believe that these two models of deterrence by international criminal trials are distinct, we conduct separate analyses of the prospects for prevention

---

[1] LE Fletcher and HM Weinstein, 'Violence and Social Repair: Rethinking the Contribution of Justice to Reconciliation' (2002) 24(3) *HRQ* 573, 585.

of future atrocities under the 'traditional' and 'expressive' deterrence models. We examine the validity of analogies to domestic criminal systems in order to analyse international courts' deterrent capacity, and rely on social science accounts of mass atrocity perpetrator motivations to consider potential offenders' ability to be deterred.

We suggest that under either model, it would be extremely challenging for international criminal justice mechanisms to produce a deterrent effect – and frankly, we are not certain they are up to the challenge. However, we argue that the difficulties presented by the traditional model and the expressive model are different. The challenge for classical deterrence arises out of the fact that prosecutions by international tribunals remain rare, and the punishments are relatively lenient, while potential perpetrators may face substantial incentives to offend. For expressive deterrence, the ability of international tribunals to shape norms and create social consequences is still in doubt, and therefore may also be insufficient to act as a counterweight to incentives to offend. We conclude with a discussion of how attempts to maximise the prospects for deterrence under these two distinct models of deterrence might indicate different directions for future prosecutorial policy.

## I. Evolving Expectations for International Criminal Law

Today's emphasis on deterrence as a goal of international criminal justice is a relatively recent development. In fact, the modern international criminal justice enterprise began, at the Nuremberg Tribunal, with a primary focus on retribution. The Tribunal's Charter listed the trial's purpose as the 'just and prompt trial and punishment of the major war criminals of the European Axis',[2] and authorised the death penalty for those convicted.[3] This, along with the 'scant attention' paid to sentencing, has led scholars such to infer that, 'insofar as a coherent penal theory can be inferred from the post-war trials, it seems to be a crude retributivism'.[4]

International criminal justice, like swing dancing, went out of vogue for much of the twentieth century, only to reappear on the scene following the end of the Cold War. At that time, consequentialist goals began to play a more central role.

---

[2]    Agreement for the Prosecution and Punishment of Major War Criminals of the European Axis, 82 UNTS 279, 8 August 1945 (Nuremberg Charter), art 1.

[3]    Nuremberg Charter (n 2) art 27; Charter for the International Military Tribunal for The Far East, Annexed to the Special Proclamation by the Supreme Commander of the Allied Powers in the Far East, Tokyo, 19 January 1946, art 16.

[4]    R Sloane, 'The Expressive Capacity of International Punishment, the Limits of the National Law Analogy, and the Potential of International Criminal Law' (2007) 43 *Stanford J Int'l L* 39, 66. See also WA Schabas, 'Sentencing By International Tribunals: A Human Rights Approach' (1997) 7 *Duke J of Comparative ad Int'l L* 461, 500 ('At Nuremberg and Tokyo, and in the various successor trials of the national military tribunals, retribution played a major role in fixing sentences, as shown by widespread use of the death penalty').

The preambular language in the Security Council resolutions authorising the International Criminal Tribunals for Rwanda and the former Yugoslavia (the 'ICTR', and 'ICTY', respectively), proclaimed the importance of incapacitation:

> Believing that the establishment of an international tribunal and the prosecution of persons responsible [for the crimes to be tried] will contribute to ensuring that such violations are halted and effectively redressed.[5]

A focus on deterrence soon followed. International criminal law scholars began to argue that international criminal trials would have a general deterrent effect. Explaining the function of accountability exercises, Cherif Bassiouni observed in 1996 that '[t]he relevance of prosecution and other accountability measures to the pursuit of peace is that through their effective application they serve as deterrence, and thus prevent further victimization'.[6] In 1998, Theodor Meron argued that:

> Abandoning the [ICTY] tribunal now would have a negative impact on the behavior of the parties to the conflict ... On the ground, those committing war crimes would infer that regardless of their past or future violations they will not be held criminally accountable by the international community.[7]

Prospects for deterrence were a major consideration in negotiations of the penalties to be included in the Rome Statute that established the International Criminal Court.[8] Some delegations lobbied for the inclusion of penalty fines on the logic that 'forfeiture of the proceeds of criminal activities could help to "remove an incentive" to engage in human rights violations'.[9]

General deterrence logic also began to feature in tribunal decisions on individual cases. In the 1998 case against Jean Kambanda, the ICTR Trial Chamber noted that the penalties imposed on the guilty must be directed at deterrence 'over and above' retribution, in order to 'dissuad[e] for good those who will attempt in the future to perpetrate such atrocities by showing them that the international community

---

[5] UNSC Res 827 (1993) UN Doc S/RES/827; UNSC Res 955 (1994) UN Doc S/RES/955.

[6] MC Bassiouni, 'Searching for Peace and Achieving Justice: The Need for Accountability' (1996) 59 *Law & Contemporary Problems* 9, 18.

[7] T Meron, 'The Case For War Crimes Trials in Yugoslavia' in *War Crimes Law Comes of Age* (OUP, Oxford 1999), 187, 196. See also Akhavan arguing in 2001 that 'individual accountability for massive crimes is an essential part of a preventive strategy' and could be expected to contribute to the promotion of international peace and security. P Akhavan, 'Beyond Impunity: Can International Justice Prevent Future Atrocities' (2001) 95 *AJIL* 7, 10.

[8] J Klabbers, 'Just Revenge? The Deterrence Argument in International Criminal Law' (2001) 12 *Finnish Ybk Int'l L* 249, 251 (general deterrence 'is one of the main reasons (perhaps the main reason) underlying the creation of the ICC: the idea is to ensure punishment and, through punishment, to deter').

[9] Klabbers (n 8) 251.

was not ready to tolerate the serious violations of international humanitarian law and human rights',[10] a sentiment that it echoed a year later, in its opinion in the *Rutaganda* case.[11]

Recently, the logic of deterrence has come to dominate discussions of the International Criminal Court's role in the international community. ICC Chief Prosecutor (and accomplished wearer of white linen suits) Luis Moreno-Ocampo has repeatedly referred to the 'shadow' of the court, and its ability to 'contribute to the prevention of massive crimes'.[12] Strikingly, neither Moreno-Ocampo nor the commentators supporting his view elaborate the mechanism by which the court will have this effect. Rather, it is taken as a given that more trials will produce more deterrence.

## II. What Is Deterrence? (Defining Some Terms)

Models of the goals and functions of criminal law are divided into three distinct categories: the retributive, the expressive and the consequentialist. The retributive, or punitive, model holds that punishment is proper if it is a fitting response to the nature of the crime, regardless of its consequences. In the retributive framework, criminals are punished because they deserve it, not as a means towards any other goal. Punishment serves to provide a moral rebalancing by making the offender suffer as the victim has. Retributive theory is most strongly associated with the philosopher Immanuel Kant, who embraced a particularly harsh version, believing that the perpetrator of a crime should be made to suffer a punishment 'which according to the spirit of the penal law – even if not to the letter thereof – is the same as what he inflicted on others'.[13] In the more modern view, retributivism restores both the perpetrator and the victim to their original positions 'by ensuring that criminal sentences proportionally reflect the impact of the criminal act'.[14]

The expressive theory of criminal justice, by contrast, sees criminal punishment as a means for society as a whole to communicate its disapproval of the criminal acts,

---

[10] *Prosecutor v Kambanda* (Judgment and Sentence) ICTR-97-23-S (4 September 1998) para 28.

[11] *Prosecutor v. Rutaganda* (Judgment and Sentence) ICTR-96-3-T (6 December 1999) para 456. The Trial Chamber stated that penalising mass atrocity could deter potential future offenders by 'showing them that the international community shall not tolerate the serious violation of international humanitarian law and human rights'.

[12] Luis Moreno-Ocampo, Keynote Address at 'Pursuing International Justice: A Conversation with Luis Moreno-Ocampo' <http://www.cfr.org/content/publications/attachments/MorenoOcampo.CFR.2.4.2010.pdf> last accessed 25 May 2011.

[13] I Kant, *Metaphysical Elements of Justice* (Part I of the Metaphysics in Morals: John Ladd (tr), Hackett Publishing, London 1999) (first published 1797), 171–172.

[14] Note, 'Victim's Justice: Legitimizing the Sentencing Regime of the International Criminal Court' (2004) 43 *Columbia J Transnat'l L* 229, 243; see also J Hampton, 'Correcting Harms Versus Righting Wrongs: The Goal of Retribution' (1992) 39 *UCLA L Rev* 1659, 1686.

and to express allegiance to the moral order. Under this theory, the punishment's effect on society, or the convicted criminal, is merely incidental to that goal. Punishment is used because it 'has a *symbolic significance* largely missing from other kinds of penalties', and is therefore 'a conventional device for the expression of attitudes of resentment and indignation, and of judgments of disapproval and reprobation, on the part either of the punishing authority himself or of those "in whose name" the punishment is inflicted'.[15] Durkheim, describing this philosophy, argues that the point of punishment is 'not to make the guilty expiate his crime through suffering or to intimidate possible imitators through threats, but to buttress those consciences which violations of a rule can and must necessarily disturb in their faith'.[16]

The consequentialist model looks at the practical consequences of punishment, such as deterrence or rehabilitation, finding 'the justification of a criminal sanction in the predicted consequences of condemning the particular defendant as a criminal and depriving him of his liberty'.[17] Rehabilitation, reconciliation, incapacitation, and specific and general deterrence are all examples of consequentialist justifications for criminal justice.

Deterrence is criminal punishment's capacity to dissuade criminals from committing crimes. Specific deterrence refers to the punishment's ability to dissuade the punished offender from committing future offences after his release. (Incapacitation, in which the offender is prevented from committing future crimes because he is in prison, can be thought of as even-more-specific deterrence.) However, the most common deterrent goal is general deterrence, in which punishment dissuades other potential offenders from committing crimes.[18] Typically, discussions of deterrence refer to general deterrence, unless otherwise specified, and this chapter follows that convention.

The traditional model of deterrence holds that potential offenders are deterred from crime by the prospect of the punishment itself – that they are rational actors reacting to an increase in the cost of criminal activity. Such arguments rest on the assumption that 'when other variables are held constant, an increase in a person's probability of conviction or punishment if convicted would generally decrease, perhaps substantially, perhaps negligibly the number of offenses he commits'.[19] Under this theory, the strength of the deterrent effect is a function of the relative certainty and severity of the sentence. If the punishment is too light, or the prospect of conviction is too remote, then potential perpetrators will not be deterred.

---

[15] Sloane (n 4) 42; quoting J Feinberg, 'The Expressive Function of Punishment' in J Feinberg (ed) *Doing and Deserving: Essays in the Theory of Responsibility* (Princeton University Press, Princeton 1970).

[16] E Durkheim, *Moral Education: A Study in the Theory and Application of the Sociology of Education* (Free Press, New York 1973) 167.

[17] GP Fletcher, *Rethinking Criminal Law* (OUP, Oxford 2000) 414.

[18] Ibid.

[19] GS Becker, 'Crime and Punishment: An Economic Approach' (1968) 76 *J of Political Economy* 169, 176.

Alternatively, a more recent literature argues that formal criminal punishment deters crime not because would-be criminals fear the punishment, but because they fear the broader social consequences of a criminal conviction. Under this model, punishment's deterrent value depends primarily on its ability to reinforce social norms, and on the severity of the informal sanctions it triggers, rather than on the severity of the punishment itself.[20] 'Official *actions* can set off societal *reactions* that may provide potential offenders with more reason to avoid conviction than the officially imposed unpleasantness of punishment.'[21]

## III. Who Are We Trying to Deter?

The foregoing suggests that international criminal tribunals face challenges in raising the costs of crime through criminal punishment. However, it is important to note that deterrence does not require that the costs meet an objective standard. Rather, the costs of committing crime must outweigh the benefits for a particular potential offender. It is therefore surprising that very little of the literature on international criminal law has undertaken any serious consideration of why individuals commit mass atrocity. This is a bit like a campaign to reduce teenage pregnancy failing to consider whether teenagers find sex appealing.

The political science literature on large-scale violence against civilians during wartime suggests two distinct – but not mutually exclusive – models of perpetrator motivation. In the first model, atrocities are 'top-down' crimes, the result of military and rebel leaders' strategic deployment of violence against civilians in order to gain an advantage in a conflict.[22] In these cases, mass atrocity is committed in pursuit

---

[20] DS Nagin, 'Criminal Deterrence Research at the Outset of the Twenty-First Century' (1998) *Crime & Justice* 1, 19.

[21] Ibid 19, 21. This effect becomes stronger for individuals with a high commitment to conventionality. For instance, in an experiment designed to determine how willing ordinary middle-class individuals were to violate tax laws, the respondents were dramatically more willing to consider tax noncompliance when they risked only a confidential monetary penalty than when they risked public criminal sanctions. '[I]f the evasion gamble also involved putting reputation and community standing at risk, our middle-class respondents were seemingly unwilling to consider taking the noncompliance gamble.'

[22] Downes has found that, in interstate wars, 'civilian victimization results from desperation to win and to save lives on one's own side induced by costly, protracted wars of attrition'. AB Downes, 'Desperate Times, Desperate Measures: the Causes of Civilian Victimization in War' (2006) 30(4) *Int'l Security* 152, 154. Studies of government violence against civilians in civil wars suggest a similar pattern. Valentino, Huth and Balch-Lindsay suggest that mass atrocities in civil wars can be a strategic choice in situations where governments face well-organised guerilla insurgencies that rely on the local civilian population, and have been unsuccessful at defeating them using conventional means. B Valentino, PL Huth and D Balch-Lindsay, 'Draining the Sea: Mass Killing and Guerrilla Warfare' (2004) 58(2) *Int'l Organization* 375, 377. Stanton suggests that this logic may apply equally to rebel groups in

of an objective that the offender is likely to consider extremely important (such as control over territory, or avoidance of military defeat). Consequently, for these potential perpetrators, the perceived benefits of offending will be very high. In order for deterrence to operate, the costs imposed by criminal punishment would have to be correspondingly high.

In the second, 'bottom-up' model, leaders do not affirmatively order the commission of mass atrocity, but rather fail to prevent their troops from committing crimes against civilians. This model suggests a more central role for individual-level decisions, and, importantly, criminality.[23] The impetus for committing crimes lies with low-ranking individuals, and the opportunity arises because their superiors are unable or unwilling to restrain them.[24] In these cases, commanders are less likely to expect extensive benefits from the commission of mass atrocity. Thus, deterring them may be achievable at a lower cost threshold.

These accounts imply that there are four distinct categories of mass atrocity perpetrators: (1) leaders or military commanders who *order or encourage* the commission of criminal violence; (2) their subordinates, who commit crimes because of that top-down pressure; (3) leaders who *fail to prevent or punish* the commission of criminal violence by their subordinates; and (4) their subordinates, who commit crimes of their own volition, due to the absence of any credible restraint from above. Because they have different motivations for offending, these groups are also likely to differ in their responses to deterrent influences. For ICTs to reduce the incidence of mass atrocity, they must significantly alter the incentive structure for at least one of these groups of perpetrators.

---

civil wars. She attributes strategic decisions to commit coercive violence against civilians to the low likelihood of achieving victory in civil wars, noting that both governments and rebel groups use violence against civilians 'to create enough military and political pressure on their opponent to force negotiations or concession'. J Stanton, *Strategies of Violence and Restraint in Civil War* (PhD Dissertation, Columbia University Department of Political Science 2009) 33.

[23] Mueller argues that violence against civilians in the former Yugoslavia and Rwanda was 'the result of a situation in which common, opportunistic, sadistic, and often distinctly non-ideological marauders were recruited and permitted free rein by political authorities'. Here, commander involvement was simply indifference to the possibility of violence against civilians, rather than active encouragement of it. J Mueller, 'The Banality of Ethnic Conflict' (2000) 25(1) *Int'l Security* 42, 43.

[24] Weinstein's work suggests a different account of leaders who, while not affirmatively choosing to employ mass violence against civilians, fail to rein in the criminal element among their combatants. He finds that rebel groups operating in the presence of abundant natural resources or external support commit higher levels of indiscriminate violence than other rebel groups. He argues that the resource environment drives the character of the rebel group through the mechanism of comparative ease or difficulty of recruitment. In resource-constrained settings, recruits join up out of ideological commitment, while in resource-rich settings, they may join out of simple opportunism. J Weinstein, *Inside Rebellion: The Politics of Insurgent Violence* (CUP, Cambridge 2007) 7.

## IV. Applying Traditional Deterrence Theory to the International Context

Much of the discussion of international tribunals' potential impact appears to presume that international tribunals will have similar effects to domestic ones. However, much like a kiwi fruit and Jemaine Clement, they are not actually very similar. The presumption that international justice will operate like domestic justice overlooks key structural differences between international tribunals and municipal justice systems. In most developed countries' criminal justice systems, prosecutors do not investigate and prosecute crimes in isolation. Rather, they are part of an institutional network that includes investigative authorities, such as police detectives or judges, depending on the legal culture in question; and enforcement officers, such as police, parole officers, and pre-trial detention monitors. Criminal trials may take place in tandem with civil actions arising out of the same subject matter. Administrative agencies may be involved at the policy level, or act in a supervisory capacity.

By contrast, international tribunals float unmoored from any such system, a sort of 'Howl's Moving Castle' of jurisprudence. They lack a police force with the capacity for forcible arrests, which has had a noticeable effect (namely, individuals with outstanding warrants who remain noticeably un-arrested). Perhaps more importantly, they lack the resources and authority to conduct investigations in the way that is expected of detectives or investigative magistrates. It is rare that they have access to 'fresh' crime scenes. They have too few staff to investigate international crimes thoroughly, and so must rely on reports from NGOs, other UN bodies, and media reports to bolster their evidence gathering. Although there is no reason to believe these sources are illegitimate *per se*, they can be expected to focus on issues within their own mandates (such as protecting refugees or selling newspapers respectively), leaving international criminal tribunals with a perspective that has been distorted by other organisations' priorities. Moreover, as evidenced by the cavalcade of problems in the ICC's trial of Thomas Lubanga, these evidence-gathering methods can also cause such serious evidentiary issues that they jeopardise the trials themselves.[25]

Similarly, because international tribunals do not have the capacity to try substantial numbers of perpetrators, and have thus largely followed a policy of trying only the 'worst of the worst' offenders, they lack the network effects that are created when prosecutions are built from the bottom up, through a series of lower-level prosecutions and plea agreements. The latter method is typical in organised crime or other large-scale criminal prosecutions in domestic courts. Although it requires compromises, this bottom-up prosecution strategy offers

---

[25] See for example *Situation in the Democratic Republic of the Congo: Prosecutor v Lubanga* (Decision on the Prosecution's Urgent Request for Variation of the Time-Limit to Disclose the Identity of Intermediary 143 or Alternatively to Stay Proceedings Pending Further Consultations with the VWU) ICC-01/04-01/06 (8 July 2010).

significant benefits. It motivates witnesses to testify, in order to avoid prosecution or to obtain more lenient sentences. It provides numerous opportunities for establishing common facts, such as senior officials' involvement in criminal acts. Also, it prevents the appearance of unfairness that results when a handful of individuals are prosecuted for criminal acts in which thousands were complicit. Because international tribunals do not have the resources to follow that strategy, they are hampered in their ability to prosecute complex crimes. This has led to peculiar results, such as Saddam Hussein being prosecuted for extrajudicial killings in Dujail, rather than mass atrocities such as the Anfal Campaign; and the Special Court for Sierra Leone's decision to attach all charges to a handful of high-level commanders under a joint criminal enterprise theory, while slightly lower-ranking individuals, who still had significant involvement in the atrocities that were committed during the civil war, were not prosecuted at all (and, in many cases, profited directly from their compatriots' trials via witness protection and compensation agreements).[26]

Finally, international accountability mechanisms have the unenviable task of attempting to mediate between very different legal cultures. In international criminal tribunals, this problem has encompassed vicious in-fighting between common law and civil law system lawyers over competing standards for rights protections, as well as quixotic efforts to render Western-style justice legible to communities with different cultural modes of accountability. At the hybrid tribunals, the need to integrate municipal substantive and procedural law with international norms and standards further complicates matters. In all cases, the lack of hierarchy of courts and uncertain role of precedent hampers the ability of the international legal system to deliver justice in a manner analogous to that of domestic legal systems.

At a more finely grained level, because international tribunals offer only a combination of unlikely prosecutions and relatively lenient punishments, they are handicapped in their ability to deter international crimes under the standard deterrence model. As a threshold matter, the ICTY, ICTR and the hybrid tribunals have strict geographic and temporal limitations, and so offer zero danger of prosecution to the vast majority of potential offenders. The ICTR, for instance, has jurisdiction over only those crimes that occurred on Rwandan territory during

---

[26] See for example J Easterday, *The Trial of Charles Taylor Part 1: Prosecuting 'Persons Who Bear The Greatest Responsibility'* (UC Berkeley War Crimes Studies Center, June 2010) 44–47 (noting that witnesses received payments for, *inter alia*, school fees, rent, 'maintenance' and 'miscellaneous', in addition to direct trial-related expenditures such as travel and hotel costs); C da Silva, 'The Hybrid Experience Of The Special Court For Sierra Leone' in BS Brown (ed) *Research Handbook on International Criminal Law* (Elgar Publishing, Northampton 2011) 245–246 (noting that the prosecution's reliance on insider witnesses who may themselves have committed war crimes 'raises questions as to whether there should have been more prosecutorial restraint on the extent of its reliance [on] such insiders to prove its case, given the fine line between indictees and insider witnesses', and pointing out that RUF commander Issa Sesay, who is currently serving a 52-year sentence after his conviction for war crimes, was originally considered as an insider witness, not an indictee).

1994.²⁷ Consequently, to the extent that any potential perpetrator elsewhere saw the creation of the ICTR as increasing their probability of conviction and punishment for mass atrocities, it would only be through the attenuated mechanism of signalling that another such institution might be created that would have jurisdiction over her own acts. This is clearly different from an individual's analysis in a domestic jurisdiction in which a new statute has entered into law that criminalises the act they are considering committing.

Although that particular concern is not present with the ICC, whose jurisdiction is potentially unlimited in geographic scope (subject to the procedural limitations on how cases may be referred to the court) and applies to any events taking place after 1 July 2002, other difficulties remain. The first requirement for a deterrent effect, that potential perpetrators believe that there is some non-negligible likelihood that they will face prosecution and punishment, poses a large hurdle for the ICC. In its eight years of operation, the court has indicted only 23 individuals for genocide, war crimes or crimes against humanity. During that same period, according to the UCDP/PRIO database, there were over 200 episodes of armed conflict, involving thousands of armed actors.²⁸ Thus, the chance of ending up on trial, although marginally greater than before the court was established, is still tiny. It is comparable to the possibility of being crushed by a falling meteor – certainly *possible*, and unpleasant if it comes to pass, but not the sort of probable life event that leads one to reconsider major strategic plans. That remote possibility is unlikely to weigh heavily in a potential offender's calculus.²⁹

Additionally, the fact that the risk of prosecution for any given potential offender is identifiably non-random may also affect cost–benefit calculations. Nearly all of the current indictments relate to conflicts in sub-Saharan Africa (in the eastern Democratic Republic of the Congo, Cote D'Ivoire, the Central African Republic, Darfur, Northern Uganda and Kenya). The single exception is Libya, which is an African country, but not a sub-Saharan one. Additionally, most of the indictees have been rebel commanders. Although the court has now issued indictments for several prominent government figures, it may still appear justifiable for potential perpetrators who are not rebel commanders in sub-Saharan Africa to discount their chance of prosecution. The average Central Asian dictator is likely to feel comfortably beyond the reach of international justice should he be seized of the urge to boil his political opponents alive.

Nor do international criminal tribunals present a credible threat of severe punishment. Mark Drumbl, in his analysis of the severity of sentencing for international crimes, has found that 'at both the national and international levels, punishment for multiple international crimes is generally not more severe than

---

[27] Statute of the International Criminal Tribunal for Rwanda, UN Doc S/RES/955, UN Security Council, 1994 ('ICTR Statute'), art 7.

[28] NP Gleditsch et al, 'Armed Conflict 1946–2001: A New Dataset' (2002) 39(5) *J of Peace Research* 615.

[29] MA Drumbl, 'Collective Violence and Individual Punishment: The Criminality of Mass Atrocity' (2004) 99 *Northwestern U L Rev* 539, 560.

what national jurisdictions award for a single serious ordinary crime'.[30] He posits that this is 'in part due to the reality that the massive nature of atrocity cannot be reflected in retributive punishment owing to human rights standards, which cabin the range of sanction'.[31]

Moreover, international tribunals fare particularly poorly when compared to the non-judicial retribution that perpetrators of atrocities already face. Notably, it was summary executions, not more lenient sentences, which were considered the primary alternative to the Nuremberg Tribunal.[32] Winston Churchill was of the opinion that the Nuremberg defendants should have simply been taken out back and shot post haste. It can hardly be argued that trials are more punitive than a hole in the head.

Similar considerations operate today. For instance, Ku and Nzelibe find that coup perpetrators in Africa 'routinely face sanctions which are likely to be more severe and certain than any meted out by any existing or future ICT'.[33] Death, imprisonment and exile (not to mention impromptu earectomies)[34] are frequent outcomes for African leaders whose policy choices meet with dissatisfaction from their constituents or rivals. Ku and Nzelibe suggest that potential perpetrators of mass atrocity are likely to face at least as dire possible outcomes.[35] They therefore conclude that the threat of prosecution is more likely a 'weaker substitute, rather than a complement, to pre-existing sanctions against likely ICT targets'.[36]

The above analysis of perpetrators' motivations suggests that commanders who affirmatively order mass atrocity are also likely to perceive high potential benefits from the commission of mass atrocity. The risk of prosecution and punishment is therefore not likely to change their decision-making calculus. However, the same might not be true of those commanders who permit the commission of, or fail to punish their subordinates for, mass atrocity. Given a high enough likelihood of facing prosecution and punishment, this set of potential perpetrators may be more easily deterrable.

However, that type of prosecution is rare. Jean-Pierre Bemba is the only ICC indictee to date who can be categorised as a commander who permitted the commission of mass atrocity, rather than affirmatively ordering it. He is on trial for

---

[30] MA Drumbl, *Atrocity, Punishment, and International Law* (CUP, Cambridge 2007) 15.

[31] Ibid.

[32] MJ Bazyler, 'The Role of the Soviet Union in the International Military Tribunal at Nuremberg and Impact on Its Legacy' <http://www.amnestyusa.org/events/western/pdf/AmnestyConference_BazylerMichaelCLE.pdf> last accessed 22 May 2011, 1.

[33] J Ku and J Nzelibe, 'Do International Criminal Tribunals Deter or Exacerbate Humanitarian Atrocities?' (2006) 84 *Washington U L Rev* 777, 807.

[34] Former President of Liberia Samuel Doe was mutilated in this way before his execution. See B Law, 'Meeting the Hard Man of Liberia' *BBC News* (London 4 November 2006) <http://news.bbc.co.uk/2/hi/programmes/from_our_own_correspondent/6113682.stm> last accessed 22 May 2011.

[35] They find that 'more than one-half of all African leaders since independence through 1991 have been killed, imprisoned, or exiled'. Ku and Nzelibe (n 33) 802.

[36] Ibid 780.

violence committed by his Congolese MLC militia against civilians in the Central African Republic while helping President Ange-Félix Patassé to put down a coup. Bemba is not alleged to have directed his troops to commit atrocities. In fact, he was not even present in the Central African Republic for most of the campaign. Rather, he is charged with failing in his responsibility to prevent or punish their crimes. The Prosecutor's opening statement alleged: 'Jean-Pierre Bemba knowingly let the 1,500 armed men he commanded and controlled commit hundreds of rapes, hundreds of pillages. Command responsibility means that the commander owns the actions of his troops.'[37] The doctrine of command responsibility applied here by the Prosecutor reflects a belief that military commanders are essentially the 'least cost avoiders' of mass atrocity, who are better placed than anyone else – including subordinates on the crime scene – to prevent such wrong. The foregoing discussion of the theory of 'traditional' deterrence and the dynamics of the commission of mass atrocity suggests that Bemba's is the type of case where the international criminal law's potential traditional deterrent bite will be strongest. Similarly situated commanders will not have overwhelming incentives to allow the commission of violence against civilians (although they may still have strong incentives, such as the need to avoid attrition, or desire to avoid expending the effort to restrain and discipline). They are also less likely to face extensive pre-existing sanctions for allowing their subordinates to offend. Thus, enforcing superiors' criminal liability for the actions of questionably controlled subordinates may induce a measurable change to their cost–benefit analysis. However, current international criminal prosecutorial policies are not likely to maximise this deterrent effect, because they rarely focus on this type of defendant.

## V. Prospects for Expressive Deterrence in the International System

Given that international criminal tribunals offer only a remote chance of relatively weak punishment, and are addressing themselves to a population who may face extremely high perceived benefits for the commission of crimes, their prospects for deterrence according to the classical model of certainty and severity of punishment outlined above seem relatively limited. A closer examination of the literature, however, indicates that the deterrent claims made by some international justice proponents may be relying on a very different mechanism than this standard general-deterrence model.

---

[37] International Criminal Court, Opening Statement of the Prosecutor (22 November 2010) <http://www.icc-cpi.int/NR/rdonlyres/30DF9EE7-E1F2-4407-BA21-D81D8C7A785C/282701/101122BembaProsecutorsOpeningStatementformatted.pdf> last accessed 22 May 2011, 3.

As noted above, the rhetoric of courts and commentators suggests an alternate theory that international criminal tribunals will deter future crimes through the strength of their *expressive* force, rather than the severity of their criminal sanctions. For instance, in the *Kambanda* decision, the ICTR asserted a belief that future potential perpetrators would be deterred by the knowledge that 'the international community was not ready to tolerate the serious violations of international humanitarian law and human rights', a statement that was repeated a year later in its *Rutaganda* decision.[38] Similar sentiments can be found in the frequent claims that international criminal tribunals are necessary because, by failing to act, the international community 'permits' the crimes to occur.

Although those statements are couched in the language of deterrence, the logic behind them is primarily expressive in nature: they are concerned with international justice as a means of expressing international norms. This hybrid expressive-deterrence theory appears to assume that if the international community expresses its disapproval of international crimes strongly enough by prosecuting perpetrators, then that disapproval will dissuade others from committing similar acts in the future. The apparent logic here is that no one wants to be known as a war criminal. In fact, rebel commanders do seem to have an obsessive need to self-define – see for example General Butt Naked (née Joshua Blahyi), General Peanut Butter (née Adolphus Dolo), and Bosco 'Terminator' Ntaganda – and are not likely to welcome an internationally-assigned identity.

A small scholarly literature addresses itself to the mechanism by which international tribunals can deter crime via the expressive value of criminal punishment, rather than through the costs of punishment itself. Robert Sloane, for instance, argues that international criminal law possesses such power to discredit and stigmatise elites that 'the mere issuance of an indictment, the very prospect of a trial, is itself the "punishment" by which [international criminal law] may deter'.[39] Likewise, Akhavan claims that 'incitement to ethnic violence is usually aimed at the acquisition and sustained exercise of power', and thus criminal punishment deters because '[m]omentary glory and political ascendancy, to be followed by downfall and humiliation, are considerably less attractive than long-term political viability'.[40]

Thus, the theory of the expressive deterrence model is that international criminal tribunals are able to deter future atrocities because they have the ability to stigmatise potential perpetrators as war criminals. For this to work, two factors must be present. First, international criminal trials must be an effective means of stigmatising perpetrators of international crimes. If they are not, then there will be no reputational consequences for potential perpetrators to avoid. Second, the consequences of that stigma must be sufficiently harsh to be worth avoiding, and to outweigh competing incentives to commit atrocities.

---

[38] *Prosecutor v Kambanda* (Judgment and Sentence) ICTR-97-23-S (4 September 1998) para 28; *Prosecutor v Rutaganda* (Judgment and Sentence) ICTR-96-3-T (6 December 1999) para 456.
[39] Sloane (n 4) 74.
[40] Akhavan (n 7) 12.

## VI. Can International Criminal Tribunals Stigmatise Potential Perpetrators?

For 'expressive deterrence' to work, international criminal tribunals must be able to effectively stigmatise the people whom they prosecute. International criminal trials do enjoy a handful of advantages in this regard. For one thing, international tribunals are performing a function that is familiar, in a familiar way – trying the accused and sentencing the guilty. The concept of criminal guilt is widely understood, so tribunals are not dealing with a novel concept, even though the specifics of particular crimes may take many forms around the world.

Likewise, courts are generally seen as legitimate institutions to deliver criminal sentences. By contrast, some other types of interventions, such as armed peacekeeping missions, have no ordinary domestic analogue. International tribunals also enjoy considerable influence on the international stage, making stigma a significant force for elites who hope to enjoy a continuing role in international politics, diplomacy, industry or finance.

Furthermore, under this model, the rarity of international criminal prosecutions may actually be an advantage. For an event to carry stigma, it must be relatively uncommon.[41] Thus, if criminal prosecutions are too frequent, then they will lose their ability to deliver social stigma, and their deterrent value will be weakened. This theory suggests that international tribunals' inability to prosecute more than a handful of criminals may not be the crippling problem that it is for classical deterrence.

However, international tribunals do suffer from significant disadvantages in their ability to stigmatise perpetrators. For a tribunal to offer a credible threat of social consequences, the relevant community must accept both (i) the validity of the norm that has been violated, and (ii) the authority and legitimacy of the tribunal. The international criminal system struggles on both counts. Firstly, the collective character of international crimes means that individual perpetrators often operate under the 'figurative compulsion of an inverted morality or collective pathology whereby ordinarily prohibited conduct starts to appear as a holy obligation, a positive achievement'.[42] In that context, perpetrators are likely to perceive international norms as irrelevant or oppressive.

Secondly, the legitimacy of the international tribunals' authority, in the eyes of perpetrators and their communities, cannot be taken for granted. Activists often seem to assume that the 'international' character of international criminal tribunals means that they will automatically be perceived as prestigious, justice-delivering institutions. However, history suggests that within affected communities, tribunals can be seen as politicised institutions with particular national or ethnic agendas. For instance, Patricia Wald notes that in a survey of Bosnian judges and prosecutors' attitudes towards the ICTY, responses were sharply divided between Bosnian Muslims, who believed the tribunal to be largely fair, Bosnian Serbs, who

---

[41] Nagin (n 20) 22.
[42] Sloane (n 4) 76.

called it a 'political body that was an instrument of Western influence rather than an independent judicial institution', and Bosnian Croats, who believed that the tribunal focused its efforts unfairly on Croatian defendants.[43] In more recent years, the ICC's focus on African crimes has led many to perceive it as a neo-colonialist institution meddling on behalf of wealthy foreign nations who can't quite kick the imperialist habit.[44]

Moreover, as a simply practical matter, it is not clear that global understanding of international criminal law has reached a high enough level to influence the audience of potential perpetrators. General confusion persists about what international tribunals are, what crimes they are able to try, and what cases they have commenced. For instance, a recent article in the *New York Times* stated that it was likely that Libya's Muammar Gaddafi would be 'indicted by the International Criminal Court in the Hague for the bombing of Pan Am 103 in 1988, and atrocities inside Libya'.[45] In fact, of course, the bombing of Pan Am 103 is outside the ICC's temporal jurisdiction, which only covers events that took place after 1 July 2002. Furthermore, because Libya is not a signatory of the Rome Statute, the court only has jurisdiction over crimes covered by the referral in Security Council Resolution 1970, which is limited to 'the situation in the Libyan Arab Jamahiriya since 15 February 2011', so most 'atrocities inside Libya' are beyond its scope.[46] The fact that the *New York Times* made such an error, despite its resources and considerable expertise, suggests that the workings of the ICC remain a mystery even to well-educated, interested observers.

Understanding among affected populations is, unsurprisingly, no better. Sara Darehshori, writing about her experiences with outreach to affected populations at a number of international tribunals, notes that international tribunals begin with a significant handicap in this regard, compared to national courts:

> In most courts, there is no need to ensure dissemination of information about the workings of justice mechanisms because the legitimacy of the courts is well established in the communities which they serve.

---

[43] P Wald, 'The International Tribunal For The Former Yugoslavia Comes of Age: Some Observations on Day-to-Day Dilemmas of an International Court' (2001) 5 *Wash U J of Law and Policy* 87, 115.

[44] See for example N Waddel and P Clark, *Courting Conflict? Justice, Peace, and the ICC in Africa* (Royal African Society 2008) 8–9 ('[T]he Court's focus on Africa has stirred African Sensitivities about sovereignty and self-determination – not least because of the continent's history of colonization and a pattern of decisions made for Africa by outsiders'); MM deGuzman, 'Gravity and Legitimacy of the ICC' (2008) 32 *Fordham Int'l L J* 1400, 1446 ('[W]ith regard to situation selection, some African populations perceive the Court's current focus on Africa as unfair, charging that it is reminiscent of colonialism. The Prosecutor's protestations that the African situations are the gravest have not stemmed this criticism').

[45] DE Sanger and E Schmitt, 'U.S. and Allies Seek a Refuge for Qaddafi' *New York Times* (New York, 16 April 2011).

[46] UNSC Res 1970 (2011) UN Doc S/Res/1970.

The courts are usually quite accessible to the local population and proceedings are conducted in the local language.[47]

International tribunals do not enjoy those advantages. Their legitimacy is not established, their proceedings often take place in a different country from the one in which the crimes occurred, and trials are conducted in English and French, rather than the local language. Darehshori notes a litany of outreach problems experienced by international criminal tribunals, ranging from the ICTY being portrayed by its opponents as an agent of ethnic persecution that mistreated its detainees;[48] to rumours in the Democratic Republic of the Congo that the ICC 'paid [non-governmental organizations] to find victims and will fabricate victims if necessary to obtain funding from the court, that President Kabila is using the court to get rid of his enemies, and that the DRC government must approve any arrest warrants',[49] and that Thomas Lubanga was only arrested because he killed 'white people' (i.e. UN peacekeepers);[50] to a belief amongst Darfuri refugees that the ICC 'would arrest all criminals in Darfur or at least the fifty-one identified by the International Commission of Inquiry', or that it was a potential peacekeeping mission.[51] Such basic and widespread misunderstandings about the activities of international criminal tribunals do not inspire confidence in their ability to deter crimes under the expressive-deterrence model.

## VII. What Are the Expected Consequences of Stigma for Potential Perpetrators?

Even assuming that indictments or convictions by international tribunals are able to create a threat of stigma for potential perpetrators, for expressive deterrence to operate, the consequences of that stigma must be significant enough to outweigh potential perpetrators' incentives to commit international crimes. Previously, we set forth four categories of potential perpetrators: (1) commanders who order or incite crimes; (2) the rank-and-file troops whom those commanders order or incite; (3) commanders who fail to restrain their troops from committing crimes; and (4) their troops, who commit crimes for personal gain.

The question, therefore, is whether potential perpetrators from any of those categories perceive the stigma of indictment or prosecution by an international

---

[47] S Darehshori, 'Lessons for Outreach from the Ad Hoc Tribunals, the Special Court for Sierra Leone, and the International Criminal Court' (2008) 14 *New England J Int'l and Comp L* 299, 300.
[48] Ibid 301.
[49] Ibid 305
[50] Ibid 305.
[51] Ibid 306.

tribunal as severe enough to outweigh the benefits of committing (or failing to prevent or punish) atrocities. At the international level, there are certainly some consequences that accompany an indictment by an international tribunal. The most obvious is that indicted individuals are unable to travel to states that are parties to the court in question, limiting their ability to act on the international stage. However, there are also other negative consequences associated with not being a member-in-good-standing of the international community. Indictments and prosecutions are also likely to be accompanied by asset freezes, targeted sanctions, and other similar international remedies that apply not only to the indicted individual, but also to his associates.

For elites who have power, and are considering attacks on civilians as a means of retaining it, such consequences may have some marginal persuasive effect by reducing the value of the power such leaders are struggling to keep. Therefore, it seems that potential perpetrators in categories one and three might be deterred, to some extent, by the prospect of the international consequences that accompany indictment and prosecution. However, for potential perpetrators in categories 2 and 4 – individual troops who might commit atrocities under orders, or for their own personal reasons – it seems unlikely that such international consequences would have much deterrent effect. Travel bans, asset freezes and other such consequences are limited to elites (as, for the most part, are international travel and the possession of significant assets).

Stigma within potential perpetrators' local communities would be more likely to have a strong effect on all categories of perpetrators – leaders because it would undermine their legitimacy, and subordinates because they would face consequences in their communities after the cessation of hostilities. However, because international tribunals have not yet been particularly successful at creating stigma within affected populations, it remains unclear whether such stigma would be strong enough to counteract the various groups' incentives to commit atrocities.

Expressive deterrence, therefore, suggests a somewhat different prosecutorial strategy than traditional deterrence does. Because international criminal tribunals are currently more able to create stigma within the international community than within affected communities, if expressive deterrence is the goal, then it makes sense for prosecutions to focus on prominent, high-level offenders who seek a continuing role in global politics. Such individuals are more likely to be deterred by the prospect of being tarred as a war criminal by the international community than lower-level offenders, who tend to be less concerned about the tone in which their name is spoken in the corridors of New York, Geneva or Brussels.

Prosecutions of prominent, high-profile offenders have the additional benefit of being newsworthy: the arrest warrant for President Omar Hassan Al-Bashir of Sudan was heavily reported around the world, while the prosecutions of less famous individuals, such as Bemba and Lubanga, have received dramatically less attention. Over time, this coverage may also have the benefit of increasing awareness and understanding of the activities of international criminal tribunals, which may also improve their expressive deterrence capabilities.

## Conclusion

The above analysis suggests that international criminal tribunals suffer from significant handicaps in their ability to produce deterrence under either the traditional or the expressive deterrence model. However, the two different models suggest different – even conflicting – strategies for overcoming those difficulties. If they wish to follow the traditional deterrence model, prosecutors will likely achieve the best results if they focus on leaders who failed to restrain their troops, rather than those who affirmatively ordered their subordinates to commit atrocities. However, under the expressive deterrence model, prosecutors are most likely to achieve a deterrent effect if they focus their efforts on high-profile, elite perpetrators whose prosecutions will be heavily reported in the media. While there may be overlap between those two categories, they are not likely to be identical. Consequently, international justice practitioners should think carefully about the goals they are trying to achieve, and the means by which they hope to do so.

# Hybrid Courts in Retrospect: Of Lost Legacies and Modest Futures

## Pádraig McAuliffe

Every manifestation of international criminal justice has occasioned a sizeable gap between the earnest expectations of their initial advocates and the disappointing reality of compromise, politics and unforeseen circumstance that ensues once they came into operation. The *ad hoc* tribunals for the former Yugoslavia and Rwanda were designed to 'put an end to such crimes' that occurred in each state and 'contribute to the maintenance of peace', but were helpless to prevent further war crimes in Kosovo and the Great Lakes region.[1] Universal jurisdiction – heralded in a brief spurt of activity in the years before the ICC as a means by which municipal courts could successfully pursue international justice in the absence of international criminal tribunal jurisdiction – has been under-utilised and criticised for jurisdictional imperialism, vulnerability to politicisation and difficulties of implementation.[2] The advent of the ICC gave rise to a sense of optimism that 'impunity has been dealt a decisive blow', but this has receded in the face of slow trials, questionable decisions and the familiar obstacles of power politics.[3] So too it has proven with the novel structure of the hybrid tribunal. Initially presumed to enjoy an inherent ability to knit the traditional preoccupations of international criminal justice to punish and deter with the more holistic aspirations of rule of law reconstruction, in practice the tribunals for Cambodia, East Timor, Kosovo and Sierra Leone have demonstrated that the imperative to punish quickly and cheaply has generally operated to the exclusion of the capacity-building and norm-inculcating functions their unique mixed structure appeared to promise.

---

[1]  UNSC Res 808 (22 February 1993) UN Doc S/RES/808; UNSC Res 955 (8 November 1994) UN Doc S/RES/955.

[2]  See for example T Moghadam, 'Revitalising Universal Jurisdiction: Lessons from Hybrid Tribunals Applied to the Case of Hissene Habré' (2008) 39 *Colum Hum Rts L Rev* 471.

[3]  Transcript of Press Conference with President Carlo Ciampi of Italy and Secretary-General Kofi Annan in Rome and New York by Videoconference, UN Doc SG/SM/8194 (11 April 2002).

As a preliminary matter, the editorial reason for focussing on these four tribunals only requires explanation. The Special Tribunal for Lebanon is clearly a hybrid tribunal, but given that it issued its first round of indictments only in late July 2011, it is excluded because it is at such an early stage in its work. Though it is clearly of mixed composition, it is worth remembering that the Bosnian War Crimes Chamber (BWCC) is merely one of three chambers of mixed-international composition operating within the Criminal Division of the State Court of Bosnia, the others being Organised Crime and General Crime Chambers. Indeed, the judges may sit simultaneously in the different chambers. Each project is intended to be fully absorbed into the national courts. Therefore, though hybrid in structure, the BWCC might best be conceptualised as a regional project of strengthening the rule of law and creating national capacity,[4] as occurs in other jurisdictions such as national courts in the Caribbean and Africa. As one observer points out, 'although it contains a significant international component, the [B]WCC is essentially a domestic institution operating under international law'.[5] This difference is worth bearing in mind by those tempted to compare its superior performance with the struggles of the other hybrid courts.

This chapter examines what indications the past practice of hybrid courts can provide us about their future, if any, in the increasingly uni-polar international criminal legal order dominated by the ICC. Beginning with a brief treatment of the optimistic theories espoused at the dawn of the hybrid court, the chapter contextualises the hybrid court experience as a one-sided battle between the traditional preoccupation with punishment or impunity and a hitherto-unrealised potential to use transitional accountability to catalyse the development of a rule of law culture. It then examines how this tension may play out in the era of the ICC's complementarity regime, where the hybrid structure may act as a complement or alternative to the body in The Hague.

## I. The Promise of Hybrid Courts

The only unifying definition of hybrid courts is that of a temporary criminal court of mixed international and domestic composition given that it may differ over the mix of law (some may try only domestic crimes, some only international but usually it is a mix of the two), physical location (domestic, foreign or both) and location within the domestic justice system (grafted onto the ordinary justice system or a special court independent of it). It is perhaps easier to say what it is not – while

---

[4] O Ortega-Martin and J Herman, 'Hybrid Tribunals and the Rule of Law: Notes from Bosnia & Herzegovina & Cambodia' (JAD-PbP Working Papers Series No 7, 2010) <http://www.uel.ac.uk/chrc/documents/WP7.pdf> last accessed 2 December 2011, 10.

[5] Human Rights Watch, 'Looking for Justice: The War Crimes Chamber in Bosnia and Herzegovina' (2006) <http://www.hrw.org/en/reports/2006/02/07/looking-justice-0> last accessed 2 December 2011, 2.

the Iraqi Special Tribunal/Supreme Iraqi Criminal Tribunal perches awkwardly between international and domestic law, the requirement to appoint foreign advisors or observers can be distinguished from the full judicial and prosecutorial roles adopted by international actors in hybrid tribunals. It is entirely *sui generis*.

Hybrid courts were constituted primarily as a response to the shortcomings of domestic courts, to whom the primary obligation to punish serious crimes attaches. It was initially predicted that the 'hybrid' element would also serve to remedy one of the main problems visible in fully international courts, namely their failure to catalyse or stimulate the revitalisation of domestic rule of law structures whose shortcomings compelled internationalisation in the first place. It was widely predicted that hybrid courts could merge the best elements of both international and domestic systems as a more successful and sustainable means of transitional accountability.[6] The potential for hybrid tribunals to mobilise holistic domestic rule of law reform was outlined in very influential and widely-cited articles by Laura Dickinson in 2002 and 2003,[7] with the critique therein refined and extended by a number of subsequent commentators.[8] The primary advantage claimed for hybrid tribunals was that their domestic staffing and location (if applicable) avoided the legitimacy deficit identified in the *ad hoc* tribunals, given the physical and psychological distance between the sites of the atrocities (in Yugoslavia and Rwanda) and the courts (in the Netherlands and Tanzania) which meant there was little or no connection between the affected population and the trials.[9] The hybrid tribunal structure was posited as a means of importing legitimacy to successor trials in politicised and hostile environments; the presence of international judges and prosecutors in either a majority or minority would alleviate fears of impartiality, while the trials would enjoy presumptive legitimacy in the eyes of the

---

[6] S Linton, 'Hybrid Tribunals: Searching for Justice in East Timor' (2003) 16 *Harv Hum Rts J* 245; see further, (n 7) and (n 8) below.

[7] The most influential is probably L Dickinson, 'The Promise of Hybrid Courts' (2003) 97 *AJIL* 295, which built on the author's earlier works, 'Transitional Justice in Afghanistan: The Promise of Mixed Tribunals' (2002) 31 *Denver J Int'l L & Policy* 23 and 'The Relationship between Hybrid Courts and International Courts: The Case of Kosovo' (2002/2003) 37 *New Eng L Rev* 1059.

[8] Most notably ER Higonnet, 'Restructuring Hybrid Courts: Local Empowerment and National Criminal Justice Reform' (2006) 23 *Arizona J Int'l & Comp L* 347; JI Turner, 'Nationalising International Criminal Law' (2005) 41 *Stanford J Int'l L* 1, and serving as the critical point of reference for SMH Nouwen, '"Hybrid Courts": The Hybrid Category of a New Type of International Crimes Courts' (2006) 2 *Utrecht L Rev* 190. Dickinson's mode of analysis was followed to a lesser extent, or referred to approvingly, in D Cohen, '"Hybrid" Justice in East Timor, Sierra Leone and Cambodia: "Lessons Learned" and Prospects for the Future' (2007) 43 *Stanford J Int'l L* 1; R Lipscomb, 'Restructuring the ICC Framework to Advance Transitional Justice: A Search for a Permanent Solution in Sudan' (2006) 106 *Columbia L Rev* 182; D Tarin, 'Prosecuting Saddam and Bungling Transitional Justice in Iraq' (2005) 45 *Virginia J Int'l L* 467.

[9] E.g. J Alvarez, 'Crimes of State/Crimes of Hate: Lessons from Rwanda' (1994) 24 *Yale J Int'l L* 365, 403.

local population as judges of their 'own kind are present as actors in the tribunal'.[10] It was anticipated that this sense of ownership would increase the relevancy of the court for the survivor populations and accord with the emerging consensus that nationally-led strategies were more conducive to sustainable peace-building.[11]

It was furthermore expected that hybrid tribunals would perform a capacity-building function by serving to instruct the domestic court system in how trials should generally be operated, and by developing the abilities of judges, prosecutors, defenders and administrators who might gradually be empowered to assume full responsibility.[12] To adopt a timeworn development cliché, while the *ad hoc* tribunals fished for justice, hybrids could teach how to fish. For example, David Cohen argued that hybrid composition 'offers unique opportunities for capacity-building in all areas of the court. Training and mentoring court actors and administrators … represent some of the most important contributions that a "hybrid" tribunal can make'.[13]

Thirdly, it was predicted that having local judges and lawyers participating in high-profile, foundational trials in their own country would have a beneficial 'demonstration effect' on emerging local legal systems, by offering exemplary standards of independence, impartiality and fair trial norms that would inculcate a cultural commitment and expectation among the public to continue to measure up to such yardsticks. Writers in the field have proposed that hybrid tribunals would allow greater opportunities for public debate,[14] construct networks between international experts and the local judiciary, encourage cross-fertilisation of international and domestic norms, and serve as a platform on which the local people 'absorb, apply interpret, critique and develop' international norms in the national criminal justice system.[15] Whereas, until now, transitional trials were approached in a retributivist manner directed primarily towards removing impunity for past acts, in the hybrid trial system the inculcation of exemplary fairness and due process standards domestically would be equally determinant of success. Hybrid tribunals would cross a psychological Rubicon; where something like the right to counsel is seen as law in one context within a state, it would assume a validity and force of its own in analogous contexts within that state in future. By the time of the UN Secretary-General's seminal 2004 'Report on Transitional Justice and the Rule of Law', hybrid tribunals had been mainstreamed as a policy choice. The Report repeated many of the academic arguments in favour of hybrid structures that emerged after their formation, arguing that 'specially tailored measures for keeping the public informed and effective techniques for capacity-building, can

---

[10] B Hall, 'Using Hybrid Tribunals as Trivias: Furthering the Goals of Post-Conflict Justice While Transferring Cases from the ICTY to Serbia's Domestic War Crimes Tribunal' (2005) 13 *Michigan State J Int'l L* 39, 57.

[11] UN SC, 'Report of the Secretary-General: The Rule of Law and Transitional Justice in Conflict and Post-Conflict Societies' UN Doc S/2004/616 (23 August 2004), para 15.

[12] Higonnet (n 8) 377.

[13] Cohen (n 8) 37.

[14] WW Burke-White, 'Regionalisation of International Criminal Law Enforcement: A Preliminary Exploration' (2003) 38 *Texas Int'l L J* 729, 737.

[15] Dickinson, 'The Promise of Hybrid Courts' (n 7) 304.

help ensure a lasting legacy in the countries concerned'.[16] By 2008, a report by the OHCHR on hybrid tribunals as a peace-building tool posited that 'substantive legal framework reform, professional development ... and raising awareness of the role of courts as independent and well-functioning rule-of-law institutions' remained at the core of their remit.[17]

However, what such claims ignore is the reality that any intention to integrate successor trials with holistic rule of law reform has historically remained at the margins of policy-making and negotiations when formulating internationalised judicial responses to gross human rights violations.[18] Those who negotiated the constituent statutes for the Nuremberg and Tokyo trials, the *ad hoc* tribunals and the ICC were more concerned with creating a global culture of accountability or non-impunity as a goal in itself than fostering the domestic rule of law. Hybrid tribunals were expected to engage with peace-building dynamics that international tribunals had hitherto assiduously avoided. The architects of the institutions of international criminal justice have historically focussed more on punishment in the immediate term than institution-building in the long term, and are at best agnostic as to whether international criminal law has a beneficial impact on the national justice system and domestic legitimacy.

> [W]hile other sectors have paid more attention to the idea of building domestic capacity and creating exit strategies, war crimes tribunals have remained largely unconcerned with these projects ... The human rights community has concerns about whether it is even normatively desirable to elevate the goal of capacity-building to the level of other goals of accountability mechanisms. This position assumes that certain important principles intrinsic to fully achieving accountability will be sacrificed if collaboration increases with domestic institutions and people.[19]

As such, while it was possible to argue that the traditionally minimalist goals of international criminal law institutions could incorporate a holistic 'rule of law reconstruction' legacy, this would constitute more of a revolution in the approach and priorities of the international community than a creative adaptation of existing approaches. Domestic rule of law development – like the harmonious development of international criminal law, rehabilitation of offenders or creation of a historical record – remains merely a secondary aspiration of those who negotiate international

---

[16] UN SC (n 11) para 44

[17] Office of the High Commissioner for Human Rights, 'Rule of Law Tools for Post-Conflict States: Maximising the Legacy of Hybrid Tribunals' (2008) HR/PUB/08/02, 2.

[18] D Joyce, 'The Historical Function of International Criminal Trials: Re-thinking International Criminal Law' (2004) 73 *Nordic J Int'l L* 461; LE Fletcher and HM Weinstein, 'Violence and Social Repair: Rethinking the Contribution of Justice to Reconciliation' (2002) 24 *HRQ* 573.

[19] V Hussain, 'Sustaining Judicial Rescues: The Role of Judicial Outreach and Capacity-Building Efforts in War Crimes Tribunals' (2004) 45 *Virginia J Int'l L* 547, 551.

criminal tribunals, by comparison with the overriding impulse of preventing impunity. For example, the Commission of Experts established by the UN to review the work of the Special Panels in East Timor judged them against what they referred to as the 'Five Core Achievements of the ICTY', namely spearheading the shift from impunity to accountability, establishing a historical record of the conflict, bringing justice to victims, accomplishments in international law and the rather nebulous strengthening of the rule of law.[20] Issues of capacity-building, the inculcation of fair trial norms and legitimacy played little role in this reckoning. Antonio Cassese's independent Report on the Special Court for Sierra Leone and a series of UNMIK and OSCE reports on the Regulation 64 panels in Kosovo concentrated primarily on the inefficiency of those bodies in fulfilling their duty to prosecute those most responsible for international crimes.[21] Issues of capacity-building and inculcation of fair trial norms were treated with incidental interest at best, notwithstanding the ostensibly more holistic initial expectations of these courts.

## II. The Experience of the Hybrid Courts

The hybrid tribunals for East Timor, Cambodia, Kosovo and Sierra Leone should be commended for establishing accountability as a standard of law and public policy where the alternative was systematic impunity. Notwithstanding their financial shortcomings and lack of diplomatic support, each tribunal contributed significantly to combating impunity in their respective theatres of operation, only struggling when it came to making the predicted cultural, normative and institutional impacts on the domestic rule of law. In Sierra Leone and Cambodia, the leading figures bearing greatest responsibility for the crimes coming within the jurisdiction of the hybrid tribunals were indicted, prosecuted or convicted by the respective courts, even if observers and victims would have preferred the net of accountability to be spread further down the ranks. The Timorese Special Panels completed 55 trials in four years, resulting in over 80 convictions, albeit not including the most senior Indonesian organisers of the violence surrounding the 1999 referendum.[22] Kosovo yielded jurisdiction to the ICTY for the prosecution of the most serious criminals from the Kosovar war, but nonetheless completed

---

[20] Report to Secretary-General of the Commission of Experts to Review the Prosecution of Serious Violations of Human Rights in Timor-Leste (then East Timor) in 1999 UN Doc S/2005/45825 (26 May 2005) para 31.

[21] Report on the Special Court for Sierra Leone submitted by the Independent Expert Antonio Cassese (12 December 2006) <http://www.sc-sl.org/LinkClick.aspx?fileticket=VTDHyrHasLc=&> last accessed 26 January 2012 and OSCE Mission in Kosovo, 'Kosovo Review of the Criminal Justice System 1999–2005: Reforms and Residual Concerns' (March 2006) <http://www.eulex-kosovo.eu/training/material/docs/KR/KR_Material/osce2321.pdf > last accessed 26 January 2012.

[22] Commission of Experts Report (n 20) para 120.

23 prosecutions that reversed or re-tried earlier ethnically-biased verdicts.[23] Notwithstanding some disparity in the numbers of indictments, prosecutions and trials, the current and completed tribunals have done something revolutionary in each society: they punished egregious breaches of human rights in state courts for the first time, when impunity of the sort that could imperil peace had previously been the norm. Beyond this retributive impulse, another limited but essential goal was achieved. By processing criminals in East Timor, Cambodia and Sierra Leone and by reversing unjust convictions in Kosovo, the influence of certain individuals and the potency of particular revanchist appeals based on political allegiance or ethnicity was reduced, and the potential for retributive attacks or instability receded in the formative years of the emerging peace. Society did not lurch back into the dominant and violent antagonisms that gave rise to the hybrid tribunals in any of the states where they were active; although the extent (if any) to which this could be attributed to the legacy of these courts becomes impossible to gauge when one considers the wide array of social, political, historical and security dynamics that will always exert more influence on a developing post-conflict society than a temporary court.

Though these outcomes fit within the parameters of what transitional criminal trials are traditionally designed to achieve, what is apparent in each tribunal is the consistent failure to go further in developing capacity, inculcating fair trial norms or becoming fully legitimate in the eyes of the survivor population. The completed hybrid courts have been subject to withering criticism in these regards.[24]

Hopes for capacity-building and for local ownership, perhaps best described by the Special Panels Judge Rapoza as the degree to which the national component acknowledge (or are allowed to acknowledge) the division of responsibility for operating the tribunal, have continually fallen short of expectations.[25] Initially, it was argued that local ownership imported by the hybrid model should be maximised to the extent compatible with fair and competent trials in the pursuit of legitimacy and capacity-building.[26] However, the reality in the years between 2000 and 2003 when hybrid tribunals were in their infancy was that UN officials were simultaneously

---

[23] UNMIK Department of Justice figures, cited in Amnesty International, 'The UN in Kosovo – A Legacy of Impunity' Index Number: EUR 70/015/2006 (8 November 2006) 5.

[24] E.g. T Perriello and M Wierda (International Center for Transitional Justice), 'Lessons Learned From the Deployment of International Judges and Prosecutors in Kosovo' (March 2006) <http://www.peace-justice-conference.info/download/Kosovo.study.pdf> last accessed 26 January 2012; C Reiger and M Wierda (International Center for Transitional Justice), 'The Serious Crimes Process in Timor-Leste: In Retrospect' (March 2006), 40 <http://ictj.org/sites/default/files/ICTJ-TimorLeste-Criminal-Process-2006-English.pdf> last accessed 26 January 2012, EE Stensrud, 'New Dilemmas in Transitional Justice: Lessons from the Mixed Courts in Sierra Leone and Cambodia' (2009) 46 *J Peace Research* 5.

[25] P Rapoza, 'Symposium: International Criminal Tribunals in the 21st Century: Hybrid Criminal Tribunals and the Concept of Ownership: Who Owns the Process?' (2006) 21 *American University Int'l L Rev* 525, 526.

[26] Cohen (n 8) 36–37; Dickinson 'The Promise of Hybrid Courts' (n 7) 307; A Cassese, 'The Role of Internationalized Courts and Tribunals in the Fight against International

vetoing negotiations with Cambodia because local participation was too great,[27] UNMIK was progressively weakening Kosovar participation in the most important trials,[28] and the Sierra Leonean government was voluntarily relinquishing ever-greater control over the bench and prosecution to internationals.[29] Though it was assumed that hybrid tribunals would be genuinely co-operative, the tendency of both controlling partners (the UN and the domestic governments) in most tribunals has been to transfer as much responsibility to international actors as possible in order to secure convictions.

The reluctance of each state (bar Cambodia) to assume ownership of the process increased the likelihood of marginalisation of national judges and prosecutors into minor assistance positions, and could only serve to further diminish any sense of ownership the local legal community may have had in the hybrid process. International dominance in hybrid courts has reinforced what Tom Perriello and Marieke Wierda call 'the spaceship phenomenon': where the court was seen by the national community as an irrelevant, alien presence.[30] While domestic authorities were largely marginalised or disengaged in each tribunal, the international staff who dominated the process were primarily focussed on the traditional goal of closing the impunity gap, at the expense of the necessarily time-consuming project of transferring their skills to domestic actors.[31] Mentoring and professional development played little role in any of the mixed tribunals, which were hybrid in form but rarely in ethos. This suggests that professional development and

---

Criminality' in C Romano, A Nollkaemper and J Kleffner (eds) *Internationalised Criminal Courts and Tribunals: Sierra Leone, East Timor, Kosovo, and Cambodia* (OUP, Oxford 2004) 6.

[27] In 2001 the Cambodian government published their domestic law on the ECCC which closely resembles the current model. It was markedly different from a draft agreement the UN negotiated. On 8 February 2002, the UN withdrew from negotiations, declaring that it had 'come to the conclusion that the Extraordinary Chambers, as currently envisaged, would not guarantee the independence, impartiality, and objectivity that a court established with the support of the United Nations must have' (UN, 'Daily Press Briefing by the Office of the Spokesman for the Secretary-General', 8 February 2002).

[28] UNMIK Regulation 2000/64 gave the accused, defence, prosecutor or Department of Justice the right to ask UNMIK to intervene in a case and assign international judges or prosecutors to it whereas the previous regulations 2000/6 and 2000/34 preserved Kosovar majorities (Special Representative of the Secretary-General, 'On the Assignment of International Judges/Prosecutors and/or Change of Venue' UNMIK/REG/2000/64 (15 December 2000)). In such circumstances, UNMIK could designate a three-judge panel of whom at least two would be international, one of whom would preside.

[29] The Freetown Government went so far as to amend the Agreement to replace the words 'Sierra Leone judges' with 'judges appointed by the government of Sierra Leone', choosing to appoint only three national judges out of the possible four appointees they could make to the Trial and Appeals Chambers (A Tejan-Cole, 'The Special Court for Sierra Leone: Conceptual Concerns and Alternatives' (2001) 1 *African Hum Rts L J* 107, 119).

[30] T Perriello and M Wierda (International Center for Transitional Justice), 'The Special Court for Sierra Leone under Scrutiny' (March 2006) <http://ictj.org/sites/default/files/ICTJ-SierraLeone-Special-Court-2006-English.pdf> last accessed 26 January 2012, 2.

[31] See generally Hussain (n 19).

mentoring will invariably suffer diminished roles where successor justice is conceptualised primarily as a matter of combating impunity.

The second main contention about the promise of hybrid tribunals was that their trials would be more legitimate in the eyes of the domestic population – relative to purely international or purely domestic trials – because of their location, the impartiality guaranteed by international involvement and the participation of national actors. However, studies of popular attitudes towards the tribunals show a lack of interest, and in some cases hostility, regarding the process.[32] It is clear that the earlier *ad hoc* tribunals failed to engage the local community in any meaningful way. Outreach, a time-consuming and costly process removed from the pursuit of convictions, was non-existent in East Timor and Kosovo, though relatively successful in Sierra Leone. Nevertheless, it appears that issues like location and outreach are less significant in terms of public satisfaction than the prosecution policy adopted; attending trials or being better-informed about the court ultimately mattered far less than whether the population agreed or disagreed with prosecutorial policy or the manner in which trials are conducted. An examination of national attitudes towards the hybrid tribunals show that neither of the divergent policies in East Timor (widespread accountability for physical perpetrators) and Sierra Leone (selective accountability for organisers of violence) met with public approval.[33] This does not reflect badly on hybrid tribunals specifically – given the inevitable selectivity mass crime in resource-strapped conditions, even the most representative or comprehensive of prosecution policies will disappoint large numbers. This disappointment will however contaminate views of the tribunal no less than in any purely domestic or purely international court.

The other argument in terms of the legitimacy of hybridised trials was that the international component would import impartiality and undermine the perception (or reality) of victor's justice or politicisation of trials. While the experience of Kosovo prior to Regulation 2000/64 suggests that in particularly polarised post-conflict states international involvement is necessary for impartiality and independence of the proceedings, the experience of the other tribunals suggests that even significant international involvement alone is not sufficient to guarantee independence. Both

---

[32] P Pigou (Asia Foundation), 'Law and Justice in East Timor – A Survey of Citizen Awareness and Attitudes Regarding Law and Justice in East Timor' (February 2004) <http://www.asiafoundation.org/pdf/easttimor_lawsurvey.pdf> last accessed 26 January 2012; DE Artzt, 'International Processes: Views on the Ground: The Local Perception of International Criminal Tribunals in the Former Yugoslavia and Sierra Leone' (2006) 603 *The Annals of the American Academy of Political and Social Sciences* 226; P Pham et al (Human Rights Centre, UC Berkeley), 'So We Will Never Forget: A Population-Based Survey On Attitudes About Social Reconstruction and the Extraordinary Chambers in the Courts of Cambodia' (January 2009) <http://www.law.berkeley.edu/HRCweb/pdfs/So-We-Will-Never-Forget.pdf> last accessed 26 January 2012.

[33] Human Rights Watch, 'Bringing Justice: The Special Court for Sierra Leone: Accomplishments, Shortcomings and Needed Support' (September 2004) <http://www.hrw.org/sites/default/files/reports/sierraleone0904.pdf> last accessed 26 January 2012, 20.

Cambodia and East Timor saw significant degrees of political interference that set a less than exemplary standard for the local society.³⁴

Advocates of the hybrid structure further contended that the very process of trying cases fairly, meeting procedural requirements, applying clear law and generating inarguably just convictions could contribute to the permeation of these legal and human rights norms throughout the national courts. Worryingly given its systematic and institutional nature, of all the elements of a fair trial, inequality of arms is the one where the hybrid courts fell most short. It may be loosely interpreted as meaning that the defence is unfairly handicapped and a fair trial is jeopardised if the defence is disadvantaged materially or otherwise to so great a degree that it cannot make a case to counter that of the prosecution. In *Kordić*, the ICTY Appeal Chamber held that 'at a minimum, "a fair trial must entitle the accused to adequate time or facilities for his defence" under conditions which do not place him at a substantial disadvantage as regard his opponent',³⁵ while in *Tadić*, the same Chamber held that 'equality of arms obligates a judicial body to ensure that neither party is put at a disadvantage when presenting its case'.³⁶

However, in most hybrid tribunals, the objective of efficiently prosecuting the mandated number of indictees took precedence over the need to provide anything more (and sometimes less) than the most rudimentary defence structures. While UNTAET passed Regulation 2000/16 governing prosecutors, there was no new legislation to regulate the provision of defence in Special Panel trials, though an under-resourced Defence Lawyers Unit was belatedly created in 2002.³⁷ As Cohen noted, '[i]t appears simply not to have occurred to the UN administration that provision had to be made for defense, particularly in the post-conflict situation where no experienced lawyers were available'.³⁸ Neither Kosovo's Regulation 2000/64 nor its predecessors provided for international defenders or a specialised hybrid defence office, even in cases related to war crimes.³⁹ At the SCSL, a Defence Office was created to centralise a number of defence functions in one location.⁴⁰

---

³⁴ P McAuliffe, 'The Limits of Co-Operation: Resolving the Question of "How Low Do You Go?" in the Khmer Rouge Trials' Bicephalous Prosecution' (2010) 30 *Tasmanian University L Rev* 99 and D Cohen, *Indifference and Accountability: The United Nations and the Politics of International Justice in East Timor* (East-West Centre, Hawaii 2006).

³⁵ *Prosecutor v Kordić* (Appeals Judgment) IT-95-14/2-A (18 September 2000) para 22, footnote 39.

³⁶ *Prosecutor v Tadić* (Appeals Judgment) IT-94-1-A (15 July 1999) para 48.

³⁷ MC Othman, *Accountability for International Humanitarian Law Violations: The Case of Rwanda and East Timor* (Springer, Berlin 2005) 103.

³⁸ Cohen (n 8) 16.

³⁹ In cases involving international judges and prosecutors, the Kosovar Department of Judicial Administration and the Ministry of Public Services paid defence teams. Sometimes private funds were used in high-profile KLA cases to get high-quality counsel (Perriello and Wierda (n 24), 24).

⁴⁰ Rule 45 of the Rules of Procedure and Evidence provided that the Defence Office was to fulfil the following functions: 'In accordance with the Statute and the Rules, provide advice, assistance and representation to suspects questioned by the Special Court and

However, even here, defence was merely an 'afterthought' created after the Sierra Leone/UN agreement to establish the Court.[41] The prosecution budget of US$83 million dwarfed the defence's US$4 million in 2005, demonstrating a greater concern to secure prosecutions than to vindicate the autonomy of the individual before the courts.[42] Provision has improved in the later Khmer Rouge trials – Rule 11 of the Internal Rules of the ECCC outlines the duties of a specialised Defence Support Section (DSS) in supporting the one foreign and one domestic Co-Lawyer each defendant is entitled to, though observers note a consistent problem of short-staffing, meaning that suspects have been interviewed without the presence of defence lawyers, while the DSS has no role in detention issues.[43]

While it is difficult to point to individual cases where an accused may have been acquitted by better defence (though the Special Panels' coercive plea-bargaining process is a possible exception),[44] the complicity on the part of the international community in the systematic weighting of the court apparatus against defendants suggests that vigorous criminal defence is seen as an impediment to the proper working of the courts rather than an essential element. In addition to inequality of arms, unduly delayed trials were a common factor across all tribunals. This too was in keeping with the shift in human rights law from a defence-based to a prosecution-based perspective, but undermined the example of the tribunals in respecting the fair trial rights of citizens tried before them.[45] All tribunals at one stage or another lacked sufficient equipment, security and administrative staffing to demonstrate competent trials in action due to lack of resources.[46] While all hybrid tribunals have been criticised for failing to exemplify commonly accepted international fair trial standards, it could hardly be otherwise given the lack of resources and the need to co-opt domestic lawyers and judges whose failure to attain such standards was the *raison d'être* of the tribunals in the first place. While the Sierra Leone and

---

accused persons before the Special Court; provide initial legal advice and assistance, as well as legal assistance ordered by the Special Court to the accused persons; provide adequate facilities for counsel in the preparation of defence; and maintain a list of highly qualified criminal defence counsel and manage the assignment, withdrawal and replacement of counsel acting for accused persons.'

[41] Cohen (n 8) 8–9.

[42] J Cockayne, 'The Fraying Shoestring: Rethinking War Crimes Tribunals' (2005) 28 *Fordham Int'l L J* 616, 671. See generally JRWD Jones et al, 'The Special Court for Sierra Leone: A Defence Perspective' (2004) 2 *JICJ* 211.

[43] R Skilbeck, 'Defending the Khmer Rouge' (2008) 8 *ICLR* 423, 440–441.

[44] See generally, S Linton and C Reiger, 'The Evolving Jurisprudence and Practises of East Timor's Special Panels for Serious Crimes on Admissions of Guilt, Duress and Superior Orders' (2001) 4 *Ybk Int'l Humanitarian L* 1.

[45] WA Schabas, 'Balancing the Rights of the Accused with the Imperatives of Accountability' in R Thakur and P Malcontent (eds) *From Sovereign Impunity to International Accountability: The Search for Justice in a World of States* (United Nations University Press, Tokyo 2004) 155.

[46] T Ingadottir, 'The Financing of Internationalised Criminal Courts and Tribunals' in Romano et al (n 26) 271.

Timorese experiences show that inadequate resourcing is not inimical to securing convictions, it is a recurring issue which will condemn to failure any process with ambitions beyond mere punishment.

It is clear that predictions about the legacy of hybrid tribunals ignored the disjunction between idealised high-standard proceedings and the emergency-driven circumstances which triggered the demand for such hybrid structures to begin with, and elided the extent to which pressing short-term exigencies motivated their creation. It remains conceivable then to argue that if sufficient resources, support and motivation were forthcoming, hybrid tribunals would prove equal to the elevated expectations made of them. Even today, a strong residual hope in the promise of hybrid tribunal structure remains undimmed by actual practice. Notwithstanding the compromised proceedings of the tribunals, there remain those who nevertheless still contend that 'the theoretical justifications for hybrid tribunals ... suggest that the hybrid approach can be more ethical, practical and sophisticated than alternative IHL accountability mechanisms'.[47] As Laura Dickinson argues, the problems endured by the tribunals are those of implementation and not of conception, 'stem[ming] more from resource constraints than from structural problems with the hybrid model'.[48] Similar arguments have been made recently by Neha Jain,[49] David Cohen[50] and Parinaz Mendez.[51]

It is certainly arguable that the experience of the last decade does not demonstrate a failure of the hybrid tribunal hypothesis. It remains conceivable that a hybrid tribunal could marry the stringent fairness of the Regulation 64 panels in Kosovo to the standards of jurisprudence in Sierra Leone and Cambodia, and could attract sufficient material support to make capacity-building and programmes to inculcate fair trial norms a reality. However, what the practice of the last 10 years does show is that the mindset that would make such promises a reality may never exist. The impact of a trial process on the domestic justice system and its legitimacy in the eyes of the population remain in a subordinate position in the normative hierarchy of priorities of those at UN and international level tasked with responding judicially to gross violations of human rights and the laws of war. Hybrid tribunals can only arise in post-conflict or repressive situations, where almost inevitably there is never time to plan for perfect solutions and where the strategic priorities of the international community are antithetical to deliberation or delay. Although it has also been argued that hybrid tribunals could achieve their more holistic promise through greater investment in resources, in the view of this author, a thorough re-orientation of purpose is what is most required.

---

[47] PK Mendez, 'The New Wave of Hybrid Tribunals: A Sophisticated Approach to Enforcing International Humanitarian Law or an Idealistic Solution With Empty Promises?' (2009) 20 *CLF* 53, 55.
[48] Dickinson, 'The Promise of Hybrid Courts' (n 7) 307.
[49] N Jain, 'Conceptualising Internationalisation in Hybrid Criminal Courts' (2008) *Singapore Ybk Int'l L* 81, 85.
[50] Cohen (n 8).
[51] Mendez (n 47) 55.

## III. The Modest Future of Hybrid Courts

Though some still maintain that 'the use of hybrid tribunal may be a more appropriate approach to accountability than the assertion of ICC jurisdiction', the model may yet prove a fleeting experiment.[52] For example, Luigi Condorelli and Theo Boutrouche argued in the initial years of hybrid tribunals that if there was in fact an international criminal court that worked and had jurisdiction over the area and perpetrators of future crimes, the mixed structure would be rendered obsolete.[53] The more likely future role for hybrid tribunals is positioned somewhere between these two poles, by retaining a useful – but largely subordinate – role in the era of the ICC in one of the following four ways:

a. as a means for a state to create a genuine domestic proceeding to preclude admissibility of a case or situation before the ICC under Article 17 where it would otherwise be found to be unwilling or unable to investigate or prosecute;
b. as a complementary mechanism to the ICC for the prosecution and trial of suspects further down the criminal hierarchy than those subject to proceedings in The Hague;
c. (c) as a mechanism for trying serious crimes for which the ICC does not have jurisdiction; and
d. as a mechanism for trying political or sui generis crimes not covered, or not covered adequately, in the Rome Statute.

As stated in the Preamble to the Rome Statute, the primary motivation for the establishment of the ICC was to put an end to impunity, noting emphatically that grave international crimes 'threaten the peace' and that the prosecution of such crimes contributes to the maintenance of international peace and security.[54] The ICC, no less than the *ad hoc* tribunals or the hybrid tribunals already examined, is based on the retributive model of exclusively trying and punishing individuals, determined 'to put an end to impunity for the perpetrators of these crimes and thus to contribute to the prevention of such crime'.[55] In this context, the Preamble recalls that it is the duty of every State to ensure 'effective' prosecution of those responsible for international crimes.[56] Only where a State proves unwilling or unable or persists in inactivity can a case be admissible before the ICC.

---

[52] L Raub, 'Positioning Hybrid Tribunals in International Criminal Justice' (2009) 41 *NYU J Int'l L and Politics* 1026, 1026–1027.

[53] L Condorelli and T Boutrouche, 'Internationalised Criminal Courts and Tribunals: Are They Necessary?' in Romano et al (n 26), 427, 435.

[54] Rome Statute of the International Criminal Court, 2187 UNTS 90, 17 July 1998, entered into force 1 July 2002 ('ICC Statute'), preamble, para 3.

[55] Ibid para 5.

[56] Ibid para 4.

Though it has been argued that the interaction of a hybrid tribunal and the ICC could help develop local capacity and foster the domestic implementation of human rights norms articulated by the latter's jurisprudence and procedures in such States,[57] there is little reason to believe these will either be primary objectives or likely by-products of what might ultimately be quite tenuous or antagonistic relationships. By virtue of its purely international character, a domestic legacy is far from central to the Court's remit. Even where it co-exists or co-operates with a hybrid tribunal, the dominant preoccupation of the ICC with the fight against impunity means that the latter will be employed only to fill gaps left by the Rome Statute regime, and so might preclude any pursuit of their interaction's much-theorised 'promise'.

## A. As a Means for a State to Create a Genuine Domestic Proceeding to Preclude Admissibility of a Case or Situation before the ICC under Article 17

Under the Article 17 complementarity regime, the ICC may only commence proceedings where the relevant State is not investigating or prosecuting the case, or purports to do so but in actuality is unable or unwilling to genuinely carry out proceedings. As such, the commencement of genuine proceedings to prevent impunity – abstracted from any of the other justifications typically associated with international criminal justice such as creation of a historical record, reconciliation, restitution, social pedagogy or wider rule of law restoration – has become the dominant criterion determining which of the two legal regimes, international or domestic, can exercise jurisdiction. In effect, genuine progress in closing an impunity gap becomes the primary or even sole purpose of any domestic proceeding, as it becomes determinative of any consideration of admissibility.

If, for example, a divided post-conflict state wishes to forestall ICC involvement but cannot demonstrate the ability or willingness of national proceedings to pursue genuine accountability (owing to concerns over security or the political make-up of the institutions of justice), then an international component could be added in a majority or minority to domestic proceedings to remedy this. States Parties or Article 13 referral states may enter into an agreement with the UN, another state or group of states, or even the ICC itself to create a hybrid tribunal that would render the case(s) inadmissible before the ICC. Though the court would be internationalised to a certain extent, location within the state and national involvement could allow the retention of a degree of ownership in order to preserve its sovereignty, even in post-conflict conditions that make purely domestic prosecutions untenable. Although the national justice system alone may be unwilling or unable to prosecute, internationalised domestic trials (even with significant foreign input) are easier for a national government to accept, because the state need not surrender that most central aspect of sovereignty, namely the jurisdiction to try its own nationals.

---

[57] Dickinson, 'The Promise of Hybrid Courts' (n 7) 309.

Indeed, the lenient state-centric nature of the complementarity regime is itself a testament to states' reluctance to cede this essential aspect of sovereignty.[58] The 'jurisdictional imperialism' critique of the ICC as a European court for African leaders has proven potent in the past, most notably employed by Sudanese and Libyan leaders who consistently indicated that none of their citizens would be handed over to the ICC for trial. Perhaps an added attraction is the possibility that where the state enters into an agreement to participate in a hybrid tribunal, the government might hope maintain some control over the process of indictment and prosecution, as in Dili and Phnom Penh.[59] It may be attracted by the greater possibility of offering pardon after trial (as happened in East Timor, for example) if ICC influence can be marginalised or excluded completely.

Article 17 requires examination of the domestic system that purports to exercise jurisdiction. The key question therefore is whether a hybrid tribunal constitutes a national court. On the face of it, hybrid tribunals might not automatically be accommodated with the complementarity regime in Article 17. Sub-sections 1(a) and (b) require investigation 'by a State' which has jurisdiction over a case, while sub-section 2(a) speaks of a 'national decision'. Article 17(3) refers to the 'collapse or unavailability of its national judicial system'. In the absence of any case-law on the matter, there is a plausible *prima facie* argument that a hybrid tribunal staffed and/ or funded predominantly by the international community applying international law might not be considered part of the State's judicial system by the Court or Prosecutor in admissibility proceedings. Certainly, the approach of the ICC in the case of the Ugandan and Congolese self-referrals suggests a Court which is jealous of its jurisdiction, and perhaps reluctant to cede it unnecessarily to a domestically-based apparatus, however well-intended. In accordance with Article 31(1) of the Vienna Convention on the Law of Treaties, whereby a treaty shall be interpreted in good faith in accordance with the ordinary meaning to be given to the terms of the treaty in light of its object and purpose, Fausto Pocar has taken a teleological view of such a possibility, arguing that 'the establishment of international courts and tribunals is aimed at ensuring a proper and effective exercise of criminal jurisdiction over crimes ... with a view to combating impunity for such crimes, even where domestic courts would not be able or willing to do so'.[60] Given that the Rome Statute's overwhelming preference is for states to take responsibility for the prosecution of international crimes – a responsibility which would arguably be manifested by an agreement to establish such a hybridised process – any level of participation by the State, be it in a leading role as in Cambodia or a subordinate

---

[58] F Mégret, 'Why Would States Want to Join the ICC? A Theoretical Exploration Based on the Legal Nature of Complementarity' in J Kleffner and G Kor (eds) *Complementary Views on Complementarity* (TMC Asser Press, The Hague 2006) 1, 30.

[59] JT Holmes, 'Complementarity: National Courts Versus the ICC' in A Cassese, P Gaeta and JRWD Jones (eds) *The Rome Statute of the International Criminal Court: A Commentary: Volume II* (OUP, Oxford 2002) 675.

[60] F Pocar, 'The Proliferation of International Criminal Courts and Tribunals' (2004) 2 *JICJ* 304, 307.

one as in East Timor, be it in mere establishment in Sierra Leone or actual operation as in Lebanon, should suffice to subsume it under the term 'national' for the purpose of Article 17.[61] Morten Bergsmo and Markus Benzing similarly contend that if a State were to discharge its duties under the Rome Statute by engaging the assistance of the international community (and in particular the UN), this would accord with the object and purpose of the Rome Statute.[62]

The principle of effectiveness is crucial. As Philippe Kirsch notes in another context, 'it is the essence of the principle [of complementarity] that if a national judicial system functions properly, there is no reason for the ICC to assume jurisdiction'.[63] It would constitute a means of preserving the Rome Statute's underlying preference for domestic trial by utilising the national legal system, but the emphasis on the 'effectiveness' of the division of labour means that any hybrid process of accountability at the domestic level is likely to have as its dominant purpose the closure of the impunity gap that originally occasioned ICC interest. The twin barriers of ability and willingness would remain to be crossed, but the international character of the proceedings should diminish the threat of an adverse finding on either criterion. The ICC would not have any authority to intervene directly in hybrid tribunal proceedings established to forestall international involvement, although the Rome Statute provides in Articles 15, 17, 18, 19, 20 and 53 that the Office of the Prosecutor will gather facts and conduct analysis in order to form arguments on whether national courts are genuinely carrying out proceedings directed towards accountability.

A more painstaking and considered process that would prioritise capacity-building or the instructional benefit of scrupulously fair trials may fall foul of the demanding 'unwillingness' tests in Article 17(2), particularly if such an approach occasioned 'unjustified delay in the proceedings which in the circumstances is inconsistent with an intent to bring the person concerned to justice'.[64] It is also considered unlikely by some commentators that lack of exemplary fair trial standards in locally-based trials would suffice to constitute unwillingness or inability for the purposes of the complementarity regime.[65] The types of post-conflict societies that find themselves unwilling or unable to prosecute would benefit most from a comprehensive and integrated approach that would maximise the possibilities offered by prosecutions of human rights violations to develop the

---

[61] M Benzing and M Bergsmo, 'Some Tentative Remarks on the Relationship Between Internationalised Criminal Jurisdictions and the International Criminal Court' in Romano et al (n 26) 412.

[62] Ibid 409; see also C Stahn, 'The Geometry of Transitional Justice: Choices of Institutional Design' (2005) 18 *LJIL* 425, 464.

[63] P Kirsch, 'Keynote Address: Symposium: The International Criminal Court: Consensus and Debate on the International Adjudication of Genocide, Crimes against Humanity, War Crimes, and Aggression' (1999) 32 *Cornell Int'l L J* 437, 438.

[64] ICC Statute, art 17(2).

[65] M Benzing, 'The Complementarity Regime of the International Criminal Court: International Criminal Justice between State Sovereignty and the Fight against Impunity' (2003) 7 *Max Planck Ybk UN L* 591, 598.

domestic rule of law, as broadly understood. However, the donors necessary to fund such a hybrid model may prove reluctant to finance any process that strays far from the ICC's dominant concern with ending impunity quickly in situations where the peace is precarious.

## B. As a Complement to the ICC for the Prosecution and Trial of Suspects Further Down the Criminal Hierarchy than those Subject to Proceedings in The Hague

Limited resources, as well as Article 17(1)(d)'s provision that the Court shall declare a case inadmissible when 'it is not of sufficient gravity to justify further action', demands that the ICC Prosecutor adopt a policy of focussing only on those few individuals who he believes bear the greatest responsibility for the most serious crimes that have been committed in each situation. For example, while the Darfur Commission's Report contained a sealed envelope with the names of 51 people the Commission determined were most responsible for the crimes committed in Darfur, thus far only a handful of people have been indicted. Responsibility for trying what would otherwise be an overcrowded docket could be devolved to a hybrid tribunal that could focus on prosecuting high- or intermediate-level figures that the ICC Prosecutor exercises his discretion not to pursue, owing to the relative lack of seniority, but whom the State in question is willing to prosecute. Along similar lines, Rule 11*bis* of the ICTY's amended Rules of Procedure and Evidence enabled the transfer of ICTY cases to national authorities by ICTY judges after considering the gravity of the crimes and whether the individual involved constituted a 'lower- and intermediate-rank accused'. As a result, a model of burden-sharing may operate where the purely international tribunal deals with the most senior (and most destabilising) figures, and a hybrid tribunal prosecutes those lower down in the scale of organisation. As the African Union High-Level Panel on Darfur noted in relation to the ICC Prosecutor's initiatives in prosecuting the case:

> This prosecutorial policy inevitably leaves the overwhelming majority of individuals outside of the ICC system and still needing to answer for crimes they might have committed … justice from the ICC, exclusively, would therefore leave impunity for the vast majority of offenders in Darfur, including virtually all direct perpetrators of the offences.[66]

Bruce Broomhall and Laura Dickinson have similarly argued that hybrid tribunals can assist the ICC by prosecuting lower-profile cases as part of a co-operative 'joint

---

[66] AU, 'Report of the African Union High-Level on Darfur (AUPD)', PSC/AHG/2 (CCVII) (29 October 2009) para 320.

venture'.⁶⁷ The ICC Prosecutor appears to foresee a role for hybrid tribunals in this subordinate role.⁶⁸

Any such hybrid tribunal may be established by agreement between the state in question and the UN, but agreement on co-operation with the ICC itself might also need to be formalised in the case of a co-operative hybrid tribunal. The complete or partial hybridisation of the ICC's jurisdiction is legally possible and has been advocated in the past.⁶⁹ Regardless of how it is established, a hybrid tribunal may be attractive given the precedent of a co-operative, if under-utilised, relationship between the ICTY and the Regulation 64 panels in Kosovo (and Bosnian War Crimes Chamber to the extent it can be considered hybrid) and the proven adaptability of hybrid processes to a variety of transitional ecologies and prosecutorial imperatives: representative accountability for 10 accused in Sierra Leone; prosecution of the upper echelon of five individuals in Cambodia; widespread perpetrator accountability in East Timor. Where impunity remains a concern, the lesser overall cost of hybrid tribunals will make them attractive by comparison, even where this acts to the detriment of the provision of a competent defence or the recruitment of qualified judges and administrators.⁷⁰

Insofar as it combats impunity for senior criminals, a co-operative hybrid model that can handle a heavier caseload might prove attractive to the ICC in future, particularly as its own workload continues to increase. Any such hybrid based locally might add more legitimacy to a government's decision to acquiesce to an accountability mechanism than a similar process based solely in The Hague. William Burke-White has argued that the success of the ICC will depend on the extent to which it can lead, complement and integrate a 'community of courts' enforcing international criminal law.⁷¹ As Carsten Stahn notes, the framework of the ICC is supportive of multi-layered accountability incorporating hybrid

---

⁶⁷   Dickinson, 'The Promise of Hybrid Courts' (n 7) 308; B Broomhall, *International Justice and the International Criminal Court: Between Sovereignty and the Rule of Law* (OUP, Oxford 2004) 104.

⁶⁸   'Sudan Accuse ICC Prosecutor of Standing Behind AU Hybrid Court Proposal' *Sudan Tribune* (Washington, 1 November 2009) <http://www.sudantribune.com/Sudan-accuse-ICC-prosecutor-of,32978> last accessed 26 January 2012. ('ICC chief prosecutor Luis Moreno-Ocampo welcomed a proposal this week from a panel of African leaders to end the conflict in Darfur, which includes the establishment of a special court to try those charged with atrocities, even though the ICC is already investigating there.')

⁶⁹   For example, Lipscomb contends that articles 3 and 4 of the Statute allow for the creation of a hybrid tribunal where the ICC acts as the instrument of international oversight in place of the UN. Lipscomb (n 8) 206–211.

⁷⁰   For example, as of December 2009 the ICTR had spent about US$1.4 billion and the ICTY cost an estimated US$1.79 billion, comparing unfavourably with even the relatively well-funded SCSL which has cost only about US$208.7 million in more than half the time (CC Jalloh, 'Special Court for Sierra Leone: Achieving Justice?' (2011) 32 *Michigan J Int'l L* 395, 430–432).

⁷¹   Burke-White (n 14) 11.

structures.⁷² However, the concern must remain that the inevitable emphasis of a hybrid tribunal established specifically to close the impunity gap for lower-level offenders would replicate prior experiences of pauperisation, inequality of arms and low-quality trials, raise concerns over dictation of policy by the international community and marginalise any potential for the prioritisation of capacity-building. Of course, any consensual division of labour between the ICC and a hybrid tribunal could offer a domestic model for enforcing international criminal law that is backed by ICC oversight which could ensure credible, impartial and effective trials.⁷³ High standards of trial procedure and actual capacity-building may emerge as a by-product of this co-operative arrangement. However, it is more likely that any hybrid tribunal created specifically for the purpose of filling the accountability gap left by the ICC's jurisdiction over the most senior criminals is unlikely to demonstrate the sea-change in attitude required for the slower, more deliberative process that would emphasise high quality of trials, outreach and capacity-building and that could finally realise the more ambitious dreams of hybrid tribunal theorists.

## C. As a Mechanism for Trying Serious Crimes for which the ICC does not have Jurisdiction

Article 24 of the Rome Statute's provision on retroactivity, coupled with Article 11's *ratione temporis* guarantee that the ICC has jurisdiction only in relation to crimes committed after the entry into force of the Statute on 1 July 2002, leaves a gap for crimes committed before that date where there is no international will to create an *ad hoc* tribunal on the ICTY model. Another significant gap is left by States not party to the Rome Statute. As of August 2011, only 115 States had ratified it. Current conflicts in non-signatory States lie beyond the ICC's jurisdiction without Security Council referral. In a number of the 'hot' areas of the world where conflicts and violent repression of human rights occur, States which are likely to commit such crimes are unlikely to be parties at present or become parties in future. A hybrid tribunal could be established in a non-Party State but the existence of such a tribunal outside the international community's preferred framework for justice may inhibit the international support necessary to realise any wider potentialities, if indeed such will was existent domestically.⁷⁴ Similarly, a hybrid tribunal could be established for crimes that occurred before 2002. While the greater distance in time for any such trials from the present-day political or security interests may be more conducive to a less rushed and more exemplary process, that same distance from

---

⁷² Stahn (n 62) 427.
⁷³ Mendez (n 47) 71.
⁷⁴ It was initially feared, for example, that support for hybrid tribunals was a means to undermine the ICC: Dickinson 'The Relationship between Hybrid Courts and International Courts: The Case of Kosovo' (n 7) 1060.

present-day exigencies may make it less likely to garner sufficient international interest and expertise to make the tribunal of revolutionary long-term utility.

## D. As a Mechanism for Trying Political or Sui Generis Crimes Not Covered or Not Covered Adequately in the Rome Statute

The STL's unique jurisdiction as the first tribunal established to adjudicate allegations of a crime targeted at specific persons,[75] the ECCC and SCSL's distinct subject matter jurisdictions over crimes specific to national conflicts such as abuse of young girls[76] or cultural crimes,[77] and the much-criticised tendency of the Timorese Panels to focus on simple crimes of murder and rape abstracted from their wider context[78] are testaments to the hybrid tribunal's flexibility to adapt to the prosecution of a wide array of crimes in a wide array of post-conflict ecologies. Article 5 of the Rome Statute on *ratione materiae* lists only genocide, crimes against humanity, war crimes and the undefined crime of aggression as crimes under the Court's jurisdiction. Acts of terrorism and assassination (as in the STL) could, so long as they were not committed as part of a widespread or systematic attack directed against any civilian population, be tackled by such a hybrid tribunal in a State that needs international assistance to buttress the capacity, legitimacy or political freedom it lacks to prosecute such crimes. However, such specific focus on any given crime may not be conducive to developing capacity or demonstrating standards of fair trial generally. The narrowly-focussed STL, for example, has no mandate in these regards.[79]

---

[75] The STL may only try those allegedly responsible for the attack on PM Hariri and other attacks connected with his assassination (Statute of the Special Tribunal for Lebanon, UN Doc S/RES/1757, UN Security Council, 2007 ('STL Statute')).

[76] Statute of the Special Court for Sierra Leone, annexed to the Agreement between the United Nations and the Government of Sierra Leone on the Establishment of the Special Court for Sierra Leone, signed on 16 January 2002 ('SCSL Statute') art 7.

[77] Law on the Establishment of Extraordinary Chambers in the Courts of Cambodia for the Prosecution of Crimes Committed during the Period of Democratic Kampuchea, 10 August 2001 with inclusion of amendments as promulgated on 27 October 2004 (NS/RKM/1004/006), art 7.

[78] K Askin, S Starr and S Frease (Open Society Justice Initiative and Coalition for International Justice), 'Unfulfilled Promises: Achieving Justice for Crimes Against Humanity in East Timor' (November 2004) <http://digitalcommons.law.umaryland.edu/cgi/viewcontent.cgi?article=1600&context=fac_pubs&sei-redir=1#search=%22Unfulfilled%20Promises%3A%20Achieving%20Justice%20Crimes%20Against%20Humanity%20East%20Timor%22> last accessed 26 January 2012, 37.

[79] STL Statute, art 1.

## Conclusion

All hybrid courts with the exception of the Special Tribunal for Lebanon were negotiated before the ICC came into operation in 2002. As such, one can only theorise about how the future relationship, if any, between the two structures will play out. However, more than a decade of divergent hybrid court experiences allows for some conclusions to be drawn. The various hybrids have helped combat impunity in their fields of operation and yielded much-needed accountability for victims in post-conflict societies in a manner that is both quicker and more efficient than the ICC's apparent current capabilities. However, pursuit of this laudable aim, which has animated all institutions of international criminal justice from Nuremberg onwards, has operated to the exclusion of the type of exemplary, co-operative and holistic approaches that might fulfil the early expectations of the potential rule of law legacy of hybrid courts. In view of the failures in this regard examined herein, it may well be argued that the promise of hybrid courts is overstated or that pursuit of any role beyond accountability is inadvisable, but it remains conceivable that the arguments made a decade ago could be vindicated if sufficient attention, resources and application were directed towards their realisation. Many of the failures of these courts can be ascribed to the primary concern for speedy and efficient convictions and the dominance of the priorities of international actors, abstracted from the needs of the local community. These tendencies will regain force in years to come as more hybrid courts are established, especially if employed either to obviate the need for the ICC's assertion of jurisdiction or to complement it. Their practice are likely to be influenced by the Rome Statute's preoccupation with non-impunity and punishment to the exclusion of all else. The ICC's inevitable distance from the emerging rule of law reconstruction process within states may do little to effect the necessary re-orientation of priorities.

# 'Political Trials'? The UN Security Council and the Development of International Criminal Law

### David P. Forsythe[1]

The development of international criminal law from the 1990s to the present is arguably the most profound current aspect of international law, and perhaps one of the most important developments of international relations more broadly. According to Professor Ken Anderson, the development of international criminal law is the signal achievement in international law after the Cold War.[2] The UN Security Council (UNSC) has been at the centre of this development. The Council is both a political and legal organisation, giving rise to a fundamental tension between these two dimensions.

On the one hand, the Council has primary responsibility for maintaining or restoring international peace and security. This role may require a creative approach not fully consistent with existing law, and/or may entail the bargaining and compromising well known in political arenas in order to advance certain security objectives. Article 24(2) of the UN Charter, in reference to Council action for peace and security, requires that the UNSC 'shall act in accordance with the Purposes and Principles of the United Nations'. It does not require the Council to act in conformity with existing international law. It is not at all clear if any public authority is authorised to review the actions of the Council to pronounce

---

[1] The author is grateful for comments on earlier versions from William A. Schabas, Steven R. Ratner, Roger Clark, Michael J. Matheson, David M. Malone, Patrice C. McMahon, Courtney Hillebrecht, Larry D. Johnson and Thomas G. Weiss. The author alone is responsible for the final version.

[2] K Anderson, 'The Rise of International Criminal Law: Intended and Unintended Consequences' (2009) 20(2) *EJIL* 331. More generally see D Tolbert, 'International Criminal Law: Past and Future' (2009) 30(4) *U Pennsylvania J Int'l L* 1281. Some legal experts think the law's attention to human rights more generally, and not just to criminal justice, is the most striking feature of contemporary legal developments.

on compatibility with law.³ The result of the broad authority given to the UNSC in the Charter scheme was that increasingly the Council was seen as having broad 'legislative' authority to create new norms.⁴ This will be evident regarding international criminal law as analysed below.

On the other hand, the Council is supposed to enhance international law, or at least not undermine it in a blatant fashion. According to the preamble to the Charter, one of the purposes of the United Nations is to 'establish conditions under which justice and respect for the obligations arising from treaties and other sources of international law can be maintained'. In Council proceedings, state members have the ample advice of many lawyers, and some of these no doubt would elevate the role of law to a more important position.⁵ In the last analysis, these two roles for the Council, the political and the legal, do not always co-exist easily.⁶

This tension is certainly evident when one examines international criminal law, or more to the point international justice, since the concept of justice may entail a broader notion of justice that departs from the criminal justice process. As is well recognised, in certain situations, a concern for doing good may result in amnesty for atrocities rather than holding individuals legally responsible for their foul deeds.⁷ Securing agreement on when this type of situation exists is no easy matter.

---

3    In 1992 the UNSC unanimously required Libya to extradite suspects in the Lockerbie terrorist bombing of 1988 for trial in a Scottish court (UNSC Res 731 (21 January 1992) UN Doc S/RES/731). Libya petitioned the International Court of Justice in resisting, claiming that its obligations under treaty law did not require such extradition (see *Questions of Interpretation and Application of the 1971 Montreal Convention arising from the Aerial Incident at Lockerbie (Libyan Arab Jamahiriya v United Kingdom)* ICJ General List No 89 (3 March 1992) <http://www.icj-cij.org/docket/files/89/7209.pdf> last accessed 31 January 2012). The Court (in *Questions of Interpretation and Application of the 1971 Montreal Convention arising from the Aerial Incident at Lockerbie (Libyan Arab Jamahiriya v United Kingdom)* (Judgment on Preliminary Objections) 1998 ICJ Reports 9 (27 February 1998)) cited the Charter of the United Nations, 24 October 1945, 1 UNTS XVI, art 103, interpreting it to mean that UNSC decisions were not only legally binding but superseded other legal obligations. Art 103 reads: 'In the event of a conflict between the obligations of the Members of the United Nations under the present Charter and their obligations under any other international agreement, their obligations under the present Charter shall prevail.' The question of judicial review of UNSC Resolutions is too large to fully cover here. Not only the ICJ but other courts like the ICTY, European Court of Justice, and the ICC have become, or may become, involved in the matter. Further discussion awaits at another time and place.

4    S Talmon, 'The Security Council as World Legislature' (2005) 99(1) *AJIL* 175.

5    See SR Ratner, 'The Security Council and International Law' in DM Malone (ed) *The UN Security Council: From the Cold War to the 21st Century* (Lynne Rienner, Boulder 2004) 591.

6    See further MC Bassiouni, 'The Perennial Conflict between International Criminal Justice and Realpolitik' (2006) 22(1) *Georgia State U L Rev* 541.

7    Policy choice after atrocities with a view to a future legal order that protects human rights is usually referred to as 'transitional justice' and has led to a publishing industry on the subject. For a summary of some of the literature, see DP Forsythe, 'Human Rights and Mass Atrocities: Revisiting Transitional Justice' (2011) 13(1) *Int'l Studies Rev* 85.

Moreover, attempting to do some good by means of retributive justice may entail, as a political necessity, exempting some actors from that process – or perhaps not.

The UN Security Council during the time under review has consisted of five permanent members with veto power who manifest different constitutional orders and different approaches to both international law in general and international criminal law in particular.[8] Still further, the policies of each may vary across time, issue and governmental change, or be so unclear or contradictory as to defy easy analysis and prediction. In what follows in this chapter, changing politics – with relatively unfettered policy choice at its centre – is seen as primary and legal obligation secondary. As Werner Levi has written, 'Politics ... settles who gets what, when, and how ... and law turns the settlement into obligatory behaviour'.[9] Thus, state policy choice about criminal law and courts is seen as primary, and resulting Security Council resolutions about criminal law, particularly a 'decision' taken in reference to Chapter VII of the UN Charter, is seen as the secondary outcome. Political choice is the independent variable and mandatory or other development of criminal law is the dependent variable. Thus politics, the struggle to exercise power to codify and implement policy choice, is primary, and specific legal wording in the form of SC resolutions is the secondary outcome. Once created, of course, legal rules are supposed to inform subsequent political choice.

A central (but not all-encompassing) dynamic is argued as follows: the three P-5 states which are liberal democracies – Britain, France and the United States – have initiated many of the UNSC developments in favour of different forms of criminal law; while China as an authoritarian polity without fully independent courts has often, but inconsistently, hesitated in following those initiatives – often joined by Russia, a state which the NGO Freedom House has put in the intermediate category of 'partly free'. This prevalent central dynamic is then cross-cut by many other considerations, to be noted in subsequent analysis. Of course the elected Council members are not without importance, but the P-5 states with their potential vetoes retain the status of *primus inter pares*.

A second fundamental political factor is that, consistent with earlier eras, the most important members of the UNSC usually approach the subjects of criminal law not primarily or uniquely with a long-term and strategic view of what should transpire for the common good in a lawful world order, but rather with strong consideration of how they can adequately manage to protect their immediate national interests (subjectively perceived, of course) given various pressures and power realities. As one scholar perceptively noticed some time ago, the major states 'have tried to use the United Nations as a vehicle for the advancement of their

---

[8] In an oft-cited analysis, Robert Kagan holds that Britain and France and the other European states place more reliance on international law than the United States. R Kagan, *Of Paradise and Power: America and Europe in the New World Order* (Vintage, New York 2003).

[9] W Levi, *Law and Politics in the International Society* (Sage, Beverly Hills 1976) 13. For a broad application of this approach see TG Weiss, DP Forsythe, RA Coate and KK Pease, *The United Nations and Changing World Politics* (6th edn Westview Press, Boulder 2010).

individual, antithetical foreign-policy interests'.[10] A British diplomat, assigned to the UN, resigned in disgust at the narrow, petty, short-term policies pursued by London (and other diplomatic capitals) in the name of national interest.[11]

Governments are often short-sighted, whether about foreign policy or budgets and finances, with the perceived exigencies and desires of the moment often overwhelming more careful strategic visions. To cite a classic example, the United States during the Congo crisis of the early 1960s argued that the (then pro-Western) UN General Assembly could legally require all member states to pay for security operations authorised by that body and not by the Council, despite the strong opposition of the Soviet Union (and France). The United States favoured the UN course of action taken in the field and so wanted automatic payment for it. The Soviet Union was opposed, since its allies were losing on the ground. With short-term considerations foremost – namely, what political actors should govern in the Congo – the United States made general legal arguments that it eventually was glad to see not prevail, once the Assembly majority came to be much more critical of the United States and other Western states.[12] The point here is that general legal arguments were the by-product of a short-term focus on power struggles in the Congo.

While there usually are some sectors of the national bureaucracy which are charged with strategic planning, and while a bureau like the State Department Legal Office may take an unusually strategic view sometimes, it remains true that many state policies in the UNSC reflect pursuit of short-term and narrow national interests (again, subjectively defined) in response to various political pressures rather than long-term strategic vision in pursuit of the common good. Abstract notions of consistent legal principle do not always fare well in the rough and tumble of routine Council politics (or national politics, for that matter).[13]

Because of these political factors – namely, the nature of the P-5 states and their often changing and short-term perceptions of national interest – the UN Security Council has compiled a rich but certainly complex record concerning international criminal law. The UNSC has: (1) helped develop certain legal norms; (2) called on states to implement those norms in national proceedings, and then sometimes supervised matters but sometimes not; (3) carved out exceptions for certain actors and situations; (4) created and sometimes supported, but sometimes not, *ad hoc* criminal courts; (5) endorsed, to varying degrees and in various ways, special criminal courts, (6) both ignored and utilised the International Criminal Court; and (7) left a thoroughly muddled record on when to prosecute individuals for crimes under international law and when to adopt a different course of action.

---

[10] JG Stoessinger, *The UN and the Superpowers: China, Russia, & America* (3rd edn Random House, New York 1973) xi–xii.

[11] C Ross, *Independent Diplomat: Dispatches from an Unaccountable Elite* (Cornell University Press, Ithaca 2007).

[12] See further Stoessinger (n 10).

[13] Strategic visions may fare better after 'hegemonic wars' when a Woodrow Wilson or a Franklin Roosevelt is presented with an opportunity to construct new organisational arrangements for the long-term ordering of international relations.

State strategic vision, pursuit of the common good, and ultimately a consistent UNSC approach to international criminal law is often in short supply. The problem is not the UNSC per se but the policies of its member states, above all the P-5.

Since the UNSC is first a political organ and only secondarily a legal one, the view persists with some reason that the criminal trials that do evolve through Council practice are political trials, rather than fully or purely legal ones as found in an independent court system. In this sense 'political trials' are a synonym for selective justice.[14] But it is a good question as to whether perfectly non-political criminal trials linked to international developments are possible in the world as it exists and given the structure of the UN as it exists. The question might then become: is half a loaf better than no bread at all, on the assumption – debatable to be sure – that improvements will occur over time.

## I. The Politics of Criminal Law in the UN Security Council

We are where we are regarding international criminal law, to considerable degree, because of US foreign policy. It was Washington that insisted on the Nuremberg Trials and companion Tokyo Trial of the 1940s (Churchill and Stalin were at first in favour of summary execution of leading Nazi officials).[15] These highly imperfect proceedings provided a foundation for later, improved developments – a point not to be dismissed too quickly by those labelling the trials of the 1940s as nothing more than victor's justice. Once some development is established, it is not always clear where subsequent decisions might lead. Among all the 'laws' at play, there is the law of unintended consequences. The road from Nuremberg to the ICC shows many twists and turns, as well as a considerable pause because of blockages from Cold War politics, but, without Nuremberg, the ICC and other aspects of international criminal law would have been more difficult to construct.

---

[14] A former UN official agrees that the Organization has contributed to selective justice. See LD Johnson, 'UN-Based International Criminal Tribunals: How They Mix and Match' (2008) 36(4) *Denver J Int'l Law and Policy* 275.

[15] It is not so well known, but relevant to subjects discussed here, that later in the early 1950s the United States backed away from the Nuremberg process, seeing it as an impediment to other foreign policy objectives such as the election of Konrad Adenauer in (West) Germany and that state's integration into NATO. This was US 'strategic legalism' with juridical matters pursued or not according to changing conceptions of the national interest. See P Maguire, *Law and War: An American Story* (Columbia University Press, New York 2010). For Justice Jackson and others who wanted to legalise international relations via the Nuremberg trials, this objective proved more difficult than they imagined.

## A. UN Ad Hoc Tribunals

Some 50 years later, it was the United States that made a decisive difference in the renaissance of international criminal justice with the creation in 1993 of the International Criminal Tribunal for the former Yugoslavia (ICTY). This is not to denigrate the contributions made in the 1990s by European and other actors.[16] But international criminal courts were resumed only when officials in Washington succeeded in convincing President Bill Clinton that such a tribunal was a desirable policy option for the western Balkans.[17] To be sure, the UNSC decided to create the ICTY under Chapter VII of the UN Charter as a mandatory peace and security measure in part because the Clinton Administration was under pressure to act in response to well publicised atrocities during 1991–2. Not wanting to put its military personnel in harm's way at that time, some on the Clinton policy-making team saw the ICTY as a feasible option that would demonstrate a response but without entailing unacceptable national blood or treasure.[18] Britain and France officially went along, even if particularly the former had doubts about the wisdom of that particular choice, since in London's view one might have to negotiate a return to peace with war criminals.[19] In the first blush of the post-Cold War world, sometimes referred to as the unipolar moment, China and Russia likewise voted yes. China, like Brazil, was not keen on a UN-mandated criminal court at the start of the deliberations, but eventually came around to the Western position.

Some independent legal experts have held that the Council's creation of criminal courts violates international law, such courts not being mentioned in either Charter Chapter VI (non-binding measures) or Chapter VII (binding measures).[20] This strict constructivist approach is surely passé now, whatever its intellectual merits, given the extensive Council action in this domain and the acceptance of, or deference to, Council policies by most if not all states. To paraphrase a hoary maxim, the life of the law has not been logic but political experience. Moreover, the ICTY Appeals

---

[16] The broad record is well traced in WA Schabas, *The UN International Criminal Tribunals: The Former Yugoslavia, Rwanda and Sierra Leone* (CUP, Cambridge 2006) 11–20 and GJ Bass, *Stay The Hand Of Vengeance: The Politics of War Crimes Tribunals* (Princeton University Press, Princeton 2000) chapter 6.

[17] One inside account is provided by the US Assistant Secretary of State for Human Rights, Democracy, and Labor at the time: J Shattuck, *Freedom on Fire: Human Rights Wars & America's Response* (Harvard University Press, Cambridge MA 2003). Other insiders maintain a slightly different version of persons and reasons involved.

[18] See DP Forsythe, 'Politics and the International Criminal Tribunal for the Former Yugoslavia' in RS Clark and M Sand (eds) *The Prosecution of International Crimes* (Transaction, New Brunswick 1996) 185 and Bass (n 16) 207. There were those in the State Department that approached the ICTY and later the ICTR as the right thing to do, morally and legally. In other circles of opinion in Washington, more expedient considerations were taken into account.

[19] See Bass (n 16) 211 *et seq*.

[20] See Schabas (n 16).

Chamber in the *Tadić* case has held that the Court was properly created under international law.[21]

Even so, US and European military leaders were decidedly unenthusiastic about arresting some of those indicted by the ICTY's Office of the Prosecutor, fearing casualties that would trigger a domestic backlash against deepening involvement in violent foreign affairs.[22] This was not an unreasonable fear, given the congressional and public backlash in the wake of the deaths of 18 US military personnel in Somalia in 1993 in a failed arrest attempt, which eventually compelled Clinton to reduce US – and UN – involvement in that failed state. So the Council might create *ad hoc* criminal courts, but making them work effectively did not follow automatically. Apparently Russia, having voted for the ICTY, then aligned with Serbia in trying to impede the workings of that court.[23]

Having created the ICTY in part for debatable reasons – namely, to avoid a military intervention to stop atrocities – the UNSC then created the International Criminal Tribunal for Rwanda (ICTR) in 1994, again as led by the United States. In part, some on the Clinton team were looking for a way to atone for their refusal to support a more robust UN security mission in the midst of the 1994 genocide.[24] It was also embarrassed by UN Secretary-General Boutros Boutros-Ghali and his contrasting the considerable Western attention to Bosnia with the lack of similar attention to the Great Lakes region of Africa. So the United States had short-term and self-interested reasons for advancing the ICTR, apart from any principled commitment to international criminal justice as a feature of the current world order – the latter being the view in the State Department Legal Office and aligned bureaus.

This time around China abstained in support of Rwanda, an elected member of the UNSC. The new Paul Kagame government voted against the creation of the ICTR in protest about the absence of a death penalty and other issues. So China in its approach to criminal law in the Council seemed to place great reliance on the views of developing countries, but at the same time China's abstention did not block what the United States wanted to do. China obviously sought to please both quarters – the United States and the West, but also African states. China itself had engaged in the Tiananmen massacre of protesting dissidents in 1989, yet it no doubt calculated that UN *ad hoc* criminal courts with limited geographical jurisdiction and a focus on war crimes rather than general human rights law posed little threat to China's – and the ruling elite's – core interests. China was not enthusiastic about

---

[21] *Prosecutor v Tadić* (Appeals Judgment) IT-04-1-A (15 July 1999).

[22] See Shattuck (n 16) regarding the Pentagon's opposition to arrests by Western military forces.

[23] Carla del Ponte, *Madame Prosecutor: Confrontations with Humanity's Worst Criminals and the Culture of Impunity: A Memoir* (Other Press, New York 2009) 113–114.

[24] Among many sources, for an excellent overview explaining why various UN and Western officials opposed further involvement in Rwanda in 1994, see MJ Barnett, *Eyewitness to a Genocide: The UN and Rwanda* (Cornell University Press, Ithaca 2002). For an excellent treatment of what transpired at grassroots level and the frustrations of unsuccessfully seeking that further, more robust involvement, see R Dallaire, *Shake Hands with the Devil: The Failure of Humanity in Rwanda* (Carroll and Graf Publishers, New York 2003).

most human rights developments at the UN, whether in the Security Council or Human Rights Commission (née Council), but it could tolerate some developments if it meant avoiding deterioration in US relations.[25]

Over time the UNSC supervised its judicial creations in many ways, creating judges *ad hoc*, dealing with petty corruption and other problems in the ICTR, pressing for a wind-up strategy for both courts, allowing an extension of the ICTY to deal with the *Karadžić* and *Mladić* cases, among others. The subject is too large for coverage here.

## B. Sierra Leone

With the two UN *ad hoc* criminal courts proving not only able to hold fair trails and convict numerous defendants but also proving slow and costly, the situation in Sierra Leone resulted in the UNSC taking a different approach. The Council started by endorsing the 1999 Lomé Accord which presumably ended the internationalised internal conflict that had been running for almost a decade between the government and mainly the Revolutionary United Forces (RUF). This accord promised an amnesty from legal prosecution for all those involved in the conflict who agreed to lay down their arms. So in Resolution 2060 (1999), the Council seemed to endorse bypassing criminal justice in the interests of the restoration of stability. A year later, however, with a changed political situation, the Council adopted Resolution 1315 (2000) authorising the Secretary-General to negotiate various arrangements with the government of Sierra Leone.

In effect, UN organs wound up negotiating with themselves, as the Security Council exchanged views with the Office of the Secretary-General, the latter also negotiating with Sierra Leone. The end result was a new criminal court, partly national and partly international both in terms of judges appointed and laws enforced, but one not financed through UN channels. Financial arrangements were opposed by the Secretary-General and did not play out very well. But at that time, there was no enthusiasm in the Council and General Assembly for financing a new criminal court. The Sierra Leone court lacked the authority derived from being created under Chapter VII of the UN Charter. The court was based on a negotiated agreement between Sierra Leone and the UN Secretariat, with a companion UNSC resolution in the background. Whereas the two UN *ad hoc* courts had supreme legal authority within their jurisdiction and could legally compel cooperation from all states, the authority was otherwise for the new hybrid court. There was also a Truth Commission.[26]

---

[25] See the excellent article by M Fullilove, 'China and the United Nations: The Stakeholder Spectrum' (2011) 34(3) *Washington Quarterly* 63. I am indebted to David Malone for calling this article to my attention.

[26] See further WA Schabas, 'The Relationship between Truth Commissions and International Courts: The Case of Sierra Leone' (2003) 25(4) *HRQ* 1035.

As the court proceeded with indictments and prosecutions, the UNSC played a supervisory role. Through Resolution 1688 (2006), for example, at the request of concerned African states, it authorised a Special Chamber of the court to sit in The Hague, utilising the facilities of the International Criminal Court, in order to try the former dictator of Liberia, Charles Taylor. Taylor was charged with authorising various atrocities in Sierra Leone. His continuing popularity in certain West African circles of opinion led to the Council decision to hold his trial in The Hague. The relevant UNSC resolution provided the Court with legal authority beyond Sierra Leone and responded to concerns by states like the Netherlands and the United Kingdom about certain jurisdictional issues.

It might be mentioned in passing that the Office of the Prosecutor for the Sierra Leone special court was David Crane, an American lawyer who had served previously in the Pentagon. This appointment, while criticised in certain circles, may have ensured a certain US interest in the operations and indeed in the success of the court. (One judge was from the United States and one from the UK.) By 2011, the United States had contributed some $80m in voluntary donations to the chronically under-funded court, including an expedited $5m to try to ensure the continuation of the Taylor trial. US support for the ICTY and ICTR, in terms of money and personnel and equipment, has also been important.

## C. Cambodia

Likewise, regarding Cambodia, the UN Secretariat engaged in protracted negotiations about the creation of a special or hybrid criminal court to deal with the residue from the Khmer Rouge atrocities during 1975–9. While some parties preferred another UN *ad hoc* criminal court as mandated by the UNSC under Chapter VII, China refused to agree to any criminal law process that would be imposed on Cambodia (as distinct from negotiated with Cambodia). China was closely aligned with the Hun Sen government there. Hun Sen had been part of the Khmer Rouge movement, and some circles of opinion did not believe he negotiated in good faith regarding the hybrid criminal court. At the end of a long diplomatic process, with mediation by the United States, a complicated and perhaps even dubious criminal court was created that started its first case only in 2009. Judicial arrangements had been approved by the UN General Assembly in 2003, with no role for the Security Council, and despite serious concerns by the Secretary-General. Once China made clear that it would not support a Chapter VII court, the Council was effectively sidelined.

## D. East Timor and Kosovo

In East Timor and Kosovo, territories for a time under UN administration, the Security Council authorised a security mission which was managed by the office of the Secretary-General. The top UN official in these missions, the Special

Representative of the Secretary-General, proceeded to create criminal courts and other legal bodies as part of his general administrative duties. The UNSC retained an oversight function which sometimes came into play when it was time to terminate or re-authorise the field missions. Judicial matters did not loom large in Council deliberations in these two cases.[27]

## E. The International Criminal Court

The Council's creation of the two *ad hoc* criminal courts facilitated diplomatic progress on the ICC, not only by demonstrating the feasibility of international criminal courts but also by indicating how much time, diplomatic capital and money was required to get them up and running. One can recall the hesitation in the Council to have the UNSC commission yet a third *ad hoc* court for Sierra Leone. Many states concluded that the time was ripe for a permanent international criminal court, if only to reduce the transaction costs involved in creating a series of *ad hoc* courts.

As states and other interested parties met at the Rome diplomatic conference in 1998 to hammer out a court statute, it being clear that such a court would need to be created by treaty and not by UNSC decision, the early assumption by the United States and certain other states was that cases would be referred to the new court by the Council.[28] Just as the UN Charter ensured that no P-5 state would ever be charged with aggression or breach of the peace by the Council, given veto provisions, so particularly most US officials assumed that the same logic would prevail at Rome. The UNSC veto would ensure that no Americans (or Chinese or Russians, etc.) would be defendants before the ICC. When that logic did not prevail, because international political culture about double standards had apparently changed since 1945, the United States decided that it could not support the final Rome Statute.[29]

---

[27] On East Timor, in addition to S Eldon, 'East Timor' in DM Malone (ed) *The UN Security Council: From the Cold War to the 21st Century* (Lynne Rienner, Boulder 2004) 551, see S Katzenstein, 'Hybrid Tribunals: Searching for Justice in East Timor' (2001) 16(2) *Harvard J Int'l L* 245. On Kosovo, in addition to P Heinbecker, 'Kosovo' in DM Malone (ed) *The UN Security Council: From the Cold War to the 21st Century* (Lynne Rienner, Boulder 2004) 537, see Human Rights Watch, *Kosovo Criminal Justice Scorecard* (27 March 2008). There was also a Special Chamber for War Crimes in Bosnia that was supervised by the UN; see Human Rights Watch, *Narrowing the Impunity Gap: Trials before Bosnia's War Crimes Chamber* (12 February 2007).

[28] Among many sources, a concise overview of the creation of the ICC can be found in BN Schiff, *Building the International Criminal Court* (CUP, New York 2008).

[29] In 1945, the prevailing opinion was that the League of Nations had been too democratic, with too much emphasis on state equality, for it and associated arrangements to work. What was needed, so it was thought back then, was more emphasis on the realities of state power even if this resulted in only partial justice. See Anderson (n 2). This 1945 view was re-evaluated in 1998 at the Rome Conference.

The reasons given for the US failure to ratify the Rome Statute have been well documented and need not be repeated here.[30] The underlying cultural and political dynamics have also been analysed.[31] It may be that some in Washington during the time of the Bill Clinton Administration did genuinely fear a rogue prosecutor and other developments that might reflect an anti-Americanism leading to politicised trials for American defendants. But particularly after the administration of George W. Bush, and in the light of US torture and other violations of international human rights and humanitarian law in US counter-terrorism policies after 9/11/2001, it seems reasonably evident that some in Washington believed that torture and other violations of law entailing individual criminal responsibility might be required in a world of dangerous enemies.[32] Moreover, more generally, throughout its political history the United States, represented by various governments of both political parties, had rarely accepted a court, or indeed any international organisation, that it could not control on important issues.[33]

China and Russia also objected to the ICC as it emerged from the Rome conference (as did Israel, among other important military powers). France and the UK did eventually sign and ratify the Rome Statute, the French obtaining some temporary concessions of interest to Paris. So here we find two modern military powers who did indeed commit their military forces abroad on occasion (e.g. Afghanistan, Iraq, Sierra Leone, Ivory Coast, Libya, etc.) but who clearly did not fear politicised trials against their nationals. It should be mentioned that there are

---

[30] See Schiff (n 28).

[31] See DP Forsythe, 'The United States and International Criminal Law' (2002) 24(4) *HRQ* 974.

[32] As a matter of policy, the US government during the George W Bush Administration engaged in enforced disappearances, torture, cruel, inhuman, and degrading treatment, and other serious violations of human rights and humanitarian law. For a summary treatment making use of broad sources, see DP Forsythe, *The Politics of Prisoner Abuse: US Policy and Enemy Prisoners after 9/11* (CUP, Cambridge 2011). Circumstantial evidence suggests that the UK was involved in the creation and implementation of many of these policies. To date, the United States has been unwilling or unable to seriously investigate, much less try in court, the high ranking authors of these illegal policies.

[33] The leading example to the contrary is US membership in the World Trade Organization. There the US has lost a number of 'cases' in Dispute Panels. But sanctioning is up to states, not the international organisation. According to Cerone, US policy on criminal law has been guided by certain goals: shield Americans from the reach of the ICC; seek accountability for others, and minimise international legal authority. See JP Cerone, 'Dynamic Equilibrium: The Evolution of US Attitudes toward International Courts and Tribunals' (2007) 18(1) *EJIL* 277–315. This analysis confirms Forsythe's earlier interpretation (n 31). On the complexity and inconsistency of US policy in the UNSC, see F Rawski and N Miller, 'The United States in the Security Council: A Faustian Bargain?' in DM Malone (ed) *The UN Security Council: From the Cold War to the 21st Century* (Lynne Rienner, Boulder 2004) 357. See also DP Forsythe, 'International Criminal Justice and the United States: Law, Culture, Power' in R Thakur and P Malcontent (eds) *From Sovereign Impunity to International Accountability: The Search for Justice in a World of States* (United Nations University Press, Tokyo 2004) 61.

safeguards against politicised trials, principally two: (1) that the ICC can act only if a state is unwilling or unable to properly investigate and, if warranted, try those suspected of genocide, crimes against humanity, or major war crimes; and (2) that the prosecutor cannot proceed to trial without the approval of a special pre-trial chamber of judges.

Once the ICC became a reality in July 2002, this affected the politics of criminal justice in the UNSC. In that same month, the Bush Administration threatened in the Council to veto a UN peacekeeping operation unless any US personnel in that security mission were immunised from legal liability under international law. Amidst much controversy, the Council eventually did as the United States desired. The same process played out the following year as well.[34] But prisoner abuse at the US-run Abu Ghraib prison in Iraq in 2003, publicised in 2004, brought an end to such US demands. Nevertheless, the Bush Administration continued to try to undermine, limit, and perhaps even destroy the ICC through various policies outside the Council.[35] The US Congress was also broadly hostile to the ICC as it emerged from the Rome Conference, passing legislation authorising the Executive to take military action to free any Americans detained in relation to ICC processes. While largely symbolic, such legislation indicated that a truculent American unilateralism was not monopolised by President George W. Bush and his UN Representative John Bolton.

Matters changed somewhat, however, in 2005. Confronted with continuing violent and abusive policies by the Sudanese government in the Darfur region, policies that then Secretary of State Colin Powell had labelled genocide, the UNSC referred the matter to the Office of the Prosecutor of the ICC, as permitted by the Rome Statute, with a view to possible investigation and criminal proceedings against certain Sudanese officials. The vote was 11-0, with the United States, China, Brazil and Algeria abstaining. Both China and the United States could have exercised a veto but did not. Thus the United States, seeing no better options, and under heavy pressure particularly by certain American religious groups to act regarding the atrocities in Sudan, decided to cooperate with the ICC rather than to undermine it. The Bush team preferred another *ad hoc* criminal court, but opinion in the Council was still set against that option. The United States again insisted on, and got, legal immunity from international liability for all personnel participating in the UN-AU field mission deployed in Darfur. Moreover, the United States dealt with ICC personnel and facilities when it facilitated the transfer of Charles Taylor from Nigeria to The Hague in 2006 to be tried before the Special Court for Sierra Leone.

---

[34] For interpretations about the UNSC modifying the Rome Statute, and state legal obligations in the event such modifications were illegal, see N Jain, 'A Separate Law for Peacekeepers: The Clash between the Security Council and the International Criminal Court' (2005) 16(2) *EJIL* 239.

[35] See further, MJ Matheson, *Council Unbound: The Growth of UN Decision Making on Conflict and Post-Conflict Issues after the Cold War* (United States Institute for Peace, Washington 2006) 210 *et seq*.

After the Prosecutor had secured arrest warrants for Sudanese President Omar Hassan al-Bashir and others, China received him on an official visit in 2011 rather than arresting him. Other states, such as Kenya, also hosted him rather than apprehending him and turning him over to ICC authorities. While there were more than 30 African states that were party to the Rome Statute, there was growing concern across Africa about the ICC.[36] In some circles of African opinion, there was a belief that the Prosecutor had not paid sufficient attention to African views about when arrest warrants were appropriate. Again one can see that Chinese policy was affected by its many African contacts: while it was reluctant to exercise a veto in criminal law matters, it was not really committed to vigorous action by the ICC and its prosecutor. Especially when developing countries were not enthusiastic about ICC actions, China limited its cooperation as well.

When, in early 2011, the UNSC unanimously referred the situation in Libya to the ICC with a view to eventual criminal prosecution of Muammar Gaddafi and his top aides, the African Union later voted to disregard the indictment that had been brought forward against Gaddafi. According to press reports,[37] the AU held that such an indictment was a barrier to its attempts to end the violence in Libya by diplomacy. This action made clear the growing rift between the ICC – or at least the Office of the Prosecutor – and many African states. At the time of writing it was not clear how events would play out, either with regard to the ICC or other matters. But as compared with Sudan in 2005, with regard to Libya in 2011, both the United States and China (along with all other Council members) voted for the referral to the ICC rather than abstaining. One important factor was that the Arab League supported the UNSC referral to the ICC. This put political pressure on China to vote in favour of the referral. By 2011, the Barack Obama Administration spoke for the United States, not the Bush Administration. The Obama team of policy-makers, while showing some continuity with some previous US policies, was generally less unilateralist than the Bush team.[38]

In the UNSC, with regard to the ICC, US policy had shifted from opposition to tolerance to support, but all the while trying to ensure that no Americans would be defendants before the Court.[39] Chinese policy on these matters was to follow rather

---

[36] For a review of criticism of the ICC by African states and by the African Union, see 'The ICC Loses Credibility and Cooperation in Africa' *The Economist* (Kampala 17 February 2011) <http://www.economist.com/node/18176088> last accessed 1 February 2012.

[37] For example, see 'Gadhafi Indictment Hinders Peace: African Union' *Canadian Broadcasting Service* (Toronto 2 July 2011) <http://www.cbc.ca/news/world/story/2011/07/02/world-african-union-gadhafi.html> last accessed 1 February 2012.

[38] See further, DP Forsythe, 'US Foreign Policy and Human Rights: Situating Obama' (2011) 33(3) *HRQ* 767. In the second term of the Bush Administration certain officials like Secretary of State Condoleezza Rice and State Department Legal Counsel John Bellinger III were not as hostile to international law in general or the ICC in particular as certain other officials like Vice President Dick Cheney or Secretary of Defense Donald Rumsfeld. See further Cerone (n 33); see also Forsythe (n 32).

[39] UNSC support for the ICC in the Libyan affair was limited. UNSC Res 1970 (26 February 2011) UN Doc S/RES/1970, para 5, asserted that 'States not party to the Rome Statute

than to lead, to avoid a veto that might antagonise the United States, but also to avoid support for criminal law developments that would irritate its friends in the developing world. Yet as long as no UNSC debates focused on Chinese repression, Beijing was content to provide some carefully calculated support for advances in international criminal law directed to others. In this it was similar to Washington. Among the P-5 only the British and French, having ratified the Rome Statute, did not try to shield their nationals from ICC jurisdiction.

One might also note the different UNSC approach to Sudan and Libya on the one hand, and other states such as Syria on the other. In 2011, Syria too was wracked by massive public protests demanding more democracy and human rights protections (and better economic opportunity). The Bashar al-Assad regime responded with primarily repression for a time, killing hundreds of protestors in the process. Yet the UNSC did not refer the matter to the ICC or call for the departure of Assad. Russia had numerous economic interests in Syria. The United States, with one eye on relations with Israel, feared an uncertain power vacuum in a fractured Syria without firm control at the top. For years Assad had not made direct or serious trouble for Israel. China once again followed the other P-5 policies concerning a state where it had few vital interests. France, the former colonial power in Syria, displayed far more concern about Libya. So the record of the UNSC in referring cases to the ICC, and in considering when such referral might complicate regime change, was highly inconsistent. The political fact seemed to be that Gaddafi was more of a pariah than Assad, in the eyes of most of the P-5 (and in the Arab League).[40] At the time of writing, European states in the Council wanted tougher action against Assad; the United States was supportive; but China and Russia blocked action. It was not clear whether the Council would eventually act in ways similar to the Libyan case, perhaps prodded by the growing opposition to Assad by particularly Turkey and most of the Arab League.

## F. Lebanon

Finally in this section one should acknowledge that the UNSC created a special criminal court regarding – primarily but not exclusively – the assassination in Lebanon of former Prime Minister Rafiq Hariri on 14 February 2005. Led by

---

have no obligation under the Statute' and in para 8 that 'none of the expenses incurred in connection with the referral, including expenses related to investigations or prosecutions in connection with that referral, shall be borne by the United Nations and that such costs shall be borne by the parties to the Rome Statute and those States that wish to contribute voluntarily'.

[40] Both the Libyan and Syrian situations were unresolved at the time of writing. As the Assad regime continued and even accelerated its repression, the UNSC finally issued a Presidential statement of criticism in later summer 2011, as even Russia began to soften its opposition to UNSC involvement and as the United States and others lost patience with an Assad who refused to moderate and reform. UNSC, 'Presidential Statement on Syria' UN Doc S/PRST/2011/16 (3 August 2011).

Britain, France and the United States, the Council voted in Resolution 1559 (2004) to demand that Syria cease its intervention in Lebanese affairs. This was followed by Resolution 1664 (2006) which advanced a focus on, and investigations about, the Hariri killing. The Western P-5 states believed that the killing was the result of certainly Hezbollah and maybe Syrian policies. Finally in Resolution 1757 (2007), the Council by a vote of 10 in favour with five abstentions approved an agreement between the UN Secretariat and Lebanon which brought the Court into being. This agreement was in some ways similar to the one that had brought the Special Court for Sierra Leone into being. But, in approving negotiated arrangements for Lebanon, the UNSC took a decision under Chapter VII, which mandated cooperation with the tribunal. Abstaining were China, Russia, South Africa, Indonesia and Qatar. Public explanations of abstentions had to do with unacceptable interference in Lebanon's domestic affairs. Politically, the Council's backing for a special criminal court, the only one dealing primarily with one killing, was widely seen as a project of the Western P-5 states, aligned with Saudi Arabia and others, designed to counter the influence of Syria, Iran and Hezbollah in Lebanon.[41]

The agreement between the Lebanese government and the UN which the Council endorsed had been negotiated in unique procedures by the Sunni Prime Minister (Rafiq Hariri was a Sunni); without the cooperation of the Speaker of the Parliament (always a Shia, and in current times affiliated with Hezbollah, which in turn was backed by Iran and Syria); and with no role for the President (always a Christian). Thus the Special Tribunal for Lebanon (STL) was entangled in the politics of the weak Lebanese state which had historically found it difficult to take decisive action in the context of disagreement among the main political groupings. In the situation under analysis here, the Lebanese Sunni were aligned with the Western states in the UNSC, as well as with Sunni Saudi Arabia outside the Council.

From one view (meaning the Western view), the STL was an attempt to break out of the chronic Lebanese stalemate by imposing an international solution to violent politics engineered by one coalition (Hezbollah–Syria–Iran). Criminal prosecution was thus intended not only to break out of impunity for political murder in Lebanon, but also to curtail the power of Syria and Iran acting either directly or through Hezbollah. Particularly China and Russia were not very keen on advancing the policy objectives of the leading Western states, but at the same time they apparently did not want to exercise their veto on a matter that did not engage what they saw as their vital national interests.

In January 2011 Hezbollah withdrew its members from the coalition government over the issue of cooperation with the STL, causing a political crisis and further instability in the country. And when, in June 2011 the STL brought four indictments against senior Hezbollah members, the crisis intensified. The leader of Hezbollah, Nasrallah, claimed that the killing of Rafiq Hariri was the work of Israel, and that the STL was nothing more than a conspiracy between the United States and Israel

---

[41] For a good analysis, see N Shehadi and E Wilmshurst, 'The Special Tribunal for Lebanon: The UN on Trial?' *Chatham House, Briefing Paper* (July 2007) <http://www.chathamhouse.org.uk/files/9408_bp0707lebanon.pdf> last accessed 1 February 2012.

to undermine the legitimate political activity of Lebanese Shia as led by Hezbollah. Naturally Nasrallah did not cite any misdeeds by Syria or Iran, his movement's primary backers. He said the four indicted would never be turned in, and it was unlikely that any organisation in Lebanon had the power to apprehend them as required by the rules of the Court.

At the time of writing it was evident that the UN Special Tribunal for Lebanon, rather than quickly breaking out of traditional Lebanese politics which had allowed for penetration by various outside parties over the years, had become enmeshed in the dysfunctional domestic politics that had produced the catastrophic internationalised civil war during 1975–90. The indictment of certain Hezbollah officials (while absolving thus far Syrian operatives) certainly contested the practice of impunity. But given the rigid reaction of the Hezbollah leadership, presumably supported by Iran (with Assad in Syria presumably preoccupied with the political uprising there), it was not at all clear that the STL was the progressive breakthrough that the Western P-5 states desired, either in legal or political terms.

## II. Evaluating the UNSC and Criminal Law Developments

The UNSC has had some *direct* influence on international criminal law, as when it puts on its legal hat and declares some norm is subject to individual responsibility and thus possible criminal prosecution. It has also played a direct role in making clear that states are legally required to cooperate with certain criminal courts. The Council has had considerable *indirect* influence in the sense that its creations, like the two UN *ad hoc* courts, have then proceeded on their own to develop legal norms and punish a number of defendants through convictions and incarceration. This indirect influence extends to the ICC when the Council refers a subject matter, and then the Office of the Prosecutor and legal chambers proceed on their own. Of course it goes without saying that in some matters the developments in international criminal law have little or nothing to do with the UNSC, as when a state such as Côte d'Ivoire accepts ICC jurisdiction and then the Prosecutor and Judges proceed independently.

### A. Norms

A classic example of the Council's direct contribution to the normative development, reinforcement or codification of international criminal law occurred in 1992 when the UNSC was dealing with Somalia. As that failed state degenerated into multifaceted violence and starvation, the Council invoked Charter Chapter VII to declare that the humanitarian crisis constituted a threat to international peace and security. Deploring the armed attacks on relief efforts that were trying to bring assistance to civilians in need, the Council declared in Resolution 794 (1992), paragraph 5, that it 'Strongly condemns all violations of international humanitarian law occurring in Somalia, including in particular the deliberate impeding of the delivery of food and medical supplies essential for the survival of the civilian population, and affirms that those who commit or order the commission of such acts will be held individually responsible for the commission of such acts'.

Now, in Somalia in the early 1990s, it has been said with only slight exaggeration that no local who possessed a weapon had ever heard of the 1949 Geneva Conventions or the laws of war. Since no central government functioned to any great extent, it was certainly not clear what judicial system would bring to legal justice those carrying out the attacks (largely for pecuniary reasons) on Red Cross and other agencies involved in assistance. Nevertheless, the Council reinforced the general principle that war crimes such as attacks on non-fighters entailed individual legal liability. While the practical significance of paragraph 5 of Resolution 794 turned out to be slight, it is very clear that certain war crimes may lead to criminal prosecution.

The Council has contributed to the normative development of international criminal law many times, in many ways, pertaining to many different situations, especially since the end of the Cold War.

## B. State Responsibility

Closely linked to normative development is the principle that territorial states have primary responsibility to enforce criminal law. Consistent with the UN Resolution containing paragraphs on the responsibility to protect[42] – namely that states have the primary responsibility to enforce human rights protections in their jurisdiction, especially to prevent genocide, crimes against humanity, major war crimes and ethnic cleansing – the Council has repeatedly called on states to exercise that responsibility.

In 2009, the Council, working closely with the International Committee of the Red Cross, the guardian of international humanitarian law, adopted Resolution 1894 which was concerned primarily with protection of civilians in armed conflict. The UNSC first recognised that 'States bear the primary responsibility to respect and ensure the human rights of their citizens, as well as all individuals within their territory as provided by relevant international law', and that 'parties to armed conflict [states and armed non-state actors] bear the primary responsibility to take all feasible steps to protect the security of civilians'. The Council then went on to say in operative paragraph 10 that it: '*affirms* its strong opposition to impunity for serious violations of international humanitarian law and human rights law and *emphasizes* in this context the responsibility of states to comply with their relevant obligations to end impunity and to thoroughly investigate and prosecute persons responsible for war crimes, genocide, crimes against humanity or other serious violations of international humanitarian law in order to prevent violations.'

---

[42] UNGA Res 63/308, 'The Responsibility to Protect' (14 September 2009).

Now, one can well doubt the efficacy of this type of general SC statement given the record of certain fighting parties in targeting civilians as part of their calculated strategy to achieve certain objectives. Unfortunately, in many contemporary armed conflicts, harm to civilians is not a matter of collateral damage but of intentional terrorising, displacement, and even killing. Nevertheless, the UNSC put itself on record in favour of the rule of law in general and criminal law in particular in a diplomatic effort to counter such unlimited and inhumane war-fighting strategies. In a number of cases the Council authorised some type of security mission to at least impede, if not confront, such abuses of civilians. In Resolution 1894 the Council laid out a general statement, including emphasis on state primary responsibility for the application of criminal law, with no practical measures attached. In the case of the UNSC and counter-terrorism, on the other hand, we find the Council not only adopting resolutions requiring states to criminalise certain terrorist actions, but also sometimes creating a supervisory process to monitor state compliance with UNSC directives.[43]

## C. The UN Ad Hoc Tribunals

If it turns out to be true that the ICTY and ICTR are generally judged to be a success, after many difficulties, in developing international criminal law and bringing to legal justice some big fish and several medium fish for their crimes, the UNSC deserves some credit for authorising these courts.[44] If it turns out to be true that these *ad hoc* courts have had some beneficial impact on national and regional political culture, peace and reconciliation, which is a much more complex and debatable consideration, then again the Council deserves whatever credit is appropriate.

Without doubt these two courts have developed or clarified a number of legal points, so much so that some legal experts think they have re-written modern international criminal law: e.g. that individual responsibility for crimes obtains in internal as well as international armed conflict; that rape can be a war crime as well as evidence of crimes against humanity and genocide, as well as evidence of other criminal acts; that legal immunity of sitting public officials does not extend to certain major crimes; that certain acts in both jurisdictions were part of genocide; that there can be complicity through a joint criminal enterprise; and so on. Of course these determinations were made by court officials and not by state representatives sitting in the UNSC. Nevertheless it was the Council that created the institutions that allowed the determinations to be made.

---

[43] See further, E Podgor, RS Clark and E Wise (eds), *International Criminal Law: Cases and Materials* (3rd edn Lexis-Nexis, Newark 2009).

[44] For support for this emerging consensus, see the entries on the ICTY and ICTR, with suggested additional readings, in DP Forsythe (ed) *The Encyclopedia of Human Rights* (OUP, New York 2009). The literature evaluating the two UN *ad hoc* courts that these entries summarise is voluminous.

Likewise, it was the Council that was at the origin of the trail of decisions that resulted in the likes of Slobodan Milošević (a high Serb official), Radovan Karadžić (a political leader of the Bosnian Serbs) and Ratko Mladić (a Bosnian Serb general) facing legal justice in the ICTY; and Jean Kambanda (a prime minister), Jean-Paul Akayesu (a mayor) and Georges Rutaganda (a high official of a Hutu militia) facing legal justice in the ICTR. This is no small record of accomplishment for modern criminal law. In the short term, some of these indictments and arrests, especially in the Balkans, led to an outpouring of support for the alleged war criminals, as an illiberal nationalism continued to rear its ugly head. In the long term, in both regions, the indictments, arrests and convictions helped to delegitimise illiberal political views and their adherents.

Particularly in the case of the ICTY, cooperation with the *ad hoc* court did not often occur because of some epiphany in favour of criminal law by heretofore recalcitrant parties. Cooperation occurred, often grudgingly over time, because an important coalition backed the court. The United States, the European Union, the World Bank, and other actors often (if inconsistently) backed the ICTY and threatened to withhold something that Serbia, or Croatia, or some other party dearly wanted – e.g. membership in the EU, foreign assistance, a loan, whatever. The UNSC was at times part of this supporting coalition that leveraged certain actors and insisted on cooperation with the court.[45]

For example in Resolution 1503 (2003) the Council urged 'Member States to consider imposing measures against individuals and groups or organizations assisting indictees at large to continue to evade justice, including measures designed to restrict the travel and freeze the assets of such individuals, groups, or organizations'. The Council then went on to name Serbia, Croatia, Bosnia and the Serb Republic in relation to the ICTY, and Rwanda, Kenya, DRC and Congo in relation to the ICTR. This resolution had the effect of putting the named states on notice that they were being watched and their cooperation or lack of same noted. The wording was fairly soft, urging rather than legally requiring, but the political effect was the same. The UNSC may not have been the key actor in the network, particularly since the compromise wording was fairly soft. Nevertheless, over time particularly the ICTY could draw on important sources of support, including the UNSC. The Council also paid periodic attention to the pace of court proceedings and the replacement of judges and prosecutors to provide continuity and smooth functioning.

The network of actors that supported the two *ad hoc* courts also ensured that the legal justice pursued would be partial justice. The ICTY Prosecutor did not pursue the subject of possible NATO war crimes in the western Balkans because: (1) NATO offered no precise cooperation with preliminary investigations and the Prosecutor

---

[45] See PC McMahon and DP Forsythe, 'The ICTY and Serbia: Judicial Romanticism Meets Network Politics' (2008) 30(2) *HRQ* 412. On the inconsistency of UNSC support for the two *ad hoc* courts, see P Kirsch, JT Holmes and M Johnson, 'International Tribunals and Courts' in DM Malone (ed) *The UN Security Council: From the Cold War to the 21st Century* (Lynne Rienner, Boulder 2004) 281.

had no way to compel that cooperation: and (2) if the Prosecutor antagonised NATO member states, that would undermine pursuit of Serb and Croat indictees, because cooperation from those states was crucial to apprehending or pressuring others to apprehend those persons. It is even clearer that regarding Rwanda, the Prosecutor was not allowed to pursue probable crimes committed by Tutsi against Hutu, and was removed from her role there, at least in part, because of wanting to do so. Both several important states and various UN officials insisted that the ICTR focus remain on Hutu atrocities, lest the Tutsi-dominated government of Paul Kagame make it impossible for the ICTR to function.[46]

## D. Special Criminal Courts

Generalised evaluation of the various special criminal courts, even of a tentative nature, is difficult, owing to the different circumstances and also the different Council role in each. Most of the proceedings remain uncompleted at the time of writing. Probably the most successful is the Special Court for Sierra Leone, if only because of the trial of Charles Taylor. While this court might not prove to have great impact on Sierra Leone itself, it might contribute over time to African rapacious dictators being more careful about their policies.

Probably the most controversial is the Special Tribunal for Lebanon, in part because it was a component of the Western P-5 states' strategy to contest the influence in Lebanon of Iran and Syria, the latter having close relations with Hezbollah. It was also the case that this Western strategy-cum-court further destabilised Lebanon, at least in the short term. It is all well and good to go on record as opposing political murder. But if the government proves unable to arrest and try those indicted, the creation of the court will have served to demonstrate yet again the weakness of the Lebanese government and state without notable advance in criminal law. Thus the STL may turn out to be a bridge too far.

The hybrid criminal court in Cambodia is likely to turn out to be a largely symbolic venture, perhaps reinforcing the principle that atrocities do entail individual criminal responsibility. But not much else is likely to come out of these judicial proceedings, given particularly the manoeuvres of the Hun Sen government to keep it a minor matter and end it quickly. The public there seems not much engaged, the defendants old and few, and the process full of resignations and other problems. The UNSC role was minimal to non-existent. The courts in East Timor and Kosovo have not figured broadly in local or regional developments. The Bosnian War Crimes Court is important in the sense that its proper functioning would allow, eventually, the well-considered closing down of the ICTY. But the arrests of Karadžić and Mladić require the continuation of the ICTY for a few more years. Again, the UNSC role in judicial matters was small and episodic.

---

[46] See particularly del Ponte (n 23) 60–63, 233–241 *et seq*.

## E. The ICC

At the time of writing, the Council has referred two matters to the ICC, Sudan/Darfur in 2005 and Libya in 2011. Neither state in question was a party to the Rome Statute. The first referral came about in part because the Council, and particularly the United States, was out of other feasible options. Various condemnations of the al-Bashir policies have already been put on record, some economic sanctions already put into place, and a Chapter VI peacekeeping mission already deployed. There was no political support for further use of military force in an enforcement action, especially since leading Western military powers were already involved, and even bogged down, in places like Iraq and Afghanistan – not to mention Libya. Hence criminal procedures, as in the Balkans in 1993, demonstrated some concrete action but avoided the more controversial notion of humanitarian intervention. But when an arrest warrant was issued for al-Bashir, to take just that example, he flaunted his status, continued to travel rather freely (but not completely so) in many places, and mobilised considerable African support by painting the ICC and its Prosecutor as a neo-colonial instrument. It became evident that despite his brutal policies, many states were not prepared to back the ICC in putting him on trial for atrocities.

The second referral was different in that a focus on the criminal responsibility of Gaddafi and his top lieutenants (including one son) was combined with military action. This combination raised the question of the wisdom of seeking criminal justice while also seeking regime change. As widely discussed, if Gaddafi had no prospect of safe haven as per Cedras when he left Haiti or brutal Salvadoran officials allowed to find safe haven in the United States or Spain, why would not Gaddafi be motivated to stay and fight to the bitter end, as indeed occurred. True, one could perhaps later bargain with the leaders of the Gaddafi regime, offering to postpone trials indefinitely in response to desired behaviour. Under Article 16 of the Rome Statute, the Council can vote a postponement of juridical proceedings for a period of one year, without limit on the number of such votes.

Since these two referrals have yet to fully play out, little can be said at this point of a definitive nature. Certainly the Sudan case demonstrates that many states that became parties to the Rome Statute, or allowed the referral to be made by the Council, were not really interested in a robust implementation of international criminal justice *per se* – particularly if it seemed to block a diplomatic solution. In the Libyan case, the ICC Prosecutor, having brought certain indictments, then met with victorious rebel officials in late 2011 and deferred to their intention to pursue criminal justice in national proceedings. The Prosecutor offered his resources to help implement proper judicial proceedings consistent with international standards.

## Conclusion

One can suppose that many observers of international relations were astounded at the renaissance of international criminal justice after the Cold War.[47] More than half a dozen internationally approved criminal courts have been created, and the ICC's Rome Statute currently has 119 state parties. Authoritarian China, semi-authoritarian Russia, and the highly nationalistic United States have all given some support to various aspects of this renaissance, as have the other P-5 states, the United Kingdom and France. Yet these developments in support of criminal law remain fragile and often controversial.

A first and persistent problem, clearly not yet overcome, is how to integrate international criminal law into other national interests as defined and pursued by states. Recall that the United States abandoned the Nuremberg process in the interests of shoring up West Germany's pro-Western democracy and NATO membership. Recall that many critics thought the criminal focus on Gaddafi unwise if one wanted to entice him to step aside and allow more responsible government to evolve in Libya. Establishing a political consensus about when to prosecute and when to go the route of seeking improved human dignity through non-juridical diplomacy is a tough nut to crack. So the first problem is how to make the exceptions to criminal proceedings principled and systematic, in such a way that the movement towards more effective criminal law is not derailed.[48]

A second and persistent problem is that double standards obviously persist. China, Russia and the United States refuse to ratify ICC arrangements that would legally regulate them, but push the ICC on others. Particularly the United States, which has been a major advocate for such measures as the UN *ad hoc* courts and the Special Tribunal for Lebanon, has sought to turn American exceptionalism into legal exemptionalism.[49] This has long been true of its policies on international criminal law. Regarding the Nuremberg and Tokyo trials, for example, the United States insisted that the notion of crimes against humanity be linked to armed conflict, lest someone take that legal concept and address the systematic attacks on

---

[47] Not the least of those surprised are conservative nationalists like Jack Goldsmith, for a time head of the Office of Legal Counsel in the George W Bush Department of Justice, who argued that the ICC could not function without US power behind it, and who assumed the United States would always contest the court. See J Goldsmith, 'The Self-Defeating International Criminal Court' (2003) 70(1) *U Chicago L Rev* 89.

[48] See especially J Snyder and L Vinjamuri, 'Trials and Errors in Strategies of International Justice' (2003–2004) 28(3) *Int'l Security* 5, who note three options: consistent trials, truth commissions, and a pragmatic reading of context leading sometimes to impunity when 'spoilers' are strong. They favour the last option and do not seem concerned that frequent by-passing of criminal justice might undermine a liberal rule of law in international relations.

[49] See J Ruggie, 'Doctrinal Unilateralism and Its Limits: America and Global Governance in the New Century' in DP Forsythe et al (eds) *American Foreign Policy in a Globalized World* (Routledge, New York 2006) 31.

African-Americans especially in the American south.⁵⁰ As shown above, the United States was part of the network demanding that Croatia and Serbia take unpopular decisions regarding the arrest of popular political and military figures, while the United States itself refused to address its own record of torture and cruel treatment of detainees in its counter-terrorism policies after 9/11.⁵¹ The United States urged Sri Lanka to do what Washington refused to do itself, namely to address vigorously the national record of alleged violations of human rights and humanitarian law.⁵² This political partiality, which certainly played out in the UNSC, undercut the notion of impartial legal justice and contributed to especially much African discontent about UNSC and ICC actions. One should also recall the abbreviated – if not aborted – attempts of Carla del Ponte to look into NATO and Tutsi war crimes. Western opposition to such inquiries sealed their fate.

One could say that the central issue regarding contemporary international criminal justice is how equal or partial that justice will be. Certainly a fundamental tenet of universal human rights is that all states are obligated to adhere to those norms, even if it is recognised that universal norms should be applied with due regard to specific contexts. Especially when looking at the UNSC and criminal law, one can see that political factors and special privileges are very much in play. In a sense, the Council's decisions leading to criminal trials have resulted in political trials, not in the sense of unfair proceedings leading to predetermined outcomes, but because those trials are selective, being dependent on political choice and political limitations. The quest for impartial criminal justice remains to be fulfilled. The question of whether that goal can be approached incrementally, with progressively less exceptionalism and relatively more even-handedness, will be answered in the future.

---

⁵⁰ See further, *inter alia*, A Clapham, 'Issues of Complexity, Complicity and Complementarity: From the Nuremberg Trials to the Dawn of the New International Criminal Court' in P Sands (ed) *From Nuremberg to The Hague: The Future of International Criminal Justice* (CUP, Cambridge 2003) 10.
⁵¹ Forsythe (n 32).
⁵² US Department of State, 'Sri Lanka: Accountability for Alleged Violations of International Human Rights Law (Taken Question)' (27 June 2011) <http://www.state.gov/r/pa/prs/ps/2011/06/167218.htm> last accessed 1 February 2012.

# Expanding the Focus of the 'African Criminal Court'

## Kai Ambos[1]

To date, all situations where investigations have been formally opened (pursuant to Articles 15(3) and 15(4) and Article 53(1) of the ICC Statute[2]) which have been initiated by the ICC since its establishment in 2002 originate in the African continent (these are: Democratic Republic of Congo [DRC], Central African Republic [CAR], Uganda, Sudan, Kenya, Libya and Côte d'Ivoire)[3], and also the ICC's first conviction as well as its first acquittal concerned African nationals[4]. This led to criticism of the ICC as an 'African Criminal Court',[5] criticism which came to a head when an arrest warrant was issued against Sudan's sitting President Omar al-Bashir.[6] Although the African Union

---

[1] I thank my research assistant and doctoral student Sabine Klein for her most valuable support in preparing this chapter. I also thank Dr Phil Clark (London/Oxford) and Dr Gerhard Anders (Zurich) for helpful comments. The paper is accurate as of 18 February 2013.

[2] Rome Statute of the International Criminal Court, 2187 UNTS 90, 17 July 1998, entered into force 1 July 2002.

[3] ICC, 'Situations and Cases' <http://www.icc-cpi.int/EN_Menus/ICC/Situations%20and%20Cases/Pages/situations%20and%20cases.aspx> last accessed 1 January 2013.

[4] See on the one hand ICC Trial Chamber I *Situation in the Democratic Republic of Congo, Prosecutor v Thomas Lubanga* (Judgment) 14 March 2012 (ICC-01/04-01/06); on the other Trial Chamber II *Situation in the Democratic Republic of Congo, Prosecutor v Mathieu Ngudjolo Chu* (Judgment) 18 December 2012 (ICC-01/04-02/12).

[5] For a survey on the debate, see M Kimani, 'Pursuit of Justice or Western plot? International Indictments Stir Angry Debate in Africa' (2009) 23(3) *African Renewal* <http://www.un.org/africarenewal/magazine/october-2009/pursuit-justice-or-western-plot> accessed 1 January 2013 and M du Plessis, 'The International Criminal Court that Africa Wants' (Institute for Security Studies, Pretoria 2010) identifying six arguments of the debate starting from vi, and analysing those arguments from 13. As an example for one of many journalistic accounts, see the cover story 'ICC vs. Africa. The Scales of Injustice' *New African* (No 515, March 2012) 10 *et seq* <http://www.newafricanmagazine.com/issues/march-2012> last accessed 2 January 2013.

[6] The first warrant of arrest for war crimes and crimes against humanity was issued by ICC PTC I in *Situation in Darfur, Sudan: Prosecutor v al Bashir* (Warrant of Arrest for Omar Hassan Ahmad al Bashir) ICC-02/05-01/09-1 (4 March 2009). After the Appeals

(hereinafter, 'AU') promoted the ICC unreservedly some years ago, calling, for example, for universal ratification of the Rome Statute in its strategic plan for 2004–7,[7] its attitude changed considerably with the issuance of the al-Bashir arrest warrant.[8] The AU Assembly and its Peace and Security Council have repeatedly, albeit unsuccessfully, called upon the UN Security Council [hereinafter 'SC'] to apply Article 16 and defer the Sudan proceedings.[9]

---

Chamber's partial overturning of this decision (*Situation in Darfur, Sudan: Prosecutor v al Bashir* (Judgement on the appeal of the Prosecutor against the 'Decision on the Prosecution's Application for a Warrant of Arrest against Omar Hassan Ahmad al Bashir') ICC-02/05-01/09-OA (3 February 2010)) a second warrant of arrest including a genocide charge was issued: *Situation in Darfur, Sudan: Prosecutor v al Bashir* (Second Warrant of Arrest for Omar Hassan Ahmad al Bashir) ICC-02/05-01/09-95 (12 May 2010). The ICC's investigations in Sudan do not end with those against al-Bashir, other cases are pending. So, in 2007, two arrest warrants against (former) Sudanese senior leaders were issued by ICC Pre-Trial Chamber I: *Situation in Darfur, Sudan: Prosecutor v Harun and Kushayb* (Warrant of Arrest for Ahmad Harun) ICC-02/05-01/07-2-Corr (27 April 2007); *Situation in Darfur, Sudan: Prosecutor v Harun and Kushayb* (Warrant of Arrest for Ali Kushayb) ICC-02/05-01/07-3-Corr (27 April 2007). In 2012, a further warrant of arrest against the current Minister of National Defence were issued by ICC Pre-Trial Chamber I *Situation in Darfur, Sudan: Prosecutor v Hussein* (Warrant of Arrest for Abdel Raheem Muhammad Hussein) ICC-02/05-01/12-2 (1 March 2012). At the time of writing all accused remained at large. Furthermore, in *Situation in Darfur, Sudan: Prosecutor v Banda and Jerbo* (Decision on the Confirmation of Charges) ICC-02/05-03/09-121-Corr-Red (7 March 2011) war crimes charges have been confirmed. In this case, both accused appeared voluntary before the Court and are awaiting trial.

[7] AU, 'Strategic Plan of the Commission of the African Union, Volume 3: 2004-2007 Plan of Action' (May 2004) 65.

[8] Reuters reported having been told by an African diplomat: 'Bashir is dividing us' and 'Those two parts caused a big fight between the delegates'. B Malone, 'African Nations divided over Bashir Genocide Charge' *Reuters* (Kampala 25 July 2010) <http://uk.reuters.com/article/2010/07/25/uk-africa-bashir-idUKTRE66O1NR20100725> accessed 2 January 2013. See recently K Mills, '"Bashir is dividing us": Africa and the International Court' (2012) 34 *Human Rights Quarterly* 404-447 (identifying four areas of tension: human rights v. sovereignty; human rights v. pan-africanism; global v. regional geopolitics; peace v. justice).

[9] See most recently AU Assembly 'Decision on the Implementation of the Decisions on the International Criminal Court (ICC)' (15-16 July 2012) Assembly/AU/Dec. 419 (XIX) para 4 (also including a request to defer the Kenyan proceedings); AU Assembly 'Decision on the Progress Report of the Commission on the Implementation of the Assembly Decisions on the International Criminal Court (ICC)' (29-30 January 2012) Assembly/AU/Dec. 397 (XVIII) para 3 *et seq*; and as an earlier example, AU Assembly 'Decision on the Implementation of the Decisions of the International Criminal Court' (30–31 January 2011) Assembly/AU/Dec.334 (XVI) para 3. See for a comprehensive account D Akande et al, 'An African Expert study on the African Union Concerns about Article 16 of the Rome Statute of the ICC' (Institute for Security Studies, Pretoria 2010) 7–24; L Oette, 'Peace and Justice, or Neither? The Repercussions of the Al Bashir Case for International Criminal Justice in Africa and Beyond' (2010) 8 *JICJ* 345, 350; R Cryer, 'The Security Council, Article 16 and Darfur' in The Foundation for Law, Justice and Society in collaboration with The Centre for Socio-Legal Studies, University of Oxford (ed) *Debating International Justice in Africa: Collected Essays, 2008–2010* (Foundation for Law, Justice

# Expanding the Focus of the 'African Criminal Court'

An African Union High-Level Panel on Darfur (AUPD) was set up in March 2009[10] mandated 'to examine the issues of peace, justice, accountability, impunity and reconciliation in Darfur'.[11] In its final report, the AUPD recommended, *inter alia*, the establishment of a hybrid court for grave crimes committed in Darfur and expressed the hope that such a court might influence the ICC's decision on complementarity.[12] Recommendations on the Bashir case were not given in the AUPD Report. Yet the AU Assembly's solidarity with al-Bashir became obvious, when it decided[13] that:

---

and Society, Oxford 2010) 80–82, considering that the Security Council would be 'lawful', but 'ill-advised' to defer the situation in Sudan; CC Jalloh, 'Universal Jurisdiction, Universal Prescription? A Preliminary Assessment of the African Union Perspective on Universal Jurisdiction' (2010) 21 *CLF* 1, 57–58, critical of the SC's silence.

[10] Following a decision by the Peace and Security Council of the AU at its 142nd meeting held at ministerial level on 21 July 2008 and subsequently reaffirmed by decision of the 12th Ordinary Session of the Assembly of the African Union held on 1–3 February 2009, the AUPD began its work in March 2009 and finished its activities in September 2009: AU, 'Report of the African Union High-Level on Darfur (AUPD)', PSC/AHG/2 (CCVII) (29 October 2009) iv; xiii.

[11] AUPD Report (n 10) xiii.

[12] The AUPD Report addresses the complex situation in Darfur on various levels. Regarding issues on justice and impunity – and especially criminal justice processes – it recognised existing instruments in Darfur being ineffective and confusing (AUPD Report (n 10) 54 *et seq*; 87) and therefore recommended national proceedings as a principal forum for delivering criminal justice for crimes committed in Darfur (ibid 86) as well as the establishment of a hybrid court with jurisdiction over 'individuals who appear to bear particular responsibility for the gravest crimes' (ibid 86–87). As to the ICC, the AUPD remains vague and points to its limited capacity and to a 'vital importance of strengthening national legal systems'. It furthermore states that the ICC, due to the principle of complementarity, is 'obliged to take into consideration the fact that a State has taken or is taking effective justice measures to deal with relevant crimes' (ibid 91). The Deputy Prosecutor of the ICC, Fatou Bensouda, however, quoted the South African President and Head of the AUPD Mbeki as having expressed a 'perfect understanding between the Panel and the ICC' (E Ankumah, 'Is Africa a Participant or Target of International Justice – An Interview with Fatou Bensouda, Deputy Prosecutor of the International Criminal Court' (2010) *African Legal Aid Quarterly* 1, 3.

[13] The decisions of the AU Assembly – as 'supreme organ of the Union' (Organization of African Unity, Constitutive Act of the African Union, done at Lome, Togo, 1 July 2000, entered into force 26 May 2001 <http://www.au.int/en/sites/default/files/Constitutive_Act_en_0.htm> last accessed 2 January 2013, art 6(2); see also arts 7 and 9) have, in principle, a binding effect. While this is not explicitly regulated in the relevant provisions, it follows from its art 23 of the Constitutive Act which provides for sanctions if a member state 'fails to comply with the decisions and policies of the Union' (para 2) – and, subject to interpretation, from the respective decision. See further, M du Plessis and C Gevers 'The Obligation of African Union States to Implement ICC Arrest Warrants' (4 February 2011) <http://www.ejiltalk.org/the-obligation-of-african-union-states-to-implement-icc-arrest-warrants/> last accessed 2 January 2013.

the AU Member States shall not cooperate pursuant to the provisions of Article 98 of the Rome Statute of the ICC relating to immunities, for the arrest and surrender of President Omar El Bashir of The Sudan.[14]

When the ICC issued a further warrant of arrest against the (meanwhile deceased[15]) Libyan leader Muammar al-Gaddafi[16], the AU produced a similar statement calling on its member states not to cooperate with the ICC in this regard.[17]
Moreover, the AU is currently trying to limit the powers of the SC with regard to Article 16: an amendment of this provision has been proposed to the ICC's Assembly of States Parties (ASP) that would transfer the power to defer a case from the SC to the UN General Assembly in case the SC failed to decide on such a request for six months.[18]

---

[14]  AU Assembly, 'Decision on the Meeting of African States Parties to the Rome Statute of the International Criminal Court' (3 July 2009) Assembly/AU/Dec. 245 (XIII) para 10; confirmed e.g. by the AU Assembly 'Decision on the Progress Report of the Commission on the Implementation of Decision' (July 2010) Assembly/AU/Dec. 270 (XIV) on the Second Ministerial Meeting on the Rome Statute of the ICC, Assembly/AU/Dec. 296 (XV) para 5; by the AU Assembly, 29-30 January 2012 (n 9) para 8 (moreover in this decision, para 9, the AU Assembly expressed 'concern over the conduct of the ICC prosecutor, Mr. Moreno-Ocampo, who has been making egregiously unacceptable, rude and condescending statements on the case of President Omar Hassan El-Bashir of The Sudan and other situations in Africa'), and last but not least by the AU Assembly, 15-16 July 2012 (n 9) para 8.

[15]  After Gaddafi deceased on 20 October 2011, ICC Pre-Trial Chamber I terminated the case against him on 22 November 2011 (*Situation in the Libyan Arab Jamahiriya: Prosecutor v Muammar Gaddafi, Al-Islam Gaddafi and Al-Senussi* (Decision to Terminate the Case Against Muammar Mohammed Abu Minyar Gaddafi) ICC-01/11-01/11-28).

[16]  ICC Pre-Trial Chamber I *Situation in the Libyan Arab Jamahiriya* (Warrant of Arrest for Muammar Mohammed Abu Minyar Gaddafi) ICC-01/11-13 (27 June 2011).

[17]  AU Assembly 'Decision on the Implementation of the Assembly Decisions on the International Criminal Court' (1 July 2011) Assembly/AU/Dec. 366 (XVII) para 6. Hereto, see HJ Lubbe, 'The African Union's decisions on the indictments of Al-Bashir and Gaddafi and their implications for the implementation of the Rome Statute by African States' in K Ambos and OA Maunganidze (eds) *Power and Prosecution: Challenges and Opportunities for International Criminal Justice in Sub-Saharan Africa* (Universitätsverlag Göttingen 2012) 194 *et seq* <http://webdoc.sub.gwdg.de/univerlag/2012/GSK24_ambos_power.pdf> last accessed 8 January 2013. On Gaddafi's role with regard to the relationship between the ICC and Africa/the AU, see K Mills (n 8) 446 *et seq* (arguing that with the death of Gaddafi one 'extremely important source poisoning the relationship between the Africa and the ICC' was eliminated).

[18]  The issue was discussed briefly at the 9th Assembly of States Parties, and a Working Group on this amendment has been installed: D Akande, 'ICC Assembly of States Parties Discusses Possible Amendments to ICC Statute' (18 December 2010) <http://www.ejiltalk.org/icc-assembly-of-states-parties-discusses-possible-amendments-to-icc-statute/> last accessed 2 January 2013. The amendment is discussed in Akande et al (n 9) 12 *et seq*; AU Assembly, 30-31 January 2011 (n 8) paras 7–8 (calling upon the AU members to actively support the amendment). D Akande 'Addressing the African Union's Proposal to Allow the UN General Assembly to Defer ICC Prosecutions' (30 October 2010) <http://www.ejiltalk.org/addressing-the-african-unions-proposal-to-allow-the-un-general-assembly-to-defer-icc-prosecutions/> last accessed 2 January 2013, links the amendment to a 'feeling on a part of some African states that African concerns

In this context, recent developments with regard to the Kenya situation are worth mentioning.[19] After the Prosecutor named six suspects in the post-election violence and applied for the respective summonses to appear in December 2010, the Kenyan parliament considered withdrawing from the Rome Statute, and the Kenyan government, supported by the AU's Assembly,[20] requested the SC to use its powers to suspend the proceedings on the basis of Article 16 in order to facilitate domestic justice mechanisms.[21] Later, the Kenyan government filed an admissibility challenge which was rejected by the ICC. PTC II argued that there were 'no concrete investigative steps regarding the ... suspects in question',[22] and that a situation of inactivity remained.[23]

---

are being marginalised and that the structure of the UN Security Council does not take sufficient account of their interest'. Plessis (n 5) 67 analyses the argument of double standards at the SC.

[19] On 'Kenya's inglorious 'fall from grace', see C Gevers and M du Plessis, 'Another Stormy Year for the International Criminal Court and its Work in Africa' (22 April 2011) <http://papers.ssrn.com/sol3/papers.cfm?abstract_id=1870965> last accessed 4 January 2013. Similarly, Kenya has been described as having 'come to the fore as the battleground for the ongoing "struggle for the soul of international law"' in M du Plessis, A Louw and O Maunganidze, 'African Efforts to close the Impunity Gap. Lessons for Complementarity from National and Regional Actions' (November 2012) 241 *Institute for Security Studies Paper* 2, citing D Tladi, 'The African Union and the International Criminal Court: The Battle for the Soul of International Law' (2009) 34 *South African Yearbook of International Law* 57. On the reasons of the difficulties in achieving domestic and international justice in Kenya: S Brown and CL Sriram, 'The Big Fish won't fry themselves: Criminal Accountability for Post-Election Violence in Kenya' (2012) 111 *African Affairs* 244-260.

[20] AU Assembly, 30-31 January 2011 (n 9) para 6.

[21] For a summary of these developments see Statement by African Civil Society Organizations and International Organizations with a Presence in Africa, 'Kenya: Civil Society Organizations Call for Support for the International Criminal Court' (25 January 2011) <http://www.hrw.org/en/news/2011/01/25/kenya-civil-society-organizations-call-support-international-criminal-court> last accessed 2 January 2013.

[22] *Situation in the Republic of Kenya: Prosecutor v Muthaura, Kenyatta and Ali* (Decision on the Application of the Government of Kenya challenging the Admissibility of the Case Pursuant to Article 19(2)(b) of the Statute) ICC-01/09-02/11-96 (30 May 2011) paras 49-65. A similar finding was reached in *Situation in the Republic of Kenya: Prosecutor v Ruto, Kosgey and Sang* (Decision on the Application of the Government of Kenya challenging the Admissibility of the Case Pursuant to Article 19(2)(b) of the Statute) ICC-01/09-01/11-101 (30 May 2011). Both decisions were confirmed by ICC Appeals Chamber, *Situation in the Republic of Kenya: Prosecutor v Muthaura, Kenyatta and Ali* (Judgment on the Appeal of the Republic of Kenya against the Decision of Pre-Trial Chamber II of 30 May 2011 entitled "Decision on the Application by the Government of Kenya Challenging the Admissibility of the Case Pursuant to Article 19(2)(b)) ICC-01/09-02/11-274 (30 August 2011), and *Situation in the Republic of Kenya: Prosecutor v Ruto, Kosgey and Sang* (Judgment on the Appeal of the Republic of Kenya against the Decision of Pre-Trial Chamber II of 30 May 2011 entitled "Decision on the Application by the Government of Kenya Challenging the Admissibility of the Case Pursuant to Article 19(2)(b)) ICC-01/09-01/11-307 (30 August 2011).

[23] *Muthaura* et al Admissibility Decision (n 22) para 66. Despite the governmental criticism against the ICC, it was scholarly argued for an enhancing effect of the ICC's activities for the process of transitional justice in Kenya, see EO Asaala, 'The International

Recent developments in Libya also revealed tensions. After the death of Muammar Gaddafi, the ICC continued investigations against his son Saif Al-Islam Gaddafi and former intelligence chief Abdullah Al-Senussi. ICC arrest warrants have been issued against both,[24] but both are now in the hands of the Libyan authorities[25] which refuse to surrender them to the ICC. In the course of a visit by four ICC officials (of the Office of Public Defence) to Saif Al-Islam Gaddafi, they have been arrested by Libyan authorities.[26] Pre-Trial Chamber I has not yet decided on the last Libyan admissibility challenge.[27]

Criticism also came from other quarters with regard to the al-Bashir arrest warrants. For Rwandan President Paul Kagame, the ICC 'has been put in place only for African countries, only for poor countries ... Rwanda cannot be part of that colonialism, slavery and imperialism'.[28] To be sure, the tone of the Rwandan

---

Criminal Court Factor on Transitional Justice in Kenya' in K Ambos and OA Maunganidze (n 17) 119 *et seq*.

[24] ICC Pre-Trial Chamber I *Situation in the Libyan Arab Jamahiriya: Prosecutor v Muammar Gaddafi, Saif Gaddafi and Al-Senussi* (Warrant of Arrest for Saif Al-Islam Gaddafi) ICC-01/11-01/11-3 (27 June 2011); ICC Pre-Trial Chamber I *Situation in the Libyan Arab Jamahiriya: Prosecutor v Muammar Gaddafi, Saif Gaddafi and Al-Senussi* (Warrant of Arrest for Abdullah Al-Senussi) ICC-01/11-01/11-4 (27 June 2011).

[25] 'Saif al-Islam Gaddafi arrested in Libya' *Al Jazeera* (19 November 2011) <http://www.aljazeera.com/news/middleeast/2011/11/20111119111936535209.html> last accessed 10 January 2012. Al-Senussi has been arrested in Mauritania, but was extradited to Libya where he continues to be detained, see 'Gaddafi spy chief Abdullah al-Senussi held in Mauritania' *BBC* (17 March 2012) <www.bbc.co.uk/news/world-africa-17413626> last accessed 10 January 2013; 'Mauritania deports Libya spy chief Abdullah al-Senussi' *BBC* (5 September 2012) <http://www.bbc.co.uk/news/world-africa-19487228> last accessed 10 January 2012.

[26] See 'Crisis deepens over Legal Team detained in Libya' *The Guardian* (London 13 June 2012) <http://www.guardian.co.uk/law/2012/jun/13/legal-team-libya-four-officials> last accessed 10 January 2013. See in more detail *Situation in Libya: Prosecutor v Saif Gaddafi and Al-Senussi* (Public Redacted Version of the Corrigendum to the "Defence Response to the 'Application on behalf of the Government of Libya pursuant to Article 19 of the ICC Statute'" ICC-01/11-01/11 (31 July 2012), para 11 *et seq*.

[27] See most recently *Situation in Libya: Prosecutor v Saif Gaddafi and Al-Senussi* (Decision requesting further Submissions on Issues related to the Admissibility of the Case against Saif Al-Islam Gaddafi) ICC-01/11-01/11-239 (7 December 2012) para 3. See also 'International Criminal Court Prosecutor calls on Libyan Authorities to ensure no Impunity' *UN News Center* (7 November 2012) <http://www.un.org/apps/news/story.asp?NewsID=43435#.UO7PebaUrUg> last accessed 10 January 2013. See also C Stahn, 'Libya, the International Criminal Court and Complementarity: A Test for "Shared Responsibility"' (2012) 10 *JICJ* 325 *et seq*.

[28] For a criticism, see N Mhango, 'No Kagame! ICC not a Tool for Colonialism and Imperialism' *The African executive* (13-20 August 2008) <http://www.africanexecutive.com/modules/magazine/articles.php?article=3430> last accessed 2 January 2013. In an interview in September 2009, Kagame further stated: 'Now, when I read about the International Criminal Court being used as a stick to whip people into line – in the world I come from, I would avoid that because it can be counterproductive' (in M Wakabi, 'Learn and Borrow, but You Must Own the Process' *East African* (Kenya 13 September 2009) <http://www.theeastafrican.

government changed with the arrest of Callixte Mbarushimana, press secretary of the Hutu 'Forces Démocratiques de Libération du Rwanda' (FDLR), in Paris in October 2010 on the basis of an ICC arrest warrant.[29] In a similar mood, Libya's former leader Gaddafi echoed, during his incumbency as chairman of the AU, that '[t]he ICC warrant to arrest President Bashir is an attempt by [the west] to recolonize their former colonies'.[30] His position obviously did not change when the ICC turned against him.[31]

The critical, even hostile attitude has not gone unnoticed in The Hague and some African capitals. Fatou Bensouda, the ICC's newly-elected Prosecutor, refers to 'rumours' about 'African disengagement'[32] and warns that the relationship between the ICC and the AU should not deteriorate further.[33] Several African State Parties, for example Chad and Kenya, defied their obligations under the Rome Statute[34] when they welcomed al-Bashir on an official State visit instead of

---

co.ke/news/-/2558/657182/-/item/3/-/dn1yqe/-/index.html> last accessed 2 January 2013). Rwanda has not yet ratified the Rome Statute, hereto CN Garuka, 'Rwanda and the ICC: a need for the ratification of the Rome Statute' in K Ambos and OA Maunganidze (n 17) 57.

[29] See 'Rwanda Offers Rare Praise to ICC Over Arrest of War Crimes Suspect' *Sudan Tribune* (France 11 October 2010) <http://www.sudantribune.com/Rwanda-offers-rare-praise-to-ICC,36556> last accessed 2 January 2013, referring to a statement of the Minister of Justice. To be sure, Kagame himself did not comment on the arrest of Callixte Mbarushimana and the parallel prosecutions of two other FDLR leaders in Germany (on the latter see the arrest warrant of the investigation judge of the German Supreme Court against Ignace Murwanashyaka of 17 June 2010, AK 3/10, partially reproduced in [2010] 30 *Neue Zeitschrift für Strafrecht* 581). The charges against Mbarushimana have, however, been dismissed by ICC-Pre-Trial Chamber I (ICC Pre-Trial Chamber I, *Situation in the Democratic Republic of Congo, Prosecutor v Callixte Mbarushimana* (Decision on the confirmation of charges) ICC-01/04-01/10-465-Red (16 December 2011) 149; confirmed by ICC Appeals Chamber, *Situation in the Democratic Republic of Congo, Prosecutor v Callixte Mbarushimana* (Judgment on the appeal of the Prosecutor against the decision of Pre-Trial Chamber I of 16 December 2011 entitled 'Decision on the confirmation of charges') ICC-01/04-01/10-514 (30 May 2012), and he is today a free man again.

[30] 'Sudan Leader in Qatar for Summit' *BBC News* (London 29 March 2009) <http://news.bbc.co.uk/2/hi/7970892.stm> last accessed 2 January 2013.

[31] See the statement of Gaddafi's lawyer: TB Langa, 'Libya: Legal Statement on International Criminal Court (ICC)' <http://www.mathaba.net/news/?x=627316> last accessed 2 January 2013. The proceedings against Gaddafi have been terminated with his death, see *Situation in Libya: Prosecutor v Muammar Gaddafi* (Decision to Terminate the Case against Muammar Mohammed Abu Minyar Gaddafi) ICC-01/11-01/11 (22 November 2011). On the AU's support for Gaddafi, see n 16 and related text.

[32] Ankumah (n 12) 3.

[33] Statement by Fatou Bensouda, ICC-OTP roundtable, 19–20 October 2010.

[34] See below (n 100). The AU Assembly (n 9) decided afterwards that Chad and Kenya 'were implementing various AU Assembly Decisions ... as well as acting in pursuit of peace and stability in their respective regions', para 5. See also W Mwangi and T Mphepo, 'Developments in International Criminal Justice in Africa during 2011' (2012) 12 *African Human Rights Law Journal* 273 et seq.

arresting him.³⁵ Chad's ambassador Ahmat Mahamat Bachir certainly expressed the general unease of African leaders when stating: 'We are with the rule of law and everybody has to pay for his mistakes and for any crime he commits, but when it will be selectively and targeting only African leaders it should not be accepted.'³⁶ In a final diplomatic snub, the AU rejected the establishment of an ICC liaison office close to its headquarters in Addis Ababa, Ethiopia;³⁷ instead a Criminal Chamber for international crimes of the African Court of Justice and Human Rights was proposed.³⁸

While the problem of the negative image of the ICC in some African quarters has only recently received more attention in scholarly writings,³⁹ it has always

---

³⁵ Associated Press, 'Kenya Defends Failure to Arrest Sudan's President Omar Al Bashir in Nairobi' *Guardian* (London 29 August 2011) <http://www.guardian.co.uk/world/2010/aug/29/kenya-omar-al-bashir-arrest-failure> last accessed 2 January 2013; X Rice, 'Chad Refuses to Arrest Omar Al Bashir on Genocide Charges' *Guardian* (London 22 July 2010) <http://www.guardian.co.uk/world/2010/jul/22/chad-refuses-arrest-omar-al-bashir> last accessed 2 January 2013. Other trips are reported to Egypt, Eritrea, Ethiopia, Libya, Mauritania, Qatar, Saudi Arabia, Zimbabwe, see 'Sudan's Bashir Planned Visit to Mauritania Kept Under Tight Wraps' *Sudan Tribune* (Sudan 19 December 2009) <http://www.sudantribune.com/Sudan-s-Bashir-planned-visit-to,33510> last accessed 2 January 2013. The AU noted that Malawi, Djibouti, Chad and Kenya were implementing various AU Assembly Decisions on non-cooperation with the ICC when receiving Sudanese President Bashir, see AU Assembly, 29-30 January 2012 (n 8) para 7; on a more general note it urged the African State Parties to the Rome Statute to counterbalance their obligations towards the African Union with the ones towards the ICC, cf. AU Assembly, 15-16 July 2012 (n 8) para 5.

³⁶ 'Bashir Warrant: Chad Accuses ICC of Anti-African Bias' *BBC News* (London 22 July 2010) <http://www.bbc.co.uk/news/world-africa-10723869> last accessed 2 January 2013.

³⁷ See ICC ASP, 'Report of the Court on the Establishment of an Office for the International Criminal Court at the African Union Headquarters in Addis Ababa' ICC-ASP/8/35 (4 November 2009) paras 15 and 46, arguing that such an office is desirable and feasible with a view to help to develop and maintain a close working relationship with the AU and to disseminate information on the Court. See also Ankumah (n 11) 4–5; K Mills (n 7) 432.

³⁸ See n 119 below, and M du Plessis, A Louw and O Maunganidze (n 18) 3.

³⁹ For an overview see CL Sriram, 'The International Criminal Court Africa Experiment- The Central African Republic, Darfur, Northern Uganda and the Democratic Republic of the Congo' in CL Sriram and S Pillay (eds) *Peace versus Justice? The Dilemma of Transitional Justice in Africa* (University of KwaZulu-Natal Press, Cape Town 2009) 320; N Waddell and P Clark, 'Introduction' in N Waddell and P Clark (eds) *Courting Conflict? Justice, Peace and the ICC in Africa* (Royal African Society, London 2008) 8. See also H van der Wilt, 'Universal Jurisdiction under Attack: An Assessment of African Misgivings towards International Criminal Justice as Administered by Western States' (2011) 9 *JICJ* 1043; E Keppler, 'Managing Setbacks for the International Criminal Court in Africa' (2011) *Journal of African Law* 1; for a different approach T Reinold, 'Constitutionalization? Whose constitutionalization? Africa's ambivalent engagement with the International Criminal Court' (2012) 10 *International Journal of Constitutional Law* 1087 *et seq* (arguing that the AU is refusing to be coopted by the system of international constitutionalism, a position part of a 'broader campaign aimed at reorganizing the relationship between different public authorities involved in global (and regional) governance'). See also HL Lubbe (n 17) 179 *et seq*.

been widely discussed in the press, especially in African newspapers.[40] Many commentators take the same view as the most critical political leaders. Chief amongst accusations are that the ICC is a (neo-)colonial legal instrument,[41] or that the African states have been used as a guinea pig for the ICC in its formative years.[42] Adam Branch adopts a completely radical position: in his view, the ICC 'refuses to listen to Africans and it intervenes only where it suits its political and pragmatic interests to do so'; moreover, it 'undermines the possibility of meaningful politics itself' and hence '[p]erhaps the best solution is for all of us, Africans and Westerners, to ignore – to forget – the ICC, because our belief in it is a major part of the problem'.[43]

In this chapter I will show that the criticism against the ICC, albeit understandable to a certain extent, is misleading for essentially three reasons. First, the African continent has been heavily involved in the creation of the ICC and continues to be so. Thus, Africa is not (at least not primarily) a target but a part of the ICC. Second, there is not one but many African voices on this matter; others, maybe less vocal, support the ICC. Third, there are objective legal and policy reasons which explain why currently most situations before the ICC come from Africa. In conclusion, the chapter will argue that the ICC is not currently limited to Africa and will in the foreseeable future also open investigations into non-African situations and cases.

---

[40] For several critical opinions in newspapers see JA Goldston, 'More Candour about Criteria: The Exercise of Discretion by the Prosecutor of the International Criminal Court' (2010) 8 *JICJ* 383, 385.

[41] ES Abdulai, 'The Standoff between the? ICC and African Leaders: The Debate Revisited' in The Foundation for Law, Justice and Society in collaboration with The Centre for Socio-Legal Studies, University of Oxford (ed) *Debating International Justice in Africa: Collected Essays, 2008–2010* (Foundation for Law, Justice and Society, Oxford 2010) 9–11; see also D Hoile, 'International Criminal Court: Africa Beware of "New" Legal Colonialism' *The Independent* (Uganda 14 June 2010) <http://www.independent.co.ug/index.php/column/opinion/86-opinion/3032-international-criminal-court-africa-beware-of-new-legal-colonialism-> last accessed 2 January 2013; D Chandler, *From Kosovo to Kabul and Beyond. Human Rights and International Intervention* (2nd edn Pluto Press, London 2006) 147–148, 155–156.

[42] On these allegations and on difficulties to source them see CL Sriram 'The ICC Africa Experiment: The Central African Republic, Darfur, Northern Uganda, and the Democratic Republic of the Congo' <http://www.humansecuritygateway.com/documents/ISA_ICCAfricaexperiment.pdf> last accessed 2 January 2013.

[43] A Branch, 'Forget the ICC: Reflections on the Bashir Arrest Warrant' *Critical Investigations into Humanitarianism Africa* blog (6 April 2009) <http://www.cihablog.com/forget-the-icc-reflections-on-the-bashir-arrest-warrant/> last accessed 2 January 2013; A Branch, 'What the ICC Review Conference Can't Fix' in The Foundation for Law, Justice and Society in collaboration with The Centre for Socio-Legal Studies, University of Oxford (ed) *Debating International Justice in Africa: Collected Essays, 2008–2010* (Foundation for Law, Justice and Society, Oxford 2010) 32–35.

## I. This is (also) an African ICC!

The ICC is, despite its universal claim, also an African court. There has been active involvement and immense support from African states for the Court since its creation.[44] Africa is – with 34 State Parties – currently the biggest regional group among the member states.[45] These 33 States are the majority of the in total 54 African states[46] and cover nearly 62 per cent[47] of the total African population. A good number of high-ranking positions within the Court are held by African nationals. Four of the 18 Judges are of African origin (Sanji Mmasenono Monageng of Botswana, Akua Kuenyehia of Ghana, Joyce Aluoch of Kenya, Chile Eboe Osuji of Nigeria).[48] In the OTP, the former Deputy Prosecutor Fatou Bensouda (Gambia) was appointed Prosecutor of the ICC in November 2011, while Phakiso Mochochoko (Lesotho) is head of the 'Jurisdiction, Complementarity and Cooperation Division'.

---

[44] On the strong African involvement in the creation of the ICC see also H Jallow and F Bensouda 'International Criminal Law in an African Context' in M du Plessis (ed) *African Guide to International Criminal Justice* (Institute for Security Studies, Pretoria 2009) 41. Similarly K Mills (n 8) 445.

[45] Thirt teen more States have signed the Rome Statute but at the time of writing had not yet ratified it – they are: Algeria, Angola, Cameroon, Cape Verde, Egypt, Eritrea, Guinea-Bissau, Morocco, Mozambique, Sao Tome and Principe, Sudan and Zimbabwe.

[46] See listing of the African Development Bank <http://www.afdb.org/en/countries/> last accessed 2 January 2013. Other sources list up to 58 African states including European departments or overseas territories (Canary Islands, Mayotte, Réunion, Saint Helena) and the disputed territory of Western Sahara, see e.g. Relief Web, administered by UN Office for the Coordination of Humanitarian Affairs (OCHA) <http://www.reliefweb.int/rw/dbc.nsf/doc103?OpenFormandrc=1#show> last accessed 2 January 2013. After the recent referendum in Southern Sudan, this territory became the 54th African State with its declaration of independence on 9 July 2011. See for the referendum's result published by the Southern Sudan Referendum Commission: <http://southernsudan2011.com/> last accessed 2 January 2013; 'South Sudan Referendum: 99% Vote for Independence' *BBC News* (London 30 January 2011) <http://www.bbc.co.uk/news/world-africa-12317927> last accessed 2 December 2011. On the declaration of independence, see 'South Sudan's Flag Raised at Independence Ceremony' *BBC News* (London 9 July 2011) <http://www.bbc.co.uk/news/world-africa-14092375> last accessed 2 January 2013. South Sudan became UN member state on 14 July 2011, see 'UN welcomes South Sudan as 193rd Member State' *UN News Center* (14 July 2011) <http://www.un.org/apps/news/story.asp?NewsID=39034#.UOQDTraUrUg> last accessed 2 January 2013.

[47] Own calculation on the basis of the population report of the Population Reference Bureau's '2012 World Population Data Sheet' (Population Reference Bureau, Washington 2012) <http://www.prb.org/Publications/Datasheets/2012/world-population-data-sheet/datasheet.aspx> last accessed 2 January 2013. According to this report, in the middle of 2011, the total African population amounted to 1,072 million. The population of the 34 African ICC State Parties adds to 663.8 million, which equals 61,92 per cent of the total African population.

[48] See <http://www.icc-cpi.int/en_menus/icc/structure%20of%20the%20court/chambers/the%20judges/Pages/the%20judges%20%20%20biographical%20notes.aspx> last accessed 2 January 2013.

The ICC also enjoys broad support among the African civil society; more than 800 African NGOs are members of the Coalition for the ICC (CICC), amounting to approximately one-third of all its member organisations.[49]

Apart from that, the fact that the OTP takes a closer look at a situation in a particular country could also entail positive effects for this country. It has the chance to become actively involved in the development of international criminal law.[50] The ICC is not only dealing with the concrete situation or case, but takes a more comprehensive, holistic approach as to the political and legal situation in the country concerned. Thus, it must assess the willingness and ability of the national judicial system to deal with the situation and analyse the individual factors substantiating the complementarity test of Article 17.[51] This requires a constant and ongoing relationship with the respective country, mainly through communications, cooperation, measures of 'positive complementarity'[52] and outreach. This relationship may also prove fruitful for the OTP and the Court to better understanding the social context concerned and to develop general policies and strategies for the Court's future investigations.

All in all then, given the strong African involvement in and commitment to the ICC, it is fair to say that there exists strong support and even a need for the Court from Africa: 'Africa is a participant, it is not a target'.[53] In the words of Kofi Annan, as stated at the ICC Review Conference in Kampala:

> When I meet Africans from all walks of life, they demand justice: from their own courts if possible, from international courts if no credible

---

[49] J Ford, *Bringing Fairness to International Justice: A Handbook on the ICC for Defence Lawyers in Africa* (Institute for Security Studies, Pretoria 2009) 19.

[50] On the significant impact of the people from Africa on the fight against impunity, see Jallow and Bensouda (n 44) 47 and du Plessis (n 6) 5 *et seq*. See also with regard to the Review Conference held in Kampala from 31 May to 11 June 2010, B Among 'Court Must Fight Impunity, say African Delegates' *Africa Renewal Online* (Kampala 6 July 2010); E Keppler, 'Strong African Support for the ICC at the Kampala Review Conference' (2010) 1 *The Forum* 33–34 (published by the Ugandan Coalition on the ICC).

[51] For such a test with regard to Colombia see K Ambos, *The Colombian Peace Process and the Principle of Complementarity of the ICC: An Inductive, Situation-based Approach* (Berlin, Springer 2010) starting at 43; for an updated, briefer version see K Ambos, 'The Colombian Peace Process (Law 975 of 2005) and the ICC's Principle of Complementarity' in C Stahn and M El Zeidy (eds) *The International Criminal Court and Complementarity: From Theory to Practice* (CUP, Cambridge 2011) 1071.

[52] In favour of positive complementarity, see also K Ambos, 'Introduction' in K Ambos and OA Maunganidze (n 17) fn 18. On a broader understanding of complementarity in the African context within the framework of positive complementarity, see M du Plessis, A Louw and O Maunganidze (n 19) 5 *et seq*.

[53] Ankumah (n 12) 5.

alternative exists ... Africa wants this Court. Africa needs this Court. Africa should continue to support this Court.[54]

## II. There is Not *One* African Position on the ICC

African governments do not speak with one voice. Despite the recent criticism referred to in the introduction to this chapter, it is fair to say that the majority of the AU members, i.e. the 33 States Parties, support the ICC. They reaffirmed their commitment recently at the Kampala Review Conference in the so-called Kampala Declaration.[55] Admittedly, the commitment of the States Parties differs in degree, but this applies to the States Parties in general and does not deny the general support for the ICC project expressed by the accession to the Rome Statute.[56]

The real split, as emerged following the al-Bashir arrest warrant, runs generally along the line of States Parties and non-State Parties. While the AU Assembly decided that its member states should not extradite al-Bashir to the ICC,[57] an aggressive anti-ICC campaign has been orchestrated by a few Arab states, led in particular by Libya,[58] whose (former) leadership condemned the arrest warrant with the following words:

> It considers this a dangerous precedent that leaves no doubt of the injustice and independency of the ICC since it is based on selectivity and double standards away from its legal capacity. The so-called ICC

---

[54] K Annan, Address at the Review Conference to the Rome Statute of the ICC in Kampala (31 May 2010) <http://www.icc-cpi.int/iccdocs/asp_docs/RC2010/Statements/ICC-RC-statements-KofiAnnan-ENG.pdf> last accessed 2 January 2013, para 35.

[55] ICC Review Conference, Kampala Declaration, adopted on 8 June 2010 by consensus, ICC-RC/4: 'We, high-level representatives of States Parties to the Rome Statute of the International Criminal Court, gathered in Kampala, Uganda, at the first Review Conference under this Statute, held from 31 May to 11 June 2010 ... (t)ogether solemnly 1. Reaffirm our commitment to the Rome Statute of the International Criminal Court and its full implementation, as well as to its universality and integrity ... 7. Further resolve to continue and strengthen our efforts to ensure full cooperation with the Court in accordance with the Statute, in particular in the areas of implementing legislation, enforcement of Court decisions, execution of arrest warrants, conclusion of agreements and witness protection, and to express our political and diplomatic support for the Court'.

[56] For a more nuanced approach, for example by focusing on the domestic dynamics as an explanation of accession to the ICC Statute see C Lauterbach 'Commitment to the International Criminal Court among Sub-Saharan African States' (2008–2009) 5 *Eyes on the ICC* 85.

[57] On AU decisions against the ICC see further (n 14). K Mills (n 8) 404-447 refers to a debate within the AU to try Bashir and therefore concludes that justice is not denied in general, but that the discussions show 'Africa arguing with itself and the international community over how best to proceed' (at 445).

[58] Annan (n 54) referred to 'a few African leaders'.

has no legitimacy or legal jurisdiction to examine such accusations against the Sudanese president Omar Hassan al-Bashir.

This order threatens security and peace in Africa and the world ... International criminal courts specialized in making such accusations at random and not based on evidences directed against leaders of African and Arab countries and third world countries other than others since it is unable to take similar measures towards the real war criminals in Iraq, Afghanistan, Palestine and former Yugoslavia.[59]

The League of Arab States (where 10 out of 22 members are African countries) called the arrest warrant 'dangerous'.[60] (North) Sudan created a High Level Crisis Committee and attacked the ICC several times.[61] Among the non-Arab African states, the accusation of Rwandan President Kagame, quoted above,[62] stands out. All in all these reactions are not surprising if one considers that an arrest warrant against a *sitting* head of state – a state which, in addition, is one of the biggest of Africa – is not just daily business of an (international) criminal court and thus with considerable certainty meets with resistance in some political quarters. It would not be much different in other continents, including Europe. Against this background, it is rather more surprising that some AU governments gave their treaty obligations precedence over solidarity with the Sudanese President. Thus, for example, Botswana officially stated that al-Bashir would be arrested if he set foot in the

---

[59] Editorial 'Libya Condemns ICC Decision as Sudan Rejects Hague Court, Expels Aid Agencies' *The Tripoli Post* (Libya 6 March 2009) <http://www.tripolipost.com/articledetail.asp?c=1&i=2911> last accessed 3 January 2013.

[60] 'Sudan Genocide Charges "Dangerous". Arab League Official says ICC Prosecutor's move will have Dangerous Repercussions' *Al Jazeera* (19 July 2008) <http://english.aljazeera.net/news/africa/2008/07/2008719201910382737.html> last accessed 2 January 2013.

[61] A 'High Level Committee to Manage the Crisis with the ICC' has been formed by the Sudanese government: see Annalisa Ciampi, 'The Proceedings against President Al Bashir and the Prospects of their Suspension under Article 16 ICC Statute' (2008) 6 *JICJ* 885. Later, warnings of increasing violence as reaction to indictments have been given: e.g. Associated Press, 'Sudan to ICC: Darfur Violence may Increase if You Indict President Bashir' *Christian Science Monitor* (Khartoum 14 July 2008) <www.csmonitor.com/World/Africa/2008/0714/p04s02-woaf.html> last accessed 2 January 2013. In contrast, the Sudanese opposition appreciated the arrest warrants: Al Jazeera, 'Mixed Reaction to ICC Ruling' *Al Jazeera* (17 July 2008) <http://english.aljazeera.net/focus/2008/07/200871784055275712.html> last accessed 2 January 2013.

[62] See (n 28) and accompanying text.

country,[63] and a similar statement was given by South Africa.[64] A substantial shift in direction was to observe in Malawi. On 14 November 2011, this country allowed a visit of al-Bashir without arresting him and was subsequently denounced by the ICC for this violation of its treaty obligations.[65] When few months later in July 2012 the 19th AU Summit was mapped to take place in Malawi, the new government under president Joyce Banda refused to host it since it did not want to receive Al Bashir again.[66] Thus, apparently, the ICC's incompliance decision and referral to the Security Council had some impact.

Apart from the divisions among the African governments, there are also disagreements between some governments, even within governments[67] and between them and the people they claim to represent. Although there is no hard

---

[63] At the AU Summit in Kampala, Vice-President Mompati Merafhe said: 'Botswana cannot associate herself with any decision which calls upon her to disregard her obligations to the ICC. Botswana intends to comply with its obligations and to cooperate with the ICC': see Botswana Ministry of Foreign Affairs and International Cooperation, 'Press Release: Botswana stands by International Criminal Court' (Gaborone 28 July 2010) <http://www.mofaic.gov.bw/index.php?option=com_content&view=article&id=567:botswana-stands-by-international-criminal-court&catid=8:latest&Itemid=241> last accessed 2 January 2013.

[64] Thandi Modise, deputy secretary of the ruling ANC party in South Africa, stated: 'If Bashir were to come to South Africa today, we will definitely implement what we are supposed to in order to bring the culprit to Hague. We can't allow a situation whereby an individual tramples on people's rights and gets away with it ... The perpetrators of war crimes should be tried at all costs', in *Sudan Tribune*, 'South Africa Says it will Arrest Sudan's Bashir Despite AU Resolution' *Sudan Tribune* (Khartoum 30 July 2010) <http://www.sudantribune.com/South-Africa-says-it-will-arrest,35817> last accessed 2 January 2013. South Africa is one among the few African countries with implementing legislation of the Rome Statute, hereto M du Plessis, 'South Africa's Implementation of the Rome Statute' in K Ambos and OA Maunganidze (n 17) 23 *et seq*.

[65] ICC Pre-Trial Chamber I *Situation in Darfur, Sudan: Prosecutor v al Bashir* (Decision Pursuant to Article 87(7) of the Rome Statute on the Failure by the Republic of Malawi to Comply with the Cooperation Requests Issued by the Court with Respect to the Arrest and Surrender of Omar Hassan Ahmad Al Bashir) ICC-02/05-01/09-139 (12 December 2011) para 47. See also W Mwangi and T Mphepo (n 34) 274 *et seq*.

[66] AU '19th African Union (AU) Summit to be held in Addis Ababa, Ethiopia' (13 June 2012) <http://www.au.int/en/content/19th-african-union-au-summit-be-held-addis-ababa-ethiopia> last accessed 2 January 2013. 'Malawi not to host Summit after Row over Sudan Leader' *BBC News* (London 8 June 2012) <http://www.bbc.co.uk/news/world-africa-18364947> last accessed 2 January 2013.

[67] A good example is Kenya where in the ruling coalition Prime Minister Raila Odinga and the ODM (Orange Democratic Movement) generally support the Court while President Mwai Kibaki (Party of National Unity, PNU) increasingly opposes it (see Daily Nation, 'Kenya: African Leaders Split on Bid to Defer Hague Trials' *AllAfrica.com* (Nairobi 27 January 2011) <http://allafrica.com/stories/201101271286.html> last accessed 2 January 2013). Such a split within a government may be typical for governments which are a product of power-sharing deals in a phase of political transition.

empirical and reliable data,[68] journalistic impressions and NGO accounts indicate that the ICC enjoys a broad support among African civil society, especially in the situation countries and regions.[69] Thus, with regard to the AU's decision not to cooperate with the ICC concerning al-Bashir's arrest, no less than 164 NGOs from all over Africa had the following to say:

> we, the undersigned civil society organizations, appeal to African ICC States Parties to reaffirm their support for the ICC and their commitment to abide by their obligations under the Rome Statute, particularly in relation to the arrest and transfer of the President of Sudan to the ICC ...
>
> Civil society across the continent has expressed concern about the AU decision. Ensuring that the determined steps to end impunity on our continent are not undermined requires a collective effort by all Africans. Instead of retreating from important achievements to date, we look to our governments to remain steadfast in their support for justice for victims of the worst crimes, including by reaffirming their commitment to cooperate with the ICC.[70]

---

[68] To the knowledge of this writer there are only a few solid studies on the attitude towards the ICC from Uganda: P Vinck et al, *When the War Ends. A Population-based Survey on Attitudes about Peace, Justice and Social Reconstruction in Northern Uganda* (December 2007) <http://www.law.berkeley.edu/HRCweb/pdfs/When-the-War-Ends.pdf> last accessed 2 January 2013 (this survey complements an earlier study on Northern Uganda: International Centre for Transitional Justice and Human Rights Centre, University of California, Berkeley, *Forgotten Voices. A Population-based Survey on Attitudes about Peace and Justice in Northern Uganda* (July 2005) <http://escholarship.org/uc/item/4qr346xh> last accessed 2 January 2013). Accordingly, 74 per cent of those who had heard of the ICC thought that it had contributed to reducing violence and 68 per cent thought that it contributed to pressuring the LRA into peace talks (ibid 37–39). For a study with a more elaborate questionnaire see UN Office of the High Commissioner for Human Rights, *Making Peace Our Own: Victims Perceptions of Accountability, Reconciliation and Transitional Justice in Northern Uganda* (August 2007) especially 49 and 61 <http://www.reliefweb.int/rw/rwb.nsf/db900sid/AMMF-763G7T?OpenDocument> last accessed 2 January 2013.

[69] See Kimani (n 5) 12. For further examples of civil society's support for the ICC, cf. M du Plessis, A Louw and O Maunganidze (n 19) 9 *et seq*.

[70] See for the statement and a list of 164 signatories: Human Rights Watch 'African Civil Society Urges African State Parties to the Rome Statute to Reaffirm their Commitment to the ICC' *HRW News* (New York 30 July 2009) <http://www.hrw.org/node/84759> last accessed 2 January 2013; see further, for a joint initiative of national and international NGOs: International Federation of Human Rights, African Centre for Justice and Peace Studies and Sudan Human Rights Monitor on the al Bashir investigations: International Federation for Human Rights (FIDH), 'Press Release: The African Union Defies the ICC and Dares Trample on the Memory of Dafuri Victims!' (Paris, Nairobi, Khartoum and Kampala 30 July 2010) <http://www.fidh.org/The-African-Union-defies-the> last accessed 2 January 2013.

Similarly, 58 organisations (originating from 17 African states) reacted to the recent Kenyan anti-ICC activities with a joint statement, urging:

> the Kenyan government and parliament to reaffirm their support for the ICC and put a stop to any attempts to undermine the Rome Statute system and the ICC's Kenya investigation, including through withdrawal or seeking deferral.[71]

Pro-ICC statements can also frequently be found in African media.[72] From the victims' perspective, concerns have been voiced as to some governments' stance towards the al-Bashir arrest warrant:[73] 'African victims deserve more than this from our Heads of State; indeed the African continent deserves more.'[74] Last but not least, the African Commission for Human and People's Rights (ACHPR), a quasi-judicial organ based on the African Charter,[75] accused the Sudanese government of committing a wide range of human rights abuses and ordered it, *inter alia*, to investigate abuses in Darfur and hold those responsible accountable.[76] The Sudanese government has even been criticised by the Special Rapporteur on Refugees, Asylum Seekers, Internally Displaced Persons, and Migrants in Africa –

---

[71] Statement by African Civil Society Organizations and International Organizations with a Presence in Africa (n 21); reactions thereto in ICC OTP, 'Weekly Briefing: 26–31 January 2011' Issue 72, 3.

[72] As examples: D Pacuto, 'Why the ICC is Important for You and Me' *Daily Monitor* (Uganda 19 January 2010) 12; K Mulli, 'We Must Not Forget the Real Beneficiaries of ICC' *The East African* (Kenya 7 June 2010) 17.

[73] See further, Statement by James Gondi, Eastern Africa International Criminal Justice Initiative in Nairobi (position 'threatens to block justice for victims of the worst crimes committed on the continent') at Human Rights Watch, 'Africa: Reaffirm Support for International Criminal Court' *HRW News* (New York 30 July 2009) <http://www.hrw.org/en/news/2009/07/30/africa-reaffirm-support-international-criminal-court> last accessed 2 January 2013; S Wandera and E Kasozi, 'Human Rights Officials want President Bashir arrested' *Daily Monitor* (Uganda 31 August 2010) <http://www.monitor.co.ug/News/National/-/688334/969732/-/view/printVersion/-/1r0b5k/-/index.html> last accessed 2 January 2013 and International Federation for Human Rights (FIDH) et al (n 70).

[74] Coalition for the ICC, 'Press Release: African Union Heads of State Approve Anti-ICC Provisions: Global Coalition Calls on African States to Honour Obligations to the Court' (The Hague 3 August 2010) <http://coalitionfortheicc.org/documents/CICC_AdvisoryAU_3August2010_final.pdf> last accessed 2 January 2013.

[75] The African Commission for Human and People's Rights (ACHPR) came into existence with the coming into force of the African Charter (on 21 October 1986; adopted by the OAU on 27 June 1981). It is tasked with promoting and protecting human rights and collective (peoples') rights throughout the African continent as well as interpreting the African Charter on Human and People's Rights and considering individual complaints of violations of the Charter (African Charter of Human and People's Rights, art 30). It reports to the Assembly of Heads of State and Government of the African Union.

[76] ICC OTP, 'Weekly Briefing 27 July – 3 August 2010', Issue 48, 1.

3 May 2011 (under President Ouattara with Gbagbo now on trial in The Hague!).[88] Although a self-referral leaves the Prosecutor with discretion over whether to open a formal investigation or not,[89] it displays a certain desire on the part of the self-referring State that the ICC should take up a prosecution. Accordingly, it does not come as a surprise that the Prosecutor initiated formal investigations post-referral[90] and that none of the referring State Parties – unlike Kenya where the Prosecutor intervened *proprio motu*[91] or Libya where the jurisdiction was triggered by an UN SC Resolution[92] – has so far challenged the admissibility of the proceedings.[93] Against this background, it can hardly be argued that the Prosecutor is pursuing a neo-colonial endeavour or is arbitrarily targeting African countries which, after all, have self-referred the situations under investigation.

The three other African situations have arisen as the result of a Security Council referral (Sudan[94] and Libya[95]) and a *proprio motu* investigation (Kenya[96]). In the latter

---

[88] ICC Press Release 'Situation in Côte d'Ivoire assigned to Pre-Trial Chamber II' (20 May 2011) ICC-CPI-20110520-PR672 ICC Press Release 'Côte d'Ivoire ratifies the Rome Statute' (18 February 2013) ICC-ASP-20130218-PR873.

[89] P Akhavan, 'Self-Referrals before the International Criminal Court: Are States the Villains or the Victims of Atrocities?' (2010) 21 *CLF* 103, 112.

[90] See ICC OTP Press Release, 'The Office of the Prosecutor of the International Criminal Court Opens its First Investigation' ICC-OTP-20040623 (23 June 2004); ICC OTP Press Release, 'Prosecutor of the International Criminal Court Opens an Investigation into Northern Uganda' ICC-OTP-20040729-65 (29 July 2004); ICC OTP Press Release, 'Prosecutor Opens Investigation in the Central African Republic' ICC-OTP-20070522-220 (22 May 2007).

[91] See n 96 below.

[92] See n 95 below.

[93] The admissibility has only been challenged by the defence in the *Bemba* trial: *Situation in the Central African Republic: Prosecutor v Bemba* (Judgment on the appeal of Mr Jean-Pierre Bemba Gombo against the decision of Trial Chamber II of 24 June 2010 entitled 'Decision on the Admissibility and Abuse of Process Challenges') ICC-01/05-01/08-962 (19 October 2010). In the Ugandan situation the admissibility was reviewed *proprio motu* on the Pre-Trial Chamber II's initiative: *Situation in Uganda: Prosecutor v Kony et al* (Decision on the admissibility of the case under article 19(1) of the Statute) ICC-02/04-01/05-377 (10 March 2009); see also on Defence appeal thereto: *Situation in Uganda: Prosecutor v Kony et al* (Judgment on the appeal of the Defence against the 'Decision on the admissibility of the case under article 19(1) of the Statute' of March 2009) ICC-02/04-01/05-408 (16 September 2009). In *Situation in the DRC: Prosecutor v Katanga and Chui*, the case's admissibility was confirmed on the Defence and not on the DRC government's request: (Reasons for the Oral Decision on the Motion Challenging the Admissibility of the Case (Article 19 of the Statute)) ICC-01/04-01/07-1213-tENG (16 June 2009); confirmed in (Judgment on the Appeal of Mr Germain Katanga against the Oral Decision of Trial Chamber II of 12 June 2009 on the Admissibility of the Case) ICC-01/04-01/07-1497 (25 September 2009). For the Kenyan admissibility challenge, see n 21 above, for Libya n 26 above.

[94] UNSC Res 1593 (31 March 2005) UN Doc S/RES/1593.

[95] UNSC Res 1970 (26 February 2011) UN Doc S/RES/1970.

[96] ICC OTP, 'Letter to the ICC's President in accordance to Regulation 45 of the Regulations of the Court' ICC-01/09-1-Anx (6 November 2009) and *Situation in the Republic*

case, the State concerned was originally willing to cooperate; in fact, the Prosecutor prepared the ground for his *proprio motu* intervention in extensive negotiations with the Kenyan authorities.[97] Similar negotiations took place in Uganda and the DRC where they led to self-referrals.[98] Only in the Sudan situation (and the Libya situation) has there always been, as already mentioned above, fierce opposition from the states concerned[99] and, indeed, these situations – especially with the case against President al-Bashir – are the main cause for the deteriorating relationship between the ICC and (some) African states. Indeed, it is, in terms of its legitimacy, the weakest situation under investigation if it is directed against a non-State Party and (even) focuses on a sitting head of state. Yet, irrespective of the complex legal question whether a SC Chapter VII referral Resolution may lift the immunity of a Head of State even in the horizontal inter-state relationship (Article 98(1)),[100] it is

---

*of Kenya* (Decision assigning the Situation in the Republic of Kenya to Pre-Trial Chamber II) ICC-01/09 (6 November 2009).

[97] ICC OTP 'Agreed Minutes of the Meeting between Prosecutor Moreno-Ocampo and the Delegation of the Kenyan Government' (3 July 2009) <http://www.icc-cpi.int/NR/rdonlyres/6D005625-2248-477A-9485-FC52B4F1F5AD/280560/20090703AgreedMinutesofMeetingProsecutorKenyanDele.pdf> last accessed 2 January 2013; ICC OTP Press Release, 'Kenyan High-Level Delegation Meets ICC Prosecutor' ICC-CPI-20090703-PR431 (3 July 2009). Both Kenya's President and Prime Minister committed explicitly to cooperate with the Court during preliminary examinations, ICC OTP 'Weekly Briefing' (30 March – 5 April 2010) Issue 31, 3; the OTP received potential evidence from Kenyan authorities, ICC OTP Press Release 'ICC Prosecutor Receives Materials on Post-Election Violence in Kenya' (16 July 2009) ICC-OTP-20090716-PR438. According to Phil Clark (statement in personal communication, 16 February 2011) the Prosecutor's initial intention was to obtain a self-referral from Kenya, and only when this was not forthcoming did he employ his *proprio motu* powers.

[98] The extent, initiatives and interests in those negotiations remain unclear. Thus, for example, as to Uganda, the Prosecutor speaks of having invited the referral to maximise cooperation with a view to most effective investigations: L Moreno Ocampo, 'The Tenth Anniversary of the ICC and Challenges for the Future: Implementing the Law', Speech at London School of Economics (8 October 2008) <www.iccnow.org/documents/20081007LuisMorenoOcampo.pdf> last accessed 2 January 2013. According to SMH Nouwen and WG Werner, 'Doing Justice to the Political: The International Criminal Court in Uganda and Sudan' (2011) 21 *EJIL* 941, 947, 'some of Uganda's foreign legal advisors suggested to both the Ugandan government and the ICC's Office of the Prosecutor (OTP) that Uganda had a situation on its own territory that would be ideal for the ICC'. In contrast, according to Clark, the OTP chased the governments of DRC and Uganda to refer the cases to the ICC in order to prove the success of the young Court with regard to global justice: P Clark, 'Chasing Cases: The International Criminal Court and the Politics of State Referral in the Democratic Republic of Congo and Uganda' in C Stahn and M El Zeidy (eds) *The International Criminal Court and Complementarity: From Theory to Practice* (CUP, Cambridge 2011) 1180.

[99] Sudan's opposition is officially mainly based on the claim that justice conflicts with peace in Darfur. Al Bashir, shielded by the State structure as the current Head of State, remains politically active and continues travelling to other countries (see n 35 above).

[100] For a convincing interpretation of the SC Chapter VII referral as implicitly making art 27 applicable to Sudan on the national level, and other non-State Parties having the right (albeit not the duty) to arrest and surrender al Bashir, see D Akande, 'The Legal Nature

not the ICC's responsibility when the SC invokes its Chapter VII powers to refer a situation concerning a non-State Party and a Head of State in the first place. In other words, the primary responsibility, at least from a 'cause and effect' perspective, for the existing tension between the ICC and some African states lies with the Security Council which, in fact, let the ICC down afterwards by not following up on its referrals as to enforcement.

In sum, it is fair to say that the current state of affairs at the ICC is not due to an arbitrary prosecutorial policy discriminatorily targeting African states. In fact, no African situation has come before the Court on the basis of singular *proprio motu* decisions of the Prosecutor. Even in the Kenya situation, the only investigation formally triggered by *proprio motu* action of the Prosecutor under Article 15 of the Statute, there had been extensive previous conversations between the OTP and the Kenyan authorities in order to ensure their willingness to cooperate once a formal investigation began.[101] Indeed, the triggering mechanisms of the Statute in Article 13 make the OTP's intervention dependant on a formal decision (such as a state or Security Council referral) or at least some form of external input (such as the reference to 'information on crimes' in Article 15(1)) which allows the Prosecutor to initiate an investigation *proprio motu*. The Kenya situation shows that the Article 15(1) information threshold is high and even if it is met – for example, by a report of an independent expert commission, *in casu* the Waki Commission report[102] – the policy of the current Prosecutor is not to initiate an investigation without further

---

of Security Council Referrals to the ICC and its Impact on Al Bashir's Immunities' (2009) 7 *JICJ* 333; R Frau, *Das Verhältnis zwischen dem ständigen Internationalen Strafgerichtshof und dem Sicherheitsrat der Vereinten Nationen: Art. 13 lit. b) IStGH-Statut und der Darfur-Konflikt vor dem Gerichtshof* (Duncker and Humblot, Berlin 2010) 364 *et seq*, and joint press release issued by FIDH, African Centre for Justice and Peace Studies and Sudan Human Rights Monitor (n 70). In contrast, considering the arrest warrant as lawful but the ICC's requests to State Parties for surrender to be incompatible with art 98(1): P Gaeta, 'Does President Bashir Enjoy Immunity from Arrest?' (2009) 7 *JICJ* 315. See also K Ambos, *Internationales Strafrecht* (3rd edn Beck, Munich 2011) 7 marginal number 106, 8 marginal number 77 with further references. On the relationship between Article 27 and Article 98 of the Rome Statute, see C Gevers, 'Immunity and the implementation legislation in South Africa, Kenya and Uganda' in K Ambos and OA Maunganidze (n 17) 85 *et seq*.

[101] See (n 97).

[102] See K Annan, 'The Kenya National Dialogue and Reconciliation: Two Years On, Where Are We?' (Nairobi, 2–3 December 2010) <http://www.dialoguekenya.org/index.php/media.html> last accessed 2 January 2013. In Kenya in early 2008, Mr Annan led the African Union's Panel of Eminent African Personalities to help find a peaceful resolution to the post-election violence.

ado but to enter into conversations, one could even say 'negotiations',[103] with the State concerned.[104]

On another note, it is worth mentioning that investigations in Africa do not mean that the suspects are necessarily Africans. The ICC Prosecution has repeatedly made clear it will also go after the persons 'who ordered and financed the violence',[105] i.e. the investigations may also focus on businessmen involved in international crimes committed on African territory.[106] If this statement of intent were to be put into practice, maybe even turned into a prosecutorial strategy,[107] the Prosecutor would deserve praise, since it has long been alleged that powers led by financial, business and other similar interests are involved in several African conflicts.[108] The supposed Western complicity in these conflicts has been considered as a disincentive for the AU's cooperation with the ICC.[109] Such a strategy may also have a preventive effect on future crimes if one assumes that these are largely profit driven.[110]

---

[103] Critical in this respect, see Clark (n 98) who sees ICC's self-interested pragmatic concerns to secure judicial results exposing the Court to manipulation by domestic elites and to the possibility that deals such as offering guarantees of insulating government officials from investigations could be done. Nouwen and Werner (n 98) 951–958 are also critical on pre-investigative activities driven by institutional interests in Uganda and Sudan but conclude rather optimistically that the ICC's activities entail an inherent political dimension, that needs to be acknowledged and understood (ibid 961).

[104] E.g. ICC OTP Press Release 'ICC Prosecutor Receives Materials on Post-Election Violence in Kenya' ICC-OTP-20090716-PR438 (16 July 2009), mentioning 'collaborative efforts', having received information on the Kenyan post-election-violence from Kenyan authorities.

[105] L Moreno-Ocampo, 'Interdisciplinary Colloquium on Sexual Violence as International Crime: Interdisciplinary Approaches to Evidence' (2010) 35 *Law and Social Inquiry* 839, 846: 'the mandate of the ICC is to go up to the chain of command to those most responsible, to those who ordered and financed the violence'.

[106] R Gallmetzer, 'Prosecuting Persons Doing Business with Armed Groups in Conflict Areas: The Strategy of the Office of the Prosecutor of the International Criminal Court' (2010) 8 *JICJ* 947, 950–951. Although no cases of business involvement have been subject in international criminal proceedings to date, this strategy has been endorsed repeatedly: see e.g. D Stoitchkova, *Towards Corporate Liability in International Criminal Law* (Intersentia, Utrecht 2010) 182; A Clapham, 'Extending International Criminal Law beyond the Individual to Corporations and Armed Opposition Groups' (2008) 6 *JICJ* 899.

[107] For a critical analysis of the ICC Prosecutor's strategy see K Ambos and I. Stegmiller, 'Prosecuting Crimes at the International Criminal Court: Is there a coherent and comprehensive prosecution strategy?' (2012) 58 *Crime, Law & Social Change* 391.

[108] For example, the war in Congo was financed with tropical wood concessions, precious metal and the exploitation of other natural resources such as coltan: UN SC, 'Report of the Panel of Experts on the Illegal Exploitation of Natural Resources and Other Forms of Wealth of the Democratic Republic of the Congo' UN Doc S/2001/357 (12 April 2001); on correlations between conflict's resources and violence in the Great Lakes Region see UN SC Res 1653, UN Doc S/Res/1653 (27 January 2006).

[109] I Eberechi, 'Armed Conflicts in Africa and Western Complicity: A Disincentive for African Union's Cooperation with the ICC' (2009) 3 *African J of Legal Studies* 53, 54.

[110] See also ICC OTP, 'Press Release' PIDS.009.2003-EN (16 July 2003) 3–4: 'investigation of the financial aspects of the alleged atrocities will be crucial to prevent future crimes and

Another explanation for the African focus of the ICC is certainly the *lack of viable regional or national criminal justice mechanisms*.¹¹¹ For grave crimes in Africa, the pursuit of justice, especially for those most responsible, has been conducted largely by international organisations and not by domestic criminal justice mechanisms justice *stricto sensu*.¹¹² Even in South Africa, with its seminal Truth and Reconciliation Commission, fully fledged criminal prosecutions were never

---

for the prosecution of crimes already committed'; similarly ICC OTP, 'Press Release' ICC-OTP-20030926-37 (26 September 2003).

¹¹¹ Pointing out a 'weakness of African national jurisdictions' and linking this to an impression of uneven justice from the ICC: TYN Wilson, 'The International Criminal Court: Creation, Competence, and Impact in Africa' (2008) 3(2) *African J of Criminology and Justice Studies* 115–116. See further, C Ero, 'Understanding Africa's Position on the International Criminal Court' in The Foundation for Law, Justice and Society in collaboration with The Centre for Socio-Legal Studies, University of Oxford (ed) *Debating International Justice in Africa: Collected Essays, 2008–2010* (Foundation for Law, Justice and Society, Oxford 2011) 11–14, calling upon the AU to work more effectively to enforce accountability. See also B Olugbuo, *The Domestic Implementation of the Rome Statute in Sub-Saharan Africa: A Discussion on the Strategies, Problems and Prospects of Fighting Impunity in the African Continent* (Lambert Academic Publishing 2011).

¹¹² Hereto, Phil Clark (statement in personal communication 16 February 2011) points out that in respect to domestic efforts – including more than 400,000 proceedings against genocide suspects at Rwandan national courts and the *gacaca* jurisdictions as well as hundreds of cases of crimes against humanity (including sexual violence) at Congolese civilian and military courts, the role of international justice has been significant, but played a limited role and has not outweighed domestic efforts. The enormous weight of these domestic proceedings will in no way be challenged here, though these proceedings are not considered as ordinary criminal justice mechanisms *stricto sensu* in the above mentioned sense. For a critical account on the ICC's complementarity decision in the *Lubanga* case in light of a 'sufficient legal system', see R Bowman, '*Lubanga*, the DRC and the African Court: Lessons Learned from the First International Criminal Court Case' (2007) 7 *African Human Rights L J* 412, 424 *et seq*. On the Rwandan *gacaca* courts, see WA Schabas, 'Genocide Trials and *Gacaca* Courts' (2005) 3 *JICJ* 879; and A Megwalu and N Loizides, 'Dilemmas of Justice and Reconciliation: Rwandans and the *Gacaca* Courts' (2010) 18 *African J Int'l and Comparative L* 1. Implementing legislation has been passed in Burkina Faso, the Central African Republic, Kenya, Mauritius, Senegal, South Africa, The Comoros and Uganda, see M du Plessis, A Louw and O Maunganidze (n 19) fn 57. For the status of national implementing legislation as to 2006 in detail, see O Bekou and S Shah, 'Realising the Potential of the International Criminal Court: The African Experience' (2006) 6 *Human Rights Law Review* 499. This implementing legislation has faced different challenges, see regarding immunities in South Africa, Kenya and Uganda cf. C Gevers (n 100) 85 *et seq*, especially 105 *et seq*; regarding implementing jurisprudence on sexual and gender based violence cf. B Meyersfeld, 'Implementing the Rome Statute in Africa: Potential and Problems of the Prosecution of Gender Crimes in Africa in Accordance with the Rome Statute' in K Ambos and OA Maunganidze (n 17) 145 *et seq*; for implications of the death penalty in DRC cf. L Ngondji Ongombe, 'The Impact of the Death Penalty in the Process of Adopting the Law Implementation of the Rome Statute in the Democratic Republic of Congo' in K Ambos and OA Maunganidze (n 17) 73 *et seq*.

an option.¹¹³ The ICC's complementarity principle guarantees respect for domestic investigations, prosecutions and trials.¹¹⁴ So far, the complementarity test led in all situation countries to a determination of admissibility due to total State inaction.¹¹⁵ Attempts to establish domestic mechanisms – for example, the implementation of a International Crimes Division at the High Court in Uganda¹¹⁶ or the establishment of a hybrid court as proposed by the AU¹¹⁷ in Sudan – did not go much beyond the drafting of the corresponding legal provisions and did not produce any concrete results with regard to possible prosecutions or trials.¹¹⁸ This is the decisive difference from the situation in Colombia, for example, where domestic activity at various levels turns the complementarity test into a highly normative exercise doomed to pass judgment on the whole criminal justice system.¹¹⁹ On a

---

¹¹³ O Fiss, 'Within Reach of the State: Prosecuting Atrocities in Africa' (2009) 31 *HRQ* 59–60 who concludes that national mechanisms have to be taken in account.

¹¹⁴ On complementarity *stricto sensu*, see Ambos (n 50) 54.

¹¹⁵ On this test, see Ambos (n 51).

¹¹⁶ See <http://www.judicature.go.ug/index.php?option=com_content&task=view&id=117&Itemid=154> last accessed 2 January 2013.

¹¹⁷ AUPD Final Report (n 9) para 246. Similarly for an assessment of lacking national proceedings in the Kenya situation: A Okuta, 'National Legislation for Prosecution of International Crimes in Kenya' (2009) 7 *JICJ* 1063 and N Wainaina and P Chepng'etich, 'Special Tribunal Enactment: Why Cabinet, MPs, are Misleading Kenyans' in The Foundation for Law, Justice and Society in collaboration with The Centre for Socio-Legal Studies, University of Oxford (ed) *Debating International Justice in Africa: Collected Essays, 2008–2010* (Foundation for Law, Justice and Society, Oxford 2010) 110.

¹¹⁸ In Uganda, quite to the contrary, the respective prosecutions received a serious blow with the suspension of the International Criminal Division's first trial against a former LRA commander after the Ugandan Constitutional Court ruled in favour of the application of the country's amnesty laws: Ugandan Constitutional Court, Constitutional Petition No. 036/11, *Thomas Kwoyelo alias Latoni v Uganda*, 22 September 2011 <http://www.ulii.org/ug/judgment/2011/10> last accessed 2 January 2013. Since the Ugandan Amnesty Law of 2000 ceased on 23 May 2012 after the Ugandan Minster for Internal affairs refrained to use his powers to extend the blanket amnesty rule for another two years (cf. Ugandan Minister of Internal Affairs, Statutory Instrument No. 34 of 2012 (23 May 2012); Ugandan Minister of Internal Affairs, Statutory Instrument No. 35 of 2012 (23 May 2012); see also Justice Law and Order Sector, 'The Statute of Amnesty in Uganda (Part 2)' (11 June 2012) <http://www.jlos.go.ug/page.php?p=curnews&id=89> last accessed 9 January 2013), it remains to be seen whether the International Crimes Division will handle post conflict prosecutions. For similar critical assessments see also Oette (n 9) 363 *et seq* (greeting the AUPD's recommendation to establish a hybrid tribunal). Recommending the expansion of domestic prosecutions to those accused of ICC crimes, see Akande et al (n 9) 24. See for the factors and/or difficulties that explain the delay in the implementation of the respective national justice mechanisms (e.g. lack of awareness, capacity shortfall, other priorities, political misgivings, political or constitutional concerns, costs, absence of domestic pressure groups) Max du Plessis 'Complementarity: A Working Relationship between African States and the International Criminal Court' in du Plessis (n 44) 134–135.

¹¹⁹ For an analysis with regard to the peace process under Law 975 see Ambos (n 51) 57; see also K Ambos and F Huber, 'The Colombian Peace Process and the Principle

supranational level, an African criminal court does not exist either, and the existing human rights bodies such as the African Commission on Human and People's Rights or the African Court of Justice and Human Rights are not equipped with jurisdiction over international crimes.[120] However, recently both the African Union and the East African Community have proposed to extend the jurisdiction of existing regional supranational judicial bodies to international crimes.[121] Under the term of 'negative complementarity' or even 'cynical complementarity', such efforts have been criticized for potentially being led by the attempt to circumvent the ICC's jurisdiction, to prepare for show-trials, and to uphold impunity.[122] The only

---

of Complementarity of the International Criminal Court: Is there Sufficient Willingness and Ability on the Part of the Colombian Authorities or Should the Prosecutor Open an Investigation Now?' Extended version of the Statement in the 'Thematic Session: Colombia' ICC OTP- GO roundtable (The Hague 19–20 October 2010) <http://www.icc-cpi.int/NR/rdonlyres/2770C2C8-309A-408E-A41B-0E69F098F421/282850/civil1.pdf> last accessed 2 January 2013. For a critical assessment of the ICC OTP's Colombia report of 14 November 2012 see K Ambos, www.asuntosdelsur.org/informe-examen-preliminar-de-la-fiscalia-de-la-cpi-al-caso-colombiano/; English version in EJIL talk! (forthcoming).

[120] On prospective regional criminal justice mechanisms and on their irrelevance with regard to complementarity see Oette (n 9) 362 *et seq*. Calling for support for the African Court on Human and People's Rights rather than referring cases to the ICC, see Bowman (n 112) 426 *et seq*.

[121] At the African Union, the Executive Council presented a draft protocol to the AU Assembly extending the African Court of Justice and Human Rights' jurisdiction to international crimes. The Assembly requested for a study of the financial and structural implications. The matter ought to be discussed again at the AU's summit slated in January 2013. Cf. AU Assembly 'Decision on the Protocol of Amendments to the Protocol on the Statute of the African Court of Justice and Human Rights' (15-16 July 2012) Doc. Assembly/AU/13 (XIX)a para 1 and 2. Hereto, see M du Plessis, 'Implications of the AU decision to give the African Court Jurisdiction over International Crimes' (2012) 235 *Institute for Security Studies Paper*. For an assessment of basis and likely problems of a criminal chamber of the African Court, see CB Murungu, 'Towards a Criminal Chamber in the African Court of Justice and Human Rights' (2011) 9 *JICJ* 1067 *et seq* (arguing that such a chamber constitutes a breach of obligations deriving from the Rome Statute).

At the East African Community (EAC) it was proposed to extend the East African Court of Justice's jurisdiction: on the recent 14th Ordinary Summit, a respective progress report of the Council of Ministers was received, and the matter shall be reported to the 12th Extra-Ordinary Summit taking place in 2013, see EAC Secretariat 'Communiqué of the 14th Ordinary Summit of EAC Heads of State' (30 November 2012) para 10. Hereto, see also E Kabeera, East Africa: EAC "Competent to Handle International Criminal Cases"' *allAfrica* (19 August 2012) <http://allafrica.com/stories/printable/201208190034.html> last accessed 3 January 2013. On both developments, see also K Ambos, 'Introduction' in K Ambos and OA Maunganidze (n 17) 11-2.

[122] M du Plessis, A Louw and O Maunganidze (n 19) 2. See also M du Plessis, 'A case of negative regional complementarity? Giving the African Court of Justice and Human Rights Jurisdiction over International Crimes' *EJIL:Talk!* blog (27 August 2012) <http://www.ejiltalk.org/a-case-of-negative-regional-complementarity-giving-the-african-court-of-justice-and-human-rights-jurisdiction-over-international-crimes/> last accessed 3 January 2013.

regional mechanism enforced is the 'Protocol for the Prevention and Punishment of the Crime of Genocide, War Crimes and Crimes against Humanity and All Forms of Discrimination', that condemns international crimes and obliges the member states to implement the respective prosecutorial measures.[123] Thus, all in all, the ICC potentially performs a necessary, potentially even pioneering role with a view to strengthening the still-incipient African human rights and national criminal justice systems.[124]

Finally, the political critics of the ICC seem to overlook that it is a *sovereign decision of each state* if it joins the ICC or prefers not to do so. The ICC is not – unlike the *ad hoc* criminal tribunals – imposing justice but, as a rule (a SC referral being the exception), simply extends its jurisdiction to the states which delegated criminal jurisdiction to it in the first place. Against this background, the reproach of legal neo-colonialism[125] is misleading. While colonialism distinguished itself by an imperialistic pretension put into practice by occupation or annexation (and would be an international crime today),[126] international criminal justice is a response to gross human rights violations and ensuing widespread impunity. In other words, the neo-colonial discourse puts the perpetration of crimes on an equal footing with the prosecution of crimes.

## IV. Expanding the Focus of the ICC: Potential Prospective Situations Worldwide

While it should be clear by now that the Court's focus on Africa is not the result of an arbitrary exercise of prosecutorial discretion but can be explained by a complex set of legal and political factors, it is equally true that the Court must expand its focus beyond the African continent in order to gain broader legitimacy and dispel existing

---

[123] Adopted by the Heads of State and Governments of the International Conference on the Great Lakes Region on 29 November 2006 as a Protocol to the Pact on Security, Stability and Development in the Great Lakes Region. On this Protocol and its regulation in more detail, see CB Murungu, *Immunity of State Officials and Prosecution of International Crimes in Africa* (University of Pretoria, 2011) <http://upetd.up.ac.za/thesis/available/etd-01252012-112603/> last accessed 3 January 2013, 162 *et seq* (furthermore concluding on p. 192 that this protocol constitutes the 'only sub-regional mechanism' against international crimes in existence in Africa).
[124] Wilson (n 111) 117.
[125] Sriram (n 40); see further, text to n 41 above.
[126] See the new crime of aggression (art 8*bis*) which as to the unlawful act of aggression (art 8*bis*(2)) draws on the definition in UN General Assembly Resolution 3314 (XXIX) of 14 December 1974 according to which such an act is directed 'against the sovereignty, territorial integrity or political independence of another State'. For a comprehensive analysis with further references see K Ambos, 'The Crime of aggression after Kampala' (2010) 53 *German Ybk of Int'l L* 463.

African concerns.[127] In this context, it is first of all important to note that the formal investigations opened at the ICC must not be confused with its overall activity. This activity goes well beyond Africa. Currently, the OTP has eight situations which are publicly under preliminary examination, i.e. they are in the first phase of the OTP's activities which serves to assess if a formal investigation should be opened.[128] Only three of these situations refer to African countries (Guinea,[129] and Nigeria), the others to situations in Asia (Afghanistan, Georgia, Republic of Korea) and Latin America (Colombia, Honduras).[130] In addition, previous preliminary examinations included Iraq, Venezuela and Palestine[131], in which the Prosecutor concluded that the requirements to seek authorisation to initiate an investigation in the situation had not been satisfied.[132]

Thus, the overall activity of the OTP, reaching well beyond Africa, gives reason for hope that in the foreseeable future the Prosecutor will open a formal investigation in a non-African situation. In any case, it is important to note that already, in the preliminary phase, a complex investigatory activity has developed within the

---

[127] On a 'double standard', see LN Sadat, 'On the Shores of Lake Victoria: Africa and the Review Conference for the International Criminal Court' (Washington 31 May 2010) <http://law.wustl.edu/harris/papers/AfricaICCAFLASpring-Final5-24-2010.pdf> last accessed 2 January 2013.

[128] See for the OTP's definition its 'Weekly Briefing: 7–13 December 2010', Issue 67, 4–5. For the structure of the pre-trial phase generally see Ambos (n 100) 8 marginal numbers 20 *et seq.* and Ambos/Stegmiller (n 107), at 395 *et seq.*

[129] ICC OTP, Press Release, 'ICC Prosecutor Confirms Situation in Guinea Under Examination' ICC-OTP-20091014-PR464 (14 October 2009).

[130] ICC OTP, 'Weekly Briefing 7–13 December 2010', Issue 67, 4. The OTP distinguishes between preliminary examinations regarding subject-matter jurisdiction (Afghanistan, Honduras, Korea, Nigeria) and regarding admissibility/complementarity issues (Colombia, Georgia, Guinea, Mali), see ICC, 'Report on Preliminary Examination Activities 2012' (November 2012) 37 <http://www.icccpi.int/en_menus/icc/structure%20of%20the%20court/office%20of%20the%20prosecutor/comm%20and%20ref/Pages/Report-on-Preliminary-Examination-Activities-2012.aspx> last accessed 9 January 2013. For the referral, see n 87 above.

[131] ICC OTP, 'Situation in Palestine. Summary of Submissions on whether the Declaration Lodged by the Palestinian National Authority Meets Statutory Requirements' (3 May 2010) <http://www.icc-cpi.int/NR/rdonlyres/D3C77FA6-9DEE-45B1-ACC0-B41706BB41E5/282845/PALESTINEFINAL201010273.pdf> last accessed 2 January 2013. For a discussion see Michael Kearney and John Reynolds in Chapter 18 of this volume.

[132] Venezuela: ICC OTP, 'Letter of the Prosecutor' (9 February 2006) <http://www.icc-cpi.int/NR/rdonlyres/4E2BC725-6A63-40B8-8CDC-ADBA7BCAA91F/143684/OTP_letter_to_senders_re_Venezuela_9_February_2006.pdf> last accessed 2 January 2013; Iraq: ICC OTP, 'Letter of the Prosecutor' (9 February 2006) <http://www.icc-cpi.int/en_menus/icc/structure%20of%20the%20court/office%20of%20the%20prosecutor/comm%20and%20ref/decision%20not%20to%20proceed/iraq/Pages/otp%20letter%20to%20senders%20reply%20on%20iraq.aspx> last accessed 2 January 2013. On an assessment of both decisions see L Gentile 'Understanding the ICC' in du Plessis (n 34) 110.

OTP.[133] The sheer number of Article 15 communications – the total number received until the end of 2010 amounts to 8,976, of which 4,126 were manifestly outside the jurisdiction of the Court – exhibits the enormous workload the OTP faces during the phase of preliminary examinations.[134] The OTP must, *inter alia*, examine the Court's jurisdiction, the existence and gravity of international crimes, possible national investigations and conflicting principles, in particular the 'interests of justice' clause.[135] Clearly, greater transparency in the process of situation and case selection would dispel concerns, not only from an African perspective, with regard to a certain degree of arbitrariness in that process.[136] The OTP's recent publications of a (draft) policy paper on preliminary examinations and reports on preliminary examination activities are therefore to be welcomed.[137] In fact, the drafting of the policy paper is explained by:

> the interest of clarity and predictability over the manner in which [the OTP] applies the legal framework agreed upon by States Parties. The Office hopes that such clarity may facilitate the adjustment of other actors (political leaders, diplomats, conflict managers and mediators, NGOs and advocacy groups) to the legal framework set out in the Rome Statute, promote cooperation and increase the preventive impact of the Statute.[138]

The paper stresses the general principles of independence, impartiality and objectivity[139] and proposes an adequate procedure to be applied during preliminary examinations. It also makes clear that 'factors such as geographical or regional

---

[133] On the 'in-house procedure' before the Prosecutor selects a case or opens an investigation see Ankumah (n 11) 6.

[134] ICC OTP 'Weekly Briefing' (21 December – 6 January 2010) Issue 69, 3.

[135] Ankumah (n 12) 6.

[136] A du Plessis and A Louw 'Symposium on "The ICC that Africa Wants": Key Outcomes and Recommendations' (Institute for Security Studies, Pretoria 2010) 4 (the symposium was held in Stellenbosch in November 2009). See also P Clark, 'Law, Politics and Pragmatism: The ICC and Case Selection in the Democratic Republic of Congo and Uganda' in Waddell and Clark (n 39) 38; seeing a 'considerable transparency' already emerging, see Ford (n 49) 20.

[137] ICC OTP, 'Draft Policy Paper on Preliminary Examinations' (4 November 2010) <http://www.icc-cpi.int/en_menus/icc/structure%20of%20the%20court/office%20of%20the%20prosecutor/policies%20and%20strategies/Pages/draft%20policy%20paper%20on%20preliminary%20examinations.aspx> last accessed 2 January 2013; see on this paper Ambos/Stegmiller (n 107), espec. 397 *et seq*; ICC OTP, 'Report on Preliminary Examination Activities 2011' (13 December 2011) <http://www.icc-cpi.int/en_menus/icc/structure%20of%20the%20court/office%20of%20the%20prosecutor/comm%20and%20ref/Pages/otp%20report%20on%20preliminary%20examinations_%2013%20december%202011.aspx> last accessed 2 January 2013; and ICC OTP, 'Report on Preliminary Examination Activities 2012' (n 130).

[138] OTP Policy Paper on Preliminary Examinations (n 137) para 20.

[139] Ibid para 33.

balance are not relevant criterion for a determination that a situation warrants investigation under the Statute'.[140] The policy paper goes in the right direction since it contributes to a better understanding of the internal selection and working procedures. Still, external observers must recognise that there is a limit to the external control of prosecutorial decisions on situation and case selection, since such decisions are based to a large extent on prosecutorial discretion which, in turn, is necessary, to a certain degree, for an effective fulfilment of the functions of any prosecutorial authority.[141]

## Conclusion: African Solutions for African Problems?

The ICC's present focus on Africa does not mean that the ICC should or will impose Western-style retributive justice on African societies without taking into account the specific local cultural environment.[142] In some aspects, African societies can be distinguished from other societies[143] but that does not mean, as protracted by old Western stereotypes, that they are uncivilised, barbaric and violent societies *per se*.[144] They are often characterised by a community-centred perception. As reaction to outlaw behaviour, so-called traditional justice mechanisms such as the *gacaca* courts in Rwanda[145] have been promoted as an alternative to the retributive vision of justice espoused by the West and the ICC.[146] These mechanisms are more focused on restorative justice, aimed at reconciling concerned communities and

---

[140] Ibid summary para 11

[141] Goldston (n 29) 383–406; similarly, see DDN Nsereko, 'Prosecutorial Discretion before National Courts and International Tribunals' (2005) 3 *JICJ* 124, 142.

[142] See also quite forcefully, du Plessis (n 5) 82–83: 'The myths of the ICC's anti Africa nature and its discriminatory singling out of African situations for investigation are an attack on an institution that deserves support'.

[143] Needless to say, it is difficult to speak about Africa as a whole – there not only exist substantial differences between Northern Africa and Sub-Saharan Africa, but circumstances differ also widely from state to state as well as between districts, tribes and clans and partly even from village to village.

[144] For a good critique, particularly with regard to the Taylor trial before the Special Court for Sierra Leone, see G Anders, 'Testifying About "Uncivilised Events": Problematic Representations of Africa in the Trial Against Charles Taylor' (2011) 24 *LJIL* 937.

[145] On these see Schabas (n 112) 879; Megwalu and Loizides (n 112); P Clark, *The Gacaca Courts, Post-Genocide Justice and Reconciliation in Rwanda* (Cambridge Studies in Law and Society, Cambridge 2010).

[146] See e.g. K Ambos, 'The Legal Framework of Transitional Justice: A Systematic Study with a Special Focus on the Role of the ICC' in K Ambos et al (eds) *Building a Future on Peace and Justice* (Springer, Berlin 2009) 48–49; on difficulties in the context of international criminal justice and non-Western cultures, see T Kelsall, 'International Criminal Justice and Non-Western Cultures' in The Foundation for Law, Justice and Society in collaboration with The Centre for Socio-Legal Studies, University of Oxford (ed) *Debating International Justice in Africa: Collected Essays, 2008–2010* (Foundation for Law, Justice and Society, Oxford 2010) 17.

re-establishing a 'social equilibrium',[147] instead of stigmatising the responsible by imposing Western-style criminal punishment. It may be questioned whether or to what extent retributive mechanisms are reasonable responses to outlaw behaviour, if the community and its members never internalise any values of retributive justice.[148] Thus, local and regional solutions should be accepted and recognised to the greatest extent possible.

As has been demonstrated elsewhere, the ICC Statute is a flexible instrument, which allows for alternative justice mechanisms as long as these entail some kind of accountability.[149] Thus, the key question is whether alternative justice mechanisms like *gacaca* (Rwanda), traditional proceedings for reconciliation and healing in Uganda (e.g. Mato Oput)[150] or the South African Truth and Reconciliation Commission[151] provide such a measure of accountability.[152] Clearly, each case must be decided on its particular merits, taking into account the nature and number of crimes committed and the possible suspects involved in terms of their status in the hierarchy of the criminal enterprise.[153] It may not be sufficient to let a senior leader who is alleged to have committed genocide merely face a traditional procedure. Where an impunity gap persists, for example where no effective national criminal justice measures exist, investigations by the ICC are justified on the basis of the complementarity principle. In this case, it is not Africa or African culture which is

---

[147] O Oko, 'The Limits of Prosecutions' in The Foundation for Law, Justice and Society in collaboration with The Centre for Socio-Legal Studies, University of Oxford (ed) *Debating International Justice in Africa: Collected Essays, 2008–2010* (Foundation for Law, Justice and Society, Oxford 2010) 21.

[148] In this sense: Oko (n 147) 21, who sees violence in Africa as a result of ethnic distrust and economic marginalization of communities and argues that Western style criminal procedures fail to address the broad range of ways in which situational cultural pressures exacerbate violence.

[149] See further, Ambos (n 125) 40.

[150] J Wasonga, 'Rediscovering Mato Oput: The Acholi Justice System and the Conflict in Northern Uganda' (2009) 2(1) *Africa Peace and Conflict J* 27, 31; J Ojera Latigo, 'Northern Uganda: Tradition-Based Practices in the Acholi Region' in International Institute for Democracy and Electoral Assistance, *Traditional Justice and Reconciliation after Violent Conflict: Learning from African Experiences* (International IDEA, Stockholm 2008) 85; EK Baines, 'The Haunting of Alice: Local Approaches to Justice and Reconciliation in Northern Uganda' (2007) 1 *Int'l J of Transitional Justice* 91, 103; Tim Allen, 'Ritual (Ab)use? Problems with Traditional Justice in Northern Uganda' in Waddell and Clark (n 39) 49–54.

[151] On truth and reconciliation commissions, see Ambos (n 147) 40: 'if a TRC operates as a (partial) substitute for justice the truth to be discovered by this TRC must, in qualitative and quantitative terms, compensate for the loss or deficit of justice'.

[152] For Clark (n 80) 342, *Gacaca* trials have been prosecutorial, punitive and conducted according to the Rwandan national criminal justice framework.

[153] Suggesting a model on complementary justice mechanisms, whereupon senior leaders should face punitive sanctions only and where traditional local justice would be allowed to those whose offences were minimal, see I Stegmiller, *The Pre-Investigation Stage of the ICC – The Criteria for Situation Selection* (Duncker and Humblot, Berlin 2011) 528–535.

being targeted by the ICC, but a culture of impunity for serious international crimes.¹⁵⁴ It should be recalled in this context that the AU, even in its most critical times with the ICC, never averted from the fight against impunity. Its representative made this clear at the ICC Review Conference, stressing 'Africa's unflinching commitment to combating impunity' and claiming that the fight against impunity would always be non-negotiable,¹⁵⁵ In addition, the AU Assembly reiterated its 'commitment to fight impunity'¹⁵⁶ in each decision concerning the ICC, notwithstanding the explicit or implicit criticism contained in these decisions.

---

¹⁵⁴ Annan (n 54) para 43.

¹⁵⁵ Statement of Ben Kioko on behalf of the AU <http://www.icc-cpi.int/iccdocs/asp_docs/RC2010/Statements/ICC-RC-gendeba-AfricanUnion-ENG.pdf> last accessed 2 January 2013. On the critical position of the AU Sudan, he re-requested the SC to defer the situation in Sudan to promote peace, reconciliation and democratic governance in Sudan. Thereby, 'the AU is in no way condoning impunity. There is no doubt ... that in order to achieve lasting peace and reconciliation in Darfur, it is imperative to uphold the principles of accountability and bring to justice the perpetrators of gross human rights violations in that region. At the same time, it is equally important to ensure that the search for justice is pursued in a way that does not impede or jeopardize efforts aimed at promoting lasting peace' (ibid 4). This speech came three weeks before the AU reiterated its call on all members not to cooperate with the ICC in respect to Al Bashir (n 114).

¹⁵⁶ Lastly, AU Assembly, 15-16 July 2012 (n 9) para 2.

# The Future of International Criminal Law and Transitional Justice

Mark A. Drumbl[1]

> Only I never saw another butterfly.
> That one was the last one.
> Butterflies don't live here,
> In the ghetto.[2]

A teenager, Pavel Friedmann, penned these poignant words while captive in the Terezin ghetto near Prague. Friedmann later perished in a Nazi concentration camp, along with 15,000 other Jewish children from Terezin. He knew he was being grievously wronged: his poetry makes that clear. But never would Friedmann have expected that his tormentors would come to face legal sanction. Moral condemnation, certainly, but courts of morality are for the afterlife. They are not courts of law for the worldly.

Friedmann's suffering – along with that of millions of others – did motivate the creation of courts of law to condemn Nazi barbarity. But these tribunals, principally situated in Nuremberg, were neither global nor permanent. Nor were they civilian. At the outset, nobody could have predicted how Nuremberg would turn out – either as a paradigmatic watershed or as a flash in the pan. History has proven kind to Nuremberg. The proceedings conducted by the International Military Tribunal (IMT) have become lionised. What is more, as Kevin Jon Heller reminds

---

[1] This chapter is adapted and updated from a commentary first published as Mark A. Drumbl, 'International Criminal Law: Taking Stock of a Busy Decade', in Volume 10 of the *Melbourne Journal of International Law* (2009). I thank the *Melbourne Journal of International Law* for permission to do so. Adaptations and updates reflect changes in current events, recent developments, and evolutions in my thinking. Lisa Markman of the Washington and Lee Law School provided stellar research assistance.

[2] P Friedmann, 'The Butterfly', quoted in H Volavkova (ed) *I Never Saw Another Butterfly* (US Holocaust Memorial Museum, Schocken Books, 1993).

us in his new book, the subsequent proceedings conducted under the auspices of the American Military Tribunal, also situated in Nuremberg, have sculpted the development of contemporary law, practice, discourse and expectations.[3] The subsequent proceedings have done so more subtly than the IMT proceedings, to be sure, but no less tangibly and, perhaps, even more nimbly.

The IMT famously held that: 'Crimes against international law are committed by men, not by abstract entities, and only by punishing individuals who commit such crimes can the provisions of international law be enforced.'[4] At the time, the IMT meant to dispel the argument made by defendants that they were not guilty because they served merely as powerless cogs in an abstract criminal state. The IMT battled to ensure that personal responsibility would not be obscured by the muck and murk of the anonymity of collective violence. Over time, however, these words have transcended this minimalist defensive posture. They have come to represent an affirmative normative preference, namely, that the pursuit of post-conflict justice is best served through the selective prosecution and punishment of individual defendants.

Events of the past decade, in particular, have vivified Nuremberg. This geographic pinpoint now stands as a metaphor for law's tensions, that is, its dual capacity to both legitimise and denounce evil. Cumulatively, these recent events have mainstreamed courts of law as the reflexive first option to hold accountable those persons responsible for the commission of extraordinary international crimes such as genocide, crimes against humanity, aggression or war crimes. International criminal law iconographically ripples through the imaginative space of post-conflict justice and, thereby, aspires to fill the sullen void of impunity.

The atrocity trial glows in this iconic status. It is the *primus inter pares* of transitional justice mechanisms. The architecture of justice, hence, involves courtrooms and jailhouses. The narrative of justice relates to individual culpability, rules of evidence, legal technique and microscopic proofs. Judges are the arbiters of guilt or innocence and assessors of right or wrong. This 'jureaucracy', in turn, serves as a stabilising beam and corrective antidote to the unprincipled desultoriness and unpredictable vacillation of politics. The frame of punishment, moreover, has become defined as sequestered incarceration along the penitentiary model.[5]

International criminal law dazzles by dint of its ambition. The claim that courtrooms can distil terribly complex episodes of collective atrocity is a bold one. So too, is the claim that the jailhouse can punish the enemies of all humankind. These tall ambitions, nevertheless, have prompted concrete action. In this chapter, I survey

---

[3] KJ Heller, *The Nuremberg Military Tribunals and the Origins of International Criminal Law* (OUP, Oxford 2011).

[4] *Trials of the Major War Criminals before the International Military Tribunal, Nuremberg, 14 November 1945 – 1 October 1946* Vol 1, Judgment (International Military Tribunal, Nuremberg, 1947–1949) 223.

[5] The IMT had sentenced convicts to death, as well, but this form of punishment is no longer operationally available under contemporary international criminal processes.

this concrete action. I examine four recent developments in international criminal law and transitional justice, following which I adumbrate six challenges for the future.

## I. Recent Developments in International Criminal Law

The four major developments are: (1) institution-building; (2) remarkable judicial and jurisprudential output; (3) trendsetting and epistemic communities; and (4) political management.

### A. Institution-Building

The past decade has witnessed tremendous institutional growth and solidification in international criminal law. Forerunner institutions such as the *ad hoc* International Criminal Tribunals for the former Yugoslavia (ICTY) and Rwanda (ICTR) have persevered in their work. In addition, many new institutions have popped up. The topography of international relations now includes the permanent International Criminal Court (ICC, currently with 121 state parties);[6] hybrid tribunals such as the Special Court for Sierra Leone (SCSL);[7] the Extraordinary Chambers in the Courts of Cambodia (ECCC);[8] and the Special Tribunal for Lebanon (STL).[9]

Victims also have become involved in the justice process. At the ICC and the ECCC, they have done so not only as witnesses, but also as participants in criminal proceedings and as claimants for reparations. For example, Rule 23 of the ECCC Internal Rules permits victims to participate in criminal proceedings brought by the ECCC Prosecutors and to seek collective and moral reparations. Rights of civil party action can be asserted before the ECCC by a victim who suffers a physical, material or psychological injury, which is the direct consequence of the offence, is personal, and has actually come into being.[10] The ICC also permits victims to

---

[6] Rome Statute of the International Criminal Court, 2187 UNTS 90, 17 July 1998, entered into force 1 July 2002 (ICC Statute).
[7] Agreement between the United Nations and the Government of Sierra Leone on the Establishment of a Special Court for Sierra Leone, 2178 UNTS 137 16 January 2002, entered into force 12 April 2002.
[8] Agreement between the United Nations and the Royal Government of Cambodia Concerning the Prosecution under Cambodian Law of Crimes Committed during the period of Democratic Kampuchea, 6 June 2003, entered into force 29 April 2005.
[9] Pursuant to UNSC Res 1757 (2007) UN Doc S/RES/1757.
[10] Extraordinary Chambers in the Courts of Cambodia, Cambodia, *Internal Rules and Regulations*, available at <http://www.eccc.gov.kh/english/internal_rules.aspx> last accessed 6 December 2011, Rule 23.

participate in trial proceedings.¹¹ Reparations, moreover, might be possible, including through the Victims' Trust Fund.¹²

Because of this kinetic institutionalism, international criminal law now is everywhere. It is newsworthy, topical and attractive. Although it has been chided for attracting an inordinate amount of the intellectual interest of international lawyers,¹³ younger international lawyers still disproportionately think about it, write about it, and push to be part of it.

## B. Judicial and Jurisprudential Output

The institutions of international criminal law are neither spectral nor illusory. They are not empty suits. They are very real. No doubt, they often move languidly, while incurring great costs and gobbling up large tranches of UN budgets. But they are living and breathing. They engage and are engaging. And they are busy. The political economy of judicialised accountability is a going concern.

As of the time of writing, the ICTY has sentenced 64 offenders, with 16 additional cases currently before the Appeals Chamber. Nineteen other cases are at trial or are in pre-trial phases. The ICTR has convicted roughly 55 defendants on charges related to the 1994 Rwandan genocide (including 19 cases that are pending appeal, and several convicts who have died or been released following completion of their sentence). Trials also continue apace at the ICTR. The ICTY has received a major legitimacy uptick now that long-term fugitives Radovan Karadžić, Ratko Mladić and Goran Hadžić have been brought into custody. No ICTY indictees remain at large – the embarrassment for the institution now has been lifted. The ICTY also has transferred 13 cases to national courts in states emergent from the former Yugoslavia. In a first, ICTR judges, too, have transferred a case to national court in Rwanda.¹⁴ The ICTR previously had transferred two cases to France.

The ICTY and ICTR do more than merely convict. They also acquit, thereby attesting to the genuineness with which they view the proof beyond a reasonable doubt maxim. Their trials are not form over substance; they showcase, but they are not for show. At the ICTR, for example, eight detainees have been acquitted, while the ICTY has acquitted 13. To date, the SCSL has concluded three cases, involving leaders of the Armed Forces Revolutionary Council (AFRC), the Civil Defence Forces (CDF) and the Revolutionary United Front (RUF). SCSL indictees – eight of whom have been convicted – are among those persons most responsible for a decade of civil war in Sierra Leone. Appeals have ended. A verdict in the fourth

---

¹¹ ICC Statute, art 68.
¹² Ibid art 79.
¹³ K Anderson, 'The Rise of International Criminal Law: Intended and Unintended Consequences' (2009) 20 *EJIL* 331.
¹⁴ *Prosecutor v Uwinkindi* (Decision on Prosecutor's Request for Referral to the Republic of Rwanda) ICTR-2001-75-R11*bis* (28 June 2011).

case, against Charles Taylor, was rendered in early 2012. The Taylor case will be the SCSL's last, other than some residual proceedings on contempt charges.

In late June 2011, the STL delivered a sealed indictment and arrest warrants to Lebanese authorities as part of its mandate to investigate the 2005 assassination of former Lebanese Prime Minister Rafik Hariri. Over 80 individuals have been convicted by another hybrid institution, the Special Panels for Serious Crimes in Timor-Leste, which – for lack of funding – closed down in May 2005. Owing to its premature closure, much of its work remains unfinished. These convictions only represent about a quarter of the total number of indictees, most of whom remain free in Indonesia. There is little will to bring these fugitives into custody.

The ECCC is busy prosecuting surviving elements of the senior Khmer Rouge leadership most responsible for atrocities that resulted in the deaths of 1.7 million persons in the 1970s. The ECCC has two cases before it. In the first case, Kaing Guek Eav, alias Duch, was sentenced to 30 years' imprisonment for crimes against humanity and war crimes arising out of his chairmanship of the Khmer Rouge's most notorious torture prison. Appeals have been filed. The second case, implicating four septuagenarian and octogenarian leaders, has just recently begun. While the ECCC's international co-prosecutor wishes to increase the number of defendants and initiate two new cases, he faces chronic resistance from his national counterpart. Claims of political interference and resultant misconduct, moreover, also have been levied – for example, by Human Rights Watch – against some ECCC judges.[15]

The permanent ICC and its organs deserve special mention. These are now at work in seven situations: Uganda, Democratic Republic of Congo (DRC), Central African Republic, Libya, Kenya, Sudan and Côte d'Ivoire.[16] Although some of these situations are long-standing, a flurry of activity has enlivened the ICC in very recent years. Its first verdict – in the matter of Thomas Lubanga, a DRC rebel leader charged exclusively with the unlawful conscription, enlistment, or use of children under the age of 15 to participate actively in hostilities – was issued in March 2012.[17] Another DRC case, against Germain Katanga and Mathieu Ngudjolo Chui, is at trial as well; so, too, is the case against Jean-Pierre Bemba Gombo arising from the Central African Republic Situation. To date, referrals have arisen through each of the three methods contemplated by the Rome Statute: by a state party, by the United Nations Security Council, or by the Prosecutor acting *proprio motu*.

On 31 March 2010, Pre-Trial Chamber II granted ICC Chief Prosecutor Moreno-Ocampo authorisation to open an investigation into the situation in Kenya. This has since led to the issuance of summonses for six Kenyans allegedly implicated in

---

[15] Human Rights Watch, *Cambodia: Judges Investigating Khmer Rouge Crimes Should Resign* (New York 3 October 2011) <http://www.hrw.org/news/2011/10/03/cambodia-judges-investigating-khmer-rouge-crimes-should-resign> last accessed 6 December 2011.

[16] The Office of the Prosecutor is also monitoring a number of other possible situations, including Colombia, Afghanistan, Palestine and Honduras.

[17] *Situation in the DRC: Prosecutor v Lubanga* (Judgment pursuant to Article 74 of the Statute) ICC-01/04-01/06 (14 March 2012).

widespread violence in the wake of the country's 2007 presidential elections. These individuals are very high-ranking members of the domestic political establishment (notably, of both the incumbent and opposition parties). With decisions on the confirmation of charges scheduled to be issued in early 2012, the intensity of this referral will amplify. An admissibility challenge brought by the Kenyan government proved futile.

The unanimous February 2011 vote by the UN Security Council to refer the situation in Libya to the ICC reflects just how far the ICC has become naturalised both within international relations and as a response mechanism to breaches of the peace. The Security Council's earlier vote on the Darfur referral, in contrast, had been far less decisive. Within days of the Libya referral, Prosecutor Moreno-Ocampo announced that he would open an investigation. On 26 June 2011, Pre-Trial Chamber I issued arrest warrants for three individuals in Libya on charges of crimes against humanity, including the country's leader, Colonel Muammar Gaddafi.[18] Proceedings against Gaddafi were terminated following his death.

But these numbers and names relate only a quantitative and descriptive story. These institutions have also generated reams of substantive law, thereby serving an important expressive, social constructivist, and jurisprudential function. Over the past decade, international criminal law has advanced rapidly in terms of codification and interpretation. Crimes, and elements of crimes, are now set out in great detail. The case law interpreting textual documents is thick, textured and robust. Processes of codification and interpretation have, for the most part, been progressive. States and judges have expanded the ground covered by law. The vitality of international criminal law has veritably boomed. Crimes committed against women and children, hitherto marginalised, have now become a focus of attention.[19] The Rome Statute directly criminalises many manifestations of gender-based violence, including persecution on the grounds of gender as a crime against humanity. Liability theories such as joint criminal enterprise, indirect co-perpetration, and superior responsibility widen the range of potential perpetrators. To be sure, these theories are controversial. They do not remain static.[20]

---

[18] The other two persons against whom arrest warrants have been issued are Gaddafi's son Saif al-Islam and Abdullah Sanussi.

[19] Several of the ICC's indictees are specifically charged with crimes against women and children; both the ICTR and the ICTY have been major forces in criminalising sexual violence. See for example: *Situation in the DRC: Prosecutor v Lubanga* (Warrant of Arrest) ICC-01/04-01/06 (10 February 2006); *Situation in the DRC: Prosecutor v Ntaganda* (Warrant of Arrest) ICC-01/04-02/06 (22 August 2006); *Situation in Uganda: Prosecutor v Kony et al* (Warrant of Arrest) ICC-02/04-01/05 (8 July 2005); *Situation in the Central African Republic: Prosecutor v Bemba* (Decision Pursuant to Article 61(7)(a) and (b) of the Rome Statute on the Charges of the Prosecutor Against Jean-Pierre Bemba Gombo) ICC-01/05-01/08 (12 January 2009); *Situation in Darfur, Sudan: Prosecutor v Harun and Kushayb* (Warrants of Arrest for Ahmad Harun and Ali Kushayb) ICC-02/05-01/07 (27 April 2007).

[20] See for example *Prosecutor v Krajisnik* (Appeals Judgment) IT-00-39 (17 March 2009); *Prosecutor v Dordević* (Appeals Judgment) IT-05-87/1 (23 February 2011).

# The Future of International Criminal Law & Transitional Justice

Although international criminal law's reach ebbs and flows, it has, for the most part, been expansionary. International criminal law regulates more and more: at times elegantly, at times tenaciously. Its place has solidified within post-conflict peace negotiations, thereby tainting the amnesty and jaundicing the pardon. The peace *versus* justice debate is becoming a relic of the past and indicative of the tempo of an antecedent generation. Regardless of whether justice thwarts peace or stimulates it, the fact remains that justice has intractably wended its way into, and now entwines with, peace discourse.

## C. Trend-Setting and Epistemic Communities

International criminal law transcends the international plane. It seeps into national jurisdictions. Over the past decade, national courts have increasingly prosecuted and punished perpetrators of genocide, crimes against humanity, and wide-scale war crimes. The iconic status of the atrocity trial remodels national legal orders and guides the micro-politics of post-conflict transitions.

In Rwanda alone, at least 10,000 individuals have come before national courts. Many hundreds of thousands more individuals have appeared – for better or for worse – in neo-traditional *gacaca* proceedings that, gloomily, have become warped by governmental ideology. Bosnia, Serbia and Croatia, spurred on by the ICTY's Completion Strategy, each have created domestic war crimes chambers.[21] Many states are combing their immigration records to ferret out suspected war criminals and prosecute them or, if the evidence has grown worn with time, subject them to less onerous denaturalisation proceedings. Quickly, prosecutors are looking to identify and charge octogenarian and nonagenarian pensioner Nazis, so that they cannot cheat justice through a tranquil death noted only in the local obituaries column.

Many states have domesticated the Rome Statute. Uganda's Parliament, for example, did so by passing the International Criminal Court Act on 9 March 2010. This Act accords the recently established Ugandan High Court (International Crimes Division) jurisdiction over Rome Statute crimes. The first case before this division implicated Colonel Thomas Kwoyelo, of the notorious Lord's Resistance Army (LRA). The LRA (now significantly weakened) has been involved in a two decades-long conflict against the Ugandan government. Proceedings against Kwoyelo had begun on 11 July 2011, but have led to a finding by Uganda's Constitutional Court that Kwoyelo was entitled to rely upon an amnesty he, and many other, LRA

---

[21] See UNSC Res 1503 (2003) UN Doc S/RES/1503; Law on Organization and Jurisdiction of Government Authorities Prosecuting Perpetrators of War Crimes 2003 (Serbia); Law on the Application of the Statute of the Interntional Criminal Court and the Prosecution of Criminal Acts against the International Law of War and International Humanitarian Law 2003 (Croatia); Law on the Court of Bosnia and Herzegovina 2002 (Bosnia and Herzegovina); Penal Code of the Federation of Bosnia and Herzegovina 2003 (Bosnia and Herzegovina).

fighters had received pursuant to official legislation upon their demobilisation.[22] The Constitutional Court ordered that the Kwoyelo proceedings be returned to the International Crimes Division and dismissed. The refusal to respect the amnesty, the Constitutional Court held, violated the equal treatment provision of Uganda's constitution. Kwoyelo had been abducted into the LRA in 1987 at the age of 15. Reportedly the LRA's fourth-in-command, Kwoyelo is the highest ranked LRA official in custody. He nonetheless invokes a narrative of helpless subservience. He told a Ugandan newspaper that his 'situation in the bush was like that of a dog and his master. When you tell a dog to do something, it will act as instructed. All orders came from [LRA leader Joseph] Kony'.[23] For his part, Kony has been indicted by the ICC. Yet he remains at large in the bush, along with two other ICC indictees, including former child soldier Dominic Ongwen. Two other ICC indictees in the Kony case have apparently been killed.[24]

Despite its contested status, universal jurisdiction remains energetic. Alien Tort Claims Act litigation in the United States persists as a cottage industry, where it inspires plaintiffs, dissents, circuit splits, concerns, and truculence. This litigation opens a fecund vein that germinates a host of other legal questions – ranging from the status of corporations as defendants to the scope of customary international crimes to the redressability of grievous harms through symbolic civil damage awards. Every week, it seems, yet another aspect of historical wrongdoing is becoming judicialised, thereby further naturalising courtrooms as the suitable locus for redress and remedy.

Over the past decade, an entire generation of lawyers has cut its professional teeth at the various international criminal tribunals. These lawyers have become specialists, whose expertise in international criminal law and procedure is no longer only of academic value. This expertise is marketable and, what is more, the market values it. Understandably, these lawyers now have an interest in husbanding the value of their expertise. Within the college of international law, an energetic, transnational and networked epistemic community of international criminal lawyers has arisen. This group is portable and mobile: in the words of Elena Baylis, its constituents 'tribunal hop'[25] from Arusha to Freetown to Phnom Penh. With it, this group brings humanitarianism, resources, jeeps, air-conditioning, fancy restaurants and cool drinks to fend off the tropical heat. Once this group exits, it hopefully leaves a new footprint, namely, some reconciliation, some infrastructure, and renewed leadership.

---

[22] See for example 'Ugandan LRA Rebel Thomas Kwoyelo Granted Amnesty' *BBC News* (London 22 September 2011) <http://www.bbc.co.uk/news/world-africa-15019883> last accessed 6 December 2011.

[23] C Ocowun, 'LRA's Kwoyelo Charged with Kidnap' *New Vision* (Uganda 4 June 2009) <http://www.newvision.co.ug/D/8/13/683670> last accessed 6 December 2011.

[24] Vincent Otti and Raska Lukwiya are both reported to have died. See Coalition for the International Criminal Court, 'Northern Uganda Information Sheet' <http://www.iccnow.org/?mod=northernuganda> last accessed 6 December 2011.

[25] E Baylis, 'Tribunal Hopping with the Post-Conflict Justice Junkies' (2008) 10 *Oregon Rev Int'l L* 361.

## D. Political Management

All international criminal tribunals touch much more than just law. They also affect domestic political structures in the countries whose tragedies they judicialise.[26] At times these effects are salutary: they inspire the rule of law, promote transparency, and hollow out reprehensible governments. In other instances, however, international tribunals might abet – whether inadvertently or consciously – incumbent governments to consolidate their own power. Borrowing a term of art from Jens Meierhenrich, then, international criminal tribunals may permit these governments to engage in patterns of 'lawfare' that shield their own illiberal practices from scrutiny while stigmatising only the human rights abuses committed by their political opponents.[27] The Rwandan and Ugandan governments have managed the ICTR and ICC, respectively, to these ends.[28] Securing justice for atrocious rebels or losers comes at the price of insulating the government or winners from justice. National proceedings also can serve ulterior purposes both in terms of who is targeted and who is *not* targeted. One example is the exclusion of the Rwandan Patriotic Front's crimes from the scope of the Rwandan *gacaca* tribunals and the inclusion of certain trials against suspects based on charges of genocidal ideology, negationism and divisionism.[29]

# II. Future Challenges

Although dazzling, the development of international criminal law also frustrates. I posit six challenges for the future: (1) (re-)nationalisation: from technique to context; (2) diversity: from law to justice; (3) scrutiny: from faith to science; (4) truths: from convenience to discomfort; (5) even-handedness: who and what is being prosecuted?; and (6) imagery: from essentialisms to nuance.

## A. (Re-)Nationalisation: From Technique to Context

Although international criminal law is everywhere, in a sense, it is also nowhere. The emergence of international criminal law as impartial technique has come at the expense of context or area studies. The pursuit of neutrality has – deliberately

---

[26] See for example W Burke-White, 'Complementarity in Practice: The International Criminal Court as Part of a System of Multi-level Global Governance in the Democratic Republic of Congo' (2005) 18 *LJIL* 557, 559.
[27] J Meierhenrich, *Lawfare* (draft monograph on file with the author, 2012).
[28] M du Plessis, *The International Criminal Court and its Work in Africa: Confronting the Myths* (Institute for Security Studies, Pretoria 2008) 1, 11.
[29] See for example S Straus and L Waldorf (eds) *Remaking Rwanda: State Building and Human Rights after Mass Violence* (University of Wisconsin Press, Madison 2011).

or inadvertently – tended to sideline traditional approaches to dispute resolution and externalise justice from afflicted communities. Now that the institutions of international criminal law are deeply embedded in the fabric of international relations, however, might they develop the confidence to better welcome the local and thereby more proximately align themselves with the place most relevant to most of us, that is, the parochial and quotidian? Happily, there are brightly positive signs in this regard. Outreach efforts, for example, have become prioritised.[30]

Chief Prosecutor Moreno-Ocampo was correct when he concluded in 2008 that 'after five years of operations the Rome Statute is modifying the way in which we think about the law at [the] national level'.[31] Now that the ICC is pushing 10 years of operation, his statement is all the more accurate. But it remains unclear whether the modernity narrative upon which international criminal law sails necessarily means that nothing is lost amid the progressive gains. The point is not so much for the technique of the international to domesticate or otherwise tame the nativism of the domestic. Rather, it is for the international to revisit its relationship with the domestic to promote synergy and inclusively foster bottom-up input. Hence, the endgame could move from domestication to renationalisation.

## B. Diversity: From Law to Justice

Together with better incorporating the local, international criminal law would do well to open up to other accountability mechanisms. Can we readily assume that liberal legalist trials, which international criminal tribunals borrow and tweak from influential national criminal justice systems, are suitable for the perpetrator of extraordinary international crimes? Such crimes are often crimes of obedience. Does the *génocidaire* really have that much in common with the transgressive and deviant common criminal? International criminal law's predicate of individual culpability and incarceration may simply not be favoured among all victim communities. Nor do all victim communities idealise the atrocity trial. Many such communities prefer other justice modalities, or an admixture thereof, including truth commissions, lustration, memorialisation, public inquiries, community service, and traditional re-integrative practices. Moreover, the collective nature of mass atrocity is such that collective forms of responsibility that target states, organisations, non-state actors and corporations may more accurately reflect the aetiology of the crime.

In the end, a challenge for international criminal law is the need to foster other justice mechanisms, rather than dissuade them or view them suspiciously

---

[30] See for example International Criminal Tribunal for Rwanda, 'ICTR Opens Two More Information Centres in Rwanda' (23 February 2009) <http://ictr-archive09.library.cornell.edu/ENGLISH/PRESSREL/2009/586.html> last accessed 6 December 2011.

[31] International Criminal Court, 'The Tenth Anniversary of the ICC and Challenges for the Future: Implementing the Law', Statement by Luis Moreno-Ocampo at the London School of Economics (8 October 2008) <http://www.iccnow.org/documents/20081007LuisMorenoOcampo.pdf> last accessed 6 December 2011, 8.

as competitors. International criminal justice should involve much more than just international criminal law. Although talking about cost may be vulgar, the fact remains that, as far as accountability mechanisms go, international criminal trials are very expensive. Primary school mathematics puts the cost of each ICTR conviction at 10 to 20 million US dollars. In Rwanda, nearly everyone lives on less than two US dollars per day. Hybrid institutions do it more cheaply, to be sure, but they, too, are still ragingly expensive from the afflicted society's perspective. The SCSL's budget already raised hackles in 2008 when it touched $150 million.

## C. Scrutiny: From Faith to Science

The driving force behind international criminal law, to clumsily paraphrase Oliver Wendell Holmes, is neither logic nor experience. Instead, it is faith — always inspired and often exuberant.[32] Faith was necessary in order to actually establish the juridical institutions. This same faith, however, also has oversold the transformative power of the atrocity trial. Criminal prosecution and incarceration for the guilty is claimed to promote a broad array of goals, including deterrence, retribution, collective reconciliation, re-integration, rehabilitation, expressivism, truth-telling and ending impunity.

Are these goals being attained? Are they even attainable? Now that the institutions are up and running, the only way to find out is to move from faith to science and treat the institutions that enforce international criminal law as subjects of study in the same rigorous way domestic scholars treat domestic courts. Happily, there has been remarkable growth in interdisciplinary and empirical scholarship that examines many aspects of international criminal law and practice. Cognate fields have also boomed.[33] The challenge for international criminal law is to encourage such study and then absorb the lessons that quality research has to offer.

## D. Truths: From Convenience to Discomfort

Although the narrative of international criminal law is often presented as a heroic struggle by lawyers, activists and organisations against state interests, the reality is considerably more sublime. Without states, there would be no institutions of international criminal law. There would be no prospect of enforcement. There would be no financing. There would, in fact, be nothing. Chief Prosecutor Moreno-

---

[32] See generally D Koller, 'The Faith of the International Criminal Lawyer' (2008) 40 *NYU J Int'l L and Politics* 1019, 1020–1022.

[33] A recent survey of the political science literature found that the 15 leading journals in the field published 36 articles about human rights in the 1980s, 60 in the 1990s, and 103 since 2000. See S Jaschik, 'Political Scientists and Human Rights' *Inside Higher Education* (Washington DC 20 January 2009) <http://insidehighered.com/news/2009/01/20/polisci> last accessed 6 December 2011.

Ocampo may have describedthe Rome Statute as 'a criminal justice system without a State',[34] but in reality the ICC exists largely *because* of state action, consent and financing.

States do get something out of the ICC, as they do with other international criminal tribunals. States – along with international organisations – have some interest in the kinds of truth-telling that international criminal tribunals achieve. The atrocity trial pins blame on the vilest and most reprehensible individuals. In reality, however, atrocity is the product of many factors. Individual action, say of leaders, assuredly is one of these. But disappeared from the truth-telling process is the involvement (or nonfeasance) of state actors and international organisations. Also disappeared is the catalytic role of benefitting bystanders, transnational capital, institutional omissions and colonial histories. The truths told by international criminal law are convenient. They are manageable. By blaming the few for the annihilation of the many, these truths comfort. They do not embarrass too much or too many. But the origin of atrocity is much more discomfiting and discomforting. If we move into a mindset where the articulated truths of international criminal law become totalising, and exclusionary of all others, then we achieve some justice, but we actually settle for a very crimped understanding of justice. One of the reasons why international criminal law may have limited transformative potential – despite its lofty rhetoric – is because it only scratches the surface of what justice actually entails following mass atrocity.

### E. Even-Handedness: Who and What is Being Prosecuted?

Within judicialised conflicts, international criminal law *prima facie* endeavours to be even-handed. So, for example, the ICTY prosecutes and punishes Serbs, Croats and Muslims. It does so differentially, to be sure: over two-thirds of its indictees have been Serbs, leading to accusations of ethnic bias. These accusations became all the more stinging in tone following the 2012 acquittals (on appeal, by a narrow 3 to 2 majority) of high-profile Croatian generals Ante Gotovina and Mladen Markač regarding crimes against humanity and war crimes that occurred during and subsequent to the Operation Storm campaign (which retook the Krajina in 1995). The ICTY also acquitted, on a retrial, Ramush Haradinaj, a Kosovo Albanian former guerrilla commander who had served briefly as prime minister and now might return to that post. The SCSL's push towards even-handedness has proved to be more fruitful, insofar as it built up three cases keyed to the three principal fighting factions, plus one case against Charles Taylor. Convictions were entered in each. Fighting for a just cause – the way many Sierra Leoneans saw, and still see, the CDF – was even dismissed on appeal as a factor in sentence mitigation. A war crime is a war crime, regardless of whether undertaken in defence of the flailing democratic state against the brutal assault of the RUF. The situation in Darfur before the ICC has likewise seen both rebel leaders and President Bashir prosecutorially

---

[34] Statement by Moreno-Ocampo (n 31) 2.

targeted, despite the evident disproportion between the two on the scales of horror. Places where judicialised even-handedness is explicitly lacking – for example, as I mentioned previously, Rwanda and Uganda – become, in the current *Zeitgeist*, critiqued specifically because of this absence of putative impartiality and historical balance.

Even-handedness may appear *within* certain individually judicialised conflicts, but does not materialise in terms of which conflicts actually become internationally judicialised in the first place. Power politics persist. So long as only conflicts within the weakest states become internationally 'jureaucratised', the operation of the law will remain uneven. This tendency is overwhelming at the ICC – all of its situations are African.

Also perplexing is the approach of the West to international terrorism. The 9/11 attacks – which I posit constitute crimes against humanity – present a stark example.[35] In the wake of these attacks, a low premium was placed on international criminal law as a mechanism to pursue justice. The thought that an internationalised court adhering to internationalised legalist procedure would mete out justice was unacceptable to US (and to many, albeit not all, Western) policy-makers. No such tribunal was created. In fact, no such proposal was ever seriously tendered; nor would such a proposal have gained traction. This silence is all the more deafening since nationals of 81 countries perished on 9/11,[36] and nationals of an array of countries were implicated, to varying degrees, in the attacks and subsequent Al-Qaeda bombings. The notion that Osama bin Laden, if caught rather than summarily killed in 2011, would have been spared capital charges was unimaginable in US discourse. The prospect that erudite judges from outside the United States would determine his culpability, and that prosecutors from outside the United States would conduct the proceedings such that Americans would have to follow through translating earpieces, would be even more unthinkable.

Little has changed under President Obama's watch in this regard. The first conviction by military commission at Guantánamo Bay – that of child soldier Omar Khadr – emerged from an outrageously flawed process.[37] It is disturbing – if not downright corrosive – when the nationality of the victims determines the perpetrators' level of due process entitlements.

## F. Imagery: From Essentialisms to Nuance

International criminal law prefers simple images: innocent victim, evil oppressor and heroic humanitarian. In this regard, international criminal law mimics Makau

---

[35] MA Drumbl, 'Judging the 11 September Terrorist Attack' (2002) 24(2) *HRQ* 323.

[36] Letter sent by Ambassador John Negroponte to Richard Ryan, President of the Security Council, as quoted in 'United States Officially Informs United Nations of Strikes' *Washington Times* (Washington 9 October 2001) A14.

[37] See for example Human Rights Watch, 'Omar Ahmed Khadr' <http://www.hrw.org/news/2010/11/02/omar-ahmed-khadr> last accessed 6 December 2011.

Mutua and David Kennedy's deconstruction of international human rights law.[38] Yet the simplicity of these images belies the vacillating nature of human behaviour in the crucible of atrocity. Captors – after all – can capture, victims can victimise, and the abused can, in turn, abuse. Primo Levi painfully grappled – without resolution – with the 'gray zone', by which he refers to the fuzzy line between connivance and courage, and obsequiousness and morality, interstitially occupied by the *kapos* in the concentration camps.[39] Hannah Arendt, to considerable controversy, also chimes in on this theme by faulting the leaders of the various *Judenräte* for cooperating with the Nazis.[40]

International criminal law evinces squeamishness with ambiguity. Its binary absolutes of guilt or innocence are ill-equipped to handle the frustrating subtlety of the human experience during episodes of collective violence. Moreover, in emphasising the crushed status of victims in order to justify onerous punishment for their oppressors, international criminal law may curry disabling stereotypes of those victims. A new generation of scholarship examines how the simplicity of victim designations, particularly in regard to women and juveniles, may come to hamper post-conflict empowerment and robust citizenship of both women and juveniles. Feminist scholars have noted how gender essentialisations of women's role in conflict – which accelerate the flow of funds to support women as victims and have been central to successful sexual violence prosecutions at the international level – inadvertently spill into post-conflict phases where they may perpetuate stereotypes of women's weak and passive civic roles.[41] In other work, I have voiced similar concerns regarding dominant portrayals of child soldiers.[42]

The recent amendment of the Rome Statute to define aggression also presents a tricky intersection with victim protection. One under-theorised aspect of criminalising aggression involves its effects on humanitarian interventions. However paradoxical, violence may stem violence; sometimes, the only way to stop a tyrant from decimating a minority population is to use force against that tyrant. No exception was included in the aggression definition regarding interventions to prevent the commission of other Rome Statute crimes. Such an exception, when proposed by the United States, was rejected by other delegates. Any exception of this genre may prove difficult to manage, to be sure. It might be prone to manipulation and abuse. Still, as Beth Van Schaack courageously points

---

[38] M Mutua, 'Savages, Victims, and Saviors: The Metaphor of Human Rights' (2001) 42 *Harvard Int'l L J* 201, 201–202, 227; D Kennedy, *The Dark Sides of Virtue: Reassessing International Humanitarianism* (Princeton University Press, Princeton 2004) 14.

[39] P Levi, *The Drowned and the Saved* (Vintage, New York 1989) 36.

[40] H Arendt, *Eichmann in Jerusalem* (Penguin Books, London 1977) 125.

[41] K Engle, 'Feminism and Its (Dis)contents: Criminalizing Wartime Rape in Bosnia and Herzegovina' (2005) 99 *AJIL* 778; R. Charli Carpenter, '"Women, Children and Other Vulnerable Groups": Gender, Strategic Frames and the Protection of Civilians as a Transnational Issue' (2005) 49 *Int'l Studies Quarterly* 295.

[42] MA Drumbl, *Reimagining Child Soldiers in International Law and Policy* (OUP, Oxford, 2012).

out, there is cause to question whether the criminalisation of aggression might chill *bona fide* exercises of humanitarian intervention.[43]

## Conclusion

The spirited development of international criminal law over this past decade belies the lingering fact that we know very little about what atrocity trials actually accomplish. To this end, instead of being bullish, perhaps we should err on the side of modesty. Some movement is afoot in this direction. The temperament of the field has become more mature. This is a positive trend. Admittedly, it may have been strategic for international criminal lawyers to aggressively tout the transformative potential of the atrocity trial in order to convince states to support institutions, donors to fund them, and persons to devote their professional lives and intellectual capital to them. But now that the institutions are solidly established, and have become the defining normative fixtures of transitional justice, perhaps the political pressure for trumpeting the transformative potential of the atrocity trial has waned. As a result, we might become more circumspect about what atrocity trials actually can do and what the skill-set of the international criminal lawyer actually can accomplish.

Although international criminal law remains the dominant accountability mechanism for episodes of mass atrocity, it awkwardly elucidates the provenance of collective violence and organisational massacre. Perhaps, then, international *criminal law* should recede and international *post-conflict justice* – a broader paradigm that includes diverse accountability modalities and a more sublime lexicon – should step up.

---

[43] B van Schaack, 'The Crime of Aggression and Humanitarian Intervention on Behalf of Women' (2011) 11 *ICLR* 477.

# Index

accessory liability 101-105, 112, 117, 126, 127, 129, 344
accused, rights of the xxi, 165-168, 172-173, 182, 184, 187, 188, 190, 191, 197, 204, 214, 252, 254, 261, 262, 272, 274, 276, 277, 278, 282, 284, 289-307
*actus reus* 48-49, 51, 103-105, 109-112, 126-127, 234, 235, 244, 371
*ad hoc* international criminal tribunals *see* International Criminal Tribunal for Rwanda; International Criminal Tribunal for the former Yugoslavia
admissibility xi, xiv, xviii, xx, xxiii, xxv, xxvi, 7, 8, 69, 167, 168, 177, 179, 182, 188, 190, 208, 212, 220, 221, 292, 301, 335, 337, 338, 342, 349, 351, 354, 358-367, 370, 372-383, 398, 399, 401-403, 465-477, 503, 504, 517, 522, 536
African Union xlv, 86, 397, 401, 469, 487, 499-501, 502, 503, 506, 512-514, 519-520, 523
aggression xxxi, xxxiii, xliii, xlv, 2, 57, 61, 63-78, 392, 402, 403, 419, 468, 472, 484, 524, 532, 544-545
aiding and abetting 101-107, 109-116, 123-131, 235, 244-249, 347
amendments to the Rome Statute 65, 67, 544
apartheid xxxvi, xliv, 61, 411
armed conflict xxvii, xxxv, xxxviii, 14, 32, 42, 45, 53-60, 75, 80, 82, 83, 88, 97, 209-210, 221, 226, 232, 248, 364, 425, 444, 491, 492, 496, 516, 520
arrest xi, xii, xiii, xv, xvii, xix, xlii, xlv, 11, 26, 27, 33, 36, 37, 38, 39, 40, 41, 43, 50, 52, 170, 172, 193, 195, 208, 219, 227, 238, 239, 248, 259, 260, 264, 269, 277, 282, 305, 316, 335, 350, 351, 359, 362, 396, 397, 399, 403, 442, 450, 451, 481, 487, 493, 494, 497, 499-502, 504-507, 510-514, 518, 519, 535, 536

Bashir, Omar Al xii-xiii, 26, 27, 33, 50, 52, 194, 195, 227, 238, 239, 350, 390, 451, 487, 495, 499-502, 504-507, 510-514, 518, 519, 529, 542
Bassiouni, M. Cherif 80, 257, 258, 259, 262, 310, 314, 437, 476
Bemba Gombo, Jean-Pierre xi-xii, 26, 27, 28, 39-40, 188, 191, 193-195, 199, 209, 211-212, 216, 275, 445-446, 451, 517, 535, 536
Bensouda, Fatou 9, 22, 39, 43, 501, 505, 508, 509, 516, 525
burden of proof 59, 66, 130, 131, 135, 173, 189, 252, 274, 277, 283, 290, 294, 377

Cassese, Antonio 31-32, 80, 82-84, 85, 94-97, 108, 133, 134, 139, 225, 232, 233, 236, 241, 243, 254, 255, 310, 312, 337, 376, 403, 458, 459, 467
Central African Republic xi-xii, 26, 28, 39, 40, 191, 193, 194, 195, 199, 211, 221, 275, 280, 363, 444, 446, 499, 506, 507, 516, 517, 521, 535, 536
Charter of the United Nations xliv, 65, 67-68, 77, 81, 390, 413, 415, 419, 475-477, 480, 482, 484, 490
Chapter VII 81, 415, 477, 480, 482, 483, 489, 490, 518, 519
Civilians 28, 37, 51, 54, 64, 66, 82, 110, 124, 125, 130, 147, 148, 149, 244, 247, 248, 249, 323, 347, 350, 371, 374, 400, 402,

403, 409, 414, 418, 419, 440, 441, 446, 451, 472, 490, 491, 492, 521, 531, 544
collateral damage 57, 492
command responsibility *see also* superior responsibility 31, 38, 101, 123, 124, 134, 211, 238, 276, 293, 344, 350, 364, 446, 536
   effective control 102, 123
   failure to prevent or punish 31, 441, 446, 451
   superior–subordinate relationship 101, 116, 123, 124, 316, 344, 350, 441, 445, 446, 452
common Article 3 *see* war crimes
complementarity xxxvi, 2, 69-71, 77, 177, 179, 206, 219, 220, 335-386, 393, 394, 403, 454, 466-468, 497, 501, 503, 504, 509, 518, 521-523, 525, 529, 539
complicity modes of participation 103, 104, 112, 114, 115, 122, 128, 324, 364, 492, 497
   aiding and abetting 101-107, 109-116, 123-131, 235, 244-249, 347
   inducing 17, 127
   instigating 123, 133, 141, 144, 157, 158, 234
   ordering 40, 53, 63, 124, 126, 157, 158, 234, 323, 374, 414, 445, 452, 520
   planning 65, 66, 104, 105, 133, 138, 139, 148, 150, 234, 414
confidentiality 12, 18, 25, 28, 187, 188, 202, 283-285, 398, 404
confirmation of charges xii, xiv, xv, xvii, xviii, xix, 13, 23, 27-30, 32-33, 35-37, 39-41, 111, 112, 137, 175-177, 194, 207-211, 213, 218, 220, 238, 296, 300, 365, 500, 505, 536
consent 74, 174, 175, 177, 193, 285, 542
conspiracy xxvi, 79, 109, 173, 227, 489
co-perpetration 109, 137, 144, 148, 536
counsel xxii, xxv, xxvi, xxxii, xxxiii, xxxiv, xxxvii, xxxviii, 15, 21, 33, 101, 129, 138, 175, 178, 189, 194, 195, 198-203, 204, 251, 253, 255, 258, 260-263, 265-267, 269, 271-276, 280-282, 285, 286, 289-291, 295, 297, 304-306, 456, 462, 463, 487, 496
crimes against humanity xxxiv, xxxvi, xxxvii, xli, xliii, xlv, 9, 10, 26, 34, 36, 37, 41, 50-52, 55, 60, 63, 71, 83, 108, 147, 166, 226, 235, 238, 248, 276, 310, 311, 318, 320, 321, 324, 325, 327, 342, 347, 358, 371, 390, 394, 411, 414, 421, 433, 435, 444, 468, 472, 486, 491, 492, 496, 499, 521, 524, 532, 535, 536, 537, 542, 543
   attack against a civilian population 37, 51
   widespread or systematic 51, 150, 156, 364, 371, 472,
customary international law 60, 64, 66-69, 77, 79-80, 83-85, 88-92, 94, 96-99, 102, 108-111, 113, 128, 130, 136, 139-140, 160, 224, 226, 232-238, 241, 246, 250, 318, 358, 425

Darfur xii-xiii, 26, 27, 31-34, 50, 52, 193-195, 200-202, 221, 227, 238, 239, 280, 335, 343, 389, 390, 401, 416, 420, 425, 444, 450, 469-470, 486, 495, 499-501, 506, 507, 511-515, 518-519, 529, 536, 542
Defence office 138, 241, 261-262, 264, 274, 277, 305-306, 462
   defences 65-66, 68, 345, 349, 352, 364
   duress 226, 235, 374, 375, 463
   military necessity 53, 57, 59, 60, 147, 151, 268
   mistake of law 68, 345
   superior orders 463
delay xxiii, xxiv, 143, 165-167, 172-175, 177-178, 183, 188, 190, 194, 199, 220, 253, 290, 293, 355, 463, 464, 468
Democratic Republic of the Congo xiii-xvii, 10-21, 24 26-29, 33, 34, 37, 111, 137, 177, 185-195, 199, 207, 209, 210, 212, 214, 215, 217, 219, 238, 252, 254, 259, 260, 272, 275, 277, 283, 296, 304, 306, 335, 362, 363, 364, 403, 442, 444, 450, 493, 499, 506-508, 516-518, 520-521, 535, 536
Detention xlv, 11, 120, 145, 151, 153, 169, 173, 248, 270, 296, 316, 326, 442, 463
Deterrence 9, 312, 313, 315, 318, 322, 329, 330, 352, 353, 388, 435-452, 541
Disclosure xv, xvi, xviii, xxvi, 7, 12-13, 18-19, 25, 34, 97, 143, 174-176, 188-190, 252, 257, 258, 260, 267, 282, 283-87, 291-297, 305, 322
discrimination 47, 50, 524
*dolus specialis see* genocide

East Timor xxxv, 55, 266, 453, 455, 458-463, 467-468, 470, 472, 483-484, 494

elements of crimes 9, 21, 33, 35, 40-42, 47-49, 51, 59, 63-68, 73, 77, 82, 84, 103, 110-111, 113, 120, 135, 139, 140-141, 145-146, 149, 152, 159-160, 207, 216-217, 219, 234-235, 241, 244-245, 253, 276, 359, 371, 394, 536

enforced prostitution *see* sexual violence
enforced sterilisation *see* sexual violence
enforcement 1, 27, 86, 168, 248, 262, 266, 286, 290, 318, 424, 442, 456, 495, 510, 519, 541

enslavement xli, 7, 11, 14, 42, 61, 104, 107

ethnic cleansing xliv, 144, 491

ethnic groups xxxvi, xlv, 10, 34, 41-42, 48-49, 63, 87, 151, 298, 308, 312, 313, 321, 441, 447-448, 450, 459, 528, 542

evidence *see also* disclosure; Rules of Procedure and Evidence; witnesses xv, xvi, xviii, xxii, xxiii, xxv, xxvi, 7, 8, 10, 11, 12-13, 14, 15, 16, 17, 19-25, 27-39, 41-43, 49, 51, 59, 83, 84, 88, 93, 95, 105, 114, 124, 128, 133-136, 138-140, 142-146, 150-151, 157, 159-160, 167, 168-171, 173-176, 178, 180, 184, 186, 188-190, 197, 206, 208-212, 213-214, 217-219, 221, 233, 237, 240, 246, 249, 252, 258-259, 263-265, 268-270, 279, 281-287, 290-296, 298-305, 327, 337, 347, 358, 371, 374, 376-377, 394, 397, 399, 403, 411, 414, 435, 442, 485, 492, 511, 518, 520, 537

European Convention on Human Rights 290

European Court of Human Rights xxvi-xxvii, xxxiii, xxxviii, 168, 279, 401

Extermination **xlv,** 42, 51, 110, 147, 151, 324

Extraordinary Chambers in the Courts of Cambodia ECCC xxxv, 34, 460-461, 453-455, 458-464, 467, 470, 472, 483, 494, 515, 533, 535

fair trial *see also* accused, rights of the xxi, 2, 17-18, 135, 165-180, 184, 190, 192, 198, 251, 253, 254-257, 259-260, 262, 271-272, 276, 278, 283, 289-306, 365, 366, 456, 458-459, 462-464, 468, 472

forced pregnancy *see* sexual violence forcible transfer 51-52, 147, 151

Gender xxiii, 8-10, 11, 12, 14, 15, 16, 21, 22-24, 25-28, 32, 33, 37, 39, 41-43, 521, 536, 544

General Assembly UN 81, 83, 85, 86, 236, 263, 267, 398, 407, 409, 411-413, 415-417, 419, 424, 427, 431, 478, 482, 483, 491, 502, 524

general principles of law 98, 241, 242

Geneva Conventions xxxvi, 53, 54, 58, 82, 102, 124, 130, 317, 325, 412, 413, 415, 431, 491
   Additional Protocol I 53-57, 59, 238, 412
   Additional Protocol II 130, 412

Genocide xxvii, xxxii, xxxv, xxxvii, xxxviii, xliii, xliv, xlv, 8, 9, 26, 33-34, 42, 47-52, 60, 61, 63, 71, 114, 128, 173, 235, 267, 311, 318-322, 324-327, 336-337, 343, 347, 349, 364, 444, 468, 472, 481, 486, 491, 492, 500, 506, 511, 521, 524, 527, 529, 532, 534, 537
   complicity 128, 324, 364
   conspiracy to commit 173
   Convention xxvii, 47, 50, 61, 128
   *dolus specialis* 33-34, 48-51
   incitement 324, 347
   mental element 33, 34
   protected groups 48-49

Goldstone, Richard 9, 13, 414-418, 419, 432

grave breaches *see* war crimes

gravity 39, 65, 67, 156, 177, 208, 221, 248, 316-318, 320, 322-325, 328, 335-337, 339-346, 349-350, 352-353, 355, 359, 360, 363-365, 369, 370, 373, 379, 393-394, 399-405, 449, 469, 526

human rights *see also* accused, rights of the; victims, rights of xxvi, xxvii, xxxi, xxxii, xxxiii, xxxiv, xxxv, xxxvi, xxxvii, xxxviii, xxxix, xli, xliv, xlv, 1, 28, 31, 32, 35, 45, 47, 61, 80, 84, 85, 89, 98, 165, 166, 168, 177, 178, 199, 207, 248, 253-255, 257, 259, 260, 262, 263, 264, 268, 274, 279, 281, 287, 290, 317, 365, 366, 378, 390, 401, 403, 407-409, 411, 414-418, 419, 421, 430, 436-438, 445, 447, 457-459, 462-464, 466, 468, 471, 475, 476, 480, 481-482, 485, 487,

488, 491, 492, 497, 500, 506, 507, 513, 514, 523-524, 529, 539, 541, 544
Human Rights Watch 11, 29, 37, 248, 266, 274, 343, 350, 399, 421, 454, 461, 484, 503, 513, 514, 535, 543
humanity, crimes against *see* crimes against humanity

impartiality 30, 36, 80, 95, 96, 455-456, 460-461, 527, 543
imprisonment *see also* detention; sentencing 53, 61, 116, 117, 122, 147, 151, 169, 170, 315-318, 321-326, 347, 349, 352, 375, 445, 535
impunity 9, 64, 217, 251-253, 270, 294-296, 329, 336, 349-350, 355, 360, 371, 377, 378, 390, 399, 411, 413, 420, 421, 425, 429, 432, 437, 453-454, 456-461, 463, 465-471, 473, 481, 484-485, 489-491, 496, 501, 503, 504, 509, 513, 515, 521, 523, 524, 529, 532, 541
*in absentia* trials 304
incitement 112, 324, 347, 447, 450
indictments xxiv, xxv, xxvi, 8, 11, 14, 21, 22, 26, 134, 135, 137-138, 140-150, 159, 168, 169, 173, 174, 175, 206, 207, 209, 240, 244, 269, 270, 271, 276, 280, 281, 286, 291, 292, 298, 302, 303, 323, 325, 326, 391, 398, 444, 447, 450, 451, 454, 459, 467, 483, 487, 489, 490, 493, 495, 499, 502, 511, 535
individual criminal responsibility 23, 33, 38, 46, 50, 52, 55, 58, 67, 123, 125, 129, 133, 137, 147, 234, 240, 244, 329, 485, 494
  accessory or secondary liability *see* accessory liability accomplice liability 104-106, 112, 128, 235, 420
  control of the crime 135
  omissions 2, 24, 91, 93, 101-132, 141, 244, 542
  principal liability 66, 105-107, 109-110, 112, 115, 125, 139, 142, 157, 158, 245, 344
*in dubio pro reo* 242
inhumane acts 7, 8, 26, 37, 41, 42, 51, 52, 147, 151, 325
instigation 141
intent 28, 33-34, 42, 47-52, 54, 55, 60, 61, 66, 84, 87, 90, 103, 105-109, 118-120, 124,

129, 130, 136, 141, 143, 149, 150, 153, 156, 158, 179, 217, 234, 240, 242, 277, 278, 338, 343, 351, 353, 359, 364, 365, 376, 401, 468, 492
Inter-American Commission of Human Rights xxvii, 257
Inter-American Court of Human Rights 281
interests of justice 174, 175, 203, 206, 228, 230, 231, 243, 276, 302, 303, 381-383, 402, 425, 526
intermediaries xvii, 16-20, 25, 28, 192, 203, 252, 253, 306, 442
international armed conflict *see* war crimes
International Committee of the Red Cross ix, 59, 182, 491
International Court of Justice xxvii, xxxi, xxxviii, 91-93, 95, 97, 128, 236, 242, 408-409, 412-414, 424, 427, 476
  Statute 95, 427
International Covenant on Civil and Political Rights 89, 166-167, 255, 268, 290
International Criminal Court *see also* Rome Statute xi-xx, xxxi-xxxiv, xxxvii-xxxviii, xli-xliv, 1, 7-43, 45-48, 50-52, 54-55, 57-58, 60, 63-71, 73-76, 103, 107-111, 123, 131, 136-137, 160, 165-168, 175-177, 179, 181-203, 205-221, 224, 226-227, 232, 238-239, 246-249, 251-256, 258-264, 268-269, 272, 275-276, 280, 282-285, 290-294, 296, 299-300, 303-307, 310, 335-355, 357-367, 369-384, 388-389, 391-395, 397-405, 407-408, 411, 414-416, 418, 420-427, 429-433, 437-438, 442, 444-446, 449-450, 453-455, 457, 465-471, 473, 476, 478-479, 483-488, 490, 495-497, 499-529, 533-540, 542-543
  Preparatory Commission 68
  Rules of Procedure and Evidence xv, 10, 11, 14, 32, 34, 182, 184-187, 192, 207-209, 221, 253, 262, 276, 285, 291-292, 299, 303-304, 345, 383, 391, 402
International Criminal Tribunal for Rwanda xxiii-xxv, xxxiii-xxxv, xlii, 8-10, 13, 33, 40, 101, 103, 110-111, 114-115, 123, 125, 129-130, 138, 140-141, 143, 146, 159, 165, 167-168, 172-174, 177, 180-181, 226, 232, 233, 251, 256, 258-259, 262, 264, 267-270, 272-274,

277-278, 280-281, 283, 286, 289-290, 292-301, 303-305, 308-320, 324-325, 328, 330, 339, 341-342, 347, 349, 352, 362, 366, 371, 373, 391, 425, 437-438, 443-444, 447, 470, 480-483, 492-494, 516, 533-534, 536, 539-541
    Rules of Procedure and Evidence 258, 283, 291-292, 294, 297-299, 304, 310, 366
    Statute xxiv, 42, 55, 103, 123, 167, 173, 232, 258-259, 269, 273, 290, 305, 310, 362, 371, 444, 457
International Criminal Tribunal for the Former Yugoslavia xx-xxiii, xxxii-xxxiv, xxxvii, xlii, 9-10, 13, 27, 31, 40, 55-56, 92, 95-96, 101, 103, 109-113, 123-124, 131, 133-136, 140-147, 150, 152, 159-160, 165, 167-168, 170-171, 178-179, 181, 207, 210, 224, 226-227, 232-233, 235, 239, 242-244, 256-260, 262-264, 267-270, 272, 274-275, 278, 283-286, 289-321, 323, 325-326, 328, 339, 341-342, 346-347, 349, 352, 371, 373, 391, 404, 437, 443, 448, 450, 456, 458, 462, 469-471, 476, 480-483, 492-494, 533-534, 536-537, 542
    Rules of Procedure and Evidence 13, 169, 171, 178-179, 207, 258, 283-284, 291-295, 297-299, 301-305, 310, 391, 469
    Statute 42, 55, 103, 123-124, 134, 144, 147, 152, 167-168, 224, 232-235, 244, 246, 258-259, 264, 269-270, 290, 298, 305, 310, 312-313, 318, 371, 457
international humanitarian law xxxv, xxxvi, 1, 54-55, 59, 82, 101, 122, 129, 133, 135, 211, 224, 226, 232, 234, 235, 246, 248, 267, 311, 315, 359, 362, 413, 424, 425, 438, 447, 462, 464, 485, 490, 491, 497, 537
laws or customs of war 147, 151, 321, 325
    principle of distinction 60
    principle of proportionality 55, 57, 60, 374, 414, 419
International Law Commission 61, 71, 108-109, 398
Interpretation xxvii, xxxvi, 14, 19, 21, 40, 42, 53, 56, 60, 72, 74, 76, 77, 96, 112, 121, 134, 156, 157, 165, 167, 186, 207, 210, 212, 213, 215, 217, 221, 223-250,

253, 277-279, 303, 307, 310, 362, 365, 367, 377,-378, 396-397, 421-423, 425, 427, 476, 486, 501, 518, 536
investigations xii, xiii, xiv, xv, xvii, xix, xxxiii, xxxviii, 2, 7-2, 15, 17-18, 20, 25, 28-32, 34, 36, 43, 69-70, 92, 143, 161, 179, 182, 185, 187, 194, 198, 206, 208, 221, 243, 248, 252, 254, 258, 261, 263-267, 270, 273, 276, 279, 280, 282-287, 291, 299, 336, 351, 354, 360, 362, 363, 365, 366, 371, 380-383, 387, 389, 392-399, 401, 402, 414-416, 431, 432, 442, 467, 486, 488, 489, 493, 499-500, 504-505, 507, 509, 513-514, 516-520, 522, 523, 525-529, 535-536
Iraq xxxviii, 49, 51-52, 54-56, 88, 400-401, 403-404, 455, 485-486, 495, 511, 525

Jackson, Robert 254, 479
joint criminal enterprise JCE xxiii, xxvi, 9, 102, 109, 112, 133-161, 228, 232-235, 249, 276, 293, 305, 443, 492, 536
judicial activism 91, 229, 233, 237, 239, 243, 250
judicial creativity xxxvi, 8, 84, 97, 123, 159, 221, 223-250, 425
judicial notice 298
jurisdiction xvii, xxi, xxiii, xxv, xli, xlii, 3, 7, 9, 10, 40, 55, 56, 60, 63, 64, 68-77, 82, 105, 107, 116, 117, 131, 140, 179, 182, 184, 185, 195, 198, 203, 208, 214, 217, 219, 226-228, 231, 234, 236, 238, 240, 241, 264, 277, 278, 285, 286, 292, 310, 328, 338, 343, 344, 354, 358-366, 371, 372, 377, 380-383, 389-395, 397, 399-402, 404, 407, 408, 411, 413, 420-425, 428, 430-433, 443-445, 449, 453, 454, 458, 465-468, 470-473, 481-483, 488, 490-492, 501, 506, 508, 509, 511, 516, 517, 521, 523-524, 526, 537, 538

knowledge 51, 54-55, 59, 66, 68, 101, 103-110, 112-113, 118, 125-127, 129-131, 144, 244-248, 279, 284, 344, 410, 446
Kosovo 171, 311, 414, 424, 453, 455, 458-459, 461-462, 464, 470-471, 483-484, 494, 507, 542

laws or customs of war *see* international humanitarian law

legality, principle of *nulla poena sine lege, nullem crimen sine lege* 89, 118, 123, 140, 222, 224, 226, 236-238
legitimacy 25, 42, 70, 81, 84, 94, 115, 123, 136, 222, 223-250, 286-287, 320, 390, 409-412, 416, 421, 448-451, 455, 457-459, 461, 464, 470, 472, 511, 518, 524, 534
*lex specialis* 212
London Charter Nuremberg Charter 7, 107, 436

Martens Clause 238
*mens rea* 34, 48-51, 66, 68, 102-103, 105, 109-110, 113, 118, 120, 129-130, 141, 157-158, 235, 245, 343-345, 364
   *dolus eventualis* 104, 106, 113
   intent *see* intent
   knowledge *see* knowledge
   negligence 20, 48, 60, 105, 118, 120, 125, 294, 297, 344
   recklessness 60, 62, 107, 112, 118-120, 128, 343
   specific intent *see* genocide wilful blindness 107
military necessity *see* defences
motive xlv, 87, 90, 104, 240, 327

non-international armed conflict *see* war crimes
non-retroactivity of offenses *nulla poena sine lege, nullem crimen sine lege* 54, 89, 123
Nuremberg Tribunal International Military Tribunal xxvii, xxiv, xli, 7, 53-54, 107, 224, 232, 253-254, 260, 265, 292, 388, 390, 436, 445, 457, 473, 479, 496, 497, 531-532

occupation xxxvi, xlii, 65-66, 400, 407-408, 428-429, 432, 453-454, 524
omission *see* individual criminal responsibility
*opinio juris* 89, 91, 93, 97, 235-237
ordering 31, 106, 124, 445, 451, 538

Palestine xxxv, xxxvi, 389, 407-433, 511, 525, 535

Persecution xlv, 10, 26, 37, 42, 51, 52, 145, 147, 151, 158, 238, 321-322, 324-326, 347, 359, 390, 450, 536
planning *see* complicity
presumption of innocence xxxii, 160-161, 254, 276-277, 290, 375
prisoners of war 126, 130
procedure *see also* Rules of Procedure and Evidence xvii, xxxv, xxxvi, xxxvii, 10, 11, 68-69, 71, 76-77, 94, 165, 172, 178-180, 190, 192-193, 196, 201-202, 204, 206, 208-210, 212, 214, 216, 218-220, 222, 240, 252, 256-258, 260, 262, 265, 273, 285-287, 291, 296, 300-301, 304, 306, 308-309, 319, 325, 327, 328, 344, 362, 365, 375, 387, 391, 393, 398, 402, 428, 466, 471, 489, 495, 526-529, 538, 543
proportionality, principle of *see* international humanitarian law
protected persons 81

rape 7-12, 14-15, 22, 25-26, 31, 33-35, 37-40, 42, 110, 114, 235, 325, 340-341, 347-349, 390, 401, 446, 472, 492, 544
*ratione loci see also* jurisdiction 481
*ratione materiae see also* jurisdiction 472
*ratione personae see also* jurisdiction xxv, 234, 372, 391
*ratione temporis see also* jurisdiction 73, 372, 394, 449, 471
reconciliation xxxviii, 235, 307-331, 435, 439, 457, 466, 492, 501, 513, 519, 521, 527-529, 538, 541
refugees xxxvi, 90, 166, 415, 429, 442, 450, 514-515
right to a fair trial *see* fair trial
right to life 166
Rome Statute of the International Criminal Court xi-xiv, xvii-xx, xxxi, xliv, 9-10, 12-14, 20, 23-24, 27-28, 30, 33, 35-36, 38-42, 47-48, 50-60, 63-78, 103, 107-111, 123, 167, 176-177, 179, 181-191, 197-198, 204-221, 227, 238-239, 246, 252-254, 258-259, 261, 269, 283-285, 290, 294, 299, 303-305, 307, 335-338, 342, 344-346, 350-354, 358-363, 365-366-367, 370-373, 376-384, 388, 390-398, 400-403, 405, 415, 420-427, 437, 449, 457, 465-468, 470-473, 484-488,

495-496, 499-500, 502-506, 508, 510-514, 516-517, 519, 521, 523, 526-528, 533-537, 540, 542, 544
Preamble xliv, 70, 252, 465
Rules of Procedure and Evidence *see* International Criminal Court; International Criminal Tribunal for the former Yugoslavia; International Criminal Tribunal for Rwanda; Special Court for Sierra Leone; Special Tribunal for Lebanon

Schabas, William A. vii, xxxvii-xxxviii, 1-3, 27, 30, 34, 61, 111, 146, 165, 207, 208, 211, 213, 215, 254, 257, 274, 307, 310, 314, 337, 378, 387-405, 418, 427, 436, 463, 475, 480, 482, 521, 527
Second World War *see* World War II self-determination 81, 87, 408, 412, 414, 423, 449
self-representation 178
sentencing xx-xxv, xxxii, 2, 8, 14, 24, 53, 101, 114, 116-117, 120-121, 125, 129-130, 151, 153, 169-170, 172-173, 208, 226, 235, 238, 267, 273, 277, 285, 298, 307-331, 335-355, 357-367, 369-384, 436, 438-439, 443-445, 447-448, 532, 534-535, 542
sexual violence *see also* rape xxxiii, 7-43, 401, 403-404, 520-521, 536, 544
  enforced prostitution 10
  enforced sterilisation10
  forced marriage xxv, 8, 14
  forced pregnancy 10
  other forms of sexual violence 10, 26, 35, 37, 39, 41-42
  rape *see* rape
  sexual slavery xxv, 8, 10-11, 14-15, 24, 26, 28, 214
Special Court for Sierra Leone xxv-xxvi, xxxiii, xxxiv, xlii, 8, 96, 103, 110, 135, 165-167, 175, 226, 253, 255-262, 266-267, 272-276, 279, 283, 285, 305, 306, 391, 443, 450, 458, 460-463, 470, 472, 486, 489, 494, 515, 527, 533-535, 541-542
  Rules of Procedure and Evidence 258, 261, 283, 462
  Statute xxvi, 103, 167, 258-259, 276-278, 305, 391, 462, 472

Special Tribunal for Lebanon xxvi, 79-99, 226, 239-243, 251, 258, 259, 261, 304, 306, 454, 472-473, 489-490, 494, 496, 533
  Rules of Procedure and Evidence xxvi, 95, 239-240, 259, 283, 304
  Statute 91, 103, 110, 206, 240-243, 258-259, 261, 472
Srebrenica 144, 244, 311, 320, 323
state practice 59, 71, 83, 93-94, 97, 108, 112, 123-124, 127-128, 131, 235-237
State responsibility 61, 67, 80, 491
stateless persons xxxvi
states of emergency xxxvi, 464
Statute *see* International Court of Justice; International Criminal Court; International Criminal Tribunal for the former Yugoslavia; International Criminal Tribunal for Rwanda; Special Court for Sierra Leone; Special Tribunal for Lebanon
strict liability 244-246
superior orders *see* defences
superior responsibility *see also* command responsibility101, 123-124, 536

Taylor, Charles xxvi, xxxiv, 8, 255-257, 266, 272, 276, 443, 483, 486, 494, 527, 535
terrorism xxvi, xxxvii, 79-99, 105, 227, 239-243, 472, 485, 492, 497, 543
Tokyo Tribunal International Military Tribunal for the Far East xli, 292, 390, 436, 457, 479, 496
torture xliv, xlv, 11, 12, 26, 37, 39-40, 42, 101, 110, 147, 151, 166, 169, 217, 248, 317, 324, 325, 347-349, 359, 485, 497, 535
transitional justice xxxii, xxxv, xxxviii, 160, 307, 330, 361, 367, 435, 455-456, 459-460, 468, 476, 503-504, 506, 513, 527-528, 531-545
treaty interpretation 96, 167, 233, 241
truth xxxviii, 30-31, 91, 186, 189-191, 204, 219, 254-255, 295, 299, 313, 322, 327, 330, 482, 496, 521, 528, 539-542

United Nations General Assembly 81, 83, 85, 86, 236, 263, 267, 398, 407, 409, 411-413, 415-417, 419, 424, 427, 431, 478, 482, 483, 491, 502, 524

United Nations Secretary-General 10, 14, 34, 69, 72, 74, 77, 224, 232, 234, 240, 243, 247, 253, 261, 311, 312, 330, 391, 407, 415, 416, 418, 419, 427, 453, 456, 458, 460, 481-484

United Nations Security Council 3, 10, 31, 32, 34, 64, 69, 76, 77, 81, 82, 85, 87, 89, 92, 93, 99, 167, 206, 224, 234, 240, 247, 248, 253, 258, 263, 264, 266, 280, 308, 310-312, 390-393, 398, 403, 407, 409, 412, 415-420, 425-428, 430, 431, 433, 437, 444, 449, 471, 472, 475-498, 500-501, 503, 512, 517-519, 535, 536, 543

United Nations War Crimes Commission xxvii, 53

universal jurisdiction 64, 69-71, 360, 361, 421, 453, 501, 506, 538

Vienna Convention on the Law of Treaties 75, 242, 425, 467

war crimes *see also* international humanitarian law xxvii, xxxiv, xliii, xliv, 7-11, 26, 33, 37, 46, 50, 53-62, 68, 71, 166, 169, 182, 193, 209, 214, 226, 235, 248, 260, 266, 302, 307, 310, 311, 326, 327, 337, 342, 347, 358-360, 364, 376, 394, 400, 411, 414, 416, 418, 421, 424, 433, 435, 437, 443-444, 453, 454, 456, 457, 462, 463, 468, 470, 472, 480, 481, 484, 486, 491-494, 497, 499, 500, 505, 512, 515, 516, 524, 532, 535, 537, 542

grave breaches 42, 317, 325, 358

international armed conflict 53, 54, 59, 82, 210, 492

non-international armed conflict xxxviii, 45, 54, 59-60, 75, 82, 232, 248

World War I1, 310, 314

World War II xxvii, xli, 1, 53, 57, 107, 109, 139, 236